In the
FOOTSTEPS
of
Take a Tram to Hampstead for this ramble

17th Century
FASHION

A Walk Through Old Hampstead's Streets of Surprise

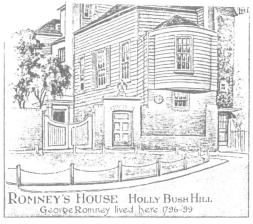

ROMNEY'S HOUSE HOLLY BUSH HILL
George Romney lived here 1796-99

FOR the heart of old Hampstead, the Hampstead of the spa, you must seek Well Walk. But on the way from Hampstead tram terminus halt in Keats Grove before a house called Wentworth Place. There, practically unaltered, is the garden where Keats wrote his Ode to a Nightingale and other poems. The house, Keats' home for two years, has a Keats museum, which contains personal relics and is open every weekday from 10.30 a.m. to 8 p.m.

In Well Walk is a chalybeate well, as a stone inscription records, "given to the benefit of the poor," in 1698 ; and Weatherall House was the Long Room of Hampstead Wells. So that on the raised footpath, shaded by elm and lime, you can imagine the belles and beaux of the 17th and 18th centuries thronging in a fashionable procession that included the literary lions of the day—Addison and Steele and, later, Dr. Johnson. At No. 40 lived the painter Constable, after quitting 2, Lower Terrace.

Spare some moments to view Church Row, in the red-brick demureness of the First George, before returning to the twisting, up-and-down streets to find other houses on the map. R. L. Stevenson lived at Abernethy House ; a retired sea-dog took Admiral's

House (as it has been called since) and equipped the roof like a man o' war and fired cannon in explosions of joy; John Galsworthy wrote and died in the adjoining house, Grove Lodge; New Grove House was the home of George du Maurier, author of "Trilby."

Now for a walk across the heath to Ken Wood. There among the woodland and lawn is an Adam mansion, where 18th century portraits and other paintings — the Iveagh bequest — hang in rooms furnished in the period. The mansion is open daily: on Wednesdays and Fridays 1/-, on other days free. See the duelling ground, walled by giant beeches and oaks at the top of the wood; see the lime avenue, which Coleridge—in his poetic fancy—called a cathedral aisle ; and, leaving woodland shade for the open heath, search the unequalled panorama obtainable on Parliament Hill. Thence it is a pleasant stroll, past bathing ponds, to Parliament Hill Fields tram terminus for services 7 and 15 to town via Kings Cross. Alternatively, by Merton Lane walk to Highgate Village, such a precious fragment of rustic London, and descend Highgate Hill by tram service 11, noticing on the right (near its foot) a railed-in stone to commemorate Dick Whittington.

✳ This map shows the situation of houses named in the article above and of some others. Note the tramway services and consult this map on your walk

THE
LONDON COUNTY COUNCIL
TRAMWAYS

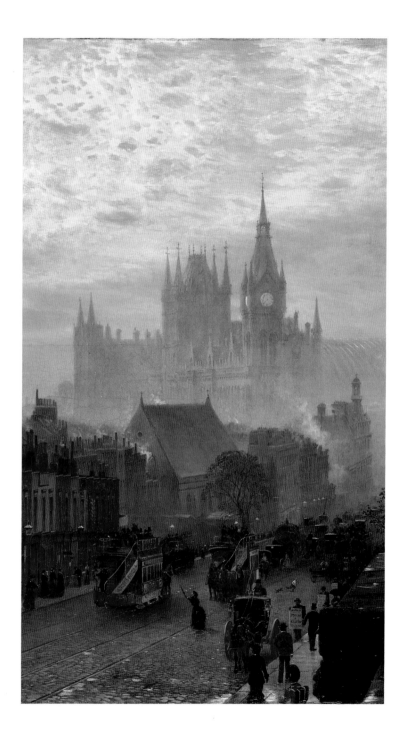

THE
LONDON COUNTY COUNCIL
TRAMWAYS

VOLUME TWO – NORTH LONDON

by

E. R. OAKLEY

Published by
The London Tramways History Group
in association with
The Tramway & Light Railway Society
and
The Light Rail Transit Association

The London County Council Tramways, Volume II
by E. R. Oakley.

First Edition, 1991.

© The London Tramways History Group.

ISBN: 0 9513001 1 3

Origination by Mosaic, London. E17 6SH.

Printed by W. J. Ray & Co. Ltd., Walsall, West Midlands, WS1 2HQ.

Published by The London Tramways History Group.

Address: 33 Mayplace Road East, Barnehurst,
             Bexleyheath, Kent. DA7 6EA. England.

Printed in Great Britain.

CONTENTS

Frontispiece: A section from the painting 'St. Pancras Hotel and Station from Pentonville Road: Sunset' by John O'Connor (1830-89). Dated 1884. The picture is reproduced courtesy of the Museum of London, where it is presently on display (1991).

Endpapers: Pages from the London Holiday Maker, a guide produced by the London County Council Tramways, 1933.

The Ballad of Fell

Do you tell me you've never heard of Fell -
Aubrey Llewellyn Coventry Fell!
Serious, now! Never heard of him? Well!
Lo, now, the East is grey!
'Tis the dawn of another day!
But as yet there is no milkman on his way.

On with the snooze, and don't pull up the blind!
But hark! Was that a snore?
Or simply a comet's whizz?
There! - nearer, clearer, deadlier than before!
Hark! for it is - it is
Fell hurtling past the door!

Fell on his way already,
Sober and straight and steady,
Thrusting and thriving!
Fell when the dawn is grey,
Fell when they've cleared away
Ledgers, and Fell all day
Steadily driving!

Fell, Fell for Waterloo,
Fell for Blackfriars too,
Fell all the dam' way through,
Doing it thorough!
Fell for Blackfriars Bridge,
Fell for Westminster Bridge,
Southwark and Vauxhall Bridge,
Fell for the Borough!

Down the Embankment (Vic),
Husband and Wife and Chick,
Cheap is their safe and quick
Transit as strawberries,
O the long ride they made!
O the small fare they paid!
When shall his glory fade?
Noblest of Aubreys!

Aubrey Llewellyn Coventry Fell!
I hear the patter of feet pell-mell!
For the day is done; they have worked their spell;
The night is dark, and the wind is snell,
But it brings a suburban dinner-smell! -
Pack 'em like oysters inside your shell!
Grasp your tiller and bang your bell,
And drive like billy-O, drive like hell!

From Vauxhall Bridge by the Wandsworth Road,
With thousands of passengers tightly stowed;
From Southwark Bridge by Newington Butts,
Roaring along in his iron ruts;
From Blackfriars Bridge by the Blackfriars Road,
From Waterloo Bridge by the Waterloo Road,
From Westminster Bridge by Westminster Bridge Road,
Lunging along with his carolling load -

Like the animals safe in Noah's Ark,
In the pouring rain and the poring dark -
Bricklayer, burglar, typist, clerk,
Steering 'em safe by Kennington Park!
By Kennington Oval and Peckham Rye,
Right out to Lewisham Fell doth ply,
Banging his bell and shouting "Hi!" -

By Kennington Oval and Balham and Tooting,
Right out to Merton Fell goes scooting,
With Metropolitan P'leece saluting;
By Kennington Oval and Brixton and Streatham,
Right out to Norbury Fell will set 'em! -
Right out to Norb'ury!
Right out to Naub'ry!
Gallantest Aubrey!

There are dinners that wait
At Kennington Gate;
There are teas that are high
At Peckham Rye;
There are wives at Catford and wives at Lee
Who sing as they dandle their babes on their knee,
"Father will come to his babe in the nest
For Fell drives safely and Fell drives best, -
Fell will bring Father again to theee!
Bring him again to thee!"

And where all the fathers of families dwell,
Whether in Wandsworth or Camberwell,
As they hear the step and the key or the bell,
I trow there is never a need to tell
Tiniest Lucy or Lucy's sister
To drop on their knees
And to murmur, "Please
Goos Bleth Mister -
Dear, Good, Kindest (and cheapest as well) -
Aubrey Llewellyn Coventry Fell.

                                    Wilfred Blair

Introduction

This volume, the second in the series, completes the history of the London County Council Tramways. The subject matter covers the founding and operation of the several horse tramway companies which were formed to work in the metropolitan area north of the Thames, and, in the case of one of them, to build and work lines extending into the County of Essex, and eventually to purchase and operate lines in Middlesex as well.

The pioneer cable tramway which was constructed from the bottom to the top of Highgate Hill is also described, which includes its eventual absorption, together with all the horse tramways in the County north of the Thames, into the LCC (Northern) Tramways, and their eventual electrification.

The period covered ranges from 1869, with details of the first of the lines to be authorised on the north side of London, to 1933, when the very efficient electric tramways of the London County Council were compulsorily transferred to the London Passenger Transport Board on 1st July of that year.

Details of the way in which the conduit and overhead wire electric current collection systems were constructed are to be found in Volume One, except for three unusual experimental arrangements which are described in these pages. The tramcar modernisation programme, or "pullmanisation" programme, by which name it is more popularly known, is also described, as is the acquisition of new cars.

Ancillary subjects that were not dealt with in Volume One are covered, including a chapter on the politics surrounding the formation of the LCC Tramways; a description of the fares and tickets system used by the Council; and also statistical information. A bibliography has also been included, which covers all sources from which information has been obtained, together with a comprehensive index.

In order to preserve continuity in the way in which material has been presented, similar standards have been employed to those used in Volume One, both for the spelling of words and the use of traditional British expressions for weights, measures, money and the description of days and dates.

Acknowledgements

The completion of Volume Two, and with it the completion of this history, gives considerable satisfaction to all the members of the London Tramways History Group, who, individually and collectively, have given hundreds of hours of their time to the task. But, firstly, with regard to Volume One of the history, it has given us all great pleasure to know how well it has been received. A number of readers have taken the trouble to write to us with their comments, almost all constructive and useful for future reference. To these readers, we express our appreciation for their interest.

So far as Volume Two is concerned, I am pleased to add the name of Brian Connelly to our list of members, and thank him for his part in the completion of the work. I would also like, once again, to stress the importance of the assistance given by Messrs. G. E. Baddeley and C. S. Smeeton in assisting me in undertaking research at a number of establishments, which has involved them both in considerable travelling and long hours of writing up the results of their labours. To Messrs. A. J. Wills and R. Elliott, I again tender my thanks for checking sections of the text and providing answers to the many questions asked in our search for accuracy. With regard to the Law Report referring to the case of Benn v Griffiths-Bedell and its subsequent outcome, we are grateful for the use of information supplied by Mr. R. M. Sexton, and presented by courtesy of Mr. C. S. Smeeton.

Appreciation and thanks must go to Mr. M. Maybin for obtaining for us the Report of Andrew Nance, Manager of the Belfast Street Tramways Company, giving his assessment of the methods employed in the operation of the London Street Tramways Company in 1892; to the Rev. P. Lidgett and the Omnibus Society for letting us photograph tickets from their collection; and Messrs. T. M. Russell and K. H. Thorpe for kindly supplying several of the car drawings. We are also grateful to the many people and official bodies who have allowed up to use photographs, and to whom we have attempted to the best of our ability to give due credit.

With regard to the affairs of the Highgate Hill Cable Tramway, I have to acknowledge the use of extracts taken from the notes of the late Mr. C. E. Lee, kindly provided by Mr. V. Goldberg. So far as the other contributors are concerned, all of whom are mentioned in Volume One, I again offer my thanks for the advice and assistance so willingly given during the long period in which research and writing up have been in progress. This again extends to the design work for the cover and contents, ably carried out by Mr. M. B. Leahy; to text checking and proof reading, undertaken by Messrs. P. J. Davis and C. E. Holland; to compilation of the index base by Mr. C. L. Withey; and to the printer and binder for their parts in presenting the completed Volume.

There is a list of people mentioned in Volume One who had an interest in the project, but were taken from our midst during the time that the work has been in progress. I must now, sadly, add two more, Messrs. G. E. ("Ted") Budden and M. L. Harper, and remember them for the contribution which they made.

A copy of the system map devised and designed by the late David Willoughby is again provided, so that you may have access to its content in whichever book you are studying. Finally, I trust that you will enjoy reading the material presented within these covers, and that it will give you a greater appreciation of what was involved in the construction and operation of what was, in its time, one of the largest and most efficient tramway undertakings anywhere in the world.

E. R. Oakley,
Hartley, Kent.
Summer 1991.

Some Useful Addresses

Museums

East Anglia Transport Museum,
Chapel Road, Carlton Colville, Lowestoft, Suffolk.

London Transport Museum,
Covent Garden, London. WC2E 7BB

National Tramway Museum,
Crich, Matlock, Derbyshire.

Societies

Light Rail Transit Association, Membership Secretary,
6 Hermitage Woods Crescent, St. John's, Woking, Surrey. GU21 IUE

Tramway & Light Railway Society, Membership Secretary,
6 The Woodlands, Brightlingsea, Colchester, Essex. CO7 0RY

Drawings

T. M. Russell, "Chaceside", St. Leonard's Park,
Horsham, West Sussex. RH13 6EG

Chapter 33
The London Tramways and Politics

A description has been given in Volume One of this history how the tramway came to the metropolis, and the many problems and difficulties which had to be overcome before and after its sometimes reluctant acceptance by various authorities, not least by many of the politicians of the day. With the formation of the London County Council in 1889, new plans were drawn up, the object of which was to gain for Londoners a public street transport system that was worthy of the name and one, it was hoped, that would be a credit to the capital. It had been intended that this should be dealt with by the acquisition and consolidation into one undertaking of the many tramway companies which operated independently of one another in the new county area. Very little, however, was said about the political aspects of these moves or of the opposition to them that came from many quarters.

Local, district and national politics continuously entered into the implementation of tramway schemes in Britain. The Tramways Act of 1870 set the seal of Parliament on the whole question of proposal, authorisation, construction, maintenance and even removal of any tramway to be operated on or off the streets in England, Wales and Scotland, with slightly different laws applying to the whole of Ireland at that time.

In the closing years of the nineteenth century it was the Purchase Clause (Section 43) of the 1870 Act that gave great cause for concern among the tramway companies' managements, but great promise for the future for members of municipal bodies who hailed the 21-year option either as a thing to be fought off at all costs, or an ideal to be realised at all costs. Consequently, it was predictable that the years after 1890 were to see battles fought over the terms of the 1870 Act, which, twenty years later, appeared to have become somewhat outdated and repressive. So far as the vast area which became the County of London was concerned, the tramway companies operating within the new County boundaries could expect, when their time came, to be swallowed up by the representatives of the ratepayers, and chose to fight the issue.

However, London was a disadvantaged county when it came to implementing tramway proposals. The complex situation that developed, due to the Borough Councils having power of veto over the LCC, permitted them to overturn many of the proposals made by the County Council in its endeavour to obtain authorisation for new tramways after 1899. This became something of a nightmare to the progressive party members, the more so as the moderates, together with central government, hacked away at the Bills put forward in the years from 1900 onwards. The only real winners were the omnibus proprietors, who flooded the streets with their vehicles, with little or no interference from any official body, together with a group of entrepreneurs from America who succeeded in obtaining Acts of Parliament to enable them to construct tube railways beneath London. In the Acts obtained by Charles Tyson Yerkes and his confederates, there was no mention of a Purchase Clause being invoked after a given number of years although members of several of the Borough Councils made such suggestions. Neither was there any mention of any control by the County authority.

To return to the early 1890s, one of the leading progressives, John Williams Benn (later Sir. J. W. Benn), made it almost his life's work to gain for London what he considered to be its just fruits; that the LCC should become responsible for the mass transit of the people, both to and from their places of work, and for their social and leisure journeys.

At the beginning of his campaign, the trams, 'buses and everything else on the roads, with a few exceptions, were horse hauled. The tramway companies were also bound by statute to carry "workmen" at low fares, which, by comparison with omnibus fares, were very much cheaper. The 'bus owners were not statutorily bound in any respect regarding fares, and most made no effort to carry "workmen", which made it plain for those who wished to see it that way that they were "superior", a ticket that remained firmly tied to them for many years to come.

A long-drawn-out argument on the merits or otherwise of municipal ownership of the tramways took place in the Council chamber, which began in 1891 and did not end until after the LCC had electrified its first lines between Tooting and the Thames Bridges. For the whole of those dozen years, the two political factions slogged it out, with an uneasy truce occasionally, when everyone realised that it was necessary to get some sense of order into the chaotic state of affairs which beset public transport in the capital. To use a modern idiom, London was "light years" behind much of the civilised world when it came to travel as the following example extracted from "John Benn and the Progressive Movement" by A. G. Gardiner will show.

"In his review of the Council in 1901, Mr. A. M. Torrance, the Chairman, gave an illustration of the affliction of travel in London. 'On returning ... from the ceremony of the opening of the new electricity generating station at Lombard Road, Battersea, the following appeared to be the quickest way of route to Highbury ... a car from the station to connect with a car to Chelsea Bridge, then a 'bus to Victoria, train to Mansion House, 'bus to Broad Street, train to Mildmay Park, then car to Highbury, or seven conveyances to go about nine miles'..."

Once, however, the idea of municipalisation became acceptable, the great debate on whether the overhead wire system or conduit system of electric power collection should be adopted, opened the way for all and sundry to air their views. Most of the road authorities, which were the local councils, made it plain that they would not accept anything other than the conduit method through their districts. But, equally, the general consensus of opinion of Benn and his Progressives, advised by Dr. A. B. Kennedy, was that, for such a large and important city, London should not be disfigured with the "festoon effect" that the overhead wire would necessarily inflict upon the capital. The conduit system, unobtrusive, but very expensive, won the day.

Benn had also advocated the construction of tramway subways in the central areas and had been to America to see several in action. He was impressed, but had difficulty in impressing the Board of Trade or Parliament. Eventually, he did win over the County Council, the result being the construction of the Kingsway Subway, but that was all, and he was too late! The "tube" railways were being bored beneath the capital at great speed.

Another battle took place when the Council attempted, between 1901 and 1906, to obtain powers to build a tramway from the terminus on the south-east side of Westminster Bridge, along and over the bridge and then along the Victoria Embankment as far as the Charing Cross Railway Bridge. At the time of the opening of the Westminster to Tooting electric tramway, John Benn apologised to the Prince of •Wales for his being unable to board the Royal Car outside the Palace of Westminster, because of the "obstructions emanating from within that place"! From then on, a continuous campaign was fought by opponents of the several tramway Bills submitted by the Council in its attempt to get tracks laid across the bridge. At long last in 1906, however, the Council did gain its Act and lost no time in laying the lines over the bridge and along the Embankment.

During the period between 1911 and 1913, the City of Manchester Tramways Department had been conducting an investigation into the Passenger Transportation Problem. The Special Committee, whose Chairman was James Bowes, were not very complimentary about the conditions prevailing in greater London. Among other things, they stated that "the defect in London's 'rapid transit system' is that there is no comprehensive plan; that the full development of the tramways is retarded, due to local causes and influences, and the use of the veto by local authorities; that the tramways are financially hampered".

The onset of the Great War brought a respite in the bickering between the various factions, but not for long! After the war, the LCC started to "pick up the pieces", and tried to arrange for extensions to be made in Central London, mainly to connect up several "dead ends", but again were baulked by objections from the police, and almost everyone else. This time it was on the premise that the roads were not suitable for tramways; that the trams were and would be "in the way of other traffic"; that the trams were obstructionist; that they were dangerous.

Many committees sat; many lengthy documents were written. In 1922 it was revealed that the "Underground Group" were negotiating with the government with regard to financial guarantees to be made in connection with the extension and development of the tube railways. This prompted the LCC to consider what were to be the first thoughts on the subject of a unified public transport system for London, in which the London County Council would take a major part. Due also to the problems associated with the vast increase in the numbers of omnibuses being put into service by the LGOC and others referred to as "pirates", efforts were made to control this influx, resulting in the London Traffic Act of 1924 making its appearance, and giving some protection - in theory at least - to the tramway undertakings which were working in the metropolitan area.

The 1924 Strike and Wages Enquiry

London tramwaymen went on strike on Saturday 22nd March 1924 for nine days in quest of an 8/- rise. LGOC busmen struck in sympathy. The independent omnibus operators - the "pirates" - took advantage of the situation and made what was reported as "a killing". Mr. Ernest Bevin, leading the Trade Unions, and his colleagues were accused of being "communists".

A Court of Enquiry which had been arranged, opened its proceedings on the first day of the strike. Headed by Sir Arthur Colefax, K.C., he had with him Messrs. G. W. Paton (Managing Director of Bryant & May Ltd) and Arthur Pugh (Secretary of the Iron and Steel Trades

Federation). Others present were A. L. C. Fell (LCCT), L. Slattery (West Ham Tramways and also Secretary of the Metropolitan District Council for Tramways), C. J. Spencer (MET, SMET and LUT), F. Pick (LGOC), E. Bevin (T&GWU), J. Beckett (Secretary of the Municipal Tramways Association and National Council for Tramways), Councillor Matthews (LCC, and who was also looking after the interests of the municipal tramways of Leyton, Ilford, Walthamstow, Erith and Bexley), E. J. Johnson (East Ham Borough Treasurer), Dr. Newnham (Town Clerk of Croydon) and Lord Ashfield.

In the first place, the representatives of most of the municipal tramways departments and the company tramways stated that this claim was beyond their means to satisfy. The general point of view held was that much of the traffic which the tramways could bear was being lost, due to the activities of the LGOC and the "pirates", who were swamping the tram routes with their 'buses. During the discussion, several comments were made by Bevin regarding the outlook of the London "combine" members, including a suggestion that they were after a monopoly, which was refuted by Ashfield.

A statement was made by Spencer that, although the company tramways were part of the combine, they could not pay the 8/- which was asked for, although it was admitted that the LGOC paid its staff almost £1 a week more than the tramwaymen received. This brought more questioning from Bevin, who asked Ashfield why this was. The answer indicated that the LGOC made a profit and he could see no reason why the busmen should not share in this.

Aubrey Fell then stated in general terms the position of the Council with regard to employment and pay, giving a set of figures for staff in all branches of the service; their pay, hours of work, extra payments and so on. He said that the LCC paid rates to the borough councils amounting to £69,500 on 163 miles of tramway, and that there were 1,116 'buses competing with LCC trams in February 1924, which figure included "pirates".

The outcome was that an immediate award of 6/- per week was made, with the other 2/- remaining negotiable as part of a cost-of-living clause included in the agreement. The small municipal operators were hard put to implement the award, but nevertheless, somehow, managed to do so.

(Extracted from an Editorial printed in the 11th June 1924 issue of the Light Railway & Tramway Journal).

Further Attempts at Unification

Several more attempts were made to form a unified transport system for London. After the earlier abortive proposals, the LCC tried, by promoting "The London County Council (Co-ordination of Passenger Traffic) Bill, 1928", to bring something positive into the discussions. The London Electric Railway Company, a constituent company of the "combine", presented a similar Bill, but neither got very far, being defeated by a new Labour Government after its election in 1929.

The document at the heart of the defeated LCC Bill, known as "The Blue Report", recommended a municipal approach to co-ordination, in which a "common fund" played a large part. This had been accepted in principle by many, including Mr. Herbert Morrison, who, at the time, was Minister of Transport in the Labour Government. Later, however, Morrison changed his mind, deciding that "a public Board, outside politics and commercial in outlook" would be more acceptable.

Meanwhile, Lord Ashfield, as head of the "combine", was busy posing "The Tramway Question" as well as the "Transport Question", this being brought out in the content of a memorandum to the Cabinet Office (CP 170 [29]), dated 24th June 1929 which reads "... It must be expected that he (Lord Ashfield) would then ask what was the attitude of government to the problem, and in what direction they were prepared to contemplate a solution ..."

At the same time, the Council was still trying to obtain a more positive attitude, with little success, with regard to the implementation of the 1924 Traffic Act, whereby much of the omnibus competition still very much in evidence, would be reduced. It again presented a Co-ordination Bill in 1929, in an attempt to get something done. It was stated by Sir George Hume for the LCC "that we had to act, because the Minister of Transport would not. If Parliament then turn down the Bills (sic), be it on the head of Government". In retaliation, Morrison suggested "that the Bills must be withdrawn or 'negatived' - I cannot ask you to withdraw, but - ". This implied that he was still intent on going ahead with his own ideas. No more was heard of the LCC Bill.

There were, however, opponents to the government proposals, including all the municipal bodies, led by the LCC, who wanted to see the "Blue Report" implemented. John Cliff and J. E. Binks went further and said that, as the Report had been originally accepted, this commitment should stand. Nevertheless, the Minister of Transport continued on his new path with a plan for "the good of London", but at the same time "commercial and non-political". His 1931 Bill proposed a Board composed of between five and seven members. There was to be no local authority involvement - that would be too political. Instead, the stage was set for a takeover by the "commercial transport people", in other words, the "combine" management, with Lord Ashfield playing a major role. Despite further accusations which were directed at the Minister and a threat of a Conservative revolt, the Bill passed through two readings. Then the Labour Government fell.

The London Passenger Transport Board

The pressure was maintained in the new parliament for the Bill to be allowed to proceed. After considerable negotiation which was said "to please all parties", the Bill was read for the third time in the House of Commons on 10th April 1933. It passed through the House of Lords two days later, and received the Royal Assent on 13th April 1933. It emerged as the **London Passenger Transport Act, 1933 (23 Geo. V. cap. 14).**

Lord Ashfield was Chairman of the Board. The other members of the first Board were:-

Sir John Gilbert, K.B.E.   Mr. John Cliff,
Mr. P. Ashley Cooper, B.A., Ll.B.   Mr. Frank Pick,
Sir Edward Holland, D.L., J.P.
Brig. Gen. Sir Henry Maybury, C.B.E., K.C.M.G., C.B., M.I.C.E., J.P.

The only representatives from the London County Council were Sir John Gilbert and John Cliff, and neither of these were directly involved in the Tramways Department. The new Board took control of all public transport (with the exception of the four main line railway companies) on 1st July 1933, in a vast area, stretching far into the countryside around London.

Except for T. E. Thomas, General Manager of the LCC Tramways, who, together with C. J. Spencer of the combine tramways, remained in authority on the tramway side, the rest of the municipal managers who stayed with the new Board only received consolation prizes, albeit reasonably well paid.

Apart from a few extensions and improvements undertaken in the 1920s, and some considerable modernisation of existing plant and rolling stock, together with the loss of two outstanding General Managers due to the stress of it all, the LCC Tramways did the best with what it had, and went down fighting in 1933, overtaken by "unification". The "combine", led by Albert Stanley, Lord Ashfield, had won the battle.

The Police Attitude

Mention has been made in Volume One of the attitude of the Metropolitan Police towards the horse tramways when they were in the ascendant. When the LCC took control and electrified, the Council expected the police to respond in a more positive "modern" manner. They were wrong! The police became, if anything, even more difficult to deal with. It resulted in Mr. Fell, together with members of the Council, complaining in 1912 to the Home Secretary of the cavalier manner in which the LCC was being treated by the Commissioner of Police, and asking for an urgent meeting, in an attempt to put the matter right.

At this meeting, it was stressed that the LCC was the tramway authority for the area, and that it operated the tramways as a statutory right; that it should be allowed to construct and work the lines in the best way possible, and with the co-operation of the police - not its obstruction. Other contentious matters were the opposition of the police to:-
1. the operation of coupled cars and trailer cars;
2. the formation of queues by waiting passengers;
3. the arrangements made to teach learner motormen;
4. the removal of disabled cars (and other vehicles) from the tram tracks after accidents, even when there was no involvement by a tramcar;
5. the carriage of standing passengers;
6. the display of printed faretables in the saloons of cars;
7. the provision of used ticket boxes on cars;
8. the practice of the police in attempting to have stopping places rearranged, usually to the advantage of the London General Omnibus Company;
9. the construction of a lay-by track at Hill Street, Peckham;
10. the opposition to four-track running on Dog Kennel Hill while track work was still going on;
11. the attempt to induce the Council to alter the position of the plough-shift at Lea Bridge Road.

Things reached such a pitch in 1913 when motormen and conductors were being harrassed, by being accused of all kinds of misdemeanours - real or imaginary - and having any comments made by them "being taken down and used in evidence ...", that Mr. Fell issued an instruction that staff were not to make any comment of any kind to police officers on any occasion. He insisted that this was to protect tramwaymen against police action. Any interviews with police would, in future, take place at the LCC Tramways Office, and nowhere else, in the presence of a Tramways Official. He also insisted that any statements made in the privacy of the office would not be used against the men for purposes of prosecution.

It was at this time that the police were at loggerheads with the LCC over the use of trailer cars. At the same time, the London United Tramways were also applying for similar powers, to which the police objected in their customary way, with the following comment made by a senior officer:- " ... to run trailers ... would cause obstruction."

An Editorial in the 9th April 1914 issue of "Tramway & Railway World" pointed out " ... and yet ... if he looked out of his door ... he would see them in use, with no obstruction". And so it went on, until greater problems thrown up by the Great War finally gave the police more important matters to deal with. But after the cessation of hostilities, the same old attitude began to emerge once again, with the Council almost always defeated in its desire to provide a comprehensive tramway system, while the police were usually to be seen on the side of the opposition. Sadly, this attitude did not change while the tramways were under the control of the LCC.

H. M. Railway Inspectorate

Authority was vested in the Board of Trade in 1840 to appoint Inspectors to carry out the duties involved in the inspection of railways, railway stations, buildings and works. This duty was extended in 1870 to tramways, with the passage of the Tramways Act of that year. Thereafter, all tramways in the Kingdom - and many outside also - were favoured with the mandatory visit of one of H. M. Inspectors, who were all Officers of the Royal Engineers. In later years, although they were drawn from the military, upon taking up appointments, they also became civil servants, although retaining their military ranks.

It was the duty of these men to check thoroughly all aspects of construction of the tracks, vehicles and, if mechanically operated, their means of propulsion. In the case of electric tramways, they would have the assistance of electrical engineers who were also civil servants attached to the Railway Inspectorate of the Board (later, the Ministry of Transport). After carrying out an inspection, a formal report would be issued, which would either recommend the issue of a Certificate authorising the use of the line or lines for public patronage, or, occasionally, refusing to issue such a Certificate until certain remedial work was undertaken and a further inspection carried out.

Some of those who had close links with the LCC Tramways and its predecessors were:-

Colonel W. Yolland,	Colonel F. H. Rich,
Major-General C. S. Hutchinson,	Colonel Sir Francis Marindin,
Lt. Colonel Sir H. Arthur Yorke,	Lt. Colonel P. G. Von Donop,
Colonel Sir John W. Pringle,	Lt. Colonel E. Druitt,
Lt. Colonel G. L. Hall,	Lt. Colonel Sir Alan H. L. Mount,
Colonel A. H. C. Trench.	

General Acts of Parliament

There were a number of Acts of Parliament which had an indirect bearing on the formation and operation of tramways in what was to become the area ultimately controlled by the London County Council. These were:-

The Metropolis Management Act, 1855, by which was established the Metropolitan Board of Works.

The Local Government Act, 1888, by which the London County Council was established, formally taking office on 21st March 1889.

The Local Government Act, 1899, by which were established the 28 Metropolitan Borough Councils.

In addition to these, the Tramways Act, 1870 fully controlled the proposal, construction, operation and even abandonment of all tramway undertakings in the metropolis. The only exceptions to this were the original Acts of Parliament obtained to enable the North Metropolitan Tramways Company, the Metropolitan Street Tramways Company and the Pimlico, Peckham & Greenwich Street Tramways Company to be founded in 1869.

Chapter 34
The North Metropolitan Tramways Company
1869-1897

The Beginning

The area known as London north of the Thames and within the boundaries of the Metropolitan Board of Works, was in the County of Middlesex until the formation of the London County Council in 1889, and was divided physically from the neighbouring county of Essex by the River Lea (or Lee, as referred to in older documents). The river rises near Sundon Park, north of Luton in Bedfordshire, meanders in a south-easterly direction towards Welwyn Garden City, next taking an easterly course, skirting Hertford and Ware. It then turns south to pass through what is now known as the Lea Navigation, and finally empties into the Thames at Poplar.

Originally a tidal waterway, the Lea was eventually enclosed by a system of earthworks, wall, locks and gates, by which it was divided into manageable streams, instead of being quite untamed at times of exceptional flood and spring tides, when it was, in places, almost a mile wide.

The Roman cities of Camulodunum (Colchester) and Londinium (London) were connected by a highway which led to either side of the River Lea at a point now known as Old Ford, which was superseded in the twelfth century by a new crossing a little to the south. The first causeway and bridge was built there over the river, and it is believed, took its name, Bow Bridge, from the shape of its arch. Over the centuries, several structures have in turn served to provide this crossing. The road out from London passed through Whitechapel, which, due to its proximity to the City, became an important centre of trade, in particular that of garden produce, hay and straw, the market for which remained in use until 1928.

On the western side of the Lea, early settlements were established, one of the best known probably being at Waltham Cross in Hertfordshire, immediately opposite Waltham Abbey in Essex. Moving south into Middlesex, Enfield Wash, Edmonton and Tottenham were all well established villages alongside the river, with Stoke Newington and Shoreditch being at the outer limit of influence of London. These two, with Islington, Finsbury, Holborn, Highgate, Hoxton and Hampstead, all well trodden ancient areas, constituted the villages surrounding the north side of the city. It is these, within metropolitan Middlesex, that this study is concerned at this stage.

Holborn, an area immediately to the west of the City of London, has had many connections with London for almost a millenium. Until 1867, when they were demolished, Holborn Bars restricted the way to and from the city. Most of the Inns of Court, the "homes" of many persons engaged in the legal profession, are situated in Holborn, with one, Gray's Inn, concerned with this tramway history. The district is named after the River Holebourne, which was one part (or arm) of the Fleet River, today enclosed as part of the storm water sewer network.

Shoreditch lies a little to the north-east of the City and has always had close links with it. Shoreditch, a corruption of "Soerdiches", was named after the Lords of the Manor in the time of King Edward III. At one time it was in possession of a Benedictine nunnery, which is commemorated by the present-day Holywell Lane. The Parish Church is dedicated to St. Leonard, the first edifice being founded in, or just before the beginning of the thirteenth century.

Hoxton, formerly known as Hogsden and variations on that name, is to the north of Shoreditch and lies between the New North Road on the west side and Kingsland Road on the east, while Stepney, otherwise known by the ancient name of "Stibenhethe" (among others) is to the east of the City. The Tower of London, Whitechapel and Limehouse are within the area. Bethnal Green lies to the north-east of Stepney, while Poplar, until 1817, was a hamlet and an appendage of Stepney.

Finsbury, Highbury, Stoke Newington and Hackney, all one-time villages surrounding the City, are now inner suburbs, while Finsbury Park, several miles to the north of Finsbury, was just outside the metropolitan area when purchased by the Metropolitan Board of Works. After landscaping, the park had cost about £16,000.

Stamford Hill, about four miles north of the City, lies on rising ground at the intersection of the Upper Clapton - Finsbury Park and London - Cambridge roads. After the formation of the LCC, it became the most northerly point in the county. It was at this prominent place that it was supposed the Lord Mayor and Corporation of the City of London met King James I on his way to London in 1603.

In the middle years of the nineteenth century, the population of metropolitan Middlesex, and of the westernmost parts of Essex had increased considerably, the villages becoming towns, and in some cases it became almost impossible to tell where one community ended and the next began, such was the rate of building. It was in these districts that the North Metropolitan Tramways Company made its first proposals for the "laying down of trams".

The Formation of the Company

In the first instance, the proposed company was referred to only by the title "The Metropolitan Tramways", and proposals were made which were eventually accepted by the Metropolitan Board of Works, the Board of Trade and Parliament. Promoted by an Anglo-American syndicate, the undertaking had as its founders John Fox, James Frazer, Nathan Randolph Vail, Charles Francis McDonald and John Thomas Pagan, together with "other persons and corporations who have already subscribed or shall subscribe".

At one of several meetings held early in the summer of 1869, Messrs. M. C. Fisher and D. Parrish Jnr, trading as Fisher & Parrish, agreed to undertake the construction of the first of the proposed lines. At the same time, the London General Omnibus Company agreed to provide the necessary horses. The first directors of the new company were three of the founders, Frazer, McDonald and Pagan, while the engineer was George Hopkins. At a meeting held on 30th September 1869 at which John Weston, a newly appointed director took the chair, Benjamin Broughton and James Corrigan accepted directorships.

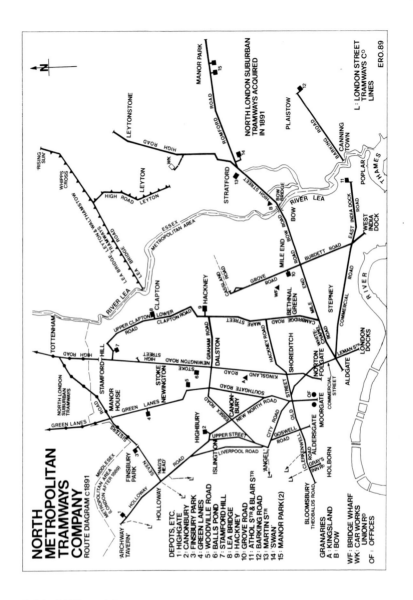

NORTH METROPOLITAN TRAMWAYS COMPANY
ROUTE DIAGRAM c1891

ERO.89

L: LONDON STREET TRAMWAYS Co LINES

NORTH LONDON SUBURBAN TRAMWAYS ACQUIRED IN 1891

DEPOTS, ETC.
1: HIGHGATE
2: CANONBURY
3: FINSBURY PARK
4: GREEN LANES
5: WOODVILLE ROAD
6: BALLS POND
7: STAMFORD HILL
8: LEA BRIDGE
9: HACKNEY
10: GROVE ROAD
11: ATHOL STR & BLAIR STR
12: BARKING ROAD
13: MARTIN STR
14: 'SWAN'
15: MANOR PARK(2)

GRANARIES
A: KINGSLAND
B: BOW

WF: BRIDGE WHARF
WK: CAR WORKS
      UNION RD
OF: OFFICES

Original Bills and Acts

During the presentation to the Metropolitan Board of Works and Parliament in 1869 of the first Bill, the contents were commented upon by the Engineer to the Metropolitan Board, J. W. Bazalgette, in the following terms:- "Metropolitan Tramways, There are two routes proposed by this Bill, the first from Upper Holloway, along the Islington and City Roads to Finsbury Pavement, and the second from High Street, Whitechapel to Stratford. The length of these lines together is sixteen miles".

Section 5 of the Bill described the proposed tramways:-

Nos. 1 and 1A. 2 mls. long, commencing in Archway Road, about 8 ch. from its junction with Junction Road, passing along Archway Road and Holloway Road, terminating in Holloway Road near Highbury Place.

No. 2. 1 ml. 2.40 ch. long, from Nos. 1 and 1A, along Holloway Road, Upper Street and High Street, Islington, terminating opposite "The Angel" Hotel.

No. 2A. 2 f. 6 ch. long, from a junction with No. 2 in Upper Street, from Holloway Road to Barnsbury Street.

No. 2B. 2.50 ch. long, a passing place in Upper Street just south of Cross Street.

No. 2C. 2 f. 7.50 ch. long, from a junction with No. 2 at the north end of Islington Green and terminating opposite "The Angel" Hotel.

No. 3. 6 f. 3.50 ch. long, commencing in Seven Sisters Road by Stroud Green Lane and passing along Seven Sisters Road into Holloway Road, terminating by a junction with No. 1A about 0.50 ch. south of the junction of Seven Sisters Road with Holloway Road.

No. 3A. 1 f. 7 ch. long, commencing in Seven Sisters Road by a junction with No. 3 near Campbell Road, passing along Seven Sisters Road and terminating by a junction with No. 3 near Russell Road.

No. 3B. 1 f. 9.20 ch. long, commencing in Seven Sisters Road by a junction with No. 3 near Hornsey Road, passing along Seven Sisters Road into Holloway Road and terminating by a junction with No. 1 just south of the junction of the two roads.

Nos. 4 and 4A. 1 ml. 3 f. 1.60 ch. long, commencing at the termination of Nos. 2 and 2C at "The Angel", passing along High Street, City Road and Finsbury Square (west side), terminating in Finsbury Place.

Nos. 5 and 5A. 2 mls. 4 f. 4 ch. long, commencing in Whitechapel Road just east of Church Lane, passing along Whitechapel Road, Mile End Road, Bow Road and High Street, Bow, terminating in High Street about 7 ch. east of Bow Churchyard.

No. 6. 1 ml. 3 ch. long, from the end of Nos. 5 and 5A, passing along High Street, Bow Bridge, High Street, Stratford and Stratford Broadway, terminating near the Gurney Memorial Fountain just west of Stratford Churchyard.

No. 6A. 3 ch. long, a passing place in High Street, Stratford, to the east side of Bow Bridge.

No. 6B. 3 ch. long, a passing place in High Street, Stratford, at the point where the road is carried over the northern outfall sewer.

No. 6C. 3 ch. long, a passing place in High Street, Stratford, where the road is carried on a bridge near the Channelsea River.

No. 6D. 6 ch. long, commencing 6 ch. from the termination of No. 6, passing along Stratford Broadway and terminating there by a junction with No. 6 at its termination.

Section 25 recommended that the capital of the company be £180,000 in 18,000 shares of £10 each.

Section 37 called for powers to borrow on mortgage a maximum sum of £60,000, and of that sum, to borrow from time to time a sum not exceeding £15,000 in respect of every £45,000 of capital.

Section 60 proposed that "not withstanding anything in this Act or the Acts incorporated herewith contained, the Company shall not be chargeable nor charged with the payment in respect of passengers carried upon and along the said Tramways, of the Government duty on passengers payable by Railway Companies, but in lieu thereof the carriages and horses used by the Company upon the said Tramways shall be subject to the payment of the same duties as are charged and levied upon Metropolitan Stage Carriages".

Of the first three tramway companies to gain a foothold in the Metropolis, the North Metropolitan Tramways Company was to become the largest in size and in area of operations, eventually embracing virtually the whole of the eastern half of Middlesex and covering most of the main roads eastwards into west Essex. It was brought into existence by the passage of the above-written Bill through Parliament, which emerged as one of three Private Acts.

The North Metropolitan Tramways Act, 1869 (32 & 33 Vic. cap. ci), received the Royal Assent on 12th July 1869, empowering the company to construct and work the tramways numbered 5, 5A, 6, 6A, 6B, 6C and 6D as detailed in the Bill, covering the route between Whitechapel and Stratford.

A total of 85 sections or clauses covered the whole of the legal requirements demanded by Parliament, of which:-
No. 6 stated "that the width of the rails be laid at a distance (reckoning from the outer edge of each rail) of five feet three inches from each other and maintained in such a manner that the uppermost surface of the rail shall be on a level with the surface of the street".
No. 42 authorised the company to raise capital to the extent of £90,000, all of which was to consist of shares of a value of £10 each.
Nos. 43 to 52 dealt with the issue of shares.
No. 54 allowed the company to borrow on mortgage a maximum of £22,500, with regulations on how that sum was to be raised.
No. 67 laid down the conditions regarding the collection of fares, which were to be charged at the rate of one penny a mile, with the proviso that the company may, for any less distance than three miles, charge a fare of threepence.
No. 69 required that at least two carriages be run each way each morning and evening on weekdays, at times not later than seven in the morning and six in the evening for carrying artisans, mechanics and daily labourers at fares not exceeding one halfpenny a mile, but at a minimum payment of one penny.
No. 81 provided for the future purchase of the undertaking by the road or street authorities after a period of twenty-one years, upon the terms of paying the full value of the tramways, works, materials, lands, buildings, property and goodwill of the company.

Even before any work started on the construction of the lines, the company, now a legal entity, placed a Bill before the Metropolitan Board of Works and Parliament for consideration in the 1870 Session. It contained a number of changes, one of which was to repeal many of the sections contained in the Act of 1869 and replace them with fresh ones. This was done partly as the result of changes made in legislation due to the passage of the Tramways Act, 1870; partly to introduce extensions to the proposed system; partly to clarify the somewhat confused situation which had developed over the description of the track gauge, which was now written as being 4 ft. 8½ in.; and partly to give this company, in common with the other two pioneer companies south of the River Thames an extra seven years' security of tenure in exchange for giving up some of their financial assurances which could be expected at the end of the period.

The North Metropolitan Tramways Act, 1870 (33 & 34 Vic. cap. clxxii) received the Royal Assent on 10th August 1870, which authorised the following tramways:-
Nos. 1 and 1A. Each 1 ml. 4 f. 4.50 ch. long, in Holloway Road, from Archway Road to a point near the end of Liverpool Road.
No. 2. 1 ml. 3 f. 3.25 ch. long, from No. 1, passing along Holloway Road, Upper Street and High Street, Islington, terminating near the

An original car of the North Metropolitan Company stands at "Archway Tavern". This scene was soon to be altered when the hostelry was rebuilt.
(Courtesy: J. H. Price)

end of White Lion Street.

No. 2A. 6 f. 4.50 ch. long, from No. 1A, passing along Holloway Road and Upper Street, terminating by a junction with No. 2 at or near the end of Barnsbury Street.

No. 2B. 4 ch. long, a passing place just south of Cross Street.

No. 2C. 2 f. 4 ch. long, commencing by a junction with No. 2 at the north end of Islington Green, terminating in High Street near the end of White Lion Street.

Nos. 3 and 3A. Each 1 ml. 2 f. 6.25 ch. long, commencing in Holloway Road at the north end of Liverpool Road by junctions with Nos. 1 and 1A, passing along Liverpool Road and terminating in High Street.

Nos. 4 and 4A. Each 1 ml. 3 f. 5.25 ch. long, commencing in High Street, Islington by junctions with Nos. 2 and 2A, passing along High Street and City Road, Finsbury Square (north side) and terminating in Finsbury Place.

Nos. 5 and 5A. Each 2 f. 7.50 ch. long, from Nos. 4 and 4A, along Finsbury Place, Finsbury Place South, Finsbury Pavement, Moorgate and Moorgate Street, terminating at or near the south end of Moorgate Street.

Nos. 6 and 6A. Each about 6 f. 3.50 ch. long, commencing in Seven Sisters Road at Stroud Green Lane, passing along Seven Sisters Road into Holloway Road, terminating just south of the intersection by a junction with Nos. 1 and 1A.

Nos. 7 and 7A. Each about 3 f. 3 ch. long, commencing in Seven Sisters Road at its junction with Holloway Road, by junctions with Nos. 6 and 6A, passing into and along Park Road and terminating at or near its junction with Camden Road.

Nos. 9 and 9A. Each about 2 f. 9 ch. long, commencing in Whitechapel Road near Church Lane by junctions with Nos. 5 and 5A (1869 Act), passing along Whitechapel Road, Whitechapel High Street and Aldgate High Street, terminating at or near the end of the Minories. ·

No. 9B. 2 ch. long, a short junction in Whitechapel High Street, commencing by a junction with No. 9 just west of Osborn Street, terminating by a junction with No. 9A opposite Osborn Street (a crossover).

Nos. 10 and 10A. Each 1 ml. 1.75 ch. long, (in substitution for Nos. 6,

6A, 6B, 6C and 6D of the 1869 Act), commencing in High Street, Bow, at the end of Nos. 5 and 5A, passing along High Street and over Bow Bridge, along High Street and Stratford Broadway, terminating just west of the Gurney Memorial Fountain.

No. 10B. 2 ch. long, a short junction in Stratford Broadway, at a point 2 ch. from the termination of the tramway.

Nos. 11 and 11A. Each about 1 ml. 2 f. long, commencing in Stratford Broadway by junctions with Nos. 10 and 10A, passing into High Street, The Grove, Maryland Point and Leytonstone Road, terminating in Low Leyton in the County of Essex in Leytonstone Road opposite "The Plough and Harrow" Inn.

Nos. 12 and 12A. Each 1 ml. 1 f. 1.50 ch. long, commencing in Stratford Broadway by a junction with Nos. 10 and 10A, passing along Stratford Broadway, High Street and Romford Road, terminating opposite the "Princess Alice" Inn at the end of Woodgrange Road.

No. 13. 2 f. 2 ch. long, commencing in Leytonstone Road by Union Lane, along Union Lane, terminating on land at Mornington Terrace, about 1 ch. from Union Lane.

No. 13A. 6.50 ch. long, commencing in Union Lane by a junction with No. 13 at Birkbeck Road, passing into and terminating in the land on the north-west side of Birkbeck Road about 1 ch. from the road.

No. 13B. 2 ch. long, a junction and curve commencing in Leytonstone Road by a junction with No. 11A just south of Union Lane, passing to and forming a junction with No. 11, then curving to and terminating in Union Lane by a junction with No. 13 near the end of the lane.

Section 31 of the Act clarified the position regarding purchase by the "local authorities" in the several areas through which the company's lines were to pass. The original intention was for the Local Boards and Vestries to carry out purchase, but as this company had powers to operate tramways within the area of the Metropolitan Board of Works and outside it, notice had to be taken of the rights of local authorities in Essex. In both cases, the security of tenure held by the company and now extended to twenty-eight years, meant that no enforced sale and purchase could take place until at least 1897.

Section 32 stated that "where any tramway in any district has been opened for traffic for a period of six months, the company may, with the consent of the Board of Trade, sell their undertaking in such district to any person, persons, corporation or company, or to the local authority of such district ..."

Section 33 extended the terms of Sections 67, 68, 70, 71 and 72 of the Act of 1869 to this Act, which authorised the company to charge fares and make charges for their services.

Section 34, dealing with the operation of special cars for artisans, mechanics and daily labourers, amended that of 1869, by stating that "the company shall, and they are hereby required, at all times after the opening of their tramways for public traffic, to run carriages each way every morning in the week and every evening in the week (Sundays, Christmas Day and Good Fridays always excepted), at such hours, not being later than seven in the morning or earlier than six in the evening respectively ... for artisans, mechanics and daily labourers, at such fares as may be from time to time fixed by the Board of Trade ..."

Section 52 increased the sums which the company were allowed to raise in capital to that not exceeding £240,000 in addition to the sums allowed by the Act of 1869.

Section 64 increased mortgage borrowing to an absolute maximum of £60,000, subject to certain conditions.

There was one minor proposal made by another group who set out to try to obtain an Act to allow it to lay tramways into the City of London at Aldgate. Known as the East London Tramways, the proposal was that a line was to commence near the "Toll Gate Inn" and take it along Commercial Road East and through a new street at Whitechapel, then into Whitechapel High Street and Aldgate High Street to the Minories; thence along the Minories to Little Tower Hill, then by a single line along George Street, and by another single line along Postern Row, both terminating at Great Tower Hill by Trinity Square. The proposed tramways were to be about five miles in length and of a gauge of 4 ft. 8½ in. and were to be laid on a level with the streets. Works were to be completed within two years, while each section was to be completed within six weeks after the street had been opened up. This proposal did not succeed.

First Construction

Work commenced in Whitechapel Road in December 1869 with, initially, one gang of about 40 men which, after about a week was increased to four gangs, making in all about 150 men employed by the site manager, M.W. Anderson, for Messrs. Fisher & Parrish, the main contractor. This firm hailed from New York and had obtained contracts of this nature in the USA. The office of the contractor was on the east side of Bow Bridge, over which a single track was laid to enable

One of the company cars, rebuilt with a "garden" seat top deck is seen passing along Whitechapel Road.   *(Commercial view)*

the cars, when put into service, to stand in their yard and from there to be drawn to and from the temporary terminus. By February 1870 about 200 men were at work on the line which, by the middle of April, was complete between Whitechapel and Bow Bridge. On Monday 9th May 1870, after an inspection had been carried out by George Hopkins on 25th April, this section was opened to traffic.

The opening may best be described in the words used in Herepath's Railway Journal of Saturday 14th May 1870. "On Monday morning the Company opened 2½ miles of line from Whitechapel Church to Bow Bridge, a double line. The rails are slightly below the level of the surrounding pavement. Vehicles can drive across the lines at any angle without being in the slightest degree incommodated (sic) by its presence and junctions are made by fixed points (no switches to go wrong). There are single line stubs at terminals.

"Cars are built by Stephenson of New York, very light and for twenty two passengers inside and twenty four out. Car bodies are 16 ft. long, with 4 ft. platforms. There are four wheels with india-rubber blocks as springs ... windows have glazed sashes and venetian blinds. A light circular ladder to the roof is fastened by hooks in rings to receive them. The break (sic) is to the driver's right hand.

"Horses are harnessed by collars and traces to two splinter bars pivoted to a cross piece and a common pole secured to the car by a bolt dropped through an opening ... the horses are walked round one side at the terminus, and the ladder is carried round the other. Fare for the whole journey until 7 a.m. is 1d, and after this, 2d, with a 1d stage between".

The Engineer employed similar methods of construction to those used on the Metropolitan Street Tramways and the Liverpool Tramways, of which he was also engineer. The design consisted of a wrought-iron grooved rail bar, 4 inches wide and $1\frac{7}{8}$ inches deep, and weighed 45 lbs/yard. This was laid upon a continuous Baltic timber sleeper, 4 inches wide and 6 inches deep. These were set at intervals into

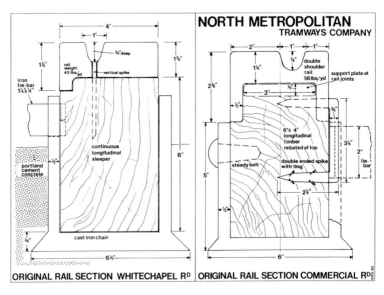

ORIGINAL RAIL SECTION WHITECHAPEL R^D | ORIGINAL RAIL SECTION COMMERCIAL R^D

cast-iron chairs, on the insides of which were dovetailed cross-ties of iron to maintain the gauge. The rails were held in place on the sleepers by countersunk headed iron spikes hammered vertically through holes in the bottom of the rail grooves. The inner edge of each rail was corrugated.

To form the foundation of the track, an excavation to a depth of nine inches was required, which extended for two feet on either side of the outer rails. Longitudinal trenches were formed, one for each rail, about 16 inches wide and nine inches deep. These were filled with concrete and made up to the level of the excavated ground to form footings for the rails, which, on their sleepers, were packed up to final level by ramming concrete beneath them. Finally, the paving setts were bedded on a layer of sand and then grouted and rammed.

The first five cars delivered were sufficient to provide about a ten-minute service on the line, with the first one running about 5 a.m. and the last just before midnight. Horses were supplied by the LGOC under contract at the rate of 6¾d per car mile and worked between 14 and 16 miles a day, doing 3 to 4 hours on the road. Eleven horses were required to work each car; five pairs on duty and one spare. The working life of an animal was between four and five years. Contract horsing continued for almost seven years.

As this was one of the "experimental" lines authorised by Parliament and built under the terms of the first Act, no mention appears to have been made of the need for a compulsory inspection to be carried out by a representative of the Board of Trade. It seems, therefore, that the inspection made by the engineer was considered at that time to be sufficient.

The First Extension

The extension authorised by the Act of 1870 allowed a line to be built across Bow Bridge and along High Street to Stratford Broadway, all of which was in Essex and outside the boundaries of the Metropolitan Board of Works. All was double line, apart from one short single section of about 160 yards not far from the terminus. However, the planned extension along Romford Road was not built at this time. At the London end, a short extension of about 29 chains was also built, which effectively brought the tramway up to the boundary of the City of London at Aldgate.

Messrs. Fisher & Parrish constructed the extensions, which were both completed at the end of 1871. This allowed a through journey of just over four miles, worked at a fare of 3d, with 2d and 1d stages between, while the workman fares were 2d and 1d.

In conjunction with the extension to Stratford, a traffic office was established in a building known as Surinam House, not far from "The Swan" public house at Stratford Broadway. Mr. John Corrigan, one of the directors was put in charge, and had as his assistant and traffic superintendent, Mr. George Ludbrook. However, after about six months, John R. Maples took over the duty.

The tracks on the short extension westwards from Whitechapel Road to Aldgate had to be laid near to the kerbs on either side of the road, as the area in the centre was used for the purpose of carrying on a daily hay market. This continued to operate right through the horse tramway era and well into the electric car age, not being finally given up until 1928, when the opportunity was taken to re-align the tracks into the more usual position in the centre of the road.

Early structural methods which had been used on these pioneer lines, employing the top-spiked rail used in conjunction with a timber sub-structure was very soon to be questioned, both for its mechanical strength and its lasting qualities. Even so, it was to be several years before any great change was made, when the company, along with others found it necessary to renew quite considerable lengths of the original lines. This, in turn, was to cause considerable expense, which the pioneer undertakings found difficult to bear. The result was a long drawn-out programme of track reconstruction, much of it carried out on a piecemeal basis.

A busy scene in High Street, Stoke Newington. Both cars are working on the Stamford Hill & Holborn service. (Commercial view)

The 1871 Bill and Act

The next Bill was submitted to Parliament with eleven lines listed. They were divided into a number of "tramways" of which there were 34, having a total length of approximately 49 miles.

The North Metropolitan Tramways Act, 1871 (34 & 35 Vic. cap. clxxix) received the Royal Assent on 31st July 1871, and gave the company powers to form the following nine lines of tramway out of the eleven sought:-

The Kingsland Road Route; Nos. 2, 2A, 3 and 3A. 3 mls. 1 f. 7.25 ch. long, from Shoreditch Church, along Kingsland Road to Stamford Hill.

The Finsbury Park (Manor House) Route; Nos. 4, 4A, 5 and 5A. 3 mls. 3 f. 1.25 ch. long, from City Road at the junction with the authorised tramway, along East Road, New North Road, Mintern Street, Bridport Place, Mildmay Park and Green Lanes to Manor House.

The Islington & Kingsland Route; Nos. 6, 6A, 7 and 7A. 1 ml. 4 f. 7.5 ch. long, from Upper Street at the junction with the authorised tramway, along Essex Road and Balls Ponds Road to Kingsland High Street (a junction with the Kingsland Road route).

The Old Street Route; Nos. 15, 15A, 8, 8A, 8B, 8C and 8D. 7 f. 7.5 ch. long, from Goswell Road at the junction with the authorised tramway, along Old Street to Shoreditch Church.

The Hackney Route; Nos. 9 and 9A. 1 ml. 1 ch. long, from Shoreditch Church, by a junction with the Kingsland Road route, along Hackney Road to Cambridge Road, at the junction with the authorised tramway.

The Mile End & Clapton Route; Nos. 10, 10A, 11 and 11A. 4 mls. 2 f. long, from Mile End Road by a junction with the existing tramway, along Cambridge Road, Mare Street and Lower and Upper Clapton

Stephenson eight-window car No. 261, with upper deck "knifeboard" seating, waits at Stamford Hill for the conductor to give the signal to begin the journey to Holborn. (Courtesy: L T Museum 1662C)

Company built car, No. 477, of seven-window body type with upper deck "garden" seats, is standing outside Stamford Hill depot prior to taking up service on the Moorgate Street line. (Courtesy: L T Museum H16725)

An early view of a seven-window "knifeboard" car, travelling along Mare Street, Hackney towards Upper Clapton. (Courtesy: D.W.K.Jones)
(H. Nicol collection)

Roads to Stamford Hill, by a junction with the Kingsland Road route.
The Limehouse & Victoria Park Route; Nos. 12, 12A, 12B, and 12C.
1 ml. 5 f. 2.75 ch. long, from Old Ford Road, along Grove Road and Burdett Road to East India Dock Road, at a junction with the authorised tramway.
The Commercial Road Route; Nos. 13 and 13A. 2 mls. 6 f. 3 ch. long, from Whitechapel High Street at a junction with the existing tramway, along Commercial Road and East India Dock Road to East India Dock Gates (Robin Hood Lane).
The Islington & Post Office Route; Nos. 14, 14A and 14B. 6 f. 6 ch. long, from City Road by a junction with the authorised tramway, along Goswell Road to Aldersgate Street.

Two lines which were deleted from the Bill were:-
No. 10, approximately 2 f. long, from Moorgate Street (authorised tramway), along Princes Street to Bank, double track throughout.
No. 11, approximately 1 f. 5 ch. long, from the authorised line in Aldgate High Street, double track to Jewry Street, then two single lines, one to Leadenhall Street, the other to Fenchurch Street.
Section 22 of the Act states "the Company shall not in the Commercial Road East, from the west side of the Britannia Bridge carrying that road over the Limehouse Cut to a point 80 yds. eastwards of the east side of Church Row, construct more than one line of tramway without the consent in writing of the Board of Works for the Limehouse District, and the Company shall construct such tramway so that there shall be a clear width of not less than 3 ft. 6 in. between the present stone tramway and the rail of the tramway nearest thereto".

The First Board of Trade Inspection

The Board of Trade was advised on 17th July 1871 that the section between Islington Green and Ropemaker Street, Finsbury was available for inspection if the Board so desired. As previously mentioned, no definite arrangements had been made for the inspection of street

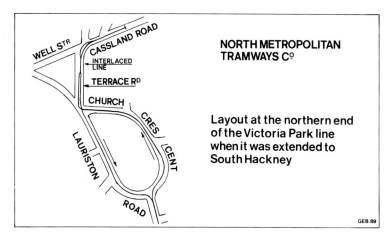

WELL S^TR
CASSLAND ROAD
INTERLACED LINE
TERRACE R^D
CHURCH
CRESCENT
LAURISTON
ROAD

NORTH METROPOLITAN TRAMWAYS C^O

Layout at the northern end of the Victoria Park line when it was extended to South Hackney

GEB.89

tramways by the Railway Inspectorate, as it had been anticipated that, as the company had to pay for the employment of clerks of works on behalf of the Metropolitan Board of Works, that would be sufficient to ensure that all work was up to standard.

However, Col. F. H. Rich of the Board of Trade thought otherwise, and he inspected the line on 19th July. In his report he stated that "grooved rails have been laid, are four inches broad and weigh 50 lbs per yard. The road is not in very good repair, being sunk on either side of the rails. But the tramway is in good working order and has been operating for the past three or four weeks". It was suggested that a certificate be issued, but at a subsequent conference held to decide upon a policy regarding "this novel subject", this was disallowed. It appears, however, that nobody told the company of the decision, and services continued for years, until December 1877 in fact, when it was "discovered that an omission" had occurred.

In the meantime, the solicitor for the company had been taken to task for allowing the line to be opened prematurely, but it appears that the attitude of the company was that, according to the terms of the relevant Act of Parliament, no mention was made of an inspection, and therefore, the view taken was that none was required. The Board of Trade, in conjunction with Parliament, however, had arranged to have a clause inserted in all Acts, requiring that all new lengths of tramway be inspected, reported upon and authorised for use before any public services were operated.

Further Construction

A report from the Engineer's Department of the Metropolitan Board of Works on 27th September 1871 stated:-
"Notice of the intention of the North Metropolitan Tramways Company to commence certain works authorised by their Act is given. Referred to in the Notice are so much of their lines numbered 6 and 6A as passed through the Seven Sisters Road and Holloway Road in the Parish of Islington.
"Under the authority of the Board of 11th ult. (Nos. 13 and 42) I signify their approval to the carrying out of the above works under the usual conditions that they be executed so far as required by the Companies' Acts to the satisfaction of the officers of the Board and at the sole

cost inclusive of the requisite supervision of the company.

(Signed) J. W. Bazalgette, Engineer."

Eventually, with 11¼ miles of lines open, the company, in its traffic return for the week ending 13th April 1872, stated that £1,737. 4.10d had been taken in fares, and it had every hope that, with the continuing extension of the network, this figure would be substantially increased later in the year. It was also said that the Commercial Road, Kingsland Road and Stamford Hill lines "were nearly complete".

On 14th August, Capt. Tyler inspected the Camden Road and Park Road extensions of the joint North Metropolitan and London Street Tramways Companies. These had been authorised under an Act obtained by the London Street company, and built by their contractor, with the intention of connecting the two systems together. The junctions, however, were not made, due to a disagreement between the two undertakings. The North Metropolitan company paid for 3 f. 2.5 ch. of the work, with the London Street company being responsible for the remaining 2 f. 8.25 ch. of line.

Double-shouldered rails with side spikes were used, subject to the following specification:
Rails: 52 lbs/yard, with side flanges.
Wrought-iron tie bars 2 in. x ⅜ in. every 6 ft.
Cast iron "shoes" (chairs).
Occasional cross sleepers, 7 ft. x 6 in. x 4 in.
Continuous longitudinal fir sleepers 8 in. x 4 in. cross section.
Capt. Tyler authorised the use of the line.

The Commercial Road East Stone Tramway
(From "Engineering", 25th March 1870)

"This granite way, designed for loads being conveyed to and from the West India Docks and the City, is a single track way on the south side of the road to Whitechapel. The stones are 18 inches wide, with a 4-foot way in between; 12 inches thick. This way was designed and built by James Walker, Ll.D; F.R.S; L & E; etc (sic), one time President of the Institute of Civil Engineers, and since 1850, in the charge of J. B. Redman. There are 5,223 stones, 4 ft. long, of which 3,631 are of Aberdeen granite, with the remainder from Herm, Guernsey, Mount Sorrell and Jersey.

Over the years, there has been continuous heavy traffic and a smooth ride is guaranteed, so much so, that by 1870, omnibuses and cabs, as well as many other vehicles are driven over the tramway. This information has been presented in an effort to show that if cast-iron 'trams' were used, a long life could be expected".

The East India Dock Line

The company laid the line to East India Dock during the summer of 1872. The section along Commercial Road as far as the beginning of East India Dock Road by Burdett Road was inspected by Capt. Tyler on 6th September and he made the following report:-
"This 2 ml. 6 f. 3 ch. line is all double with the exception of 80 yards at Limehouse Church where the road is only 30 ft. wide. Until August 1871, the road was in the hands of the Road Trustees, after which the various Vestries and the Whitechapel District Board of Works took control". After commenting on the differences in the various sections of road surface, he authorised the use of the tramway. The track, constructed by Fisher & Parrish, used rail of the double-shouldered

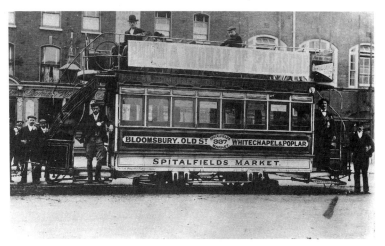

Car 337 stands at the Poplar terminus of the Bloomsbury service. This car has had the top deck converted to "garden" seating. (R. Elliott)

type. Messrs. Mowlem & Co. of Greenwich sub-contracted for paving, with each Vestry insisting upon the use of granite setts of a different size.

1. Whitechapel Road   3 in. x 9 in.
2. Vestry of St. George in the East   4 in. x 2 in.
3. Vestry of Mile End Old Town   3 in. x 7 in.
4. Limehouse District Board   4 in. x 7 in.
5. Poplar Board of Works   3 in. x 6 in.

More Lines Inspected

The next inspection was of the lines in Essex Road, Balls Pond Road, Stoke Newington Road, Kingsland Road and Old Street to City Road. The request was made by the company on 20th September 1872, and Capt. H. W. Tyler visited the lines on 14th October. Constructed by Messrs. Fisher & Parrish under the supervision of George Hopkins, the works were, according to the Inspector, "well carried out". Most of the lines were paved with granite cubes, except for about 170 yards outside Shoreditch Town Hall in Old Street, where Val de Travers asphalte macadam was used. Capt. Tyler authorised the use of the line and the certificate was issued on 17th October.

The last section to be completed in 1872 was the half-mile line along Goswell Road between "The Angel" Islington and Old Street. On 6th December, the secretary to the company, Frederick Mosley Watts, informed the Board of Trade that the work was complete and ready for inspection. On this occasion Col. Yolland was appointed to carry out this duty and visited the line on 16th December. In his written report of his findings, he wrote that the line appeared to be well constructed and, being satisfied with what he saw, he authorised its use for public traffic as from 19th December. There was, however, a one furlong section at the south end of the line, between Old Street and the City of London boundary near Fann Street which was still being dealt with by the contractor, and therefore could not be inspected until a later date.

The 1873 Proposals

The year 1873 saw an interesting crop of proposals from:-
  (a) The Corporation of the City of London.
     (The North East of London Tramways and Columbia Market Approaches)
  (b) The South Hackney Tramways.
  (c) The North Metropolitan Tramways Company.

(a) The Corporation of the City of London Bill

Entitled "The Columbia Market Approaches and Tramways", the Bill was intended to seek authorisation for the construction of an additional tramway to that authorised by the Columbia Market Approaches & Tramways Act, obtained in 1871.

The Columbia Market had been financed by and built for The Baroness Angela Georgina Burdett Coutts in 1866 as part of a comprehensive redevelopment of a large site near Hackney Road, not far from Shoreditch Church, which had been a notorious slum area. After completion, the market was presented as a free gift to the City of London Corporation, who then wished to obtain a direct connection to it from the Great Eastern Railway by means of a "tramway". Section 13 of the proposed Bill sought powers for the use of locomotive steam engines on the tramway. Due to the refusal of the Metropolitan Board of Works and Parliament to sanction proposals made by the North Metropolitan Tramways Company, described below, the City Corporation decided not to proceed with the tramways portion of the Bill.

(b) The South Hackney Tramways Bill

A proposal was put forward for the construction of a single line of tramway from the sanctioned line of the North Metropolitan Tramways in Cambridge Heath, to pass along Victoria Park Road to the Broadway, then along Grove Street and around the Church of St. John, South Hackney, (later Lauriston Road and Church Crescent). This too, was refused.

(c) The North Metropolitan Tramways Bill

The company was still looking to further expansion of the system and submitted the following proposals to the Metropolitan Board of Works for their consideration.
1. From the existing tramway at Goswell Road at Fann Street, along Aldersgate Street and St. Martin's le Grand to Newgate Street.
2. From the terminus of the tramway at Finsbury Place, along South Place, Eldon Street, Bloomfield Street and Liverpool Street to New Broad Street,
3. From the terminus of the proposed line at the south end of Moorgate Street, along Princes Street to the Bank, with a short branch line from the end of Moorgate Street into Lothbury.
4. Along Aldgate High Street from the terminus of the authorised tramway, together with a loop line around Aldgate Pump.
5. From the authorised tramway in Hackney Road at Shoreditch Church, along High Street Shoreditch to Norton Folgate at White Lion Street.

Due to the refusal of both the Board of Works and the City of London to allow any extensions to take place at that time, these were struck out of the Bill which had been presented to Parliament. This only left the company with power to extend the time allowed for the construction of certain of their already authorised lines. **The North Metropolitan Tramways Act, 1873 (36 Vic. cap. lxxviii),** Royal

Assent date 16th June 1873, gave an extension for one year from the date of expiry of the original powers, to the time allowed to complete the construction along Finsbury Place and Moorgate Street of Tramways Nos. 5 and 5A, together with portions of Tramways Nos. 9 and 9A in Aldgate High Street, authorised by the Act of 1870. The new date given was 10th August 1874.

More Completions

Further sections of the lines authorised by previous Acts were completed during 1873, with the Board of Trade Inspectors being called upon no less than four times during that year. On 31st March, the 5 f. 4 ch. of single line and loop along Grove Road from Mile End Road to Victoria Park was successfully inspected by Col. Yolland, and the certificate authorising its use was issued on the same day. Two weeks later, on 15th April, Col. Yolland inspected the section from Mile End Road, along Burdett Road to Commercial Road (this was missed out of the original request) and authorised the issue of a certificate.

On 18th June 1873, Col. Yolland inspected:-
(a). Goswell Road, from Old Street to City boundary, 41 ch.
(b). Old Street, from City Road to Goswell Road, 12 ch.
(c). Hackney Road, from Shoreditch Church to Cambridge Road, 1 ml. 3 ch.
(d). From Hackney Road, along Cambridge Road, Cambridge Heath Road, Mare Street, Lower and Upper Clapton Roads to Clapton Pond, 1 ml. 70 ch.
(e). Cambridge Road, from Hackney Road to Mile End Road, 75 ch. All lines were found to be in good order and a certificate was issued Finally, Col. Yolland inspected the 30 ch. length of line from Clapton Pond to Lea Bridge Road on 23rd July, and certified it fit for use.

No. 219, a Stephenson seven-window car with upper deck "knifeboard" seating, is seen in Upper Clapton Road.   (Courtesy: L T Museum 1663C)

Another of the eight-window cars, No. 244, fitted with corrugated metal dashplates, stands at Clapton terminus.   (Courtesy: L T Museum 1666C)

Management Changes

It was not long after the constitution of the Board that the first changes were made. After meetings of shareholders held on 27th December 1869 and 11th January 1870, it was agreed that the directors would be J. Weston (chairman), R. J. Carpenter, J. J. Corrigan, C. Fisher (contractor), G. Firth, J. Frazer, C. F. McDonald, E. W. Pearson and P. G. Pound. The remainder of the Board consisted of W. L. Mitchell (solicitor), G. Hopkins (engineer), G. W. Weston (auditor) and E. T. Weston (secretary). This was followed on 29th April 1870 by the election of Corrigan as managing director.

During the next two years, several changes took place. On 10th February 1871, by which time Firth had become chairman, George Richardson joined the board as director and deputy chairman, and B. Broughton became a director. This was followed on 4th February by the appointment of F. Mosley Watts as secretary, a position he was to hold for many years. Several more changes took place during the autumn of 1871, including the resignation of Richardson on 5th October. This was followed by the resignation of Firth on 3rd January 1872 and the re-election of Richardson as director and chairman. On 7th October 1872, C. Beard joined the board.

The next major change came on 1st February 1873, when Messrs. Corrigan and Beard resigned their positions, and J. M. Gillies (of the London Tramways Company) and John Goddard took their places.

On 22nd December 1873, a crisis of confidence in the company was seen to appear, when the directors were accused of not observing the terms of the Railways Act, 1860, with regard to the presentation of company accounts. The Board of Trade was drawn into the affair, and the company was told to comply with regulations. At a meeting held on the same day, two of the shareholders questioned the "excessive" sum of £21,000 per mile of double track which had been incurred in the construction of the first sections of the company's tramways. They demanded to see the company books and records, and also stated that they wished to see the Inspectors called in.   The management denied the accusation, at the same time refusing to allow the books to be inspected by the shareholders.   At subsequent meetings, the same question was directed towards the management, and it was several months before the difficulty was finally overcome.

The Act of 1874 and More Completions

The company presented a Bill in 1874 which, in essence, was only concerned with requesting a further extension of time in which to complete works authorised by the 1873 Act.   **The North Metropolitan Tramways Act, 1874 (37-38 Vic. cap. xlv)** received Royal Assent on 30th June 1874 and authorised an extension until 10th August 1877.

More lines were completed and opened during 1874 and 1875.   The lines in East Road, New North Road, Mintern Street, Bridport Place, Southgate Road, Mildmay Park, Stoke Newington Green and Green Lanes as far as Highbury New Park, all double track and granite paved, was satisfactorily inspected by Maj. Gen. Hutchinson on 9th May 1874, and the certificate was issued on 11th, even though the line had been opened to traffic on 7th.

The final section authorised by earlier Acts (except for several City-end lengths) was the 1 ml. 20 ch. line along Upper Clapton Road between Clapton Pond and Stamford Hill, which was inspected by Hutchinson on 3rd April 1875 and authorised for immediate use.   The certificate was received by the company on 5th April.

The 1877 Act

The next proposals were submitted to Parliament in 1877 and were partly aimed at filling up some of the gaps then existing in the network. There was, however, one line which was to cause controversy and was not proceeded with.   This was from Hart Street, Bloomsbury, along Theobalds Road, and then along "Kings Road, Liquor Pond Street, the authorised new street through Clerkenwell and Wilderness Row" (all this later became Clerkenwell Road).

The North Metropolitan Tramways (New Works) Act, 1877 (40-41 Vic. cap. cxi), received Royal Assent on 23rd July 1877 and authorised the construction of the following additional tramways:-
The Kingsland Road & City Route; Nos. 1, 1A to 1D, consisting of 7 ch. 11 yds. single and 4 f. 7 ch. 11 yds. double line, from Shoreditch Church to Bishopsgate Street, Without (5 ch. south of the end of Sun Street).
The Highbury & City Road Route; Nos. 2, 2A to 2H, consisting of 1 f. 8 ch. single and 7 f. 8 ch. double line, from the south end of Holloway Road, along St. Paul's Road, Canonbury Road, Canonbury Square and New North Road to Mintern Street.
The Limehouse & Hackney Route; Nos. 3, 3A to 3D, consisting of 3 f. 1 ch. 11 yds. single and 4 f. 2.5 ch. double line, from the junction of Grove Road and Old Ford Road, along Grove Road, Grove Street and Terrace Road to Cassland Road.
The Limehouse & Bethnal Green Route; Nos. 4, 4A to 4E, consisting of 1 ml. 3 ch. single and 1 f. 3.5 ch. double line, from Hackney Road, along Prospect Place, Bishops Road, Sewardstone Road, Bonners Road and Old Ford Road to Grove Road.
The Balls Pond & Hackney Route; Nos. 5, 5A to 5F, consisting of 1 f. 6.5 ch. single and 5 f. 5.7 ch. double line, from Balls Pond Road,

along Dalston Lane and Graham Road to Mare Street.

Tramway No. 6, a single line, 3 ch. long, in Cazenove Road.

It was stated that no part of Nos. 1, 1A and 1B south of Bethnal Green Road should be constructed without the consent of the Board of Works for the Whitechapel District, and that the terminus at Sun Street should not be built without the agreement of the Commons and Servers of the Court of Common Council for the City of London. A number of other conditions were imposed, a few of which are reproduced.

Section No. 5:- So much of Tramways Nos. 5 and 5A by which junctions are formed at Mare Street, shall be used only for access for the depot and not for through traffic, except with the consent of the Board of Works for the Hackney District.

Section No. 22:- Regarding the tramway in Prospect Place and Old Ford Road, the company shall not construct the lines in Prospect Place until it is widened. Three years are allowed in which to complete the work, the company to pay one-quarter of the cost, or £3,000.

Part of Section 24:- The company shall, as far as possible, work the Highbury and City Route as part of the through route between City and Upper Holloway. The company shall not use the tramways at Highbury Corner as a terminal stopping place.

The company had, in most cases, to pay for laying granite cubes or setts (or do it themselves) for the whole width of the roads, or in the case of Hackney and St. Mary, Stoke Newington, a 20 ft. width for single lines and 28 ft. for double. The raising of additional capital up to £80,000 in £10 shares was also authorised.

On completion, the various sections were completed on the dates shown and authorised as fit to be used:-

Kingsland Road & City Route.
    14th October 1878 (part) by Maj. Gen. Hutchinson.
    5th August 1879 (part) by Maj. Gen. Hutchinson.

Highbury & City Road Route.
    25th March 1879 by Maj. Gen. Hutchinson.

Limehouse & Hackney Route.
    23rd July 1879 by Maj. Marindin.

Balls Pond & Hackney Route.
    5th August 1879 by Maj. Gen. Hutchinson.

Limehouse & Bethnal Green Route. Not built.

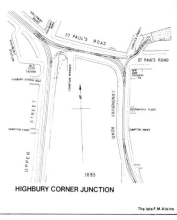

NORTH METROPOLITAN TRAMWAYS

1894

HIGHBURY CORNER JUNCTION

1893

T&LRS

The late F. M. Atkins

528

An Approach by the London Street Tramways Company

During 1875, the London Street Tramways Company appeared to be in a crisis. The financial return for the second half of the year showed an unsatisfactory trend, so much so that overtures were made to the North Metropolitan Tramways Company management in an effort to obtain their assistance in getting the undertaking into a healthy state once again.

In correspondence to John Morris, solicitor to the London Street Tramways, dated 15th November 1876, the North Metropolitan Company chairman, George Richardson made an offer to purchase the ailing undertaking and all its assets at a price sufficient to take up 10,000 LST Co. shares at a premium of 10/- for each £10 share, and the remaining 3,500 at par. He also offered to take over the 5% debenture debt up to the sum of £25,000, free from any liability whatsoever. As the shares of the London Street Company stood at £10 each, the offer made was effectively £140,000 for the complete undertaking, provided that the sale and purchase was satisfactorily completed by or on 30th June 1878. In the meantime, an offer was made to take a lease on the London Street Company, commencing on 1st January 1877 "if it can be legally done", at a rental sufficient to pay interest charges on the debentures and a dividend of £5 per cent on the capital of the company.

Lastly, Richardson noted that the track was apparently in a very bad condition, and this would have to be put right. He also stated that the offer made was a generous one, and that "we are paying an enormous price for it and especially so when we take into consideration that for four-fifths of your line we shall only have about seventeen years' possession, while the North Metropolitan have twenty-three years yet to run on the best portion of their lines".

The Board of Trade, however, discounted the leasing arrangement, stating that it was not a legal possibility and therefore could not take place. This put the whole idea in jeopardy, even though discussions went on for another two years. In November 1879 the company tried again, but this time it was suggested that a Parliamentary Bill be raised to allow the purchase to take place. Although preliminary negotiations were instituted, it got no further than that. In the end, the matter was dropped, the two companies agreeing instead to co-operate in connecting up several of their lines and running through services.

1877 Reconstruction

By 1877, much of the Northmet track was also in an extremely bad condition, due, in the main, to the original structure and the method of construction being of a primitive nature, where the top-spiked rails were laid on to timber longitudinals. Six years of use, coupled with the pounding received from the wheels of many other types of road vehicles running over and along the tramway, together with the detrimental effects suffered from the weather and a poor road surface, left the whole installation in such a state that complaints were levelled at the company from many sources.

Eventually, the Board of Trade Railway Inspector became involved, leading to Col. Rich of that department being appointed to investigate the complaints. On 21st December 1877, he made a particular check of the Ropemaker Street to Islington Green section, which was reported as being one of the worst parts affected, and discovered that many rails and spikes were fractured or broken, and that the roadway in places was between one and two inches lower than the level of the rails. He said that, in his opinion, while the tramway was not unfit for public traffic, it was potentially dangerous to other road users.

In his report of 5th January 1878, he stated that the line had been opened in 1871 prior to any inspection having taken place and, although it was later visited by himself, he declined to issue a certificate as "certain works were still outstanding". He also stated that, at the time, he forbade the company to open any other tramway without first having an official inspection undertaken. But, it appears, he did not instruct the company to cease operations until the outstanding works were completed. Therefore, he said, the line continued to be used "to the present day".

The Vestries were informed of the position and asked to ensure that lines in their areas were properly maintained, and it was also hinted that some of the blame for the bad state of some roads was due to a measure of disinterest on the part of the Vestry managements. In reply to this, the secretary of the Vestry of St. Luke complained that congestion was caused on the roads because too many cars were in use on the services.

An instruction was then issued to the company that all lines must be put into good repair, or a closure notice could be placed upon all operations of the undertaking. Mention was again made of the Islington lines, including the offending one to Ropemaker Street, together with those in Liverpool Road, Holloway Road and Seven Sisters Road.

An admission was made by an Assistant Secretary of the Board of Trade that it was "a curious case", but, as the Board Inspectorate itself had "slipped up", closed the matter by admonishing the company engineer and instructing him, again, that all the lines of the undertaking must be put into good order.

Many months were to go by with very little repair work being carried out. On 25th July 1878, the company secretary informed the Board of Trade that the engineer, George Hopkins "was seriously ill and in bed" and, until he was able to resume duty, the company would be obliged to leave the matter in abeyance. However, on 19th August, it is recorded that Wiliam Page, assistant to Hopkins, had meantime been instructed to deal with the problem, and advised the Board of Trade that 1,390 yards of double track had been entirely reconstructed with steel rails, and considerable repair carried out on other sections. And so, over a period of about two years, most of the track mileage was attended to, the company taking advantage at the same time by using more up-to-date rails and other equipment, together with new methods of construction which had been developed.

During the course of reconstruction work, an experiment was carried out involving the use of toughened glass sleepers developed by Frederick Siemens of Dresden, and introduced into England by Hamilton Lindsay Bucknall. It is reported that a number of these were laid during 1879 on the line in High Street Stratford, but the outcome of the experiment is not recorded.

Money Matters

The company was in the habit of making loans to other tramway undertakings for various purposes. In one case, the London Tramways Company took a loan in 1879 for use as a deposit in connection with a Parliamentary Bill. Difficulties occurred in the processing of the Bill, in which the North Metropolitan Company became involved.   After much discussion, the London Company agreed to repay the sum to the Northmet "in due course".   Several other undertakings making use of this "banking facility", which was to be repaid at one-half of one per cent above Bankers' Rate, were:-

25th February 1880	Wolverhampton Tramways Company, £2,500.
	Repayment: London Street Tramways, £6,000.
4th August 1880	Wolverhampton Tramways Company, £1,500.
2nd February 1881	Provincial Tramways Company, £3,000.
23rd March 1881	Repayment: Provincial Tramways Coy. £3,000.
21st December 1881	Wolverhampton Tramways Company, £4,500.
	Belfast Tramways Company, £2,500.
18th January 1882	Belfast Repaid £1,500.
15th February 1883	Provincial Tramways Company, £2,500.
	Belfast Tramways Company, £1,500.

During the course of this activity, the company itself made mortgage agreements, by which, it was hoped, £20,000 would be raised for making extensions, for reconstructions and various other purposes.

A Reminiscence

The following notes from recollections penned by Inspector T. Davey, late of the Metropolitan Electric Tramways, are recorded as originally presented to the T. O. T. Magazine, March 1928.

"I joined the London Tramways Company in March 1880 and worked as a driver on a 'money-box' car which ran on the Blackfriars - Brixton and Borough - Clapham services.   The flat fare was 2d, and use was made of a "Beatle's Money Box and Change Gates".   On entering the car, passengers dropped coins through a slot on to an enclosed tray and as each one did so, the driver pulled a cord which rang a bell and worked an indicator that recorded the number of people who had paid. The rear door of the car was controlled by a lever fitted just above the driver's head, and could not be opened by the passenger.   No tickets were issued.   Each driver had £1-worth of change, made up in small packages.   The money-box car was patronised by what may be termed as 'good class passengers' and regular riders waited for it.   The flat fare of 2d probably kept the artisans away.

"I went then to the North Metropolitan as a conductor working from Stratford yard under 'Yankee' Smith.   Pay was 4/6d per day to start, then 6/- after two years.   The conductor was expected to provide a tip and a couple of drinks for the driver - or the driver made things hard.   The timekeeper and regulator expected 3d or so each evening, as did the ticket inspector, and coins were 'put under the band' of the waybill.

"The driver was expected to tip the horsekeeper - up to 1/- a day.   There was a separate waybill for each journey, at the end of which the money was paid in.   Spare men were lucky if they got two or three days work a week.   A £5 deposit was paid to the company when taken on for work - it was 'lost' if you were dismissed.   It was almost necessary to 'fiddle the bag' for the conductor to pay all the other people their spoils.

"On 3rd April 1881, I went to Major Hill of the London Street Tramways for a job as a conductor and was taken on.   Ticket punches were introduced about 1879, and there were 1d, 2d and 3d fares.   To induce people to ride 'on top' in winter, a 1d fare was introduced 'outside only' on the Euston - Camden Town Station run".

The New North Road Line

On 28th March 1879, the tramway in New North Road was opened to traffic, but shortly afterwards claimed its first victims when "several children were run down by the cars and killed". It is reported that the families, heartbroken, were, in common with many in those days, very poor. Although the company did not admit liability in any way, they did agree, on 9th April, to provide a ten guineas (£10.10s) gift of money for "Funeral expenses and mourning suitable to the position in life of the parents"! On 23rd April, the Rev. Mgr. Canon Smith made a plea to the company management for this sum to be increased, resulting in the payment of another 5 gns. to the bereaved parents.

Into The Eighties

The North Metropolitan Tramways Act, 1880 (43-44 Vic. cap. xcvii) received Royal Assent on 2nd August 1880 and empowered the company to construct new works and raise further money, and also make certain arrangements with the London Street Tramways Company. The new tramways authorised were:-
The Leytonstone Lines, Nos. 9, 9A to 9D, consisting of 2 f. 3.6 ch. of single line and 5 f. 6.6 ch. of double line, commencing in High Road Leytonstone, by junctions with the existing tramways, and passing along High Road to terminate about 1 ch. north of the "Green Man" Inn, Leytonstone. The work was completed during the summer of 1881 and inspected by Maj. Gen. Hutchinson on 12th August, who certified them fit for traffic.

Section 33 of the Act gave powers to the company and the London Street Tramways Company, subject to the provisions of Part III of the Railway Clauses Act, 1863, which was to apply as if the company and the London Street Tramways Company were railway companies, to make and carry into effect agreements with respect to the working, use, management and maintenance by the company of the tramways of the London Street Tramways Company or any part thereof.

North Metropolitan car No. 470, seen late in 1906 after being sold to Leyton District Council Tramways, and working on the short service between Borthwick Road and "Green Man". (Courtesy: L R T A)

During the winter of 1880, the weather was very severe, so bad in fact that snow clearing became a great problem. In order to pay the casual labourers who had to be employed, fares were raised during the period of bad weather. What was normally a 2d fare - from Holloway to London - was raised to 3d. The company stated that "as the Vestries would not clear the streets, the company had to do it to keep the services operating".

Even so, the local authorities charged a considerable sum each year in rates to maintain the roads. As an example, the Parish of St. Mary, Islington, rated the lines in that area at £1,461 (which included £300 for cleaning and repairing the roads). The total assessment for Islington was £6,067 in 1880 and £7,703 in 1881. The company decided, in this case, to appeal against their assessments, commenting in correspondence that "if friends of the vestrymen rode in the cars (meaning those who voted them into power), as the vestries put up the rates, these 'friends' would have to pay higher fares"!

The arguments about the company having to pay rates on their tracks was the cause of considerable acrimony, the more so when the management stated that the omnibus proprietors paid no rates, which brought forth a comment from the representatives of that body. The railway faction then joined the discussion, with Sir. E. Watkins adding that tramway companies paid no duty to the state as did the railway companies. This, in turn, again raised the hackles of the directors of the North Metropolitan Tramway Company sufficiently to reply in some detail, pointing out that the company paid out £897 in the year 1880 merely for licenses and duty payments. And so it went on.

On 3rd August 1881, the 23rd half-yearly meeting of the company took place, with George Richardson in the chair, assisted by Frederick Mosley Watts, the company secretary. The chairman commented that the extension of the line to "Epping Forest" (Leytonstone) from Harrow Green, built under the authority of the 1880 Act, was almost ready for use and would hopefully be worked by a "Beaumont Locomotive" instead

The line between "Green Man" and Stratford was at one time worked by company cars as a complete service. Here, an eight-window car is seen in High Road, Leytonstone. (Commercial view)

of by horse power. With regard to horsing costs, these, at 5.44d per car mile was 1¼d less than was charged by the LGOC.

There was, however, one aspect of operation that was worrying. "Compensations" appeared as a regular debit on each year's accounts, and almost all tramway companies suffered them. It had, according to Richardson, become almost a "pastime" by some unscrupulous persons to attempt to obtain money fraudulently in this way. In common with other companies, the North Metropolitan began contesting each attempt at this practice, taking the claimants to law in order to prove or disprove their cases.

Labour Commission Evidence, March 1882

At a session of the Labour Commission, R. L. Adamson gave facts about the company during his evidence to that body. A dividend of 8½% was paid in 1881, while 75,323,000 passengers were carried. The number of employees was 1,800, for which the wages bill was £145,256. Pay of drivers on engagement was 4/6d a day, rising to 6/- after twelve months, while conductors received 3d a day less. Horsekeepers were paid between 24/6d and 28/- for a week of seven days, with 1/- extra for night work.

Average hours of work for all staff were less than 12 a day, while at holiday periods, men were paid 1/- extra for three days. Deductions made for loss of equipment averaged 0.86d per person per week. No person was dismissed for being a member of a union, while there were no fines and no strikes. Average discharge rate was two drivers a week out of 450, mainly for drunkeness, accidents, carelessness or cruelty. Many of the servants had been with the company for many years.

Further Acts Obtained

The company next obtained **The North Metropolitan Tramways Act, 1882 (45-46 Vic. cap. cxxxvi)**, which received the Royal Assent on 12th July, authorising:-
The Green Lanes Lines, Nos. 2 and 2A, consisting of 6 f. of double line, commencing in Green Lanes by junctions with the existing tramways at or near the entrance to the company's Highbury New Park depot, and then passing northwards along Green Lanes to terminate at the junction of Green Lanes with Seven Sisters Road. The work was completed at the end of August 1883 and inspected by Maj. Marindin on 4th September, who authorised the issue of a certificate.

Two more years were to pass before the company obtained its next Act. **The North Metropolitan Tramways Act, 1884 (47-48 Vic. cap. clxviii)** received Royal Assent on 28th July, authorising:-
The Great Eastern Street Line, Nos. 1 and 1A, consisting of 3 f. 6 yds. of double line, commencing in Old Street by junctions with the existing tramways, at or near the (western) end of Great Eastern Street and terminating in High Street Shoreditch by junctions with the existing tramways at or near the (eastern) end of Great Eastern Street.
The West India Dock Road Line, Nos. 6 and 6A, consisting of 2 f. 4.25 ch. of double line, commencing by junctions with the existing tramways at or near the south end of Burdett Road, then passing into and along and terminating in West India Dock Road at or near the crossing by the London and Blackwall Railway.
No. 7, a crossover, 3 ch. long, at the western end of Commercial Road.
The Romford Road Line, Nos. 8 and 8A, consisting of 2 mls. 7.75 ch.

The Romford Road line, while being connected to the rest of the system at Stratford, was often worked as a separate service. In this view the car is travelling towards Stratford. (Courtesy: C. Carter)

of double line, commencing in High Street Stratford, by junctions with the existing tramways at or near "The Swan Hotel", passing along High Street on the south-east side of Stratford Church, into and along Romford Road, Ilford Road and Great Essex Road, terminating in Great Essex Road near the junction with White Post Lane.

The Barking Road Line, Nos. 9, 9A to 9H, consisting of 2 f. 3 ch. of double and 1 ml. 0.75 ch. single line, commencing in Barking Road about 2.50 ch. west of Victoria Dock Road, then along that road and terminating about 6 ch. east of Greengate Street. Provided that the company shall not, without the consent of the West Ham Local Board, construct any part of Nos. 9 and 9A west of the end of Burnham Street.

The following conditions were also imposed. "In lieu of constructing the double line of tramway consisting of parts of No. 9 and of Nos. 9E and 9F, the company shall construct a single line only in the centre of Barking Road and the company shall be at liberty to construct a passing place in the said road adjacent to the end of Balaam Street, provided that no rail shall be laid less than 9 ft. 6 in. from the footpath on either side of the road. The passing place on the bridge of Barking Road over the northern outfall sewer shall, notwithstanding anything shown on the deposited plans, be constructed only of such length as is absolutely necessary to permit two cars passing each other.

In addition to the tramways shown on the deposited plans, the company shall, for the purpose of affording through communication by car between the City and the West India Docks lines, make and maintain junctions between the tramways numbered 6 and 6A by this Act and the existing tramways in Commercial Road".

Section 49, in dealing with fares, stated:- "The company is not to demand or take more than 2d on the Romford Road line between the "Princess Alice" and St. John's Church, Stratford, or 1d between the "Princess Alice" and White Post Lane, while Section 50 stated that "on the Barking Road line, a maximum fare of 1d will apply".

On completion, the various lines were inspected on the following dates:-

Great Eastern Street, Nos. 1 and 1A, 12th September 1888 by Maj. Marindin. Certificate issued on 14th.

West India Dock Road, Nos. 6, 6A and 7, 30th March 1885 by Maj. Gen. Hutchinson. Certificate issued on 9th April.

Romford Road, Nos. 8 and 8A, 28th May 1886 by Maj. Gen. Hutchinson. Certificate issued on 1st June.

Barking Road, Nos. 9, 9A to 9H, 6th September 1886 by Maj. Gen. Hutchinson. Certificate issued on 9th, but Nos. 9A and 9F were not mentioned.

The year 1885 saw the publication of another Act on behalf of the company. **The North Metropolitan Tramways Act, 1885 (48-49 Vic. cap. xxvi)** received Royal Assent on 21st May 1885 and authorised the following lines:-

The Clerkenwell Road Line, Nos. 1, 1A, 2 and 2A, consisting of 5 f. 2 ch. of double line, commencing at the west end of Old Street by junctions with the existing tramways, and passing in a westerly direction across Goswell Road into and along Clerkenwell Road, terminating opposite Holborn Town Hall.

The Act specified that steel rails weighing 90 lbs/yard were to be used. These were to be in lengths from 20 ft. to 30 ft., with a groove 1 inch wide and ¾ inch deep. Steel fishplates, 20 inches long and weighing 24 lbs/pair were to be used in conjunction with the rails.

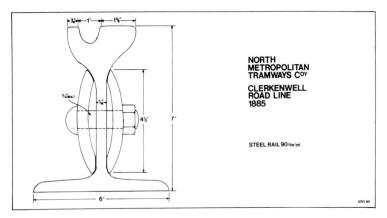

Section **40** of the Act was most important, authorising the company, at its works in Union Road, Leytonstone, to construct rolling stock for its own use, or for sale to other undertakings; together with harness, fittings and appliances for use with the cars. This license, however, was to be renewed by Parliamentary authority after five years.

On 10th September 1885, the company manager, R. L. Adamson, asked for an inspection of the completed lines. Maj. Gen. Hutchinson undertook this duty on 22nd, and authorised their use.

Two years later, the company obtained **The North Metropolitan Tramways Act, 1887 (50 Vic. Session 2, cap. xii)** which received Royal Assent on 29th March. It authorised the company "to lay down and maintain" new tramways in Clerkenwell Road, Theobalds Road, Gray's Inn Road and Commercial Street, and to construct a double line of tramway in lieu of a single line in a part of Goswell Road. Two Bills had been submitted to Parliament for this work, entitled The North Metropolitan Tramways (No. 1) Bill and the (No. 2) Bill, and during the course of their progress, they were combined into a single Act.

Also included was power for the Board of Trade to grant licenses to the company to enable operation by electrical power on the portions of line lines in the Borough of West Ham and in the Parishes of East Ham and Leyton in the County of Essex. The following tramways were authorised:-

No. 1, a double line, 2 f. 7 ch. long, commencing at the existing line in Clerkenwell Road at Holborn Town Hall, then running in a westerly direction across Gray's Inn Road into Theobalds Road, terminating at the east side of Devonshire Street.

No. 2, a line, 1 f. 8 ch. double and 1.50 ch. single, from a junction with the existing line in Clerkenwell Road at Holborn Town Hall, into and along Gray's Inn Road, terminating at its south end.

No. 3, a line, 2 ch. double and 1.25 ch. single, from the existing line in Clerkenwell Road to the west of Farringdon Road, into and along Farringdon Road in a northerly direction, to a junction with Tramways Nos. 25 and 251 authorised by the London Street Tramways (Extensions) Act, 1885 at or near their respective terminations.

No. 4, a line, 2 f. 6 ch. double and 2 f. 4.50 ch. single, from Great Eastern Street at or near its eastern end by junctions with Nos. 1 and 1A (Act of 1884), into and along Commercial Street, to a junction with the existing tramways at or near the junction of Commercial Road with High Street Whitechapel.

No. 10, a double line, 6 ch. long, in lieu of the existing single line in Goswell Road between Percival Street and Compton Street, but it shall not be constructed until the widening of the carriageway has been completed on the west side.

Section 6 stated " ... the company ... shall make a single line of Tramway No. 4 where it crosses High Street Shoreditch, together with other passing places where agreed in Commercial Street. The rails to be used are to be made of steel, weighing 90 lbs/yard, in lengths from 24 ft. to 30 ft., with fishplates 20 in. long and weighing 40 lbs/pair. The groove in the rail is to be 1 in. wide and ¾ in. deep".

Section 9 was included for the protection of the hay and straw salesmen in the Whitechapel Hay Market. "In Commercial Street, between Wentworth Street and High Street Whitechapel, Tramway No. 4 is to

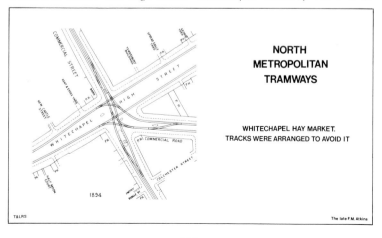

NORTH
METROPOLITAN
TRAMWAYS

WHITECHAPEL HAY MARKET.
TRACKS WERE ARRANGED TO AVOID IT

T&LRS   The late F.M. Atkins be built as a double line, with two crossovers at the south end of Commercial Street so as to admit of cars being shunted from one line to the other, and between the hours of 7 a.m. and 12 noon on Tuesdays, Thursdays and Saturdays of every week, the hay and straw salesmen shall be entitled to occupy the site of the westernmost line with their carts, etc., with the eastern line only being entitled to be used by the tramway cars".

Inspections and agreements for these lines were:-
No. 1, inspected by Maj. Gen. Hutchinson, 2nd September 1887.
Certificate issued on 5th September.
No. 2, inspected by Maj. Gen. Hutchinson, 5th July 1887.
Certificate issued on 6th July.
No. 3, (Limited to agreement with the London Street Tramways Co.)
No. 4, inspected by Maj. Marindin, 12th September 1888.
Certificate issued on 14th September.
No. 10. (Limited to widenings issue).

To round off the bulk of their proposed network north of the City of London, the company made application to the Board of Trade for a Provisional Order **(The North Metropolitan Tramways Order, 1888)**, the content of which was confirmed in the **Tramways Orders Confirmation (No. 3) Act, 1888 (51-52 Vic. cap. cxxii).** This authorised the company to construct one tramway:-
No. 1, a line 3 f. 7.50 ch. long, of which 1 f. 9.5 ch. was to be double, commencing in High Street Whitechapel by a junction with Tramway No. 4 (Act of 1887) at or near the end of Commercial Street, and passing into and along Leman Street and Dock Street to terminate at its south end. The double line sections were to be at the following places:-
Between its commencement and apoint opposite Nelson Stret.
Between points 1 ch. north and 1 ch. south of Great Alice Street.
Between Great Prescot Street and a point 5 ch. north of its terminus.

As in the previous Act, a special Section or Clause was written into the Act for the protection of the hay and straw salesmen working in the weekday market. "The company ... shall construct ... two crossovers near the north end of Leman Street to admit cars going in either direction being shunted from one line to the other. The north end of the crossovers shall not be more than 70 ft. from the north-west corner of Leman Street and ... between 7 a.m. and 12 noon on Tuesdays, Thursdays and Saturdays in every week, hay and straw salesmen shall be entitled to occupy the western line with their carts, etc., and the eastern line shall be only entitled to be used by cars".

Plans were submitted to the Board of Trade on 1st June 1889, and the line was completed at the end of October 1890. Inspection was undertaken by Maj. Gen. Hutchinson on 3rd December, and in his report he remarked "the line ... is one chain short of the authorised line. It is double throughout, although authorised as a single line in the Act ... and ... means some very narrow pavements, but I do not object to it as it is in accordance with an amended plan. It is well laid". He authorised its use and the certificate was issued on 6th December.

North Metropolitan and London Street Tramways Joint Services

In January 1882, the company was approached by the secretary of the London Street Tramways Company, J. Barber Glenn, suggesting that consideration be given to joint and through running along Caledonian Road, but was opposed by the North Metropolitan Company Board, who decided that such services were not required.

The next approach was made in August 1886, when, on 4th, a joint service was agreed, with cars running between Finsbury Park and King's Cross as from 16th. Of the twelve cars working on weekdays, eight were provided by the London Street, while on Sundays, with fourteen cars on the service, nine were provided by the London Street. The service was short-lived, however, as on 17th November, the two undertakings had a disagreement with regard to the pooling of fares, and this, coupled with the comment from the London Street Company that the bad weather and the fact that cars "had to be ramped at Nag's Head to get them from one set of tracks to the other", resulted in the London Street withdrawing from the agreement. After a meeting between Adamson and Barber Glenn, the service resumed.

In April 1887, it was the turn of the North Metropolitan to insist that the joint service be withdrawn "for service reasons". However, on 10th February 1888 the joint workings were once again resumed, and harmony reigned until 6th June 1894, when the North Metropolitan once again gave notice to the London Street to stop working on the lines to Finsbury Park.

One other arrangement concerning cars of one company running over the tracks of the other occurred on 1st May 1889, when an agreement was made to allow the Gray's Inn Road line to be used by cars of both undertakings. The North Metropolitan was to pay rent of £187 per annum; half of fares taken; half of maintenance costs of £550 per annum and half the cost of reconstruction.

After 1889

Subsequent to the formation of the London County Council in 1889, the Chairman of the Highways Committee let it be known that, as the successor to the Metropolitan Board of Works, it would be considering the purchase of all the tramway companies within its area as they fell due under the terms of the 21-year rule as stated in the Tramways Act of 1870. For the company, this meant that those lines constructed under authority of the Act of 1871 would fall due for consideration for purchase in 1892. (The 1869 and 1870 Acts of the company were safeguarded until 1897 and 1898 under a separate 28-year rule).

Almost immediately, the management responded with a protest that the short sections of line involved, on their own, would be of no use to the LCC and, if purchased, would only serve to break up the system, which would be detrimental to both parties. However, the principle of purchase had already been established, as the Council was already in negotiation with the London Street Tramways Company, whose first lines, authorised in 1870, were to become due for purchase in 1891. In April 1892 however, the North Metropolitan took over the North London Tramways Company, who operated lines from Finsbury Park to Ponders End and Wood Green, with a connection from Stamford Hill to the latter point. Details of this company are given elsewhere.

Under the North Metropolitan Company Act of 1871, about 19 miles of line, together with certain depots, stables and other works facilities would fall due for purchase. At the end of September 1892, both sides prepared for battle. On 6th October, the company secretary advised the Board of Trade that the LCC had again stated its intention to purchase the sections of line as they fell due. He followed this up with the publication of a statement pointing out the 'error' of such a move 'which would divide up the system'.

On 14th November, Godfrey suggested to the Board of Trade that arrangements should be made with the LCC to consider purchasing the whole undertaking and lease it back to the company to operate, and to postpone the original course of piecemeal purchase for a further period to allow discussion to take place. The LCC disagreed, pointing out that, under the terms of the Tramways Act and the relevant Act of the company, the time by which the Notice would expire on 31st January 1890 was too short to alter the arrangements. It was, however, prepared to agree to the appointment of an arbitrator, which appointment could then be postponed "if negotiations rendered such a course desirable".

On receiving the Notice of Intent, which was dated 7th December 1892, the company again made the proposal that the Council purchase all the lines and lease them back to the company to operate, and, although discussions took place between the two, the Council eventually decided to continue with the outright purchase of the nine sections of line which were included in the following routes:-

1. Kingsland Road	5. Hackney Road
2. Finsbury Park	6. Mile End & Clapton
3. Islington & Kingsland	7. Limehouse & Victoria Park
4. Old Street & Old Street Road	8. Commercial Road
	9. Islington & Post Office

The actual sections of track concerned were:-

Goswell Road and Aldersgate Street;   Old Street;
Essex Road to Upper Street;   East Road;
Bridport Place, Southgate Road, Mildmay Park and Green Lanes (to the depot);
Kingsland Road, High Street Kingsland, Stoke Newington Road, Stoke Newington High Street, Stamford Hill;
Hackney Road;
Cambridge Road, Mare Street, Lower and Upper Clapton Roads;
Commercial Road East, East India Dock Road;
Burdett Road, Bow Road.

The war of words continued into and through 1893, with the LCC on 18th November finally sending another Formal Notice of Intent to purchase further sections of line which had been authorised by the North Metropolitan Tramways Act, 1872. This time, however, it stated that, after purchase, the lines might be leased back to the company to operate.

To this, the company replied on 24th November that, having due regard to the provisions of the various Acts obtained by it, the Council had no power to any part of its property until after 21 years from the date of the last of such Acts. This delaying tactic brought the response that the LCC was applying to the Board of Trade for the appointment of a referee, as also provided for in the Tramways Act of 1870. In January 1894, Sir Frederick J. Bramwall, Bt. undertook to arbitrate in the dispute, to which Arthur Godfrey objected, saying that he thought that Bramwell was prejudiced. Despite this, the whole matter became even more delayed by legal proceedings in which the London Street Tramways Company and the LCC were involved. In this case, the company had appealed to the High Court of Justice in an effort to have set aside an arbitrator's award of 22nd January 1894.

The North Metropolitan, following the lead set by the London Street Tramways, took its complaint to the High Court, in order to obtain a judgement on whether or not the LCC could legally take possession of the assets of the company. A decision was given on 17th May

1895 in favour of the LCC, which resulted in the company stating that it would appeal against the decision. On 13th December 1895, a judgement was again given in favour of the LCC.

There was still very much concern at the prospect of a piecemeal takeover by the LCC, with a preference instead for a negotiated settlement, whereby the Council might be persuaded to purchase the whole of the undertaking within the metropolitan area. This was again put to the Council in conjunction with a proposal that the remainder of the London Street Tramways be purchased at the same time at an agreed sum, the whole of the two undertakings then being leased back to the North Metropolitan to operate for a fixed initial period. In this way, both companies would hope to obtain a reasonable price for their assets, together with a level of security for several years to come, both in preserving the integrity of their companies and, as important, keeping their shareholders happy.

On 17th December 1895, comment was made in the Council chamber that the approach to the matter of purchase, so far, together with the lack of any result, was very disappointing. The Highways Committee was then given authority to consider any positive proposals that might be made by any tramway company regarding purchase by the Council. By this time, the purchase of the first 4¼ miles of the lines of the London Street Company had been dealt with, including a leasing arrangement whereby the lines were to be worked by the company on behalf of the LCC.

It was then that H. T. Butler, F. Davies, F. H. Morris, E. Church, L. Blum, J. Mitchell and W. G. Turnbull proposed forming "The County of London Tramways Syndicate Limited" with a capital of £50,000, and suggested to the LCC early in 1896 that one large tramway company be formed, by uniting all the London undertakings. The object of this appeared to be to ward off the purchase of them all by the LCC, or else to enable the syndicate to negotiate with the LCC for running rights over all lines. In this case, the Council rejected the proposal out of hand, but it was to act as a spur to the North Metropolitan to come to terms with the Council.

Hugh C. Godfray, solicitor, acting for both the North Metropolitan and London Street Tramways, again asked the Council whether the Highways Committee was yet ready to reconsider the proposal for the immediate sale to the LCC of the tramways of both companies within the county and for a subsequent lease to be constructed with the Northmet to allow it to operate all lines. The reply was very different from the original one, with the Highways Committee agreeing that an arrangement could now be considered and, after minor amendments were made to the proposal, all parties finally came to terms.

One of the peculiar aspects of the purchase of these lines is that, due to the irregular configuration of the boundary of Middlesex with London, two isolated pockets of land within the LCC area through which tramways passed were still deemed to be in Middlesex. These short lengths were:-
    (a) 267 yards in Green Lanes between Kings Road and Riversdale Road,
    (b) about 272 yards in Stoke Newington Road and High Street,
    (c) a small portion between Green Lanes and Mildmay Park,
and these had to be specially negotiated upon, It was agreed that, as an exception, these should be purchased and leased so that continuity could be afforded to the operation of the system on behalf of the LCC.

On the other hand, and probably as a gesture of goodwill by the Council, several short lengths of line at the outer London ends, which formerly belonged to the North London Tramways, would be excluded from the purchase, so that the company, still operating in Middlesex, could have acess to reasonable terminal points. These were:-

(a) Stamford Hill terminus to the County boundary at Craven Park Road, 133 yards,
(b) Manor House to the County boundary at Hermitage road, Green Lanes, 280 yards,
(c) Manor House to Amhurst Park County boundary, 480 yards,
(d) Finsbury Park Station to Manor House, approximately 880 yards.

It was arranged that the LCC should purchase the lines at the rate of £10,000 per mile of double track, and £5,000 per mile for single. Buildings used for all purposes were also to be purchased at an agreed price, with the company paying a reasonable rent for their continued use. The sale and purchase process began in the summer of 1896. The agreement provided for the North Metropolitan to take a comprehensive lease on all lines for 14 years as from 24th June.

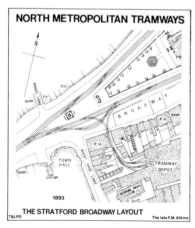

The "Swan Hotel", Stratford in the 1890s, with two cars on the Bow Road service. The track layout may be more easily appreciated by referring to the track plan.
(Commercial view)

542

Chapter 35
The North London Tramways Company

The North London Suburban Tramways Company

This title belonged to a company which operated in Middlesex, outside the area of the Metropolitan Board of Works, and was registered on 14th December 1878.   Authorised by a Board of Trade Provisional Order, confirmed by **The Tramways Orders Confirmation Act, 1879 (42-43 Vic. cap. cxcii)**, the company was to be able to construct a long single line with 32 passing places, commencing just inside the boundary of the metropolitan area at Stamford Hill, then over the boundary and along High Road, Tottenham and northwards through Edmonton and Enfield to Cheshunt in Hertfordshire, a total of 9 mls. 2 f. 3.30 ch. in all.   Horse traction was to be employed.   Under **Section 31** of the Act, the company was to be able to enter into traffic agreements with the North Metropolitan Tramways Company, but this was not to be achieved.

Construction begain at Tramway Avenue, Edmonton, for which £38,000 had been allocated, and with many interruptions, Stamford Hill was eventually reached.   Maj. Gen. Hutchinson inspected the section between Tramway Avenue and Lower Edmonton on 12th April 1881, and authorised its use for horse traction only.   This was followed by the remainder of the line southwards, the section to the Edmonton boundary on 16th May and the remainder to Stamford Hill on 7th June 1881.

The next section to be tackled was from the northern end, from Tramway Avenue to Ponder's End, just south of the Enfield boundary. It was inspected by Maj. Gen. Hutchinson on 5th January 1882 and

An engraving showing the Eades Reversible single deck, single ended car, which was to work on the system.   (Courtesy: C. S. Smeeton)

opened two days later. This was also to be the last section to be built by the company. Due to serious financial problems, it was also to be the end of the company, for three weeks later, on 30th January, a Bill was submitted to Parliament which had the effect of proposing to dissolve the company. **The North London Tramways Company Act, 1882, (44-45 Vic. cap. cxciv)**, which received Royal Assent on 10th August, replaced it with a statutory undertaking.

It had been anticipated that further lines would be built, and a Provisional Order had been obtained by the old company to allow the construction of lines along Seven Sisters Road from Tottenham to Finsbury Park, and in Green Lanes from Manor House to Wood Green. Although a Section in the 1882 Act authorised the transfer of the Order, any extensions had to wait until the new company was in a position to make the necessary arrangements.

The North London Tramways Company

Chairman of the new company was W. J. Carruthers Wain, who also had interests in other tramway undertakings, as well as in other commercial spheres. The directors were named as Christopher James, John Beattie, Henry Lee Corlett, Thomas O'Hagan and Arthur Randolph Robinson.

A provision introduced into **The Tramways Orders Confirmation Act, 1879 (42-43 Vic. cap. cxcii)** empowered the Board of Trade, by Section 3, to grant licenses, by way of experiment, to the use of steam or any mechanical power upon tramways in certain cases and for limited periods. No license, however, could be granted or renewed except with the consent of the "local" and "road" authorities.

The North London Tramways Act, 1883 (46-47 Vic. cap. cxlii), empowered the company (among other things) to abandon the section of line north of Ponder's End, and to use steam or other mechanical power including compressed air and electricity, but only in the area outside the metropolis and for a period of seven years in the first instance. It was this condition that in later years was to be the cause of confrontation with the Metropolitan Board of Works.

Fourteen "Economical Class" steam tram engines fitted with "steep gradient motors" were ordered during 1884 from Merryweather & Sons of Greenwich, London, for which up to £15,000 had been allocated, together with twenty double-deck open top bogie trailers from the Falcon Engine & Car Works Ltd. of Loughborough. This was followed in 1885 by the purchase of another Merryweather engine, this one more powerful than the rest. All these engines were inspected by Hutchinson on 31st March 1885, before being allowed to be used in service.

Even at this early stage it was becoming clear that, assuming that all parts of the lines, when completed, could provide a steam operated service, there were three sections within the area of the Metropolitan Board of Works, at Stamford Hill, in the middle section of Seven Sisters Road, and about three furlongs in Green Lanes where these would not be allowed to go. After asking permission of the Board of Trade, who agreed, and the Metropolitan Board of Works, who declined, the company decided to obtain authority from Parliament in an authorising Act, to overcome this hurdle.

The Bill met with considerable opposition from the Metropolitan Board, whose Engineer, Sir Joseph Bazalgette, together with the Deputy Chairman of the Works Committee, W. J. Selway, considered that

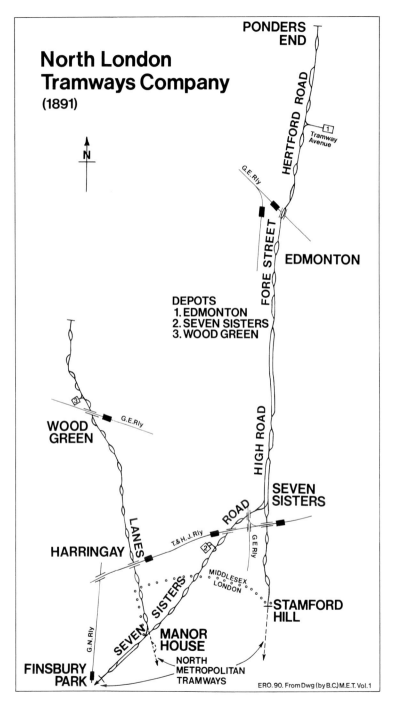

North London Tramways Company
(1891)

N

PONDERS END

HERTFORD ROAD

1
Tramway Avenue

G.E.Rly

FORE STREET

EDMONTON

DEPOTS
1. EDMONTON
2. SEVEN SISTERS
3. WOOD GREEN

HIGH ROAD

3
G.E.Rly

WOOD GREEN

SEVEN SISTERS

LANES

ROAD

T.&H.J.Rly

2
G.E.Rly

HARRINGAY

MIDDLESEX
LONDON

SEVEN SISTERS

STAMFORD HILL

G.N.Rly

MANOR HOUSE

FINSBURY PARK

NORTH METROPOLITAN TRAMWAYS

ERO. 90. From Dwg (by B.C.) M.E.T. Vol.1

it should be the Metropolitan Board and not the Board of Trade who should have the right to allow or refuse the company's request. After an enquiry, the company was eventually authorised to use steam tram engines over the whole of its undertaking.

Early in 1885, construction of the authorised extensions between Seven Sisters Corner and Finsbury Park, and between Manor House and Wood Green began and, after completion of the line between Seven Sisters and Manor House, Maj. Gen. Hutchinson inspected the eastern part of it on 24th October 1885, following this with his inspection of the remainder to Finsbury Park on 12th December.

The sections between Manor House and Wood Green, however, were the subject of some disagreement between the company and the local authorities and, although Hutchinson inspected the line on 10th August 1887, it was to be 21st December before it was opened to traffic. To work this line, ten Dick, Kerr steam tram engines and seven Falcon-built trailers were acquired, but even so, it is recorded that, at times, horse cars were used to supplement the steam cars so that a regular service could be provided.

By the end of 1888 it was becoming noticeable that the company was in some financial difficulty, and early in December 1889 it went into liquidation. Wain became the Interim Liquidator as from 15th December, but even this was to be the cause of of some disquiet from the Official Receiver, who took several more weeks in making up his mind that Wain could continue in that capacity.

The permit to enable the company to use steam power was due to expire on 2nd August and, despite objections from several of the local authorities who were concerned about the state of the roads and the engines, the company asked the Board of Trade for a renewal of the license. Hutchinson agreed to this, but only until 30th October 1890, and only then if certain repairs were undertaken to bring the engines "up to standard". This gave little time for the company to do very much, and in any case, there was very little money available with which to do anything. After two further inspections by Hutchinson on 3rd and 10th November, he issued the company with what in reality was an ultimatum:- "If £1,200 per annum can be found to repair the engines, then another license will be issued. If not, find a buyer, or reconstruct the company". These harsh terms were modified after representations by the company. It was agreed that, for a deposit of £600, paid to the Board of Trade as a guarantee of proper maintenance, a six-month license would be given. Alternatively, for a payment of £100 per month, a monthly license would be forthcoming until the expiration of the six month period. The company took the "easy payments" option, literally to stay in business! Nevertheless, the decision was taken to put it up for sale.

After an abortive effort by Wain, together with others, to form "The London Electric Tramways Company Limited", the North Metropolitan Tramways Company was approached on 13th June 1891 by the Middlesex County Council, who asked whether the Northmet would be prepared to work the lines on a temporary basis, by horse power, to which the company agreed. In view of this, the Board of Trade issued a final free license for steam operation, which was to expire on 1st August. From this date, the steam locomotives were taken out of service.

Instead of just taking on the operation of the lines, the North Metropolitan Company management decided to purchase the undertaking outright, agreeing on a price of £22,000, with the transfer date to be

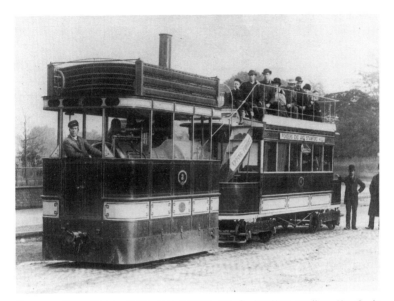

Merryweather steam tram locomotive No. 2, hauling trailer No. 6, is seen here working on the Ponders End and Stamford Hill service. The clean and tidy condition of both vehicles indicates that the cars had not been long in service. The notice posted on the stair stringer gives the indication that the service worked "Near To Epping Forest", which, at Ponders End, began about a mile to the east. (C. S. Smeeton)

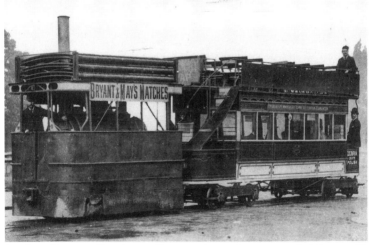

Another Merryweather locomotive, number unknown, coupled to car 25, working on the Finsbury Park and Edmonton service. In comparing the condition of the engine to that of No. 2 in the top photograph, it would appear that it had seen considerable service and was possibly nearing the end of its days in service. (C. S. Smeeton)

12th April 1892. Thus, the only steam worked tramway in the area of Greater London passed into oblivion, after about seven or so years of fitful working.

Following the takeover, a thorough check and survey of the lines caused the management to decide to close sections as necessary and relay them. One of these was the Stamford Hill to Tottenham boundary line, which was completely renewed, re-opening to traffic on 13th June 1894, using pair-horse cars working on a 14-minute headway throughout each day of the week.

A description of this company has been compiled in conjunction with C. S. Smeeton, who has kindly allowed the reproduction of some parts of his work as described in "Metropolitan Electric Tramways" Volume I.

After the North London Tramways Company was purchased by the North Metropolitan Tramways, services reverted to horse car working, and a car is seen standing at the end of Tramway Avenue, Edmonton.
(Commercial view)

Chapter 36
The London Street Tramways Company

Early Days

Another of the early starters, the company first appeared in the districts of the metropolis now referred to as inner north west London, when proposals were put before the Metropolitan Board of Works, the Board of Trade and Parliament for the laying down of tramways in these areas, also at Kilburn, Southwark and the City of Westminster.

Most of the proposed lines were immediately to the north of the "new" road which stretched from the Bank of England in the City of London to Paddington by way of Islington, Euston and Marylebone. It was on this road that the first "short stage" vehicles were to be seen in the 1830 s, these being the predecessors of the early omnibuses. At this time the road was more or less the northern boundary of the built-up Metropolitan area. The inner districts, Euston, St. Pancras, King's Cross and Islington were all well established; the southern parts of Camden Town and Kentish Town, the area to the north of Islington and in Upper Holloway much the same, but just a little more into "the open air"; while Hampstead and Parliament Hill were almost out into the country - but not quite!

At one time just outside the environs of early London, Kentish Town was, at the time of Domesday, known as Kentistoune, or something similar. By the end of the nineteenth century, the whole area was quite built up, becoming in the process an important centre of the pianoforte manufacturing industry. Camden Town, to the south, was drawn into the urban sprawl of the Capital by the construction of the Regents Canal, which brought industry to the district. The first terminal station of the London and Birmingham Railway was built there, followed in later years by a large locomotive and carriage depot, which served this important main railway line.

Euston became prominent by the construction, in 1754-56, of the "new" road and with the siting, three-quarters of a century later, of the final railway terminal of the London and Birmingham Railway. King's Cross, about half a mile to the east of Euston, is also the site of a large railway terminus. Until 1836, the area was known as Battle Bridge, from a bridge of that name which crossed the Fleet River and which, it is said, may have been the scene of a battle between the forces of Suetonuis Paulinus and those of Boadicea (Boudicca), although there is doubt about its authenticity.

Standing astride the boundary of the City of London, Farringdon was once a nondescript area through which the Fleet River flowed on its way to the Thames. This river, polluted to a great degree by the activities of the local population, was finally enclosed when the highway now known as Farringdon Street was built over it. The area rose to some prominence in the mid-nineteenth century with the construction

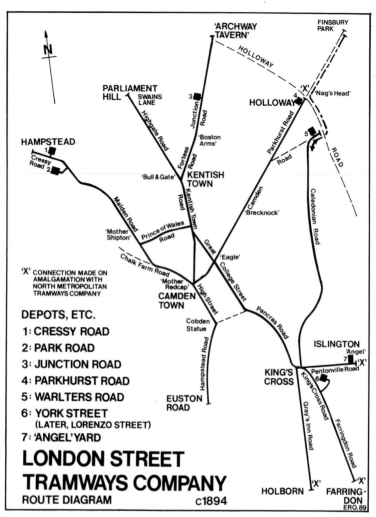

'ARCHWAY TAVERN'

FINSBURY PARK

N

PARLIAMENT HILL — SWAINS LANE

3 Junction Road

HOLLOWAY

'X' 'Nag's Head'

HOLLOWAY 4

Highgate Road

'Boston Arms'

Parkhurst Road

5

ROAD

HAMPSTEAD

1 Cressy Road 2

Fortess Road

'Bull & Gate'

KENTISH TOWN

Kentish Town Road

Road

Camden Road

'Brecknock'

Caledonian Road

Malden Road

'Mother Shipton'

Prince of Wales Road

Great College Street

'Eagle'

Chalk Farm Road

'Mother Redcap'

CAMDEN TOWN

High Street

'X' CONNECTION MADE ON AMALGAMATION WITH NORTH METROPOLITAN TRAMWAYS COMPANY

Cobden Statue

Pancras Road

ISLINGTON
'Angel'
7 'X'

DEPOTS, ETC.

Hampstead Road

KING'S CROSS

Pentonville Road
6

1: CRESSY ROAD

2: PARK ROAD

3: JUNCTION ROAD

4: PARKHURST ROAD

King's Cross Road

Gray's Inn Road

Farringdon Road

5: WARLTERS ROAD

6: YORK STREET
(LATER, LORENZO STREET)

EUSTON ROAD

7: 'ANGEL' YARD

LONDON STREET TRAMWAYS COMPANY

ROUTE DIAGRAM   c1894

HOLBORN 'X'   FARRING-DON
ERO.89

---

of the Metropolitan Railway, and with it, warehouses of many trades.

Hampstead, situated about four miles to the north west of the City, has been a settlement since Roman times and a Manorial Seat since 798 A.D. It was once well known for its spa waters, heath and highway robbers. While today, the spa waters and highway robbers are of little consequence, the heath is still well known and rightly famous. Together with Parliament Hill Fields to the east and Golders Hill to the north west, it provides one of the "lungs" of the metropolitan area.

Islington, just over a mile north of the City, like Hampstead, once boasted a spa, but this one had the delightful name of Sadler's Wells. The well is still there, but is now enclosed within the structure of a theatre. A little further up the road, the "Angel Inn", standing at the corner or Pentonville Road and Upper Street, was once a hostelry of considerable local importance. The building is still there, but now houses a bank, among other things.

The First Tramway Proposals

The London Street Tramways Company was promoted by John Humphries, William White, William Morris, William Sheldon and Elias de Pass, and it was these people who subsequently became the first directors after it was formed.

The proposals made were quite comprehensive, and to some degree impinged upon some of those made by the North Metropolitan Tramways Company as well as by the Metropolitan Street Tramways Company and the Pimlico, Peckham & Greenwich Street Tramways Company, which were all intent on obtaining consent to lay tramways, both north and south of the Thames. These were put before the Board of Trade for inclusion in the 1870 Session for Parliamentary Bills, and were described as follows:-

"The starting point of the proposed tramway is near the "Archway Tavern" and its route from thence is along the Holloway Road to Highbury; thence along Upper Street, Islington, to the City Road and along the latter road, terminating at Finsbury Pavement.

"Opposite Camden Road a junction will be formed in the Holloway Road, and a line of tramways run along Camden Road to Camden Town; thence along High Street, Hampstead Road and Tottenham Court Road, to New Oxford Street, being the same routes as those proposed to be taken up by the North Metropolitan Tramways.

"Another line of tramway is to start from Kilburn Bridge, by the North Western Railway, passing along Edgware Road to Oxford Street; thence along Oxford Street to Tottenham Court Road, and along High Holborn to Holborn Circus, passing along· New Charter-House (sic) Street, and terminating in Victoria Street.

"Also a line from Leighton Road, along Kentish Town Road, Great College Street and St. Pancras Road to King's Cross; thence along Bagnigge Wells Road and Victoria Street to Farringdon Street, continuing on and over the New Bridge, to and along Blackfriars Bridge Road to St. George's Circus, thence along Westminster Bridge Road to Belvedere Road.

"It is also proposed to lay down a double line of tramway along Queen Victoria Street, from Blackfriars Bridge to the Mansion House. Also a line from Holloway Road, along Liverpool Road, joining the proposed tramway at High Street, Islington.

"Also a line from the City Road, near the "Angel", passing along the Goswell Road and Aldersgate Street, to the General Post Office. Also a single line from Farringdon Road, along Clerkenwell Green, Aylesbury Street, part of St. John Street, along Northampton Street, Percival Street to Goswell Road; and a branch from Goswell Road, running along Compton Street to St. John Street. Also a tramway from the Great Northern Railway, along Caledonian Road, Roman Road and Offord Road to the Liverpool Road.

"These tramways will be about 53 miles long, and are to be constructed with two rails laid at a distance of 4 ft. 8½ in. from each other, and laid on a level with the surface of the street. The tramways are to be completed within three years, and each section is to be finished in six weeks after breaking open the street for that purpose".

Competition came almost immediately by proposals from another group calling themselves the North London Tramways Company, who wished to lay lines in part of the area and along some of the streets already mentioned; in fact, in much the same way as the London Street

Tramways Company was asking for powers to build and operate in areas in which other companies were interested. This, however, failed.

From the proposals of the London Street Tramways Company, a Bill was constructed and presented to Parliament in time for the 1870 Session. At the same time, Parliament was busy dealing with a general and far-reaching Bill, which subsequently became law on 9th August as **The Tramways Act, 1870.** On the following day, **The London Street Tramways Act, 1870 (33-34 Vic. cap. clxxi)** was passed, authorising the company to make or "form" the following tramways.

Nos. 9 & 9A, a double line, 2 mls. 5 f. 2 ch. long, commencing in the Holloway Road about 1 ch. from the junction of Camden Road with Holloway Road, into and along Camden Road, High Street and Hampstead Road, terminating at the south end of Hampstead Road.

No. 14, a single line, 1 ml. 5 f. 6 ch. long, commencing in Kentish Town Road at the bridge carrying the road over the Midland Railway, passing along Kentish Town Road, Chesnut Row, Monte Video Place, College Terrace, Great College Street North, Great College Street, the north side of Goldington Crescent, Old St. Pancras Road and Battle Bridge, terminating in Pentonville Road opposite the main entrance to King's Cross Station (Metropolitan Railway).

No. 15, a line 2 f. 8.5 ch. long, in Kentish Town Road, commencing at the bridge over the Midland Railway and terminating near Bartholemew Road.

No. 16, a single line 1 ml. 3 f. long, commencing at Monte Video Place, and running along College Terrace, Great College Street North, Great College Street, the north side of Goldington Crescent, Old St. Pancras Road and Battle Bridge (with No. 14 making a double line).

No. 17, a line 1.5 ch. long, commencing by a junction with No. 14, 2 ch. south of the junction of Alpha Place with Monte Video Place, terminating with a junction with No. 16.

A condition laid down by **Section 44** of this Act gave the company an initial tenure of 21 years, as against the 28 granted to the three other early companies, after which, within six months from 10th August 1891, the Metropolitan Board of Works were empowered to purchase the authorised 6 mls. 1 f. 7 ch. of line, provided that the Board of Trade agreed. This condition was to have far-reaching effects, as these sections of line were to be the first to be considered for purchase, not by the Metropolitan Board, but by its successor, the London County Council. **Section 48** of the Act authorised the raising of capital up to £100,000 in £10 shares, with an additional £25,000 to be raised in debenture stock. By **Section 84,** the Metropolitan Police had power to license vehicles, drivers and conductors.

Section 86 empowered the company to enter into traffic arrangements with the Pimlico, Peckham & Greenwich Tramways Company and the Metropolitan Street Tramways Company, which powers passed to their successor, the London Tramways Company in 1873. Under this section, the company could, in whole or in part, work the lines of the other, or any portion of them.

Meanwhile, further proposals were being made for extensions to the authorised lines of the company, and were presented to the Board of Trade and Parliament in time for the Session of 1871. They were quite comprehensive and were grouped under several headings.

1. London Street Tramways (Extensions).
a. From Edgware Road Station, along Edgware Road to Oxford Street.
b. From The Grove, Hammersmith, along Uxbridge Road to Edgware Road, then along Oxford Street, Holborn and Charterhouse Street to Farringdon Road. A branch line to run over Holborn Viaduct to the

Old Bailey, then along Giltspur Street and Charterhouse Street to connect with the proposed line to Farringdon Road.

c. From "The Crown" public house, Bayswater Road, then along Grand Junction Road, Marylebone Road, Euston Road and Pentonville Road to the "Angel", Islington.

d. From the authorised line in Hampstead Road, along George Street to the proposed line in Euston Road.

e. From Camden Town, "Mother Redcap", in two lines:-
   (i) Along Park Street to the "York & Albany" public house.
   (ii) Along High Street, Wellington Street, Gloucester Crescent and Road, where the two lines will run parallel to the Regents Canal, which will be crossed by a single line to Albany Street; then along Albany Road by a double line, Marylebone Road, round Park Crescent, through Portland Place to Regents Circus, Oxford Street.

f. From Hampstead Road near Euston Road, along Tottenham Court Road to Oxford Street.

g. Along Bagnigge Wells Road (King's Cross Road), Farringdon Road, Farringdon Street, New Bridge Street, over Blackfriars Bridge, to make connection with the authorised lines of the Pimlico, Peckham & Greenwich Tramway.

h. From City Road, along Goswell Road and Aldersgate to the G.P.O.

i. From Farringdon Road, along Clerkenwell Green to St. John Street, along Compton Street to Goswell Road. A branch line at Compton Street to run along Northampton Street and Percival Street to join the proposed line in Goswell Road.

j. From Blackfriars Road, along New Southwark Street, Borough High Street to near the railway bridge, thence one line along the railway approach and Denman Street to form a loop line to the tramway in High Street.

2. London Street Tramways (Kensington, Westminster and City Lines Extensions), Hyde Park and Charing Cross Branch.
To commence at Hyde Park Corner, along Piccadilly, Haymarket, Pall Mall East to the west side of Trafalgar Square, along Charing Cross to Nelson Column. It will then return past Charles I Statue, along Cockspur Street, Pall Mall, Waterloo Place and Regent Street to Piccadilly, forming a loop line between Charing Cross and Regents Circus.

3. London Street Tramways (Caledonian Road Extension).
The proposed tramway will commence in Camden Road near the Holloway Road to form a junction with the authorised North London Street Tramways; it will then run along Caledonian Road to Pentonville Road near King's Cross.

4. London Street Tramways (Euston Road Extension).
From Hampstead Road by a junction with the authorised line, along Euston Road to King's Cross where it will join another authorised line in Pentonville Road.

5. London Street Tramways (Kensington, Westminster and City Lines).
Nos. 1 & 1A, commencing near Russell Road, Kensington, along Kensington Road to High Street, then continuing along Kensington Road to the cab stand east of Victoria Road.
Nos. 2 & 2A, short lines from Addison Road Station to join Nos. 1 & 1A.
Nos. 3 & 4, a continuation westwards of Nos. 1 & 1A, along Kensington Road to William Street and along that street.
Nos. 5 & 5A, an eastwards continuation of Nos. 1 & 1A along Kensington Road to Knightsbridge, then on to Grosvenor Place, Hyde Park Corner.

Nos. 6 & 6A, a continuation of Nos. 5 & 5A, along Grosvenor Place, Grosvenor Gardens, part of Vauxhall Bridge Road to Victoria Street, with a junction with the Pimlico Company lines which will, when laid, extend from Vauxhall Bridge Road, along Victoria Street to Artillery Row. Then along Victoria Street to Broad Sanctuary, Westminster.

Nos. 7 & 7A, a continuation of Nos. 6 & 6A, along Broad Sanctuary, Bridge Street and Victoria Embankment to Bridge Street, Blackfriars.

Nos. 8 & 8A, a continuation of Nos. 7 & 7A, from Bridge Street, Blackfriars to Cannon Street along a new street.

No. 9B, a continuation of Nos. 8 & 8A along eastern Queen Victoria Street to Mansion House, then along King William Street, returning to Queen Victoria Street by Cannon Street.

Nos. 9 & 9A, commencing opposite the G.P.O. and running along St. Paul's Churchyard to Cannon Street, thence eastward, joining Nos. 8 & 8A in Queen Victoria Street.

No. 10, commencing on Victoria Embankment by a junction with No. 7A, along a new approach road, then through Whitehall Place, along Whitehall to Charing Cross, returning to the Embankment by the same route.

Nos. 11 & 12, junctions on Victoria Embankment connecting Nos. 10, 7 & 7A.

Nos. 13 & 14, junctions with Nos. 6 & 6A and the Pimlico Tramway in Vauxhall Bridge Road by Victoria Street.

Nos. 15 & 16, junctions from Westminster Bridge with Nos. 7 & 7A on Victoria Embankment.

Nos. 17 & 18, junctions from Bridge Street with Nos. 8 & 8A.

No. 19, a short single line connecting the proposed tramways in Cannon Street by Victoria Street.

Much of the foregoing was outside what became the "home ground" of the operations of the company. A large part of it overlapped the proposals made by other bodies, both the established companies and other entrepreneurs, while a portion of it was for tramways on unchallenged ground, mostly in the "West End", which was to remain as an unattainable prize in the tramway stakes.

By the time that the Metropolitan Board of Works had made a study of these proposals, a general hardening of attitude in Government circles had taken place. The Board of Trade, Board of Works and Parliament had become concerned over what they termed the "mania" allegedly showing itself with regard to the many proposals for building tramways. Control was achieved by means of an Act entitled **"The Metropolitan Tramways Provisional Orders Suspension Act, 1871 (34-35 Vic. cap. lxviiii),** which effectively put a stop for two years to the passage of all Bills through Parliament where they affected tramways in the Metropolis.

Track Construction

One of the problems associated with track construction in the early days of street tramways in Britain was the difficulty experienced in fixing the rail sections to the timber longitudinals. The most common method in use was for vertical spikes to be hammered through prepared holes in the bottom of the grooves of the cast iron bar rails which, apart from this fixing, merely rested on top of the supporting timbers, or sometimes had a projecting lip or flange extending over one edge of the timber.

After a year or so of use, the rails became loose, due, in the main, to the shocks imparted by the car wheels to the rail joints and to the

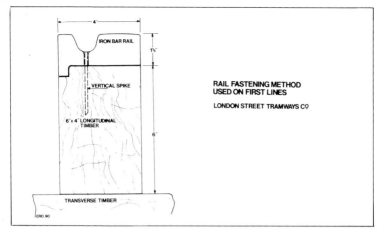

IRON BAR RAIL

4"

1½"

VERTICAL SPIKE

6" x 4" LONGITUDINAL
TIMBER

6"

TRANSVERSE TIMBER

ERO.90

RAIL FASTENING METHOD
USED ON FIRST LINES

LONDON STREET TRAMWAYS CO

stresses imposed upon the rail sections by other road vehicles. Once loosened, spikes lifted and were promptly hammered down again by the passage of the wheel flanges of the next tramcar to pass over the track. This caused the holes made by the spikes in the timbers to open up. Wet and freezing weather did the rest. Wandering rails, dropped joints, loose and missing spikes, all caused premature wear to car wheels, springing and bodywork, and, to say the least, gave a rough ride, if not exactly a dangerous one. Complaints of one kind or another were hurled at the tramway companies, who soon saw their good name and, as important, their business sadly going down to a low level. Several engineers had been looking at this problem with varying degrees of success, with one, Jorgen Daniel Larsen producing something which worked satisfactorily and which was employed in the construction of the London Street Tramways track.

The Larsen Fastening

As a result of the authority given under the Act of 1870, work commenced early in 1871 on the section of line from Euston Road, along Hampstead Road, Camden High Street and Kentish Town Road to the Midland Railway Station, the contractor being Mr. Sewell.

In the construction of this section, J. D. Larsen employed his special design of rail, which, after modification, he eventually patented. The rails were four inches wide, weighed 60 lbs/yard and were double flanged. They were fixed upon the tops of longitudinal sleepers six inches in depth by means of side fastenings, which at first consisted of three pieces, an iron strap 3¼ in. long, ⅝ in. wide and ⅜ in. thick and two spikes which were driven horizontally into the sleeper through a hole at each end of the strap. The upper spike also passed through a hole made in the flange of the rail. In some cases, the fastenings could be taken right through the sleepers, to fit into holes in the flange on the opposite side. Subsequently, in his patent design, he reduced the number of pieces to two on each side of the rail.

The excavation for the foundation was carried down to a level of four inches below the underside of the sleepers, for the whole width of the way. An even bed of concrete, four inches thick, was placed in the bottom and the longitudinal sleepers laid directly upon it. The timbers were placed in cast-iron chairs at the joints, and the gauge was

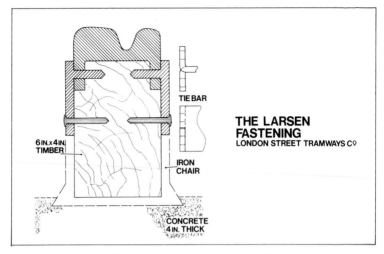

THE LARSEN FASTENING
LONDON STREET TRAMWAYS Cº

TIE BAR

6 IN. x 4 IN.
TIMBER

IRON
CHAIR

CONCRETE
4 IN. THICK

fixed by means of 2 in. by ⅜ in. flat bar-iron ties, "split and kneed" both ways at the ends, and fixed to the sleepers by bolts or spikes. Flat fishplates, 9 in. x 3 in. x ½ in. were placed beneath each rail joint. A two-inch layer of sand or gravel was distributed over the concrete surface to form a bed for the paving, which was laid and grouted in the usual manner.

Hampstead Road Completed

The line was reported in "The Standard" as having opened to traffic on 27th November 1871. It was, however, strictly unofficial, as no request had been made by the company to the Board of Trade for the work to be inspected. This resulted in an Assistant Secretary of the Board, W. R. Malcolm telling J. Barber Glenn, the secretary of the company, that the opening was totally out of order, indeed illegal. On 1st December, Glenn made a profuse apology, adding " ... as secretary of the company, I overlooked the fact that such an inspection was necessary ... "

On 4th December, Malcolm appointed Col. Yolland to carry out an inspection, which took place on 7th. Yolland reported that there was no plan to check the work against; that the road, although generally well laid, had sunk in places; and that there was so much mud about, particularly at Monte Video Place (later, after road widening, becoming an extension of Great College Street at the junction with Kentish Town Road) that he could not even find the rails! At one place, "according to the conductor of the car", there was not sufficient room between the sets of rails for the cars to pass one another.

The Colonel then referred to Clause 7 of the company's Act " ... where the distance is less than the (statutory) 9 ft. 6 in. between the footpath and the outer rails of a double line of tramway, the company shall, and they are hereby required, to construct a passing place or places connecting one tramway with the other and by means of such place or places the traffic shall, when necessary, be diverted from the one tramway to the other". As, in his opinion, this Order had not been complied with, he declined to issue a certificate, instructing the company to apply this procedure with respect to the lines in Monte

Video Place. He also adversely commented on the condition of the roadway.

Even though the Board's approval was not forthcoming, it did not, it seems, debar the company from continuing to operate; a service was being provided and continued to be provided, the company saying that the Act of Parliament was unclear on this point. Neither were they challenged, as under the terms of the Act, there appeared to be no requirement that they should inform the Board, or ask for an inspection.

The response from Barber Glenn was not long coming, when he wrote:- "I find that at Monte Video Place where there is a double line of tramway with a less width between the outside of the footpath and the tramway than 9 ft. 6 in., the company has constructed a passing place connecting the one tramway with the other as directed by the section referred to". Yolland retorted on 22nd December that "it was not there when I made my inspection". This led to an impasse which was only broken by a re-inspection of the line by Yolland on 5th January 1872, when he said - " ... the paved road ... is much improved ... and needs to be looked after. The double line in the narrow part of Monte Video Place is authorised to be so laid by the deposited plans, and a passing place exists at this narrow part, to cross from one line to the other as prescribed by Clause 7. It must have been covered up with mud when I went over the line before, as the gentleman, Mr. Ayres, who accompanied me, nor myself, could trace it, although we searched for it. The conductor was in error (referring to the cars being unable to pass) in his statement regarding the narrow part of Monte Video Place". He then recommended that the sanction of the Board be given and a certificate issued, although he noted that "the opening has already taken place". The certificate was issued on 9th January 1872. The depot for this section of the line was between Nos. 36 and 42 Kentish Town Road, on the east side, just south of Kentish Town Wharf on the Regents Canal.

More Completions

The next section to be completed by Sewell was from Camden Town Station (NLR) to the "Brecknock Arms" in Camden Road, and on 19th January 1872 the company secretary informed the Board of Trade that they were ready for an inspection, enclosing a specification of the works:-
"The line is 5 furlongs in length, all double line, using best rolled iron grooved rails on 6 in. by 4 in. longitudinal sleepers of best red Baltic timber. Rails are 18 ft. long, joined by cast-iron shoes and fishplates, 9 in. by 3 in. by ½ in. thick. The ground is excavated to a depth of 17 in. by 17 in. wide. The whole width of the roadway is macadamised on a 9 in. bed of concrete, with 6 in. by 3 in. Mount Sorrel granite setts between the rails, well grouted and rammed with liquid mortar".

Col. Yolland carried out his inspection of the lines on 25th January 1872 and stated that, while the ride he experienced was smooth, he could not tell whether the road was laid with granite or macadam as there was so much mud lying about. Nevertheless, on the following day he authorised the line for public use. The certificate was received by the company on 29th January. On 29th February, he inspected the line between Camden Town Station and King's Cross via Great College Street and Pancras Road. However, he declined to authorise its use until the condition of the road surface had been improved, criticising the contractor and the local authority for not clearing the road of mud. Following this, a gang of 50 men set to work to carry out repairs, while the Local Board was prevailed upon to clear up the rest of the mess. A second inspection was carried out by Yolland on 21st March and, apart from commenting on a few minor repairs which he considered should be dealt with, he authorised the use of the 1 ml. 3 ch. of line.

Meanwhile, the Great Northern Railway Company, by agreement with the local authority, had closed the part of Pancras Road between the Great Northern Hotel and King's Cross and had made a diversion to another road running alongside the Midland Railway Station. The tramway was laid on the new alignment, but this meant that it also had to have a section in Euston Road, which required the authority of the Board of Trade, which was obtained by issuing a Provisional Order.

King's Cross Station and its environs on a busy day. Car No. 622 is making its way out of Pancras Road to join the main stream of traffic in Euston Road. *(Commercial view)*

The last 2 f. 8.25 ch. of the original line to be completed was from Brecknock Road northwards along Camden Road and Park Road. At this point, ownership of the next 3 f. 2.5 ch. of line to Holloway Road was vested in the North Metropolitan Tramways Company who contracted with the London Street Company to carry out its construction. The specification for this portion was identical with that used for the other sections. As stated elsewhere, the tracks of the two companies should have been connected, but this was not effected at this time.

Capt. Tyler was appointed to inspect, undertaking the task on 14th August 1872. He reported favourably on both sections, the certificate authorising the company to use the line being received on 19th August. Public service, however, did not commence for several weeks. It is believed that it was on 1st October that the first cars ran on the line, terminating just short of Holloway Road, close by the depot, which was in Parkhurst Road, not far from the "Nag's Head".

Even though all further development on tramways in the Metropolis had been brought to a standstill by Parliament, the company decided to press for extensions in the 1872 and 1873 Parliamentary Sessions.

In 1873 they were successful, as the bar had been lifted on the passage of "London" Bills, with those in suspension being processed as they were originally presented. So far as the company was concerned, both the 1871 and 1872 Bills were heard, and later in 1873, authority was given by two further Acts to continue expansion, even if only in a limited way. These were:-

a. **The Metropolitan Tramways Orders (Confirmation) Act, 1873 (36 - 37) Vic. cap. ccxv),** which received the Royal Assent on 5th August, and gave powers for the construction of junction lines from St. Pancras Road into Euston Road, past King's Cross Station and into Pentonville Road (being the subject of the Provisional Order previously obtained.

b. **The London Street Tramways (Further Powers) Act, 1873 (36-37 Vic. cap. ccxxi),** also received Royal Assent on 5th August and empowered the company to have transferred to it the tramway that had been built in Park Road for the Northmet Company. The Act also gave authority for the two companies to enter into through running agreements, subject only to the approval of the Board of Trade.

In 1874, the company was still looking towards making further extensions to its system, and included an application again for some of the routes not authorised by the 1873 Act. These were:-
1. From Leighton Road, Kentish Town Road, along Junction Road to Holloway Road.
2. From Camden Road at Park Road, then along Hillmartin Road to Caledonian Road.
3. From Caledonian Road, along North Street to Pentonville Road.

The Metropolitan Board of Works and the Board of Trade received the proposals in 1874 which were to form the basis of a Provisional Order granted by the Board of Trade and confirmed in **The Tramways Orders (Confirmation) Act, 1874, (37-38 Vic. cap. clxxxiii),** to which the Royal Assent was given on 7th August. The authorised lines were:-
No. 1, a double line 6.75 ch. long, from Kentish Town Station Bridge at

The "Archway Tavern" was the terminus for cars of both the London Street and the North Metropolitan companies. The car on the left is on the Clerkenwell service; the right-hand one on the Moorgate service. Compare this view with that on page 513.   *(Commercial view)*

559

an end-on junction with the existing tramway, into Fortess Road near Blandford Place.

No. 2, a single line 2 f. 8.30 ch. long, along Fortess Road, from Blandford Place to Brecknock Road at the "Boston Arms".

No. 3, a passing place 2.50 ch. long, in Fortess Road by Lady Somerset Road.

No. 4, a single line 4 f. 9.70 ch. long, along Junction Road from the "Boston Arms" to Archway Road.

No. 5, five short junction lines (passing places), of a total length of about 1 f. 5 ch.

The method of construction was to be with transverse ties of fir, 4 in. by 6 in., laid at 6 ft. intervals, with concrete packed to the top of the sleepers. Longitudinal sleepers, 4 in. by 6 in., with preformed tops to be laid on the transverse timbers and fixed to them by means of side angle brackets of wrought iron. The 55 lbs/yard wrought iron rails to be fastened to the longitudinals by side fixings every 3 ft. Flat metal plates to be placed under all rail joints. All macadam used outside the rails to be well rammed.

Maj. Gen. Hutchinson inspected the section between Kentish Town Station and the "Boston Arms" on 23rd April 1874 and, after a discourse on a discrepancy over the size of the "flat plates" employed, authorised its use. The final length, from the "Boston Arms" to the "Archway Tavern" was satisfactorily inspected by Col. Yolland on 28th May. The depot for the whole line was in Junction Road near Poynings Road.

By 1875, the company had expended £94,900 on capital account. Receipts for the year were £43,497, expenses £34,860, with 5,350,000 passengers being carried during the year. A dividend of 7¼% was declared.

Along Caledonian Road

In 1877, the company put forward another extension proposal to the Board of Trade in respect of a line in Caledonian Road. In this case, there was opposition from a body calling itself "The London Central Tramways Company", which was attempting to obtain powers to build this line, as well as several others eleswhere. It was, however, the London Street Tramways Company that was successful.

Royal Assent was given on 10th August 1877 to **The London Street Tramways (Caledonian Road Extension) Act, 1877 (40-41 Vic. cap. ccxix)** for a double line of tramway to be constructed from Pentonville Road, along Caledonian Road, there to make a junction with the lines of the North Metropolitan Tramways at Holloway Road by Camden Road, a distance of 1 ml. 6 f. 7 ch., to be known as **Tramways Nos. 1 and 2.**

Construction commenced in the spring of 1878, but during the work, the North Metropolitan Company objected to a connection being made, whereupon the London Street Company provided a stub-end terminus at the end of Caledonian Road, which made the total length of the lines some 4 chains (88 yards) shorter than shown on the plans. The completed work was inspected by Maj. Marindin on 20th September, and he authorised its use. Services began on Monday 28th September.

The Company in Difficulty

As has previously been mentioned, the company found itself in some difficulty in 1875 and turned to the North Metropolitan Company in 1876 for assistance. A lease and purchase proposal was made by George

Richardson, chairman of the North Metropolitan to George Morris, solicitor to the London Street Company on 15th November 1876.

On 16th November, Morris conveyed the terms of the offer to the directors, indicating that he had every confidence that the sum of £10. 10s, mentioned as being the likely maximum price that the North Metropolitan would pay for each of the 10,000 London Street shares under discussion, could be increased to £11.

With regard to the difficulty being experienced, the London Street Company had been involved in litigation over a very serious accident which had occurred in 1875, and although the matter had been settled in Court, the company was under the impression that the plaintiffs were about to ask for a retrial of the case. This threat, however, was removed when the Court decided not to allow this.

Although discussions continued over the next two years, the proposal to lease the company to the Northmet came to nothing, as the move was declared to be illegal. This, in turn, caused the North Metropolitan to reconsider its position with regard to purchase, although from time to time the matter was raised in both companies' boardrooms.

The company was again in trouble in 1880. At a meeting held on 20th February, with G. F. Fry in the Chair, a proposition to reconstruct the Board was discussed, as some shareholders had become displeased with the way in which the affairs of the company had been, in their view, dealt with. This resulted in a call for the resignation of one of the directors, Mr. Erichson, and also that of Mr. Sheldon. Erichson went, Sheldon stayed. There was also a difference of opinion regarding the way that the duties of manager and secretary were being conducted and it was reported that another of the directors, Mr. Bacon, made the point that both duties should not be covered by the same man, in this case, Mr. J. Barber Glenn. In his view, the manager should be out of doors and the secretary in the office. Eventually, this matter was resolved by the appointment of Maj. Hill as manager.

The 1879 and 1882 Acts

On 24th July 1879, **The London Street Tramways (Extensions) Act, 1879 (42-43 Vic. cap. clxxxix)** was obtained, authorising the company to construct a double line, 7 f. 2.9 ch. long, from a junction with the existing tramway in Kentish Town Road, along Prince of Wales Road, Malden Road and Southampton Road, to terminate at Circus Road, Hampstead, and known as **Tramways Nos. 1 and 1A** in the originating proposal. Another section of the Act gave authority to the company to increase its share capital to a maximum of £24,000 and to increase borrowing powers on mortgage up to £6,000. There were also the usual protective clauses included. Work was completed during April 1880, and the line was inspected by Maj. Gen. Hutchinson on 30th, who approved its use for traffic. Services commenced on 10th May. A number of other extensions had been proposed, including lines in Marylebone and St. John's Wood, but these were not allowed.

In 1880 and 1881, the company tried to obtain authority to construct a number of additional lines in and around St. Pancras, Bayswater, Marylebone, Islington and Holborn, but met with stiff opposition, which resulted in the proposals being dropped, some at least for the time being. In 1882, they tried again, this time with a little more success, as a double line along Pentonville Road between King's Cross and the "Angel", Islington, a distance of 5 f. 3.5 ch., was authorised by **The London Street Tramways (Extensions) Act, 1882 (45-46 Vic. cap. clxiii)**, which received Royal Assent on 24th July.

One of the small double deck cars built by the Falcon Engine & Car Works Ltd. for use on the Pentonville Road line.   *(Brush Co. photo)*

By **Section 6** of the Act, authority was given to raise new capital up to £55,000, while by **Section 8**, extra borrowing on mortgage up to £18,500 was permitted, but none of this was to be borrowed until the whole of the additional capital was issued and half paid-up.

At the King's Cross end, it had been arranged that a connection with the existing line could be made, while at the Islington end, a single line stub-end was provided. The type of rail suggested was to incorporate a wrought-iron "standard", upon which the rail-head was to be keyed. However, Maj. Gen. Hutchinson recommended that, instead of keying the rail-heads to the uprights, they should be firmly bolted, to make them much more rigid. This done, the completed work was inspected by him on 23rd June 1883 and the authorising certificate issued on 25th.

In January 1882, the company deposited a proposal in an attempt to obtain a Provisional Order to enable them to construct a tramway in the Hampstead area from Adelaide Road, along Haverstock Hill as far as Heath Street, a distance of about 1 ml. 6. f. This raised a storm of protest, both with the members of the Hampstead Vestry and sundry other individuals and groups. The tone set by these people, some of whom were known as "influential persons" in the area, can be seen in the Notice circulated in the name of the Permanent Committee of Hampstead Residents.

Mainly due to vociferous opposition raised, the line was never authorised. But the company did not give up all that easily. In 1884, it was still proposing to build lines in the Hampstead districts of Chalk Farm and Haverstock Hill. These were:-
1. From Park Street, Camden Town, along Chalk Farm Road to the "Adelaide Tavern", Haverstock Hill.
2. Along Haverstock Hill to the west end of Prince of Wales Road.
3. Along Prince of Wales Road to the existing tramway at Malden Road.
4. Along Ferdinand Street.

OPPOSITION TO
HAVERSTOCK HILL & HAMPSTEAD TRAMWAYS

Application is about to be made to Parliament for a private Bill to authorise the construction of Tramways, on the public highway, up Haverstock Hill to Hampstead Heath, through High Street and Heath Street, to be worked by Cable, Locomotive, or other mechanical or motive power, in addition to, or in substitution for animal labour.

The promoters of the Bill propose to obtain a concession of the greater portion of the chief highway in Hampstead, for the purpose of laying down rails, and thus appropriating the main road to the almost exclusive use of a speculative Company with nothing but selfish and pecuniary interests to serve.

It is earnestly hoped that all the inhabitants of this favourite suburb will do their utmost to resist this bold encroachment on their rights.

A permanent Committee of Hampstead residents has been formed in order to protect the interests of the inhabitants, and now urge upon their consideration the following reasons for protesting against the infliction of the proposed Tramways.—

I. Tramways are unsuitable to the road proposed to be traversed by them. The road is narrow in many places, the gradients are exceedingly steep, and the ordinary traffic would in consequence be impeded by the trams, which would in many places monopolise the road.

II. The injury to the horses and vehicles of residents in the town by the rails on our hilly road would be a daily loss to the owners. Horses with laden wagons have to climb our hills in zigzag fashion, and would constantly cross and re-cross the tramways, involving the liability of collision with descending trams.

III. The irritating annoyance caused by the vibration of the cars or locomotives, and the constant jingling of the bells to warn the public, would be a serious nuisance day and night to the residents in the line of road, and would drive away the best ratepayers.

IV. The still greater damage in depreciating the value of property all along the route traversed by the trams calls for very serious consideration, before granting a concession of our valuable roads to such a monopoly.

V. It is submitted that the Queen's highway should be, and was designed to be, for the common use of all Her Majesty's subjects, without favour or prejudice to any. It is a violation of our common rights, notwithstanding trams in other districts, to sanction such a monopoly of the best part of our highway to the proposed schemes.

VI. It is a well-known fact that, wherever trams are permitted in the suburbs, the result is the gradual decline of the neighbourhood in residential and commercial importance, as witness Islington, Brixton, and Clapham, in the last named of which places many large houses are deserted, and will remain so. Trams will vulgarise Hampstead, and lower its tone as a superior residential suburb.

VII. The trading interests of Hampstead contribute largely to the metropolitan rates and to local taxation, and have a just claim to be considered in this matter. The establishment of tramways would be peculiarly injurious to traders, because their customers would avoid the business thoroughfares on account of the injury done to their horses and carriages by the tramways. The tradesmen feel that a grievous loss would be sustained by them if this monopoly were permitted to be placed on the roads of this Parish.

VIII. It is an important fact that there are already seven Railway Stations belonging to four different Companies in the Parish of Hampstead, besides the omnibus service of the London General Omnibus Company, and there is a probability of another Railway Station being opened on Haverstock Hill. There is, therefore, ample accommodation for all in the various parts of the Parish, and no need for the proposed tramways.

IX. The road proposed to be traversed by the trams is not a *through* artery for continuous traffic. It practically stops short at Hampstead, so that there is the less need for additional means of transit.

X. Our Sundays are now comparatively orderly and quiet in the main road. But if trams were permitted, they would bring crowds of the most objectionable classes to disperse in the midst of our town, with all the noise, drinking, and other unseemly behaviour of many Sunday excursionists. This would be a very grave evil, and should be thoroughly appreciated by those to whom Sunday is a sacred day of rest.

XI. It appears a monstrous and unreasonable thing that a speculative company should, unasked by the residents, with only selfish interests to serve, be clothed with powers to injure permanently the comfort and rights of the inhabitants, the property along the road, and the commercial interests of this town, which would assuredly be the case if this favourite suburb were invaded by tramways.

The energetic action of the Vestry and this Committee in opposing this scheme at the Board of Trade in January last, was successful in defeating it. *The promoters of this injurious speculation have now changed their tactics, and are going direct to Parliament for a private Bill.* But to obtain this, the consent of the Road Authorities having jurisdiction over two-thirds of the proposed route is necessary under the Standing Orders of both Houses. And we have great hopes that we may induce the Vestry to withhold their consent.

Signed on behalf of the Permanent Committee:—
JAMES HEWETSON, *Hon. Secretary & Treasurer,*
Nov. 23rd, 1882.   11 & 12, High Street, Hampstead, N.W.

A Memorial to the Hampstead Vestry in support of the arguments above set out will shortly be sent to the Residents for Signature.

5. Doubling along Fortess and Junction Roads.
6. An extension of the Pentonville Road line beyond King's Cross to Charterhouse Street, a distance of about 1 ml. 2 f.

In this case, only a small part of the presented Bill managed to survive in Parliament, the remainder of which emerged as **The London Street Tramways (Extensions) Act, 1884 (47-48 Vic. cap. xciv)**, which received Royal Assent on 3rd July, and referred to doubling the line running from Fortess Road into and along Junction Road, about 9 chains in length.

From the terms of the report it appears that there was an element of "horse trading" by various Boards of Works in their dealings with the company. In the instance of the doubling in Junction Road, one of the conditions laid upon the company in exchange for the sanction of the Islington Board was that it should "cube" (i.e. lay stone setts) for the whole width of the road.

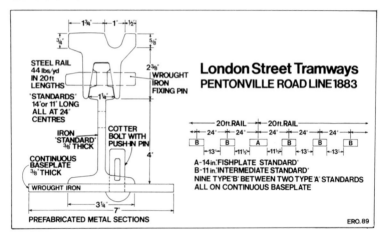

The Acts of 1885, 1887 and 1888

Mention was again made in 1885 of the London Central Tramways in connection with proposals to lay tramways in Holborn, Clerkenwell and Islington. There were, however, many objections and none of the proposals were proceeded with. At the same time, the London Street Tramways Company sought authority to make a considerable number of extensions to the system, involving, in all, 25 "tramways", of which some were doublings of existing single sections. **The London Street Tramways (Extensions) Act, 1885 (48-49 Vic. cap. cxv)** received Royal Assent on 22nd July and authorised the construction of the following:-
No. 1, a single line, 4 f. 4.30 ch. long, commencing in Southampton Road by a junction with the existing tramway opposite Circus Road, along and into Fleet Road, terminating at South End Green.
Nos. 1B to 1E, four passing places in Fleet Road.
No. 1F, a terminal line 0.80 ch. (18 yards) long, at South End Green.
Nos. 2 & 2A, a double line 1.60 ch. long, at Junction Road near Vorley Road.
Nos. 3 & 3A, a double line 7.70 ch. long, along Fortess Road from opposite No. 152 to Lady Somerset Road.
Nos. 4 & 4A, a double line 1.60 ch. long, along Fortess Road near Fortess Grove.

A line of cars seen standing at the South End Green, Hampstead, terminus, and being made ready for their return to various central London destinations. (Commercial view. Courtesy: J. B. Gent)

No. 6, a single line 3 f. 4.60 ch. long, along Kentish Town Road from Rochester Road, into High Street Camden Town, to terminate opposite the "Mother Redcap".

No. 6A, a single line 1 f. 0.85 ch. long, in Kentish Town Road, commencing by a junction with the existing tramway near Rochester Road and terminating by a junction with No. 6 just south of Clarence Road.

No. 6B, a single line 3.50 ch. long, in Kentish Town Road near Hawley Road.

No. 6C, a single line 2 ch. long, in Kentish Town Road near Hawley Crescent.

No. 6D, a single line 4.40 ch. long, from a point just south of Bank Street, into High Street, Camden Town, terminating opposite "Mother Redcap".

No. 25, a single line 6 f. 8.10 ch. long, in Pentonville Road, by a junction with the existing tramway, 1.75 ch. west of North Street, into and along King's Cross Road and Farringdon Road, terminating 1.25 ch. north-west of Farringdon and Clerkenwell Roads.

No. 25A, a single line 2.40 ch. long, from 1.75 ch. west of North Street, along Pentonville Road into King's Cross Road and terminating by a junction with No. 25, 2.75 ch. north-west of Field Street.

Nos. 25B to 25E, passing places in King's Cross Road.

Nos. 25F to 25I, passing places in Farringdon Road.

It was stipulated that girder rails were to be used, 7 inches high, from 20 to 30 feet in length, made of best steel and connected together with steel fishplates 20 inches long, weighing 24 lbs/pair.

Work commenced on Tramway No. 6 and the passing places, Nos. 6A to 6D in Kentish Town Road in the early spring on 1886, and were ready for inspection by Maj. Gen. Hutchinson on 26th May. Apart from a few minor alterations to be made to the rail fastenings, the lines were declared fit for use. This was followed in June by the completion of Tramways Nos. 1 and 1B to 1F. They were inspected by the Major General on 16th and opened to traffic on the following day.

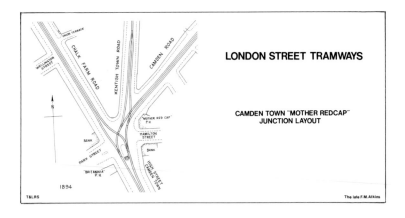

LONDON STREET TRAMWAYS

CAMDEN TOWN "MOTHER REDCAP"
JUNCTION LAYOUT

On completion of the lines designated Nos. 1 etc., the contractor moved on to King's Cross Road and Farringdon Road to begin work on Tramways Nos. 25, 25A and the passing places 25B to 25I. By mid-October, a considerable amount of work had been completed, in fact, much more than had been authorised by Parliament. Some sections shown as single lines with passing places had been effectively doubled by extending some of the loops by a sufficient length that they were joined together. A complaint by a Mr. L. Vickers to this effect on 16th October moved the Board of Trade sufficiently to ask the company for an explanation.

The reply from J. Barber Glenn confirmed that the additional work had been carried out, explaining that, as the Vestries had agreed to this while road widenings were being carried out, the company decided to instal the additional tracks at the same time. Glenn also asked the Board to inspect the completed lines, which Maj. Gen. Hutchinson did on 29th October.

Hutchinson authorised their use as they were well laid and well sited, but added a rider that, due to the divergence from the terms of the Act, the company must, if any complaints be made regarding the positions of the rails at any time in the future, agree to relay the lines as cited in the Act if called upon to do so. The company was also advised to confirm the departures from the 1885 Act by securing a further Act. Thus assured, Hutchinson recommended the issue of a certificate on 16th December 1886. The complaint from Mr. Vickers was "left on the table" until the company had obtained the necessary authority.

When the line was opened in Great College Street between Kentish Town Road and Camden Road in mid-June 1886, it provided an alternative route from Camden Town into Kentish Town Road, and all services ceased to use the original short length of track in the southern part of Kentish Town Road. The tracks remained in situ for many years, eventually being taken over by the London County Council with the rest of the assets of the company. Upon electrification of the Camden Road lines, a conduit junction was installed and temporarily connected to the horse car tracks, as the LCC at first had decided to electrify the line, but rescinded this later. The spur remained until about 1910, with the occasional statutory horse car maintaining the rights of the Council.

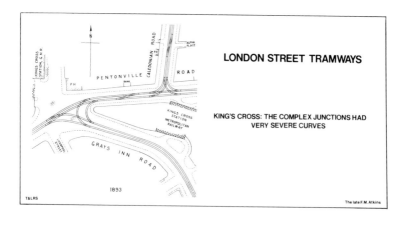

LONDON STREET TRAMWAYS

KING'S CROSS: THE COMPLEX JUNCTIONS HAD
VERY SEVERE CURVES

Two more Bills were presented to Parliament in 1887 and 1888, both of which resulted in further Acts being obtained by the company. The first, **The London Street Tramways Act, 1887 (50 Session 2 cap. iv),** to which Royal Assent was obtained on 29th March, authorised the following tramways:-

The Highgate Road Lines.
No. 2, a line 4 f. 9 ch. long, of which 2 f. 9 ch. is single, commencing in Kentish Town Road by a junction with the existing tramway, passing into and along Highgate Road to near Woodsome Road.
No. 2A, a line 1 f. 5.3 ch. long, of which 9.8 ch. is single, from No. 2 to its termination near Swains Lane.

The Chalk Farm Lines.
No. 3, a double line 3 f. 2 ch. long, from the existing tramway in High Street Camden Town just south of Park Street, passing along High Street, across Chalk Farm Road Bridge into and along Chalk Farm Road to just south of Ferdinand Street.

King's Cross in the 1890s, with a car bound for Hampstead. Pentonville Road (left) and Gray's Inn Road (centre) was where the severely curved junction line was laid, as shown in the plan above. (L T Museum U3921)

567

No. 3C, a double line 1 f. 9.7 ch. long, commencing in Chalk Farm Road at Tramway No. 3, passing into and along Ferdinand Street and Malden Crescent, crossing Prince of Wales Road into and terminating in Malden Road opposite the "Mother Shipton" tavern by a junction with the existing tramway.

The Crowndale Road Line.

No. 4, a line 2 f. 2 ch. long, of which 8.5 ch. is single, commencing at the existing tramway in High Street Camden Town opposite the Cobden Statue, passing into and along Crowndale Road and St. Pancras Road, terminating by a junction with the existing tramway just east of Great College Street.

Doubling of Existing Lines.

No. 5A, in Kentish Town Road.

Nos. 5B to 5E, all in Junction Road.

The South End Green Line.

No. 6, a double line 2.75 ch. long, from the end of Tramway No. 1 in Fleet Road (1885 Act), to a terminus at the end of a new road to be constructed across South End Green.

The Gray's Inn Road Line.

No. 8, a double line 5 f. 8.5 ch. long, commencing at King's Cross at the existing tramway opposite Liverpool Street, passing into and along Gray's Inn Road, terminating at a point opposite Henry Street.

No. 8A, a double line 9.6 ch. long, commencing at No. 8 in Gray's Inn Road, passing along and terminating in Gray's Inn Road, 0.5 ch. south of Theobalds Road.

Steel girder rails weighing 90 lbs/yard and of a length between 24 ft. and 30 ft. were specified, together with steel fishplates, 20 inches long, weighing 40 lbs/pair.

By **Section 13** of the Act, new capital stock to the value of £60,000 was authorised, while by **Section 15,** borrowing powers were given up to a maximum of £15,000.

After construction of these sections of line, they were inspected by Maj. Gen. Hutchinson on the following dates.

Nos. 2 and 2A.	16th June 1887.
Nos. 3 and 3C.	28th September 1887.
Nos. 5A to 5E.	Presumably not inspected.
No. 6.	16th June 1887.
Nos. 8 and 8A.	16th May 1889.
Tramway No. 4 was not built.	

The last Act obtained by the company before the LCC came into office was entitled **The London Street Tramways Act, 1888 (51-52 Vic. cap. lxxviii),** which received Royal Assent on 5th July, and which authorised the following tramways:-

Nos. 2 & 2A, junction lines from Pentonville Road to Gray's Inn Road, 1.5 ch. double, and from Caledonian Road to Pentonville Road, 2.5 ch. double.

Nos. 7 & 7A, a line 1 ml. 5 f. 8 ch. long, of which 1 ml. 1 f. 2 ch. is single, from the north end of Junction Road, along Archway Road to High North Road.

On completion, the junction lines Nos. 2 and 2A were inspected by Maj. Gen. Hutchinson on 16th May 1889. Tramways Nos. 7 and 7A were not built.

The London County Council Involvement

Unlike the first three companies to obtain authorising Acts, the London Street Tramways was not protected with a 28-year security of tenure. Consequently, very soon after taking office, the new County Council armed itself with a complete dossier consisting of all the Acts obtained and of the financial and working history of the company, with the intention of purchasing what became available to it under the 21-year clause when it fell due. The receipt of this news was viewed with alarm and bad feeling by the management, with acrimonious statements being made by those in control, as well as in the tramway industry generally and, indeed, among some of the members of the new County Council. Under the terms of the Tramways Act, 1870, it could be interpreted that the sale and purchase of undertakings to municipal bodies could, if a hard enough bargain was driven, be obtained at what was described as "scrap iron" prices, and this is what appeared to the company to be the attitude displayed by the LCC.

On 15th June 1891, the first blow was struck. The LCC formally proposed that the first sections be purchased, amounting to just over 4¼ miles and consisting of the lines from Kentish Town to King's Cross and from "Nag's Head" Holloway to Euston Road. This was about one-third of the total mileage owned and operated by the company. The management took exception to being "threatened" in this way as, in its opinion, it would have been extremely difficult to divide the assets in such a way that services could be maintained and that each partner would obtain a fair deal. In any case, as each section fell due for purchase at later dates, the whole procedure would necessarily have to be gone through again and again. This was one of the first lessons to be learned about the content of the 1870 Act; the problems which would arise 21 years later were not appreciated when the Act was constructed.

However, after delivering its proposal, the LCC found itself divided over the issue. In June and July 1891, the full Council met to consider the matter, but the division among the opposing factions was so deep, that both these occasions passed without a formal procedure being agreed to. On 29th October, the matter was once again brought up in the Council chamber and, after more acrimonious discussion, which resulted in a number of the "moderate" members walking out, the motion was finally passed that the Council take steps to acquire the first lines belonging to the company, together with two depots, plant, equipment and tools necessary to maintain that part of the system, as allowed by the Tramways Act. This decision was notified to the Board of Trade on the following day.

Notice was served upon the company on 12th November and, at the same time, it was invited to send in an assessment and claim as a basis for negotiations with the Council. This appeared to have had little effect as, in February 1892, the chairman of the Highways Committee, Mr. Bassett Hopkins, stated that no progress had been made "as the company will not come to terms". Eventually, at the end of the month, the company did respond with a claim for £604,090, which was totally rejected by the Council. In turn, the company rejected the right of the Council to purchase at anything less than this sum and demanded that an arbitrator be appointed to sort the whole problem out. Sir Frederick Bramwell was, by the authority of the Board of Trade and with the agreement of both parties, appointed to the task which was the first of its kind in the metropolitan area.

The hearing commenced during the last week of June 1892 and went on until 14th July. As the session of 30th June, the Engineer, George Hopkins, gave a detailed report of the state of the company as at that date. The directors at this time were W. R. Bacon (Chairman), G. F. Fry, John Greig, J. M. Gillies and C. Q. Henriques. The secretary was

J. Barber Glenn and the traffic manager was Maj. A. Hill.

Ten services of cars were worked:-
1. Highgate "Archway Tavern" - Euston, worked from Junction Road depot.
2. Holloway - Euston, worked from Parkhurst Road depot.
3. Hampstead - "Angel", worked from Cressy Road and Pentonville Road depots.
4. Hampstead - Euston, worked from Cressy Road depot.
5. Hampstead - Holborn, worked from Cressy Road depot.
6. Highgate Road - Holborn, worked from Junction Road depot.
7. Caledonian Road - Holborn, worked from Warlters Road and Parkhurst Road depots.
8. Caledonian Road - Clerkenwell, worked from Warlters Road depot.
9. Caledonian Road - King's Cross, worked from Parkhurst Road depot.
10. (Finsbury Park) - Caledonian Road - then as 9.

This six-window car, working on the Hampstead Heath and Euston Road service has a display on the waist panels proclaiming "Park Street for Zoological Gardens".   *(Courtesy: L T Museum U22246)*

Arbitration

In the meantime, Mr. Andrew Nance, manager of The Belfast Street Tramways Company had been called upon to undertake an impartial assessment of the company and its methods of operation. His evidence was presented to the arbitrator in December 1892, in which he pointed out the options and economics of working the 4¼ miles of line under discussion, both as part of the remainder of the system and also as a separate entity.

Eventually, on 11th March 1893, Sir. F. Bramwell announced his award, fixing the sum payable by the LCC for the 4 miles 2 furlongs 7.70 chains of line at £64,540; two depots at Cressy Road and Parkhurst Road, together with eight houses in Parkhurst Road at £37,258, and a proportion of the plant, machinery, tools and sundries at £32,000, which included 68 cars, 649 horses, 649 collars and head stalls (including logs and chains), 108 cloths for changing and 108 sets of harness (two cloths and two sets of harness for every 12 horses). Stable utensils were 54 each of feeding baskets, rope halters, curry combs and oil brushes, together with 108 dandy brushes.

Despite the findings of the arbitrator, the company would not agree to the terms and decided to take the case to law. At the Divisional Court, judgement was given in favour of the company. Piqued, the LCC took the matter to the High Court of Appeal where battle was joined yet again. In this case, the hearing lasting five days, was a long-drawn-out affair, with almost every nut, bolt, stone and piece of timber in use being discussed. Many "experts" were called upon to give evidence, but in the end the company lost its argument. Even this, however, was not to be the final round. The company took the case to the House of Lords, whose judgement was given on Monday 30th July 1894, just three years after the LCC made its first move.

Lord Watson (Lord Chancellor) and Lord Shand found against the company, while Lord Ashbourne dissented from the judgement of the other two. In the words of a newspaper report of the day (Kentish Mercury, Friday 3rd August 1894) "the decision will not be regarded with satisfaction by those who have invested their savings in tramway shares, who will not, unnaturally, consider that in this instance, strict law is not synonymous with justice".

The LCC Takes Over

Meanwhile, the LCC as legal owner of this small part of the London Street Tramways Company system was considering how best to deal with its new acquisition. One of the conditions laid down in the award was that the lines were to be offered back on lease to the London Street Company. Legally, this meant that the Council had to advertise the leasing by tender, which it did on 4th January 1895, with 10 o'clock in the morning of 24th January being the latest time for the completed tender forms to be delivered to the Council. The final paragraph in the form of tender also stated that "The Council does not undertake to accept the highest or any tender". This apparently meant that, as it was bound by the remarks of the arbitrator, only the tender of the London Street Tramways Company would be considered. Sir Frederick also stipulated that such a lease back should take place simultaneously with the sale and purchase, in order not to inconvenience the public by the necessity of ceasing services during the period of the change of ownership. In fact, from the time the final agreement had been made, the company acted as agent for the LCC until the new lease had been negotiated. In return, the machinery, cars and horses were to be left in the hands of the company as part of its assets.

Terms of the lease included a payment by the company of £5,729 per annum for rent of the lines and depots, to be made at the monthly rate of £477. 8. 4d. There was to be no increase in fares on Sundays and Holidays; all employees were to work a maximum of 60 hours a week, or 11 hours in any one day, or, in two consecutive days, no more than an average of 10 hours a day. Finally, the lessees were to run an increased service of workmens' cars between 7 and 8 a.m. This agreement was to remain in force until 31st December 1900, the LCC having power to determine after 31st December 1898. The lease was exchanged on 1st August 1895. The leasing back agreement caused the management of the North Metropolitan Tramways Company to get very concerned, as they could foresee some of their company's assets going the same way.

During this period of pressure, the LCC realised that, although it was aiming towards complete ownership of the London tramways, it had no power to operate such a network, as the terms of the Tramways Act of 1870 did not allow for this. The directors of the London Street and North Metropolitan companies then suggested to the Council that, if the LCC were to negotiate the purchase of the remainder of the London Street and all of the North Metropolitan mileage within the County and lease the lot back to the North Metropolitan to operate, the Council would fulfil its ambition to own the network, leaving an established company to run a coherent and complete undertaking.

Although the Council accepted this idea, it also set in train the necessary legal formalities which would eventually lead to it obtaining an Act of Parliament enabling it to operate its own tramways. This instrument, known as **The London County Tramways Act, 1896, (59-60 Vic. cap. li)**, armed the Council with the weapon that it needed most, which allowed it to set about making further proposals for the compulsory purchase of other tramway undertakings in the London area. At the same time, negotiations were continued with the London Street and the North Metropolitan regarding the purchase and leasing back to the North Metropolitan, and for that company to operate the whole lot for a period of 14 years.

During the period under discussion, the Council notified the London Street Company on 19th December 1895 that it formally proposed to purchase a further 1 mile 2 furlongs of company line in Junction Road. The company agents, Messrs. Ashurst, Morris & Co., considered that the Council was out of order, by saying that, as the line was rebuilt in 1887, with much of it being doubled at the same time, it would not fall due for purchase until 1908. The LCC refuted this statement, while the Board of Trade was not sure and had need to take Counsel's opinion from Henry Sutton of the Temple, who said that, in his view, the Council could purchase under the terms of the original Act by which the line or lines were constructed.

So far as the purchase and lease back of the remainder of the London Street Tramways were concerned, protracted negotiations with the two companies took almost another two years to complete. The agreements were finally concluded on 27th January and 27 May 1897 in the following form:-
"The lines are to be sold at the price of £10,000 per mile of double line, single line being paid for at the rate of £5,000 per mile; the depots and granaries to be sold at a price to be settled by agreement ... or ... arbitration ...; the North Metropolitan Company also to sell the major part of their undertaking on the same terms. After the completion of the purchase, a lease is to be granted by the Council to the North Metropolitan Company of the lines and depots purchased from both companies, including those already purchased from this company, for a term expiring at midnight at Midsummer 1910, the existing lease to this company being surrendered as from the date of commencement of the new lease to the North Metropolitan Company.
"An agreement has also been made between the North Metropolitan Company and this company; provided that from the date of the completion of the purchase by the County Council until the expiration of the term of the lease to the North Metropolitan Company, the North Metropolitan Company shall pay to this company a yearly sum, equal to 5% on the capital of this company remaining after deducting the amounts received on the sale of all its lines and depots to the Council, and of its cars, horses, plant, stores and effects to the North Metropolitan Company ... and, in addition, a yearly sum of £1,800, these

After LCC takeover and during electrification, short working services were introduced. Here, car No. 228 is working between "Nag's Head" and Holborn via Caledonian Road. (Courtesy: Tramway Museum Society)

sums to be paid quarterly. That the cars, horses, harness, plant, tools, stable utensils, materials and stores of this company shall be purchased by the North Metropolitan Company at a price to be agreed or ... to be settled by arbitration.

"With regard to the Junction Road line from Kentish Town to the "Archway Tavern", the Council contend that the whole line became purchaseable in 1895 and gave notice accordingly. The company do contend that the line is only purchaseable in sections as indicated. This question forms ... litigation between the company and the Council but ... these proceedings have been suspended for the negotiations which have led to the arrangement now submitted ...

"The remaining lines fall in as follows: Caledonian Road in 1898; Malden Road and Prince of Wales Road in 1900; Pentonville Road in 1903; King's Cross Road, Fleet Road and part of Kentish Town Road in 1906; Chalk Farm Road, Highgate Road and Gray's Inn Road in 1908. It will thus be seen that, when the County Council can become possessed of Caledonian Road, the heart of the system is lost to the company, leaving only outlying connections which by themselves would probably be unremunerative.

"With reference to the agreement for sale to the County Council, the price to be paid for the permanent way has been settled at £82,750. The price to be paid for the depots, stabling and granaries has been agreed at £34,000. The properties covered by the sum of £34,000 stand in the company's accounts as follows:-

Leasehold properties	£39,241.17. 1d
Machinery account	1,411. 6. 0d

	£40,653. 3. 1d
Deduct leasehold redemption fund	7,279.15.11d

	£33,373. 7. 2d

It will therefore be seen that the price agreed is somewhat in excess of the book value of the depots, etc.

"The Holloway Road property purchased in connection with the Warlters Road depot is not included in this sale. The company have also £10,500 on loan and £5,729 deposited with the County Council, both of which sums will be available for distribution among the shareholders.

"The lease to the North Metropolitan Company will be for 14 years from 24th June 1896. This is until 24th June 1910 and until that date the North Metropolitan Company will make to the London Street Company the payments referred to ...

"Out of the proceeds of the sales which have been made to the County Council the whole of the company's debentures have been paid off and a return of 10/- per share has been made to the shareholders. The directors anticipate that the arrangements made ... will enable them to make a further return to the shareholders of £6 per share and they estimate that the annuity payable by the North Metropolitan Company will be worth nearly £2 per share. This makes a total return to the shareholders including the 10/- per share already repaid, of about £8.10s per share.

"Provided that the scheme met with the shareholders' approval, the result would be that within a few months they would have returned to them £6 per share, making, with the amount already returned, £6.10s per share, and on the remaining £3.10s they would receive about 6%".

Completion and final conveyance of the company was formally carried out on 13th October 1897. At the same time, the lease of 1895, by which the company worked just over four miles of line on behalf of the County Council, was surrendered. To enable the LCC to make all its payments, it was necessary to obtain a special Act of Parliament, allowing the Council to have the necessary borrowing powers. This came by way of **The London County Council Money Act, 1897.**

After the dust had settled on this transaction, which had effectively rendered the London Street Tramways Company inoperative, it only remained in existence to discharge its duties as a holding company for the benefit of its shareholders. The last few years were therefore uneventful. As things transpired, the lease to the North Metropolitan company was terminated by the LCC in April 1906. Therefore, the last years are described as part of the history of the North Metropolitan Tramways Company.

The Cars

The earliest cars of the company were similar to those used by the North Metropolitan Tramways, the Metropolitan Street Tramways and the Pimlico, Peckham & Greenwich Street Tramways companies.

They were of double deck formation and iron ladders were provided to enable passengers to obtain access to the knifeboard-type seating provided on the open top decks. This arrangement did not last for very long, however, being replaced by what became the usual standard by having permanently fitted staircases at either end of each car.

Earliest records of the company do not show very much in the way of rolling stock detail, but only give the number of cars in use on the system, so it is exceedingly difficult to identify car types. It is very likely that the builders of the first batches of cars were either Starbuck of Birkenhead or the Metropolitan Railway Carriage & Wagon Co. Ltd. of Birmingham, who usually supplied these vehicles at a cost of between £175 and £195 each.

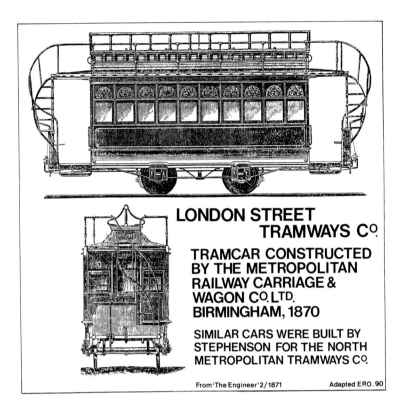

It is almost certain that the company used only double decked vehicles on their rather small system. Apart from an artistic print dating from 1871, showing a large ten-window car which would have seated up to 46 passengers and reproduced above, a photograph of about 1883 shows a small five-window double deck knifeboard seat car, which had the hallmark of the Falcon Engine & Car Works Ltd., and which held about 32 persons. Each small car probably cost between £150 and £175.

In later years the fleet was gradually increased in number as new sections of track were opened. From a total of 75 cars in 1883, the number had risen to 110 in 1888, to 124 in 1890, and to the final figure of 139 in 1897 when the company was taken over by the North Metropolitan Tramways Company.

All repair and maintenance work was undertaken at first at works situated in each depot, but eventually, all this was transferred to Cressy Road depot at Hampstead, where a specialised workshop was provided. It was here that, over the years, most cars were reconstructed to some degree. This rather substantial rebuilding work was essential, as the timber used in the construction of the cars had to stand up to very heavy wear and tear on the rather primitive tracks, where pitching and swaying was almost continuous.

Parts of a London Street Tramways car have survived and this faretable with it, referring to the service working between Swains Lane and Holborn. (Photo: N. Taylor)

Fares

The company charged fares on all services at the rate of one penny per mile. In common with other early undertakings, this could be interpreted in one of several ways, in that the company could, if it wished, charge a minimum of 2d, or the throughout fare for every journey. It eventually became policy to charge fares on a sliding scale, depending upon how far the passenger wished to travel, which soon resulted in a system of 1d, 2d and 3d fare stages being introduced, followed in later years by the limited introduction of a 1½d fare.

Statutory obligations required the company to charge "artisans, workmen and daily labourers" a different scale of fares, in most cases being at the rate of 1d for any one journey of any distance on any one car. To qualify for this, these people had to get up very early in the morning to travel on the few special "workman" cars that were provided. In order to obtain the same privilege on the return journey in the evening, it was necessary to present the morning ticket to the conductor on the special car to obtain the concessionary fare. In later years, special return tickets, which were used in conjunction with "exchange" tickets, were on issue to these people.

With regard to travel on Sundays and Bank Holidays, the London Street Tramways, in common with most others, charged premium fares to all. In most cases, this was the through single fare, usually 2d, but occasionally 3d. There were no special reduced fares for children.

Routes and Services

The company published a list of "Routes, Distances & Fares" in 1892, an extract of which is reproduced on page 577. It was used for display in and on the cars, and in public places served by the cars of the company. The full table shows the workings of the undertaking at its greatest extent.

Tickets

The arrangements made were in some measure similar to those made elsewhere. Almost from the beginning, tickets produced by

HAMPSTEAD HEATH AND EUSTON ROAD LINE.

Yellow Cars, Yellow Lights.

Via Hampstead Road, High Street, Camden Town, Chalk Farm Road, Ferdinand Street
Malden Road, Southampton Road.   Distance : 2¾ miles. Time : 30 minutes.

First Car from Hampstead Heath	...	...	...	
Last ,, ,, ,,	...	...	...	
First ,, Euston Road ...	...	...	...	
Last ,, · ,,	...	...	...	

FARES.

Hampstead Heath and corner of Chalk Farm Road and Ferdinand Street						...	1d.
" Gospel Oak Tavern " and " Red Cap "	...	...	...	...			1d.
" Red Cap " and Euston Road	...	...	...	...	...	...	1d.
Hampstead Heath and Euston Road	...	...	...	...	...	...	2d.

NAG'S HEAD, HOLLOWAY ROAD, & EUSTON ROAD LINE.

Green Cars, Green Lights.

Via Hampstead Road, High Street, Camden Town, " Brecknock," Camden Road, " Holloway
Castle," Parkhurst Road.   Distance : 2¾ miles. Time : 26 minutes.

First Car from " Nag's Head "	...	...	...	
Last ,, ,, ,,	...	...	...	
First ,, Euston Road ...	...	...	...	
Last ,, ,,	...	...	...	

FARES.

" Nag's Head " and " Brecknock "	...	...	...	...	...	...	1d.
" Brecknock " and " Britannia "	...	...	...	...	...	...	1d.
" Eagle Tavern " (Camden Town Station, (N. L. Rly.) and Euston Road	...			...	1d.
" Nag's Head " and Euston Road	...	...	...	...	...	...	2d.

An extract from the "Routes, Distances & Fares" chart of 1892.

T. J. Whiting of London were used, which continued until the company was absorbed into the North Metropolitan Tramways undertaking. They were quite distinctive in appearance, boldly displaying the name

LONDON STREET TRAMS
COMPANY

across the tickets immediately beneath the serial letters and numbers. Fare stage names or other destination information was either printed "landscape" on the sides of the ticket, with the fare value printed large in a central box, or "ladder fashion" to the right of the fare value, which was printed either upright or "landscape".   Some tickets also bore fare stage numbers.

The original colours adopted by the company for the tickets did not appear to conform with any set pattern.   Examples seen of early issues of the 1d value show some to be white, with others buff, green or orange.   Similarly, some 2d values were pink, with others blue, green or white.   From about 1874 the colour scheme seemed, more or less, to become 1d white, 2d pink, orange or blue, and in some cases, white, according to which service the car was being worked on, 3d mauve or green, and in one case, pink, in conjunction with a 2d blue for the same journey between "Archway Tavern" and Euston Road.   The 3d value would probably have been the Sunday fare and the 2d the weekday version.   Many tickets also carried a large capital letter overprinted in red.

After 1896, when the North Metropolitan Company assumed control, the ticketing arrangements, including colours, followed that of the new operator, and all reference to the old company disappeared.   The 1d value became blue, 1½d green, 2d white, while the orange exchange ticket, issued in conjunction with workman two-journey tickets was buff.

The type of ticket punch used, made a hole a full quarter-inch in diameter, which was similar to the original machines supplied to the North Metropolitan Company by J. H. Small.   From ticket specimens examined, it does not appear that the later type of Bell Punch was used until the North Metropolitan took over the operations and assets of the London Street Company.

Some of the car crews who worked at Cressy Road depot in 1898.
(Courtesy: L T Museum U38975)

Depots

At the end of company operations, it was possessed of seven car depots and stables. During the formative years of the undertaking, four sites were acquired, one each at Junction Road, Kentish Town, Warlters Road and Parkhurst Road, both in Holloway, and Park Road, Hampstead. Additionally, there were two depots which were centrally sited, at York Street, King's Cross, which also housed a granary, and "Angel Yard", Islington. At a later date, another depot at Cressy Road, Hampstead was built, where the workshops became established.

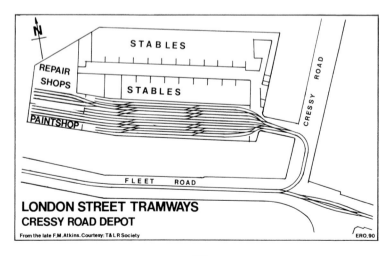

LONDON STREET TRAMWAYS
CRESSY ROAD DEPOT
From the late F.M.Atkins.Courtesy: T&LR Society

Mechanical Traction - The Mekarski Car

The Mekarski compressed air car was developed by M. Mekarski of Paris in 1872, and vehicles of this type were used in France for a number of years. A car was seen by Sir Frederick Bramwell, an English Engineer, who brought the idea to Britain. For use here, however, his company, known as the British Mekarski Improved Air Engine Co. Ltd., had devised the Mekarski Automobile Car, with a method of control which could be used on double-ended cars. The result was a four-wheeled vehicle resembling a standard horse car in most respects, except that the platforms and floor were built upon a steel channel frame and was higher than on a horse car. The 38-seat double deck car body, with "knifeboard" seating on the top deck, was said to have been built by the Lancaster Wagon Company, while the mechanical equipment was supplied by Clayton & Co., Preston, Lancs.

One pair of wheels was connected to the driving mechanism, which consisted of two cylinders of 5¼ in. diameter by 10 in. stroke, driven by a mixture of compressed air and steam. Air was supplied from a stationary pumping engine (compressor) to a maximum of 450 psi, into tanks beneath the car body. A "special feature" was that air was passed through one of two "hot pots" which contained boiling water and steam at 60 psi pressure. This caused the air to expand (and which also prevented "snow" from forming in the cylinders and exhaust). The moisture in the air also acted as a lubricant in the slide valves and pistons.

Air pressure could be varied for working purposes from 120 psi down to 50 psi, by means of a variable valve consisting of a piston which, by means of a hand wheel and screw was forced into or raised from a vessel in which the water and air were contained. The bottom of this vessel was fitted with an india-rubber diaphragm which was connected to a valve, opening against the pressure of the steam and air in the pot. When the piston was forced down into the vessel in which the water was contained, the diaphragm was pressed downwards and the valve was opened, allowing the steam and air to escape from the hot pot to the working cylinders. This valve gear gave the driver what was described "as a most delicate and beautiful means of varying the pressure", and it was, in addition, automatically regulating.

One of the hot pots with its regulating valve on it was placed at each end of the car, and means of entrance and exit for passengers was provided in such a way that when the terminus was reached, "the driver took his reversing handle and the wheel of the regulating valve to the opposite end of the car, the conductor changing ends as on an ordinary horse car".

It was said that the car made no noise from the engine exhaust; there was no steam visible; no smell of fire or hot oil or other lubricant from the engines. It was for vehicles to this specification that Messrs. Ashurst, Morris & Co. requested a license on 8th March 1882, to enable them to work on the Caledonian Road line as an experiment.

Letters from the Vestry of St. James & St. John, Clerkenwell on 16th December 1881 and from St. Mary, Islington on 8th March 1882, agreed to a trial taking place, in the first instance for three months, to which the Metropolitan Board of Works agreed. On the same day, Ashurst, Morris asked for a twelve month license. Arrangements were made for an inspection to be carried out by a Board of Trade Inspecting Officer, and was dealt with by Maj. Gen. Hutchinson on 16th March 1882, who approved the route and also the facilities provided in a stables at the Holloway Road end of the line for charging the tanks

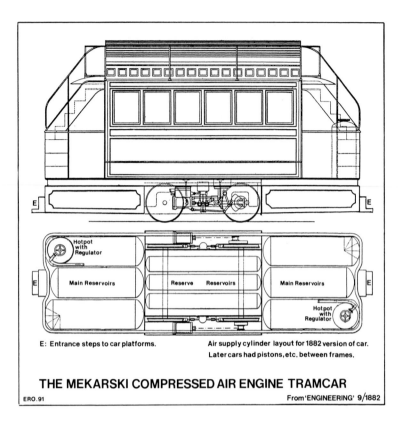

E: Entrance steps to car platforms.   Air supply cylinder layout for 1882 version of car.
Later cars had pistons, etc. between frames.

THE MEKARSKI COMPRESSED AIR ENGINE TRAMCAR

ERO.91   From 'ENGINEERING' 9/1882

and attending to the engines, but was unable to see a car at that time "as one was not quite ready", but, in fact, neither the car nor the depot to house it were yet constructed.

It was not until 2nd February 1883 that a car was said to be ready for inspection. Trial runs - with the consent of the police - were apparently carried out at night. It is stated that the car was governed to a maximum speed of ten m.p.h. Messrs. Ashurst, Morris made an application to the Board of Trade for another inspection to be carried out. On 18th May, Maj. Gen. Hutchinson again visited the installation. In his report, he said "I have inspected the working of the Mekarski Automobile Compressed Air Car for use on Caledonian Road. The depot for compressing the air is at the Holloway Road end of the line. The car is an ordinary tramcar with four wheels, one pair only of which is used for driving. Weight is 6½ tons and, with 38 passengers, about 9 tons loaded.

"Reservoirs, nine in number, are fixed under the floor, of which seven are in regular use and two in reserve. Air pressure at fifteen atmospheres or 450 lbs/sq. in. (sic) is charged at the depot. On its way from the reservoirs to the cylinders of the cars, the air passes through boiling water and steam at 110 lbs. pressure, contained in a "hot pot", which is charged at the depot at the same time as the reservoirs.

"Working pressure in the cylinders, which are 5¼ in. in diameter with 10 in. stroke, is between 50 and 120 psi, regulated by a valve. It is stated that enough air is available to drive the car between eight and ten miles under favourable circumstances, i.e. about two complete round journeys. A governor and speed indicator are provided; there is no emission of smoke or fumes and the machine is very quiet. The break (sic) power is prompt in its action and is applied either automatically by governor action, or by air pressure, or by the use of a foot treadle. No means have yet been arranged for turning the car at termini - and provision has been made for driving the car from either end. I pointed out the necessity for covering the tops of the hot pots with cages, to prevent unauthorised persons from tampering with the machinery, and also to prevent persons burning their hands on the hot metal. I recommend a three-months' license be issued". This was sent to the company on 23rd May 1883.

On 7th August 1883, J. Barber Glenn, on behalf of the "Compressed Air Engine Company" asked for the renewal of the license for another one year and nine months for the "several" cars then said to be working. It is not clear whether or not any new license was forthcoming. If it had been renewed, it would only have been for three months, as on 17th November 1883 the company again asked for a renewal. As all the local Boards had agreed to a 12 months' extension, the Board of Trade agreed to the same period, subject to an inspection being carried out on any new cars.

Four years later, on 13th August 1887, an inspection "of new cars", which were stated as standing at Warlters Road depot, was requested by the company. The answer from the Board of Trade was short and to the point - "This is not a renewal - it must be considered as a new request - it is four years since the last one - ". This meant that the company had to go to all the local authorities and the Metropolitan Board of Works for their approval, and it was not until 30th January 1888 that the Board of Trade agreed to an inspection. This was carried out by Maj. Gen. Hutchinson on 14th February, after which he authorised the issue of a license for six months, which enabled up to six cars to be used. At this point, on 22nd February, the police declined to fit license plates until a copy of the original license was produced. This was eventually provided by the Board of Trade. At the end of this period, no more applications seem to have been made for renewal.

Chapter 37
The North Metropolitan Tramways Company
1897-1906

An agreement dated 27th May 1897 completed the sale, purchase and lease between the company and the LCC, also providing for a Parliamentary Bill to confirm it, which was deposited to legalise the situation. The Bill also included proposals to construct certain new lines, mainly short connecting junctions between the lines of the two previous companies. Several of these were not allowed, including a line from Holborn Town Hall to join the existing line near the "Angel", from the "Angel" to St. John's Lane (sic), and from Theobalds Road to Oxford Street. In the second Bill, powers were sought to place traction wires over the lines for the purpose of electrifying the system, but due to opposition from the local authorities through whose areas the lines passed or were to pass, this part, with others, were struck out. Both Bills were then combined.

Purchase price of the North Metropolitan lines was £340,000, and of the London Street lines, £82,750; lands, depots, stables, etc. of the North Metropolitan, £233,831, and of the London Street, £34,000; while the first portion of the London Street lines had cost £64,540, the depots £37,258 and loans and other charges, £7,097. In turn, the Northmet was to purchase from the London Street all harnesses and other miscellaneous items for which £32,500 was set aside.

Full details of the leasing arrangements were:-
"Under a conveyance or indenture of 14th October 1897 made between the London County Council and the North Metropolitan Tramways Company, the lessees deposited £50,000 with the LCC as security for rents, etc.
"A yearly rent of £45,000 is to be paid in quarterly instalments together with £14,244.14s, which is 5% of the sum paid by the LCC for the freehold properties, plus 6% of the sum paid for leasehold properties. Yearly rent is to be paid on 25th March each year of 12% on the amount by which the gross receipts during the year ended on the previous 31st December exceeded gross receipts for 1895 (£616,872. 5. 7d) plus other such sums on demand including fire insurance not exceeding £6,000 with indemnities.
The company:
a. to observe the by-laws, maintain sufficient horses and cars and keep them in good condition. Only horses are to be used, except by special permission.
b. to allow the Council to use the tramway between the hours of 1 a.m. and 5 a.m. for the removal of dust, refuse, etc.
c. only to carry passengers.
d. to run workman cars between 3 a.m. and 8 a.m. at specified rates of 1d for a single journey and 2d for return.
e. not to raise existing fares on Sundays or Bank Holidays.
f. to keep rails clear and remove snow, but not by chemicals.
g. to restrict hours of work and wage levels to an agreed average.

h. to repair and maintain the tramways and buildings.
i. to provide funds towards renewals, etc. of initially not less than £37,000, followed by £12,500 per annum.
j. to insure depots, observe all covenants, repair roads.
k. not to underlease any part of the undertaking.
l. to yield up the undertaking at the end of the term."

North Metropolitan Tramways Company. Freehold buildings.

Stamford Hill depot	£ 51,600
Mare Street depot	53,920
Highgate depot	22,000
Canonbury depot	12,220
Woodville Road depot	8,300
Lea Bridge, part depot and part stoneyard	12,325
Finsbury Park, part depot	17,350
Athol Street, part depot	4,800

	£ 182,515

Leaseholds.

Part Lea Bridge depot	29th September 1874	99 years
Part Finsbury Park depot	24th June 1880	85
Part Athol Street depot	24th June 1872	90
Blair Street, Poplar depot	24th June 1874	99
Green Lanes depot	25th March 1876	76
Grove Road depot	25th March 1873	40
Kingsland Granary	29th September 1877	70
Metropolis Wharf (adjacent to Kingsland Granary)	29th September 1893	21
Balls Pond stores and workshop	25th December 1872	40
Bridge Wharf stoneyard	29th September 1885	21

London Street Tramways Company. Freehold building.
Cressy Road depot

Leaseholds.

Parkhurst Road depot	24th June 1872	51
Junction Road depot	25th December 1874	99
22 Poynings Road	25th March 1880	90
25 Tremlett Grove (residence)	24th June 1884	21
Park Road depot and		
57 Park Road	24th June 1879	71
59 Park Road	24th June 1883	67
York Street depot		
(later Lorenzo Road)	29th September 1885	42
Warlters Road depot and		
377 Camden Road	24th June 1866	56
"Angel" Yard depot and		
4 Pentonville Road	24th June 1883	21

180 Great College Street traffic offices, yearly from Christmas on terms of an expired lease.

Other sections and clauses written into the Act and extracted from the lease included:-
"The lessor has the right and privilege 'to interfere' with the roads and tramways for sewer and other public works.
"Provision ... for experiments with mechanical traction by the lessor.
"The lessor may be required to purchase certain stock at the end of the term upon expiration or sooner determination from any cause of this lease, the lessor will, if required by the lessees by notice in writing to be given to the lessor, two calendar months at least before such de-

termination, purchase from the lessees the horses, cars, harness, stable utensils, tools and plant in use upon the tramway and belonging to the lessees under the conditions which would be applicable if the purchase were made under Section 43 of the Tramways Act, 1870."

Services operated by the North Metropolitan Tramways Company within the County of London on 27th May 1897.

Service	Cars Run	First Car a.m.	Last Car p.m.	Service Minutes min.	max
Highgate & Moorgate via Upper Street	26	7.00	11.08	4	8
Highgate & Moorgate via Liverpool Road	14	7.03	11.06	7	9
Finsbury Park & Moorgate	26	7.04	11.05	4	8
Manor House & Moorgate	26	7.00	11.00	3	5
Stamford Hill & Moorgate	23	7.00	11.08	4	6
Stamford Hill & Holborn	29	7.04	11.00	4	6
Seven Sisters Road & London Docks	12	6.53	10.56	10	11
"Swan" Clapton & Dalston Lane	4	7.40	11.28	12	12
Lea Bridge & Bloomsbury	30	6.52	10.58	4	5
Well Street & Aldgate	7	7.25	11.10	8	9
Hackney & Aldersgate	24	7.00	11.12	3	5
South Hackney & West India Docks	9	7.00	10.58	7	8
(Stratford), Bow & Aldgate	47	6.15	11.25	2	3
Poplar & Aldgate	20	7.00	11.30	3	5
Poplar & Bloomsbury	17	7.03	10.42	7	8

Services operated by the London Street Tramways Company.

Service	Cars Run	First Car a.m.	Last Car p.m.	Service Minutes min.	max
Holloway & Clerkenwell via Caledonian Road	7	7.46	10.45	9	9
Highgate & Euston Road	23	6.45	11.35	3	6
Hampstead Heath & "Angel"	13	7.38	11.11	5	6
Hampstead Heath & Euston Road via Chalk Farm Road	13	7.05	11.42	5	7
Hampstead Heath & Holborn	5				20
Holloway & Euston Road	20	7.00	11.49	3	5
Holloway & Holborn via Caledonian road	7	7.25	10.52	9	9
Swain's Lane & Holborn	10	7.36	11.03	9	9
Holloway & King's Cross	5	6.46	12.10	6	11
"Shipton" & "Angel"	10	p.m. 3.59	9.17	6	11

Special Workings: Workman Cars.

Hampstead & Holborn	5 journeys
Highgate & Euston Road	3 journeys

Conditions of Employment

Grade	Daily Hours	Wage Rates
Ticket Inspector	12	42/- to 47/- week
Timekeeper	11	42/- week
Driver and Conductor	11½	4/6d day, 1st 4 months
		5/- day, next 5 months
		5/6d day, next 3 months
		6/- day, thereafter

Horsekeeper	10½	3/6d day, 1st 3 months
		3/8½d day, next 3 months
		4/- day, thereafter
Washer	9	as for horsekeeper
Trackman	10½	as for horsekeeper
Pole Turner	11	3/6d day
Point Shifter	11	2/6d day
Trace Boy	8	2/- day
Granary Carman	10	5/- day, 1st 6 months
		5/6d day, next 6 months
		6/- day, thereafter
Granary Labourers, Cutters,		
Mixers, etc.	10	4/- day, 1st 3 months
		4/2d day, next 3 months
		4/4d day, thereafter
Farrier and Fireman	9	7/- day
2nd Fireman	9	5/10d day
Doorman	9	5/4d day
Car Factory Employee		Usual Trades Union Hours and
		Rates of Pay for the District

In the many conditions and restraints imposed upon the company by its leasing agreement, was one that was intended to safeguard the position of employees in a more positive way than had been the custom hitherto. Although the company paid lip service to the intentions of the Council, it was still to be seen that an arbitrary approach was often taken with regard to problems involving the lower grades of staff. In most cases of this kind, instant dismissal seems to have been considered normal as the punishment for almost any misdemeanour, even the most minor.

Later Days

After the merger of the two companies, steps were taken to connect up several lines so that better services could be provided between the two. The Bill presented in 1897 also sought powers to enable the company to extend other lines in Middlesex. After the passage of the Bill through Parliament, **The North Metropolitan Tramways Act, 1897 (60-61 Vic. cap. ccxxxix)** received Royal Assent on 6th August and empowered the company to construct these new tramways.

No. 5, a double line 2 ch. long, from Parkhurst Road, crossing Holloway Road to Seven Sisters Road.

No. 6, a double line 2 ch. long, from Camden Road northwards into Holloway Road.

No. 7, a double line 9 ch. long, in Newington Green and Green Lanes, between Albion Street and a point 1 ch. west of Lidfield Road (already constructed).

No. 11, a line 2 f. double and 1 f. single, from No. 11A, along Upper Clapton Road, to the existing tramway 10 ch. south-east of Portland Avenue.

No. 11A, a double line 2 ch. long, from Stamford Hill, along Upper Clapton Road to No. 11.

No. 15, a double line 1 ml. 3 f. 2 ch. long, in lieu of the present single line with passing places in Seven Sisters Road from Green Lanes to a junction with Tottenham High Road.

No. 16, a double line 2 mls. long, in lieu of the present single line and passing places in Green Lanes, from Manor House to Wood Green.

Unnumbered, a double line between Pentonville Road and Goswell and City Roads.

St. Pancras Station in the 1890s. The car in the foreground is travelling from Hampstead to Holborn via Gray's Inn Road. *(Commercial view)*

As the company had sufficient materials in stock and the necessary labour available to carry out the work, it was agreed with the LCC that within the County of London, the company should act as agent for the construction, after which the Council would purchase the lines at the same price as it had cost the company to lay them.

It was also agreed that, for this and any future work, the company would use the more modern girder rail. It was also the hope of the company that a more substantial type of rail could be used in conjunction with any electrification programme that it may be involved in.

The first of the new connections was completed on 22nd February 1898 when the tracks were joined up at the "Nag's Head" between Parkhurst Road and Seven Sisters Road, to be followed on 4th April by the junctions at the "Angel" between Pentonville Road and City Road and the Holloway Road/Camden Road connection. A further 3 ch. of single line in Green Lanes was also doubled at a cost of about £567.

A dispute arose in September 1898 between the management of the company and a number of its employees, culminating in a strike, one of the results of which was the dismissal of five men for belonging to a trade union. The LCC alleged that under Clause 14 of the company lease, these dismissals should not have taken place, as the terms of the clause protected employees who belonged to a "lawful trade organisation", and complaints had been made on behalf of the dismissed men to this effect.

The company was invited to comment, but chose not to do so, saying that it would meet any charges of the nature indicated before a proper tribunal. This was arranged in due course, with Lord James of Hereford as Arbitrator. The enquiry took place on 12th December; on 14th, Hereford announced that, in the opinion of the tribunal, the company had, in breach of the covenants in the lease, dismissed the five men referred to "for belonging to a lawful trade organisation". He directed that the company should pay £50 for each of the five breaches, plus the costs of the LCC, of the Agreement for Reference, of the arbitration and the award, and should also bear its own costs. In addition to the £250 already mentioned, the company had to pay

£62. 3s. for the Arbitrator and £149.12.10d to the Council. There is not, however, any mention made of the five men getting their jobs back!

Workman and All Night Cars After 1896

One of the improvements insisted upon by the LCC was that existing services should be improved where possible and that the operation of special cars for workmen should be maintained and, if possible, improved. At that time, nothing was said about all-night services. However, shortly after taking over the London Tramways Company in 1899, the Council instituted the first of a number of all-night car services. At the same time, it arranged with the Northmet to do the same. The first of these worked between Holborn and Hampstead, between Holborn and Stamford Hill and between Aldgate and Stratford. Soon afterwards, services commenced running between the London termini and "Archway Tavern". In each case, they operated at nominal half-hourly intervals throughout the night, and linked into the early morning workmen services which worked from these points.

A difference of opinion arose in February 1902, when the night services between Holborn, Hampstead and Highgate were discontinued by the company. After representations by the Council and other bodies, the company restored the services, but would not guarantee maintaining them until the end of the lease, as was asked for by the Council.

The night service timetable for October 1902 showed that cars left "Archway Tavern" for Holborn at 15 and 45 minutes past every hour between midnight and 3 a.m. From this time on, the half-hourly service continued until 6.45 a.m. as workman cars. All return journeys from Holborn began at 27 and 57 minutes past each hour.

During the years remaining to the company, a number of variations were made to the schedules, almost all of which were objected to by the LCC. In one case, as from 5th November 1902, the daily service between Hampstead and Moorgate, said to be uneconomic, was cut back to work only between Hampstead and "Angel" Islington. In this case, only the workman service to Moorgate was maintained, and the first left Hampstead at 5.10 a.m.

From the beginning of 1903, the pattern of workman services, together with the timing of the first car on each is shown below.

From	To	Time
Hampstead	Euston Road	5.12 a.m.
Highgate		5.00
Manor House		5.00
"Nag's Head"		5.05
Hampstead	Holborn	4.01
"Archway Tavern"		3.57
Finsbury Park		5.15
Stamford Hill		2.59
Lea Bridge	Bloomsbury	3.05
Hackney		3.13
"Archway Tavern"	Clerkenwell	3.20
"Archway Tavern"	Aldersgate Street	3.00
Finsbury Park		3.15
Hackney		5.42
Hampstead	Moorgate Street	5.10
"Archway Tavern"		N/I *
Manor House		N/I *

Stratford   Aldgate   N/I *
Poplar   N/I *

Average service between 25 and 35 minutes.
* No information. These services not investigated.

The Twentieth Century

Early in 1900, a piece of land in Holloway Road near the "Nag's Head" public house was offered freehold to the company for £4,500. Further stabling was urgently required to accommodate extra cars and horses for the rapidly increasing traffic. It was agreed that buildings be erected under the control and to the satisfaction of the Council's architect at an estimated cost of £15,000, to provide accommodation for 24 cars and 246 horses. The company were to erect the buildings and pay 5% of the cost of the buildings per annum as rent to the Council. Other stabling had been erected on freehold land adjoining Lea Bridge depot at a cost of £22,077 and the usual 5% annual payment to the Council was also to apply in this case.

In 1900 and 1901, more connections were completed. On 22nd August 1900, authority was given for a north to south connection to be made at Manor House, and also for a link between Stamford Hill and "The Swan", Upper Clapton, while junction lines were constructed in Great Eastern Street, Commercial Street, Commercial Road and High Street, Shoreditch.

Two most important Acts were obtained by the LCC in 1900, by which authorisation was obtained to enable it to construct new tramways, alter existing tramways and work the lines by electric traction. In one of these, **The London County Tramways Act, 1900, (63-64 Vic. cap. cclxx),** which received Royal Assent on 6th August, the following new lines, all on the northern system, were authorised.
No. 1, a line 2 f. 7.60 ch. long, with 9.10 ch. double, from a junction with the existing tramway in South End Road, along Constantine and Agincourt Roads to Southampton Road.
No. 2, a double line 8.25 ch. long, along Prince of Wales Road between Maitland Park and Malden Road.
No. 2A, a double line connecting curve 2.60 ch. long, connecting Malden Road with Malden Crescent.
No. 3, a double line 3 ch. long, along Crowndale Road, from Cobden Statue to Great College Street.
No. 6, a line 5 f. 5.4 ch. long, with 3 f. 9.2 ch. of it double, along St. Paul's Road, from Canonbury Road to Balls Pond Road.
No. 8, a line 7 f. 6 ch. long, with 6 f. of it double, along Church Road, Evering Road, Brooke Road, Nightingale Road and Kenninghall Road, from High Street, Stoke Newington to Upper Clapton Road.
No. 8A, a double line connecting curve 2.60 ch. long, at the eastern end of Kenninghall Road.
No. 9, a double line 5 f. 5.5 ch. long, along Rosebery Avenue from Clerkenwell Road to St. John Street Road (sic).
No. 10, a double line 6 f. 6.5 ch. long, along St. John Street Road and St. John Street, from the "Angel", Islington to Smithfield.
No. 11, a line 3 f. 4.30 ch. long, with 1 f. 1.85 ch. of it double, from the existing line in Cassland Road to Dagmar Road.
No. 12, a double line 4 f. 5.5 ch. long, from the existing tramway at Poplar to the County boundary at Barking Bridge Road.
A period of five years allowed for the completion of all work associated with the Act.

Despite the comprehensive nature of the content of the Act, only one line was built by the company on behalf of the Council. No. 1, which was an alternative line between the Hampstead terminus and the south end of Fleet Road was inspected by Col. H. A. Yorke on 25th June 1901, after which he authorised its use for horse traction only. It was intended to be used as the "up" line from Hampstead, while the original line along Fleet Road was to be the "down" line.

Last Days of the Northmet

From about the turn of the century, other factors began to emerge with regard to the position held by the company in the areas outside London. As the LCC had effectively used the powers given to it by the Tramways Act of 1870, so other authorities outside London were beginning to appreciate that they too, could have a share in what was becoming a desirable local asset.

One of the first to realise this was Leyton UDC when, on 31st December 1899, that body resolved to purchase the lines in their area, although this did not take effect until 1906. The Middlesex County Council, together with the County Borough of West Ham, the Urban District of East Ham and the Urban District of Walthamstow followed soon afterwards. So far as the company was concerned, it was realised that it was only a matter of time before what assets it had left would be compulsorily purchased by these bodies, or, as in one case, by a representative company on behalf of Middlesex County Council.

On 1st July 1903, West Ham Corporation took over the lines in that area. On 9th August 1905, the "Swan" depot at Stratford was let to the LCC, as was the Union Road, Leytonstone Works at a rental of £1,320 p.a., and in due course the LCC utilised the Works to build some top covers for a number of class A and D electric cars, together with 50 bodies for class E/1 cars.

A company known as "The Metropolitan Tramways & Omnibus Co. Ltd." was formed and registered on 21st November 1894, its objects being to construct and operate electric tramways in Middlesex and Hertfordshire. Proposals were made for extensions to existing horse car lines as well as for the construction of new lines. Nothing very

A general view of Stratford Broadway with cars standing in the layby outside the "Swan Hotel". (Commercial view)

589

much was done until October 1901 when the British Electric Traction Group assumed control of the previous company and changed its name to "The Metropolitan Electric Tramways Limited". The remaining lines of the North Metropolitan Company in Middlesex were taken over by the MET Ltd. at the same time, but were leased back to the Northmet to operate for the time being. As Middlesex County Council was also interested, the new company lost no time in coming to an agreement with the County Council and with Hertfordshire. On 30th July 1902, the Royal Assent was given to an Act which would enable the lines in Middlesex to be electrified, and on 26th November, operations of the company in that county were taken over by the MET Ltd.

With regard to company activities in London, during 1903 there was animosity between it and the LCC over the proposed provision by the company of overhead wires in the Stoke Newington district. Many of the worn-out horse car rails were being replaced at this time and it was this that was at the root of the problem. In the last Act of Parliament obtained by the company, powers were included to allow the lines to be electrified, and it seems that the Northmet was intent on trying to head off the LCC in its plans for conduit working, the more so as it now was allied to the activities of the M E T Ltd.

On 30th September 1903, in a long-running argument with the LCC regarding the attitude of the Council to the reconstruction of the lines in Theobalds Road, the company stated that "... with regard to the powers that the company possess ... for adoption of the overhead wire system ... the company has already practically completed the construction of an overhead system on their lines in Stoke Newington and Hackney and that the work has been done with the approval of the Board of Trade ..."

This provoked the Council to action and things reached such a pitch that a writ was issued against the company, in an effort to stop any electrification work being carried out. Following this, and after further discussion, the Council agreed to withdraw the writ provided that the company complied and had the offending overhead fittings removed.

In December 1904, a communication was received by the LCC from the Town Clerk of the Borough of Shoreditch regarding the operation of what he referred to as "motor tramcars". "This is a suggestion which, I believe, will have all the advantages of both the overhead and conduit systems of electrification without their ... disadvantages and effect a very large saving of the ratepayers' money as well as benefit the travelling public. It is recommended that a car of the type in use between Hatfield and Hertford (Great Northern Railway) be tried. This vehicle has two 4-cylinder Daimler 72 h.p. engines. The total weight of the machinery is only two tons, about one-third of the weight of a petrol-electric tramcar.

"The existing rails and depots may be used and disruption of roads and trade is avoided. Also avoided is the possibility of all traffic being stopped by a power failure. In fact, the cost of the power station itself is avoided, i.e., £337,000 for a power station to operate 600 cars on the system north of the Thames. The cost for a similar station south of the river would be even greater, for 1,000 cars are operated there (sic). Petrol tramcars cost about £1,300 each, whilst electric cars cost half that. It is also foreseen that money paid to tramway companies might be put to establishing competing omnibus services".

What the writer meant in the last sentence is open to conjecture, but could be interpreted to mean that the tramway companies, after having been bought out by the LCC, could attempt to start up 'bus services with the money paid to them. The Council, however, appeared to have taken little notice of either the content or meaning of the correspondence.

On 1st April 1906, the LCC terminated the company lease and assumed direct control of all operations within its area. This had already been precipitated by the construction of a new electric tramway situated in a subway beneath the new London thoroughfare of Kingsway, the history of which is dealt with in another chapter.

The leases held by the North Metropolitan Tramways on behalf of their own operations in London, together with those of the late London Street Tramways would require to be carefully foreclosed, so that neither the staff and employees involved, the shareholders of the company, nor the LCC would be open to legal action or in danger of losing jobs or money, and the whole process took several years to achieve. The lines in Leyton were eventually taken over by the UDC on 25th June 1906, while lastly, the short line along Romford Road from Manor Park to Green Street, in East Ham, was taken over by the Corporation on 24th April 1908.

In preparation for final closure, the company had obtained **The North Metropolitan Tramways (Winding-up) Act, 1906,** with George Richardson and James McLeod appointed as liquidators. Finally, on 21st February 1912, at an ordinary half-yearly meeting at which 20 shareholders were present, it was agreed "that the company be wound-up voluntarily in accordance with Section 5 of the winding-up Act". At the final general meeting held on the following day, it was resolved "that the remuneration of the liquidators for services rendered ... including services provided by the MET Ltd. in Middlesex ... be fixed at £250". The company was then declared closed.

For a time after takeover by the LCC, the only noticeable differences were that the staff were given the same conditions as the tramwaymen already employed by the Council, and that the cars were now seen to belong to a new owner. Behind the scenes, however, things were very different, as almost immediately, plans were being made for the electrification of the system, some of this work having been started even before the company relinquished control. Conversion to electric traction took place over a number of years, until, in 1914, the only lines not attended to were those in Liverpool Road, which was closed and abandoned, and between Cassland Road and West India Docks, which was forcibly closed at the start of the Great War, when the horses were requisitioned by the War Department. It was not until 1921 that this line was eventually electrified.

Early Rolling Stock

The company, influenced to some extent by American practice, turned to the USA for the first of the cars to be used on the system. These were ordered from John Stephenson & Co. of New York. All were of double-deck pattern, with access to the open top deck being by a portable iron ladder which could be carried round the car at the terminus. This type of car, with a body sixteen feet long, had eight windows on each side, each topped with a semi-circular light, while a clerestory with ventilator lights was incorporated into the ceiling of the saloon. A platform at either end of the car, each four feet long, had a single step to give passengers access to it. Dashplates were made from sheet iron plates and had entrance steps on either side of each platform.

Each car had places for 22 persons in the lower saloon on two cushioned benches, and were protected from the glare of the sun by Venetian blinds which were fitted at all windows. On the open top deck, 22 passengers could be accommodated on two longitudinal "knife-board" seats, and two more on single seats fitted above the canopy ends. The next batch of cars ordered from Stephenson were a little larger than the earlier vehicles, with ten windows on either side of the car body, and with places for 24 passengers inside and 26 outside. It is difficult to separately assess the cost of these, but it appears that the price paid for each vehicle was about £195.

On 4th October 1871, George Hopkins, the Engineer, was authorised to purchase twenty more cars, "but to be of smaller dimensions than those now in use", resulting in the purchase of cars with seven windows on each side and carrying 36 or 38 passengers. The next recorded orders were on 11th March 1873 when four "small" cars were ordered from Stephenson at an estimated price of £1,000, and in March 1875 when six more "large" cars were placed on order. The next order for four cars was made in 1876.

In March 1877, the company authorised the construction by Messrs. Boyce at a cost of £1,047, of its new repair and car building works at Union Road, Leytonstone. Once completed, the first task of the staff there would be to overhaul thoroughly all existing vehicles.

Meanwhile, an engineering firm by the name of Hughes & Co. had developed a new type of axle unit which incorporated roller bearing boxes. The directors of the North Metropolitan agreed on 24th October 1877 to supply them with an up-to-date double deck car for the purpose of evaluating the efficiency of the new axle unit. One of the recent batch of cars received from Stephenson was to be sold to Hughes for £250, subject to all expenses being paid by Hughes and a new car to be ordered to replace it. However, the minutes dated 28th March 1878 mention that the car sold to Hughes had been bought back for £220. A number of the improved axle units were also purchased for fitting to the cars of the company.

It was in 1878 that the cost of new cars began to fall slightly. On 17th April, it was resolved to purchase 25 more cars from Stephenson at £253 each, and five from Starbuck at £220 each. Six months later, another five were purchased from Stephenson, but at £235 each.

This was followed between 1879 and 1883 by another 65 cars being purchased at considerably reduced prices, but this time they were all fitted with "garden seats" on the open top decks. Messrs. Hughes had also gone into the car building business. The list of purchases is given below.

12th March 1879	Stephenson, 3 at £190 each.
	Hughes, 3 at £190 each.
2nd April 1879	Stephenson, 4 at £195 each.
	Hughes, 4 at £195 each.
3rd September 1879	Stephenson, 12 at £200 each.
5th November 1879	Hughes, 2 at £190 each. *
23rd March 1881	Starbuck, 4 at £190 each. **
	Hughes, 2 at £180 each (was £185).
23rd November 1881	Hughes, 3 at £192.10s each.
	Starbuck, 3 at £195 each.
22nd February 1882	Hughes, 10 at £192.10s each.
	Starbuck, 5 at £195 each.
8th March 1882	Hughes, 4 at £190 each.

An original ten-window car of 1871, No. 248, with "knifeboard" upper deck seating, is standing at the Clapton Common terminus. Unusually, the dashplates on this batch of cars were fashioned from corrugated metal sheeting. The cars were considerably rebuilt in later years.
(Courtesy: L T Museum 1664C)

Working on the same service as the car shown above, is a seven-window car with "knifeboard" upper deck seating. Many of these vehicles were subsequently reconstructed, the old top deck seating being replaced with reversible forward facing "garden" seats. (Courtesy: L T Museum 1665C)

26th October 1882	Company to construct 4 single deck cars at no more than £125 each.
5th April 1883	Company to build 2 "full size" cars.

Notes: * Hughes contacted the North Metropolitan Company stating that two cars had been "built in error" for the company, and asked if the Northmet would be prepared to purchase them. This was agreed to at the stated price.

    ** Starbuck had quoted £200, but the directors of the Northmet forced the price down by £10.

At this time too, it was realised that some of the first cars which had been purchased were showing signs of "old age". On 28th June 1882 the decision was taken by the Board that cars "not worth repairing" were to be broken up, but there is no indication which cars were chosen for this treatment. What is certain, is that a number of the new cars purchased in the early 1870 s were almost completely rebuilt within a few years of the Union Road Works opening.

Mechanical and Electrical Experiments

Almost from the beginning of the use of horse-drawn tramcars, ways and means were continually being sought to find a more efficient means of locomotion for the vehicles. The stated average number of horses needed to haul a tramcar over its route throughout one working day was ten, although some of the smaller companies managed with less. Apart from the huge numbers of horses needed to provide the motive power, the organisation required to house, feed and maintain the animals was, for most of the London companies, very considerable and costly.

The North Metropolitan company experimented with mechanical means of traction of several types. Compressed air, battery electric, and steam was tried, with the battery driven vehicles showing the most promise. But none survived for more than about three years.

The Beaumont Locomotive

An experiment took place in 1881 when a Beaumont compressed air locomotive ran for a time between Stratford and the "Green Man", Leytonstone. Designed by Col. F. E. B. Beaumont and built by Messrs. Greenwood & Batley, the vehicle had two air reservoirs, each of 110 cu. ft. capacity, which were charged to a pressure of 1,000 lbs/sq. in. The air, when released, drove a small engine which transmitted power to the wheels through gearing. The compressor had a compound engine with a high-pressure cylinder of 12 inches diameter, cutting off at half stroke; the low pressure cylinder was 20 inches in diameter and the boiler pressure was 95 lbs/sq. in. The compressor itself was built on the multi-stage principle, air being passed through a series of cylinders of decreasing diameter and finally through 250 ft. of 1½ inch diameter iron pipe to a filling hydrant in Stratford Broadway. The air reservoir was filled by means of a flexible hose and the plant worked only while the air tank was being charged. The line chosen for the experiment was about 2½ miles long, with a rise of about 82 feet between the ends of the line. Both the steepest gradient of 1 in 25 and the sharpest curve of 50 ft. radius were near Maryland Railway Station.

It was reported at the February 1881 meeting of the company that Beaumont had made an approach with the object of trying out his locomotive on a working tramway. The company agreed to this, to be paid for by Beaumont at the rate of 6d per mile, which included

A print of a Beaumont compressed air car taking on air at Stratford.

the wages of the driver. The North Metropolitan Company then wrote to the Board of Trade on 2nd May 1881 asking that a license be issued to allow a compressed air engine to be worked between Stratford and Leytonstone for a period of one year. In response, the Board stated that consent of the local authorities would have to be obtained. On 17th May 1881, it was reported to the Board of Trade that the West Ham Local Board had agreed to a one month trial.

The Board of Trade then reminded the company on 25th May that Leyton and Islington Local Boards were involved. On 12th July it was reported that Islington Vestry had no objection, whilst on 6th October, the Leyton Local Board agreed to a six-week trial. As part of an agreement for extended running rights of the car, the Northmet and Col. Beaumont exchanged letters of indemnity on 3rd August, in which Beaumont made himself responsible for his own affairs. After further discussion between the parties it was decided that the car would be allowed to run in service after 19th October.

On 25th October, Maj. Gen. Hutchinson inspected the locomotive and installation at the depot of the company, and in his report he said, when referring to a test run on the locomotive, "... no governor or speed indicator fitted, but it is so well under control that I think it may be licensed. There are 2½ miles of double line; the engine is mounted on four wheels and weighs 8½ tons; two air reservoirs charged to 1,000 lbs. pressure, filled with air in the depot close to the terminus at Stratford. It is easy to manage, simple and effective, but does not comply with regard to the governor and speed indicator. About half the air was exhausted on the double journey. No noise to indicate the escape of steam. Passed for one month with effect from 28th inst., provided it is driven by a skilled mechanic, but only between Stratford and 'The Plough & Harrow' at Low Leyton".

On 28th October, the printed license form was issued, which stated:-
"Must be free from:- (blast), noise or clatter;
all fire concealed from view (not applicable);
(speed) not to exceed 8 m.p.h.;
air reservoirs shall not exceed 1,000 p.s.i.;
no smoke or steam emitted".

On 14th November, the West Ham Local Board acknowledged the receipt of the copy of the certificate for operation between Stratford Broadway and the "Plough & Harrow", Low Leyton. Three days later, the Board of Trade commented that they might be willing to consider an extension of the license for one month, but only if all the local authorities concerned also agreed.

In a letter from the Beaumont Company to the Board of Trade on 28th November, a request was made for an extension of the license in the belief that the local boards would agree. This was further reinforced on 1st December by a similar request from the Northmet company, the answer from the Board of Trade to both being that they must produce written consent from the local boards. From this date, the records are silent about the renewal of the license.

That the locomotive operated is evidenced by a letter from the West Ham Board to the Board of Trade, complaining about the noise coming from the engine, and also a letter written to the Board of Trade on 28th November 1881 from H. E. Reynolds, a "fireclay tobacco pipe manufacturer" of 245 Old Ford Road, who complained that the engine frightened his horse, and requested that damages be paid.

Had the system been installed permanently, four combined engines and cars would have been used, the estimated fuel consumption being reduced to between 9 and 10 lbs. per car mile. Col. Beaumont had other interests in air driven machinery and, in fact, his boring machines were used in the test tunnels for the original Channel Tunnel scheme. In addition, he advocated the use of air to drive the trains in the completed tunnel.

An Early Experiment in Electric Traction
The Faure Accumulator Car

Union Road, Leytonstone, was the scene of an early experiment in electric traction. In 1882, a series of trials was carried out with a Faure Accumulator Car by Mr. Radcliffe Ward on behalf of the Faure Accumulator Company. This is the first known example of electric street traction in the U. K. The vehicle was a normal horsecar with 30 cwt. of batteries stowed under the seats, and it was fitted with an electric motor and pinion gear drive. It was apparently erected at the Union Road Works, the batteries also being charged there. In running order, the vehicle weighed five tons, and on its first run, on 4th March 1882, it was said to have reached a speed of between 7 and 8 m.p.h. and to suffer from very loud gear noise. The battery capacity was said to be "equal to 25 horses for one hour, or 5 horses for 5 hours". There is no evidence to show that it ran in public service.

The Elieson Battery Electric Car

A much longer series of experiments was carried out with the electric tramcar locomotives designed by C. P. Elieson. In all, six of these were built by the Electric Light (sic) & Power Company at the North Metropolitan Tramways Company depot at Stratford, with the intention of using them on the line between Stratford and Manor Park.

The type of electrical equipment used was unusual, as the motor was connected to the axles by a vertical shaft and bevel gears, and was of curious design. It rotated on its axis and picked up current through brushes wiping a pair of copper rings. Current was supplied to a 4 h.p. motor by an 80-cell accumulator having plates of lead and asbestos.

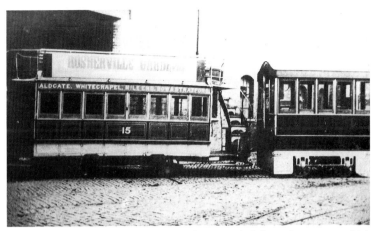

An Eliesen battery electric locomotive, coupled to a horse car which normally worked between Poplar and Aldgate. (Courtesy: L R T Ass'n)

With this arrangement, the locomotive could run (in theory) for about six or seven hours. In working order, it weighed 6 tons 17 cwts.

On 5th December 1885, the North Metropolitan Tramways Company asked the Board of Trade for permission to use the electric engine between Stratford and Aldgate, but this appears not to have been forthcoming. On 8th December 1885, it is recorded that an agreement was concluded between the West Ham Local Board and the Electric Locomotive (sic) & Power Company, that the locomotive may be run on the lines within the district of West Ham, subject to the Board's right to terminate it at 24 hours' notice. A license to operate was granted for three months as from 1st January 1886. An inspection of the locomotive was made by Maj. Gen. Hutchinson on 25th February. However, the first recorded run took place on 6th July 1886 from Stratford to Forest Gate, when the locomotive towed a car carrying more than 20 passengers at an approximate speed of 6 m.p.h. At first, trial runs were made every Thursday, and in August 1886 they were extended to the Manor Park terminus, where there was a stub-end with a crossover, which enabled the locomotive to run round its car.

The agreement to operate was made with the Electric Light & Power Company, and the Northmet took steps to legalise its position by promoting as Private Bill in which it asked for sanction to operate cars worked by electric power. There was some delay, owing to the dissolution of Parliament, but authority was finally obtained on 26th February 1887. As soon as the Bill was enacted, the electric loco-motives ran daily, and a report made in June 1887 stated that there were electric cars running alternatively with horse cars, attaining an average weekly mileage of 500, and carrying 5,000 passengers a week. However, they were not a lasting success, probably due to the incidence of a number of breakdowns, and the last Elieson locomotive ran on 8th July 1888. During the course of the experiments, the Electric Light & Power Co. had applied for extended constructional facilities at Stratford depot, and also for financial assistance to build a depot for the locomotives at Manor Park, but neither of these requests were granted.

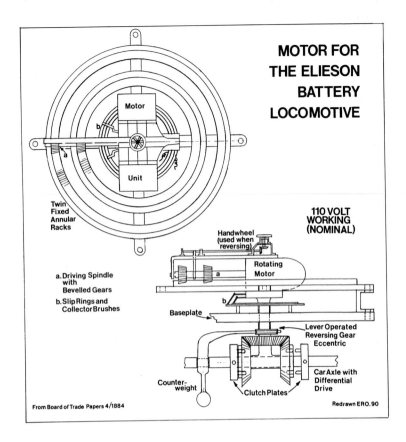

MOTOR FOR
THE ELIESON
BATTERY
LOCOMOTIVE

Motor

Unit

b

a

Twin
Fixed
Annular
Racks

110 VOLT
WORKING
(NOMINAL)

Handwheel
(used when
reversing)

Rotating
Motor

a

b

Baseplate

a. Driving Spindle
with
Bevelled Gears
b. Slip Rings and
Collector Brushes

Lever Operated
Reversing Gear
Eccentric

Car Axle with
Differential
Drive

Counter-
weight

Clutch Plates

From Board of Trade Papers 4/1884

Redrawn ERO.90

The Lironi Battery Car

The other experiment in which the North Metropolitan Tramways Company was involved concerned the use of six battery cars on the isolated Canning Town and Plaistow section. These were the property of the General Electric Traction & Power Company; each was driven by a 10 h.p. Immisch Motor on one axle. Each car seated 52 passengers and the first four were recorded as being in service on 14th June 1889. Shortly after this, an explosion occurred on one of the cars and all were temporarily withdrawn, but after a Board of Trade inspection, they all returned to service within a matter of days.

It was agreed that the Northmet should pay 4½ d per car mile for the use of these machines, this charge continuing until April 1892, when the power company asked that a fresh agreement be struck, and the rate per car for the six cars then in use be increased to 6½ d per car mile. On 11th May, after further discussion, the company agreed to accept 5½ d. However, the new agreement was not to be maintained for long, as the cars were finally withdrawn on 27th July 1892, after having completed 76,398 miles in North Metropolitan service. The reason given for their withdrawal was the deterioration of the track, which was possibly caused by the comparatively heavy weight of the batteries carried.

A Lironi battery electric car, used on the isolated section along Barking Road, between Canning Town and Greengate Street.

(Courtesy: L T Museum)

The Merryweather Locomotive Experiment

A less than successful experiment concerned the use, in 1877, of a Merryweather steam tram engine, which ran for only a few weeks in service between Stratford and Leytonstone, towing a normal horse car. The North Metropolitan Tramways Co., while already looking for a possible replacement for the horse, apparently considered that this form of motive power was not suitable for their requirements, and the engine was returned to the manufacturer.

The Merryweather steam tram engine towing Starbuck car No. 238 during the period of the experiment. *(Courtesy: L T Museum)*

Car Colours as at 31st May 1895

Ordinary Services

Service	Colour	Fare
"Archway Tavern" and Moorgate via Liverpool Road	White	2d
"Archway Tavern" and Moorgate via Upper Street	Blue	2d
Finsbury Park and Moorgate via Upper Street	Yellow	2d
Finsbury Park and Moorgate via Canonbury	Brown	2d
Finsbury Park and Edmonton	Blue	5d
Finsbury Park and Wood Green	Yellow	2d
Poplar and Bloomsbury	Brown	3d
Poplar and Aldgate	Yellow	2d
Poplar and Canning Town (omnibuses)	Red	1d
Canning Town Stn and "Green Gate" Barking Road	Red	1d
Stamford Hill and Dock Street	Yellow	3d
Stamford Hill and Holborn	Green	3d
Stamford Hill and Moorgate	Red	3d
Stamford Hill (Amhurst Park) and Edmonton	Yellow	4d
"Swan" Clapton and Lea Bridge Road	White	1d
Hackney, Well Street and Aldgate	Red	2d
Hackney and Aldersgate Street	Green	2d
Lea Bridge Road and Bloomsbury	Yellow & Blue	3d
Manor House and Moorgate	Green	3d
Leytonstone, Stratford and Aldgate	Blue	3d
Manor Park and Stratford	Red	2d
West India Dock and South Hackney	Yellow	2d

Workman Services

Service	Colour
Manor House and Aldersgate	Yellow
"Archway Tavern" and Aldersgate via Upper Street	Blue
Poplar and Aldgate	Yellow

Car Depots

In the early days, no arrangements were made to place the cars under cover when not in service. In fact, it appears that, apart from temporary accommodation which was provided at Bow Bridge by the contractors, no off-street standing was provided for some time. An entry in the minutes of the company for 4th October 1871 states that "rails had been laid in Ridsdale Road, Holloway, for 18 carriages". The fact that there were no covered depots was mentioned by the secretary of the company on 21st February 1872, when he asked the contractors to provide them as the cars were being subjected to damage during the winter weather conditions. From then on, suitable sites were obtained upon which to build car depots. The following list gives details of all buildings which were taken over by the LCC in 1906.

Depot	Location
"Angel", Islington	Pentonville Road
Camden Town	Parkhurst Road
Canonbury	St. Paul's Road
	Park Street
Dalston	Balls Pond Road
Finsbury Park	Seven Sisters Road
Hackney, Mare Street	Bohemia Place
Hampstead	Fleet Road
	Park Road (Parkhill Road)

Depot	Location
Highbury, New Park	Green Lanes
Highgate	Holloway Road
Holloway	Francis Terrace (stables)
	Junction Road
	Bowman's Place (stables)
King's Cross	York Street (Lorenzo Street)
Lea Bridge	Clapton Road
Lower Holloway	Warlters Road
Mildmay Park	Woodville Road
Poplar	Blair Street
	Athol Street
Stamford Hill	Portland Avenue
	Dunsmore Mews
Stratford	"Swan", Broadway
Victoria Park	Grove Road
Bow Granary	
Kingsland Granary	
Union Road Works	

The Union Road, Leytonstone Works

By **Section 40** of the North Metropolitan Tramways Act, 1885, the company was authorised to build cars at its Union Road Works, both for its own use and for other undertakings. It was expected that costs could be substantially reduced, an example being £140 for a double deck vehicle as against £190 for a similar car built by a specialist firm.

Cars & 'Buses Built and Rebuilt for N M T Service

1885/6	66 cars	1891	26 cars	1897	22 cars		
1887	44 "	1892	42 "		10 buses		
1888	20 "	1893	32 "	1898	40 cars		
	6 buses	1894	36 "		4 punch vans		
1889	18 cars	1895	48 "	1899	40 cars		
1890	38 "	1896	50 "				

Cars Converted From Old Pattern to "Garden Seats"

1899	12	1900	12	1901	12

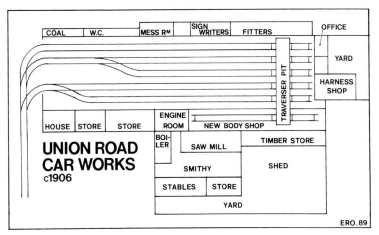

UNION ROAD CAR WORKS c1906

ERO.89

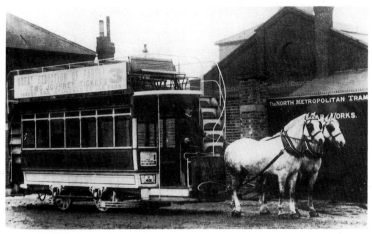

A North Metropolitan car, built at Union Road works, being returned to Stratford depot after renovation, c1890.   *(LCC photo)*

Vehicles Built For Other Undertakings

1885/6	38 cars	1892	1 car Glasgow Corporation tramways
1887	1 "	1893	1 car Glasgow Corporation Tramways
1888	6 "		3 cars Harrow Road & Paddington Tramways
1889	27 "		10 cars Portsmouth Provincial Tramways
1890	14 " *		4 cars Southampton Corporation Tramways
1891	7 "	1894	12 buses Glasgow Tramway & Omnibus Company
			3 cars S.E. Metropolitan Tramways
		1895	1 car Plymouth Tramways Company
		1896	5 electric car bodies, Dublin Southern Tramways Co.
		1902/4	21 buses
		1904/5	1 single-horse punch van, M E T Ltd.

* Including seven for the South Eastern Metropolitan Tramways Co.

As can be seen from the tables above, the company workshops staff were kept quite busy in repairing and building cars, both for its own use and for other companies. With regard to outside work, it was quite unusual for a tramway undertaking in the metropolitan area to be allowed to carry out this function, and even more so for the company to build omnibuses. Additionally, Union Road Works also provided and repaired carts and vans which were used in servicing its own undertaking.

When the Council assumed control of the company, the two were at odds with regard to the price to be paid for the 533 cars which were allocated to it. The Chief Officer of the LCC, A. L. C. Fell, together with Mr. G. Woolley had agreed to value the cars themselves, and had supposed that this could be carried out without the intervention of an arbitrator. The company, however, thought otherwise, which resulted in Sir Edward Boyle, who was already engaged in the task of deciding upon the valuation of the horses, undertaking the task. He concluded that the figure to be paid by the Council for the cars would be £41,754.

Advertising

Advertisements placed on horse cars were generally dealt with by an agent. For many years this function had been carried out on behalf of the company by R. Frost Smith, and he continued to work in this capacity after the undertaking was taken into full LCC ownership. In this case, it was agreed that he should maintain responsibility for advertising until all horse cars were disposed of, and that he would continue to deal with that on electric cars "for the time being", subject to certain conditions. Eventually, all advertising matter which was received, was dealt with by a section of the Tramways Department.

The Horse Age

It will be appreciated that, before the advent of the steam engine and later, the motor vehicle, the horse, as well as being the main source of traction for use on farms and in country areas generally, was also the only means of locomotion that could be used for travelling long distances. Different breeds of animal were developed over the centuries in order to obtain the most efficient horse for whatever purpose it was required. Heavy draught animals, such as those used for drawing farm ploughs or lorry drays, were totally unsuitable for the purpose of carrying a rider for any great distance, or of being used as the motive power for a passenger conveyance which was required to travel at a reasonable and sustained speed. Therefore, for riding and coaching, special animals were bred and developed which were admirably suited to this arduous task.

Probably the most commonly used was the Hackney, an old breed, the records of which go back to the thirteenth century A D. Also known colloquially as a "nag", it originated from a cross between an early racehorse and a heavy carthorse. It was developed for riding because of its stamina and high stepping action, but later was used for driving, being free running and proving to be a very adaptable animal. On the other hand, the Yorkshire Coach and the Cleveland Bay were horses which were both eminently suitable for coaching purposes. The Cleveland was the forerunner of the Yorkshire, although both were bred in Yorkshire. The Cob, a shorter animal, was sometimes used for driving work, although its main purpose was for riding.

As horses of the Hackney breed were the most commonly used animals for hauling carriages and the most popular to be hired by stud owners for this purpose, it was seen by the managements of the tramway companies to be probably the right type of animal for their purposes, although other breeds were used also.

With regard to the word "Hackney", being associated as it was with the breed of horse bearing that name, it became with common usage also associated with the types of vehicles pulled by the animals, and the term "hackney carriage" was coined. From this, many vehicles plying for hire, particularly taxi-cabs, became known by this term, the name persisting long after the horses had been replaced by motor vehicles.

Horsing the Tramway

Upon the formation of the North Metropolitan Tramways Company, horses were hired from the London General Omnibus Company on an initial five-year term which could be terminated by either party on giving one year's notice. Very stringent conditions were laid down by the omnibus company with regard to the miles run each day by each horse; at what average speed and how many hours each horse should run before being rested; how much feed each animal could be allocated. After the first year or so, and as more lines were opened, the tramway company agreed to provide stabling for many of the hired horses, but at the same time was looking at the economics of horsing several of its future lines itself. The first of these took place upon the opening of the Commercial Road line between Poplar and Aldgate, when Messrs. Fisher & Parrish were instructed to purchase sufficient animals, at eleven horses per car, to work the line, while arrangements were being made to stable the animals at Poplar. After this experiment, a Board agreement, made on 6th August 1872, decided to allow the LGOC to continue horsing the remainder of the lines for the next five years, mainly because of the high prices then being paid for suitable animals. Even so, it was costing the company approximately £1,500 a month for hiring horses from the omnibus company.

On 11th April 1877, the Board resolved to approach the LGOC about setting up a new horsing agreement, to run for three years at the rate of 6½d per mile run, provided that several of the clauses which were considered to be "objectionable" were removed. The reply from the LGOC on 2nd May rejected the new proposals out of hand. This resulted, on 20th June, in the company giving the LGOC notice that the horsing contract was to be determined as from 30th June 1878.

Towards the end of 1877, the company began to make plans to set up its own horse stud, and in the first instance asked the LGOC if it was prepared to sell to the company many of the animals being used on the tramways. The LGOC response was that it would sell up to 700 at £46 each, to which the tramway company replied that the figure it had in mind was £40 per horse, which in turn was rejected by the LGOC. The company then resorted to employing agents to buy in suitable animals from the United States of America, Ireland and even as far away as South America, all at an average price of £42.10s each.

Extensive new stabling accommodation was acquired, to house up to about 1,000 horses at that time, which was to increase as further extensions were made to the tramway network. "Double Tramway Harnesses" were required, 300 sets being purchased at £4. 2s. per set from John Leckie & Co. in February 1878, together with 700 extra collars at 8/6d each. A granary and sick horse hospital were built, and a qualified veterinary and stables staff taken into employment to go with them.

On 9th May 1878, the company announced the timetable for the change-over of the first sections to the use of its own horses. These were:-

23rd May:	Green Lanes lines.
30th May:	Victoria Park line.
13th/20th June:	Clapton and Highgate to Moorgate lines.
23rd June:	Hackney to Aldgate lines.

Other lines followed as soon as possible thereafter, and by the end of 1878 all lines were horsed by the company.

In many undertakings, the animals were identified by name. In the case of the Northmet, however, a numbering scheme was adopted, which number was branded on to the flank of the animal. A detailed record was kept of the performance of each animal throughout the time that it was in tramway company service. With regard to numbering, it was the practice in early days to allocate a unique number to each animal, but in later years, when a horse was disposed of by sale or slaughter, the number would be re-allocated to another recently bought-in animal.

With such a large stud of horses to care for, the company decided to set up a rest home for them, both for those who were recovering from sickness and for "holiday" accommodation for the remainder. After a long search, a lease was taken on 20th March 1889 at £240 per annum on Loughton Hall Farm in Essex, and plans were made to provide sufficient stabling for the hospital. The farmhouse was given over as accommodation for the Tramways Manager, Mr. Adamson, which he occupied until October 1901, when possession of it was given up.

On transfer to the LCC in 1906, the company expected that the horses then in the stud would be purchased by the Council at about £27.10s. each. Mr. Bruce, the veterinary officer of the LCC Tramways was instructed to examine a selection of animals at each of the stables, and advise upon the price he thought should be paid. He stated that a large proportion of the animals were either old or of inferior type and were not worth more than about £16 each. The company refused to accept this valuation and, after more discussion, £20 was offered, which was again rejected. With the agreement of both parties, Sir Edward Boyle, Bt. K.C.,M.P., who was an acknowledged authority on horses was appointed to arbitrate in the dispute. After consideration, the award was announced on 27th March that the LCC was to pay £120,796 for the 5,571 horses (£21.13.6d each) which were to be transferred to the Council.

Fares and Tickets

Fares

In common with the policy set out in the Tramways Act of 1870, the earliest Acts of the company authorised the payment of fares by passengers at the rate of one penny a mile, but allowing a charge of 2d, or even 3d to be made for any journey of up to two or three miles, although on most sections, 1d stages were introduced. Nevertheless, this "concession" did not apply on Sundays or Bank Holidays, when often, the full throughout fare of 2d or 3d was payable. There were no reduced fares for children either. After the purchase of the lines by the LCC, one of the conditions imposed was that the practice of charging higher fares on any day must cease.

Fares for workmen were rather different. This section of the community had been catered for in a special way, by legislation being introduced which made it mandatory for the tramway company to provide special early morning and late evening cars for the use of "artisans and daily labourers" only. These people were carried at the rate of ½d up to about two miles, provided that they travelled between 3 and 4 a.m., with a maximum of 1d for a single journey of any length on any one car at other times before 8 a.m., or 1d or 2d for a two-journey ticket. In this case, the two-journey ticket was given up to the conductor on the return journey, the passenger then being issued with an exchange ticket valid for the second journey. In later years, workmen were carried on some return journeys on ordinary service cars, although on the Poplar route, special cars for workmen were in service at regular intervals throughout the day.

An unusual practice began early in 1881, when the company made an agreement with the LGOC on the level of fares to be charged on tramcars and omnibuses traversing the same routes. It all started when Mr. Maples of the NMT Co. and Mr. Church of the LGOC agreed, on 26th January to put up fares "due to the recent severe weather" affecting receipts, with each agreeing to charge the same fares for similar journeys. It appears that, from then on, the representatives of both undertakings advised each other of any proposed changes. Routes and services not affected by this agreement were the Stratford, Poplar, Victoria Park, Green Lanes and Balls Pond lines.

Ticket Styles and Colours

Until March 1874, tickets for the undertaking had been supplied by a firm named Greenaway, of which very little else is presently known. Subsequently, a set of tickets was designed and supplied by T. J. Whiting of London, who then held the contract for about nine years. In June 1883, however, a long association began with the Bell Punch Company, with the supply to the company of tickets used and the punches through which they were issued to passengers.

The first tickets used were probably similar to those used by other pioneer companies, notably the Metropolitan Street and the Pimlico, Peckham & Greenwich tramways. The tickets were quite simple in design and most likely torn from a pack. The ticket serial numbers were duplicated on the stubs, which were used to account for the tickets sold and cash taken. Initially, there was only one fare of 2d on the car service between Whitechapel and Bow, with a special rate of 1d for workmen early on weekday mornings. However, with the introduction of extended and new services, it became necessary to devise a more practical system of ticket issue.

Fortunately, by this time, ticket design had become much more standardised. In the case of the North Metropolitan, two main types came into common use. On one style, the fare stages were displayed in geographical form "ladder fashion" from top to bottom of the tickets, while the serial letters and numbers were printed across the tops. On the second type, all information was printed "landscape" along the tickets including fare stage numbers but with the serial letters and numbers still along the tops, in what had now become the traditional position. All printing was in black ink.

In general, ticket colours for ordinary fares were 1d blue (although some issues were orange), 2d white and 3d magenta. Workman tickets, however, were primrose for ½d single, cream or blue for 1d and orange - later white for 2d. Fares of 1½d were added later, tickets being green, while ½d tickets for use on the local services outside the metropolitan area were primrose. Exchange tickets were usually of buff tint. Each service on each route had its own set of tickets. In almost every case, the tickets were either 2¼ or 2½ inches long by 1¼ inches wide. All were issued to passengers after being passed through a registering punch, which made a circular hole in the ticket.

After extension of company services over the lines lately belonging to the North London Suburban Tramways, two more values were added, the 4d being coloured salmon, the 5d being light sage green. Exchange tickets were coloured buff or light brown. The backs of the tickets were usually given over to advertising, mainly for commodities such as Pear's Soap, Lipton's Tea, Peark's Stores or similar emporia.

The North London Tramways Company had employed a simple ticketing system, which showed the sections of a line of route in a diagonal manner on the ticket, with the serial number and fare value printed in the centre of the fare stage information. Upon acquisition by the North Metropolitan, tickets of similar style to those used on the rest of the system were introduced.

With the purchase of the lines by the LCC and its lease back to the company to operate, the same arrangements continued with the Bell Punch Company with regard to the supply of tickets and punches. Even when the Council took over completely, the agreement with Bell Punch was to continue well into the electric car era.

Ticket Control and Ticket Punches

The first mention of any form of control being exercised over the conductors of the company regarding fare collection was made on 3rd May 1871, when the directors resolved to use "Mr. Bibra's system of checking conductors and to employ for that purpose, boys of the Corps of Commissionaires". How this form of control was exercised - if it was - is not explained, but the impression gained is that some form of simple checking of waybills may have been introduced, with the "boys" of the Corps acting as inspectors.

This arrangement appears to have been less than successful, as it was stated on 20th August 1873 that the directors were seeking a better form of fare collection. One system favourably looked at, involved the use of a registering ticket punch, and an experiment conducted with machines of this type apparently resulted in an increase of 25% in money handed in by conductors!

Next, an agreement was made with Mr. J. H. Small on 27th March 1874 for hire to the company of "Patent Alarm Registering Punches for Tickets" at the rate of 1/- a car a day. This introductory offer, which was accepted, was for a period of six months as from 31st March, with an option after this of a further agreement being made, but at double the cost! However, on 28th August, a new agreement was struck allowing the company to use these machines for a period of two years at a charge of 8d a day for each car, and was to take effect as from 1st October. Included in this charge was a sum to meet the expenses of "detectives" and their offices for superintending the use of the punches.

The Foreign Cancelling Punch Company next appears in the records of the North Metropolitan Tramways, when it was stated, on 30th August 1876, that the company had been trying to obtain a reduction in royalty payment for the use of these machines. It was apparently unsuccessful, as "a further agreement was proposed to extend the present contract for another year on existing terms". From researches undertaken, it appears that "Foreign Cancelling" and "Patent Alarm" may have both been part of the undertaking in which Small had the controlling interest.

The formation of the Bell Punch Company Ltd., registered on 11th July 1878 was made by an agreement dated 5th July 1878, when Capt. John Marshall Gillies, one of the directors of the North Metropolitan Tramways (and, at that time also, chairman of the London Tramways Company), agreed with others to purchase the interests of Walter Rathbone Bacon (possibly a patent agent), who, in turn, had purchased a ticket punch manufactory together with the patents and rights of George Haseltine, and later, other patents the property of William Robert Lake. At the same time, a part interest in the Foreign Cancelling Punch Company, also held by Bacon, was secured.

In 1881, Bacon purchased the remainder of the foreign business of J. H. Small and "Patent Alarm". Included in the purchase were 1,300 ticket punches, which were let on hire to a number of undertakings, of which the North Metropolitan was one. On 7th June 1883, Bell Punch purchased the ticket printing business of John Melton Black, of 3 Bell Yard, City Road, London. Following this, the supply of tickets and provision of ticket punches to the Northmet was undertaken by Bell Punch. On 1st January 1888 a new agreement was signed between the two, whereby for a sum of £500, Bell Punch was to equip the tramway company with between 400 and 500 new ticket punches. The association between the two then continued throughout the remainder of the existence of the tramway company.

Chairman of Bell Punch at the time was Joseph William Greig (a director of the North Metropolitan Tramways), and secretary was C. E. Greig. Some shareholders were J. M. Gillies (NMT Co.), D. Reid, H. C. Godfray (solicitor to the NMT Co.), W. R. Bacon, J. M. Black and J. Kincaid. The original registered offices were at Nos. 1 & 2 Great Winchester Street Buildings, City.

Cash Collection

Large quantities of small value coins were paid in by conductors at the end of each journey, this money being collected and taken to head office, after which it was banked. On 6th June 1877, the company was informed by the Consolidated Bank that no more 3d or 4d pieces could be accepted for the time being. As a result, conductors were asked not to pay in any more of these coins than was necessary, and to dispose of as many as possible by offering change en route. It was also decided by the company to use these coins when paying wages!

In common with the policy adopted by most of the other tramway undertakings operating in the metropolis, cash collected in fares was generally paid to clerks situated in special cash offices at the end of each half journey. There was, however, a problem concerning this arrangement, when the cash offices were closed late at night. It had been the practice for conductors on late cars to retain overnight the cash taken on the last journeys, and this particularly applied to staff at Green Lanes, Canonbury, Highgate and Finsbury Park depots. To obviate this "difficulty", it was decided in August 1881 to provide safes at all depots, to be under the control of the night inspectors, where all moneys were to be deposited.

An ex-North Metropolitan Tramways horse car standing at the northern end of Liverpool Road, and working a "shuttle" service to Upper Street. The line was never electrified. (*LCC official view*)

Horse Car Operation by the London County Council

Upon acquisition of the company by the LCC in 1906, arrangements were made to maintain services in a similar manner to that already in operation, and in many places to improve facilities. However, it was not long before it was seen that, with electrification of the north London system, many changes in the pattern of working would have to take place.

Cars began to appear in various types of LCC livery; car crews were gradually fitted out with some items of uniform clothing; while the fares structure was modified, mainly in reducing fares to some degree. Services were improved where possible, but very soon, the old cars and their horses began to make way for the new electric tramcars. This process continued until August 1914, but the Great War finally put a stop to horse car operation.

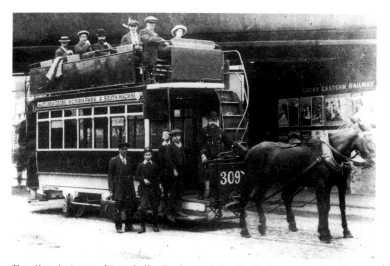

The line between West India Docks and South Hackney was the last on the northern system to be worked with horse cars. No. 309 is seen by Grove Road Railway Bridge in September 1913. (LCC photo)

Chapter 38
The Smaller Companies

THE HARROW ROAD & PADDINGTON TRAMWAYS COMPANY

In "Metropolitan Electric Tramways, Vol. I" (LRTA/TLRS 1984, £12), the author, C. S. Smeeton introduced the Harrow Road & Paddington Tramways Company as the predecessor of a part of the Metropolitan Electric Tramways system, although about two-thirds of the line lay within what became the County of London after 1889. Although the line was expertly described, it is felt that it would not be out of place here to provide the reader with an introduction into the area, together with a short version of that work.

Paddington today is a very crowded area on the western edge of the City of Westminster, but 150 years ago it was a village in Middlesex, surrounded by other similar communities such as Maida Vale, Tyburnia and Bayswater. The ancient manor, which was "attached" to Westminster Abbey, was given to the Bishops of London by King Edward III.

Harrow Road leads out from London, starting at a point about 400 yards north of Hyde Park Corner, where it leaves the Edgware Road to strike out in a westerly direction, passing through Paddington, Kensal Green and Harlesden on its route to Harrow and, eventually the West Midlands.

The district came to some prominence when, in the 18th century a branch of the Grand Junction Canal and its terminal point at Paddington Basin was developed. This was followed by the construction of the London terminal of the Great Western Railway, this monument to the Brunels being completed in 1856. During the construction of the canal, the Harrow Road was breached in two places. Bridges were erected by the canal company to restore the continuity of the road, the easterly one being over the entrance to Paddington Basin, while the western-most bridge, known as Lock Bridge, was close by the "Lock Hospital". The title of the hospital and the bridge, incidentally, has nothing at all to do with the seemingly obvious meaning - that of a canal lock. There was not one at this point. The term was originally applied to institutions set up to deal with those people who suffered the scourge of leprosy. A hospital for women sufferers was built in 1745 in Harrow Road, to which a "rescue home" was added in 1787, and which by then, was more concerned with the treatment of diseases other than leprosy. The term, "Lock Hospital", however, was retained.

By the middle of the nineteenth century the area was becoming quite built-up as a suburb of the metropolis, with housing spreading along both sides of Harrow Road, as far out as Harlesden. It was this potential that the tramway promoters were anxious to tap.

Tramways were first proposed in 1874 by the Edgware Road & Maida Vale Tramways, who suggested that a line be built along Edgware Road from Church Street Paddington to the Edgware Road Station of the Hampstead Junction Railway, a distance of about two miles, but this came to nothing. Next, in 1879, a Provisional Order was obtained by the North-west Metropolitan Tramways, to construct a line over more or less the same ground, but with short extensions at either end. This, too, perished. The same promoters tried again in 1885, but this time failed to obtain a Provisional Order.

Proposals were made in 1886 under a different title. In this case, "The Cricklewood, Kilburn & Harrow Road Tramways" sought powers from Parliament to construct the following tramways:-
No. 1. In Edgware Road for 1 ml. 4 f. 9 ch. northward as far as Kilburn (L&NWR) Station.
No. 2. In High Road Kilburn from No. 1 and into Cambridge Road and Chippenham Road to terminate in Harrow Road by a junction with No. 3, a distance of 1 ml. 3 ch.
No. 3. Commencing at Harlesden Green ("Royal Oak"), along Harrow Road to Chippenham Road, making a junction with No. 2, a distance of 2 mls. 2 f. 6.35 ch., part single.
No. 4. From a junction with No. 3 in Harrow Road, then eastwards along that road to Royal Oak (GWR Station), 1 f. 2 ch. double and 1 ch. single line.
Tramway No. 1 was removed from the Bill during its passage through Parliament, while Nos. 2 & 4 were only partly authorised. No. 3, was retained as written.

The Bill received Royal Assent on 25th June 1886, becoming known as **The Harrow Road & Paddington Tramways Act, 1886 (49-50 Vic. cap. civ)** and authorised the construction of the following tramways:-
No. 2, commencing in Cambridge Road, then along Cambridge Gardens, Cambridge Road South and Chippenham Road to Harrow Road, a distance of 6 f. 0.5 ch., part single line.
No. 3, commencing in Harrow Road at Harlesden Green, then easterly along Harrow Road to a point near the south end of Chippenham Road, 2 mls. 2 f. 6.35 ch., part single line.
No. 4, from its junction with No. 3, along Harrow Road to the Lock Hospital Bridge, 1 f. 3 ch. in all.

The first directors were John Kerr, Frederic Manuelle, John Metcalf, Benjamin Nowell and Joseph Robson. The secretary was Arthur Blunt and the engineer was George Hopkins. Work on the line began after approval of the plans on 5th January 1888. Authorised share capital was £60,000 in £10 shares.

Built by the Contract Construction Company, the line was quickly completed. On 15th June 1888 the secretary requested an inspection; on 2nd July, Maj. Gen. Hutchinson passed the line as fit for use; the Board of Trade certificate was issued on 9th, two days after services commenced. However, the line along Chippenham Road was built only as far as the "Prince of Wales" public house, the last 300 yards being finally abandoned. In the same way, the last 15 yards at the Harlesden end of the line was not built.

In 1888 and 1889 further powers were sought to make extensions to the lines, but no Acts were forthcoming. In 1891, they tried again, this time obtaining **The Harrow Road & Paddington Tramways Act, 1891** to authorise the construction of an extension eastwards, over Lock Bridge to Edgware Road, together with a line from Harrow Road at Walterton Road to Chippenham Road. Neither were built by the company. Two further Acts were obtained in 1893 and 1894 with the intention of extending the time allowed to build the extensions, but the work was never carried out. With the coming of the LCC on

One of the Falcon cars of the company stands at Harlesden terminus.
(Courtesy: C. Carter)

21st March 1889, the line along Harrow Road, became in large measure transferred from Middlesex to London, but even this depended upon which side of the road it was on in many places.

The Chippenham Road line proved to be a liability and, after 1891, only statutory cars ran at about three-monthly intervals to maintain the rights of the company. Even after the LCC became the owner, with the lines leased to the MET Ltd. to operate, the statutory car continued to be worked. Harrow Road & Paddington Car No. 1 was reserved for this function, and was specially preserved and housed at Stonebridge depot of the MET, from where it was brought out, hauled to Chippenham Road, there to be dragged across the road after the junction had been removed in 1907. Carrying its obligatory fare-paying passenger, it was then run the length of the line and back, after which it was taken back to Stonebridge to await the next occasion. Finally, in 1912, the LCC agreed to the removal of the line.

By 1892, the management, with the exception of George Hopkins, had changed. S. E. Buttenshaw was secretary, while the directors were C. C. Cramp, J. W. Greig, H. E. Jacks, A. Love and W. Peacop. Early in 1900 the company was beginning to experience a considerable drop in profits. By the end of 1902, the first signs of an agreement with, and sale to the MET were to be seen. In the spring of 1903, the company asked for Parliamentary powers to electrify its main line.

On 13th June 1903, the company, the MET, the Middlesex County Council and the London County Council made a preliminary agreement with regard to the sale, and later a Bill was presented to Parliament. On 11th August, the company received its authorising Act, which was followed on 22nd July 1904 by its sale to the MET. Now a subsidiary of the Metropolitan Electric Tramways Ltd., the company continued to operate the horse tramway for another two years, until finally, on 16th August 1906, in exchange for £36,921, the Harrow Road & Paddington Tramways Company disappeared into history. Subsequent events surrounding the line are recorded in "Metropolitan Electric Tramways, Vol. I", while details of the short-lived LCC electric car service appear in Volume I, page 251 of this history.

The Depot

The site upon which the depot and stables were built was held on lease from John Williams, William Henry Wallington and others for a 99-year period as from 25th December 1887 at an annual rent of £168. Situated in Trenmar Gardens, not far from the junction of Harrow Road with Scrubs Lane, it had a main single storey building 250 ft. long and 75 ft. wide, together with stables and other outbuildings. It had three depot roads, two of which went right through the building, out at the back and ended at a turntable. There was also a single line along the length of Trenmar Gardens which also ended at the turntable.

The Cars

These were supplied by two manufacturers. The first batch of twelve came from Milnes and were of 7-window, double deck type, with "knifeboard" seating on the upper decks. The remainder were from the Falcon Works and were of 6-window, double deck style, with "garden" seats upstairs. The Milnes cars were in a livery of red, while the others were brown. Unusually, "foot warmers" were provided in all cars during the winter months, which item consisted of a zinc box inside which a "smokeless and odourless fuel block" was placed. It was stated that one charge of fuel would be sufficient to keep the box comfortably warm for up to 15 hours.

THE WEST METROPOLITAN TRAMWAYS COMPANY

This undertaking worked in the area west of Hammersmith and Shepherds Bush, and during its existence maintained its independence from the affairs of the LCC. It eventually became known as the London United Tramways Ltd. and the system was electrified in 1901. It was not until 1922 that the LCC purchased the sections of line within London, and these have been described in Vol. I of this history. A complete historical description of the London United Tramways and its predecessors, researched and written by C. S. Smeeton is to be published jointly by the LRTA/TLRS during 1991/1992.

THE LEA BRIDGE, LEYTON & WALTHAMSTOW TRAMWAYS COMPANY

A full account of this company and its activities is given in "The Tramways of East London" by "Rodinglea" (LRTA/TLRS, 1967). As, however, a short length of the line came within the County of London after 1889, it is necessary to include an abbreviated description of the undertaking within this work, the more so as in later years, the section became part of a through route to Leyton and beyond.

By **The Lea Bridge, Leyton & Walthamstow Tramways Act, 1881 (44-45 Vic. cap. clxx)** the company was empowered to lay down and maintain a single line of tramway 3 mls. 3 f. 8.1 ch. long, from "Lea Bridge Corner" (by Upper Clapton Road) to Leyton "Rising Sun".

Capital of £65,000 was authorised and the first directors were George Denton Cardew, Benjamin Cooke and one other not named. Secretary was T. E. Crocker. Most of the line was to be situated in the county of Essex, with only about one half mile in Middlesex. The

A Leyton UDC car just entering the depot. The overhead wires for
electric traction are just visible.   (The late L. A. Thompson)

line was constructed by Messrs. B. Cooke & Co., who appears to have
been one of the directors.   The first sections to be built were on the
Essex side of the River Lea, and after inspection on 7th May 1883,
opened to traffic on 12th, but within three years the company was
bankrupt.

On 19th October 1888, a new company known as the Lea Bridge,
Leyton & Walthamstow Tramways Co. Ltd., was formed with an authorised capital of £20,000, and William Griffiths, Henry John Carter and
James Aynsley were its first directors.   J. Barber Glenn was secretary.
After further legalities, a statutory company bearing the same name
took over from the limited company and, among other things, laid
an extension westwards from the River Lea to Upper Clapton Road,
which was opened to traffic on Easter Monday 1892.   Although it had
been intended to connect the line with that of the North Metropolitan
Tramways Company in Upper Clapton Road, this was not carried out at
that time. On the formation of the LCC, this 34 ch. length of line
came within the new county area, but the company was allowed to
continue to run its services as before.

Eventually, on 13th April 1905, Leyton UDC purchased the lines in
its area with the intention of electrifying them, which work was completed late in November 1906.   Public service began on 1st December.
So far as the short length in London was concerned, this continued
to be worked for the next two years with horse cars shuttling up and
down between the River Lea and the western end of the line. Finally,
on 10th December 1908, this short length having been purchased by the
LCC for £8,040, and reconstructed for overhead wire working, the
Leyton electric cars were extended over the new tracks.   Following
this, the LCC arranged to connect the line with the rest of the network
by laying conduit tracks round the corner from Lea Bridge Road and
provide a ploughshift a few yards from the junction with Upper Clapton
Road.   This was completed during June 1910 and opened on 1st July,
allowing through services to be instituted as described in the chapters
dealing with routes and services.

A peaceful scene at the Clapton terminus of the Lea Bridge Road tramway. *(Chas. Martin)*

The Cars

The first ten cars to be purchased by the company were built by Merryweather & Co. of Greenwich, London in 1883, of which eight or nine were of the single deck type. These, of 5-window formation, each seated 16 passengers on two wooden benches. Livery was said to be red and white. The eastern terminus of the line, described as "Epping Forest" was prominently displayed on the waist panels of the cars, with the legend "Lea Bridge, Leyton, Whips Cross & Walthamstow" (sic) signwritten above the saloon windows.

Later cars were of double deck pattern, some very similar in style to those of the North Metropolitan Tramways Company, and having "knifeboard" seating on the upper deck. Others supplied by the Electric Railway & Tramway Carriage Co. in 1899 had "garden seats" outside. Livery of both batches was said to be red and white. At first, the cars were horsed by Thomas Tilling, but in later years the company maintained its own stud and stables.

The Depot

The original depot and stables was in Russell Road, on the north side of Lea Bridge Road, but this was soon replaced by another building on the south side of Lea Bridge Road to the west of the "Bakers Arms" junction and next to Westerham Road.

Chapter 39
The Highgate Hill Cable Tramway

Mainly Historical

The village of Highgate stands at the top of a hill and is about five miles to the north of the City of London and about one mile north-east of Hampstead Heath. From these heights an exceptionally fine view may be had of London and its inner suburbs. Highgate is well known for its legendary connection with Dick Whittington and his cat, now immortalised in pantomime. At the foot of Highgate Hill stands the Whittington Stone, marking the spot where he is said to have first heard Bow Bells.

At one time, Highgate was a village in a forest in Middlesex, and its history goes back to at least the fourteenth century A D. It is also supposed that the area became a favourite hunting ground for the pleasure of King Henry VIII. Many fine houses have been built in the district over the centuries, some of which still proudly stand today. By the middle years of the nineteenth century, most of the surrounding districts had been made accessible by railway, but due to its lofty position, none went nearer than about half a mile to the east of the village.

By 1873, horse tramways were beginning to spread across the metropolitan area, reaching the "Archway Tavern" at the foot of Highgate Hill. Services were provided by two companies, the North Metropolitan Tramways and the London Street Tramways, the second of which was to get nearer still by building a line along Highgate Road as far as Swains Lane. But there it terminated, unable to go any further.

The First Cable Worked Tramway in Europe

Andrew Smith Hallidie of San Francisco was a manufacturer of wire rope and in 1873 he introduced the idea of using an endless rope hauled by a steam winch to convey streetcars up and down the tortuous hills in his native city. The idea consisted of placing the rope beneath the roadway and between a pair of running rails and, by means of carefully placed pulley wheels, the rope could be guided to precisely the right positions for it to be taken up or dropped by the drivers of the cars, who used a specially designed mechanism fitted to each car for the purpose. This means of propulsion had been seen by many people, among them it is said, by Sir Sydney Waterlow. As Hallidie wished to exploit his idea in every way possible, he naturally thought of introducing it into Europe and so, with the aid of Waterlow, decided on exploring the possibility of constructing an experimental line on the steep Highgate Hill, between the "Archway Tavern" and the centre of the Village, a distance of about five furlongs. It was in 1880 that the seeds of the idea were sown.

The proposed area of operations lay within the boundaries of three

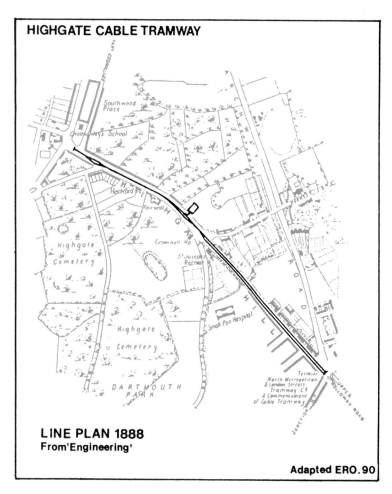

HIGHGATE CABLE TRAMWAY

LINE PLAN 1888
From 'Engineering'

Adapted ERO.90

authorities; the Parish of St. Pancras, the Parish of Islington and the Parish of Hornsey, and the division was to create problems in later years. In any event, even the knowledge that a cable tramway was being considered at all engendered opposition as, while the authorities in St. Pancras and Islington were generally in favour of such a scheme, Hornsey certainly was not! In fact, throughout the life of the line, even after it was built, Hornsey was almost always in opposition to anything that was proposed or undertaken.

The Formation of the Company

The undertaking that was eventually formed for the purpose of constructing and operating the line suffered almost from the beginning with problems of under capitalisation, inexperienced management and bad luck. It was no better under any one of the several successor companies, of which, in all, there were five. The first of these was incorporated on 23rd December 1881 under the terms of the Companies'

Acts of 1862 and later, and was entitled The Steep Grade Tramways &
Works Company Limited. In the Memorandum of Association, the
first subscribers, with one share each, were named as:-

A. Stanley Felton, Agent: M. Eugenius Birch, C. Eng:
Frank R. Robinson, C. Eng: Edward Harrison, C. Eng:
George Mertens, Solicitor: Robert Fowler, Solicitor:
Hunsell Joseph Neale, Clerk to Solicitor:

Capital was to be £100,000 in 20,000 shares of £5 each, together with
500 Founders' shares at £1 each, 200 of which were to be subscibed by
and allocated to the Founders, the remaining 300 to go to subscribers
of the first £30,000 of ordinary shares in the proportion of one share
to each subscribed sum of £100. Mertens and Fowler were named
as the first directors of the company. The office was at Victoria
Mansions, Victoria Street, London.

It was the Steep Grade Company who, using the title "The Highgate
Hill Tramways" applied for and eventually received a Provisional Order
from the Board of Trade to enable it to begin planning and engineering
the line, which was to be 5 f. 7.30 ch. long.

Parliamentary confirmation was given in the **Tramways Orders
Confirmation (No. 2) Act, 1882 (45-46 Vic. cap. lxx)**, which received
Royal Assent on 3rd July 1882. It specified that the tramway was
to be powered "by wire ropes placed underground and to be worked
by stationary engine power upon the Hallidie System of Cable Tramways" and the following lines were authorised:-

No. 1, commencing in Highgate Hill about seven yards from the south-
east corner of the "Archway Tavern", passing in a northerly direction
along Highgate Hill, and terminating in High Street, Highgate, about
eight yards from the centre of the entrance to Fairseat House.

No. 2, commencing at the termination of Tramway No. 1 and passing
along High Street and terminating at a point in the side street opposite
the south-east entrance to Southwood Lane.

Clause 32 of the Act stated that "the tramway may be used for
the purpose of conveying passengers, animals, goods, minerals and
parcels", while clause 34 stated that animals, etc. were to be conveyed
in separate carriages or in separate parts of carriages. Another list
was published giving the proposed charges and tolls to be levied in
all the different categories.

Passenger fare, either way	2d
Horse, mule, ox, cow, bull or head of cattle	6d each
Calf, pig, sheep or other small animal	3d each
Coal, coke, dung, and all sorts of manure	3d per ton
Sugar, grain, corn, flour, hides, dyewoods, timber, non-ferrous metals, nails, chains, etc.	6d per ton
Cottons, wools, drugs, fish, articles, matters or things	6d per ton
Two wheeled carriages	1/-
Four wheeled carriages	1/6d

Parcels: up to 7 lbs.   3d
          7 lbs. to 14 lbs.   5d
         14 lbs. to 28 lbs. 7d
         28 lbs. to 56 lbs. 9d
         over 56 lbs. as promoters think fit.

Articles of great weight; boilers, machinery, over 4 tons and up to
8 tons, as promoters think fit, but not more than 2/- per ton.

The company set up to construct this 3 ft. 6 in. gauge tramway,
still had only seven shareholders as at 6th July 1882. Even at this early

An early view of tractor car No. 6 and trailer No. 3 standing at the top end of the line. (*Courtesy: L T Museum U18933*)

stage there were signs of trouble. Due to its financial problems, the Steep Grade Company management recommended in December 1882 that the assets be transferred to the Hallidie Patent Cable Tramways Corporation Limited, which was agreed to. Meanwhile, the Steep Grade Company continued in existence as best it could, with a small room at the depot for use as an office, instead of at Victoria Mansions.

The Hallidie Patent Cable Tramways Corporation Limited was also a company limited by shares. James Clifton Robinson was Manager, with Henry William Shaw as Secretary. Registered office was also at Victoria Mansions. The Articles of Association of the company stated that its objects should be to adopt and carry into effect an agreement made on 18th December 1882 between it and the Engish, Foreign & Colonial Patent Tramways Company Limited. These were to acquire, construct, alter, modify, equip and work with wire rope ... tramways, railways and works in the U.K. etc., and to carry on the business of a tramway and railway company as a carrier. The E. F. & C. P. T. Co. Ltd. were to be able to purchase patents of the Hallidie Patent Cable tramways Corporation Ltd. (in course of formation) through Henry William Shaw (Trustee). At the same time, a further agreement was reached between Hallidie and Henry Farnsby Mills, granting Mills the right of purchase of certain inventions made by Hallidie, while Mills was, in turn, to assign these to the English & Foreign Company. Lastly, there were further complicated rules and conditions imposed regarding finance, and also the sale and purchase of the inventive ideas of Hallidie.

As at 2nd May 1883, the financial situation of the Hallidie Patent Company was that, of the one million shares offered at a nominal £10 each, only 20,006 had been taken up, of which 7,000 were deemed to be fully paid up. The remainder had been the subject of a call of £5 each. At the end of December, there was a share exchange and an indenture written between the two companies.

The Highgate Hill Tramways Company was the next to appear. At this time there was still no sign of any construction work taking place along the line of route, and this company had been brought into existence to take over the working of the line when it had been built. The secretary, George D. Mertens (who has been mentioned elsewhere) wrote to the Board of Trade asking for extra time to be given to enable work on the line to be carried out. A problem had arisen, it was said, when an American Engineer, who had been engaged to prepare plans etc., did not make satisfactory progress, resulting in another engineer being engaged to carry out the work. Capital had been raised and arrangements made for the diversion of water pipes along the line of route, while premises had been taken for use as a depot and engine house, and these were in course of being cleared to make way for the new buildings. The Board of Trade authorised an extension of time for six months, to take effect as from 28th June 1883.

Land at Nos. 6 & 8 High Street had been purchased on lease from William Robert Walker, who in turn had taken a lease on it from the freeholders, The Governors of Christ's Hospital (or to give it its full title, 'The Hospitals of Edward, late King of England the Sixth, of Christ, Bridewell, and St. Thomas the Apostle'), who were the Mayor, Commonalty and Citizens of London. This method of purchase was resorted to as the company had no powers of compulsory purchase granted to it under the terms of the Provisional Order or its subsequent enabling Act. The engine and winding house, together with the depot and other accommodation and engines had cost over £6,000. Over-generous provision had been made in both the size of the engines and in their accommodation in anticipation of extensions, which, in the event, did not materialise.

Construction Begins

In the case of this line, the idea was so new to British eyes that every aspect of the work was closely studied by the Board of Trade Railway Inspector, Maj. Gen. Hutchinson, before anything could be done. After he was satisfied, authority was given for the City of London Contract Corporation Ltd. to begin work, which commenced in October 1883 and carried on throughout the winter and into the spring of 1884, being finally completed early in May. A trial trip was made on the full length of the line on Saturday 10th May, at which many local dignitaries were present.

The Track

Steel rails of "Barker" type were laid, being held to the gauge of 3 ft. 6 in. by chairs 2 ft. in length, spaced 3 ft. 6 in. apart. The centre slot and slotway, within which the cable and its supporting pulleys were housed, was formed with cast-iron "frames" or yokes which were 6 in. thick and 6 in. wide with a measurement of 1 ft. 8 in. across the flat base. The slot rails, of "Z" formation were bolted directly to the inner faces of the tops of the yokes, and gave a width of just over ¾ inch between the tops to allow the passage of the car gripper mechanisms.

The yokes were buried in concrete 12 inches thick at the base and six inches at the sides, with extended concrete platforms to support the running rails. Access holes with removable covers were provided above the fixings upon which the pulleys were mounted, and which were vertically placed at intervals of about 25 ft.

There were a number of curved sections on the line and at these

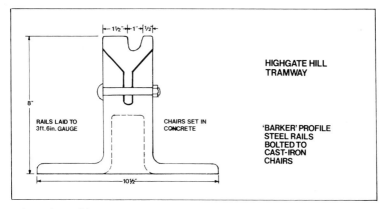

HIGHGATE HILL
TRAMWAY

RAILS LAID TO
3ft. 6in. GAUGE

CHAIRS SET IN
CONCRETE

'BARKER' PROFILE
STEEL RAILS
BOLTED TO
CAST-IRON
CHAIRS

points the cable was supported by special wide pulleys mounted at an angle of 45°, and spaced at varying distances apart depending upon the severity of the curvature. At the terminal points, the cable was carried round two sheaves or pulleys 8 ft. in diameter, mounted in the horizontal plane, with the one at the upper terminus being upon a fixed axis, while that at the lower end mounted on a moveable carriage which was counterweighted to enable the cable to be maintained at uniform tension. Sumps were provided at suitable locations to allow for efficient drainage, connections being made into the main sewer for the discharge of rainwater.

The Cable

This was an "endless" cable, the first of which was manufactured by Scott of Stockport in conjunction with Bullivant & Co. of Millwall, London. Total length of the cable before splicing was 8,000 feet; the main joint was a splice of some 60 feet long; diameter of the cable when new was $1\frac{9}{16}$ inch; weight was 4 tons 9 cwts 32 lbs. The stranded cable was made up from 114 wires drawn from crucible steel, each strand of 0.005 inches in diameter, these being woven into six strands of 19 wires each, these then being wound or formed into the finished cable. It was designed to withstand a test strain of approximately

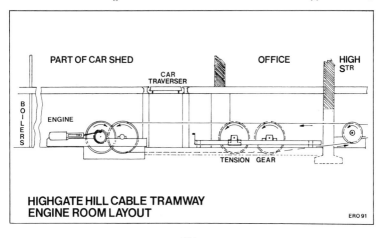

HIGHGATE HILL CABLE TRAMWAY
ENGINE ROOM LAYOUT

ERO 91

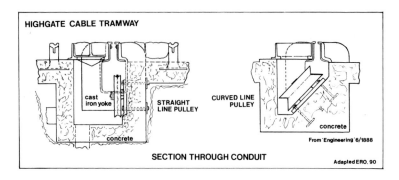

HIGHGATE CABLE TRAMWAY

cast iron yoke
STRAIGHT LINE PULLEY
concrete
CURVED LINE PULLEY
concrete
From 'Engineering' 6/1888

SECTION THROUGH CONDUIT

Adapted ERO. 90

34 tons, which was about ten times the expected strain of about three tons. Subsequent cables were manufactured by George Cradock & Co. of Wakefield.

The Engines

These, in duplicate, were by Jessop of Leicester from designs by Grafton of London and Vulcan Works, Bedford and consisted of two machines, each of 25 n h p (nominal horse power, an assumed figure to denote the power output from a steam engine and only used as a comparative indicator). Each engine consisted of two cylinders of 14 inches diameter and 28 inches stroke, placed horizontally and driving through ordinary connecting rods and "bright balanced discs", with a 2½ ton flywheel on the mainshaft driving the winding gear. The machines, of the "horizontal reversible" type were capable of being worked separately or together, as required.

The mainframes of the engines consisted of two hollow castings secured to the foundations by long bolts, the whole weighing a total of ten tons. Each engine was provided with a governor in a locked cage (to prevent them being tampered with) which controlled the speed of the cable to a maximum of six miles per hour. A cable tensioning device was installed in the engine house. The cable was driven by a Grant & Ritchie "grip pulley" and after leaving the engine house, ran left down the hill, over the terminal wheel, up the hill and over the upper terminal wheel, then back to the engine house. On the double track sections the cable was carried midway between each track, but on the single line sections, the "up" and "down" cables ran side by side, about four inches apart.

The Boilers

These were manufactured by Babcock & Wilcox of Glasgow and New York (at that time) and consisted of two 50 n h p tubular boilers fitted with "turnballs" and patent safety valves, 3½ inch main steam stop valves, water gauges and three test cocks to each boiler, together with blow-off, feeder and injector valves. Steam could be got up to working pressure from cold in less than 40 minutes.

The Board of Trade Inspection

The installation was inspected by Maj. Gen. Hutchinson on 21st May 1884, after which he authorised its use subject to severe restrictions. In his report he stated:-

A view of Highgate Village terminus taken in the first years of the twentieth century.   *(Courtesy: J. B. Gent)*

"Tramway No. 1 is a double line 41.30 ch. in length, up the hill from 'The Archway Tavern'.
Tramway No. 2 is a single line, a continuation of No. 1, with a passing place, to terminate at Southwood Lane.
Gradients vary from 1 in 28 to 1 in 11. The cable is 8,000 feet long. It is carried on pulleys 25 feet apart, but closer on curves. All is well on the double line, but, on the single line, two cable sheaves side-by-side on the curves make things difficult. To overcome some problems, the Engineer has re-aligned the single line section, which is illegal, even though the Local Board have agreed. A further Provisional Order will have to be obtained, or an Act of Parliament to legalise this.
Rolling Stock. (a). 'Ordinary' (trailer) cars attached to dummies.
              (b). Self-operating bogie cars.
The dummies carry passengers and both are double decked and carry roof passengers. It is regrettable that all cars are not of the self-contained bogie pattern, because:-
1. All break (sic) power would then be under the control of the driver and no coupling chains would be required.
2. No chance of accidents at reversing points.
3. No risk of broken couplings.
4. More stability.
There are three of each type of car. Brakes, blocks and slippers are applicable by the driver or conductor. All are of good workmanship. A modification of the gripper wheels is suggested.
The following rules are to apply:-
1. Speed to be no more than six miles per hour.
2. A complete stop to be made before facing points, until better points are devised.
3. When dummy cars are in use, on the up journey the conductor must never leave the rear platform or car.
4. Passengers are not to enter or leave the cars on the wrong side.

5. Dummies and cars not to descend the hill by gravity alone. They must always be attached to the cable, except when stopping and when passing the engine house where the cable is dropped and picked up again.
6. Engines should have speed regulators of an automatic pattern to prevent 'racing' in case the load gets out of hand.
7. Engines should have a work register (speed or revolution counter) to ensure that speed is not exceeded.

(signed) C. S. Hutchinson,
Maj. Gen. R. E.
21st May 1884".

An additional restriction was later applied with regard to speed through points. This was not to be more than four miles per hour.

After the successful inspection, arrangements were made to have this rather small but very important tramway, the first of its kind in Europe, ceremonially opened by none other than the Lord Mayor of London, Sir Robert Fowler, on Thursday 29th May 1884. The line was in Middlesex and the City of London could be said to be within the boundaries of Middlesex. As also the links with the City, Highgate and Dick Whittington were so strong, and as the previous Lord Mayor, Sir Sydney Waterlow resided in Highgate, there was probably no good reason why the Lord Mayor should not undertake this pleasant duty. No doubt, local dignitaries also became very much involved in the celebrations.

The Lord Mayor was met at the "Archway Tavern" by J. C. Robinson, after which the whole entourage, accompanied by the City of London Artillery Band, moved on to the tramway to begin the ceremony. This consisted of the party riding up to the terminus at Southwood Lane, then making a visit to the engine house, followed by celebrations at the Waterlow residence. After the opening, the rest of the day was taken up by the company giving free rides to all and sundry. Public service commenced on the following day, Friday, 30th May. The sum of £18,111 had been spent, which included the cost of the cars, while the engine house and machinery cost a further £31,889.

A carnival atmosphere is seen at Highgate Village on the occasion of the ceremonial opening of the cable tramway.   (Courtesy: T & L R S)

The Cars

The tractor cars and trailers were constructed and equipped at the Falcon Iron Works, Loughborough. The initial fleet consisted of three tractor cars with seats for passengers, three double deck trailers each seating 20 passengers inside and 22 outside, and two self contained bogie cars equipped with grippers. Two more self contained bogie cars were ordered from Falcon on 27th July 1884 "to be exactly the same mechanically as the others". On delivery, the Board of Trade Inspector was asked to check the vehicles, as the Metropolitan Police had stated that they would only be licensed if the Board was satisfied as to their condition. The Inspector was, and duly authorised their use on 12th August 1884. The company reported that the number of passengers carried during the first 17 days of operation was 50,583, while the sum of £421.10. 6d was taken in fares. The average number of passengers per journey was 40.

The Cable Gripper

On this pioneer line, the cable was driven at a steady six mph, and had need to be "picked up" and "dropped" from each car every time a vehicle was started or stopped. The gripper mechanism was firmly suspended from one axle of each car by adjustable bearings and was controlled by the driver by means of a screw-operated linkage working upon a "wedge-piece", which raised or lowered the grip mechanism as required.

On coming into service, each car was moved from the depot by horse power, and when standing in the road outside, the gripper gear was operated so that the cable was brought between the jaws of the gear. The reverse procedure was carried out when a car was taken into the depot. This method of operation was eventually to be the cause of problems.

Braking on Cars

All cars were fitted with what was described as "continuous" braking arrangements, which, on the self-contained vehicles consisted of brake shoes on all wheels which were controlled from the driving position, together with "slipper brakes" which were faced with elongated wood blocks which could be screwed down on to the rails if required. On coupled cars, a linkage was incorporated into the drawbar mechanism, which automatically applied the brakes on the trailer when the linkage was in compression with the tractor car.

Legal Problems

On 8th October 1884, the Steep Grade Company, together with the Patent Cable Tramways Corporation Ltd., was put into the hands of two Trustees, Sampson Hanbury and Charles Kemp Dyer. New mortgage debentures were authorised, with the Trustees being made responsible for their administration, together with liability for any extensions made to the line which might have been built and worked from the original engine house.

About eight months later, on 19th June 1885, the Patent Cable Tramways Corporation Ltd. again made an appearance. This was the company which had been reconstituted from the Hallidie Patent Cable Tramways Corporation. A Deed was constructed, authorising the Trustees to retain control, and was to remain in force until more

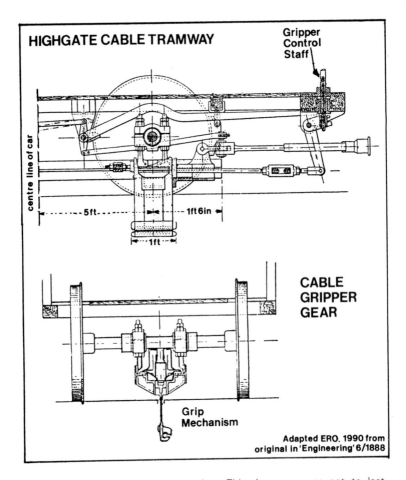

HIGHGATE CABLE TRAMWAY

Gripper Control Staff

centre line of car

5ft

1ft 6in

1ft

CABLE GRIPPER GEAR

Grip Mechanism

Adapted ERO, 1990 from original in 'Engineering' 6/1888

formal arrangements could be made. This, however, was not to last. After legal proceedings, instituted as a result of an accusation that "capital had been lost", the Steep Grade Company was ordered to be wound up on 5th June 1886.

The next date of note was 6th August 1889, when a company known as the Highgate & Hampstead Cable Tramways Company was incorporated, to enable the Deed of June 1885 to be formalised. Like all other activities of the companies involved from time to time, this arrangement proved to be not very straightforward. In the years between 1889 and 1892 the undertaking was sold and re-sold, and for much of the time was in the hands of a Receiver. On 20th December 1892, a Liquidator was appointed, and it agreed that the company should be sold yet again to another to be set up under the title of The Highgate Hill Tramways Ltd.

It was anticipated that the transfer could be made within a few weeks and, as the operating license was to expire on 31st December, application was made to the Board of Trade for its renewal, which body informed the company that a further inspection would have to

"Gripper bogie car" No. 9, when new, at the top terminus of the line.
(Courtesy: Tramway Museum Society)

be made of the installation before a new license could be issued. At this time, the tramway was carrying about 680,000 passengers and running some 85,000 miles annually, and seemed to be set to be able to continue in this way. However, on Monday 5th December 1892 a car ran back down the line and collided with a stationary tractor and trailer standing at the terminus. The rearmost car was pushed off the end of the track and ran down Holloway Road for some 200 yards, coming to rest near Elthorne Road. Miraculously, no-one was killed, although one lady was badly cut by broken glass.

This accident happened just two weeks before the "new" company was to be set up, causing something of a setback. The Board of Trade ordered that the line should be closed until a further inspection had been undertaken, and after suitable repairs had been carried out on the lines and engines. This was not done; the license was not renewed; the line stayed closed and was to remain so for the next four years.

An effort was made to reform the "new" company by the incorporation of the Highgate Hill Tramways Company Ltd. on 9th June 1893. Nominal capital was to be £8,000 in 1,600 shares of £5 each. The new body was authorised to carry into effect the agreement made on 20th December 1892. Repairs were carried out to the installation and an inspection asked for. Evidently, after Maj. Gen. Hutchinson was consulted, he insisted on further repairs being carried out, after which the sum of £500 be deposited as security with the Board of Trade. He further ordered that two men be in the engine house together at all times when the line was working.

It was at this point that a representative of the Hornsey Local Board entered into the discussions by making an objection to a further inspection taking place. The line stayed closed. It was also made known that the "new" company had not complied with the terms of the agreement of 20th December 1892 regarding certain financial obligations.

"Gripper bogie car" No. 8 this time, at the "Archway Tavern" terminus, standing in company with North Metropolitan and London Street horse cars. *(Courtesy: Tramway Museum Society)*

In April 1896, the London County Council made an offer of £2,000 for the line as it stood, stating that a further £3,000 would be required to put it in order. The vestries of Islington and St. Pancras agreed; Hornsey did not. The offer was not proceeded with. Meantime, efforts were still being made to set up another company in order to get the line working again. The Highgate Tramways Limited was formed in May 1896, but even this was of no assistance in getting things working again. Hornsey still objected, asking that the line be permanently closed.

Finally, The Highgate Hill Tramways Limited was formed on 11th May 1896 and represented by E. B. Dawson and A. J. Secretan. The object was to purchase the insolvent company from E. D. Oppert, who had been prominent in the many previous dealings. Cost was stated to be £2,500. Dawson was a complainant in the affairs of the previous company, while Secretan was an accountant engaged by Dawson for the purpose of purchasing the undertaking. On 14th August 1896 the tramway was transferred to the new company.

At last something was seen to be done. The rehabilitated line was inspected by Maj. Marindin in March 1897 and again on 12th April. It re-opened to public traffic under the watchful eye of the engineer and manager, W. N. Colam, on Easter Monday 19th April, after the issue of a license for three months. A 4-minute service was provided. Unfortunately, at about 6.30 p.m. on that evening, a steam pipe in the engine house fractured, with the result that the service had to be suspended for the rest of the day. After repairs, the line was put into use on the following day, and ran uneventfully for a number of years, with the license to operate being renewed as necessary.

The Metropolitan Electric Tramways Limited had established a line which worked between Finchley and the "Archway Tavern" at the foot of Archway Road, the last 400 yards or so running on metals belonging to the London County Council. On Saturday 21st June 1906, one of the cars belonging to the M E T Ltd. ran away out of control down Archway Road, causing a nasty accident. In the aftermath of the disaster, the Board of Trade withdrew the license to operate from the Highgate Hill Tramways until the company could assure the Board that it had seen to it that the brakes of all cars were suitable to deal with all eventualities. After a period, with an assurance that all was well, the line was allowed to be re-opened. From then on, licenses were renewed the last one being on 25th August 1907, which was valid for three years.

The London County Council again became involved in the affairs of the company in 1909 when, after further discussion, an agreement was signed on 5th May which allowed the Council to purchase the undertaking for £13,000. On 24th August the line and all its assets were conveyed to the Council. It was closed to traffic on the same day. However, Hornsey, by now an Urban District Council, objected to the sale and purchase, but on being re-assured by the LCC that it would not seek to provide depot accommodation for electric cars in the old cable station, it relented and agreed to the change. The LCC arranged for the line to be reconstructed to conduit standards. It re-opened for service on 25th March 1910.

Looking back with hindsight on the fortunes and misfortunes of this small undertaking, it was perhaps inevitable that it would suffer problems; five-eighths of a mile is not very far, even if it is on a steep hill, and to have all the trappings of a full-blown steam-powered cable tramway was probably asking too much of those responsible for it. It must also be remembered that, in the beginning, these people were pioneers and as such, could have looked for a better future than they actually obtained.

Goods Haulage

Finally, on a different theme, but one bearing heavily upon the fortunes of the undertaking, was a complaint made on 3rd May 1890 that loaded coal carts were being hauled up the hill behind passenger carrying service cars. The policy of the company was explained by Mr. Colam in a statement to the Board of Trade and the police, saying "we must do it; it is part of our business and we have always done it". This aspect of operations was quite legal, as has been described in the Act authorising the line, except that special vehicles should be used for this purpose.

The Board of Trade replied by prohibiting the practice, the company taking this to mean that service cars could not be used, but special cars without passengers could be, and they were. On 10th January 1891, an intending passenger complained that he was not allowed to board a special car being used to haul a cart up the hill. This resulted in the Board of Trade totally forbidding the practice, stating that it was dangerous, and pointing out that no towing of other vehicles was permitted. Despite this, evidence suggests that coal carts and other vehicles were still "helped" up the hill from time to time!

Traffic Accidents

Throughout its existence the line was beset by accidents, many minor, but with several rather unpleasant ones as well. The first reported case occurred at the bottom of the hill on 31st July 1884 at 9.45 p.m., when "dummy" No. 6 and car No. 3 were descending. The conductor moved on to the dummy to collect fares and shortly after- wards the driver called to him to go back to the trailer to put the brake on, as the car was increasing in speed. The conductor fell off the car as he was attempting to move back; the driver could not stop the vehicles and they collided at the bottom of the hill with dummy No. 5 and car No. 1. One lady was seriously cut from flying glass. It was said that the accident happened because of the failure on the part of the conductor to connect the brake of the trailer to the controls of the dummy, together with the failure on the part of the driver to pick up the cable on the downward journey as the car passed the engine house.

On 4th September 1884 at 2 p.m., car No. 9 suffered a broken gripper at the bottom of the hill. The drivers of two other cars, Nos. 7 and 10, left their vehicles to assist the crew of No. 9. It then seems that the brakes "came off" No. 10, which was the rearmost vehicle in the line, causing it to run into the other two, damaging all three. Fortunately, no-one was hurt.

Four months later, on 8th January 1885, car No. 8 ran away down the hill, causing damage to a standing cart. The enquiry disclosed the fact that the car was being worked by gravity from the depot to the road, which was quite improper. The driver then stopped the car for the gripper to be fitted and then ran the vehicle back down the hill for a short distance to pick up the cable on the uphill side. He failed, and the car continued to run back. In this case, both the driver and conductor jumped off the moving vehicle, allowing it to run away out of control. It was said that the move allowing the car to be run down to the single line to avoid making a "useless" journey was made as the car was to begin its schedule at the top end of the line, and it was considered to be wasteful to run it to the bottom of the hill and back first. It also meant that the sandbox was at the wrong end, but, even if it had not been, it was useless as it was empty!

There was another incident which occurred on 31st August 1889, when cars Nos. 7 and 2 ran away down the hill. It seemed that these had been left standing on the hill outside the depot and, it was stated "that some boys released the brakes". The outcome of this occurrence is not known.

Tractor car No. 5 with trailer car No. 3 at the "Archway Tavern" terminus, c1900. *(Courtesy: Greater London Photograph Library)*

Chapter 40
The London County Council Tramways, Northern Section

Concurrently with the plans adopted for the electrification of the south side services in 1902, the Council was considering the implement- ation of a similar programme for the lines on the northern system. Due to the fact that the North Metropolitan Tramways Company was operating the car services on lease from the LCC, and that powers had been secured by the company to enable it to electrify certain lines, the Council found itself in something of a quandary. Should the company be allowed to undertake the reconstruction, it could then logically expect to obtain securty of tenure for a far longer period than the remaining eight years left on the lease, and this the Council did not want. On the other hand, should the LCC decide to do the work itself, it would be committed to a very large financial outlay, both with regard to the costs of reconstruction and in the amount of comp- ensation the company would expect to receive in exchange for loss of income while the work was going on.

In March 1902, the Valuer to the Council stated in a memorandum that the company had been approached, and an offer had been made with regard to the surrender to the Council of the lease, in return for a sum based on the average profits made over the past four years. The reply from the Solicitor to the company, Mr. Hugh C. Godfray was to the effect that the sum offered was not sufficient in view of the benefits that would be likely to accrue from electrification.

The intention of the company had been that it would electrify its lines using the overhead wire system, and possibly purchase its power from local electricity undertakings. With respect to 'the use of over- head wires, the Council had already decided that, on the south side, conduit would be used exclusively, and expected that broadly similar arrangements would apply to the north, although it reserved the right to look at the use of overhead wires where suitable. The conclusion had also been reached that local electricity undertakings north of the Thames may not have sufficient capacity to provide a load for tramway operation. In fact, several of the municipalities had no facilities at that time for generating electricity.

In November 1902, the Council published its plans for north side electrification, which did contain a mixture of conduit and overhead wire working. It suggested that the lines between Leman Street and Bloomsbury and those in Cambridge Road, Hackney Road, Kingsland Road, Gray's Inn Road (lower), Moorgate Street and Shoreditch High Street be conduit worked, while those in Commercial Road, East India Dock Road and Bow Road be equipped for overhead wire working. It was also expected that all power would be supplied from Greenwich generating station when it was commissioned. Following this, it was stated that the rest of the lines on the north side would be conduit equipped. At the same time, the Council considered that, in its opinion, the tracks in the area worked by the company, which embraced those lately belonging to the London Street Tramways Company were all "practically worn out" and would probably cost upward of £65,000 to replace for the continued use of horse traction.

On 3rd December 1902, it was announced that the Council was having second thoughts on electrification "for the time being". It did not want the Northmet to do it, and decided that it was itself sufficiently committed on the southern system for some time to come, and recommended that consideration "be postponed for the present".

The LCC Takes Over

In November 1905 the Council again published its plan for the electrification of the northern lines, once it had obtained possession of the lease which was held by the company. An advance estimate was given for the conversion of the first 22½ single track miles of line, which was:-
1. From Theobalds Road via Clerkenwell Road, Old Street, Great Eastern Street, Commercial Street and Leman Street to London Docks.
2. From Shoreditch via Kingsland Road to Stamford Hill.
3. From Aldgate via Commercial Road and East India Dock Road to Poplar.
4. From Moorgate via City Road to Old Street.
5. Along Gray's Inn Road between Holborn and Theobalds Road.
6. Along Old Street from Great Eastern Street to Shoreditch.

Car sheds and sub-stations	£112,000
Roadwork and platelaying *	£415,600
Cars, cables and machinery	£250,000
Alterations to buildings	£ 26,000

	£803,600

* Acid steel rails from
  Bolckow, Vaughan & Co., £31,131.13s.

By this time it had become obvious to the Council that most, if not all, of the reconstruction work would have to be done using conduit equipped tracks, although there were still hopes that some Borough Councils would allow the use of overhead wires. A general description of both methods has been given in the first volume of this history, but in the light of experience with installations on the south side of the Thames, new standard dimensions for conduit track construction were being employed. Yokes, as before, were placed at 3 ft. 9 in. intervals, but alternate standard and extended types were used, so giving more stability to the whole installation. The conduit slot width was also set at one inch. Rails were manufactured in lengths of 45 ft., while anchor plates were placed at joints and at points between them.

There were to be two departures from the normal construction method; an experimental side-slot section was laid in Kingsland Road, while on Highgate Hill a greatly strengthened centre-slot double track was laid. A third arrangement, employing power collection by means of the "stud contact" method was also tried out on the Bow Road line for a short period. All of these are described in later chapters.

The LCC area north of the Thames was quite small by comparison with the south, being just over one-third of that on the other side of the river. What it lacked in area, however, was more than made up for by the concentration of properties, population and streets. Almost all of the main roads radiating out from the City of London were already served by tramways, or would be when the LCC came to electrify the network, and this was to complicate the way in which the lines and junctions were dealt with.

The Lease Revoked

The lease held by the company was foreclosed as from 1st April 1906. In a report dated 1st March, A. L. C. Fell stated that if the 22½ miles of lines concerned were worked by horses from then until the end of December, and then by electric traction for the remainder of the Council accounting year, there would be likely to be an estimated gross profit of some £43,000. If the lines were closed down during this period of reconstruction, the gross profit on horse traction would be lost, but the lines would be finished two months earlier and the gross profit from electric traction could be about £46,000. To this, however, would have to be added capital charges for two months on the new construction, depots and sub-stations.

He also said that if the lines were closed down, 1,776 horses would have to be sold. With regard to staff, 450 conductors and drivers would have to be laid off for six or seven months, while 25 washers, 20 farriers, 200 horsekeepers and firemen, together with 20 granary men would have to be discharged seven months earlier than planned. A total of 750 men would be thrown out of work during construction. Lastly, the roads would have to be given up to the omnibuses and tube railways, whereas if horse cars kept running, the cars would still be able to take business from the "opposition" and the LCC would retain a large number of its regular riders. He then recommended that the Highways Committee give instructions to proceed on the basis that, while the construction of the tracks might be deferred until the end of the year, construction of the car sheds, sub-stations and cars could begin at earlier dates on some of the routes. This would necessitate the discharge of only a few men.

It was next necessary for arrangements to be made for the delivery and storage of the huge quantity of materials required with which to undertake the conversion. A site on vacant land owned by the Salvation Army in Kingsland Road was secured at a rental of £25 per month, on which to store rails and other associated iron and steel items, with another at Mare Street to be used for the storage of earthenware ducts.

The decision was finally taken to deal first with the Poplar to Aldgate and Bloomsbury route and that to Stamford Hill via Shoreditch. While the Poplar line can be considered to be the first truly northern route to be dealt with, the conduit system had already been installed in the Kingsway Subway and northwards to the "Angel", Islington in advance of the Council foreclosing on the North Metropolitan Tramways Company lease. This necessitated the agreement of the company, and one in which the Council had to pay a penalty for loss of revenue resulting from the early closure of the services along Theobalds Road and Gray's Inn Road while new junction layouts were installed.

THE KINGSWAY SUBWAY
The First Section

The idea of constructing underground tunnels or subways beneath city streets, through which electric tramways operated, was used in America in the closing years of the nineteenth century. In the United States, the standard tramcars were almost all of single deck construction, and the subways were built to suit this type of vehicle.

In 1899, Mr. J. Allen Baker, the vice-chairman of the LCC Highways Committee, went to America at his own expense to see for himself what these subways were like. He came back suitably impressed and reported his findings to the Council, who decided to take the matter further by sending an official delegation headed by Dr. A. B. Kennedy, whose members were charged with the duty of making a detailed report on the subject. Upon their return, favourable comment was made on the use of such subways, and they recommended their use in London. These should, in their opinion, be electrified on the conduit system.

A second delegation visited America in 1901, when the Tramways Manager, Mr. Alfred Baker, together with J. Allen Baker and John H. Rider, the electrical engineer to the Council, visited New York and Boston to inspect and report on the subways then in use and under construction in those cities.

Resulting from the recommendations made in their report and the fact that it was decided to build a new thoroughfare from Bloomsbury at Theobalds Road to the Strand, at that time an area of old and decaying properties, it was arranged to incorporate a tramway subway into the works. At that time, the Council was attempting, against stiff opposition, to obtain powers to extend the tramway which terminated on the Surrey side of Westminster Bridge, across the bridge and along Victoria Embankment, hopefully to connect with the proposed subway line.

Authorisation was given for the construction of the subway by the **London County Council (Subways & Tramways) Act, 1902 (2 Edw. 7. ch. ccxviii)** dated 8th August 1902, at an estimated cost of £282,000. The route was between Theobalds Road, Southampton Row, where the ramp down to the subway was to begin; then beneath new roads to be known as Kingsway and Aldwych, and then beneath the Strand and Wellington Street to Victoria Embankment. Powers were only given at this time, however, to build a double track tramway in the subway from Southampton Row as far as the north side of the Strand. As designed, it was only possible for single deck cars to be used, a decision which was soon to be regretted, as it became almost immediately a restricting factor in the provision of services, together with the transfer of cars between the north and south sides of the system.

The greater part of the subway was constructed close to the surface of the street, using the cut-and-cover method and employing mass concrete for the walls, in conjunction with the use of glazed bricks and tiles in some places. The double track tunnel beneath Kingsway was 20 ft. wide and about 14 ft. 6 in. from floor to roof, which in turn was approximately 3 ft. beneath the road. The northern entry was on a descending gradient of 1 in 10, which carried the two tracks. Once at a sufficient depth, twin cast-iron tubes 14 ft. 5 in. in diameter and 225 ft. long and bored with the aid of a Greathead Shield down to a depth of about 31 ft. at rail level, carried the tracks below Holborn and a number of sewers and other obstructions, before rising and meeting the cut-and-cover section at the first of the two island-platform stations, initially named Great Queen Street, later Holborn.

Due to the enormous scale of demolition of properties along and across the proposed line of route of Kingsway, the only practical way in which the trench could be excavated was to do the work in two parts, the eastern side being dealt with first. The section beneath Kingsway was designed and built in conjunction with the provision of two 10 ft. high by 7 ft. 6 in. wide pipe subways and two sewers, one on either side of the tramway tunnel, together with a considerable

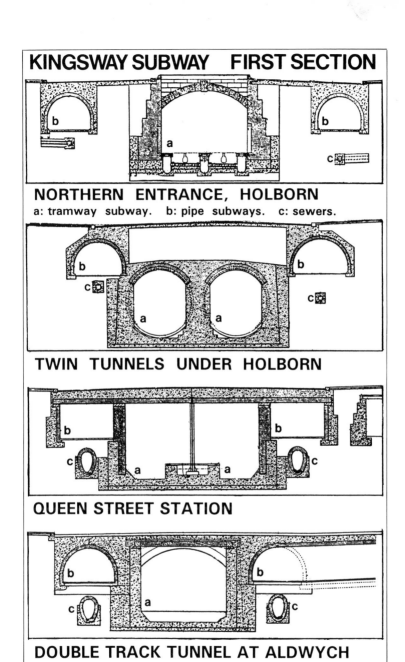

KINGSWAY SUBWAY   FIRST SECTION

NORTHERN ENTRANCE, HOLBORN
a: tramway subway.   b: pipe subways.   c: sewers.

TWIN TUNNELS UNDER HOLBORN

QUEEN STREET STATION

DOUBLE TRACK TUNNEL AT ALDWYCH
From T&RW1/1906

The diagrams show the complexity of the structural arrangements
employed in different parts of the original section of the subway.

635

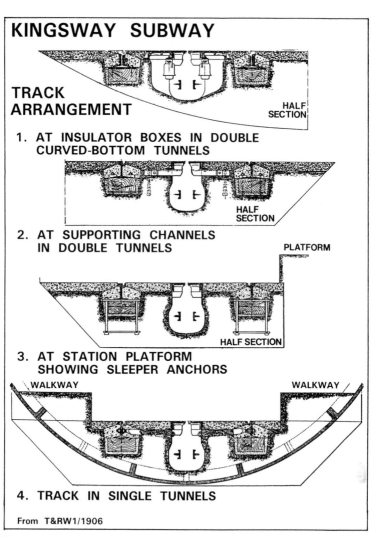

KINGSWAY SUBWAY

TRACK ARRANGEMENT

HALF SECTION

1. AT INSULATOR BOXES IN DOUBLE CURVED-BOTTOM TUNNELS

HALF SECTION

2. AT SUPPORTING CHANNELS IN DOUBLE TUNNELS

PLATFORM

HALF SECTION

3. AT STATION PLATFORM SHOWING SLEEPER ANCHORS

WALKWAY   WALKWAY

4. TRACK IN SINGLE TUNNELS

From T&RW1/1906

The unusual method employed in track construction is to be seen here.

number of pavement cellars or vaults. These extended southwards for the full length of Kingsway - just over half a mile - to Aldwych, where the second station was built.

From here, the double track brick-arched tunnel turned to the right to pass beneath the western arm of Aldwych on a falling gradient of about 1 in 20, gradually levelling out beneath the Strand at a depth of about 30 ft. and by then in twin single-track cast-iron tubes once again. As at Holborn, the presence of a large number of pipes, sewers and mains below the Strand was partly the reason for going to this depth, but also, the floors of the tubes were in alignment with the road level of Victoria Embankment so that, when the line could be extended along the Embankment from Westminster Bridge, all would be ready to make the comparatively easy connection to those tracks. During the original planning of the works, allowance had been made for a third station to be sited beneath Wellington Street, but this proposal was not proceeded with due to the depth of the subway at this point, the proximity to Aldwych Station and the expenditure it would incur.

Construction costs were estimated to be:-

1. Subway north of the Strand, half mile long, £209,000, to be carried out by the direct employment of labour by the LCC Works Department. Initial clearance work commenced in 1903.
2. Subway south of the Strand beneath Wellington Street, one quarter of a mile long, £8,650.
3. Acquisition of properties, and negotiations regarding "interference" with various properties in Savoy Street and beneath Wellington Street, with claims settled, an estimated £50,000 passed and agreed, 25th July 1905.
4. Constructing the walls of the subway between Bloomsbury and Aldwych by direct LCC labour, £5,000 agreed on 6th June 1905.
5. Wiring of the subway for lighting, contracts to the value of £1,500 agreed 1st August 1905.
6. Low tension cables, in the subway, and beneath the streets to Islington. Work by Callendars Cables, Ltd., £4,025. 4. 4d, agreed 21st October 1905.
7. Cable ducts beneath the streets to Islington and in the subway laid by J. A. Ewart, £2,813.14s. agreed 24th October 1905.
8. Switch-gear at Great Queen Street Station temporary sub-station by Evered of Birmingham, £275 agreed 24th October 1905.
9. Construction of the tramway in the subway from Southampton Row to the Strand by LCC Works Department labour, authorised 11th July and 17th October 1905 at a cost of £17,300.
10. Special work for cross-overs and junctions, between Aldwych and the "Angel", Islington, by Messrs. Hadfield for £8,335, agreed on 1st August 1905.
11. Cable ducts for the first sections of the northern tramways (other than the subway), supplied by G. Skey & Co. Ltd., London, £3,193.15s. and Stanley Bros, Nuneaton, £6,800.
    Slot rails by Steel, Peech & Tozer, Sheffield, £16,055.
    Conductor tee-rails by Frodingham Iron & Steel, £8,250.

In contrast to the method of construction employed elsewhere, conduit yokes were not used in the subway, except where crossovers were located. Due to the need to build the tracks up from the floor of the structure, a special concrete base was laid. The running rails were then laid on to longitudinal 12 in. by 6 in. timbers laid flat and were bolted to them at 7 ft. 6 in. intervals. In turn, the timbers were fixed to the concrete base. Short tie-bars, connecting the running rails to the angle-bar edges of the conduit were also fitted at intervals of 7 ft. 6 in.

The conduits were formed in the concrete foundation in the central position between the rails, and were 16 in. wide and 21 in. deep, with the sides almost vertical. They were strengthened by channel-bar supports embedded in the concrete, which took the place of the more usual yokes. The conductor rails were suspended from insulators which were encased in cast-iron casings, which in turn were bolted to the channel-bars. Cast-iron plates, 7 ft. 6 in. long were laid over the conduits and were prevented from moving by being locked into place by special flanges located into recesses in the castings. When laid,

A section of Kingsway tramway subway and its associated pipe subways seen during construction. *(Greater London Photograph Library)*

the plates formed the 1 in. conduit slot. However, in the places where crossovers were provided, the usual method of construction using cast-iron yokes embedded in the base concrete was employed.

Use of removable flat metal plates allowed the engineering staff to get easy access to the running rails, insulators and conductor rails for maintenance or replacement purposes when necessary. In the sections of the subway constructed from curved cast-iron segments, walkways were provided on either side of the tracks.

At the Aldwych stub-end, depot storage space was provided for the cars which were to be used on the first section, where inspection facilities, including pits were provided. For this purpose, the conduit tubes and tee-rails were omitted. Consequently, the ploughs had to be removed from the cars when they were over the pits, prior to being shedded. It then became necessary to provide power to the cars by the use of a flexible cable with a special plug on the end, which was connected to each car as required. Beyond the pit area, the whole width of the "road" surface was made flush with the running rails, enabling maintenance staff and car crews to move about easily and safely.

The Theobalds Road Line

To make the line serve a useful purpose, it was resolved that the horse tramway from Theobalds Road to the "Angel" be reconstructed on the conduit system at the same time as the subway was built. Horse cars working along Theobalds Road had to be suspended while the work was going on, and the LCC agreed to pay the company £25 per day during this period. Particularly difficult reconstruction work at Holborn Town Hall involving the installation of a complex junction layout meant the suspension of services from 17th September to 21st December 1905, a total of 94 days, which cost the LCC £2,350.

The transition from double track tunnel to single track tube at the south end of Kingsway is illustrated here.   (Tramway Museum Society)

Reconstruction was to prove to be expensive. Due to large numbers of pipes and other obstructions laid beneath Theobalds Road, it was necessary to construct a complete new road over the old one, using a form of cast-iron bridge or viaduct to carry it. The contracts were let to John Mowlem & Co. Ltd., who carried out all road and track work, firstly in St. John's Road and Rosebery Avenue, authorised on 31st January 1905 at a cost of £27,925, then in Theobalds Road, authorised on 1st August at a cost of £18,489. Apart from the special

No. 552, the prototype car of class F stands in Aldwych Station, while a group of passengers waits to board.   (Courtesy: C. Carter)

works in Theobalds Road, which required the use of purpose-made yokes, the conduit track laid elsewhere was to the new specification which called for alternate standard (short) and extended yokes to be placed at 3 ft. 9 in. intervals along the road.

When all work was completed, the subway line was offered to the Board of Trade early in December 1905 for inspection. This was carried out by Col. Yorke on 29th December, it being confidently expected that service would commence within a few days. The remainder of the line from Southampton Row to Islington was inspected at the same time. Due, however, to the fact that the Inspector was unsure of the suitability of the special cars ordered for working upon the line, together with an insufficient number of cars to work a proper service, he undertook a further inspection on 23rd February 1906. The public, however, had to wait until after the official opening ceremony, which was performed by John Williams Benn, Chairman of the Highways Committee, on Saturday 24th February, when he drove a car painted blue and gold through the subway, then on to the "Angel" and back to Aldwych Station. Once the public were admitted, the fares charged were:- Aldwych Station to Holborn Hall, 1d

Holborn (Great Queen Street) to "Angel", 1d

Throughout fare, 1½d

These were soon to be reduced to ½d for each section, with 1d for the through fare.

Extension to the Embankment

Although construction of the subway was authorised for its full length by the provisions of the London County Council (Subways & Tramways) Act, 1902, these powers did not extend to the construction of the tramway any further than the Aldwych Station. The London County Council (Tramways & Improvements) Act, 1906 gave authority to the Council to construct a tramway along Victoria Embankment and also to complete the subway line to meet it. The delay was caused by the intransigence of Parliament but, having finally received the necessary powers on 31st July 1906, the Council immediately started work.

Mention has been made of the general outline plan of the section of the subway beneath Wellington Street from Aldwych Station to the Embankment. This street was, at that time, the raised access roadway to Waterloo Bridge which left ground level just a few yards south of the Strand and, by means of sixteen brick piers and arches, carried the road to meet Waterloo Bridge at a level of just over 40 ft. above the Victoria Embankment. To construct the tramway tunnel through these, it was necessary to undertake considerable underpinning, both beneath and above the proposed subway. The 200-yard section from the Strand to the Embankment was probably the most expensive piece of tramway ever built in Britain; at about £80 per foot run, the total cost was approximately £55,000.

The entrance to the subway was to be in the west wing wall of the portal of the bridge, which was extended for the purpose. Due to the requirements of the estate managers for the Duchy of Lancaster, beneath whose ground the subway was to be constructed, a slight deviation from the original deposited plan was necessary to reduce the area under that authority's premises that the subway would impinge upon. Claims made on behalf of the Duchy for "interference" to the cellars and sub-structure of its offices in the sum of £9,400, and by C. Richards & Co. for £12,500 to extinguish their rights of interest in

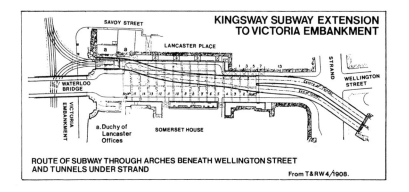

ROUTE OF SUBWAY THROUGH ARCHES BENEATH WELLINGTON STREET
AND TUNNELS UNDER STRAND

From T&RW 4/1908.

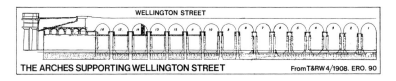

THE ARCHES SUPPORTING WELLINGTON STREET

From T&RW 4/1908. ERO. 90

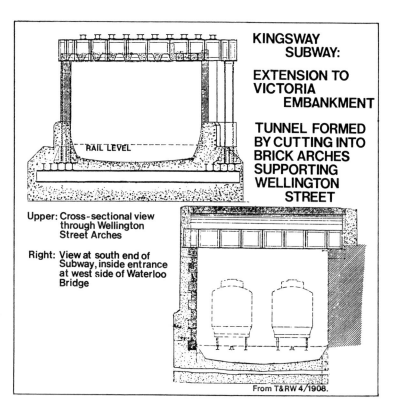

KINGSWAY SUBWAY:

EXTENSION TO VICTORIA EMBANKMENT

TUNNEL FORMED BY CUTTING INTO BRICK ARCHES SUPPORTING WELLINGTON STREET

Upper: Cross-sectional view through Wellington Street Arches

Right: View at south end of Subway, inside entrance at west side of Waterloo Bridge

From T&RW 4/1908.

At the south end of the subway, cars were able to travel in either direction, although service via Blackfriars was shortlived. The car seen is heading for Kennington via Westminster.   (LCC official view)

the arches beneath Wellington Street were paid from an allotment of £50,000 voted for the purpose by the Highways and Finance Committees on 25th July 1905.

Once the alignment of the subway was agreed and the legalities settled, the Council would have no further special requirements to be met or authority to be sought, as the bridge and its approaches were owned and maintained by the LCC already. At the same time as the main work was being processed, a double junction layout was taking shape at the entrance to the subway from the Embankment.

This extension involved very complicated engineering structural works to get the tunnels incorporated into the existing brick arches which supported Wellington Street and, at the same time to align the tracks in such a way that they were carried from beneath the centre line of Wellington Street to a position just west of it, to enable the tracks to emerge on Victoria Embankment. A description of the engineering work involved may best be taken as an extract from the issue of "Tramway & Railway World" for 2nd April 1908.

"The approach road on the bridge along Wellington Street is supported by a series of brick arches, on piers of the same material, floating for the most part on mud by means of a timber grid. This was found to be in such excellent condition that not a single crack was discovered in the whole of the structure. As the foundations of some of the piers were above the level of those in the new works, it is evident that the piercing of a large hole through these piers, and the necessary underpinning was a very ticklish business; but so carefully and skillfully has this been done that the brickwork is not disturbed in any way, nor has any settlement taken place. It was found that the massive wing of the bridge rested on an old river wall; owing to the wing wall having to be extended to make room for the large arch, which takes place of the one over the steps (now done away with), the new work projected beyond the old river wall and three large screw piles have been driven to support the lengthened wing wall. The appearance of this wing has, if anything, been improved, and most of the huge granite blocks were used again, but had to be supplemented with additional ones; these,

The subway tracks regained street level at Bloomsbury by means of a ramp, seen while still under construction. (LCC official view)

until begrimed with London smoke and dirt will present a rather patchy appearance.

"On leaving the old brick arches and for a length of about 60 ft., the overhead construction is altered, and the whole of the work rests on a massive raft of concrete reinforced by deep joists. In order to cut the holes for the subway through the old brickwork, stanchions were first erected on each side of the piers. On the tops of these, the main girders were fixed parallel to the piers. At the level of the top of the cross girders, needle joists were passed through holes cut for the purpose, resting on the cross girders and just below a stone course forming the springing of the arches. The raft of concrete already mentioned, formed the foundation of these stanchions and of the old brickwork piers where their footings were above it; these all rest on longitudinal joists laid on top of those reinforcing the concrete. All this work had to be done very gradually and carefully before the old supports to the brick arches could be cut away entirely. The spaces between the piers are covered by ceilings level with the top of the stanchions, partly of corrugated troughing and partly of concrete, strengthened by expanded metal between the reinforcing joists. The invert of the subway was carried up the sides so as to form a retaining wall for a certain height, above which a brick wall was built up to the ceiling, so that the subway is cased in all round".

It will be evident from the foregoing that at one time, long since past, the whole area over which Wellington Street was built was once the bed of the much wider River Thames. Until the enclosure of the river by the Victoria Embankment in 1870, the water lapped almost up to the Strand. The diagrams show, in some detail, the methods by which construction was carried out.

After completion of tunnelling work, which was undertaken by the LCC Works Department, the tracks were laid by the Tramways Department. Construction was similar to that already used on the earlier sections of the subway. Once the tracks were completed as far as the Embankment, they were connected to the double junction layout,

This view shows the first stage of cutting through the brick arches supporting Wellington Street.   (Greater London Photograph Library)

thereby giving access to the lines on the Embankment in both easterly and westerly directions.   After an inspection by Col. Yorke on 9th April 1908, connecting services began running the next day.

In 1930, it was decided to reconstruct the subway to accommodate double deck cars, and for this purpose a new fleet of tramcars was purchased.   A full description of these and the rebuilt subway is given in a later chapter.

Chapter 41
Electrification,
East and North East London

THE POPLAR & BOW SECTIONS

The small area from Bloomsbury in the west to Aldgate in the east, bounded on its north side by Theobalds Road, Clerkenwell Road, Old Street, Great Eastern Street and Commercial Street was nowhere more than about half a mile from the boundaries of the City of London. The west-to-east tramway constructed along these roads eventually contained a concentrated set of junctions and crossings where routes coming from the northern and eastern suburbs crossed this northern City ring road at seven points, which included the very complicated track layout at what became known as "Gardiners Corner", Whitechapel. It was into this area that electrification of the first section of the north side system was undertaken, when the northward extension of the new line in Kingsway Subway was projected as far as Islington, via Theobalds Road, Rosebery Avenue and the northern part of St. John Street.

Six of the seven tramways crossing the ring road terminated at the City boundary; the exception was the one from Shoreditch, which although its original terminus was at Norton Folgate, was eventually extended for about two hundred yards into City territory as far as Liverpool Street Station. All of these, in Gray's Inn Road, Farringdon Road, St. John Street, Goswell Road, City Road, Bishopsgate and High Street Whitechapel were constructed or reconstructed in conjunction with other sections of line. However, the main work of installing the crossings and junction layouts for them was undertaken when the first of the main contracts was let for the line from Poplar to Whitechapel and Bloomsbury.

The Poplar Line

The contract for the reconstruction of the lines between Poplar, Aldgate and Bloomsbury was let to Messrs. Dick, Kerr & Co. Ltd. on 6th March 1906 for £238,045.12. 8d, which sum included the reconstruction of all the junction and crossing work, including a layout at Burdett Road, Limehouse where horse car tracks leading to West India Dock crossed those in Commercial Road.

The intention of the Council at that time was to extend the line beyond Poplar near Blackwall Tunnel to the County boundary at the River Lea Bridge at the commencement of Barking Road. They were thwarted in this, however, by the attitude of the proprietors of the East India Docks, who refused to allow the dock entrance gates and the associated walls to be relocated, so that the road could be widened at these points. Therefore, the eastern terminus of the line was in East India Dock Road, adjacent to Aberfeldy Street, where a branch line was constructed to lead to the newly-built Poplar car shed.

Class E car No. 676, bound for Aldgate, approaching the request stop at Upper North Street. *(Commercial view, Courtesy: A. D. Packer)*

Construction along East India Dock Road and Commercial Road between Poplar and Gardiners Corner was completed early in December 1906, inspected by Col. Yorke on 12th and opened on 15th. The opening of the sections between Gardiners Corner and Theobalds Road, together with a short spur line in the lower part of Gray's Inn Road to Holborn followed on 16th January 1907, after an inspection by Col. Yorke on 12th. Lastly, the short lines between Gardiners Corner and Aldgate, along Leman Street and in City Road between Moorgate and Old Street were inspected by Col. Yorke on 26th March 1907 and opened to traffic on 29th, together with the line between Shoreditch Church and Norton Folgate (north). The remainder of Norton Folgate up to the City boundary opened two weeks later, on 9th April.

At last, in 1912, arrangements were made with the East India Dock authorities to move the obstructive gatehouse and wall, to allow road widening to take place. The Council were then able to extend the line eastwards to the County boundary, at a point known as "Canning Town Fire Station", at a cost of £17,155.11. 3d. Sanction for its use was given by Col. Yorke on 19th December and the line opened on 20th. On this short section, which was in the Borough of Poplar, the overhead wire system was used, a ploughshift being installed near Abbott Road. At the same time, arrangements were made with West Ham Corporation for the two sets of tracks to be connected, allowing through services to be operated by both undertakings.

Just west of the crossing with the horse car tracks at West India Dock Road, a double junction into single track spur line was installed and brought into use on 11th January 1915, which was to act as a lay-by for cars working short from the London end of the line.

The Gardiners Corner Layout

Situated where Commercial Road, Commercial Street and Leman Street cross High Street Whitechapel, and about 200 yards from the City of London boundary at Aldgate, Gardiners Corner was one of

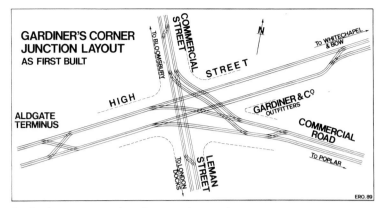

the busiest tramway junctions on the northern system. In complexity, it rivalled its opposite number on the south side at the "Elephant & Castle", the more so as, when it was constructed, account had to be taken of a hay market which, by authority of an Act of Parliament, stood in the centre of High Street Whitechapel on both sides of the junction. To be laid clear of the market area, the tracks were spaced at a distance of some 24 feet apart for the whole length of the High Street, right up to the terminus at Aldgate, where a conduit "scissors" crossover provided the means of turning the cars.

The new conduit tracks were placed in exactly the same positions as were the horse car rails that they replaced. With the use of the conduit system, consideration had to be given when designing the layout, that the motormen of the cars being driven across it were given a reasonable chance of getting through the special work without getting "stuck on the dead". This phenomenon could cause pandemonium at a busy traffic junction, and one that was all to easy to invoke, especially

The layout at Gardiners Corner, Whitechapel was probably the busiest on the northern system. The wide spacing between the tracks in High Street is clearly visible. (L.T. Museum, U 16497)

647

if an unsympathetic point duty policeman or an uncaring driver of another vehicle should cause a tramcar to be stopped astride one of the many "dead" sections on the junction layout. The only way then was for the car to be pushed by the one in rear, with the hope that both got across the rest of the layout without another enforced stop.

The Bow Road Line   The Surface Contact System

By Section 23 of the **London County (Electrical Powers) Act, 1900 (63-64 Vic. cap. ccxxxviii)**, the LCC was unable to use the overhead wire system of current collection unless it first gained the consent of the local authorities through whose areas the lines passed. This, so far, had not been obtained from any of those in the inner areas. It was this, coupled with an astute political move, that prompted the Council to look to other possibilities in its search to reduce the expenditure that was being incurred on the conduit system.

After experience in the construction and maintenance of many miles of conduit tramway, the Council came to the conclusion in May 1907 that the cost of trackwork (excluding cables, etc.) using overhead wires was about £9,500 per mile of single track, while a mile of single conduit-equipped track cost £17,000. On this basis, it was decided that an experiment should be undertaken using one of the proprietary surface contact systems then being devised. It was thought that costs would be more in line with the overhead wire method, but not having the capital outlay incurred with poles and wires and its subsequent maintenance expenditure. The Council had been advised that such a surface contact system would probably cost about £10,500 per mile of single track. The line along High Street Whitechapel, Mile End Road and Bow Road was chosen for the experiment.

In a book published in 1925 by A. G. Gardner, "John Benn and the Progressives", he states:- "Up to February 1907, the Progressive Party was in power in the LCC. On 17th January 1907, an article was printed in a newspaper accusing the Council of giving tramway contracts 'to friends'. Meantime, the way was being cleared for the LCC election in February. At the same time, the Progressives took legal action against the newspaper, which resulted in an apology being received and all costs being paid by the owners of the paper.

"By this time, however, the election had been held and the Progressives were ousted. These reported 'dirty tricks' appeared to ensure that the Moderates, who opposed the considerable spending by the Progressives on the electrification of the tramways, stood a very good chance of gaining the balance of power, and in this they succeeded. The Moderates, committed to reducing this expenditure, then proposed that the surface contact system be installed along Mile End Road 'for about a mile', as it would be very much cheaper than conduit. Benn and the Progressives bitterly opposed this move, stating that the conduit system or overhead wire method should be used, but in this they were defeated".

After much discussion and a visit by members of the Highways Committee to Lincoln, where the Griffiths-Bedell system - or "G.B." system as it was popularly known - had been in use in that city for about a year, the Council decided to carry out this experiment. The method employed metal studs sunk into the road surface, all of which were capable of being connected to the power supply, but normally "dead" until a tramcar, fitted with special equipment, passed over them.

Several reasons were given by the Council for the choice of Mile End Road and Bow Road for this experiment. In the first place, the Borough of Stepney absolutely refused to allow overhead wires to be erected in their area. Secondly, the route was, at that time, self-contained and would not interfere with other routes and services. Thirdly, that owing to the small amount of cover between the roof of the underground railway passing beneath the route of the Aldgate and Bow tramway and the surface of the road, extensive alterations, which would include rebuilding the roof of the tunnel so that conduit tracks could be laid, would prove to be extremely expensive.

On 23rd July 1907, the Council approved an estimate of £72,210 for the use of the "G.B." system, and authorised Messrs. Dick, Kerr & Co. to carry out the roadwork, and the G.B. Surface Contact Co. Ltd. of London to instal the stud mechanisms. An agreement was also made with G.B. for the installation of the collector equipment to 48 cars for £3,360, while the Council were to pay royalty fees to the company for the use of the system at the rate of £500 a mile of single track for up to 30 miles and then £250 per mile over this figure. This sum was expected to cover all patent rights involved in its use, but was not to be paid until twelve months after the opening date of the line to public traffic, and then only if it worked in a satisfactory manner, and the Council decided to retain it. The Board of Trade approved the use of the system on 1st November 1907, and work began on its installation on 7th.

The changeover point from the conduit system to stud-contact was near Whitechapel Church and was quite primitive. The centre slot at this point was run out from the outgoing track, and was continued across the inner running rails in the form of a balloon-shaped curve to become the conduit for the ingoing track.

The Griffiths-Bedell Method

This current collection method was one of a number of similar arrangements offered to tramway undertakings as an alternative to the overhead wire system, which was considered by some to be unsightly, or to the underground conduit system, which by any standards was very expensive to construct and maintain. In general, the method involved laying a power conductor cable centrally beneath each tramway track, the cable being connected at regular intervals to metal studs laid flush with the road surface. Return current from the cars was through the wheels and running rails as with the overhead wire system. The various methods advertised employed basically the same idea, but used different mechanical arrangements within the studs, in order to present power to the tramcar passing above.

The mechanism on the car consisted of a long "skate" or chain made up from a number of iron links or "shoes" fixed to a wire rope with pinch-bolts, the whole assembly suspended at intervals by springs, all of which was under the influence of a powerful magnet. Each end of the wire rope was made off to an insulated end-shackle. As the links passed over the studs, they were attracted to the iron heads, and, at the same time, the magnetic influence of the skate caused the mechanisms within the studs to make electrical contact with the power cable. The collector was long enough to ensure that there were always two studs in contact with the chain, which in turn ensured that a continuous supply of traction current was available.

The system as laid in Bow Road employed 6 in. by 5 in. egg-shaped stoneware pipes laid centrally between the tracks, except at one place

The G. B. Surface Contact line under construction at Bow Road. The stud heads have yet to be placed. (Greater London Photograph Library)

at Whitechapel, where the roof of the underground station was only just over six inches beneath the road surface and where special arrangements for laying the cables had to be made. At six-feet intervals throughout the length of the line, specially shaped lengths of pipe with vertical openings were laid to accommodate the contact studs and act as cable connection boxes. The stud heads were made of cast iron and were 10 in. long by 2½ in. wide, and these were supported by granite blocks 16 in. by 8 in. in size. A mechanism was suspended within each contact box and, when the electro-magnet on the car passing above it energised a moveable soft iron armature fitted within the body of the stud, it was attracted to the stranded galvanised iron power cable. At each contact point a galvanised steel sleeve was fitted round the cable, which served to protect it against electrical arcing when the contact was broken.

There were two parts to each armature. The soft iron core was suspended from the cast iron shank by a strong spring and electrically coupled to the shank and stud head by flexible copper leads. The lower part of the mechanism, which carried the carbon contact block, was contained within the core of the armature and was also electrically connected to it. After the passage of a car, the magnetic influence was removed, which allowed the whole mechanism to be drawn upwards by the spring. To effect a clean electrical disconnection and to over-

650

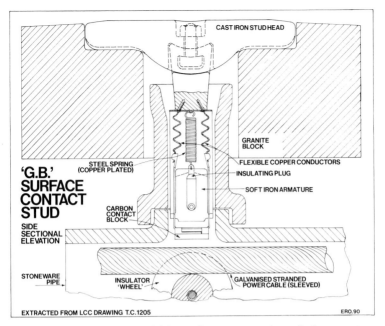

'G.B.' SURFACE CONTACT STUD

SIDE SECTIONAL ELEVATION

CAST IRON STUD HEAD

GRANITE BLOCK

FLEXIBLE COPPER CONDUCTORS

INSULATING PLUG

SOFT IRON ARMATURE

STEEL SPRING (COPPER PLATED)

CARBON CONTACT BLOCK

STONEWARE PIPE

INSULATOR 'WHEEL'

GALVANISED STRANDED POWER CABLE (SLEEVED)

EXTRACTED FROM LCC DRAWING T.C.1205

ERO.90

come the possibility of "sticking", the outer portion of the armature moved up just prior to the remainder. About halfway on its ascent, it pulled the inner section clear of the power cable. By this time, power needed to drive the car would be drawn from studs in advance.

Construction and Installation

In December 1907, the LCC decided that there would be difficulty in installing the collector gear as supplied by G.B. on to the cars without certain modifications being carried out, which would necessitate alterations being made to the contract. The company declined to enter into such an arrangement under the terms of the original contract, which resulted in the Council deciding to fit the equipment to the car trucks by direct labour under G.B. supervision. A new contract was entered into, in which G.B. supplied the gear at the same cost as before, but were to receive an extra £250 for supervisory work.

Early in July 1908, it was found that, owing to the length of the cars and the fact that they were of bogie type, special alterations would have to be made to the collectors so that they did not foul the plough carriers of the cars, which in turn meant that two skates would be required for each car. As this would necessitate even more expenditure, it was decided to equip three cars, later extended to six, with the modified gear as an experiment. A set of equipment consisted of two collector chains, each about eight feet long, and these were fitted beneath the centre line of each of the bogie trucks.

Difficulties arose almost immediately after the completion of the line and even before an inspection by the Board of Trade Officer was contemplated. "Sticking" studs appeared to be the main problem, resulting in stud heads remaining "live" after the passage of a car, or staying "dead" when a car magnet failed to actuate the stud mechanism.

Car No. 910, specially adapted to work on the G. B. system, is seen in service in Bow Road.   *(Commercial view)*

To deal with the former problem, a special mechanism connected to a "safety brush" was mounted on the car for the detection of studs remaining "live" after the skates had completed their passage over each stud. The mechanism incorporated an alarm, which gave notice of a "live" stud. Should this occur, the conductor was instructed to hit the offending stud with a rubber-headed mallet! If this treatment did not effect a cure, a special warning marker was to be placed over the stud, which then received the attention of the maintenance staff.

The Line Opens and Closes

Eventually, after much testing, some failures and considerable apprehension, the line was inspected by Col. Yorke and Mr. Trotter on 22nd June 1908. Although a certificate was given to enable it to be worked for a six-month period, all was not well. Another spectre had appeared in the guise of gas explosions! Even before the official inspection, this phenomenon had occurred on a number of occasions. Due to leakage, both at pipe joints and through cracked mains, town gas in considerable quantities was finding its way into the tramway installation. With the sparks generated by the making and breaking of the contacts in the studs, a rather terrifying series of minor explosions occurred, which forced the gas company to investigate and undertake repairs to the pipes. At the same time, the gas company persuaded the LCC into providing fan blowers throughout the installation, to drive out gas before it could accumulate sufficiently to be dangerous.

The line opened to traffic on 25th June 1908, with three cars equipped to work upon it, but it was doomed to failure, due in part, it was said, to the modified collector gear beneath the cars being not very efficient, and to considerable electrical arcing occurring within the studs, which caused them to remain "live". Difficulties continued, and on 21st July, the service, such as it was, came to a halt. After much hard work on the part of the LCC and G. B. engineers, together with Mr. W. M. Mordey, president-elect of the Institution of Electrical Engineers, the line was persuaded to work again - on and off - until 31st July when the LCC closed it down and reinstated a horse car service.

A War of Words and an Investigation

Acrimonious correspondence ensued between the Council and the gas company, with similar communications passing between the LCC, the Board of Trade, the Borough of Stepney and the unfortunate owners of the G.B. Company who had supplied the equipment. In the meantime, John Williams Benn was making comment on the unsuitability of the system, which was the cause of concern to many. Litigation was threatened and eventually occurred.

Benn's comments in some measure took the form of a catalogue of failures, including the fact that, from the opening date on 25th June, there were 927 cases of "live" studs being detected after the cars had passed. Apparently, there was one case of a person receiving electric shock and several other cases of animals getting the same treatment, while one horse was killed when it stepped on a "live" stud. Benn also accused the Moderates of "being enamoured of paying royalty to a company"! The company, meanwhile, were accusing the Council of altering the system in such a way that it would harm the efficient working of it, and that the LCC had no right to do this.

An investigation and enquiry into the affair was ordered, and on 20th October 1908 a special maintenance grant of £350 was agreed to by the Council to cover the cost of it. Mr. Mordey was retained at a fee of 250 guineas, and he conducted further exhaustive tests on the system in an effort to overcome the difficulties. His long and detailed reports and recommendations made on a number of occasions between October 1908 and March 1909, while factual, could offer nothing to overcome the real problem; that the system as devised by the inventors and modified by the Council, could not apparently cope with the added stresses of big city streets. "Questions" were asked in Parliament, while many more were asked in other places, and in particular in the LCC Chamber, where more than £10,000 was tied up in what was rapidly appearing to become a farce.

From the details recorded by Mr. Mordey, it appears that the studs which were installed were not able to stand up electrically to the

Car No. 910 seen this time in some difficulty while working on the stud contact system, and needing help to get it moving. (Commercial view)

653

large quantities of glutinous mud which accumulated in Bow Road, due to the very heavy flow of horse-drawn vehicles. The problem of finding an efficient way of insulating the electrical parts was thoroughly looked into, but it seemed that the only way to overcome some of the difficulty was to use studs of a modified design. In Lincoln, where a similar system was in use, this problem did not arise, due mainly to the paucity of horse-drawn traffic and the consequent lack of "street mud", together with the ability of the authorities to keep the streets in a cleaner condition to that prevailing in London. The use in that city of 4-wheeled cars also made it easier for the standard G.B. collector gear to be fitted.

A Further Reconstruction

By the end of 1908, the Council was beginning to reconsider its use of the system, and was making the first moves to attempt to obtain the support of the local authorities. Stepney Borough Council was again asked in December to allow the overhead wire system to be used. Again Stepney refused. However, after more discussions, Stepney finally gave way in April 1909, when the Borough Council grudgingly permitted the use of overhead wires over that part of the lines east of Grove Road, where a ploughshift was installed, with conduit track to the west of it.

On 6th April, Messrs. Dick, Kerr & Co. Ltd., was given the job of ripping up the surface contact line and replacing it as agreed, to be done as an extension to an existing contract (the Upper Clapton - Hackey electrification). Reconstruction commeneced on 24th May 1909 and was ready by the middle of July. Col. Yorke inspected the line on 29th July and it re-opened on 31st. The conduit section cost about £30,000; the overhead wire section £2,511, 5. 2d.

The car shed was situated in Fairfield Road, just to the west of St. Mary's Church, Bow. This church stood to the north side of the original Bow Road, which was very narrow at this point. Another road had been cut round to the north of the church, effectively placing it on an "island", and this became the outbound section of the Bow Road in the middle years of the nineteenth century. The electric tram tracks were laid on either side of the church and its ground.

Litigation

One of the unpleasant results of this affair was that the G.B. Company took Benn (who by now was Sir John Williams Benn) to law, accusing him of uttering libellous statements and ruining the company. The case opened in November 1910 in the King's Bench Division before Mr. Justice Ridley and a special jury, who found Benn guilty of the charge, also indicating that he was actuated by malice. Benn was ordered to pay £12,000 in damages for libel and defamatory statements. He at first refused to give security for this payment and was again taken to court. Eventually, he did agree to security in the sum of £5,000 before Mr. Justice Ridley.

There was, however, a "twist in the tail" regarding this unhappy action. Benn took his case to the Court of Appeal, where, in March 1911, Counsel for Benn stated that it was considered that the jury in the original case had been misdirected. This was upheld by Lords Justices Moulton and Buckley, while general comment afterwards indicated that Benn, in attacking the system was making an attack on the Moderates, who had brought all this about; he was not attacking the

G. B. Company. He had based his criticism on the premise that what the Moderates had done was wrong, and it had cost the ratepayers a lot in wasted money. The award of damages of £12,000 against him was quashed.

This episode, together with a fiasco over the operation by the LCC of a service of Thames Steamboats, probably did considerable harm to the cause of the Council in its constant quest for idealism as displayed by the Progressives. In this case, however, it did no good to the cause of the Moderates either, as they were dismissed at the next election! The problem was no doubt compounded by the uncompromising attitude of some members of Stepney Borough Council, but, who, by the time that the system had been installed and found wanting, also objected to its continued use!

THE STOKE NEWINGTON SECTION

The Kingsland Road Line

At the same time as the decision was taken to electrify the Poplar route, the Council arranged to do the same on the trunk route north from Shoreditch to Stamford Hill via Kingsland Road, Dalston Junction and Stoke Newington. It was suggested to the LCC by Stoke Newington Borough Council on 13th October 1904, that when consideration was being given to converting the lines in that area, it would be favourably looked upon if the LCC would construct the tracks on the side slot conduit system "as was done in Bournemouth". The Borough Council also "advised" the LCC that, in their opinion, there would be less likelihood of the slot closing up in adverse conditions. This was a suggestion that the LCC was later to regret.

When the time came to consider the work of reconstruction, the Council decided in March 1906, as an experiment, to equip the double track in Kingsland Road, between Basing Place and Bentley Road, about one mile in length, with the side slot system, where the groove of the inner, or off-side rail of each track was "open" and formed the slot through which the car ploughs could be drawn.

As the remainder of the route was to be laid using the normal conduit system, side slot construction would have to be made compatible with the standard centre slot arrangement, as the side slot would have to revert to the central position at points and crossings, and where the lines were to pass over the Grand Union Canal, as well as at either end of the section. The Board of Trade agreed to this experiment in May 1906, subject to the usual inspection and public safety arrangements. If the system was successful, it would quite likely be used elsewhere.

Like other "experimental" sections of track and operation, such as has been and is described elsewhere, the heavy duty conduit system used in London could not be readily adapted or modified to any degree without expensive changes being made, both to the track and to the equipment on the cars. In the case of the Kingsland Road line, it was also to restrict for a number of years the through running and joint working arrangements envisaged by the LCC and Metropolitan Electric Tramways. It also proved to be troublesome and very expensive to maintain.

Construction work was entrusted to Messrs. J. G. White & Co. Ltd. as part of the complete contract for the Shoreditch to Stamford Hill reconstruction. Contract price for centre slot conduit throughout was £141,399. 6. 9d, with an extra supplemental estimate of £21,000 (which was later reduced to £20,000) "to try the system of side slot conduit working". The special slot rails were obtained from Messrs. Frodingham Iron & Steel Co. Ltd. of Doncaster for £2,750, fishplates for the slot rails from The Continuous Rail Joint Co. for £523, and the special yokes and castings from the Anderston Foundry Co. Ltd. of London. Special pointwork was to come from the Lorain Steel Co. of Ohio. It was agreed that the original centre slot equipment was to remain on order, to be available elsewhere as and when required.

A particular difficulty arose where the tracks crossed Canal Bridge. Here, the road surface had to be raised some six inches to avoid having to cut into the bridge arch when excavating for the conduit tube. The road surface on either side of the bridge also had to be progressively raised to give a reasonable gradient on each approach.

There were two sections of single track on the line. At the south end of Kingsland Road, where it met and crossed Hackney Road and Old Street, there was an unusual arrangement of a single track square crossing with a single line turnout leading into single line in Old Street. Here, the usual centre single slot was used. On the other hand, a single line section with double conduit was constructed in High Street, Stoke Newington.

Work was completed at the end of January 1907 and was inspected by Col. Yorke on 1st February. Public service commenced throughout on 6th February, using cars of class E which were fitted with specially modified plough carriers.

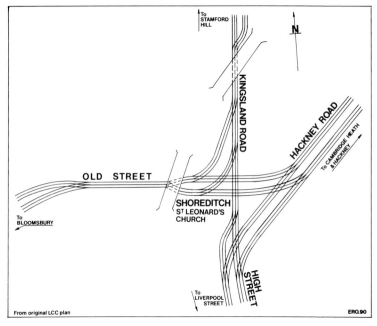

From original LCC plan

ERO.90

The conductor tee-rails beneath the side slots were about one inch lower than those in the normal central position. Consequently, the plough channels on the cars were slightly bowed so that the ploughs would be in the correct position when working on the side slot section. There was also a modification to the way in which the channels were

656

fitted to the carrier sides, resulting in a much more rigid structure. With these restrictions, only long-lead ploughs were at first used.

When constructed, the deviation radius of the slot rail from the side to centre position at all points was 40 feet, which was soon to cause trouble, as car ploughs became jammed at the radius points. Delays to service were sometimes of extended duration while jammed or damaged ploughs were removed, and while repairs to the track were effected. The Council decided on 3rd November 1908 to replace the 19 ft. 3 in. lengths of 40 ft. radius curves with 32 ft. 8 in. lengths of 200 ft. radius, of which twelve sections would be required at an approximate cost of £1,000. Before embarking on the main work, it was decided to deal with the two diversions on the "down" track at Downham Road as an experiment at a cost of £170. Eventually, all the deviation curves were dealt with, but even so, there were a number of failures which occurred over the ensuing years.

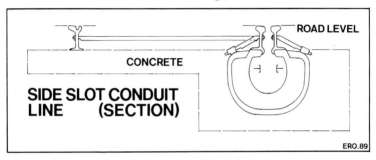

ROAD LEVEL

CONCRETE

SIDE SLOT CONDUIT LINE   (SECTION)

ERO.89

In April 1911 the Council published its findings with regard to the operation of the side slot section, setting out the points for and against its use. Those favourable to its operation were:-
1. Less metal in the road.
2. Cheaper to construct.

Conversely, those against its continued use were:-
3. The width of the slot progressively became greater as the car wheels caused wear, especially on curves.
4. Car wheel wear caused a difference in levels of the check action of the inner rail.
5. Additional costs incurred in equipping the cars to work over both centre slot and side slot sections, "as the conductor bars are slightly lower in the side slot, special cambered plough carriers have to be fitted to the cars running on both systems. Also the greater wear of ploughs occurs, together with more problems with plough breakages".
6. Increased maintenance costs.

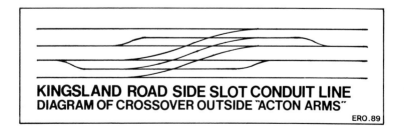

KINGSLAND ROAD SIDE SLOT CONDUIT LINE
DIAGRAM OF CROSSOVER OUTSIDE "ACTON ARMS"

ERO.89

The side slot conduit showing the special yokes
which were used.   (LCC official view)

The side slot reverted to the central position when carried
over the Canal Bridge.   (LCC official view)

Authority was given on 20th February 1912 for 130 tons of replacement special rails and fastenings to be purchased from the Frodingham Iron & Steel Co. Ltd. at £11.15s per ton, which were used during the following years. Problems continued, and by February 1916, the Council came to the conclusion that a detailed investigation be carried out and a report compiled showing the condition of the track.

It had also been expected that eventually the Metropolitan Electric Tramways would be able to participate in through services working via Kingsland Road. If this occurred, modified plough carriers would be required for these cars also, and it was not considered to be practical or desirable at the time. Due to restrictions which were beginning to take effect with regard to through working with the MET as a result of wartime conditions, it was decided that no further action be taken for the time being.

Maintenance costs for this section of the line were calculated as being four times that of the normal rate for centre slot conduit and were expected to rise. The table shows what the Council anticipated in costs and charges during the four years from 1915.

1915	1916	1917	1918	1919
£2,100	£2,300	£2,300	£2,700	£2,900

Instead, the decision was taken to replace the experimental section with standard centre slot work which, at 1915 prices, was expected to be about £12,000. By this time, it was becoming more difficult to undertake anything other than essential construction and maintenance. The conversion had to wait until after the war, when resources would be once again available to carry it out. The system at Bournemouth, however, had been replaced by the use of overhead wires early in 1911.

At last, on 26th July 1921, it was agreed that the work should be carried out as part of the track renewal programme, at a post-war estimated cost of £46,500 - very nearly four times the 1915 price. The cost was to be spread over the 1921/22 and 1922/23 financial years, with trackwork at £31,000 being covered in the first year and paving, etc. at £15,500 in the second. The work was done under the powers obtained in the London County Tramways (Electrical Powers) Act, 1900, after the authority of the Ministry of Transport as successor body to the Board of Trade had been obtained.

Standard yokes were ordered from the Anderston Foundry for £1,210, while the conversion was carried out by the Tramways Department direct labour force. It proved to be very difficult, as it was stipulated that the car service was to continue during reconstruction. This meant that the side slot arrangement had to remain in use while new standard yokes and track were laid, which was no mean feat.

All cars were eventually equipped with standard plough carrying gear, although for a number of years, specially shaped bus-bars were fitted to the existing gear, with which sliding contact ploughs could be used.

From Shoreditch to Norton Folgate and Liverpool Street

The horse tramway along High Street, Shoreditch between St. Leonard's Church and Great Eastern Street and along Norton Folgate to the City boundary was included in the original reconstruction plan for the area. Here, as in the case of the bridge over the canal at Kingsland Road, the road had to be raised by about six inches, but this time to allow room for the conduit slots without cutting into the tunnel walls of the Great Eastern Railway. There was, however, a "price" to be paid to the Borough of Shoreditch to enable this work to proceed. The LCC had to agree to lay wood blocks in the roadway, instead of the more usual granite paving blocks.

The lines were closed to traffic on 28th January 1907 to enable work to start and, two months later, on 26th March, the new double line along High Street was inspected by Col. Yorke, and was re-opened to traffic on 29th. This was followed by the opening of the short section to Norton Folgate on 9th April, so allowing electric cars to be worked on a through service to and from Stamford Hill.

After considerable discussion with the members of the City of London Corporation during 1912, the LCC finally made an agreement which would allow the line to be extended from Norton Folgate to a new terminus at Liverpool Street Railway Station. The cost for this short section of double track, just under half a mile in length, was very high at £18,747, due to the Corporation insisting that all pipes and ducts situated beneath the road be re-located in a new special-purpose trough before any track construction could begin. Messrs. Dick, Kerr & Co. carried out the whole work, which was completed early in March 1913. On 19th March, Sir. H. A. Yorke undertook the usual inspection on behalf of the Board of Trade, and on the following day the line was opened to traffic.

A Proposed Lay-By at Stamford Hill

Following the reconstruction of the tracks at Stamford Hill, the Council attempted to arrange with the local authority that cars turning there could do so at a point away from the busy traffic route. To this end, a double junction was installed which would lead the cars to and from the proposed standing space in Amhurst Park. Due to many difficulties, not least the onset of the Great War, the extension was never constructed, and when the track layout was re-arranged in August 1920 and a lay-by stub-end terminal track installed to the east of the main line, the double junction pointwork was removed.

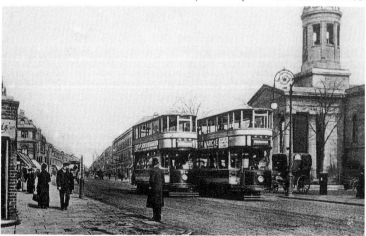

Cars Nos. 611 southbound and 614 northbound, standing at the stopping places at West Hackney Church.   *(Tramway Museum Society)*

Stamford Hill terminus, seen with class E car No. 613. Unusually, passengers are boarding before the car is reversed. Note the overhead wire traction poles of the M E T Ltd. *(Tramway Museum Society)*

The Cazenove Road Spur

During the ownership of the lines in Kingsland Road by the North Metropolitan Tramways Company, it had always been the intention to provide a connection between the north end of Stoke Newington High Street and Upper Clapton Road via Cazenove Road. While a junction spur had been provided at the Stoke Newington end, it got no further than that, and the single track stub end was used as a turning point for cars terminating at the "Weavers Arms". With the electrification of the line, the L C C decided to provide a double junction and single track stub end line into Cazenove Road, for use as a lay-by for short working cars. It was brought into use in November 1911.

No. 707 of class E, bound for Moorgate, standing at the stop opposite Brighton Road. *(Commercial view, Courtesy: A. D. Packer)*

THE HACKNEY & DALSTON SECTION

This part of the network lay mainly to the east of Kingsland Road, and included the lines in Hackney Road, Cambridge Road, Mare Street, Lower and Upper Clapton Roads, Lea Bridge Road, Graham Road and Balls Pond Road.

The Hackney Road Line

The first section to be reconstructed for electric traction was along Hackney Road between Shoreditch Church and Cambridge Road, and was opened to traffic on 18th May 1907, after inspection by Col. Yorke the day before. There was one single track section by Columbia Road. This work was carried out as part of a contract awarded to Messrs. Dick, Kerr & Co. for a total sum of £136,957.18. 1d, and which also included the lines in City Road between Old Street and the "Angel" Islington and those along Holloway Road between Highbury Corner and the "Archway Tavern".

Class E car No. 611 working between Cambridge Heath and Bloomsbury, entering the single track section by Columbia Road. (Commercial view)

Along Lea Bridge Road

Leyton UDC Tramways had been formed from the lines of the Lea Bridge, Leyton & Walthamstow Tramways Company and included a tramway along Lea Bridge Road. The Corporation electrified its lines on the overhead wire system during 1908, and agreed to construct the portion of the isolated line at the west end of Lea Bridge Road, which was in London, on behalf of the LCC. Road work was carried out by Mr. W. Manders for £1,400, while Leyton dealt with the overhead wire installation at cost price plus 10%. The work was inspected on 8th December 1908 and opened to traffic on 10th. A service from the terminus at Cornthwaite Road to Leyton and beyond was provided by Leyton UDC.

After the completion of the reconstruction of the lines in Upper Clapton Road, a connection was made with the Leyton tracks. This was carried out by Messrs, Dick, Kerr at a cost of £1,990, who constructed the conduit section junction and a ploughshift and also built the short connecting overhead wire section between the two systems. The new work was inspected by Col. Yorke on 22nd June 1910 and opened on 1st July, so allowing through services to be operated between the two undertakings.

Cambridge Road to Upper Clapton and Stamford Hill

The lines along Cambridge Road, Mare Street and through Upper Clapton were reconstructed for conduit working by Messrs. Dick, Kerr & Co. at a contract price of £149,443, the work being undertaken in three parts. There were three single track sections along the route; at the south end of Cambridge Road by Headland Road; at the north end of Mare Street; and beneath the railway bridge in Upper Clapton Road. After an inspection by Col. Yorke on 29th July 1909, the section between Hackney Road and Mare Street opened to traffic on 31st July. The line northwards to Stamford Hill was inspected by Col. Yorke on 21st September and opened on 23rd, together with a diversionary single line in Amhurst Road and Dalston Lane, which had been built to provide a double line through Hackney, as it had not been possible to widen the northern end of Mare Street. Finally, the length of Cambridge Road between Whitechapel Road and Hackney Road was inspected on 4th January 1910 and opened on 6th.

The Green Lanes Lines

A contract to reconstruct the lines along Green Lanes and Mildmay Park between Manor House and the south end of Southgate Road, and to construct a new link along Baring Street from Southgate Road to New North Road was awarded to John Mowlem & Co. at a cost of £88,195. 2. 2d. It also included the installation of a complex junction layout at the Balls Pond Road crossing and a short length of single line in the western part of Balls Pond Road to make a connection with the Essex Road lines, which had been rebuilt in 1909. The road in the vicinity of Newington Green included a tortuous bend and, just north of this, was quite narrow. At one point, near Clissold Park, a short single track section was laid. Otherwise, the remainder of the rebuilt track was all double.

Having just left Manor House and bound for Moorgate Street, No. 1272 is seen at the Lordship Park stop, with the Metropolitan Water Board Works in the background. (*Tramway Museum Society*)

At the southern end of this section, a new connection was made from the south end of Southgate Road into New North Road by way of Baring Street, replacing the horse car tracks which ran through Bridport Place and over the very steep and narrow Regents Canal Bridge. In its reconstruction programme for the lines in New North Road, the LCC was committed to rebuilding a bridge over the canal at the west end of Baring Street, and decided to use this bridge to carry the tracks to serve both routes, in order to avoid the necessity of rebuilding both bridges.

Reconstruction between Manor House and Balls Pond Road was completed by the end of July 1912 and, after inspection by Col. Yorke on 2nd August, the line opened to traffic the following day. On 22nd November, Col. Yorke returned to inspect the remainder of the line as far as New North Road, together with the single track spur in Balls Pond Road. Both sections were opened to traffic on 26th November.

Balls Pond Junction and Dorset Road

Further reconstruction took place in the area during the early months of 1913, when junction work was completed, to allow cars an easier passage between Essex Road and Green Lanes or Dalston Junction, and Southgate Road and Green Lanes or Dalston Junction. At the same time, a single line was laid in Dorset Street, to give direct access to Mildmay Park and Green Lanes by cars coming up Essex Road. This in turn allowed the use of the original single line in Balls Pond Road for cars travelling towards Essex Road, effectively providing one-way working, albeit in "reversed" form. The line in Dorset Street was inspected by Maj. Pringle on 25th July 1913, and it opened to traffic on the following day, while the tracks in the eastern part of Balls Pond Road were authorised by Maj. Pringle and opened on 6th March 1914.

Along Graham Road

The line in the west end of Dalston Lane and Graham Road between Kingsland Road and Mare Street was authorised to be reconstructed in 1911 and the contract was awarded to Messrs. Dick, Kerr & Co. at a cost of £37,110.16. 9d. About one mile long, the line had one short single track section about 100 yards east of Kingsland Road. Trackwork was completed early in March 1913 and, after Sir. H. A. Yorke had inspected it on 19th March, it opened to traffic on 20th. A single track connection was made into Mare Street to allow cars access from and to the car shed. It was not until 11th January 1915 that a double track junction was installed, which then allowed a car service to be provided to Lea Bridge Road and beyond. Special work for the junction was supplied by Messrs. Hadfield at a cost of £4,858.

Chapter 42
Electrification,
North and North West London

THE HOLLOWAY SECTION

This part of the system was very likely the most congested and busiest. It covers the area from the County boundary at Archway Road and the terminus of the Highgate Hill tramway; from Manor House and along Seven Sisters Road to the "Nag's Head" Holloway; along Holloway Road and its parallel highway, Caledonian Road; from the lines in Upper Street from Highbury Corner to the "Angel"; along Essex Road, Canonbury Road, New North Road and East Road; and the many roads leading into the termini scattered around the north side of the City of London.

Highgate and the Metropolitan Electric Tramways

The first electrified line into the north side of the capital was constructed for use by the Metropolitan Electric Tramways Ltd. when the company reached agreement with the LCC to allow it to extend its tracks down Archway Road as far as the "Archway Tavern", the last half-mile being in the London area. All the lines of the company were built to the standards set by the use of overhead wires to carry the power supply, and a special dispensation had to be obtained from the members of the LCC and the Borough of Islington to allow this form of power collection to be used.

William Griffiths & Co. Ltd. was the contractor for the road work, while the MET Ltd. installed the overhead wiring. On completion, the Board of Trade inspection was carried out by Maj. Pringle on 30th May 1905, and public service commenced on 7th. After completion, the line was leased to the company, in the first instance for three years, using a scale of payments ranging from £1,500 for the first year and followed by £2,000 then £2,500. The terminus, at the foot of Archway Road, was to remain isolated for a number of years.

From "Angel" to Highbury Corner

Following the construction of the extension of the Kingsway Subway line to the "Angel", the Chief Engineer advised the General Manager on 1st March 1906, that it would be possible and economical to extend the line along High Street, and to make a new terminus at the Myddleton Statue, near the Agricultural Hall, where the road was wide enough to accommodate a double track and a lay-by for up to three cars. This would then be followed by a further extension to Highbury Corner. The main contract for the whole of the line was let to Messrs. Dick, Kerr & Co. for £26,538.16.11d., who then sub-let the roadwork for the short section between "Angel" and Agricultural Hall to Messrs. Mowlem & Co. and the remainder to Messrs. R. W. Blackwell. Upon completion, the work was inspected by Col. Yorke on 10th November 1906, the line being opened to an extended service of single deck subway cars on 16th November.

The Liverpool Road Line

It had been intended that this short line, in common with the rest, would be electrified. Due, however, to the success of the electrification of the Upper Street tracks in carrying most of the traffic, it was decided on 21st June 1910 eventually to close it and remove the rails, together with the conduit junctions that had been installed at either end. The line closed to traffic on 19th July 1913.

The Extension to "Archway Tavern"

It was to be the end of November 1907 before the lines in Holloway Road were completely reconstructed. Messrs. Dick, Kerr & Co. had agreed to do this work as part of a substantial contract obtained in connection with the reconstruction of the lines in Hackney Road and City Road. The new lines were double throughout a length of about 2½ miles, terminating at the junction of Holloway Road with Highgate Hill, Junction Road and Archway Road. At the north end, just under half a mile from the terminus, a branch line was laid in to serve a large new car shed in Pemberton Gardens.

Junction layouts were provided at High Street Islington and in Holloway Road at either end of Liverpool Road, with the intention of eventually reconstructing the horse car tracks in that road (although this work was never carried out). Another layout was provided at the point where the line from Caledonian Road joined Holloway Road, while finally a crossing and junction network was laid in about 300 yards further north, at the "Nag's Head".

During reconstruction, the horse car services were maintained as far as possible, although in some cases it was more practical to divert some cars to adjacent roads. One such diversion involved the use

Looking into Seven Sisters Road at "Nag's Head", car No. 930 is seen, bound for Moorgate Street via "Angel".   (Tramway Museum Society)

of Liverpool Road while the considerable road and bridge works were being carried out at Highbury Corner. The line, with the exception of the short section on Highbury Bridge, was completed during the early part of November 1907; Col. Yorke inspected it on 22nd November and it was opened to traffic on 28th. Trackwork on Highbury Bridge was completed and inspected on 17th December 1907, allowing car services to commence on the following day. At the same time, the cars employed on the Kingsway Subway service were transferred to the new car shed at Holloway from temporary accommodation at St. Paul's Road, Highbury.

While the work in Holloway Road was being carried out, Messrs. Blackwell and Dick, Kerr were involved in laying new conduit tracks along St. John Street between Rosebery Avenue and Smithfield; along Pentonville Road between the "Angel" and King's Cross; throughout the length of Goswell Road from the "Angel" to Aldersgate and along Gray's Inn Road between King's Cross and Clerkenwell Road at a cost of £84,513. The line in City Road from Old Street to the "Angel" was also being dealt with by Dick, Kerr within the terms of their original contract for the Hackney Road and Holloway Road lines. The dates of inspection by Col. Yorke and their subsequent opening dates were:-

St. John Street, between Clerkenwell Road and Smithfield	- 24th July 1907: 29th July.
Pentonville Road	- 24th July 1907: 29th July.
City Road throughout	- 24th July 1907: 29th July.
Goswell Road throughout	- 22nd November 1907: 27th November.
Gray's Inn Road	- 22nd November 1907: 5th December.

The lines in the remainder of St. John Street between Clerkenwell Road and Rosebery Avenue, although inspected by Col. Yorke on 24th July 1907, continued to be used by horse cars for almost another year. Electric cars finally took up service on 9th July 1908.

The Caledonian Road Line

In March 1908 the Council accepted the £56,888.11.6d. tender of Messrs. Dick, Kerr & Co. as the main contractor for the reconstruction of the lines along the full length of Caledonian Road and for those in Seven Sisters Road between Holloway Road and Finsbury Park Station. Costs of power cables, rails and considerable alterations to bridges in Caledonian Road were to add another £21,920 to the bill. During the work, temporary turnouts were used so that the horse car services could be maintained by single line working, and cost the Tramways Department another £400 to provide.

Reconstruction of the bridge carrying the Caledonian Road over the Regents Canal, of another which carried a railway line over the road just north of Offord Road, and of a third near North Road carrying the road over a railway had also to be carried out. A double junction was installed at the Holloway Road end, while for the time being, a single track junction curve connected the Caledonian Road line with that in Pentonville Road. After completion, the line was inspected by Col. Yorke on 13th August 1908 and opened to traffic on 15th.

Along Swinton Street

The first mention of this line was made on 31st July 1907, when an estimate of £5,840 was given as the figure required to carry out the construction of the 1 f. 4.65 ch. of single track. Its purpose was to enable cars to have greater freedom of access across the junction layout at the top end of Gray's Inn Road, when travelling towards King's Cross Road and Farringdon Street, and was authorised under the terms of the LCC (Tramways & Improvements) Act, 1908. It was built by Mr. W. Manders as part of a contract for other works in the Camden Town area and along King's Cross Road. With these, it was completed in May 1909 and opened to traffic on 28th, after inspection by Col. Yorke on 26th.

The King's Cross Bridge

A direct connection between the southern end of Caledonian Road and Gray's Inn Road, which was intended to simplify movements across this junction was proposed as early as 1907. However, this would require the construction of a new bridge over the Metropolitan Railway, sufficiently substantial to support a conduit tramway. Negotiations were entered into, and eventually the LCC (Tramways & Improvements) Act, 1908 gave the authority to carry out the work.

After completion of the bridge, work started on the tramway on 11th March 1912, when preparations were made for the laying-in of the junction on the Gray's Inn Road side of the bridge. This was followed during the next few weeks with the construction of the trackwork by Messrs. John Mowlem & Co. On completion, the lines on the bridge were weight-tested between 1.30 a.m. and 7 a.m. on Sunday 23rd June. The test consisted of drawing "transport wagons" carrying weights equal to two fully-loaded tramcars on to the bridge. Maj. Pringle inspected the line on 28th June, and it was opened to traffic on 1st July 1912.

Along Seven Sisters Road

It was hoped that access to Seven Sisters Road could be gained from both Holloway Road and Parkhurst Road, and also a connection between Parkhurst Road and Holloway Road in the northern direction. It was also thought by the LCC that arrangements could be made with the Metropolitan Electric Tramways Ltd. for through services to be worked by both undertakings over each other's tracks.

The MET line between Manor House and Finsbury Park Station was constructed for use with cars having trolley poles only. These terminated by Blackstock Road, just north of the railway bridge, where a double track stub-end, with scissors crossovers was situated, the lines having been disconnected from the old horse car tracks when the MET electrified its system.

Reconstruction of the section in the LCC area, however, used the conduit system. A three track terminal layout was provided at the end of the LCC line, and although at the north end of this the tracks of the two systems were connected together, there was no possibility of through running by either party for the time being. After being inspected by Col. Yorke on 7th July 1908, the conduit tracks were opened to service cars on 9th.

Purchase of the Metropolitan Electric Tramways Line

With the setting up of the London County Council, the County boundary was drawn along the centre of the road between Manor House and Blackstock Road, Finsbury Park. This, together with several other anomalies in the boundary system, was to cause some difficulty to both the LCC and MET Ltd. in their efforts to provide electric car services.

It was also the cause of a legal argument when the LCC wished to exercise its rights of purchase and electrification of several of the disputed sections. These were:-

The 608 yards of double line in Green Lanes, northwards from Manor House to the County boundary.

The 968 yards of double track in Seven Sisters Road between Manor House and Amhurst Park Road.

The 220 yards of double track between Stamford Hill and the County boundary at Egerton Road.

One track of the double line between Manor House and Finsbury Park and known as the "boundary tramway".

Meanwhile, the MET, with the permission of the Board of Trade, had been allowed, on 30th December 1903, to purchase the sections in dispute from the North Metropolitan Tramways for £10,000. Even though the LCC still objected, it was agreed that the Council would not exercise its right of compulsory purchase of the "boundary tramway" until after 10th April 1910, this being the date that the lease of the North Metropolitan Company was expected to expire. With regard to the others, the MET obtained security of tenure until 31st December 1930.

On 1st April 1906 the lease to the Northmet was foreclosed by the Council, which brought the whole matter to a head once again. As the LCC could now purchase the whole of the "boundary tramway", even though one track was in Middlesex, the Council intended to replace the overhead wire lines with conduit track, and put in a ploughshift at Manor House to enable cars of both systems to work on the through running services.

At that time, none of the MET cars were capable of being used on the conduit system; it was expected that they would all have to turn at Manor House, except for any subsequently fitted with plough gear. This did not please the MET or Middlesex County Council, and the company sought, by a Bill prepared for the 1912 session of Parliament, to gain authority to construct a private tramway inside the boundary fence of Finsbury Park. Despite objections from the LCC, the Bill proceeded through two readings.

At this point, in March and April 1912, A. L. C. Fell for the LCC and J. Devonshire for the MET agreed that, although the LCC would reconstruct the line for conduit working, it would retain the overhead wires between Manor House and Finsbury Park Station, to allow MET cars not equipped with plough carriers to reach the latter point.

It was also agreed that a temporary ploughshift was to be installed at Finsbury Park, until such time as track reconstruction work had been completed, which was expected to be within two years. Later in April, it was announced that, under the terms of an arbitration award, the LCC was to pay the MET the sum of £7,350 as the purchase price of the "boundary tramway". The company, in turn, agreed to pay the LCC 6½d per car mile for all journeys worked by cars turning at Finsbury Park. The ploughshift was constructed during the summer months of 1912 and, on 1st August, the first car ran through from Euston Road to Enfield. This was followed by the inauguration of several other through workings, which are described in the chapters dealing with routes and services.

Reconstruction of the line to Manor House commenced during the sumer of 1914, which caused some dislocation to MET services, as the cars were unable to terminate at Finsbury Park due to the lack of a suitable crossover, and had to be turned at Manor House. After representations by the MET in January 1915, the LCC agreed that cars of the company could, for the time being, be turned on a temporary crossover which had to be specially installed at a point about 100 yards on the London side of the ploughshift, and the overhead wires extended to the same point. Reconstruction was completed in April 1915, and included the provision of a new ploughshift at Manor House. With the commissioning of the new line, the original ploughshift at Finsbury Park was removed and the track layout altered to form a through double track with a third lay-by line placed on the north side of the road, and sufficiently long to hold three cars.

The Essex Road Line

Reconstruction of this line between Islington Green and Balls Pond Road was undertaken by Mr. W. Manders as part of a larger contract, involving lines which will be described in the Hampstead Section. Essex Road is about one mile long, and about midway along its length it crosses Canonbury and New North Roads. A double junction at Islington Green connected the lines with those in Upper Street, while at the other end, they joined the Balls Pond Road layout. After the line had been completed it was inspected by Col. Yorke on 29th July 1909 and opened to traffic on 31st.

E/1 car No. 880, although showing Aldersgate Street on the indicator, is travelling northward towards Dalston.   *(Tramway Museum Society)*

The Archway Road Connecting Line

This short link line was constructed during the autumn of 1909 to connect the lines leased to the Metropolitan Electric Tramways to those of the LCC. It was inspected by Col. Yorke on 26th November and officially opened to traffic on 30th. But for all that, it could not be used for regular services for several more years, when a ploughshift was provided at the foot of Archway Road during March 1914 at a cost to the LCC of £750. Following this, the LCC became responsible for providing electric power for the half mile section at the lower end of Archway Road. Feeder cables were laid in during February 1915, and power fed from Holloway LCCT sub-station. Cost of this work was £650.

M E T car No. 77 of type A, in original condition, descending Archway Road to its terminus at "Archway Tavern" and just about to move into the LCC area. (Commercial view)

The Highgate Hill Line

This short cable operated line was the last of the original companies working within the LCC area to be acquired. On takeover on 24th August 1909, the line was immediately closed down for reconstruction to the standard gauge electric conduit system. The cable cars were sold to Messrs. George Cohen & Co. on 15th December 1909 for £12 and the cable for an unspecified sum. An unfortunate side effect of this piece of electrification was that, of the 25 men employed by the Cable Tramway Company, only seven were re-employed by the LCC, of whom four became electric car motormen, two as conductors and the other as a car washer.

This line was to be one with a difference. Due to the gradients encountered on the hill, which at its steepest part was 1 in 11, the LCC Highways Committee decided that special 4-wheeled cars should be used, these to be of either open or covered top type, whichever was considered the more suitable. A special braking system was also called for, which was to be fitted to all cars using the hill, and a form of "gripper" brake was finally decided upon. This was to be able to be used in conjunction with specially strengthened slot rails consisting of steel bars weighing 36½ lbs/yard, and shaped rather like bullhead rail but of only half section vertically, with a flat bearing surface at the bottom. These were to be rivetted to the undersides of the slot rails, and against which the lower face of the slot brake was to bear when in use.

The slot rails were of a slightly softer type of steel than was used for the running rails, but rolled to the standard section adopted on the remainder of the system, and weighed 61½ lbs/yard. Joints in the slot rails and strengthening bars were staggered so that there was an overlap of 11¾ in. at each slot rail joint. At these places, the bars were fixed to the slot rails by three rivets placed 3¾ in. apart, while for the remainder of the length of the rail, rivets were placed at 6 in. centres. Slot rail joints were made immediately above the yokes.

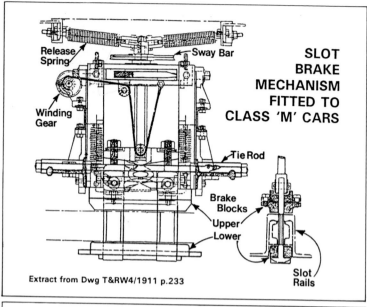

SLOT BRAKE MECHANISM FITTED TO CLASS 'M' CARS

Release Spring

Sway Bar

Winding Gear

Tie Rod

Brake Blocks

Upper

Lower

Slot Rails

Extract from Dwg T&RW4/1911 p.233

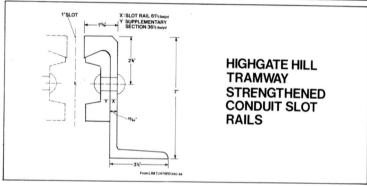

1" SLOT

X: SLOT RAIL 61½ lbs/yd
Y SUPPLEMENTARY SECTION 36½ lbs/yd

HIGHGATE HILL TRAMWAY STRENGTHENED CONDUIT SLOT RAILS

From LR&T J4/1910 ERO.88

To add further to the strength of the installation, the extended and standard yokes were placed at 3 ft. centres instead of the more usual 3 ft. 9 in., while the concrete surrounding the yokes was increased, both in thickness and width, and was composed of a 5 to 1 mixture instead of the standard 6 to 1.

The new line was constructed by Messrs. A. N. Coles, at a total cost of £17,452, and when completed was handed over to the LCC for the purpose of making special tests, particularly with regard to the braking efficiency of the cars. Car No. 255, of class C, still in its open-top unmodified condition was used for the first tests. After this, the slot brake mechanism was specially tested and inspected by Col. Yorke on 3rd March 1910, after which he made a second, general inspection on 23rd March, which was successful. The certificate was issued on 24th and the line was opened to traffic on 25th, with three cars in service. Two were of class B, Nos. 184 and 187, and one of

One of the specially adapted class M cars standing on the "down" track on Highgate Hill. (Tramway Museum Society)

class C, No. 277, each of which had been specially fitted with a carrier at one end of the Brill 21E single truck to accommodate the slot brake mechanism. These three cars worked between the "Archway Tavern" and Southwood Lane terminus only, and this arrangement lasted until sufficient cars of a new design, which were 4-wheeled and designated class M, were available to take over the service.

It had been the habit of the Highgate Hill Tramways Company to haul heavy coal carts up the hill by the cable cars. This provided a small, but regular income to the company, at the same time providing a useful service to the coal purveyors. With the re-opening of the line, the LCC was asked to provide the same facility. After a discussion with Col. Yorke of the Board of Trade, A. L. C. Fell advised that no such arrangement could be countenanced.

The line had not been working many days when one of the cars failed at the top terminus. The gripper mechanism of the car fouled a trap in the conduit slot near the end of the line, which resulted in the breakage of the carrier. The police intervened, and refused to allow the car to be moved "until it had been inspected" by an officer from the Public Carriage Office. The "inspecting officer" duly arrived after several hours, and carried out his "inspection" of the car, pronounced his approval of his "inspection" and agreed to the removal of the car.

At this point, Mr. Fell, who had been informed of the incident, decided that the car was not to be moved until it was convenient for the LCC to do it. He explained that it would not be in the interests of the Council to do this at a specified time, in order not to upset the service which was being worked with the two remaining cars. He also pointed out that as one of these would be required to assist in removing the damaged car down the hill, it would not be right to leave only one to work the service. Lastly, he hinted that, to ensure as far as possible that there would be no adverse publicity surrounding the move, it would be better to undertake the task after dark, when there would be very little risk of persons trying to take photographs of the stricken vehicle. Eventually, the car was taken away in the early hours of the following morning, assisted at the front end by one of the other cars acting as a "brake van".

A condition placed upon the LCC was that, after the line was reconstructed for electric traction, the portion in Hornsey should be purchased by Middlesex County Council for £5,909.12.10d. and then leased back to the LCC for its exclusive use for a period of 30 years at an annual rent ot £357. 3. 3d. to be paid quarterly. There were also a number of other conditions put upon the LCC "and their successors", basically for the good working of the line, in return for which Middlesex agreed to allow the LCC to "peaceably use the said part of the tramway during the said period without any interruption from the Middlesex County Council or any person lawfully claiming under them".

The LCC was also made liable to maintain virtually the whole width of the road that lay in Middlesex. However, this burden was eventually extinguished on 27th August 1925 when, in return for London paying Hornsey £2,250, the more usual arrangements regarding maintenance of the roads would apply, with the LCC only being liable for looking after the roadway within and between the tracks and for some 18 inches on either side of the outermost rail.

In 1931, the cars of class M were replaced over a period of several months by new totally enclosed double deck bogie cars of class HR/2. These had been specially designed for use on very steep hills and, after suitable trials and an inspection by the Ministry of Transport Inspector had been carried out, they were passed fit for use on Highgate Hill. After considerable discussion, including a statement by the LCC that the special slot rails "were practically worn out", an agreement was reached with the Ministry that the use of the special - and expensive - slot brake be dispensed with. It was not necessary to modify the method of track construction, as all parts were to standard dimensions, but when normal maintenance replacements were made, the opportunity was taken to use standard equipment.

Highgate Village terminus with class M car No. 1463, soon after the inauguration of through services to Moorgate Street. (Commercial view)

The Canonbury and Hoxton Line

Horse cars continued to traverse the route between Highbury Corner and City Road via Canonbury Road, New North Road and East Road until 23rd June 1913, when the route was finally closed to allow reconstruction to take place. The line, about 1½ miles long, crossed the Essex Road tracks on a four-square crossing with the addition of a double junction curve linking the south end of Canonbury Road with the west side of Essex Road. Just south of this, two single track sections were laid through a very narrow part of New North Road. The next special work to be encountered was at the end of Baring Street, where a double junction connected with the lines in the southern half of New North Road. Finally, at the City end of East Road, a double junction led these tracks into the lines in City Road.

Track reconstruction was carried out by Mr. A. N. Coles at a cost of £49,052, which included the provision of the special work at the junction with New North Road, and four crossovers along the line of route. The tracks in East Road and the lower part of New North Road were inspected by Maj. Pringle on 8th April 1914, but continued to be used by horse cars for another ten weeks. The remainder of the lines in New North Road, St. Paul's Road and Canonbury Road were inspected by the Major on 23rd June and opened for service cars on 25th. This was the last section to be reconstructed for electric traction on the north side of the Thames prior to the outbreak of the Great War and, with the exception of the Victoria Park line, completed the main electrical reconstruction programme.

The junction from New North Road into Baring Street was situated on Canal Bridge. No. 1224 is on the direct service to Finsbury Park via Highbury and "Nag's Head". (*Tramway Museum Society*)

THE HAMPSTEAD SECTION

The districts dealt with under this heading were those where almost all of the lines constructed by the London Street Tramways Company were situated. Reconstruction for conduit electric working began early in November 1908, when Mr. W. Manders started work on the first part of the route between Camden Town Station and "Nag's Head", Holloway

Road via Camden Town and Parkhurst Road. This was followed in December by the short section from Camden Town Station, along High Street and Hampstead Road. A double junction was laid in by Camden Town Station in advance of the reconstruction of the line along the northern end of High Street and the route to Hampstead.

On completion, the line along Camden Road to Holloway Road was inspected by Col. Yorke on 9th April 1909 and opened to traffic on 11th. The remainder, to Euston Road, was inspected on 26th May and opened on 29th. Total cost was £81,050.11. 2d. At the same time, the line along King's Cross Road and Farringdon Road as far as Clerkenwell Road, was inspected and opened to electric car traffic. This work had also been undertaken by Mr. Manders as part of a larger contract involving the reconstruction of the lines in Essex Road and laying the new line in Swinton Street. Completion of the final section of the Farringdon Road line was carried out at a cost of £8,437.18. 6d by Messrs. Dick, Kerr & Co. during March and April 1910. It was inspected by Col. Yorke on 12th May and opened to traffic on 14th.

During the course of all this work, Mr. Fell urged that it be dealt with "at all speed, as a frequent service of motor omnibuses to work in opposition to the tramways is likely to be put on at a very early date, and in order that those omnibuses may not get hold of the traffic, four electric cars are run through from Finsbury Park to Euston Road as soon as possible". He also urged that work on the completion of the junctions at "Britannia" and at Camden Town Station be expedited, and suggested that day and night work be done.

The next line to be reconstructed was the one from King's Cross, via Pancras Road as far as Crowndale Road. At the same time, the construction of a new length of double track in Crowndale Road was being undertaken, which was intended to provide a direct route between King's Cross and Hampstead via Camden Town and Chalk Farm. All this work was dealt with by Messrs. J. Mowlem at a cost of £47,584. After completion, these were inspected by Maj. Pringle on 17th July 1909 and opened to traffic on 22nd.

In the meantime, the tracks via Great College Street, Kentish Town Road and Prince of Wales Road were being dealt with by Mr. Manders, who completed the work early in September 1909. An inspection was carried out by Col. Yorke on 8th and the line opened to electric cars on 10th. The section between the "Britannia" and Hampstead via Chalk Farm Road was dealt with next by Mr. Manders, who started at the Hampstead end. During the course of this work, horse car services were maintained at a cost to the LCC of £2,800, which went mainly on the provision and maintenance of temporary turnouts and crossovers. This was in addition to the £35,100.18. 4d. paid for the main work. On completion, this work, all double track, was inspected by Col. Yorke on 26th November 1909 and opened on 30th.

During this time, Messrs. J. Mowlem & Co. were rebuilding the line along Kentish Town Road, Fortess Road and Junction Road to "Archway Tavern" at a contract price of £47,862. On completion it was inspected by Col. Yorke at the same time as the Chalk Farm Road section and opened in conjunction with it. This 1½ mile long line had a short single track section just before a double junction which had been inserted to serve the horse tramway running along Highgate Road to Parliament Hill Fields. A junction was also provided to give access into Monnery Road and Holloway car shed.

The last line to be reconstructed was along Highgate Road as far as Swains Lane, Parliament Hill Fields just mentioned, the work being carried out by Messrs. Kirk & Randall. There were two short single track sections just north of the junction with Fortess Road. After completion early in May 1911, the line was inspected by Col. Yorke on 19th and opened for electric services on the following day.

Hampstead car shed had been built on the site of the old horse car depot, but in course of construction had been greatly enlarged. Access to and from the shed was by way of a single line in Cressy Road which was connected to the "up" single line in Agincourt Road. To provide better facilities, a second single line connecting Fleet Road with the car shed entry track was authorised by the Council on 16th July 1912 and was eventually constructed at an estimated cost of £1,350.

There were several railway overbridges and underbridges in the area which required rebuilding to some degree, and most of this work was entrusted to Mr. Manders and Messrs. Mowlem at a total cost of almost £20,000. In one case, the road had to be lowered beneath the railway bridge at Camden Town Station in order to obtain sufficient height for double deck cars to be able to negotiate it safely.

A sylvan scene in Highgate Road near Swains Lane terminus, with car No. 755 beginning its journey to Holborn.   *(Commercial view)*

Chapter 43
Post War Reconstruction and Extension

After 1918

When the Great War finally ended, most of the system was in a somewhat run-down condition and considerable effort was required to rehabilitate much of the track mileage. Nevertheless, the Council, ever mindful of its obligation to the travelling public, decided to press for authority to extend the network still further and to complete the electrification programme which had been interrupted by the war.

The Victoria Park Line

The self-contained line between West India Docks and South Hackney via Burdett Road and Grove Road traversed a rather quiet, residential area. It was also the last line on the northern system to be worked by horse traction. The LCC had wanted to electrify the route using the overhead wire system, but despite several attempts to obtain the good-will and authority of the Borough Councils through whose areas the line was laid, no such permission was forthcoming.

As recounted in Volume I, the Council decided in 1913 to develop a self-propelled petrol-electric car with the intention of operating this type of vehicle on the Victoria Park line. However, this was not a success and horse cars continued to work until, on 19th August 1914, the horses were requisitioned by the War Office, causing the line to be closed. The Council then set about making plans to electrify it, still with the intention of using overhead wires. This time it was H.M. Treasury who put a stop to that idea, as the Lords of the Treasury on 2nd February 1915, stated that they would not sanction such expenditure while the country was in a state of war.

This produced an interesting if somewhat difficult situation for the Council to deal with. If the line was not used, and no statutory car ran at least once every three months to reserve the rights of the LCC, it might seem to be implied that all rights to work the line had been surrendered. Due to the alleged bad condition of some of the track, the several local authorities through whose areas the line was laid, were expressing concern for the safety of other road users and were making overtures to the LCC about having the tracks removed. If sections were removed because of the concern for public safety, the Council would be prevented from running statutory cars, which would give the impression that there was no further interest in working the line. This in turn would render possible an application to be made to the Board of Trade by "another party" for an Order, under Section 41 of the Tramways Act, 1870, declaring the powers of the Council to be at an end with respect to these tramways.

This situation prompted the LCC to ask the Board of Trade if it would give an assurance that no such Order would be made while the

LCC was prevented by the Treasury from incurring the capital expenditure necessary to reconstruct the lines for electrical working. The
first three of the Boroughs through whose areas the line was laid,
Poplar, Hackney and Bethnal Green, readily agreed to this without
any pre-conditions being attached. The fourth, Stepney, agreed, with
the proviso that they wished to see conduit track being laid when
conditions allowed. Having obtained the agreement of all parties, if
somewhat conditional, the Board of Trade gave the assurance that
no Order would be issued.

From what evidence is available, the line was not lifted, although
road repairs were carried out without too much regard for the presence
of the rails. In February 1920, Hackney Council had cause to ask the
LCC to attend to the rails in Cassland Road, due to the poor state of
these and the setts surrounding them. There were no doubt other
incidents as well.

After the war, the question of reconstructing the line for electric
traction again arose. This time, despite the previous pressures from
Stepney Borough Council to use the conduit system, agreement was
reached with all local authorities that the line should use the overhead
wire system. Eventually, a capital estimate was raised on 28th June
1920 for £244,370 to cover the total reconstruction of the existing
lines, together with some new construction, and which also included
£6,190 for power cables, ducts and feeder pillars. Work on the 2 miles
7 furlongs of track was carried out by the Consolidated Construction
Co. Ltd. at a contract price of £202,275.19. 9d. of which £176,320 was
allocated for trackwork. The overhead wiring was erected by Messrs.
Clough, Smith & Co. Ltd. A departure from pre-war arrangements
was that instead of turning right at the top end of Lauriston Road
into and terminating at Cassland Road, South Hackney, it would turn
left into Well Street, and continue along that road to Mare Street,
where a junction was to be formed with the existing tramway.

As the decision had been taken to use the overhead wire system, it
was necessary to obtain the authority of the Ministry of Transport, as
successor to the Board of Trade, which was obtained in November
1920. Wayleaves to allow traction poles to be planted where necessary
were also required. It was usual at that time for local authorities
to charge a nominal sum for each pole installed. An alternative was
for the local Council to be granted the facility of fitting street lamps
to the poles in exchange for the wayleave, which is what occurred
in Bethnal Green. On this route, however, it was also necessary for 20
of the poles to be planted inside the grounds of Victoria Park, for
which the LCC Parks Department charged the Tramways Department
the sum of 1/- per annum for each pole planted!

The line was inspected and opened in two parts. On 26th July 1921,
Maj. G. L. Hall inspected the main section between West India Docks
and Well Street, except for the outer conduit curve between Burdett
Road and East India Dock Road. The line was opened to traffic on
28th July. On 1st December 1921, the ploughshift at Well Street and
the double junction into Mare Street, together with the conduit junction
at the south end of Burdett Road was opened to traffic after inspection
by Maj. Hall.

Much of the line in Grove Road between Mile End Road and Canal
Bridge was laid as single track with several passing places, while on the
section between the south end of Church Crescent and Well Street,
separate tracks for "up" and "down" services were laid in two streets,
both with severe curvature, because of the impossibility of effecting

Car No. 1625 on service 77 bound for Aldersgate via Hackney, seen on the unusual track layout at Lauriston Road, at its crossing with Church Crescent.   *(The late G. N. Sutherden. Courtesy: P. J. Davis)*

road widenings. The result was a sort of "figure of eight" formation, whereby cars going towards West India Docks, after leaving a single track section in Well Street, continued along Cassland Road for a short distance before turning right into Terrace Road. At the end of this road they crossed the northbound line on a four-square crossing, to proceed along Lauriston Road to meet the northbound track again on a "wrong-way" junction at the end of a short length of single line. Once through this single line, the cars gained the left hand track to continue on their journeys. Those in the opposite direction, after navigating the single section in Lauriston Road, turned right into Church Terrace, crossed the other line coming from Terrace Road, proceeded along the north end of Lauriston Road, to be faced with a single line in Well Street.

The Amhurst Park Line

There had been a number of proposals made to construct a tramway along Amhurst Park, from its junction with Seven Sisters Road to Stamford Hill, with a connection into the line which was laid along Clapton Common to Lower Clapton and Hackney. It had also been proposed before the Great War to connect the tracks at Stamford Hill with those to be laid in Amhurst Park, and a double junction was provided in readiness for connecting up. However, this part of the proposal was never carried out, and the pointwork was eventually removed.

The situation at this point was that half the road was in the LCC area, the other half in Middlesex, which meant that special arrangements would have to be made with the MET as well as with Middlesex County Council.

The proposal was again made after the end of the Great War and, because of the insistence of both Hackney and Stoke Newington Borough Councils, the LCC came to the conclusion that conduit track would have to be provided and would probably cost about £80,000. In the event, both councils modified their demands, which allowed the LCC to use the overhead wire system. The existing tramway along Seven Sisters Road between Manor House and Tottenham, even though part of it was in London, was owned by the MET and worked on the overhead wire system. It was also used by cars of both undertakings which worked on the through services to Tottenham, Edmonton and Waltham Cross.

An allocation of £54,535 was made on 1st August 1922 to allow the work to be undertaken, and construction of this double track line began on 14th August 1923. The road and trackwork was carried out by the LCC at a cost of £45,622. 6. 5d, while Messrs. Clough, Smith & Co. supplied and erected the overhead wire equipment for £2,071. 0. 8d. The LCC also supplied an electric point machine of the "Turner" type, which was purchased from the Council by the MET at its cost price of £103.10s, and installed at the Seven Sisters Road end of the line.

The completed line, together with a junction between Upper Clapton Road and Stamford Hill was inspected by Lt. Col. Mount on 20th March 1924, after trial runs by the LCC on 17th. It had been intended that the line should have been opened to traffic on 21st March, but this had to be postponed owing to a strike of tramwaymen beginning on that day. The first service cars to run were those on the night service of 31st March, to be followed by a full day service of cars numbered 53, working between Aldgate and Euston Road (Tottenham Court Road) via Hackney and Finsbury Park.

One of the unusual aspects of this line was, although it was just within the boundary of the County of London, it was considered to be outside for the purposes of the fare structure of the service working upon it. After the introduction of the shilling-all-day ticket in 1925, the length of track in Amhurst Park was excluded from the area of availability and remained so for a number of years.

OTHER MAJOR CONSTRUCTION WORKS

The Stamford Hill Connection

It had been necessary for LCC cars to obtain access to Stamford Hill car shed by running over a very short section of track also used by MET cars at their terminal point. In 1920, an agreement was concluded between the two authorities for LCC cars to work through to Edmonton, and for this it was necessary to construct a ploughshift to enable the cars to work through on to the trolley wire sections. As it was also necessary to retain conduit working into the car shed, a conduit point mechanism was incorporated into the outbound slot by which the plough attendant at the change point was able to divert the plough out of a car or leave it in, as required.

With the provision of the ploughshift, the crossover which used by MET cars turning at Stamford Hill had to be removed, and a new one provided by the LCC some way north of the ploughshift. All the work was completed in time for the commencement of through workings of LCC service 49 on 2nd June 1920.

Another improvement concerned the provision of a lay-by terminal track on the south side of the road junction, for use by cars which terminated at Stamford Hill, allowing them to stand clear of the main tracks. This was brought into use on 28th August 1920. Lastly, with the construction of the new tracks in Amhurst Park and a ploughshift just before the Stamford Hill intersection, a new four-square crossing, together with a double junction between Clapton Common and the

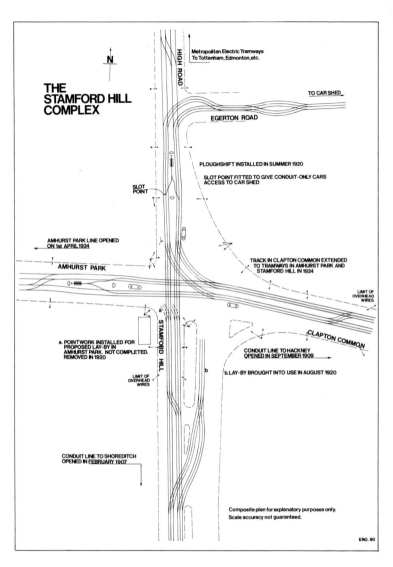

THE
STAMFORD HILL
COMPLEX

N

Metropolitan Electric Tramways
To Tottenham, Edmonton, etc.

HIGH ROAD

TO CAR SHED

EGERTON ROAD

PLOUGHSHIFT INSTALLED IN SUMMER 1920

SLOT POINT FITTED TO GIVE CONDUIT-ONLY CARS
ACCESS TO CAR SHED

SLOT
POINT

AMHURST PARK LINE OPENED
ON 1st APRIL 1924

AMHURST PARK

TRACK IN CLAPTON COMMON EXTENDED
TO TRAMWAYS IN AMHURST PARK AND
STAMFORD HILL IN 1924

LIMIT OF
OVERHEAD
WIRES

CLAPTON COMMON

STAMFORD HILL

a. POINTWORK INSTALLED FOR
PROPOSED LAY-BY IN
AMHURST PARK. NOT COMPLETED.
REMOVED IN 1920

CONDUIT LINE TO HACKNEY
OPENED IN SEPTEMBER 1909

LIMIT OF
OVERHEAD
WIRES

b. LAY-BY BROUGHT INTO USE IN AUGUST 1920

CONDUIT LINE TO SHOREDITCH
OPENED IN FEBRUARY 1907

Composite plan for explanatory purposes only.
Scale accuracy not guaranteed.

ERO. 90

north side of Stamford Hill was laid in, giving east-west, north-south and east-north connections, all of which were brought into use on 1st April 1924 with the commencement of services along Amhurst Park.

The Kingsland Road and Old Street Crossing

A considerable re-arrangement of the carriageway, pavements and tram tracks was undertaken near to and at the junction of Kingsland Road and Old Street during the latter part of 1927 and the first months of 1928. This rather complex junction layout with its lengths of single track crossing double track was the cause of considerable delay to services. To overcome the problem, the single track section at the eastern end of Old Street was doubled, together with the short length of single line between High Street Shoreditch and Kingsland Road.

The junction of Old Street and Kingsland Road, with the additional track laid in 1927 seen on the left. Class E car, No. 647, on the right, is on service 55 to Bloomsbury. No. 795, on service 49, is bound for Liverpool Street.   (The late G. N. Sutherden. Courtesy: P. J. Davis)

Whitechapel High Street Reconstruction

Probably the largest track reconstruction programme ever to be undertaken by the LCC Tramways took place in 1929. In 1925, the Ministry of Transport stated its concern about the chronic traffic congestion which occurred daily at Whitechapel Road and High Street all the way to its entrance to the City of London. It was suggested to the LCC and the Borough of Stepney that a complete re-arrangement of the tram tracks should be undertaken in conjunction with other road works, and the removal to another place of the daily hay market which carried on business in the middle of the road at this point.

Two conditions had been imposed upon the North Metropolitan Tramways Company when constructing the tramway in High Street in 1871. These were that the tracks had to be laid sufficiently far apart to allow the hay market to continue to operate in the centre portion of the road, and that the full width of the road outside the tram rails, but not in the market area in the centre, be paved by the company to the satisfaction of the Local Board of Works. This restriction passed to the LCC when it took over the lines of the company, and still applied when the line was electrified.

The first move was made on 9th June 1925 by the Engineer to the London Traffic Advisory Committee, Major H. E. Aldington of the Roads Department, Ministry of Transport. He asked J. K. Bruce, who was Acting General Manager of Tramways at that time, what his views were on a re-arrangement of the tram tracks, to place them in the more conventional positions in the centres of the roads, and what costings were likely to be "whether or not the road would be widened". A sum of about £40,000 was considered to be (at that time) a realistic figure to use, to which, apparently, the Ministry of Transport agreed.

The haymarket in Whitechapel High Street, with E/1 car No. 1169 on service 63 on its way to Aldgate terminus. Of interest, is the horse-drawn van advertising "Cheese Sandwiches, 2d"! (Commercial view)

Since the hay market had been instituted by Charter, it required an Act of Parliament to extinguish the rights of the market operators and traders. It fell to the Improvements Committee of the LCC to introduce such legislation as was necessary to enable this to be dealt with. The Council proposed that it should be introduced into the 1927 Session of Parliament as part of a General Powers Bill, which would also include the proposals for altering the tramway layout. A question then arose whether the tunnel of the Metropolitan District Railway would be likely to be affected by any alterations made, but fortunately this proved to be not the case. At worst, it was considered that, if necessary, the use of shallow conduit sections would overcome any obstacles below ground level.

Trial borings were made and trenches dug in October and November 1926, to determine the suitability of re-aligning the tracks in the positions suggested. Next, Stepney Borough Council and the LCC prepared estimates for the paving works required and, as was probably to be expected, these differed considerably. However, after discussion, a common figure of about £5,500 was suggested.

Regarding the obligation of the LCC to pave a large part of the roadway, an agreement was made on 22nd November 1926 that the Council be relieved of this responsibility by paying £5,900 to Stepney in lieu of 18 years life of the new paving, and then for Stepney to take total responsibility thereafter.

During 1927, the many agreements and other arrangements were being made with all concerned, including on 8th November completion of the agreement for the extinction of the market rights, for which compensation money at an estimated £18,000 was to be paid. The necessary Act of Parliament was also obtained during 1927. The next

Some idea of the massive work involved in re-locating the tram tracks at Whitechapel is seen in this view. *(Courtesy: J. H. Price)*

year saw the completion of the general arrangements and the announcement that reconstruction work would commence in the second half of 1929.

During the early months of 1929, tenders were invited for the many items required for use in the work. One of the side effects of the reconstruction was that all existing special work at the junction layout at Gardiners Corner would no longer be of any use and all would have to be completely renewed. The main contract for the road works was taken by the Tramways Department, with direct labour conditions, at a total estimated cost of £46,266.13s. The contract for the new track assembly was awarded to Messrs. Hadfield at a cost of £8,239, while the sub-surface iron and steelwork, such as yokes and other supporting items, from the United Steel Companies Ltd. cost another £2,062.

Arrangements were then made for the operation of car services while the work was in progress, and it was decided to terminate cars temporarily at the following points:-
Whitechapel to Bow route, at the crossover opposite St. Mary's Church.

Bloomsbury to Whitechapel route, at the crossover at the southern end of Commercial Street.

Poplar to Whitechapel route, at the crossover at the western end of Commercial Road.

Leman Street, service to be discontinued as no car shed facilities were available for this short section of line.

It was expected that the work would take between ten and twelve weeks, after which normal services could be resumed. Starting date was set for Wednesday 7th August 1929. The completed work was inspected by Col. A. C. Trench on 3rd October 1929, and he authorised its use for public traffic. The whole job was completed by the end of October. A maximum speed of 8 m.p.h. was permitted where the cars crossed junctions and points, while compulsory stopping places were prescribed for at all entry points to and exit points from the layout.

A detailed breakdown of the allocation of finance required to carry out the works programme was:-

Removal of underground obstructions:	£ 3,391. 1. 1
Supply of rails and fastenings:	1,578. 6.11
Reconstruction of tracks:	16,072.16. 6
Electrical equipment (excluding tee rails)	1,694.10. 9
Reconstruction of carriageway breasts, etc.	
(but excluding tramway area):	7,048.10. 5
Extra work in carriageway foundations, etc:	347.16. 7
Supply of special trackwork castings:	10,354.18. 5
Petty payments, photographs, advertising, etc:	161. 1.10

These figures show net costs; recovery by sales of old materials having been credited.

Materials Used in Reconstruction

Iron Castings

200 Standard short yokes
160 Standard long yokes
110 Standard shallow short yokes
107 Standard shallow long yokes
107 Special wide yokes
  6 Plough hatch short yokes
 12 Plough hatch long yokes

4 Plough hatch shallow short yokes
8 Plough hatch shallow long yokes
9 Sump box frames
9 Sump box covers
25 Mud box frames
25 Mud box covers

Steel Castings

20 Plough hatch frames
20 Plough hatch covers
32 Rail drain frames
32 Rail drain box covers

20 Double insulator frames 22-inch
110 Double insulator frames 26-inch
110 Double insulator covers 26-inch
250 Insulator pit covers

Wrought Iron and Steel Fittings

2900	Bolts, yokes 3⅜ x ¾ in. sq. rd. hex. mild steel
2200	Bolts, tee head 3½ x ¾ in. m.s.
900	Bolts, hex. rd. hex. 1¾ x ½ in. 3% nickel
2200	Washers, flat, ⅞ in, hole, wrought iron or mild steel
2900	Washers, shaped flat, w.i. or m.s.
2900	Washers, p.q. taper m.s. (item a.)
850	Washers, p.q. taper m.s. (item c.)
170	Fishplates, slot rail m.s.

Work in progress on the construction of the terminal stub layout looking towards Gardiners Corner. All operations were performed by manual labour with little or no mechanical aids, including the placing of rail lengths by gangs of 8 or 10 men, as is seen here. The old, abandoned tracks, to be removed after completion of the main work, can be seen outside the new layout.   *(Courtesy: J. H. Price)*

850	Clips, retaining bar, w.i. or m.s.
1000	Bars retaining m.s. 3 ft. 2¾ in. x 3 in. x ½ in.
550	Bars short retaining m.s.
800	Tie bars, slot to yoke
650	Tie bars, slot to track
50	Tie bars, special, m.s.
1100	Clips rail, for extended yoke, m.s. stamping
1100	Wedges, clip, for extended yoke, m.s. stamping
550	linear ft. Pipe w.i. screwed and socketted, 3 in. dia.

Miscellaneous

650	Packings, seasoned teak, 7 in. x 6⅞ in. x ⅜ in. thick
210	linear ft. Kerbing, straight, Aberdeen granite, 12 in. x 8 in. (stones not less than 3 ft. or more than 6 ft. long)
6	Refuge ends. Kerbing, curved, Aberdeen granite, 12 in. wide x 8 in. deep, semi-circular to 2 ft. 6 in. o/s radius
32	Special stoneware pipes
510	linear ft. Standard stoneware drainpipes, 9 in. dia.
225	linear ft. Standard stoneware drainpipes, 6 in. dia.

Paving Materials

635 tons 3 in. x 6 in. Guernsey granite setts
1500 tons 3 in. x 6 in. Aberdeen granite setts
1500 cu. yds. Thames ballast
400 tons cement

Enlargement of the Subway

Not long after the subway was completed in 1906, voices were being raised about the wisdom of constructing it for use by single deck cars only. By then, the north side network, except for the Highgate Hill line, had been taken into LCC ownership and the first moves made to electrify the lines on the conduit system.

It had been hoped that other overland connections would be made between the two halves of the system so that all cars on the north side, amounting to about one-third of the fleet, would be able to be taken for repairs and annual overhauls to the new Central Repair Works at Charlton, then under construction, but this was not to be. By then it was too late to change things, but in subsequent years the proposal was regularly made that the subway be enlarged. At last, on 31st July 1928 a capital estimate for £326,500 was approved to enable the subway to be rebuilt to take double deck cars, and for the 50 single deck cars to be converted to double deck pattern by placing new bodies on the existing bogie trucks.

It was proposed that, to obtain the 16 ft. 6 in. headroom required, the floor of the existing subway would be lowered at the south end beneath Wellington Street (which was later to be known as Lancaster Place) and the Strand, and through the length of Kingsway as far as Holborn Station. From there on, it was intended that, in the main, the additional height would be gained by raising the roof of the subway. The mothod of reconstruction of the main sections south of Holborn Station involved breaking up the track bed and, after digging out the old floor, the walls were extended downwards. Standard conduit track, employing yokes and slot rails set in concrete was then put in place throughout the line on the new level. Several crossovers were also incorporated into the trackwork.

The tender of Messrs. John Cochrane & Sons Ltd. was accepted on 23rd July 1929 for the structural work, at a price of £171,246.15s. Preparatory work commenced at the Bloomsbury end on 11th September 1929, when the tunnel was opened up at this point to enable a new roof to be provided over a new double width section, which in turn was to replace the two single deck car tubes. At the same time, the Council disconnected and removed the eastbound junction at the Embankment end of the subway at a cost of £325.

Single deck cars ran through the subway for the last time during the early morning of Monday 3rd February 1930. A temporary omnibus service, numbered 175, operated by the LGOC on behalf of the Council and working between Bloomsbury and Embankment (Charing Cross) via Northumberland Avenue (southbound) and Embankment, Temple Station and Kingsway (northbound) replaced the cars on that day and the subway was handed over to the building contractor. A second, temporary weekdays-only 'bus service, numbered 161, was put on as from 14th May, to work between Islington and Waterloo.

The two stations at Holborn and Aldwych were virtually rebuilt, for which a supplementary capital estimate of £6,000 had been authorised on 29th July, and also included the complete modernisation of the island platforms, which were retained. The continued use of these would mean that passengers alighting from and boarding the cars would have to use the front platforms and stairs, for which activity the motormen would be responsible. Also, the old method of actuating the signals at the northern end of the line was replaced by installing sets of contactors placed in the conduits and operated by the passage of the car ploughs.

Car No. 1931, resplendent in its special livery, stands at the entrance to the deepened subway on opening day.   *(LCC Official view)*

It had been intended that the rebuilt subway would be available for service during December 1930, and initial preparations had been made for HRH The Prince of Wales to perform the opening ceremony, using class E/3 car No. 1930 suitably painted in royal blue and gold. In the event, the subway was not available until early in January 1931, when, on 5th, the first trial and test runs were made. So far as the official opening was concerned, this was undertaken by the Chairman of the London County Council, Major Tasker on 14th January, using E/3 car No. 1931, painted in white and lined out in blue, and supplemented for the remainder of the party by the use of another class E/3 car and a class E/1 car, No. 1506. The use of 1506 is interesting for several reasons. In the first place, wooden bodied cars were not permitted in the subway on public service, but as the official opening ceremony was not a public occasion, there apparently was no reason why it should not be there. Secondly, the car was fitted for the occasion with "K-Ray" indicator boxes, complete with the "via Kingsway Subway" legend clearly showing, while special number plates had been made up, as the car showed "33" as its service number. Lastly, it was the only LCC car fitted with vestibule screens at that time, and was probably on show with the idea of convincing the assembled company that the new cars of class E/3 should be fitted with screens, as indeed they were a short time afterwards.

After all the ceremony and speeches, the subway was left in peace for the rest of the day. Very early on the following morning, however, the first of a frequent service of cars entered upon it. Three services were worked; 31, Hackney and Wandsworth via Shoreditch, Westminster and Battersea Park Road; 33, Highbury Station and Brixton, Water Lane via Westminster and Kennington; 35 "Archway Tavern" and New Cross Gate via Highbury, "Angel", Westminster and Kennington. All services were worked by the new class E/3 cars, and it is reported

The official party examine the surroundings at Holborn Station during the opening ceremony. Car No. 1979 is on the northbound track, with Nos. 1931, 1506 and another E/3 on the other. (LCC official view)

that up to 5,000 journeys through the subway were made each week. Total cost of the work, including the "reconstruction" of the 50 old cars was £312,875, which showed a "saving" of £13,625 over the original estimated costs.

With regard to the special liveries applied to cars 1930 and 1931, it seems that No. 1930 was quickly repainted in the "new brighter red and pale yellow" instead of the 1926 "Pullman" livery of "signal red and pale yellow". No. 1931 retained its white livery until sometime in March 1932, when it too was repainted in the later red livery adopted by the Council.

Leyton District Council Tramways

The tramways owned and operated by Leyton Urban District Council met the LCC Tramways at the western end of Lea Bridge Road at the County boundary. With the electrification of the LCC section of the line westwards from the River Lea and the installation of a plough-shift, it became possible for both authorities to operate through services across the boundary. These began on 1st July 1910, and were increased in scope over the next few years.

Problems brought about by the Great War affected Leyton tramways to a considerable extent. The undertaking suffered severe shortages of spare parts, which was to force it to lay up many of the cars, which in turn caused a partial cessation of the services provided by that authority. This culminated in December 1920 in Leyton Council setting up a committee to enquire into the problem, and also to appeal to the LCC for advice and assistance. A series of meetings was held between members of the two councils, with a view to some sort of arrangement being established which would, once again, allow Leyton to take its full part in the operations.

The LCC suggested that it take over the entire working of the Urban Council Tramways, but this was rejected by Leyton, who wanted to keep some control over the system. But the LCC was adamant. It would be prepared to work the tramways as part of its own system without capital payment for a period of ten years from the date of an agreement. This would extend to the maintenance of all rolling stock, permanent way and overhead wiring, but Leyton was to relay and rewire all sections in its area as soon as it could. Any money surplus or deficit should be shared in proportion to the nominal capital value of the undertakings' interest in the lines. Leyton agreed to these proposals, and 1st July 1921 was the date settled upon for the takeover. To finance the operation, the Council authorised the allocation of £132,387, which was raised by means of a Maintenance Vote. A joint committee was set up to administer the agreement, while it was also agreed that if Leyton wished to continue with the agreement, it would be expected to put 25 new cars in service by 30th June 1931, and have another 25 on order at the same date.

One advantage which was to be gained by the LCC was that a considerable saving in "dead" mileage would be possible after the implementation of the agreement. In order to provide the Council's share of the service, it was necessary to run several cars up to Leyton from Hackney car shed to take up service in the mornings, and then to run cars back from Leyton to Hackney at night, with little, if any remuneration. Under the new scheme, it would be no longer necessary to do this, as the Council intended to transfer several cars to Leyton car shed to work from there.

On a close inspection of the Leyton cars, the Council found that Nos. 1, 13, 16, 18, 21, 25, 27, 34, 35, 36, 39, 43, 48, 49, 61, 63, 65, 68 and 70 were totally unfit for further service. They were taken away to Hampstead car shed, where they were put into store, and remained there for the next ten years. They were replaced by twenty class E/1 cars, Nos. 1164-1170, 1281-1288, 1290 and 1345-1348, while the remainder of the Leyton four-wheeled cars were sent to the LCC Works at Holloway car shed for a thorough and complete overhaul.

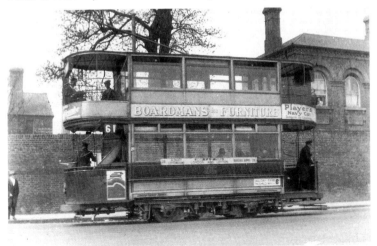

An original Leyton car, worked by the LCC on service 61, still displays the District Council monogram. (A Whitcombe photo. Courtesy: T.M.S.)

As the Leyton track was in a very bad condition, the LCC almost immediately set about relaying large sections of it on behalf of the Urban District Council. During 1922, Leyton began their share of the work, by replacing the remainder of the track and overhead wiring, and for the rest of the time that the LCC had an involvement in its operation, the system effectively became part of the LCC network.

Staff Arrangements

All staff were given the opportunity of being taken into the employ of the LCC, but for some it meant changed working conditions. With regard to the management, Mr. J. Duncan, the Leyton Traffic Superintendent was offered the post of LCC District Traffic Superintendent, while the Leyton Car Shed Superintendent, Mr. E. J. Hammett, was offered the post of LCC Car Inspector.

Other Service Re-arrangements

Leyton had been taking part in the services between Chingford, Leyton "Bakers Arms", Stratford and V & A Docks, worked jointly with West Ham and Walthamstow. Due to the shortage of suitable four-wheeled rolling stock, an agreement was reached with West Ham for that authority to work the service, while the LCC provided more bogie cars to work on service 61 between Aldgate and "Bakers Arms". Eventually, Leyton UDC financed the new cars of class E/3 which replaced the earlier vehicles, and which are fully described elsewhere. Several other changes and additions to the joint services also took place in later years, which are described in the chapter dealing with Routes and Services.

Corrugations on Lines

This phenomenon was to be the cause of considerable investigation. The problem was quite widespread on electric tramways and the London system was not to be spared. On 3rd October 1907, in an article in "Tramway & Railway World", Mr. Fell commented:-

"Corrugation on the Brixton line was noticed soon after the opening of the electric line. The phenomenon never occurred on horse drawn lines, nor on steam locomotive hauled railways, but has on steam tramways, as it does on electric tramways. Many theories have, and are, put forward for the presence of this unwanted problem. In my opinion it could be caused by:-

Original roughness of rails after rolling;
Cold rolling of rails by car wheels;
Soft rails and heavy cars;
Sand and grit on the head of the rails;
Rapid acceleration.

It takes about three years to develop on a new system, but only about three weeks on a relaid section. On straight lengths it is equal on both rails; on curves, short waves are on the outer rail, long waves on the inner. London is no exception.

It has been proved that carborundum blocks attached to cars specially used for the work and rubbed along the rails, grind out the corrugations, and they either take a long time to re-appear, or do not re-appear at all. Magnetic brakes fitted to the cars help to keep the problem within reasonable bounds".

The last statement was only true where there was a heavy service of cars, such as in London. Otherwise, the braking conditions on a lightly served line would only smooth the rails at recognised stopping places. During the whole of the time that electric cars ran in London the problem remained to some degree, necessitating the use of special cars to "scrub" the rails.

After the Great War, and with the replacement of large quantities of rail, it was hoped that the problem would be kept under control. However, it still continued to show and, in June 1920, an experiment was carried out on sections of rail on Victoria Embankment, whereby certain lengths were treated by applying the "Sandberg in-situ" rail hardening process.

A length of about 300 yards of single track near Cleopatra's Needle, which had the tendency to corrugate despite repeated "scrubbing", was thoroughly cleared of blemishes, after which alternate lengths of rail were treated. Those sections which had been attended to were to remain in good condition for upwards of three years, despite the passage of over two milion cars, while the untreated portions again showed corrugation after about a four month interval. Early in 1923, more sections of heavily used track, where the problem had regularly shown up, were dealt with by the Scholey Construction Company Ltd. using the "Sandberg" process.

Wartime Staffing Difficulties

As the war progressed, so the problems associated with the staffing of the many departments increased. It became obvious to the travelling public that there were difficulties with regard to the numbers of traffic staff available. What may not have been so noticeable was that there were normally about 800 men employed on track maintenance and other outdoor works, and their numbers were also very much depleted. In 1917-18, road gangs accounted for between 400 and 500 men. Of those who had not been called for military service, many had found more remunerative employment in other industries doing "war work", with its higher rates of pay. Consequently, track repairs and renewals were down to the absolute minimum and this, coupled with the severe shortages of replacement rails and other track items caused the system, consisting of 109 single track miles on the north side and 172 on the south side, to become in a very run-down state.

It was not until 1920 that things began to return to what could be described as "something like normal", when returned servicemen, and some of those who had been employed in "war work", began to take up vacancies in the various departments of the LCC. On the north side, 26 gangs, each made up of about 12 men, and on the south side, 44 similarly constituted gangs, were available to tackle the backlog of work.

Post War Track Works

Three main tasks were undertaken. The first concerned "high check rails", which became prominent because of the continuous wear that took place on the running surfaces of the rails, together with the constant grinding action of the insides of the wheels on the checks. These were dealt with by burning them off with oxy-acetylene flame cutters. In 1920, an electrically driven reciprocating grinder/planer, known as the Woods-Gilbert Rail Remodelling Machine appeared, and proved to be of great value in eradicating this nuisance. It was also instrumental in effecting a reduction of about 65% in the number of complaints received and of accidents that had allegedly occurred as a result of "high checks".

The second task, the curse of rail corrugation, was tackled with renewed vigour, with the assistance of electrically driven rail profile grinding machines. In the year 1921-22, an average of between 120 and 140 yards of single track could be dealt with in one shift duty. This resulted in a total of 37,740 yards of track being attended to on the north side with one machine, and 108,535 yards on the south side using three machines.

The third important task involved the renewal of sections of worn-out rails and, indeed, quite a lot of complete track sections as well. Until 1922, this part of the programme was undertaken in a very limited way as, not only was there still a shortage of new rails and other metal parts, but industrial relations generally between employed and employer were at a very low ebb. During the war, wages went up by the addition of a "war bonus", depending on the level of a "cost of living index". From 1921, according to the index, the "cost of living" fell to some extent, resulting in employers cutting wages to suit, which was the cause of great discontent. So far as the LCC was concerned, the cuts resulted in a "saving" of £11,742 in the four months between the beginning of May and the end of August 1921.

Once prices and wages stabilised, however, a more regular pattern in the way in which renewal work was dealt with was to be seen. In 1923, for example, 11.05 miles of single line was renewed on the north side, together with 9.40 miles in the south, but good though these results were, they were not good enough. The tracks appeared to be wearing out at an alarming rate, in part due to the fact that the expected average life of a length of rail was between 13 and 15 years, while much of that in use was approaching its twentieth year of service.

During 1925, considerable emergency reconstruction was called for, a large part of it on the north side tracks, due not only to excessive wear on the rails, but also to sections of roadway sinking and taking the tramway foundations down as well. These subsidences were the cause of many rail breakages and even fractures to the cast-iron yokes. Examples of this were to be seen at Aldgate, East India Dock Road, Commercial Road, Green Lanes and Seven Sisters Road. In several places where the yokes had fractured, resort was made to connecting slot rail fastenings to track rails by the use of cantilevers, until such time as the yokes could be replaced. Such was the rate of deterioration that during 1925 a mobile repair gang using a motor lorry for transport was formed on the south side, to be shortly followed by one in the north, in an effort to deal more expeditiously with problems as they arose. It has also been recorded that, in many cases, when the affected rail sections were removed, they were in such poor condition that many of them literally fell to pieces.

A minor change in procedure, but one which was to increase costs to some degree was, that in June 1924, the Commissioner of Police for the Metropolis introduced new regulations regarding the "watching and lighting" of road works during the hours of darkness. Until this time, oil lamps showing a red aspect had to be placed at 20 ft. intervals along the road works, which in the case of tramways, meant that a line of lamps had to be placed on either side of the track works. The new regulation stated that, in future, lamps must be placed at no more than 12 ft. apart, which effectively doubled the number required, and doubled the quantity of paraffin oil used in them. At this time also, electric floodlights were introduced, which obtained their power from the tramway supply, either by the use of special "ploughs" which were lowered into the conduits, or by long bamboo poles with connectors at the top, being hung on to the overhead wires.

Unfulfilled Proposals

Over almost the whole period of operation of the LCC Tramways, proposals were made for the construction of lines in both halves of the system, which, had they materialised, would have resulted in a much more cohesive network than actually was constructed. In central and inner London, there were plans for several subways, of which Kingsway Subway was one. Another was proposed between Hyde Park Corner and Marble Arch, with yet a third beneath the City of London streets and St. Paul's Cathedral. Due, in the main to political opposition, Kingsway remained as the only example to be seen.

The LCC also attempted on a number of occasions to penetrate into the "West End" of London, but were always thwarted by opposition from the members of the Borough Councils of Kensington, Fulham and St. Marylebone, together with the City of Westminster, Parliament and the Metropolitan Police, and to some degree, the London General Omnibus Company. The same thing can be said of the attempts of the Council when it tried to make a connection between Blackfriars and Farringdon Road, this time being blocked by the City of London.

One of the more long-drawn-out arguments, however, was connected with a proposal to build a line from Forest Hill to Crystal Palace via Sydenham, and another from Crystal Palace to West Norwood. The first mention of extending the line forward from Forest Hill came in 1908, and was raised at regular intervals thereafter, but was always thwarted by the attitude of the members of local authorities, who refused to give permission as required by the Tramways Act of 1870.

After the Great War, the Council tried again, but this time decided to extend the project in two ways. In the first place, it proposed to use "trolley vehicles" instead of tramcars, and secondly, the line applied for in the 1921 Session of Parliament was from West Norwood to the Crystal Palace, Catford and Lee Green via Knights Hill, Central Hill, Crystal Palace Parade, Sydenham Road, Bell Green, Catford Hill, Rushey Green, Brownhill Road and Burnt Ash Road. This also failed.

The next applications were in 1924 and 1927 for which the Council asked for powers to construct a tramway between West Norwood and Crystal Palace, but again, because of the obduracy of Camberwell Borough Council, the proposals got nowhere. Meantime, Lambeth Council had agreed and expressed its regret at the attitude of the Camberwell Borough, to which the LCC replied: "In view of the attitude of the Camberwell Metropolitan Borough Council it does not appear that any further steps can be usefully taken at the present time to promote legislation for the construction of new tramways to the Crystal Palace ..." The line was never built!

Other Tramway Proposals

Over the years, the LCC proposed many extension schemes which, for one reason or another, failed to obtain the support of the local authorities, parliament or the police. The following list gives details of all those known.

Farringdon Road - Ludgate Circus via Farringdon Street
Ludgate Circus - Blackfriars
Gray's Inn Road - Farringdon Road via Charterhouse Street
Theobalds Road - Bloomsbury Square via Hart Street
Waterloo Road - Blackfriars via New Cut
Wandsworth - Roehampton via West Hill
Forest Hill - Bell Green via Perry Vale

Southend (Bellingham) - Bromley via Bromley Road
Over St. Paul's Bridge (a new bridge proposed, but not built)
Chalk Farm - Childs Hill
Victoria Station - Westminster
Victoria - Edgware Road via Marble Arch
Marble Arch - Shepherds Bush
Paddington - King's Cross
Bloomsbury - Charing Cross

Trackless Trolley Vehicles

The following routes were proposed, but never built.
Camberwell Green - Crystal Palace via College Road
West Norwood - Lee Green via Central Hill and Perry Hill
Highbury Corner - Dalston Junction via St. Paul's Road

Chapter 44
Rolling Stock
Classes E, F, G, E/1 & M

The first electric cars used on the LCC Tramways on the south side services were commercially produced vehicles, those of classes A and D, of which there were 100 of each, being double deck open top bogie cars. Similarly, the 100 each of classes B and C were double deck open top single truck vehicles. While, at first, these were thought to be satisfactory, it was soon discovered that, having open top decks, it was sometimes difficult, particularly in bad weather to adequately cope with the numbers of passengers who wished to travel, as many people did not want to ride on the open upper deck of a car in the pouring rain. The result was that arrangements were fairly quickly made to introduce a plan for providing the cars with top covers.

Class E Cars (Nos. 402-551: 602-751)

As described in the first volume of this history, the class E cars were introduced in 1906. As their history is so closely interwoven with those that followed and known as class E/1, and as, unlike cars of earlier classes, many of them worked on the north side tramways, the main details are again recorded here.

Mr. Fell, dissatisfied with the problems affecting the modernisation of the 400 original cars, was looking for ways to provide a type of car which could be used on any part of the network, or for future extensions and reconstructions. There was already a pressing need to operate covered top cars on the Tooting route, precluded at that time by the presence of two low railway bridges at Clapham and Balham. The use of cars carrying Milnes, Voss or early LCC top covers was also out of the question - they were too high.

In conjunction with his design team and Messrs. Hurst, Nelson & Co. of Motherwell, the class E car was to emerge. The first batch of 150 was destined to be put to work in south London, many of them on the Tooting services, as they were able to negotiate those two low bridges safely. It must be remembered that at that time, no cars of the LCC carried trolley poles, leaving the roof spaces completely uncluttered.

The specification called for the car body to be constructed upon a steel girder underframe, which was strengthened with heavy tie-rods extending up inside the body framing. Rigid cross transoms and corner truss plates completed the frame. The double deck body with a totally enclosed top deck and direct staircases was built using various timbers, but the main wood employed was ash. The door pillars of the lower saloon were of white ash and/or oak, while the sliding doors had oak frames, panelled in the lower halves with oak. Waist panels were of mahogany in three lengths and rocker panels of bass wood or canary white wood in two lengths. End quarter panels were of Honduras

Class E car, No. 712, fitted with a special modified plough carrier for working on the Kingsland Road route.   (Courtesy: L T Museum U26686)

mahogany.   The lower saloon floors consisted of one-inch thick pine boards, suitably protected with wearing slats.

Uprights were, in general, made up from ash, while the carlines for both the lower and upper ceilings were of English oak strengthened by steel angle irons, to which the ceilings, made of alternate pitch pine and satin walnut tongued and grooved strips, were fixed.   All timber sections were strengthened by the use of suitably shaped steel or brass stampings.

Interior panelling in the lower saloon was mainly of oak, while in the upper saloon the sides were cased with alternate boards of white pine and satin walnut.   Outside upper deck panels were of ash.   The exterior of the roof was covered with unseamed waterproof canvas, well stretched and bedded in a mixture of white lead and linseed oil. The windows, four on either side of each saloon, were of ¼-inch plate glass in the lower and 32-ounce sheet glass in the upper saloon, all bedded in moulded india-rubber strips.   Horizontally sliding windows were placed in the sides, at each end of the roof cover, for the use of the conductor.   The direct staircases were shaped from galvanised steel sheet side stringers, the deal board treads covered with protective tread irons.   Draught screens with full length stairhead doors were not fitted initially, but were installed later as described in Volume I.

The end platforms, carried upon rolled steel angle sections were of one-inch pine boards, upon which floor slats of pitch pine were screwed. The outer ends of the steel sections carried the collision fenders, made up from 5 in. by 3 in. by ⅜ in. channel steel sections bent to shape. Dashplates were of steel sheet of 14 s.w.g. thickness, capped with round-top steel section and supported at the bottom on mahogany 2⅜ in. thick crown boards.   Platform steps of the "Hurst, Nelson patent movable type" with metal frames, had wooden panels and iron treads. "Hudson Bowring" lifeguards were fitted beneath each platform.   Each car was also equipped with a box of tools and a car lifting jack, which were stowed beneath one of the staircases.

Lower deck seats were formed from slats (known as "slat and space" seats) in four sections, made from ash and arranged in such a way that each could be lifted out to enable the underseat ancillaries, such as sand hoppers, to be attended to. The seats in the main body of the upper deck were of the two-and-two transverse "garden" pattern, also made up from open slats, with the reversible seat backs made from one-inch by half-inch section, set in metal end frames, which gave equidistant gaps between the struts, while the curved end seats over the canopies were of the slat and space type.

The 76-seat bodies were carried on a pair of Mountain & Gibson maximum traction bogies with swing bolsters and one quadrant plate to each bogie, which gave an easy riding quality. Each bogie was powered by one British Westinghouse type 200 motor of 35 h.p. Westinghouse 90M controllers were fitted to 25 of the cars, with Westinghouse type T2A controllers to the remainder. Certain records show that the first 25 of the class, Nos. 402-426 were fitted with the 90M version, but photographs taken at that period show that No. 407 had type T2A, while Nos. 433 and 445 had 90M.

As delivered, none of the 25 cars with 90M controllers were fitted with magnetic track brakes, the motormen having to rely upon less efficient electric rheostatic braking backed up by the handbrakes. It was not long, however, before Westinghouse magnetic brake equipments were fitted, together with all cars of the earlier classes, as has been described in Volume I. Car weight was 15 tons 7 cwts 1 qtr.

Main dimensions were:-

Overall length	33 ft. 6 in.
Overall width	7 ft. 2 in.
Overall height	15 ft. 6 in.
Length of lower saloon	21 ft. 0 in. (outside)
Height of lower saloon	6 ft. 3 in.
Height of upper saloon	6 ft. 2 in.
Truck wheelbase	4 ft. 6 in.
Total wheelbase	14 ft. 6 in.
Pivotal centres	13 ft. 4 in.
Bolster centres	10 ft. 6 in.
Wheel diameter (driver)	31¾ in.
(pony)	21¾ in.

Cost of the 150 cars was:-

Hurst, Nelson bodies	£63,525
Mountain & Gibson trucks	£18,000
British Westinghouse electrical equipment, including magnetic brakes and ploughs	£43,300

a total sum of £124,825, or £832. 3. 4d per car for Nos. 402 to 551.

With regard to the colours carried by the cars, these were variously described by the manufacturers and the LCC as being of "midland red and light cream" or "deep purple lake and primrose", depending upon which authority was discussing it at the time. Neither were consistent! The finishing arrangements were:-

Red: Four coats best priming
Five coats filler
One coat stain, then rubbed down
Two coats lead colour
Three coats midland red
One coat colour varnish
One coat undercoating body varnish,
    lined and lettered gold, then
One coat undercoating body varnish

	Two coats finishing body varnish.
Cream:	Four coats priming
	Five coats filler
	One coat stain, then rubbed down
	Four coats colour
	One coat colour varnish,
	then lined and lettered, then
	One coat undercoating body varnish
	Two coats finishing varnish.
Interior:	All work stained and varnished.

Delivery of the first 40 cars was scheduled for 15th January 1906, with a further 40 by 15th February, 40 by 15th March and the balance on or before 15th April. Almost immediately, the Council authorised the purchase of another 150 cars of the same class, as an extension of the first contract. Magnetic track brakes were also specified as part of the contract. Cost of the work was £819.13. 4d per car, making a total of £122,950, while, this time the LCC provided the ploughs.

The second batch, numbered 602-751, was purchased for use on the first sections of electrified track on the isolated system in north London (and were to be assembled and housed in new car sheds being built at Poplar and Stamford Hill). Deliveries were planned to take place as from July 1906, but the first came in December. Mr. Fell had been complaining, in October, about the non-delivery of the cars, which in theory put Hurst, Nelson into a penalty situation, but he then went on to say that, even if they had been delivered on time, there was nowhere to assemble them, as the car sheds were not ready for use! This was probably a ploy to avoid invoking the contract penalty clause, at the same time hinting to Hurst, Nelson that they could stay at Motherwell for the time being.

Some were fitted with special plough carrier channels, to enable them to be worked on the Kingsland Road side slot line, and they retained these for a number of years after the side slot tracks were relaid as normal conduit. Eventually, many of the cars acquired trolley poles for use on parts of the greatly expanded network, which included journeys into the areas of other undertakings.

A limited upgrading of equipments was undertaken in 1912, when several of the cars which had 90M controllers were re-fitted with type T2A controllers and type 220 motors of 42 h.p. rating. No. 415 was one of those included in this programme. Nevertheless, it was not until a comprehensive schedule was implemented in 1923, that the last of thr 90M controllers and their associated type 200 motors were taken out of service.

In common with the rest of the fleet, all cars of the class were fitted with service number equipment in 1912-13, while in 1922-23, service number boxes were installed on either side of every car which included adjustable red aspects. Many of the 402-551 series also were equipped with trailer drawgear after 1914, retaining these until no longer required in the early 1920s.

The LCC ordered 125 new cars of class E/1 in 1921. The first of these arrived at the end of the year to work on the southern system and, with the prospect of a large new fleet of cars being made available, together with extensions and alterations to existing services, a considerable re-arrangement of rolling stock was undertaken. This included the transfer of 40 cars from the southern to the northern system, when class E cars Nos. 512-551, after having their trailer drawgear removed, were taken to Hampstead car shed from Clapham.

In almost new condition, No. 608 of class E, working between Stamford Hill and Shoreditch, is seen at the stopping place outside West Hackney Church, Stoke Newington. (Courtesy: Tramway Museum Society)

Many other experiments were carried out in the years between 1925 and 1929, including "one-off" arrangements in 1927-28, when cars 440, 444 and 445 appeared in red livery, but retained the longitudinal seating in the lower saloons, fitted with cushions. The interior woodwork of all three had also been brightened up. No. 444 received black lining on the outside panels, while No. 445 sported a warning triangle on the nearside of each dashplate, and No. 440 had "gold" lining. All were "pullmanised" between 1927 and 1930, as is described elsewhere.

"Stop" Signals Fitted

The members of the Highways Committee, meeting on 17th July 1924, authorised the General Manager to carry out experiments with "stop signals" and report the results. On 29th January 1925, he reported on trials made with two experimental sets obtained from the General Supply Co. Ltd. This was followed up on 9th July 1925, when he stated that class E cars, Nos. 628 and 629 had each been fitted with a set of signals at a cost of £75, and that he would again report in due course on the performance of these.

The signals were of two types. On No. 628 the equipment consisted of a red semaphore arm displayed against a white screen (presumably on the dashplate), while the one on No. 629 is described as being a revolving cylinder which displayed "stop" and "slow". The lettering on both was illuminated, and their operation was interworked with the controllers, magnetic brakes and handbrake gear. They were offered to the Council at £40 per car set for the semaphore device and £60 for the cylinder type. The equipment was submitted to the police for their comments, but the Commissioner declined to approve either type and asked for their removal "forthwith".

Single Deck Cars

The Kingsway Subway was built with the intention of utilising only single deck cars, which called for the provision of special vehicles to

701

be constructed, with considerable restriction being imposed upon the Council by the Board of Trade with regard to the methods employed and materials used. However, in July 1905, the Tramways Manager considered purchasing 15 single deck cars from Sheffield which, he thought, would conform to the stringent conditions. The price of £5,000 was discussed, but things got no further than that, the LCC finally deciding, after all, that they would not be suitable for the work that they would be called upon to do.

One of the restrictions imposed was that any cars to be used in the subway were to be as fireproof as possible. Consequently, the bodies of the vehicles were to be almost totally constructed of metal sections. Where other materials were used, for instance in the linings between the windows and bodywork, they were to be specifically of "non-inflammable" type. Ultimately, cars of special design were placed on order, 16 of these to be known as class F and the other 34 to be of class G.

Class F Cars (Nos. 552-567)

The first car of the initial order for 16 was delivered to the Council in time for the official inspection of the subway on 29th December 1905. Numbered 552, it was the prototype of the batch, but was different from the others, being fitted with a door at each of the platform entrances. When the doors were folded back at the rear end of the car, they formed an enclosed vestibule and, at the same time, a linked mechanism caused the step below each door to be raised when that door was closed. They did not remain on the cars for very long, being removed before it went into public service.

An order was placed with Messrs. Dick, Kerr & Co., the bodies being constructed by the United Electric Car. Co. Ltd. of Preston, and the main dimensions were:-

Overall length:	33 ft. 9 in.
Overall width:	6 ft. 10 in.
Overall height:	10 ft. 11¼ in.
Length of body over corner pillars:	24 ft. 10 in.
Platform length:	3 ft. 8½ in.

Bogie details as for class E cars.
Buffer channel sections were spring loaded.
Seating capacity was for 36 passengers.
Cost was £750 each.

Underframes were fabricated entirely from steel angle and channel sections, upon which steel end and side frames were fitted. Body outer panels were of sheet steel, riveted to the angle sections. Interior panels were made entirely of aluminium, with coloured patterns etched on them. The bulkheads were of steel plates and were unglazed, while

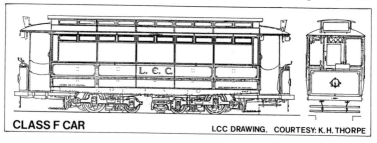

CLASS F CAR
LCC DRAWING. COURTESY: K.H. THORPE

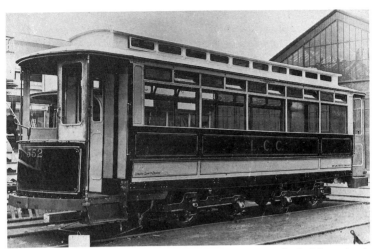

Built by the United Electric Car Co. Ltd. with Mountain & Gibson bogie trucks, car No. 552 was the prototype for a fleet of single deck cars with all-metal bodywork for use on the Kingsway Subway services, the first 16 of which were known as class F. The incomplete car is standing in the works yard of the UEC Co. Although the vestibules were open to the elements, unglazed doors were fitted, but there were dashplate headlamps. After delivery to London and following test runs, the doors were removed. At the same time, headlamps were fitted into the dashplates. (LCC photo. Courtesy: P. J. Davis)

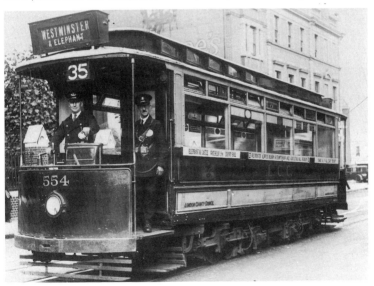

The other fifteen cars of class F were identical to this one, which is seen at the "Archway Tavern" terminus in the late 1920s. The offside platform entrances were for use by passengers at Kingsway Subway stations. (Science Museum W5163. Courtesy: D. W. K. Jones)

the saloon doors were also made from steel plates, glazed on the top half, with panels of aluminium on the lower half.

Inside each car, longitudinal benches, each seating 18 passengers, were manufactured from "non-inflammable Pantasote", consisting of specially treated oak slats (to make them "fireproof"), screwed to steel supports, while the floor covering, laid on to a steel sheet floor was of fire-resistant "Litosilo". There were five equally spaced windows on either side of each car, with two ventilator lights above each main window, while the clerestory roof also contained an equal number of opening ventilators, exactly in line with those above the main windows. Trolley planks were not fitted. Each car was fitted with two oil lamps, one in either bulkhead, placed there in case the power failed while a car was in the subway, but these were removed at an early date, being replaced with extra electric lamps.

The bodies were mounted on two trucks of the Mountain & Gibson (McGuire type 3) maximum traction centre-bearing type of 4 ft. 6 in. wheelbase. Dick, Kerr controllers and electro-magnetic brakes were specified. Lifeguards were of the Hudson-Bowring swing-gate pattern. The normal colour-light indicator boxes were suspended from the canopy ends, with the destination boxes fitted above, while projecting from the roof at both ends were metal rods, whose purpose was to strike signal indicator rods at either end of the tracks between Theobalds Road and Holborn Station, which put a signal at red while the car was on the up or down ramp, and cleared it to green once the car had left the ramp section.

Most of the cars of this class had been fitted with Westinghouse 220 motors at some time prior to 1925, with the exception of Nos. 552, 556, 560, 563 and 567, which retained D.K. type 3A motors for at least another year.

Class G Cars (Nos. 568-601)

On 21st November 1905, the Council accepted the tender of the Brush Company to construct another 34 single deck cars to be known as class G, and similar in most respects to those of class F. The maximum traction bogie trucks were, as before, to be supplied by Mountain & Gibson, with electrical equipment by British Westinghouse. Details of costs were:-

34 car bodies, The Brush Company, Loughborough, £14,280 (£420)
M & G (McGuire type 3) truck sets,
electrical equipments and assembly, ploughs and
magnetic brakes, British Westinghouse,   £13,481 (£396.10s)

                                            £27,761 (£816.10s)

There were minor differences in the details of the bodywork as compared with the cars of class F, the most pronounced being that this group had end bulkhead windows, offset saloon doors, and the canopy bends were rounded off. All had trolley planks fitted on the clerestory roofs, but in no case were they ever used.

Difficulties were experienced by the contractors in supplying a number of the earlier batch of cars on time, due to the Council not providing sufficient information on detail at an early stage of the contract; to a number of alterations which had to be made to the specification; to a shortage of suitable steel; and to lack of space when erecting the cars after delivery, which had to be done in cramped conditions in Kingsway Subway. On 22nd June 1906, A.L.C. Fell

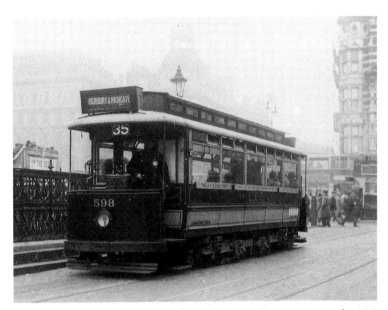

Upper view. No. 598 was one of the 34 class G cars, most of which normally worked on the subway services. The southern terminus of service 35, was, during the 1920s, at the eastern end of St. George's Road, close to the "Elephant & Castle" junction.   (LCC official view)

Lower view. The two class G cars which were involved in the coupled car experiment, Nos. 575 and 572, photographed while still undergoing trials.   The cable which electrically connected the control systems together was suspended between the canopies of the cars.   Additional equipment was also provided to enable all four motors to be controlled from either end of the set.   (Courtesy: Tramway Museum Society)

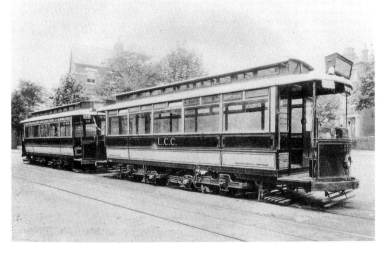

recommended that late delivery penalties, in theory incurred by Dick, Kerr be waived, and this was agreed to.

Apart from the installation of service number plates at the end of 1912, no other major structural alterations appear to have been made to the cars of these two classes. After replacement in 1930 by new bodies of double deck pattern which were placed upon the existing trucks, the old car bodies, with the exception of one, were disposed of. The exception, No. 600, remained in Holloway car shed, standing on baulks of timber, in use as a store.

There was one experiment which occurred in 1911, and concerned the use of two class G cars which were connected mechanically and electrically to form a coupled unit. A description of this has been given in chapter 23 in the first volume of this history, but since its publication it has been established that the fleet number quoted of one of the two cars used was incorrect. Photographic evidence has established that cars 575 and 572 were used.

In this experiment, a complex electrical arrangement was designed, with each car having its own plough. It was expected that this arrangement would take account of all driving conditions that the motormen would be likely to experience. A description of the method employed, given by J. D. Markham Esq., has been published in the Light Rail Transit Association booklet, "The LCC Trailers".

Classes F and G Cars. Out Of Service and Disposal Dates

Car	Withdrawn	Sold	Car	Withdrawn	Sold
552	May 1929	Aug 1929	577	Feb 1930	Feb 1930
553	Feb 1930	Feb 1930	578	Feb 1930	Feb 1930
554	Jan 1930	Feb 1930	579	Feb 1930	Feb 1930
555	Nov 1928	Jun 1929	580	Feb 1930	Feb 1930
556	Feb 1929	Jun 1929	581	Feb 1930	Feb 1930
557	Jan 1930	Feb 1930	582	Feb 1930	Mar 1930
558	Feb 1930	Feb 1930	583	Dec 1929	Feb 1930
559	Feb 1930	Feb 1930	584	Feb 1930	Feb 1930
560	Jan 1930	Feb 1930	585	Feb 1930	Feb 1930
561	Feb 1930	Feb 1930	586	Feb 1930	Feb 1930
562	Apr 1929	Aug 1929	587	Apr 1929	Apr 1929
563	Dec 1929	Feb 1930	588	Feb 1930	Feb 1930
564	Feb 1929	Jun 1929	589	Feb 1930	Feb 1930
565	Jan 1930	Feb 1930	590	Jan 1930	Feb 1930
566	Apr 1929	Aug 1929	591	Feb 1930	Feb 1930
567	Jun 1929	Aug 1929	592	Jan 1930	Feb 1930
568	Feb 1930	Feb 1930	593	Feb 1930	Feb 1930
569	Sep 1928	Jun 1929	594	Jan 1930	Feb 1930
570	Feb 1920	Feb 1930	595	Feb 1930	Feb 1930
571	Feb 1930	Feb 1930	596	Feb 1930	Feb 1930
572	Feb 1930	Feb 1930	597	Jan 1930	Feb 1930
573	Feb 1930	Feb 1930	598	Feb 1930	Feb 1930
574	Jan 1930	Feb 1930	599	Feb 1930	Feb 1930
575	Feb 1930	Feb 1930	600	Apr 1929	§
576	Feb 1930	Feb 1930	601	Feb 1930	Feb 1930

§ Car 600 body retained at Holloway car shed for use as a tool store.

(When taken out of service, all cars, except for No. 600, were taken to the Central Repair Depot where the bodies were lifted off the trucks, all electrical equipment removed, and the bodies stacked, prior to being sold to anyone who wanted any of them).

Class E/1 Cars (Nos. 752-1676)

The 300 cars of class E had proved that standardisation of the future fleet was an aim to be met and, as it had been anticipated that about 1,000 more cars would be required within a few years, the LCC Tramways team, led by Fell, set to work to carry out improvements to the design. It had been found that when magnetic brakes were fitted to the class E cars, their action was to prove that the car body trussing was insufficient to hold the bodywork rigid. A new, improved method of trussing was designed to overcome the problem, and was to be installed in the next batches of cars to be ordered. Together with other improvements, this led to the eventual introduction of cars of class E/1, which were to become a legend in tramway history.

An order for 250 of these, to be numbered 752-1001, was placed with Messrs. Hurst, Nelson on 21st February 1907, with the proviso that deliveries commenced as from 20th May. These were to have improved, lengthened and strengthened bodywork, the most noticeable visible difference being in the width of the corner pillars of the lower saloons, each of which was seven inches wider than those on the class E cars. This extra body length was sufficient to allow one more passenger to be squeezed on to each long bench seat in the saloon, making 32 seats available, but still with 46 upstairs.

As in the case of the class E cars, the bodies were mounted upon maximum traction bogie trucks, manufactured by Mountain & Gibson, and which were known by them as Type 3 or 3L (on which the truck side plates were one inch deeper), but collectively known to the LCC as Class 4. As ordered, only the last 25 of the consignment were to be fitted with trolley poles, for use on the isolated lines between Putney, Hammersmith and Scrubs Lane, cars for both services being housed at Hammersmith car shed, as described in Volume I. Before long, however, more cars were trolley fitted to allow them to be used on the Streatham-Norbury section.

The specification for the materials to be used in the bodywork was generally very similar to that employed for the earlier cars, but the results of the improvements made meant that the E/1 cars weighed 16 tons 6 cwts each, as against the 15 tons 7 cwts 1 qtr of the others.

At the same time as the 250 cars were being constructed, another 50, to be numbered 1002-1051, were authorised by the Council to be built, but this time by LCC direct labour at the Union Road Works at Leytonstone. This agreement, made on 7th February 1907, also contracted with Hurst, Nelson to supply many of the parts required to complete the car bodies. However, much of the timber was available from stocks which had been purchased by the LCC from the North Metropolitan Tramways Company and held at the works.

Costs of the 300 cars were:-

250 bodies from Hurst, Nelson, £122,375 (£489.10s each)

50 bodies by LCC with some parts bought in, £23,150 (£463 each)

50 steel underframes, Hurst Nelson, assembled by LCC, £1,759 (£35. 3. 7d each)

300 sets, maximum traction class 4 trucks, Mountain & Gibson, £49,350 (£164.10s per set) .

300 sets, electrical equipment, British Westinghouse, £100,950 including ploughs, also trolley poles where required, (equipment for one car, £316.10s; erection cost per car, £8; trolley pole for one car, £12)

300 sets, car ploughs (two per car) from LCC as sub-contractor to British Westinghouse, £3,600 (£6 per car)

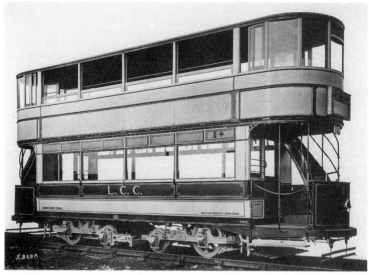

The first of the class E/1 cars, No. 752, standing on a railway siding track at the Hurst, Nelson works at Motherwell. Cars of this class proved to be the standard to which 1,000 were ultimately built for the London County Council. (Greater London Photograph Library)

Details of the cost of some of the component parts:

Item	Supplier	Cost per Car Set
Sanding Gear	Hurst, Nelson	£ 4.19. 0
Moveable Steps	-do-	£ 4. 7. 6
Lifeguards	-do-	£ 4. 5. 0
Window Operating Gear	-do-	£12.10. 0
Ventilator Operating Gear	Hoskins & Sewell	£ 3. 0. 0
Brake Gear	United Electric Car Co.	£ 4.10. 0
Sun Blinds (8 per car)	Hurst, Nelson	£ 5.17. 0
50 American Oak 3 in. planks	-do-	£ 2. 4. 0 each

Measurement details for the class E/1 cars:-

Length overall	33 ft. 10 in.
Length outside body	22 ft. 2 in.
Width over guard rails	6 ft. 10 in.
Width over roof	7 ft. 2 in.
Height overall	15 ft. 6¾ in.
Height in lower saloon	6 ft. 2¾ in.
Height in upper saloon	6 ft. 2 in.
Truck wheelbase	4 ft. 6 in.
Pivotal centres	13 ft. 6 in.
Bolster centres	10 ft. 6 in.

Deliveries of the 250 cars commenced in the summer of 1907 and continued throughout the second half of the year, with the last of the order being completed early in 1908. The last of those from Union Road were put into service at much the same time. When new, these cars were fitted with "upper deck communicating gear" (signal bells), but were soon considered to be less than successful, due to the danger of conflicting signals being given to the motormen from both decks at the same time, but more importantly, by the motormen not being able to tell whether the conductor was downstairs or upstairs. The practice was not perpetuated, while those cars so fitted eventually had the top deck equipment removed. As a matter of interest, in October 1928, the experiment was tried again, with several cars working on service 32 being fitted with upper deck bell pushes, but again, this did not last for very long.

The next order was for 175 cars, which were to be numbered 1052-1226 and used on extensions both north and south of the river. A capital estimate was approved on 26th May 1908 for £179,450 to fulfil this order. Contracts were let to:-

Car bodies	Hurst, Nelson	£72,450
Truck sets	Heenan & Froude	£27,037.10s
Electrical equipments	British Westinghouse	£55,387.10s
Magnetic brakes	British Westinghouse	£ 9,975.

On completion, batches of E/1 cars were loaded on to railway wagons at Motherwell for dispatch in train loads to London. On arrival, they were conveyed in sections to the car sheds to be assembled. Car Nos. 777 and 762 are on the nearest wagons. (*LCC official photo*)

Work on these cars commenced almost immediately and continued throughout the remainder of 1908, with the last 50 or so being delivered early in 1909. Some had trolley poles, but the number is uncertain. Meanwhile, the electrified services were expanding at a prodigious rate and, requiring what appeared to be an ever-increasing supply of, by now, standard bogie cars, the Council approved a capital estimate of £237,500 for 200 more class E/1 cars on 29th June 1909. There were also to be 50 cars of a 4-wheeled type for use on hilly routes, which will be described elsewhere. The contracts for the 200 bogie cars were fulfilled by:-

Car bodies	Hurst, Nelson	£78,000
Truck sets	-do-	£23,900
Electrical equipments	British Westinghouse	£63,650
(Trolleys by Watlington or Brecknell, Munro & Rogers)		
Magnetic brakes	British Westinghouse	£11,400

Numbered 1227-1426, the cars began to appear during the autumn of 1909, and deliveries continued throughout the remainder of that year at an approximate rate of seven or eight a week. All were trolley fitted, with four of them, Nos. 1350-1353, each receiving two poles, presumably for use on the Woolwich - Eltham line. Hurst, Nelson supplied and fitted about 75 trolley sets, with the LCC fitting the remainder. After the Great War, more were fitted with two poles each when the double overhead wire line was extended from Eltham to Lee Green.

These two views show the rather austere finish to the interior of a class E/1 car, possibly No. 1120, standing in wintery surroundings at Pemberton Gardens, Holloway. The transverse wooden reversible seats on the upper deck, each gave accommodation for two persons. In the lower saloon, the highly polished wooden benches gave adequate, if firm, support to the passengers. When first in service, the cars were fitted with sunblinds, but these were soon removed. The faretable indicates that the car was working on the Finsbury Park and Euston Road service.   (L T Museum. 16443 & 16442)

The last batch of 200 bogie cars to be ordered prior to 1914 had tenders that called for completion during the remainder of 1910 and into 1911. A capital estimate for these was raised on 3rd May 1910 for an expenditure of up to £237,500, which also included the provision of another 50 cars of a 4-wheeled type. In this case, the order for the cars was fulfilled by:-

Car bodies	Brush Engineering	£75,500
Truck sets	Heenan & Froud	£22,800
Electrical equipments		
(including trolley poles)	British Westinghouse	£67,050
Magnetic brakes	British Westinghouse	£11,400

This batch of cars, numbered 1477-1676, had cost £883.15s each as against £970.10s in 1907-08 and £942 in 1909. With regard to the last two orders, costs incurred in the construction of the 4-wheeled cars, to be known as class M, have been deducted and will appear with the description of that class of car.

Despite the ravages of the years, the cars of class E/1 provided excellent service to the people of London, leading what can only be described as a steady existence. However, in one instance early in 1921, car No. 981 was "seized" in Camberwell car shed by a bailiff, upon an Order of Court for an alleged non-payment by the Council of an account. A "stop" notice was placed upon the car until the matter had been settled!

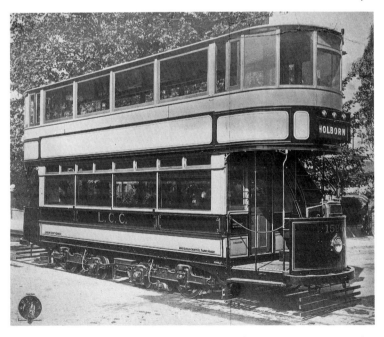

This Brush-built car, No. 1594, is seen soon after being put into service and indicates the high standard that was reached in its construction and finish. (L C C/Brush photo)

The Post War E/1 Cars (Nos. 1727-1851)

The General Manager of Tramways initiated the arrangements for obtaining an increase in the number of cars required for post-war services. In the words of his report to the Highways Committee on 24th March 1920 he stated that "... Due to the amplification of services and the opening of the new authorised extensions asked for in the Parliamentary Session of 1920, a special investigation has been made with the following findings.

Total number of cars in stock	1,663 cars +	158 trailers
Less spares held for overhaul	205	19
Less accident proportion	83	9
Average for service	1,375	130

"Therefore, 1,320 cars and 120 trailers will be required to run the estimated 56 million miles during the year 1920-21, for which 1,375 cars and 130 trailers should be available. If there are no delays, etc. there will be an additional 55 cars and 10 trailers for the authorised extensions. When all the new extensions are complete, about 80 extra cars will be required, therefore 25 more cars will be needed, and as additional cars are required to meet anticipated traffic growth, an order should be placed for an extra 100 cars over the 25 mentioned above, making 125 in all.

"Experiments such as coupled cars, modified lighting, platforms, seating, trucks and staircases are in course of preparation in design for consideration. If car weights are (to be) reduced, consideration will have to be given to the use of light alloy sections, for which at present delays of up to three years may be expected. Therefore, for a quick increase in stock, cars of class E/1 should be purchased, with up-to-date requirements. All patterns and dies are available. An estimate of costs for 125 cars is £362,500, with £2,500 for plough gear and ploughs.

(signed)   A. L. C. Fell."

At this time, a competition was proposed whereby a suitable, new design of tramcar would attract a prize of £1,000 for the successful designer. Mr. Fell, as Manager of the undertaking, laid down stringent conditions for the conduct of the competition, with 20 sub-paragraphs of instructions and many limitations and, while welcoming competitors, as good as told the Highways Committee "... all very well and good - but get me 125 extra class E/1 cars - quickly ..."

The estimate given by Fell was somewhat low in view of the huge increases in prices which had occurred in the six years since 1914. Nevertheless, he was quite optimistic that these cars would be required in conjunction with considerable anticipated expansion of the system. A more realistic estimate of £548,000 was eventually compiled after discussions with the manufacturers and, on that basis, tenders were called for. The results of these were interesting, as Hurst, Nelson only quoted for 50 bodies, but for all 125 sets of trucks, while Metropolitan Vickers and English Electric shared the contract for electrical equipments. The final contracts let for the 125 cars were:-

50 bodies, Hurst, Nelson, £2,230 each	£111,500
75 bodies, Brush, £2,245 each	£168,375
125 truck sets, Hurst, Nelson, £600 per set	£ 75,000
50 sets, electrical equipment, MetroVic, £1,300.10s set	£ 65,025
75 sets, electrical equipment, Eng. Elec. £1,306.10s set	£ 97,987.10s
125 magnetic brake sets, MetroVic, £175 set	£ 21,875

	£539,762.10s

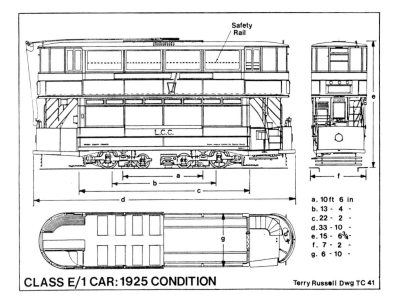

Safety Rail

L.C.C.

a.	10 ft 6 in
b.	13 - 4 -
c.	22 - 2 -
d.	33 -10 -
e.	15 - 6¾-
f.	7 - 2 -
g.	6 - 10 -

CLASS E/1 CAR: 1925 CONDITION

Terry Russell Dwg TC 41

The contracts were taken by MetroVic as the successor to British Westinghouse, which was taken over by Metropolitan Vickers in 1920. On 11th October 1921, Fell reported that a total reduction of about 5% had been agreed to, which, at £21,880, made the cost of the 125 cars £518,882.10s. To this, £1,071 must be added to account for the cost of 375 ploughs, three for each car, and manufactured by the LCC.

Estimates had also been prepared for the construction of an equal number of car bodies, which were quoted as being of "class E/2", which were - hopefully - to incorporate a number of additional improvements. The extra cost, at £120 per car, appeared to be unrealistic and this class of car never materialised. The class number was only used in conjunction with an experiment carried out during the early 1920s, when one car (probably No. 1235) was fitted up as a "pay as you enter" vehicle.

Delivery of the first of the new E/1 cars was planned to begin at the end of September 1921, a period of 42 weeks after the contracts were exchanged, and each complete car was to be erected, tested and available for service three weeks after that. Delivery rate was to be six a week for the first 100 cars and then three a week for the remaining 25. An inspection of a complete new car was made by the Highways Committee on 27th January 1922. By the end of March 1922, 40 were in service, the remainder being commissioned as and when ready. The 50 Hurst, Nelson cars, Nos. 1727-1776 were assembled at Rye Lane depot, while the 75 Brush cars, Nos. 1777-1851 were dealt with at New Cross car shed. The trucks for these were numbered into the LCC inventory as Nos. 4001-4250, the odd numbers referring to the ones carrying the plough gear.

Cars numbered 1727-1776 were each fitted with two MV 121 type motors, stated as being nominally of 51 h.p. rating, together with MV T2C (late British Westinghouse) controllers, while Nos. 1777-1851 had DK 31 C motors, rated at 63 h.p. and EE DB1-L5 controllers. The original idea was to give greater drawbar pull when towing trailer cars,

A specially posed, but poor view of a post war class E/1 car when new. *(LCC official view)*

but it also gave exceptional acceleration when the car was worked without a trailer.

Each of these cars was to be fitted with two trolley poles, so as to give a quicker and easier turnround at terminal points; better lighting; an improved mechanism to raise and lower the platform steps and their associated lifeguards, patented by W. E. Ireland; and underframe body bolsters of new design. Improved ventilation was provided in the lower saloon with the installation of a set of louvres over each of the end bulkhead windows, and on the top deck by fitting extended weather strips on the sides of the roof, to allow the four opening windows on either side to remain continuously open by just under one inch. Extractor ventilators were also fitted over the ceiling light fittings to draw foul air and tobacco smoke out of the seating area. The upper deck doors were also modified, with "hit and miss" ventilator panels replacing part of the glazed area of each door.

Timbers used in body construction were almost identical with those employed in the earlier cars and, at the time, were considered to be quite satisfactory. Many years later, however, certain defects appeared which tended to point to the use of some less or poorly seasoned woods, probably an indirect result of the effects of wartime shortages during 1914-18. The cars built by Hurst, Nelson, who mainly used ash in the construction of the bodies, fared worse than those built by Brush, who used teak.

General dimensions of cars of this class were:-

Length over fenders	33 ft.	10 in.
Length of body over corner pillars	22	2
Width over guard rails	6	10
Extreme width at roof	7	2
Width over body frame	6	8
Height to top of roof	15	7¼
Extreme height over trolley	16	1
Height inside lower saloon	6	3

Height inside upper saloon	6	2
Wheelbase	14	6
Truck pivotal centres	13	4
Body bolster centres	10	6

Livery was the standard "lake and cream" with gold lining, the metal underparts in red oxide, inside of dashplates and floors in grey, while the interiors were of varnished natural wood finish in "wainscot and quartered oak", but with the ceilings in white enamel to improve visibility in the cars at night. One other noticeable difference was that the service number plates in the windows at the upper saloon ends were placed at the top of the window space, close to the roof, while the end opening lights were moved to the tops of the windows to the left of the number plates, as viewed from outside.

It was intended that these cars should be distributed quite widely over the system on both north and south sides. On 25th October 1923, Fell stated that some would be housed in the new car shed then under construction at the top of Brixton Hill. The proposed allocations were:-

Abbey Wood	10	
Brixton Hill	45	(some for Croydon through workings, when open)
Hampstead	49	
Holloway	20	(or all 69 on the north side at Hampstead for the Amhurst Park line when open)
		This left one car not allocated, possibly for maintenance replacement purposes

As is now known, all 125 remained on the southern system, while other cars were transferred north.

New Cross	60*	In this case, Fell was attempting to get authority to purchase another 60 cars of class E/1, to replace 80 old class B and C 4-wheeled cars. An estimate was prepared, but no further action was taken.

At about this time, the Metropolitan Police regulation stating that all cars should be painted and overhauled once every year was modified, to allow of a repaint every other year. This was expected to effect a great saving in time spent by the cars in the works. It also allowed for a theoretical reduction in the number of cars required, which probably cancelled out the need for an extra 60 cars.

With regard to the result of the competition for the design of a new type of car, none of the entries submitted was considered to be of practical use and, after some discussion, the whole matter was closed and no award was made.

The "Reconstructed Subway" Class E/1 Cars (Nos. 552-601)

The last batch of cars to be classified as E/1 were those built in 1929-30. On 19th July 1928, it was proposed that, as the Kingsway Subway was to be closed for reconstruction to take double deck cars, the class F and G cars, by now 22 years old, would become surplus and could effectively be "reconstructed" by placing new double deck bodies on to the existing bogie trucks and using the existing electrical equipments to drive and control the "new" cars. Contractor for the 50 new bodies was the English Electric Co. Ltd. whose price for the work was £102,025 (£2,040.10s each).

A prototype body had been designed and constructed during 1928 at the Central Repair Depot, and used in conjunction with a pair of equal-wheel bogies as an experimental car classified "HR/1", for use on the

Dog Kennel Hill services to and from Dulwich. The main departure from previous designs was that the upper deck assembly was of "Alpax" aluminium sections. Separate half drop windows by G. D. Peters, of "Windsor" pattern, were fitted instead of the mechanically operated window sets previously used, as were ten-inch external stencil pattern service number plates, improved lighting, padded seats and backs of G. D. Peters pattern and two-by-two staggered reversible seats.

Body construction of the lower saloon, while it followed previous practice in being timber framed and panelled on a steel underframe, included the provision of wide vertical centre pillars which were reinforced with steel plates, to give added strength to the body.

Seating on the new cars was of the G. D. Peters pattern and, where the HR/1 car No. 1852 had four sets of transverse two-and-one seats in the main part of the saloon and two longitudinal seats at either end, each for four passengers, the "reconstructed" cars had the more usual "pullmanised" E/1 layout, consisting of five sets of transverse seats in two-and-one formation, together with four longitudinal seats, each for three passengers. "Ashanco" ventilators were fitted above the main windows in each corner of the saloon.

Non-slip "battleship" linoleum covered the floors of both decks. There was a one-piece ⅜-inch thick heavy duty plywood roof, manufactured by the Tucker Armoured Plywood Co. Ltd. of Crayford, Kent. The ceilings on both decks were made from heavy duty plywood, with the usual strap fitments. Many of the cars were fitted with "K-Ray" indicator boxes at either end, together with the "1922" pattern lifting steps and associated lifeguards. The colour scheme used was "pullman" style red and cream, with "imitation gold" fleet numbers, black lining on the side panels and the County coat of arms placed centrally on each waist panel. Interior decor was white for ceilings and upper woodwork, with lower panels in natural grained finish.

The trucks and electrical equipments were reconditioned at the Central Repair Depot before being used again. Any controllers of type T2A were replaced by those of type T2C. Two trolley poles were fitted to each car, one to be used for each direction of travel.

One interesting aspect to the introduction of this batch of cars was that numbering into the fleet did not appear to be consistent. As these were "reconstructed" from earlier cars, they carried the same fleet numbers - or should have done - but at least one class E/1 car carried the same number as a single deck car for a time. The first recorded use of the new cars was on a shortened version of service 35, working between Bloomsbury and "Archway Tavern" in the spring of 1930 after the subway had been closed for reconstruction. Distribution of the cars also appears to have been quite haphazard as the following examples show:-

No. 555 on service 40 at Abbey Wood
    559 on service 26 at Victoria Embankment
    562 on service 14 at Victoria Embankment
    575 when new at C R D Charlton (with splashboards fitted to the truck sides)
    578 on service 40 at Embankment
    581 with service 40 boards at C R D
    589 at Holloway car shed showing service 29
    594 at Woodford on service 81
    600 on service 38 at Abbey Wood

The new "Alpax" upper deck structures proved to be useful as replacements for original top decks of some cars which had been in

The Holloway based "1929" class E/1 car, No. 589, seen at Enfield terminus early in 1933. The mainly metal top deck structure closely resembled those on HR/2 and E/3 cars. (Courtesy: M. J. O'Connor)

involved in collisions and other incidents. Four of these, No. 1120, which was damaged in a fire in April 1929, re-appeared on 9th October; No. 454 was fitted with a new top deck early in 1930; No. 989, damaged in April 1920, came out again with a new top deck on 19th June; while No. 1081, also fire damaged in December 1930, took to the road again on 29th May 1931.

Class E/1 Cars Loaned to Metropolitan Electric Tramways

Under the terms of an agreement concluded on 12th August 1912, between the London County Council, the Metropolitan Electric Tramways and the County Council of Middlesex, the LCC was to loan a number of class E/1 cars to the MET for an initial period of one year. This was done to enable the company to take part in through running services with the LCC, while cars of its own fleet were being fitted with plough carrying gear. Of the 30 cars which were authorised to be sent, only 15 went in the first instance, these being Nos. 1590-1604. Five of these were returned to the LCC in October 1916. The ten cars which remained were later joined by Nos. 1607-1619, 1639 and 1640 and used by the company until April 1918, when they were all returned to the LCC.

Class E/2 Car

Little is known at present about the details of this class of car. It is supposed that it was to have been an improved version of the E/1, after the decision was taken after the Great War, to call for designs for a new type of car.

There has been mention of several experiments, one of which is contained in a sketch which purports to show a front-entrance rear-exit double deck car. A double width entrance was provided at each of the front ends, one for each direction of travel, with a single width exit at each of the rear ends. Access to the upper deck was by means of a quarter-turn staircase leading from the "off-side" of each platform. Lower deck body length was 22 ft. 2 in. (as for an E/1 car), while overall length of the car was 35 ft. 10 in. Seating capacity was said to be 32 in the lower saloon and 42 in the upper. The motorman was provided with his own operating space, gated off from the passenger area. He also had control of the front steps, which he could close off by a set of "rising gates". In whichever way the car was travelling, the "off-side" steps were also closed off to passengers. There is no evidence that the experiment went any further than that.

"Pay As You Enter" Car

At some time shortly after the end of the Great War, it is believed that a "mock-up" of a "p.a.y.e." car was assembled, and it has been stated that car No. 1235 may have been used for this experiment. If it was, this must have taken place between May 1920 and September 1923 when the car was out of public service.

This idea, however, if it occurred, was pre-determined in 1913 when the first thoughts for the use of this facility were apparently being considered. A drawing, supposedly approved in April 1913, shows a car platform modified in such a way that passengers boarded at the rear end of the back platform of the car, paid fare to a conductor seated on the platform, and then passed either into the lower saloon, or by way of a type of reversed staircase to the upper deck. Alighting passengers would leave the car by the exit gate at the front end of the rear platform. From the diagram, it would seem that progress of the car would be necessarily slow, particularly with regard to exit, as only one passenger at a time could leave the car. It is not known whether this arrangement was ever tested in practice, or whether it remained only as an idea to be exploited.

Class M Cars (Nos. 1427-1476 & 1677-1726)

With the need for more cars to provide services on the expanding system and the requirement for cars preferably powered on all axles for use on hilly routes, the Council explored the possibility in 1909, of using a special type of vehicle of more modern design and appearance than those of classes B and C which were then in use.

At that time, the double overhead wire line between Woolwich and Eltham was under construction, while the Highgate Hill cable tramway was being replaced with an electric conduit tramway. The gradients encountered on both these were quite severe, the more so on Highgate Hill, and it was decided to adopt the same arrangements as were being used on the line between Camberwell and Dulwich via Dog Kennel Hill. An additional reason for using 4-wheeled cars at Woolwich was that, for the time being at least, it was not expected that large, bogie cars would be required on what was then seen as a semi-rural route, although four cars of class E/1 had been - or were being - fitted with twin trolleys, which could only have meant that they were to be used if required.

Car No. 1427

With the success of the class E and E/1 cars, the first of which had been introduced in 1907, the Tramways Department was authorised on 29th June 1909 to construct a specimen 3-window double deck open

The class M car bodies had component parts interchangeable with class E/1 cars. This vehicle, one of ten allocated to the Eltham service, is standing at Abbey Wood. (LCC official view)

top car body at the Union Road, Leytonstone, Works. Numbered 1427, the saloon body for this car was to be virtually a shortened version of the E/1 class. This was to be the beginning of the class M series of cars.

Arrangements were made with Hurst, Nelson & Co. on 14th July, to construct a special 4-wheeled truck with steel plated sides, which would accept two sets of mechanical slot brake equipment (one at either end), together with plough carrying gear beneath the centre of the truck. Cost was agreed at £210, and the work to be considered as an extension of an existing contract. Before long, however, the management had a change of policy and decided that the car should be fitted with a totally enclosed top deck, similar in design to and with parts interchangeable with cars of class E/1. A total of £396 was allocated for this work, together with an allowance for certain modifications to be made to the special underframe.

The single truck had pressed steel side frames and two plough carriers. The slot brake gear fitted into the centre section. (LCC official view)

The LCC Class 5 Swing Bolster 4-wheeled Truck

On 28th April 1910, an agreement was concluded with the Board of Trade that the production truck decided upon for the Highgate Hill line need only have one special slot rail brake mechanism fitted permanently at the centre of the truck frame, instead of as originally intended, a set at either end. With the displacement of the plough carrier from its probable position in the centre of the truck, there was only one other place that it could go, and that was on the end of the truck frame. In fact, one was provided at either end, but only one plough could be used at any one time.

This most unusual type of truck, of which 100 plus spares were eventually used by the LCC, had very strongly made pressed steel side frames, with extension pieces at either end to accommodate the plough carriers. One of the advantages claimed was, that by using the swing bolster method of suspension, there was plenty of room between the truck and body at the centre point where the special slot brake mechanism could be mounted. One of the features of a class M car was its riding quality; it appeared to "float" above the truck, the body moving freely in all directions, which tended to give it a gentle swaying motion.

The "Woolwich" Cars (Nos. 1428-1437)

After having decided on the definite specification to be adhered to in the construction of these cars, the next move was to place an order with Hurst, Nelson for ten cars of the class, complete with the modified trucks, but without the slot brake gear or plough carriers (only the outer channels of the carriers were fitted) for use on the Woolwich - Eltham line. Each car was also to be fitted with two trolley poles for use on that unique line. Costs of all components for these cars, Nos. 1428-1437 were:-

Hurst, Nelson & Co. bodies	£3,550
Hurst, Nelson & Co. swing bolster trucks, 4-wheel type	£1,137.10s
British Westinghouse electrical equipment and assembly	£3,322.10s
British Westinghouse magnetic brakes	£ 570

	£8,580

Twin trolley fitted class M car No. 1435 at the Eltham terminus of the line to Woolwich, c 1912.   *Commercial view)*

or £858 each. The cars were delivered to Abbey Wood car shed for assembly and testing in time for the opening of the Woolwich and Eltham line on 23rd July 1910.

Measurement details for the class M cars:-

Length overall	29 ft.	4 in.
Length outside body	17 ft.	8 in.
Truck wheelbase	7 ft.	6 in.
Bolster centres	11 ft.	6 in.

Other measurements as for class E/1 cars.

The "Highgate Hill" Cars (Nos. 1438-1476)

When the order for the 200 class E/1 cars, Nos. 1227-1426 had been placed with Hurst, Nelson & Co., provision was made for the production of another 50 cars in multiples of ten, to be either Class E/1, M or of a single deck bogie design referred to as class N, whichever type was required by the Council. Ten class M cars for the Eltham line had been decided upon, and this was followed by a decision to continue with the production of class M cars, these for use on the Highgate Hill line. As one car body had already been built by the LCC, another 39 were ordered, together with 40 class 5 trucks. On 19th April 1910, the contractors agreed to carry out the construction of these, which incurred the following costs:-

Hurst, Nelson, 39 bodies	£14,040
Hurst, Nelson, 40 swing-bolster 4-wheel trucks	£ 4,980
British Westinghouse, 40 sets electrical equipment	£12,753

The Highgate Hill line was re-opened to electric cars on 25th March 1910, but it was to be several months before the new class M cars took over the complete working of the line.

The Slot Rail Brake

This special item was designed by Tramways Department staff for specific use on cars working on Highgate Hill. The purpose of the brake was to ensure that, should it become necessary, a car could be stopped in a very short distance by literally clamping it to the top and underside of the conduit slot rail. The brake mechanism itself, consisting of a main frame into which all components were firmly fitted, was permanently fixed into the space between the centre of the truck and the underside of the body.

The mechanism was only used while a car was actually on the Highgate Hill section; at all other times it was wound up to its resting place beneath the car body. At the point at the foot of the hill where the brake was brought into use, a special hatchway was provided in the conduit slotway on the "down" or uphill track, which could be opened and closed by means of the operation of a lever at the side of the track. It was the duty of a "brakesman" to deal with the fixing and stowing of the brake mechanism on each car. Once the hatch had been opened, the brake gear was wound down into the slot by the brakesman, who did this by placing a standard controller handle on to the end of a rod extending from the mechanism to the side of the car body. Having lowered the brake into position, the car was moved forward and the hatch closed.

Special linkages were permanently connected between the brake mechanism and handwheels fitted beneath the handbrake handles at either end of the car. To use the brake, the motorman at the leading end, or the brakesman, who travelled on the rear platform to apply

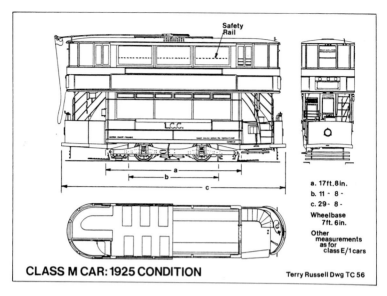

Safety Rail

L.C.C.

a. 17ft. 8 in.
b. 11 - 8 -
c. 29 - 8 -

Wheelbase
7ft. 6 in.

Other
measurements
as for
class E/1 cars

CLASS M CAR: 1925 CONDITION

Terry Russell Dwg TC 56

the brake in case of emergency, only had to turn the handwheel in a clockwise direction, which action, through a series of rods and cams, moved the two brake blocks, one above and one below the strengthened slot rail, towards each other until they made contact with the rail surfaces. This very powerful brake was also used on the downhill journey to control the speed of the car to no more than six m.p.h., while at the several stopping places, the magnetic brake was used in conjunction with the normal handbrake. The slot brake was still available to exert more pressure on the slot rail should an emergency arise.

On the return journey from Highgate Village, on arrival at the foot of the hill, the car was stopped over the hatchway in the "up" or London-bound track, where the slot brake was wound out of its working position to its resting place beneath the car body. It had originally been intended that the special brake would be used in conjunction with a lever, operated by the brakesman, who would ride up and down the hill on the front platform of each car with the motorman. This, however, was replaced by the arrangement described above.

The brake blocks were specially made for the purpose; those used on the top of the slot rail were made from grey cast iron, those on the bottom being of hard chilled white iron with a steel backplate about ⅛-inch thick, cast on to the iron block. The backplate was considered to be necessary as a precaution against fracture and breakage of the iron block.

The "Dulwich" Cars (Nos. 1677-1726)

On 19th July 1910, the tender of the Brush Electrical Engineering Co. Ltd. was accepted for the construction and delivery of 50 more bodies of class M for £17,625 (£352.10s each) and 50 class 5 trucks for £5,950 (£119 each). British Westinghouse contracted to supply the electrical equipments as part of an order for 250 car sets at £335 per car set, which included £12 each for ploughs (which were sub-contracted to the LCC) and also for trolley poles if required. British Westinghouse were also to supply sets of magnetic brakes at £57 per car set, later reduced to £55.10s. Cost of each car was therefore £862.

In this case the cars were to be fitted with a supplementary braking arrangement which was operated by a handwheel placed below the handbrake staff. When the wheel was turned in a clockwise direction, the magnetic brake shoes were mechanically screwed down on to the track to act as a "slipper" brake.

The new cars were intended for use on the steeply graded lines between Camberwell, Dulwich, Peckham Rye and Forest Hill, and which included the notorious Dog Kennel Hill. It was expected that they would replace some of the older cars in service, mainly those of class B, which were considered not to be really suitable for the arduous duties that they were expected to undertake on these lines.

Some of these cars, which initially were not fitted with trolley poles, eventually received one each, while Nos. 1708 and 1713-1726 were each given two for use on the Eltham service. No. 1427 was later taken to Camberwell car shed, from where it worked on the Dulwich services for several years, until it was transferred to Abbey Wood in the late 1920s.

Subsequent Alterations

A number of complaints were received from members of the public during the early 1920s over the alleged rough riding of the four-wheeled cars working in south London. Much of this came from passengers using the services working over Dog Kennel Hill, where cars of classes M and C were employed.

A shock absorber unit known as the Houdaille Hydraulic Suspension Apparatus were in use on heavy motor vehicles, and it was to this that the Council turned in an effort to overcome the problems inherent in four-wheeled double deck tramcar design, whereby the heavy bodies tended to cause a measure of vertical instability. The item was first described by the LCC as an "anti-sway" device and, early in 1925, the first moves were made to obtain fifteen sets of these to fit to six class M cars working over Dog Kennel Hill, two cars of class C on the same route and seven class M cars on Highgate Hill. The results of the tests were not very encouraging. Although swaying was reduced for a time, the apparatus soon showed signs of wear and proved to be unsuitable for this purpose.

Meantime, the Rolling Stock Engineer, Mr. Ireland, had devised and developed an apparatus to control vertical oscillation, which was tried on class M car No. 1690 and on two class C cars, Nos. 226 and 278. After several months in service, the experiment was pronounced a success, and the decision was taken on 2nd September 1925 to equip six more class C cars, together with three of class M working on the southern system and three working on the north. It was agreed that a three months' test should be undertaken, to ascertain the effectiveness of the apparatus, before any more cars were fitted.

With the apparent success of the latest experiment, the decision was taken on 23rd March 1926 to fit this device on to all the remaining cars of classes M and C at an estimated cost of £5,250, of which £455 was allocated for the wages of LCC staff involved in the installation work. The Kilmarnock Engineering Company and Messrs. Hurst, Nelson supplied the equipment for £3,376, of which £2,560 went to Kilmarnock Engineering. The first of the class C cars to be dealt with was No. 250

in April 1926 and, by the end of March 1927, about half the rolling stock had been fitted with the apparatus. The remainder were dealt with by the end of that year.

By 1930, it was the end for cars of class C and the beginning of the end for cars of class M so far as their hill climbing activities were concerned. The appearance of new cars of class HR/2 on the Dog Kennel Hill and Highgate Hill services meant that the four-wheeled cars would be relegated to less arduous duties. They had already been replaced on the Woolwich and Eltham service (44) by additional cars of class E/1, although a few remained at Abbey Wood, working where and when required.

Some were taken to Leyton in 1930 to take over duties from the old Leyton four-wheeled cars. Included in these were Nos. 1427-1430 from Abbey Wood, which were transferred in September. A number were also taken to Hampstead, Chiswick and Hammersmith car sheds and stored, and from where a few appeared from time to time to work on extra services such as those between Putney and Hammersmith on Boat Race Days. Those that went to Leyton and Hampstead were taken over the LCC western area and MET lines via North Finchley. The excursions over MET metals cost the LCC £4 per car.

At Leyton, the class M cars began working on ex-Leyton services 7 and 8, running between Chingford Mount, Leyton, Stratford/Forest Gate and Victoria & Albert Docks, in company with some cars belonging to West Ham Corporation. In September 1931, the last of the old four-wheeled cars of the Leyton fleet were replaced by class M cars.

Three of the class, Nos. 1441, 1444 and 1446 were selected by the LCC as candidates for rebuilding into standard length bogie cars, at first to be known as class ME/1, later changed to ME/3. In the case of Nos. 1441 and 1444, the bodies were cut in two and lengthened by one standard length window bay and placed on new underframes. The completed bodies were then mounted on standard class 4 bogies, and were fitted with body-mounted plough carriers, straight body sides, drivers' vestibule screens, and one trolley pole each. Internally there were new white enamelled plywood ceilings, linoleum covered floors, individually operated upper deck windows and fully upholstered seating on both decks. The first to be attended to, No. 1444, was completed

An LCC class M car on Leyton service 7, in Walthamstow territory at Chingford Mount. *(Courtesy: Tramway Museum Society)*

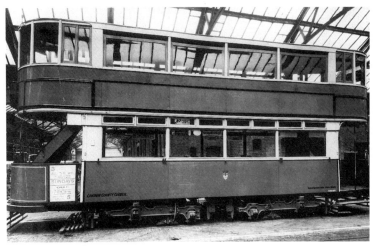

Car No. 1441 of class ME/3 in 1932.   (Courtesy: L T Museum U31320)

in May 1932, and the second, No. 1441, made its appearance in February 1933. Both were allocated to Telford Avenue car shed.

The third car, No. 1446, while being lengthened in the same way as the other two, fitted with more modern internal appointments and mounted on a pair of class 4 bogies with a body-mounted plough carrier was, from then on, treated rather differently.   In the first place, it received a new tapered-sided top deck, incorporating individually opening windows, together with a one-piece "Alpax" aluminium domed roof of much the same pattern as the one used on the new car of 1932 ("Bluebird").   One-piece straight side panels were fitted to the lower deck, while large roller blind boxes for both the destination indicators and service numbers were fitted into the space above the drivers' screens.   One trolley pole was mounted centrally on the roof. The final alteration was that of its number!   Class E/1 car, No. 1370 overturned at Kennington on Saturday 3rd June 1933 and was severely damaged.   It was taken to the Central Repair Depot to await repair. On 1st July 1933, the LCC Tramways were taken over by the LPTB. On 2nd July, No. 1370, ex-1446 entered service.   As a matter of interest, No. 1446, ex-1370, reappeared in 1934 as LPTB No. 2.

Similarly, No. 1444 was also troubled by accident damage.   Shortly after its May 1934 overhaul, it sustained considerable damage when it ran away down the ramp at Telford Avenue car shed, derailed on the catch points and overturned.   It was taken into the CRD for attention, and eventually received a new top deck, complete with a domed roof and other improvements.

Another experiment of note was undertaken.   The problem with bouncing and "jazzing" was still a worrying feature of the class M cars and, in a further attempt to overcome the difficulty, experimental four-wheel trucks were supplied and fitted to three cars.   The English Electric Company example went beneath No. 1715, one from the EMB Company was placed beneath No. 1726 in March 1932, while No. 1723 was fitted with one built by the Brush Company in May 1933.   Drivers' vestibule screens were also fitted to Nos. 1723 and 1726.   All three cars continued to work in the Leyton area after the formation of the London Passenger Transport Board.

Chapter 45
Modernisation and Pullmanisation

After the introduction of the "1922" class E/1 cars, A. L. C. Fell, through his deputy, J. K. Bruce, suggested that another 60 be purchased to bring the fleet up to strength. He also initiated a series of measures aimed at improving the standard car still further. On 15th November 1923, he issued a report on his findings which, if introduced would be:-

Additional ventilation,

Four additional lamps in each saloon,

Service number improvements - the end number plates to be brought forward from their present positions as far as the limitation of the overall extreme length of the car would allow.

He also commented upon the "poor" lighting on the cars, particularly in foggy conditions, suggesting various possible remedies, including the installation of voltage regulators and storage batteries, but these were soon to be discounted.

On 24th January 1924 he introduced a set of end number plates, similar in design to those used on the sides of the cars, but larger. This was intended to make things easier for passengers, when looking out for the service number of the car that they wished to board.

Upon the retirement of A. L. C. Fell at the end of 1924, the legal changes to the named license holder on behalf of the LCC Tramways had to be undertaken. This included obliterating the name of the previous licensee by fixing printed metal strips over it bearing the name "Joshua Kidd Bruce, Acting General Manager". The work was done at all car sheds on the night of 31st December 1924 at a cost of about £95. Bruce, in his role as Acting General Manager, in a search for a new image for the LCC Tramways, initiated a radical modernisation programme.

The First Modernisation Plans

The subject of modernisation had been raised several times since the end of the Great War, and more frequently in the mid-1920s, when the London General Omnibus Company were making great strides in providing comfortable cushioned seating for their passengers, at first in the lower decks of the 'buses and later, with the introduction of covered tops, upstairs as well. The Metropolitan Electric Tramways was also already following this trend in finding ways of improving cars on that system. Sadly, the LCC had lagged behind, because the then General Manager, A. L. C. Fell, had resisted suggestions that he should instal transverse cushioned seating in the lower saloons of the cars. He considered that it was not possible to fit seating of this type into conduit-equipped cars, due to the need to have the floor hatches kept free from obstructions, to allow the works staff to have access to the many pieces of equipment on the trucks and beneath the car floors. He was also opposed to reducing the inside seating capacity to provide transverse seats.

During 1925, after the retirement of Fell, a scheme was produced by Bruce which would allow transverse reversible seats to be installed and, at the same time, leave the floor space clear of obstruction by fixing the new seats firmly to the steel side truss-plates of the cars and carrying them on cantilevers over the floor space. A problem to be overcome was that all power cables would have to be placed into side panels running the length of the car, instead of, as in the case of a car with longitudinal seats, the cables lying beneath the benches.

With the approval of the Council he next wrote a specification for the complete renovation of a standard car, including the installation of the proposed new seating. In the meantime, the decision was taken to improve the lighting inside the cars by introducing lamps of higher wattage in conjunction with the application of white enamel to the ceilings.

On 16th July 1925, authority was given for the experimental use of heaters in the lower saloons of several cars. In the first place, one car at Hampstead was fitted up and a trial conducted between Friday 4th and Tuesday 8th December 1925. On 5th, a series of thermometer readings showed that the inside temperature was between 42°F and 44°F, while a reading taken from a thermometer on the wall of a building showed that the outside temperature was 28°F. The results prompted J. K. Bruce, who was present during the experiment, to extend it to eight cars, all of which were still equipped with longitudinal seating. The use of heaters on these cars continued until the end of March 1927, after which the experiment was abandoned.

Agreement was reached on 4th June 1925 that 50 cars should be fitted with certain improvements to service number plates and indicator boxes. This number was later reduced to five, and on 16th July, Bruce was authorised to fit these cars up at a cost of £81. No. 1235 was additionally used in the first instance, and later was put to work on service 54 with all improvements.

The experiment consisted of installing large, externally mounted service number plates with 9-inch, 10-inch or 12-inch figures, which were illuminated from behind, together with "reflective" lamps for illuminating destination indicator boxes from the front (which was rather like a cowl fitted over the top of the front of the box, with three lamps beneath it). Other cars fitted were Nos. 1056 (26th June 1926), 1547 (5th June), 1578 (6th March), 1688 (11th June), 1172 (date not known). On 19th July 1927, the 10-inch version was chosen as being the most practical.

Car No. 627 was painted in an experimental livery of orange with black ironwork in April 1926, but was repainted red in May 1927, while No. 962 was fitted up at the CRD on 21st May 1926 with air operated bells of the NUMA pattern, having four bell pushes installed on the ceiling of the lower saloon and one on each platform. The car then went into service from New Cross car shed.

Car No. 1235

This car seems to have been chosen as the vehicle upon which many experiments were carried out. In the first place it was used to demonstrate new, large service numbers early in 1924, together with "cushion spring seats" in the lower saloon. Subsequently, it became the "travelling display stand" for a number of improved items. It had already been fitted with reflective light units in April, and appeared in June 1926 with the following modifications:-

A re-arrangement of seats in the lower saloon:
Upholstered seats in the lower saloon:
Improved ventilation:
Various styles of opening windows in the lower saloon, including "Watlington" types:
A means of minimising the ingress of rainwater through the tops of the upper saloon windows during bad weather:
The provision of additional lamps:
New designs of interior lamp reflectors:
Additional methods of preventing draughts:
Ceiling handrails for passengers on the upper decks:
Additional safety handles on the staircase doors:
Modifications to upper deck windows to remove existing obstructions to passengers' line of sight:
Various types of service number indicators (again):
An entirely new form of roof construction
(one piece marine plywood):

With regard to window modifications, some agitation had occurred during the summer of 1925 for more efficient ventilation to be provided in the lower saloons of the cars of classes E and E/1, with a suggestion that they be provided with opening main windows similar to those used on the cars of classes A and D. This resulted in the modifications being made to No. 1235, on which each corner window was replaced with one of a different type, and in each case, the window was made in two parts. All special windows were supplied by Messrs. Watlington. In the first arrangement, the top section of the window was hinged to drop inwards and downwards, there to be secured to the uprights.

The second type was for a sliding drop window in two parts, where the top section slid down to a maximum depth of eight inches. In the third arrangement, the window was divided vertically, and one half was made to slide sideways, while the fourth window was divided horizontally, the top half of the assembly sliding downwards.

After being in service for several months, the car was presented to the Highways Committee at Stangate on 21st December 1926. A discussion followed, at which the General Manager said that the revenue from advertisements on windows was about £13.10s for all eight fixed windows on bogie cars and £10. 2. 6d for all six on 4-wheeled cars. This would be lost, passengers' line of sight would be likely to be obstructed, while the police would most probably object!

Gross revenue from window advertisements in 1923-24 was £9,607, while the cost of alterations would be approximately £4.15s per window, or £38 per car. A statement made on 2nd May 1927, suggested that, while the principle of new window arrangements was sound, in view of the estimated cost, which was expected to be about £35,000 to convert the whole fleet, no further action should be taken. By this time, the Council had embarked on a complete programme of modernisation, to be carried out on all cars, except those of classes A to D. Only No. 1235 carried the experimental windows for several more years.

The "Pullmanisation" Programme

The Pullman Car Co. was of American origin. George M. Pullman designed, built and operated railway carriages which were furnished to lavish standards, and the idea was brought to Britain where similar

728

The new and the old! No. 1222 newly repainted, at CRD in March 1931, stands with 1361 looking much the worse for wear. Behind that, a class D car awaits scrapping.   *(Photo: H. C. Casserley)*

high standards were implemented. In some measure, if in name only, the style still survives. It was this name, "The Pullman Car", that was adopted by the LCC when it embarked upon its tramcar modernisation plan in 1926.

Although the official term used was "Tramway Improvements", it was nevertheless to become publicly known as the "Pullmanisation" programme. The term was also used in literature provided by the LCC Tramways after the completion of the work, in a series of booklets known as "The Pullman Review", in which it states "every tram a Pullman".

Authorisation was given on 28th April 1926 for one car to be fitted with transverse lower saloon seats and "improved floor covering" as an experiment, the work to be undertaken at the CRD, using Tramways Department labour.   An estimate of £145 had been given for the work which, with later additions, finished up by being £250.12. 3d.   Car No. 1817 of the "1922" class E/1 series was selected and was taken into CRD at the end of May 1926. The Highways Committee inspected it on 17th June and, being impressed, decided that 100 cars of class E/1 should be similarly equipped.   On 21st June, No. 1817 entered public service from Clapham car shed, resplendent in a new "signal red" and "pale yellow" livery, lined in black, and sporting the coat-of-arms of the County of London centrally on each waist panel.

The remainder of the improvements as suggested by Bruce were:-
1. Lower saloon seating; longitudinal cushioned seats, each for three passengers, fitted at each corner.
   Five transverse double seats of "walkover" pattern on the "left-hand side", five transverse single seats on the "right-hand side".
   Accommodation for 27 passengers.
2. Upper saloon seating; no change.
3. Flooring; cork carpet in lower saloon. (As this was an experiment, the Metropolitan Police raised no objection but stated "not strictly

*A "child's eye" view of the uphostered
transverse seating in the lower saloon
of No. 1778.   (LCC official view)*

in accordance with police requirements ... as, some efficient means,
by battens, or otherwise, to be provided to raise passengers' feet
above the floor of the carriage".
Upper saloon; no change.

4. Lighting, lower saloon; ten lamps, an increase of four, with new
   pattern enamelled plate reflectors.
   Upper saloon; no change.

5. Signal bells; NUMA type air operated bells with four pushes in the
   lower saloon and one on each platform. (This was later increased
   to two on each platform, one by the door, the other under the
   canopy by the car entry steps).

6. Ceiling hand rails; lower saloon, modified to be almost identical
   in length to the corner seats and to be fitted with leather hand
   grab straps. Additional passenger support given by the use of grab
   handles on the corner of each of the transverse seats.
   Upper saloon; two continuous rails provided throughout the length
   of the saloon.

7. Interior decor; lower saloon, new polished plywood panels down
   from waist level.
   Upper saloon; dark paintwork on lower side and end panels.
   Both saloons to have white ceilings, window stiles, etc.

Specification and Costs

In addition to the normal renovation charges, assuming that 100 cars
were to be dealt with, costs were estimated to be:-

"1. Seating. 'The Walkover', a proprietary item so designed that the
   full width of each seat is available for use by passengers, irrespec-

tive of the direction in which passengers wish to sit, with a corresponding increase in comfort. The 'special backs' on these seats
also give 'an economy of space'. The installation of the new seats
involves a re-arrangement of the power cables within the sides
of the car body.

£163. 5s per car.

"2. Lighting.   £7. 9.11d per car.
If a similar improvement was effected at the same time on the
upper deck, the inclusive cost would be:-

£17.17.11d per car.

"3. Signal bells.   Provision and fixing of four ceiling and two doorway
bell pushes and one bell at either end.

£11. 9. 6d per car.

(This was later increased to take account of the additional bell
pushes installed).

"4. Ceiling handrails.   Modifications to lower saloon rails and provision
in the upper saloon.

£4. 2. 4d per car.

"5. Interior decor.   Provision of panellings, mouldings, and additional
decorative works.

£8. 2. 0d per car.

"6. External decor.   Complete car, lower and upper saloon.   Additional
cost over the normal renovation.

£9. 6. 0d per car.

"Total cost per car: £242. 3. 2d.

"The additional cost, amounting to £9. 6. 0d over normal renovation
could be charged to the Revenue (Publicity) Account, so reducing the
estimate to £232.17. 2d.

"If the cork carpet was omitted, a reduction of £18.10. 0d per
car would be possible, in which case the estimate could be:-

£214. 7. 2d per car.

"Therefore, a likely estimate of £232.17. 2d could be made if cork
carpet was used, or £214. 7. 2d if battens were used on the car floor.
This would mean a total of approximately £23,000 net, of which £17,000
was for materials and £6,120 for LCC labour".

J. K. Bruce then recommended that:-
"1. A capital estimate of £23,000 be obtained.
"2. Work is done by direct labour.
"3. Tenders in the usual manner to be obtained by the Chief Officer
of Tramways.
"4. The terms of years of repayment ... shall be the unexpired period
of the debt on the cars for which the improvements are installed".

An extract from the London County Council minutes of 27th July
1926 (page 231) states:- "... an estimate, No. 9776 ... be approved as
an estimate of costs, debt or liability under Section 80 (3) of the Local
Government Act, 1888".   On the same day, Mr. Bruce was authorised
to modernise 100 class E/1 cars as agreed, but costing £23,300, and
a recommendation for the work to be undertaken by direct labour.

On 7th October 1926, the Finance Committee intimated that a
fifteen year term for repayment would be better.   Therefore, it was
recommended that the Council make application to the Treasury for
sanction to be given to a special period for repayment of fifteen years.

Several cars received experimental features such as the truck sideframe covers as seen on this class E car, which worked in the Hammersmith area in 1930. They were soon removed. (*LCC official view*)

The main visible difference in the refurbished cars, apart from the obvious one of change of livery was in the internal appointments in the lower saloon, especially in the new grey-patterned moquette-covered spring seating supplied by G. D. Peters & Co., which set a new standard of comfort on the tramways of London. However, the floors were not carpeted in cork; the time-honoured timber battens remained.

The sample car, No. 1817 was an immediate success. The next four to be completed went into service during November and December 1926, being followed by one or two cars at intervals of a few days, until on 16th April 1927, the last of the 100 cars, mainly from the "1922" series had been dealt with. The lower saloon seating for these actually cost £118 per car set.

The next deficiency to be dealt with concerned the use by the passengers of the bell pushes fitted to the sides of the platform door pillars. It had been intended that these were for conductors' use, but passengers coming from the upper deck had to use them. This meant that notices advising passengers how to use them were required, and these were to be designed and provided for from the "saving" made on the estimate, as was the provision of an additional bellpush at either end, mounted under the end canopy, near the entrance/exit steps. At a meeting on 26th October 1926, it was agreed that the Equipment & Engineering Co. would supply all the necessary material, including the additional pushes for the sum of £536.

Meanwhile, in an official minute of 16th February 1927, authority was sought to deal with another 250 cars as a follow-on, at an expected cost of about £54,000, to which the Treasury agreed. G. D. Peters again obtained the contract for the seats, this time at £80 per car set, with Nettlefold & Sons supplying 250 sets of NUMA type air bells, but with the Equipment & Engineering Co. also supplying 45 additional sets at the previous price.

In the contract for the refurbishment of this batch, a number of class E cars went into the schedule. Additional work on these entailed fitting truss plates of the type in use on E/1 cars before new seating could be installed. The revised arrangement for seating in this type of car was also different from that of the E/1s, due to the slightly shorter body length. Instead of the four longitudinal seats each accommodating three passengers, those on the class E cars seated four passengers, while only three sets of transverse seats could be fitted in. Peters agreed to a change in the terms of their contract to allow for this, by increasing the cost of the end seats by £3.17.6d per car set, but decreasing the cost of the sets of transverse seats by £21.9.0d per car, making the total cost per class E car £62.8.6d as against £80 for an E/1.

Prior to July 1927, no consideration had been given to improving the upper saloon seating - the passengers still had to put up with slatted wooden seats upon which to rest their weary buttocks! With this in mind, a point was made by Bruce that £3,800 had been "saved" on the estimate for reconditioning the first 100 cars as a result of not using cork carpet, instead retaining the slatted batten floors. Using the same philosophy with regard to the next 250 cars, but this time with reference to the reduction in the cost of the lower deck seats, a total of £14,750 would be "saved". He stated that this sum could and should be used in providing spring cushion upper deck seats in place of the wooden ones, but retaining the slatted wooden backs in all the 350 cars attended to and about to be dealt with. The Council, having agreed to this approach, then called for tenders. G.D. Peters obtained this contract at a price of £32.19.6d per car set for all 350 cars, which showed a "saving" of £3,208 on the estimated capital cost of the work. At a meeting held on 6th March 1928, it was agreed to re-seat and improve both saloons of a further 500 class E and E/1 cars at an estimated £108,500. Nesta Ltd. provided the seats.

And so the programme continued. Another 350 cars were dealt with in the 1928-29 financial year, later extended to take in 500, during which the first of the class M cars, No. 1472 was completed on 6th March 1929. The provision for these involved yet another change in the contract arrangements, as in this case the seating consisted of four longitudinal end seats, each accommodating four persons, with two sets of two-and-one transverse seats in the centre of the saloon. Cost of a car set was £51.14s. The last 50 cars, consisting of class E, E/1 and M cars were dealt with during the 1929-30 financial year. Seat contracts were shared between G.D. Peters & Co. and Nesta Ltd. and by now also included the provision of spring cushion seating in the upper saloons, while the orders for the air-bell equipment were shared between Nettlefold & Sons and Equipment & Engineering.

During the progress of the improvement programme, many cars which were not trolley fitted had this item included when they were in the CRD. An example shows that 100 were dealt with towards the end of October 1926, when authority was given to purchase the trolley poles for £5,470, and fit them for £780. The last improvement came when, on 31st May 1929, the Highways Committee agreed that all cars should be fitted with platform mirrors for use by the motormen, and for this, 1,399 pairs, together with spares were purchased for £1,680.

The cars already fitted with cushion seats needed better cleaning facilities. This resulted in the installation of vacuum cleaning plant in the car sheds and at the CRD and, as more cars were re-seated, the facility was increased to suit.

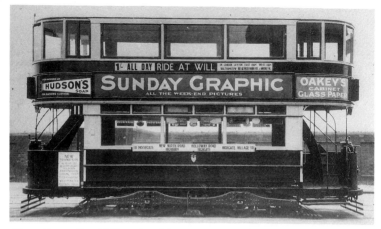

Class M car No. 1440, painted in the dark red livery when "pullmanised" in April 1930. (*LCC official view*)

The Painting Specification

On 5th August 1927, the specification for painting the outsides of the cars was published.

Sides:

From the underside of the top deck roof to the bottom of the window rail, primrose yellow. Below this rail to the bottom line of the main saloon roof, vermilion red. Framing and panelling from the underside of the main saloon roof to the bottom of the window rails, primrose yellow. Below this rail, the panels to be in vermilion red down to the underframe solebar which is to be black. The rounded edge of the corner pillars to be primrose yellow.

Relief line in black:

Round the edges of the top deck roof; the bottom of the light rail moulding; full width of the advertisement mouldings; on the edge of the lower saloon roof boards; on the drip rails above the lower saloon windows; on the edging of the moulding of the bottom window rail; on the guard rail capping iron; near the ends and about two inches from the top to bottom edges of the rocker panels.

Car ends:

End panels, staircases and dashplates (except for the advertisement spaces which are to remain grey) in vermilion red. Fender and platform bearers and underframe members in black, and underside of canopy roof boards and rails in enamel white.

Relief lines in black as follows:

On dashplate cappings and beadings; at bottom of dashplates; on end panel mouldings; on staircase beadings.

Lettering, etc:

Car numbers on dashes in imitation gold, shaded black and red. The Council coat-of-arms in satandard form and colouring, to be placed in the centre of each side waist panel.

The term "vermilion" was applied to the colour of the red paint used shortly after the programme began, being described as of slightly lighter shade than the "signal red" first used. In September 1931, the description (and no doubt the colour) was altered yet again, when it was decided to use the "new standard brighter red and pale yellow" in place of the "1926 Pullman livery of signal red and yellow".

The Pullmanisation Programme

Car	Date	Car	Date	Car	Date	Car	Date	Car	Date
402	24.10.29	469	24.11.28	536	23.08.29	646	29.07.29	709	08.06.29
403	22.10.28	470	11.03.29	537	12.12.28	647	09.01.30	710	20.01.30
404	23.06.28	471	05.07.28	538	01.12.28	648	06.07.29	711	30.11.29
405	21.09.28	472	29.01.29	539	13.03.30	649	22.01.30	712	04.07.29
406	01.08.28	473	25.02.29	540	06.04.29	650	27.04.29	713	16.01.30
407	19.02.29	474	28.07.28	541	06.08.28	651	28.12.29	714	19.02.30
408	23.03.29	475	20.10.28	542	05.01.29	652	06.06.29	715	18.04.29
409	07.07.28	476	30.05.28	543	20.01.29	653	28.08.29	716	01.20.30
410	11.12.28	477	12.02.29	544	26.01.29	654	14.12.29	717	19.06.29
411	08.12.28	478	27.10.28	545	08.09.28	655	06.11.29	718	31.12.29
412	16.02.29	479	30.10.28	546	11.09.28	656	13.12.30	719	27.07.29
413	23.02.29	480	04.10.28	547	09.06.28	657	03.06.29	720	17.08.29
414	14.02.29	481	17.09.29	548	09.03.29	658	07.02.29	721	11.10.29
415	15.08.28	482	30.10.28	549	16.07.28	659	29.01.29	722	05.03.30
416	23.02.29	483	22.04.29	550	16.09.29	660	23.01.29	723	27.05.29
417	01.09.28	484	03.11.28	551	12.04.29	661	08.11.28	724	30.05.29
418	05.09.28	485	18.09.28			662	07.02.29	725	22.05.29
419	28.06.28	486	05.11.28	*	* *	663	02.08.28	726	24.04.30
420	20.07.28	487	27.09.29	602	13.06.27	664	07.03.29	727	10.07.29
421	14.12.28	488	14.03.29	603	13.06.27	665	23.06.28	728	06.02.30
422	26.01.29	489	18.10.28	604	31.08.28	666	28.03.29	729	24.08.29
423	28.11.28	490	23.01.29	605	27.06.27	667	28.02.29	730	20.03.29
424	16.06.28	491	28.11.28	606	09.06.27	668	19.12.28	731	15.02.30
425	06.04.29	492	08.12.28	607	08.06.27	669	11.06.28	732	15.01.30
426	12.07.28	493	16.11.28	608	19.07.28	670	15.09.28	733	15.11.29
427	23.08.28	494	10.11.28	609	29.09.28	671	21.03.29	734	15.04.29
428	19.01.29	495	18.06.29	610	29.12.28	672	27.10.28	735	08.02.30
429	17.11.28	496	25.08.28	611	20.03.29	673	01.12.28	736	22.02.30
430	18.01.30	497	05.07.28	612	02.05.29	674	28.03.29	737	04.04.30
431	26.01.29	498	14.12.28	613	07.02.30	675	05.05.28	738	02.04.30
432	15.09.28	499	27.10.28	614	28.06.29	676	06.11.28	739	13.06.29
433	07.07.28	500	02.11.28	615	21.09.29	677	06.04.29	740	10.07.29
434	17.12.28	501	21.08.28	616	09.10.29	678	25.10.28	741	21.12.29
435	05.07.28	502	06.10.28	617	26.09.29	679	11.10.28	742	15.06.29
436	05.01.29	503	06.05.28	618	20.04.29	680	16.07.29	743	12.02.30
437	12.05.28	504	05.12.29	619	10.01.30	681	17.08.29	744	26.10.29
438	21.03.29	505	11.03.29	620	13.05.29	682	28.02.30	745	24.04.29
439	15.03.29	506	22.03.29	621	14.11.28	683	07.11.29	746	20.06.29
440	02.06.28	507	15.02.29	622	13.07.28	684	23.11.29	747	20.11.29
441	21.03.30	508	04.04.29	623	08.01.29	685	01.02.30	748	22.07.29
442	11.05.29	509	06.06.28	624	04.06.27	686	24.01.30	749	12.07.29
443	13.10.28	510	06.12.28	625	16.06.27	687	27.01.30	750	02.11.29
444	05.05.28	511	02.07.28	626	16.06.27	688	08.02.30	751	13.05.29
445	26.05.28	512	29.04.29	627	20.04.26 a	689	08.01.30	752	01.07.29
446	18.09.28	513	06.01.30		23.05.27 b	690	04.05.29	753	29.04.29
447	23.03.29	514	12.12.28	628	26.07.28	691	13.02.30	754	06.09.29
448	18.03.29	515	24.07.28	629	22.08.28	692	12.03.30	755	31.12.29
449	23.12.28	516	28.08.28	630	22.09.28	693	23.11.29	756	20.11.29
450	04.05.28	517	09.03.29	631	26.05.28	694	22.10.29	757	29.04.30
451	10.10.28	518	21.12.29	632	21.06.28	695	17.08.29	758	23.01.30
452	01.01.29	519	26.07.28	633	23.06.27	696	27.11.29	759	29.03.30
453	14.06.28	520	17.04.30	634	17.10.28	697	28.09.29	760	02.10.29
454	05.02.29	521	09.09.28	635	17.05.27	698	22.02.30	761	06.09.29
455	15.01.30	522	31.12.28	636	21.05.27	699	13.11.29	762	06.11.29
456	22.11.28	523	15.06.28	637	16.05.28	700	04.05.29	763	15.02.30
457	23.05.28	524	28.03.29	638	12.01.29	701	21.09.29	764	06.09.29
458	24.11.28	525	02.08.28	639	08.09.28	702	02.10.29	765	17.08.29
459	04.10.28	526	28.09.29	640	02.09.28	703	28.02.30	766	07.02.30
460	22.03.29	527	02.06.28	641	14.03.30	704	26.09.29	767	15.07.29
461	04.01.29	528	22.11.28	642	19.03.30	705	30.08.29	768	17.04.29
462	20.11.28	529	23.02.29	643	06.12.29	706	29.03.30	769	06.07.29
463	02.11.28	530	07.04.29	644	22.06.29	707	08.05.29	770	07.06.29
464	14.02.29	531	03.04.29	645	27.06.29	708	25.07.29	771	24.06.29
465	18.06.29	532	12.07.28						
466	02.03.29	533	22.08.28						
467	15.11.28	534	05.03.29						
468	26.05.28	535	16.03.29						

Car 627 (a) Orange livery
(b) Red livery

Car	Date	Car	Date	Car	Date	Car	Date	Car	Date
772	22.10.29	839	10.05.28	906	02.11.28	973	31.01.30	1040	08.09.27
773	01.02.30	840	16.12.27	907	07.12.29	974	26.06.29	1041	30.08.27
774	02.04.30	841	13.08.27	908	06.02.30	975	24.10.29	1042	03.09.29
775	19.06.29	842	24.12.27	909	08.02.30	976	25.04.29	1043	20.08.29
776	09.11.29	843	14.01.28	910	30.12.29	977	10.10.29	1044	08.08.29
777	15.05.29	844	19.12.27	911	22.06.29	978	17.04.30	1045	27.06.29
778	30.11.29	845	01.12.27	912	26.08.29	979	14.09.29	1046	12.06.29
779	17.10.29	846	15.09.27	913	25.04.29	980	11.01.30	1047	24.07.29
780	11.10.29	847	29.07.27	914	17.02.30	981	23.11.29	1048	30.11.29
781	20.07.29	848	22.09.27	915	20.01.30	982	30.01.30	1049	17.10.29
782	28.11.29	849	11.11.27	916	22.03.30	983	09.12.29	1050	11.11.29
783	28.02.30	850	26.07.27	917	19.10.29	984	27.08.29	1051	02.05.29
784	07.03.30	851	14.04.30	918	10.05.28	985	18.05.29	1052	08.01.30
785	09.12.29	852	13.12.29	919	25.07.29	986	22.02.30	1053	01.02.30
786	14.09.29	853	26.03.30	920	23.07.29	987	24.09.29	1054	20.02.30
787	07.05.29	854	24.10.29	921	26.02.30	988	28.09.29	1055	26.07.29
788	15.05.29	855	14.11.29	922	28.12.28	989	25.04.29	1056	26.09.29
789	06.07.29	856	21.12.29	923	05.05.28	990	22.03.30	1057	10.03.30
790	06.09.29	857	19.03.30	924	02.06.28	991	21.11.29	1058	02.08.29
791	29.04.29	858	11.09.29	925	14.07.28	992	19.05.29	1059	04.07.29
792	11.11.29	859	27.05.29	926	11.05.29	993	01.06.29	1060	17.07.29
793	21.02.30	860	13.11.29	927	28.11.29	994	18.05.29	1061	13.06.29
794	02.10.29	861	05.08.29	928	08.06.29	995	10.03.28	1062	31.03.30
795	28.10.29	862	19.09.29	929	17.06.29	996	18.05.29	1063	17.12.29
796	25.05.29	863	01.11.29	930	03.07.28	997	17.04.29	1064	23.10.29
797	07.11.29	864	01.03.30	931	13.11.28	998	30.08.29	1065	25.10.29
798	05.12.28	865	29.06.29	932	09.02.29	999	18.10.29	1066	06.01.30
799	01.09.28	866	22.02.30	933	21.02.29	1000	05.12.29	1067	05.02.30
800	22.12.28	867	27.11.29	934	19.07.28	1001	13.06.29	1068	13.12.29
801	30.06.28	868	31.08.29	935	09.04.29	1002	18.11.29	1069	08.03.30
802	17.01.30	869	17.07.29	936	20.10.28	1003	14.09.27	1070	11.12.29
803	28.11.29	870	01.01.30	937	12.02.30	1004	11.10.28	1071	22.10.29
804	01.08.29	871	21.11.29	938	28.07.28	1005	04.11.29	1072	15.03.30
805	28.09.29	872	30.10.29	939	18.04.29	1006	31.05.29	1073	13.01.30
806	13.05.29	873	28.09.29	940	17.12.29	1007	16.11.28	1074	08.07.29
807	19.02.30	874	03.09.29	941	14.11.29	1008	13.12.28	1075	13.07.29
808	30.07.29	875	02.08.29	942	06.06.29	1009	29.11.28	1076	20.03.30
809	29.04.29	876	07.10.29	943	04.01.30	1010	21.01.29	1077	01.09.27
810	22.05.28	877	04.03.30	944	17.10.29	1011	28.09.28	1078	24.11.27
811	23.02.29	878	10.02.30	945	25.10.29	1012	07.09.28	1079	17.10.27
812	12.05.28	879	22.04.29	946	30.11.29	1013	12.06.28	1080	21.03.28
813	05.03.29	880	24.07.29	947	15.06.29	1014	16.06.28	1081	28.05.27
814	16.06.28	881	07.12.29	948	25.11.29	1015	18.10.28	1082	08.12.27
815	19.09.28	882	19.12.29	949	26.09.29	1016	30.01.29	1083	20.01.28
816	20.07.28	883	14.12.29	950	25.01.30	1017	25.09.28	1084	31.12.27
817	07.06.28	884	02.12.29	951	02.11.29	1018	19.09.28	1085	21.11.27
818	14.12.28	885	25.09.29	952	01.05.29	1019	17.12.28	1086	07.05.27
819	14.12.28	886	05.08.29	953	02.03.28	1020	30.04.28	1087	20.01.28
820	27.10.28	887	11.12.29	954	05.07.29	1021	21.07.28	1088	05.12.27
821	19.01.29	888	28.08.28	955	10.10.29	1022	27.06.28	1089	12.01.28
822	23.10.28	889	03.05.28	956	03.07.29	1023	05.09.28	1090	25.02.28
823	01.01.29	890	22.09.28	957	27.01.30	1024	22.06.28	1091	15.08.27
824	18.09.28	891	06.12.28	958	14.10.29	1025	16.06.28	1092	06.10.27
825	01.02.29	892	09.02.29	959	12.12.29	1026	13.09.28	1093	04.06.27
826	14.03.29	893	26.06.28	960	07.01.30	1027	02.05.28	1094	04.10.27
827	16.03.29	894	06.10.28	961	12.10.29	1028	27.03.29	1095	14.07.27
828	18.10.28	895	07.07.28	962	13.04.29	1029	09.03.29	1096	29.09.27
829	15.01.29	896	26.01.29	963	11.01.30	1030	15.09.28	1097	28.10.27
830	26.05.28	897	22.11.29	964	05.09.29	1031	14.11.28	1098	15.10.27
831	22.11.28	898	09.06.28	965	30.12.29	1032	11.03.29	1099	14.10.27
832	07.12.28	899	10.07.28	966	20.09.29	1033	18.04.28	1100	09.12.27
833	02.06.28	900	31.08.28	967	05.12.29	1034	18.08.27	1101	11.06.27
834	21.08.28	901	10.07.28	968	29.01.30	1035	25.08.27	1102	02.01.30
835	24.11.28	902	21.12.28	969	28.09.29	1036	23.06.27	1103	18.11.29
836	24.04.29	903	09.03.29	970	08.06.29	1037	28.10.27	1104	07.11.29
837	22.02.30	904	14.02.29	971	08.02.30	1038	05.01.28	1105	22.07.29
838	10.01.29	905	09.03.29	972	10.01.30	1039	28.11.27	1106	04.10.29

Car	Date	Car	Date	Car	Date	Car	Date	Car	Date
1107	13.06.29	1174	10.10.27	1241	12.09.27	1308	19.11.29	1375	28.11.28
1108	05.12.29	1175	01.03.28	1242	27.07.27	1309	28.10.29	1376	19.05.28
1109	13.02.29	1176	09.01.28	1243	08.03.28	1310	18.07.29	1377	12.02.29
1110	15.11.29	1177	04.01.28	1244	16.03.28	1311	21.06.29	1378	05.10.28
1111	18.09.29	1178	02.01.28	1245	23.08.27	1312	18.05.29	1379	19.12.28
1112	27.03.30	1179	17.05.27	1246	24.06.27	1313	23.01.30	1380	21.08.29
1113	05.06.29	1180	17.04.28	1247	05.05.27	1314	15.07.29	1381	29.01.30
1114	18.09.29	1181	27.07.27	1248	19.11.27	1315	11.05.29	1382	11.07.29
1115	08.05.29	1182	03.12.27	1249	28.01.28	1316	08.07.29	1383	31.07.29
1116	06.01.30	1183	05.05.28	1250	07.05.27	1317	05.06.29	1384	30.11.29
1117	02.01.30	1184	21.09.28	1251	23.02.28	1318	05.10.29	1385	20.04.29
1118	06.02.30	1185	06.09.28	1252	08.06.29	1319	12.09.29	1386	01.02.30
1119	04.12.29	1186	13.11.28	1253	27.07.29	1320	18.01.30	1387	18.07.29
1120	09.10.29	1187	14.04.28	1254	05.10.29	1321	16.09.29	1388	06.05.29
1121	07.10.29	1188	27.12.28	1255	12.03.30	1322	18.12.29	1389	18.02.30
1122	02.01.30	1189	14.03.29	1256	09.10.29	1323	20.04.29	1390	15.03.30
1123	23.01.30	1190	15.08.28	1257	09.05.29	1324	14.11.29	1391	29.01.30
1124	04.01.30	1191	30.10.28	1258	29.09.28	1325	14.11.29	1392	11.01.30
1125	19.06.29	1192	08.12.28	1259	31.10.28	1326	11.12.29	1393	10.06.29
1126	20.10.28	1193	25.10.28	1260	13.06.28	1327	23.08.29	1394	26.09.28
1127	24.01.29	1194	18.08.28	1261	27.04.29	1328	26.09.29	1395	21.04.28
1128	23.05.28	1195	22.12.28	1262	23.03.29	1329	11.12.29	1396	28.04.28
1129	04.08.28	1196	23.06.28	1263	21.02.29	1330	15.08.28	1397	08.04.29
1130	12.02.29	1197	28.03.29	1264	26.02.29	1331	14.02.29	1398	13.06.28
1131	03.10.28	1198	19.04.28	1265	26.09.29	1332	19.01.29	1399	13.09.28
1132	01.12.28	1199	26.04.28	1266	27.02.30	1333	01.07.29	1400	06.04.29
1133	23.05.28	1200	01.01.29	1267	03.07.28	1334	25.08.28	1401	02.05.28
1134	04.01.29	1201	24.01.29	1268	18.12.28	1335	14.06.28	1402	08.06.28
1135	23.05.28	1202	14.07.28	1269	18.08.28	1336	21.02.29	1403	02.10.28
1136	11.06.28	1203	24.07.28	1270	11.04.29	1337	17.11.28	1404	27.10.28
1137	12.01.28	1204	02.08.28	1271	11.09.29	1338	28.04.28	1405	23.02.28
1138	20.07.27	1205	07.02.29	1272	11.09.28	1339	23.02.29	1406	09.11.28
1139	21.12.27	1206	30.10.28	1273	09.01.30	1340	14.08.28	1407	05.07.28
1140	23.09.27	1207	29.11.28	1274	08.06.28	1341	02.06.28	1408	05.04.28
1141	01.06.27	1208	04.10.28	1275	11.09.28	1342	04.10.28	1409	13.04.28
1142	06.01.28	1209	28.11.28	1276	23.03.29	1343	12.04.28	1410	25.04.28
1143	05.09.27	1210	30.06.28	1277	02.02.29	1344	16.06.28	1411	02.03.29
1144	17.03.28	1211	09.08.27	1278	03.11.28	1345	14.06.28	1412	16.02.29
1145	08.09.27	1212	18.06.27	1279	11.07.28	1346	17.04.28	1413	13.10.28
1146	18.01.28	1213	08.02.28	1280	08.06.28	1347	04.04.29	1414	22.01.29
1147	28.06.28	1214	23.03.28	1281	21.07.28	1348	13.04.29	1415	10.11.28
1148	11.09.28	1215	21.01.28	1282	05.12.28	1349	06.10.28	1416	30.03.29
1149	08.06.28	1216	28.05.28	1283	28.08.28	1350	02.06.28	1417	04.07.29
1150	20.11.28	1217	02.05.28	1284	21.06.28	1351	10.01.28	1418	02.07.28
1151	09.10.28	1218	04.08.28	1285	03.06.29	1352	15.02.29	1419	16.10.28
1152	19.05.28	1219	08.12.28	1286	26.01.29	1353	19.05.28	1420	30.03.28
1153	16.06.28	1220	06.11.28	1287	17.07.28	1354	15.02.29	1421	20.08.27
1154	01.12.28	1221	17.07.28	1288	26.04.28	1355	12.01.29	1422	28.07.27
1155	04.09.28	1222	23.03.28	1289	12.09.29	1356	31.07.28	1423	03.02.28
1156	12.10.28	1223	03.08.27	1290	26.04.28	1357	17.11.28	1424	22.10.27
1157	12.10.28	1224	20.08.27	1291	22.11.29	1358	01.09.28	1425	03.11.27
1158	30.08.28	1225	02.05.27	1292	27.02.30	1359	20.04.28	1426	24.05.27
1159	13.12.28	1226	03.12.27	1293	09.01.30	1360	14.09.28	1427	01.10.29
1160	19.03.29	1227	16.07.27	1294	21.12.29	1361	07.04.28	1428	25.10.29
1161	18.08.28	1228	01.10.27	1295	21.09.29	1362	02.03.29	1429	29.11.29
1162	24.11.28	1229	25.01.28	1296	30.09.29	1363	12.07.28	1430	19.10.29
1163	23.02.29	1230	09.03.28	1297	04.09.29	1364	09.05.28	1431	04.09.29
1164	12.05.28	1231	09.08.27	1298	09.05.29	1365	20.04.28	1432	26.06.29
1165	22.01.29	1232	02.07.27	1299	17.04.30	1366	27.02.29	1433	03.08.29
1166	25.03.29	1233	08.10.27	1300	29.08.29	1367	04.10.28	1434	18.02.30
1167	30.06.28	1234	30.12.27	1301	22.07.29	1368	21.08.28	1435	08.02.30
1168	12.05.28	1235	07.09.28	1302	15.04.30	1369	02.03.29	1436	18.01.30
1169	26.06.28	1236	30.04.27	1303	21.06.29	1370	16.08.28	1437	28.12.29
1170	05.01.29	1237	12.08.27	1304	03.02.30	1371	07.03.29	1438	17.10.29
1171	16.12.27	1238	26.03.28	1305	21.12.29	1372	28.01.29	1439	31.08.29
1172	21.12.27	1239	28.04.27	1306	14.03.30	1373	28.02.29	1440	10.04.30
1173	16.02.28	1240	14.07.27	1307	30.07.29	1374	23.06.28	1441	19.09.29

Car	Date	Car	Date	Car	Date	Car	Date	Car	Date
1442	01.08.29	1509	14.06.29	1576	05.03.27	1643	13.04.29	1710	12.02.30
1443	24.12.29	1510	20.11.29	1577	17.03.27	1644	31.05.28	1711	17.07.29
1444	32.01.30	1511	18.07.29	1578	11.02.28	1645	25.08.28	1712	25.07.29
1445	14,10.29	1512	15.01.30	1579	21.07.27	1646	19.12.28	1713	05.09.29
1446	02.11.29	1513	04.12.29	1580	14.02.27	1647	12.04.28	1714	16.01.30
1447	25.09.29	1514	21.09.29	1581	05.06.29	1648	30.06.28	1715	11.07.29
1448	12.09.29	1515	31.12.27	1582	22.10.27	1649	25.10.28	1716	29.03.30
1449	02.11.29	1516	29.10.27	1583	28.04.28	1650	11.07.28	1717	19.03.30
1450	29.06.29	1517	15.12.27	1584	02.03.29	1651	17.09.27	1718	24.01.30
1451	22.08.29	1518	28.03.28	1585	01.11.28	1652	03.02.27	1719	11.05.29
1452	12.06.29	1519	20.08.27	1586	23.10.28	1653	01.06.29	1720	16.11.29
1453	08.07.29	1520	07.09.27	1587	29.12.28	1654	21.09.27	1721	24.10.29
1454	03.09.29	1521	15.12.27	1588	26.07.28	1655	05.02.27	1722	02.04.30
1455	01.06.29	1522	22.12.27	1589	25.09.28	1656	29.01.27	1723	08.06.29
1456	25.09.29	1523	29.10.27	1590	26.01.27	1657	30.07.27	1724	20.12.29
1457	01.08.29	1524	28.07.27	1591	24.01.27	1658	08.07.27	1725	29.01.30
1458	05.02.30	1525	01.12.27	1592	12.10.27	1659	29.09.27	1726	20.04.29
1459	02.11.29	1526	07.01.28	1593	22.03.27	1660	28.10.27	1727	14.01.28
1460	19.02.30	1527	06.10.27	1594	12.02.27	1661	27.08.27	1728	21.01.28
1461	31.08.29	1528	24.10.27	1595	07.11.27	1662	17.03.27	1729	04.05.27
1462	08.03.30	1529	12.11.27	1596	09.11.27	1663	24.08.27	1730	27.01.28
1463	08.03.30	1530	10.12.27	1597	14.10.27	1664	02.08.27	1731	27.01.28
1464	29.06.29	1531	14.03.28	1598	19.09.27	1665	29.07.27	1732	04.02.28
1465	14.10.29	1532	30.09.27	1599	25.02.27	1666	22.05.29	1733	11.02.28
1466	12.07.29	1533	16.02.28	1600	04.07.27	1667	19.11.27	1734	18.02.28
1467	12.07.29	1534	11.08.27	1601	07.11.27	1668	12.07.27	1735	25.05.27
1468	06.11.29	1535	16.11.27	1602	03.03.27	1669	19.10.27	1736	01.03.28
1469	08.03.30	1536	16.09.27	1603	24.11.27	1670	10.09.27	1737	30.07.27
1470	05.04.30	1537	18.07.27	1604	31.01.27	1671	02.09.27	1738	29.04.27
1471	01.11.29	1538	03.02.28	1605	07.01.29	1672	27.08.27	1739	21.04.27
1472	06.03.29	1539	09.02.28	1606	06.04.29	1673	28.11.27	1740	26.04.27
1473	24.06.29	1540	20.09.27	1607	26.07.28	1674	03.09.27	1741	26.04.27
1474	28.12.29	1541	23.07.27	1608	09.01.29	1675	06.12.26	1742	06.07.27
1475	19.12.29	1542	17.06.27	1609	10.10.28	1676	06.07.28	1743	08.07.27
1476	19.12.29	1543	08.03.28	1610	18.10.28	1677	23.01.30	1744	28.06.27
1477	04.05.29	1544	31.08.27	1611	12.01.29	1678	23.05.29	1745	25.02.28
1478	05.10.29	1545	17.11.27	1612	24.12.28	1679	04.10.29	1746	23.04.27
1479	14.10.29	1546	30.06.27	1613	16.08.28	1680	20.09.29	1747	09.05.27
1480	13.11.29	1547	21.07.27	1614	01.09.28	1681	12.02.30	1748	16.05.27
1481	23.05.29	1548	09.09.27	1615	28.05.28	1682	29.05.29	1749	04.05.27
1482	26.06.29	1549	13.09.27	1616	23.05.28	1683	19.02.30	1750	18.05.27
1483	26.07.29	1550	16.05.27	1617	02.01.29	1684	07.01.30	1751	20.05.27
1484	12.10.29	1551	15.03.28	1618	14.01.29	1685	08.11.29	1752	20.05.27
1485	02.11.29	1552	16.01.28	1619	28.06.28	1686	01.01.30	1753	28.05.27
1486	12.04.30	1553	04.02.28	1620	07.02.29	1687	11.12.29	1754	26.05.27
1487	21.12.29	1554	17.05.27	1621	02.02.29	1688	23.05.29	1755	27.05.27
1488	07.11.28	1555	13.08.27	1622	07.04.28	1689	18.09.29	1756	18.06.27
1489	29.09.28	1556	25.11.27	1623	08.11.28	1690	20.11.29	1757	20.06.27
1490	05.02.29	1557	05.11.27	1624	11.12.28	1691	25.07.29	1758	21.06.27
1491	27.09.28	1558	18.02.28	1625	03.01.29	1692	26.10.29	1759	29.06.27
1492	26.04.28	1559	15.04.29	1626	23.08.28	1693	27.08.29	1760	01.07.27
1493	20.07.28	1560	26.02.28	1627	14.07.27	1694	26.06.29	1761	12.07.27
1494	08.01.29	1561	05.07.27	1628	15.06.29	1695	04.10.29	1762	16.07.27
1495	16.02.29	1562	08.10.27	1629	21.10.27	1696	03.07.29	1763	09.07.27
1496	10.12.28	1563	05.03.27	1630	11.11.27	1697	21.09.29	1764	16.07.27
1497	04.07.28	1564	21.09.27	1631	14.11.27	1698	28.09.29	1765	03.06.27
1498	24.01.29	1565	23.02.27	1632	18.10.28	1699	04.05.29	1766	20.07.27
1499	20.09.28	1566	17.01.27	1633	21.03.29	1700	03.07.29	1767	24.12.27
1500	04.02.29	1567	29.05.29	1634	16.03.29	1701	24.10.29	1768	22.07.27
1501	28.11.28	1568	24.07.28	1635	12.07.28	1702	25.05.29	1769	12.08.27
1502	15.11.28	1569	07.02.27	1636	31.01.29	1703	04.10.29	1770	06.08.27
1503	08.11.28	1570	22.01.27	1637	11.04.29	1704	26.10.29	1771	17.08.27
1504	16.01.29	1571	18.05.29	1638	28.05.28	1705	14.01.30	1772	17.08.27
1505	21.09.28	1572	23.03.27	1639	27.03.29	1706	03.09.29	1773	24.09.27
1506	21.11.28	1573	20.01.27	1640	08.08.28	1707	20.12.29	1774	26.09.27
1507	28.07.28	1574	19.03.27	1641	01.11.28	1708	10.07.29	1775	22.07.27
1508	01.06.29	1575	18.02.27	1642	31.08.28	1709	15.06.29	1776	02.11.27

Car	Date	Car	Date	Car	Date	Car	Date	Car	Date
1777	11.03.27	1792	15.01.27	1807	19.02.27	1822	28.02.27	1837	10.03.27
1778	16.03.27	1793	07.02.27	1808	19.02.27	1823	16.04.27	1838	24.03.27
1779	18.03.27	1794	04.02.27	1809	23.02.27	1824	26.02.27	1839	09.04.27
1780	20.12.26	1795	05.02.27	1810	21.02.27	1825	28.02.27	1840	12.04.27
1781	07.01.27	1796	10.02.27	1811	21.02.27	1826	07.03.27	1841	02.04.27
1782	07.01.27	1797	10.02.27	1812	24.02.27	1827	03.03.27	1842	25.03.27
1783	10.01.27	1798	11.02.27	1813	24.02.27	1828	04.03.27	1843	26.03.27
1784	16.12.26	1799	12.02.27	1814	28.01.27	1829	08.04.27	1844	29.03.27
1785	10.01.27	1800	14.02.27	1815	02.03.27	1830	05.03.27	1845	30.03.27
1786	10.01.27	1801	31.03.27	1816	25.02.27	1831	09.03.27	1846	01.04.27
1787	14.01.27	1802	16.02.27	1817	21.06.26	1832	09.03.27	1847	05.04.27
1788	17.01.27	1803	10.02.27	1818	02.03.27	1833	10.03.27	1848	18.02.27
1789	21.01.27	1804	17.02.27	1819	19.03.27	1834	12.03.27	1849	06.04.27
1790	31.01.27	1805	16.02.27	1820	09.02.27	1835	14.03.27	1850	07.04.27
1791	03.02.27	1806	17.02.27	1821	13.04.27	1836	16.04.27	1851	22.11.26

LONDON COUNTY
COUNCIL TRAMWAYS

The
PULLMAN
REVIEW
Issued in connection with
Efficiency Meetings and
Essay Competition 1932-33

The Review, published to present up-to-date information on the system.

Chapter 46
Rolling Stock
Classes HR/1, HR/2 & E/3

On 23rd November 1927 in a report to the Highways Committee, J. K. Bruce stressed the necessity for steps to be taken to develop a type of car that was suitable for replacing the original four-wheeled cars of class C, by then about 24 years old, many of which were still working over the route between London, Camberwell and Dulwich via Dog Kennel Hill. He gave the following reasons for his decision. In the first place, they were becoming quite expensive to maintain, in the same way as those of classes A and D. Secondly, 48 of these were needed to provide the services and, by increasing car speed to an average of 9¾ miles per hour on this route between Camberwell Green and Catford, as had been achieved on the remainder of the south side system, the work could be performed by 45 cars.

It was also desirable to take into account the fact that new cars would carry 74 passengers as against the 58 carried by the four-wheeled cars, and if revenue was increased by just one penny per mile, the annual gain, using 45 cars would be approximately £8,000. Together with a saving in operating expenses of some £6,200, a total improvement in finances could be about £14,200, considerably more than would be required to meet the new interest and sinking fund charges of about £10,000. At this time also, there were the first thoughts of making arrangements to reconstruct Kingsway Subway to take double deck cars.

The Experimental Class HR/1 and HR/2 Cars (Nos. 1852 & 1853)

Bruce then suggested that, in the first instance, two experimental double deck bogie cars be designed and built, these to be specifically for climbing steep hills. Preliminary plans drawn up included developments and improvements to be seen on car No. 1235 when it was shown to the Council at Camberwell car shed on 14th February 1924, and which were approved for inclusion in future batches of new cars.

Tenders and orders for component parts for the new cars were prepared in March and April 1928. It was also agreed that the two cars, to be known as class "HR" (hilly route), should be constructed by Tramways Department staff at the Central Repair Depot.

The first car, to be numbered 1852 and known as a class HR/1 car, was described as a "normal construction" type of bogie car, similar in design to the latest class E/1 cars, with a wooden lower deck body mounted upon a solebar and underframe supplied by Hurst, Nelson at a cost of £92.10s (plus up to £12.10s for extra work) in the same manner and style as applied to class E/1 cars, except that several more modern features were to be incorporated.

Body construction of the lower saloon, timber framed and panelled on a steel underframe, differed however, in having the centre verticaal pillars widened to 10½ in. to give added strength to the body, by being reinforced with a continuous steel channel section which went up from fixings on the truss plates on either side of the car body, and over the roof of the lower saloon. By this means, it was expected that lateral movement of the bodywork would be prevented and the use of truss rods would be unnecessary. The wide pillars also proved to be suitable places upon which to fit the lower saloon ventilator operating handles, each of which employed a sliding mechanism instead of the more usual rack and pinion screw arrangement. To allow for access to the four-motor equipment, the floor hatches were re-arranged, which made it necessary for four sets of transverse seats to be provided, with the four longitudinal end seats each accommodating four passengers, so making provision for 28 passengers. All other fittings were to be similar to those used on the improved or "pullmanised" cars.

The top deck structure and fitments were of the same style as were subsequently specified for the "reconstructed subway cars", consisting of strengthened "Alpax" aluminium sections which supported eight independently operated main side windows and four "conductors' sliding windows", with a sheet metal-clad totally enclosed top cover over the fully upholstered turnover transverse seats and fixed end canopy benches, which were furnished in deep maroon leatherette, and which provided places for 46 passengers on a level floor.

Numbered 1853 and to be known as class HR/2, the second car body was stated as being "mainly metal" in construction, and for this a complete steel underframe and body shell structure was supplied by Hurst, Nelson for £280 plus up to £12.10s for extra work. In this case, the lower saloon was of steel plate box formation, with four equally spaced windows and, being completely straight-sided, gave a slightly wider floor space in the lower saloon. Seating was as for No. 1852. The upper deck structure was also similar to that used on the HR/1.

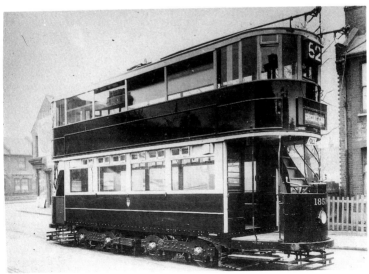

The first all-metal double deck car in the LCC fleet, No. 1853, ran on equal-wheel bogies, with the plough carrier bogie mounted. It was destroyed by bombing during the 1939-45 war. (LCC official view)

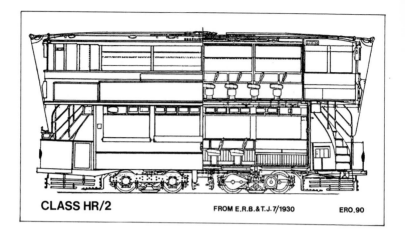

CLASS HR/2   FROM E.R.B.&T.J. 7/1930   ERO.90

Each set of main upper deck fitments, supplied by G. D. Peters & Co., consisted of:-

8 balanced windows for upper decks,	£38.14. 8d per car set.
4 conductors' sliding windows,	£ 8. 2. 0d per car set.
Seats for lower saloons,	£67. 3. 0d per car sets.
Seats for upper decks,	£118.15. 0d per car set.

Sets of swing-bolster equal-wheeled bogie trucks with steel plated sides were specified for both cars, each with a plough carrier bolted to one truck of each set. Roller bearing axleboxes constrained by hornways were fitted, together with magnetic track brakes, the shoes of which were also to be capable of being used as mechanical slipper brakes, with interconnection between the magnet shoes and handbrake wheel blocks. Hurst, Nelson supplied these items at £505 per car set, plus up to £25 for extra work.

On 20th December 1927, an initial capital estimate for £6,500 was approved, to enable construction of these two cars to proceed. Ultimately, another £560 was voted for additional work which had to be undertaken.

Two sets of electrical equipments were supplied by Metro-Vickers Electrical Co. Ltd. at a cost of £1,383 per set, with a £50 contingency allowance for any extra work required. Each set consisted of:-

Four motors of type MV 109, each of 35 h.p. complete with gears.
One set of magnetic brake equipment with four magnets.
One run-back prevention device.
Two controllers of type MV OK29B.
Three automatic circuit breakers.
One Interlock circuit breaker.
One choke coil.
Two two-way inter-connected power changeover switches
    (plough to trolley).
One lighting changeover switch.
One set of plough collector gear.
One set of main resistances.
One set of battens and screens for resistances.
One set of cables and hoses.
Two trolley booms and bases.

Both cars had similar main dimensions, even allowing for the HR/2 body being straight sided. These were:-

Length over fenders	33 ft. 10 in.
Length over top covers	32 ft. 5 in.
Length over body, lower saloon	22 ft. 2 in.
Width over guard rails	6 ft. 10 in.
Height, rail level to underside of trolley base seating	15 ft. 7¼ in.
Pivotal centres of bogie trucks	11 ft. 0 in.
Truck wheelbase	5 ft. 0 in.
Extreme wheelbase	16 ft. 0 in.
Wheel diameter	2 ft. 2½in.
Estimated weight, fully loaded	20 tons

In both cases the new, large, ten-inch external service number plates were fitted.

Two 35 h.p. motors were fitted into each bogie, both designed to work at half the normal line voltage and permanently connected in series. On these two cars, the motors were supported by springs fixed to the bogie frame, but in the case of the later production batch they were suspended on solid bearings.

All axle and motor bearings were of the roller type, supplied by the Skefco Ball Bearing Co. and these were designed to have a working life of at least 500,000 miles, with 20,000 miles run between attention for lubrication.

The controllers were specially modified to be suitable for four-motor operation. An electrically operated run-back preventer was also provided, which was a device which automatically controlled the "run back" speed of a car to between one and two m.p.h. when the driving controller was in the "off" position and the reversing key in the normal position for going forwards. Use of the handbrake was considered to be sufficient to bring the car to rest.

On the two experimental cars, the wheelbase of the trucks at 5 ft. gave insufficient clearance between the inner ends of the truck frames to allow body mounted plough carriers to be fitted, whereas on the main batch of cars, later described, the wheelbase was set at 4 ft. 9 in.

The two new cars were paraded at Stangate on 26th February 1929 for inspection by members of the Council, after which they went back to Charlton to have the finishing touches put to them. After an official inspection by Col. A. H. C. Trench at Camberwell car shed on 17th April 1929, the two cars were then taken to Dog Kennel Hill, where brake tests were carried out. Resulting from the inspections, both cars were licensed for service on 25th April for an initial period of six months. The only condition placed upon the Council was that both cars should be fitted with back-sanding gear. This was a device, controlled from an extra foot pedal on the driving platform, which allowed the motorman to apply sand to the track from the rear sand-hoppers in the event of a run-back. Both cars went into public service on 26th April, and were entirely successful.

Meanwhile, in a statement issued to the Highways Committee on 29th January 1929, Bruce set out the position with regard to the state of the rolling stock and what he considered to be future requirements. He noted that after the "reconstruction" of the 50 single deck subway cars to double deck form, 304 cars would still need to be replaced. After explaining the financial implications involved in the provision of new cars, he came to the conclusion that the principle of obtaining 300 should be adopted, but a first order for 150 at an estimated cost of £140,000 should be aimed at. Such an order would consist of 50 cars of class HR/2, together with 100 of another new class.

The Class E/3 Car

With the success of the new all-metal body style, the Council agreed to introduce a new class of car to be known as E/3, in which the bodies would be mounted on class 4 maximum traction bogie trucks on an improved design. Seating arrangement would be identical with that on the HR/2 cars. It was also intended that cars of this class would be used on the subway services once reconstruction was complete.

The Main Orders
Class HR/2 Cars (Nos. 1854-1903) & Class E/3 Cars (Nos. 1904-2003)

The Council anticipated that the Development and Unemployment Schemes, Development (Loans Guarantees and Grants) Act, 1929, which authorised H.M. Treasury to guarantee certain loans, would underwrite the venture to the estimated £140,000, which was eventually agreed.

On 17th March 1929, the Council agreed to call for tenders for:-
100 bodies for new maximum traction bogie cars to be known as E/3:
50 bodies for new equal wheel bogie cars to be known as HR/2:
100 sets of bogie trucks (LCC class 4) for E/3 cars:
50 sets of bogie trucks (LCC class 6) for HR/2 cars:
150 sets of electrical equipments:
150 sets of magnetic brake equipments.

On 30th July, the prices quoted for the new cars were published, and dealing firstly with the class HR/2 cars, the contracts subsequently agreed upon were:-

50 double deck bodies, English Electric Co. Ltd.	£ 87,400
50 sets of class 6 centre bearing swing bolster equal wheel trucks, Electro-Magnetic Brake Co. Ltd.	£ 15,600
50 complete sets of electrical equipments and assembly, Metropolitan Vickers Ltd. (Trolley equipment to come either from the EMB Co. or Brecknell Willis & Co.)	£ 60,000
50 sets of magnetic track brakes, Estler Bros.	£ 2,717.10s

	£165,717.10s

Cost on this basis was to be £3,314. 7s per car, but the final cost for the 50 cars worked out at £3,450 per car, or a total of £172,500.

With regard to the cars of class E/3, the contract prices quoted were:-

100 bodies, Hurst, Nelson.	£172,200
100 sets of class 4 centre bearing swing bolster maximum traction trucks, fitted with roller bearing axleboxes, Electro-Magnetic Brake Co. Ltd.	£ 24,900
100 complete sets of electrical equipments and assembly, English Electric co. Ltd. (Trolley equipment to come either from the EMB Co. or Brecknell Willis & Co.)	£ 83,750
100 sets of magnetic track brakes, Estler Bros.	£ 5,435

	£286,285

Cost on this basis was to be £2,862.17s per car, but the actual cost worked out at £2,990 or a total of £299,000. The 150 new cars cost the Council £471,500.

One of the reasons for the introduction of new cars with all metal bodies, was that they would be suitable for use on any part of the system, including, if necessary, the Kingsway Subway, once it had been deepened to accommodate double deck cars. The class HR/2 car, was developed, however, primarily as a "hill climber", using four motors and equal wheel trucks, and were put to work on services operating over Dog Kennel Hill, Dulwich. Car No. 1883 is seen at the terminus at Peckham Rye. *(Courtesy: R. Elliott)*

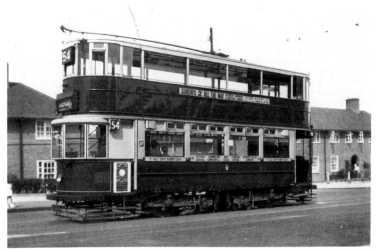

The other class of car, the E/3, was fitted with a pair of maximum traction trucks, each containing one motor, and became the standard car used on the new services working through Kingsway Subway in 1931. Some, however, were worked on other services at times, and No. 2002 is seen on service 54, standing at the terminus in Downham Way, Grove Park. *(Courtesy: R. Elliott)*

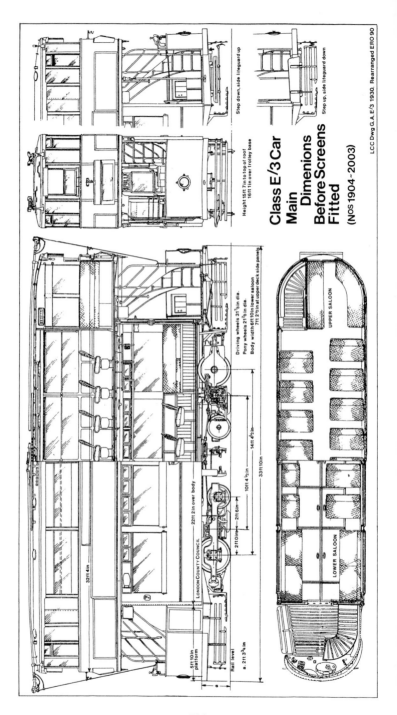

Class E/3 Car
Main
Dimenions
Before Screens
Fitted
(Nos 1904-2003)

LCC Dwg G.A.E/3 1930. Rearranged ERO 90

Step down, side lifeguard up

Step up, side lifeguard down

Height 15ft 7in to top of roof
16ft 1in over trolley base

Driving wheels 31⅝in dia.
Pony wheels 21⅝in dia.
Body width 6ft 10in lower saloon
7ft 2½in at upper deck side panels

14ft 4½in

33ft 10in

LONDON COUNTY COUNCIL

22ft 2in over body

32ft 4in

10ft 4½in

2ft 6in

2ft 10in

6ft 10in
platform

Rail level
a. 2ft 3¾in

UPPER SALOON

LOWER SALOON

746

On both types of car, plough carriers were body-mounted. This allowed the use of truck frames which were not specially made to carry ploughgear.

The final addition to the class E/3 cars was to be the fitting of "Alpax" vestibule screens, manufactured by Lightalloys Ltd., Willesden, London, and making use of metal alloy sections in which to place the panes of safety glass. Quoted cost as at 6th November 1930 was £157 per car, which was later reduced to £120 per car set. The fitting of screens required the approval of the Ministry of Transport, while the Metropolitan Police had to issue special licenses before cars so fitted could be operated in public service. In anticipation of this, the Council had applied to the police in January 1930 for a special license to experimentally operate cars in service fitted with drivers' screens. In the first instance, only a three-months' license was issued, but this was later extended, and finally the requirement for a license was removed althogether.

Rear view mirrors for the use of motormen were also fitted outside the staircases. In the case of open-fronted cars, these were arranged in such a way that they could be adjusted and left in position during the journey. However, with the use of vestibule screens, the mirrors would need to be adjusted to such an angle that they may have been hit by vehicles passing on the near side of the tramcars. To overcome this, each mirror was spring loaded and provided with an extended handle, by which the motorman could bring it to the required position at stopping places.

More Class HR/2 Cars (Nos. 101-160)

With the success of the class HR/2 cars on the steep Dog Kennel Hill, the General Manager, by then T. E. Thomas, made a request on 23rd September 1930 that more be ordered for use on Highgate Hill. One car had been taken over from Camberwell on 3rd September (via the long route through Hammersmith and the MET lines) for special tests to be made, at which Col. Trench and Lt. Col. Woodhouse were present from the Ministry of Transport Railway Inspectorate. The tests were successful and approval was given for the use of this type of car on the hill.

The reasons given for the request were that, in the first place the downhill track on Highgate Hill was "worn out". Renewal of the special slot rail for emergency braking would require the closure of the line while the work was being carried out. Secondly, cars of class M, which were smaller than the standard car, meant that more cars were needed to maintain a satisfactory service than if bogie cars were used. Lastly, a number of brakesmen were required to insert brake gear into the slot conduit at the bottom of the hill and then travel with the cars on the hill, to apply the brake from the rear platform if an emergency arose.

Col. Trench, in his report, stated that " ... back sanding equipment has been added, worked by a separate foot pedal, and the control of the car has been somewhat altered. The run-back preventer ... operates without the motorman altering his controller key and, if there is a power failure, it automatically comes in if the controller is in the 'off' position. If it is on the 'series' notches, the controller must be switched to 'off' or to a braking position. It has been tested up and down the hill under all conditions of traffic and weather and is satisfactory. Under these conditions, it would not be necessary to retain the slot brake arrangement".

*Cars of classes E/3 and HR/2 proved to be successful, both on the
Kingsway Subway and the Dulwich services.   Once the E/3 cars had
been fitted with vestibule screens, as is seen on No. 1935, they became
the model upon which the last new batch of HR/2 bodies was based.
Apart from differences in truck design, braking equipment detail and
the fact that no trolley poles were fitted to the HR/2 cars, the bodies
were almost identical as is shown on No. 139.
(Courtesy: [left] L T Museum. U37687: [right] Tramway Museum Society)*

Resulting from this, the Council agreed to purchase 60 more new
cars of class HR/2, built to standard measurements, as an extension of
existing contracts and at an expected price of £182,500, which included
£7,200 for supplementary air brakes (if required) and £1,300 for any
incidental payments.   In this case, the cars were to be allocated fleet
numbers made vacant by the disposal, several years earlier, of the
cars of class B. They were to be Nos. 101-160.

Actual detailed costings were:-

60 bodies with vestibule screens, Hurst, Nelson	£ 89,000
fog lamps, two per body	£ 300
plough carrier channels and brackets	£ 1,100
miscellaneous extras	£ 1,500
60 sets of class 6A centre bearing, equal-wheel	
swing bolster, radial arm trucks, the EMB Co.	£ 21,000
miscellaneous extras	£ 1,500
60 sets of electrical equipments, Metropolitan Vickers	£ 49,800
trolley poles (two per car)	£ 3,000
assembly,	£ 2,700
plough collector gear	£ 900
miscellaneous extras	£ 2,100
60 sets of magnetic track brakes, Metropolitan Vickers	£ 3,240
incidentals	£ 300

	£176,550

Cost per car was £2,942.10s.

The final batch of class HR/2 cars, numbered 101-160, incorporated several new features, including an electric run-back brake and very powerful slipper brakes. The bodies were also mounted on a new type of four-motor equal wheel truck. (Courtesy: Tramway Museum Society)

However, as trolley poles were not supplied by contract, and plough gear was instead provided by the LCC, the following changes to costs were made.

Deduct:	non-provision of trolley poles	£ 3,000
	non provision of plough collector gear	£ 900

	New sub-total	£172,650
Add:	provision of ploughgear by LCC	£ 420

Cost per car, £2,884.10s.		£173,070

Deliveries commenced early in 1931 and by the end of the year nearly all the new cars were in service. Although mainly intended for use on the Highgate Hill line, an allocation was made to Camberwell car shed for use on the Dulwich services. As the cars were to be used only on conduit equipped tracks it was not considered to be worthwhile that trolley poles should be fitted; that could come later, if required. Similarly, the supplementary air brakes were not fitted, reliance being placed upon the magnetic track brakes in conjunction with the use of slipper brakes and run-back-preventers.

There were slight variations made in the style of livery adopted for this batch of cars. Whereas on other cars of classes HR/2 and E/3, black lining had been applied to the side panels, this was omitted on Nos. 101-160. The other main difference was that the trucks were given a protective red-oxide finish instead of black or grey.

The Class 6A Equal-Wheel Bogie Truck

The trucks were unusual in that, instead of the usual hornways and springs which supported the axleboxes, they were contained on the ends of radial arms, which were pivoted to the truck sides. During the

A radial-arm suspended axlebox was developed by the Electro Magnetic Brake Company, which was applied to the equal wheel bogie trucks used under HR/2 cars Nos. 101-160.   *(E M B photograph)*

course of construction by the Electro-Magnetic Brake Co. Ltd. of the initial batch of 100 sets of equal-wheel trucks, experiments were conducted on one set with a view to reducing wear on the axlebox sides and hornways fitted to the truck frame, which in turn would be instrumental in reducing the amount of noise generated by movement of these parts.

This experiment consisted of omitting the sideframe hornways altogether, and substituting radial arms to carry the wheel axles. New axleboxes were made and heavy forged pins were bolted through the sideframes co-axially with the pinion centres of the motors. On each side of each wheelset, a cast-steel radial arm was bolted to the axle-box, which in turn was bushed and pivoted to the forged pin. As no hornways were fitted, there was ample clearance between the axleboxes and frame. Wearing plates were fitted on the inside faces at the moving end of the arms and also on the outside faces of the frame, which eliminated end thrust from the axles. The motors were rigidly bolted to the frame of the truck, while the geometric design of the radial arms ensured that the gear centres were accurately maintained.

Further Proposals

With regard to proposals which were made to cover the 1931-32 programme, an estimate was given for the purchase of a further 150 new cars, as follows:-

120 of class E/3 at £2,990 each including £130 each for vestibules	£358,800
30 of class HR/2 at £3,570 each, including £130 each for vestibules	£107,100
Plus £2,100 for general work and engineering	£ 2,100
	£468,000

The reasons given for this proposal were, that when the Eltham to Grove Park line was completed, for which the Council was obtaining the necessary Parliamentary authority, 13 more cars would be required while, if class HR/2 cars were used on Highgate Hill, eight less than the class M cars "now in use" would reduce the deficiency to sixty.

The remainder would be sufficient to cover the withdrawal of the last of the old cars of classes A and D, and provide a positive reserve of rolling stock.

It had been hoped that an unemployment grant would be made available with which to purchase the proposed additional cars, but this, however, was refused. Nevertheless, on 24th February 1931, the Highways Committee and General Manager decided to go ahead with preliminary work necessary with regard to the tendering process, in the hope that deliveries could start at the beginning of April 1931. This, however, was a forlorn hope. A new experimental car then under construction, caused, in the first place, a reconsideration of the car building policy. At the same time, the uncertainty surrounding the proposal that an all-embracing passenger transport board should be formed, caused the project to be at first postponed and then cancelled.

The Body-Mounted Plough Carrier

There was one aspect in the provision of new cars which proved to be of benefit to the Council. With the construction of the two new cars of class HR/2, it was not found possible to incorporate a new device for carrying the car plough. It had long been realised that something better than the truck-mounted carrier, then in general use, should be considered and, as a result, the body-mounted carrier was developed. On 12th May 1931, an order was given to Messrs. Higgs & Hill to supply 500 new carriers, which were to be used to replace the older items on cars of class E and E/1, and to provide for sufficient to go on the new cars.

The new carrier consisted of a metal framework which contained the plough channels and bus-bars, and was a completely self-contained unit. It was bolted to the channel iron sole bars of the standard class E and E/1 cars, being fitted slightly off-centre so that the existing bogie trucks could continue to be used without further modification.

This plough carrier assembly was designed by the LCC to enable it to be fitted to the solebars of wooden bodied cars, and to the base frame of metal bodied ones. (*L T Museum. H11530*)

The Experimental Car of 1932: No. 1, "Bluebird"

The first indication that the LCC was about to embark on the design of a completely new type of tramcar came in a reference made by the General Manager on 24th October 1929 in the following words. "As to an experimental type of double ended bogie tramcar for service on rails with wide rack spaces" (sic). Expenditure to a maximum of £5,000 plus £150 for incidentals was authorised. It was also intended that the second batch of 150 new cars which were being considered at that time (and which never materialised) would also be to the new design. The idea seemed to be to make up something approaching the more modern image of "Bluebell" or the "Felthams" of the Company Tramways, but due to depot traverser clearance problems, the LCC was forced to keep to a maximum length of 36 feet, but at the same time, to provide a realistic number of seats in the car. The idea of a new type of car was restated in Highways Committee minutes dated 3rd July 1930, at the same time as mention was made of the use of concealed lighting in cars, and an experiment was proposed.

It was also intended to design an equal-wheel bogie car employing only two motors to drive the four axles, instead of the four-motor design of cars of the HR/2 class. A set of bogies was ordered from the EMB Company, while Hurst, Nelson was to provide the steel framework of the lower deck and the Alpax Aluminium Company would provide the framework for the upper deck. This eventually proved to be an error of judgement, as the aluminium in contact with the steel of the lower saloon set up corrosion of the upper deck pillars. After about two years they all had to be strengthened with gusset plates.

The Body Structure

The lower deck of the car body was built up from mild steel plates, welded together by the electric arc process. Vertical and lateral loads were taken on channel sections, which continued vertically above the normal level of the lower saloon roof to the height of the bottom rails of the upper saloon window frames. The frames for the windows

The final development of the LCC tramcar was to be seen with the appearance in 1932 of experimental car No. 1 ("Bluebird"). It was also to be the only one of its class.   (Courtesy: Tramway Museum Society)

in the upper saloon were each cast as a complete unit from "Alpax" aluminium alloy, and bolted into position near to the top edges of the main steel side structures, the underside rails of the roof and to each other. The upper saloon was constructed of aluminium alloy castings and bolted to the edges of the main steel side structures. The roof cover consisted of a single sheet of steam-shaped plywood, while the lower saloon roofsticks, or carlines, were fabricated from mild steel angle pieces laid transversely, making the upper saloon floor almost flat in profile.

The lower saloon and platforms were constructed on one level, necessitating the use of a new design of headstock. Made of cast steel, this was to allow the platform bearers, in the event of a head-on collision, to pass through the main frame, so reducing the chance of buckling the frame. A layer of "Insulwood" was provided between the timber floor and the linoleum, in order to reduce the level of noise coming from the motors and trucks.

Interior Arrangements

Seating was for 28 passengers in the lower saloon and for 38 in the upper, with all seats of the "armchair" type, in pairs and with reversible backs. The row of seats on one side of the car was staggered in relation with those on the other, to facilitate passenger movement. Upholstery in both saloons was of blue moquette with panels of rexine, while the floors were covered in blue "battleship" linoleum. Drop windows in the lower saloon provided for improved ventilation in warm weather, while louvres on the windows were so arranged that the air was changed with sufficient frequency under all conditions.

There were no doors or bulkheads in the lower saloon, which allowed free access to the upper saloon from either end of the car via the straight "easy tread" staircases. The large space at the front end was also useful in accommodating standing passengers during the rush periods. When the car was in service, the rear door was kept open and the front door closed. At terminal points (or in the Kingsway Subway) the front door, under the sole control of the motorman, was operated by him by means of an air control valve, which also raised and lowered the step. Fully screened vestibule cabins were provided for the motorman, from which point he had a clear view of traffic, while facilities included a seat, air brakes, electrically-operated warning gong, air-operated windscreen wiper and sanding gear.

Main dimensions were:-

Length overall	36 ft. 0 in.
Lenght of body at floor level, including cabs	43 ft. 9 in.
Width, outside, lower saloon	7 ft. 3 in.
Width, outside, at cantrail of upper saloon	6 ft. 11 in.
Height from rail to top of lower saloon floor	2 ft. 5 in.
Height from rail to top of roof at centre	15 ft. 3 in.
Height, rail to top of trolley base cover plates	15 ft. 11 in.

Lighting

Diffused lighting was employed in both saloons, with specially designed reflectors giving a more efficient distribution of available light. In traditional manner, during the hours of darkness the car displayed two "police lights" at the leading end, together with one headlamp centrally mounted in the dashplate. A single off-side red rear light was also displayed. All window frames and other bright parts were chromium plated.

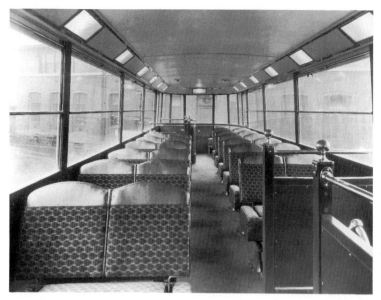

The upper saloon of No. 1 was of completely new design, with well upholstered reversible seating. The traditional stairhead draughtscreens were also dispensed with. (Greater London Photograph Library)

Pairs of comfortable transverse double seats of reversible pattern were installed in the lower saloon. Concealed lighting provided adequate illumination at night. (Greater London Photograph Library)

The Experimental Trucks

As the special trucks would need to be fitted beneath the car in a different way to those used beneath class HR/2 cars, it was decided that they would be first placed beneath another car for testing. An E/3 car, No. 1986 was used, and its underframe specially modified to take the new trucks, whose design was such that, instead of using spur drives, chain drives were substituted, but were unsatisfactory, as they kept breaking when under load. A modified set of chains was fitted, but these continued to give trouble, resulting in the decision being made to modify the truck by lengthening the radial arms of the axleboxes, which would bring the pivotal points of these nearer in line with the motor armatures. This was carried out in an attempt to try to prevent the chains "snatching" when the car was very lightly or heavily loaded, but was also unsuccessful, and the trouble persisted. It was then noticed that the car bolsters were becoming damaged, which in turn affected the underframe of 1986, resulting in the car vibrating badly when rounding curves. It was at this point that the experimental trucks were discarded.

One of the pair of experimental chain drive bogie trucks used beneath E/3 car No. 1986. The chain casing, which acted as an oil bath is to be seen in the foreground. (Greater London Photograph Library)

The Trucks

Within two months of the date of the beginning of the Tramways & Light Railways Conference which was to be held in London in May 1932, for which the car was to be the centre piece, the LCC still had no suitable bogies to put under it. It was then that a pair of class 6A bogies, each with two 35 h.p. motors were taken from HR/2 car No. 160, fitted with air brakes and placed beneath No. 1.

Electric Brake Equipment

With the use of four-motor equipment, where two pairs of motors are permanently connected in series, the use of cross-field braking connections became possible. This was a departure from the standard practice of having the motors connected in parallel with an equaliser, and overcame the possibility of setting up out-of-balance currents, a condition which could cause brake failure.

Another benefit obtained when using this method of wiring, was that electric "run-back" braking was obtained on the parallel notches, the "off" position and brake notches of the controller without the need for the motorman to "throw" the reversing key. (This arrangement was not recommended for use with two-motor equipments, as in the event of an open-circuit or earth fault on one motor, no electric braking would be available).

Livery

A distinctive livery of royal blue and white was adopted, with both colours being applied in such a way that a "streamlined" effect, so much in evidence during that period, was imparted to the appearance of the car. As this was also to have been the first example of another generation of LCC cars, it was given the number "1" and given the name "Bluebird", which it bore all through its days in service in London (even though it was eventually repainted in red livery by the LPTB).

Destination Equipment

In a complete departure from the traditional LCC style of providing information to intending passengers, all details were displayed on roller blinds. The destination and service number blinds at either end of the car were contained in composite inset boxes, while the route inform-ation, normally displayed on long wooden boards on either side of a car, was provided in "window" boxes fitted into the body of the car beneath each staircase.

In Service

Owing to the short time which was available after completion of the car and before it was to be used during the Tramways & Light Railways Conference in May 1932, testing had to be carried out at night, which may have accounted for the fact that tramway observers of that period thought that a new "night car" was about to be brought into service. After the Conference, at which No. 1 was an outstanding success, the car went into public service in July, working from Holloway car shed on subway services 33 and 35, and was taken charge of by a special cadre of motormen and conductors, who took great pride in their vehicle.

Having got the new car in service, the LCC was left with two cars without trucks, Nos. 160 and 1986. As No. 160 was undamaged, the underframe of the car was modified to accept the original trucks from 1986, and thus 160 became the only E/3 car without trolley poles. The damaged frame of 1986 was subsequently made good and a spare set of class 4 trucks was made up at the CRD and fitted to the car, which, in the opinion of some of the works' staff, became the best riding car of the E/3 class. After the end of the Second World War, a spare set of trucks of the proper type became available from a bomb-damaged car, and were fitted beneath 1986.

The Leyton Class E/3 Cars (Nos. 161-210)

One clause in the agreement made between the LCC and the UDC was to the effect that Leyton should, within a period of ten years, provide sufficient new cars to maintain the working stock used in the area. In 1929, the LCC indicated that it thought that Leyton should purchase 50 new cars up to the latest standard, in order to place them on an equal footing with London. Eventually, this was agreed to, and 50 class E/3 cars were ordered. The fleet numbers allocated to them were from 161 to 210, carrying on the new arrangement whereby the numbers of the cars which had been disposed of from the LCC fleet would be used again.

Contracts were formally agreed to on 26th November 1930 for the construction and delivery of these, which were to be assembled and tested at the Central Repair Depot, at an additional cost of £1,275.

Details were:-

50 bodies, English Electric Co. Ltd.	£ 89,375
50 sets, class 4 centre bearing swing bolster maximum traction trucks, EMB Co. Ltd.	£ 13,225
50 complete sets, electrical equipments and assembly, British Thomson-Houston Co. Ltd. (trolley equipment as for previous new cars)	£ 40,675
50 sets, magnetic track brakes, Metropolitan Vickers	£ 2,537
	£145,812

Cost on this basis was to be £2,916. 4. 10d per car.

As the cars were nominally the property of Leyton, the Urban District Council coat-of-arms was displayed on each side of every car. Bogie truck sides on some of the cars were fitted with decorative panels in an attempt to present a pleasing appearance, but these were very soon discarded. Vestibule screens made of "Alpax" alloy sections, with toughened glass panels, were supplied as part of the main contract.

An agreement was made on 2nd July 1931 that the car ploughs (at three per car) be supplied to Leyton by the LCC for £9. 9s. per set and complete body mounted plough carriers at £7. 7s. each, making a total of £840 for these items, which made the total cost £146,652, or £2,933. 0.10d per car. It was stipulated that 25 were to be available by the end of June 1931, with the remainder in service no more than one year later. The new cars were placed on service 61, working between "Baker's Arms" and Aldgate via Whipps Cross and Stratford, service 55 between Bloomsbury and Leyton Station via Hackney, and service 81 between Bloomsbury and Woodford via Essex Road and Hackney, and upon which they normally worked until after the undertakings were taken over by the LPTB.

In conjunction with the purchase of the new cars, Leyton also agreed that a re-arrangement of the Leyton car shed should take place, at the same time installing a traverser into the layout. This machine was purchsed from Messrs. Holt & Willetts for £425, plus another £275 for the electrical equipment, and £1,225 for the construction of the traverser pit. Work was completed on this part of the project by the end of June 1931.

One extra charge imposed upon Leyton was that the UDC increase the quantity of power available for running the cars up to 2,250 kW on normal weekdays, and 2,500 kW on Bank Holidays and Sundays between Easter and 30th September of each year. Finally, the LCC/Leyton agreement was extended on 1st July 1931 for another 25 years.

CLASS &	FLEET Nos.	YEAR	BUILDER	TRUCKS TYPE	& CLASS	MOTORS	CONT-ROLLERS	SEATS LS	SEATS US	LENGTH		WIDTH OVERALL		HEIGHT TO ROOF		WHEELBASE TRUCK		WHEELBASE TOTAL		WEIGHT T	C	Q
E	402-426	1905	Hurst Nelson	2 x M & G	4	2 x W 200	W 90M	30	46	33 ft	6 in	7 ft	2 in	15 ft	9¾ in	4 ft	6 in	14 ft	6 in	14	8	0
E	427-551	1906	Hurst Nelson	2 x M & G	4	2 x W 200	W T2A	30	46	33	6	7	2	15	9¾	4	6	14	6	14	8	0
F	552, 556, 560, 563, 567	1906	Dick, Kerr	2 x M & G	4	2 x DK 3A	DK DB1D	36		33	6	6	10	11	0	4	6	14	6	14	8	0
F	553-5, 557-9, 561, 562, 564-6	1906	Dick, Kerr	2 x M & G	4	2 x W 200	DK DB1D	36		33	6	6	10	11	0	4	6	14	6	14	8	0
G	568-601	1907	Brush	2 x M & G	4	2 x W 200	W T2A	36		33	6	6	10	11	0	4	6	14	6	14	8	0
E	602-751	1906	Hurst Nelson	2 x M & G	4	2 x W 200	W T2A	30	46	33	6	7	2	15	9¾	4	6	14	6	14	8	0
E/1	752-1001	1907	Hurst Nelson	2 x M & G	4	2 x W 220	W T2A	32	46	33	10	7	2	15	9¾	4	6	14	6	14	14	1
E/1	1002-1051	1907	LCC	2 x M & G	4	2 x W 220	W T2A	32	46	33	10	7	2	15	9¾	4	6	14	6	14	14	1
E/1	1052-1226	1908	Hurst Nelson	2 x H & F	4	2 x W 220	W T2A	32	46	33	10	7	2	15	9¾	4	6	14	7	14	14	1
E/1	1227-1426	1909	Hurst Nelson	2 x H N	4	2 x W 220	W T2C	32	46	33	10	7	2	15	9¾	4	6	14	6	14	14	1
M	1427	1908	LCC	H N	5	2 x W 220	W T2C	24	38	29	4	7	2	15	9¾	7	6			13	14	2
M	1428-1437	1910	Hurst Nelson	H N	5	2 x W 220	W T2C	24	38	29	4	7	2	15	9¾	7	6			13	14	2
M	1438-1476	1910	Hurst Nelson	H N	5	2 x W 220	W T2C	24	38	29	4	7	2	15	9¾	7	6			13	14	2
E/1	1477-1676	1910	Brush	2 x H & F	4	2 x W 220	W T2C	32	46	33	10	7	2	15	9¾	4	6	14	6	14	14	1
M	1677-1726	1910	Brush	H & F	5	2 x W 220	W T2C	24	38	29	4	7	2	15	9¾	7	6			13	14	2
E/1	1727-1776	1922	Hurst Nelson	2 x H N	4	2 x MV 121	MV T2C	32	46	33	10	7	2	15	9¾	4	6	14	6	14	17	0
E/1	1777-1851	1922	Brush	2 x H N	4	2 x EE 31C	EE DB1	32	46	33	10	7	2	15	9¾	4	6	14	6	14	17	0
	Leyton 11-70	1906 1907	Milnes, Voss	M & G Radial		2 x W 200	W 90M	22	34	(Taken over by LCC for operational purposes in 1921)												
HR/1	1852	1929	LCC	2 x H N	6	4 x MV 105	MV OK29B	28	46	33	10	7	2	15	9¾	5	0	16	0	17	14	0
HR/2	1853	1929	LCC	2 x H N	6	4 x MV 105	MV OK29B	28	46	33	10	7	2½	15	7	5	0	16	0	18	0	0
E/1	552-601	1929	English Elec.	2 x M & G	4	2 x W 220	W T2A/T2C	27	46	33	10	7	2	15	9¾	4	6	14	6	16	8	0
HR/2	1854-1903	1930	English Elec.	2 x E M B	6	4 x MV 109	MV OK29B	28	46	33	10	7	2½	15	7	4	9	15	9	17	7	0
E/3	1904-2003	1930	Hurst Nelson	2 x E M B	4A	2 x EE126A	EE CDB2/K	28	46	33	10	7	2½	15	7	4	6	14	4½	16	6	0
HR/2	101-160	1931	Hurst Nelson	2 x E M B	6A	4 x MV109Z	MV OK37B	28	46	34	8	7	2½	15	7	4	9	15	9	17	9	0
E/3	161-210	1931	English Elec.	2 x E M B	4A	2 x BTH 116AY	MV OK38B	28	46	34	8	7	2½	15	7	4	6	14	4½	16	13	0
Exp	1	1932	LCC	2 x E M B	6A	4 x MV109Z	MV OK37B	28	38	36	0	7	3	15	2	4	9	15	9	20	6	0
ME/3	1441	1932	LCC	2 x M & G	4	2 x EE301A	W T2C	28	46	34	4	7	2	15	9¾	4	6	14	6	16	18	0
	1444	1933								34	8									18	18	0
	1446									34	4									18	18	0

BTH: British Thomson-Houston Co.
DK: Dick, Kerr & Co.
EE: English Electric Co.
EMB: Electro Magnetic Brake Co.

Exp: Experimental.
H & F: Heenan & Froude.
HN: Hurst Nelson & Co.
LCC: London County Council.

M & G: Mountain & Gibson.
MV: Metropolitan Vickers.
W: Westinghouse Electric.

PASSENGER CARS.
DETAILS WHEN NEW.

Car Allocations

One of the complications involved in recording the whereabouts of the huge number of cars in the LCC fleet at any particular time, is the fact that only part of the recorded information has survived over the years. The position with regard to the locations of cars of classes A to D when new, has been discussed in Volume I, but for the sake of continuity, a recapitulation is given.

Cars of class A, originally at Clapham, Rye Lane and New Cross (which included the temporary car sheds in use before New Cross was opened), and later mainly at New Cross, Abbey Wood and Jews Row.

Cars of class B, originally at Streatham, Camberwell and Rye Lane, were later mainly at Camberwell and New Cross.

Cars of class C, originally at Streatham, Camberwell and Rye Lane, were later at Camberwell and New Cross.

Cars of class D, originally at Jews Row and New Cross, remained mainly in these locations, but with a few possibly at Abbey Wood.

So far as cars of later classes were concerned, what information is available is presented, although incomplete. The original allocations of class E cars, Nos. 402-551, were to Clapham where they replaced older cars, New Cross and Streatham. For a time, Jews Row car shed had an allocation, but these were soon to be replaced by class D cars. With regard to New Cross, the additional cars were needed to cater for the increasing number of services being worked from there.

This situation prevailed until 1921, but with a few of the cars being moved to other sheds, notably Hammersmith. At the end of 1921, a great upheaval occurred, when 40 class E cars, Nos. 512-551, were transferred to the northern system, to be shedded at Hampstead. This mass movement was undertaken to provide the north side with extra cars, and also to make room at Clapham for the arrival of the first of the new "1922" class E/1 cars. The second batch of class E cars, Nos. 602-751, were delivered new to north side sheds, mainly Poplar and Bow, but some were soon to be transferred to Stamford Hill. Subsequently, they were to be seen in all parts of north London.

With regard to the single deck subway cars of classes F and G, these, when new, were housed at the temporary depot space in the subway and at Canonbury. They were moved into Holloway car shed upon its completion, but later, several of them were sent to Jews Row and Clapham for use on the short line between Chelsea Bridge and Lavender Hill. After the withdrawal of the single deck cars, their "reconstructed" replacements, classified as E/1, were dispersed to several parts of the system.

The cars of class E/1 were to be seen on both halves of the system, and every car shed had an allocation at some time. In contrast to this, however, the class M cars were divided into three batches, the smallest at Abbey Wood, where cars 1428-1437 were shedded; at Holloway, where the remainder of those numbered in the 14xx series were housed; and at Camberwell, where all 50 of the 16xx and 17xx series of cars were on shed.

The first batch of the new cars of class HR/2 went to Camberwell in the first instance, but a few strayed to New Cross for a time. Cars in the second group went to Holloway and Camberwell. With regard to the class E/3 cars, the first ones went to New Cross, Abbey Wood, Streatham and Holloway, although after a short period they worked from Camberwell, Jews Row, Norwood, Hackney and Holloway. The Leyton E/3 cars were shedded at Leyton, then additionally at Bow and Hackney. Many re-arrangements were subsequently made.

759

Cars on Road, 30th July 1930

Ser-vice	A.M.												P.M.											
	12-1	1-2	2-3	3-4	4-5	5-6	6-7	7-8	8-9	9-10	10-11	11-12	12-1	1-2	2-3	3-4	4-5	5-6	6-7	7-8	8-9	9-10	10-11	11-12
2/4	28	9			1	10	25	29	29	29	30	30	30	30	30	30	30	30	30	30	29	29	28	
2/4EX							5	18	18	17	2			1	9	15	22	22	22	18	12	12	6	
2A/4A																								
22/24							19	46	46	46	20				25	48	48	47	28	3				
22/24EX								6	6	6	1													
6	7					1	8	19	21	21	22	22	22	22	22	22	23	23	23	23	22	20	15	14
8/20	11					4	19	31	31	31	29	27	27	27	27	28	32	33	33	33	30	26	24	20
10	10	2			3	8	19	25	25	25	22	17	17	17	17	21	26	27	27	27	20	14	13	
12	13	1	1	1	5	15	21	21	21	21	21	21	21	21	21	21	21	20	18	15	15	13		
14	5				2	8	16	18	18	18	17	17	17	17	17	18	19	19	18	18	16	10	9	
14EX						1	8	8	8					2	6	6	6	6						
16/18	14	6	1	1	5	8	20	30	30	30	30	30	30	30	31	31	31	31	31	31	28	22	19	
16/18EX							2	24	31	31	9				2	24	27	27	17					
26	19	4			5	16	24	29	29	29	29	29	30	30	30	30	30	30	28	28	22	21		
26EX							10	18	18	18	5			6	20	21	21	16						
28	13	1				8	28	28	28	28	27	24	24	24	24	24	27	29	29	28	26	23	19	16
30	18	2			6	20	28	28	28	28	23	20	20	20	21	24	29	29	29	28	24	22	20	
32	3				2	5	5	5	5	5	5	4	4	4	4	4	5	5	5	5	5	4	4	4
34	16	3			3	10	25	31	31	31	31	31	31	31	31	31	31	31	31	31	29	29	26	
36/38	18	2			4	31	72	76	76	76	56	52	52	52	53	63	77	77	77	68	54	42	37	28
40	17	8		1	11	28	38	39	39	39	33	28	27	27	27	31	41	41	41	29	31	28	24	23
44							3	5	7	8	8	7	1				2	6	6	6	6	5	2	
46	18	5	1	2	2	19	32	33	33	33	33	33	33	33	33	33	33	33	33	30	24	21	21	
50						1	9	9	9	9	8	8	8	8	9	9	9	9	8	2				
52				1	1	1	7	21	22	22	22				5	26	26	26	20	3				
52EX																	2	2						
54	16	3			7	15	40	45	45	45	42	42	42	42	42	48	49	49	49	40	33	26	24	
56/84	9				2	11	17	27	27	26	20	18	18	18	18	22	27	27	27	25	21	20	20	17
58	17				8	16	22	29	29	29	27	26	26	26	26	27	31	31	31	29	28	20	19	19
60						1	5	10	10	9				4	10	10	10	10						
62	12				3	13	18	18	18	18	14	14	14	14	14	15	16	16	16	16	16	16	16	16
62EX								1	1	1	1			1	1	1	1	1						
64							3	6	6	6					9	10	10	2						
66/72	20	1		1	4	10	20	22	22	23	24	25	25	25	25	25	23	23	23	23	22	22	22	
66/72EX							9	13	13	13	1													
68					4	7	15	15	15	15	15	15	15	15	15	15	15	15	14	13	12	10	10	
70	3	5	1		3	9	20	26	26	26	14	12	12	12	13	25	25	25	19	10	9	7	7	
74	5				1	12	24	24	24	24	15	15	15	15	19	24	24	24	19	13	13	13	11	
74EX							2	4	4	4	4													
76/80	10	1			8	12	23	27	27	26	26	26	26	26	26	27	27	27	27	27	25	21	20	
78	4				2	7	15	15	15	11	11	11	11	11	12	16	16	16	16	10	8	8	8	
89	1					7	9	9	9	7	7	7	7	8	9	9	9	9	9	9	7	7	7	
Night																								
2A/4A																								
22/24	4	6	6	6	6	5	4																	
14	1	1	1	1	1	1																		
26	1	1	1	1	1	1																		
36	3	3	3	3	3	2	1																	
66	2	2	2	2	2	2	1																	
Total	323	62	16	21	102	317	679	889	901	899	671	604	603	605	617	704	896	909	908	818	651	561	487	440

Total number of cars in service, southern system.

Cars on Road, 30th July 1930

Ser-vice	A.M.												P.M.											
	12-1	1-2	2-3	3-4	4-5	5-6	6-7	7-8	8-9	9-10	10-11	11-12	12-1	1-2	2-3	3-4	4-5	5-6	6-7	7-8	8-9	9-10	10-11	11-12
3	4					2	4	10	10	10	11	11	11	11	11	11	11	11	10	8	8	8	5	
5	5				1	5	16	17	17	17	17	17	17	17	17	17	17	17	16	11	9			
7	5			1	2	3	8	8	8	7	7	7	7	7	8	8	8	8	8	6	6	6		
8L	5				1	10	16	16	16	16	16	16	16	16	16	16	16	16	16	16	16	14		
9	9	1			1	5	11	12	12	12	13	13	13	13	13	13	13	13	13	13	12	12	12	
11	4				1	7	20	23	23	23	23	23	23	23	23	23	23	23	23	19	14	11		
13			2	2	2	6	10	10	10	5		1	1	2	10	10	10	9						
15	4					9	11	11	11	10	9	9	9	10	11	11	11	11	11	9	8	8		
17	3				2	6	16	16	16	16	16	16	16	16	16	16	15	9	7	7	6			
21	11	7		1	3	7	19	28	28	28	24	22	22	23	25	28	29	29	28	24	22	22	19	
25	3					2	5	5	5	5	5	5	5	5	5	5	5	5	5	5	5	5		
27						8	10	10	10	6		6	6	6	9	10	10	10	10	6	1			
35	9	3			4	7	11	12	12	12	12	12	12	12	12	12	12	12	12	12	12	10	9	
37						3	9	9	9	2		4	9	9	9	8								
39	1					4	17	17	17	17	14	13	13	13	13	14	17	17	17	17	15	9		
41	3	1			2	4	20	22	22	22	16	15	15	15	18	22	22	22	17	10	6	5		
41EX						4	6	6	6	3		3	4	4	4									
43	7	2			3	4	8	20	22	22	15	15	15	15	15	16	16	16	16	13	9	8		
43EX						2	6	6	6	5														
45					1	4	7	7	8	8	8	8	8	8	8	8	8	8	5					
47	4			1	3	13	21	23	23	23	23	23	23	23	23	23	23	21	21	15	10			
49	12	2		2	10	25	33	33	33	17	15	15	15	17	33	33	33	20	15	14	14			
49EX						4	4	4	4															
53	12	1		4	16	22	22	22	22	22	22	22	22	22	22	22	22	21	21	21	21			
55	8		2	6	9	20	25	25	25	20	19	19	19	19	23	27	27	25	18	15	12	12		
55EX						9	16	17	17	8		5	5	5	6	15	15	15	12					
57	6				4	17	23	23	23	13	12	12	13	13	18	19	19	17	10	8	7			
61	15	1		1	4	12	29	30	30	30	26	26	26	26	27	33	34	34	32	32	31	28	17	
61S							3	3	3	3	3													
61EX						3	4	4	4	4		1	4	4	4	4	1							
63	9				5	12	14	14	13	8	8	8	8	12	15	15	15	13	10	10	10			
63	8			2	9	36	39	39	44	42	42	42	42	39	43	43	43	36	31	20	19	17		
63EX						10	35	35	34	3		3	3	3	26	31	31	23	9	8	6	6		
67	5			3	5	7	7	7	7	7	7	7	7	7	7	7	7	6	6	6	6			
67EX						3	3	3	3	3	3	3	3	3	3	3	3	1						
69					4	12	12	12	7		7	7	7	7	12	12	12	12	4					
71	12	5		4	14	18	18	18	16	15	15	15	17	19	19	19	19	17	15	15				
75					2	8	12	12	12	11	11	11	11	11	12	12	12	9	8	7	5			
77	3	1		4	10	16	22	24	24	24	24	24	24	24	24	24	24	21	16	13				
81	8	2		3	18	23	23	23	18	18	18	18	19	27	27	27	24	23	18	15				
81EX						2	9	9	9			3	8	8	8									
83					1	11	11	11	10		10	10	10	10	11	11	11	11	4					
Night																								
3	1	1	1	1	1	1	1																	
13	1	1	1	1	1	1	1	1																
43	2	2	2	2	2	2	1	1																
65	2	2	2	2	2	2	1																	
Total	181	31	6	14	54	164	452	644	653	656	500	478	479	480	493	543	648	655	655	612	477	388	341	294

Total number of cars in service, northern system.

Chapter 47
Modifications and Improvements

High Power Motors

A post-war improvement involved fitting a number of cars with traction motors of higher power output. The new "1922" series cars of class E/1 came into service fitted with motors described as being either of 51 h.p.* (Nos. 1727-1776) or 63 h.p.* (1777-1851) rating, which were considerably more powerful than those fitted in any of the other cars, which had:-

Class				
A	100	double bogie cars		2 x 35 h.p.**
B	41	single truck	"	2 x 25 h.p.
C	100	single truck	"	2 x 30 h.p.**
D	100	double bogie	"	2 x 35 h.p.**
E	300	double bogie	"	2 x 42 h.p.
F	11	double bogie	"	2 x 42 h.p.
F	5	double bogie	"	2 x 35 h.p.
G	34	double bogie	"	2 x 42 h.p.
E/1	875	Double bogie	"	
		(excluding "1922" series cars)		2 x 42 h.p.
M	100	single truck cars		2 x 42 h.p.

 * This description is given at the "one-hour" rating.
** Variously described as 30 h.p., 35 h.p. (or 37 h.p.), depending upon whether the description was for the "continuous" or for the "one-hour" rating.

In a statement made by the General Manager on 12th February 1923 that it was not necessary to re-equip all the fleet, he indicated that only the cars on the south side would be dealt with, unless the other authorities working into London on the north side decided to upgrade their cars. It was not intended to deal with the older 4-wheel cars either, as these were considered to be near the end of their useful lives. He proposed that 200 car sets of 60 h.p. motors together with their associated electrical equipments be purchased, and that cars at Clapham, Streatham and Norwood be fitted, so enabling a large self-contained section in south-west London to be worked at higher speeds.

The older equipments could then be re-used on the 100 cars of class A, and the 100 of class D, which were to remain in service for several more years. This would allow a large part of south London services to be retimed, only leaving several routes working with old cars, "which could be practically isolated" from the rest. He estimated that the work would cost £144,000, which included an allowance of £1,700 for the sale as scrap of the old motors etc. from the class A and D cars, and £2,000 for re-fitting these cars with the equipments from the E/1 cars.

A lengthy report, outlining the financial obligations and advantages in re-equipping, was presented to the Highways Committee and the proposal was agreed to. Two points relevant to the discussion were that average car speeds would be increased from 9.13 to 9.24 m.p.h. using the "1922" cars as the basis for this calculation, and that the estimated annual mileage for the 400 dealt with (200 E/1, 100 A and 100 D class cars) would be 16 million, and that an additional farthing per car mile taken in fares would amount to £16,000 in a year.

The General Manager next outlined his estimated financial results of the proposal, and said that, together with reductions in other costs and charges, a gross annual saving on the revenue account could be as much as £19,000. This took account of probable debt redemption charges and of the fact that the Unemployment Grants Committee would pay a proportion of the interest costs incurred on the capital required for the new equipment. He also said that, ultimately, £1,000 would be accounted for by the disposal of the old equipments taken from the class A and D cars.

From all this came an estimate that the cost would be £142,000, repayable at £10,746 per year until the debt was repaid, while other savings would accrue from more efficient operation, with the need for less rolling stock maintenance, cleaning and oiling to approximately £34,690 annually. So far as the economy of re-using the motors taken from the E/1 cars was concerned, he pointed out that maintenance costs on the older cars with their existing motors was such that, if they were replaced with 42 h.p. secondhand motors, a reduction of approximately £5,000 in these costs could be achieved.

Lastly, any question which might arise regarding increased power consumption would be more than compensated for by the increased patronage commensurate with an increase in the speed and regularity of the services, and would not require the provision of additional plant at the generating station. Due to the higher efficiency of new, ventilated motors, overheating and excessive power consumption would be avoided. With the introduction of the 125 new cars, no increase had been registered. Similarly, the Central Repair Depot would not have any increase in its workload - probably less - due to the higher efficiency of the new plant.

At the same time, the sum of £269,800 was included in the capital estimates for 1923-24, to allow for the £144,000 for 200 sets, and the possible balance for a further 200 sets to be purchased should the Council so decide. The tenders for the new equipment were examined by the Council on 31st July 1923, resulting in the English Electric Co. Ltd. and Metropolitan Vickers Electrical Co. Ltd. sharing the contract, by each supplying 100 sets at half the total contract price of £165,200. (They both tendered in the same amount). The agreement included the delivery of the first five sets from each manufacturer within 18 or 20 weeks, and five sets a week thereafter.

Authority was given in March 1924 to obtain a second 200 sets as extensions of the contracts for the first 200. Again, the Unemployment Grants Committee approved of financial assistance amounting to 50% of the interest for 15 years on the cost of the first 200 sets, provided that work on the second series began on 15th March 1924 and was completed within nine months, on an agreed date of 15th December. A breakdown of the figures indicates that one car set cost £800 plus a provisional sum of £20 per car to cover the cost of any extra work, if required. Total main cost was £164,000, which was shared equally between the two companies, plus another £2,500 for other incidental charges.

Class 4 trucks by Mountain & Gibson, Heenan & Froude and Hurst Nelson, used under classes E, E/1, F and G cars.

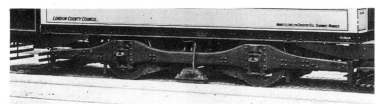

Class 5 trucks for class M cars, supplied by Hurst Nelson and the Brush Electrical Engineering Company.

E.M.B. improved class 4 trucks as used under the LCC class E/3 cars.

E.M.B. class 6 trucks as used on the first series of HR/2 cars.

E.M.B. class 6A trucks as used under the second series of HR/2 cars.

Trucks as fitted to classes E, E/1, F, G, M, HR/2 and E/3 cars.

The English Electric equipment consisted of 200 pairs of DK31C split-frame 525 volt, 63 h.p. motors and 200 pairs of controllers of type CDB2-C fitted with run-back preventers. The cars which received these were:-

840	959	979	1006	1026	1527	1547	1567	1595	1656
841	960	980	1007	1027	1528	1548	1569	1596	1657
842	961	981	1008	1028	1529	1549	1570	1597	1658
843	962	982	1009	1029	1530	1550	1571	1598	1659
844	963	983	1010	1030	1531	1551	1572	1599	1660
845	964	984	1011	1031	1532	1552	1573	1600	1661
846	965	985	1012	1032	1533	1553	1574	1601	1662
847	966	986	1013	1033	1534	1554	1575	1602	1663
848	967	987	1014	1515	1535	1555	1576	1603	1664
849	968	988	1015	1516	1536	1556	1577	1604	1665
850	969	989	1016	1517	1537	1557	1578	1627	1666
851	970	990	1017	1518	1538	1558	1579	1628	1667
937	971	991	1018	1519	1539	1559	1580	1629	1668
952	972	992	1019	1520	1540	1560	1581	1630	1669
953	973	993	1020	1521	1541	1561	1582	1631	1670
954	974	994	1021	1522	1542	1562	1590	1651	1671
955	975	995	1022	1523	1543	1563	1591	1652	1672
956	976	996	1023	1524	1544	1564	1592	1653	1673
957	977	1003	1024	1525	1545	1565	1593	1654	1674
958	978	1004	1025	1526	1546	1566	1594	1655	1675

All work on these cars was carried out at New Cross car shed.

The Metropolitan Vickers equipments were 149 pairs of MV121A (split-frame) motors and 51 pairs of MV124 (box-frame) motors, all of 525 volt, 61 h.p. at the one-hour rate, together with 200 pairs of OK4B controllers. These were fitted to cars numbered:-

1034	1089	1144	1224	1244	1362	1382	1402	1425	1495
1035	1090	1145	1225	1245	1363	1383	1403	1426	1496
1036	1091	1146	1226	1246	1364	1384	1404	1477	1497
1037	1092	1171	1227	1247	1365	1385	1405	1478	1498
1038	1093	1172	1228	1248	1366	1386	1406	1479	1499
1039	1094	1173	1229	1249	1367	1387	1407	1480	1500
1040	1095	1174	1230	1250	1368	1388	1408	1481	1501
1041	1096	1175	1231	1251	1369	1389	1409	1482	1502
1077	1097	1176	1232	1350	1370	1390	1410	1483	1503
1078	1098	1177	1233	1351	1371	1391	1411	1484	1504
1079	1099	1178	1234	1352	1372	1392	1412	1485	1505
1080	1100	1179	1235	1353	1373	1393	1413	1486	1506
1081	1101	1181	1236	1354	1374	1394	1414	1487	1507
1082	1137	1182	1237	1355	1375	1395	1415	1488	1508
1083	1138	1211	1238	1356	1376	1396	1419	1489	1509
1084	1139	1212	1239	1357	1377	1397	1420	1490	1510
1085	1140	1213	1240	1358	1378	1398	1421	1491	1511
1086	1141	1214	1241	1359	1379	1399	1422	1492	1512
1087	1142	1222	1242	1360	1380	1400	1423	1493	1513
1088	1143	1223	1243	1361	1381	1401	1424	1494	1514

Most of the work was carried out at Rye Lane depot, but it is believed that a few cars were dealt with at Brixton Hill car shed.

Due to undisclosed problems associated with the controllers, which were stated "as not capable of fulfilling the requirements imposed upon them", erection work on the first 100 cars of both batches was halted and not started up again until the middle of August. In an effort to make up for lost time, both companies increased their rate of output, English Electric to between 14 and 16 a week, Metropolitan Vickers by 10 to 12 a week, and although both companies asked that more cars be set aside for modification, the Council were unable to agree to this approach. The only alternative left was the the job to "run late", which meant that the Unemployment Grants Committee would have to agree, to enable the Grant conditions to be fulfilled. As the manufacture of the motors and controllers was completed on time, the Grants Committee confirmed that the qualification would stand. Work was completed on the cars fitted with English Electric equipment on 31st January 1925, while Metropolitan Vickers completed on 8th March 1925.

During the course of the work, a question was put to the Manager regarding the 15-year term of finance, and whether the new motors and controllers would last that long. His answer was a definite "yes", and he commented that, if cars became obsolete, the motors could be used on new cars. He stressed that they were self-contained units and interchangeable.

The only older cars left to be remotored were those of class C and the Leyton 4-wheelers. As surplus 42 h.p. motors and T2A controllers were then available, it was decided in October 1924 to re-equip 61 class C and some of the old Leyton cars. The remainder of the single-truck cars were to be disposed of. It was estimated that this work would cost £1,210. Regarding the cars of class F which were fitted with earlier equipments, together with the few class E cars which retained type 90M controllers, it is understood that these were updated during the course of normal overhaul from stocks of controllers and motors held in store.

During the early months of 1925, the British Thomson-Houston Co. Ltd. had developed a new type of traction motor known as BT-H504A, and, in a request made on 2nd June 1925, sought the co-operation of the LCC in testing it. The Council agreed to this on condition that there was no promise of purchase. The experimental motors, together with a pair of BT-HB521A controllers were installed on class E car No. 511, which was shedded at New Cross at the time and went into service from there on 27th September. During the next two years, the car ran approximately 75,000 miles in passenger service, with the motors etc. being modified as necessary. On 5th September 1927, BT-H asked whether the Council would be prepared to purchase the equipments at a discount price of £610, which was agreed to.

Apart from occasional replacements, the only other large order placed by the LCC for traction motors, except for those supplied with the class E/3 and HR/2 cars, was for 50 sets of English Electric 301R/1A, 525 volt, 57½ h.p. on 25th June 1932 and fitted to the cars numbered:-

785	794	802	810	818	826	833
786	795	803	811	819	827	834
788	796	804	812	820	828	835
789	797	805	813	821	829	836
790	798	807	814	823	830	837
791	799	808	815	824	831	838
793	800	809	816	825	832	839
			817			

One extra set was ordered on 12th November 1932 and two more on 25th January 1933, which were placed on cars 1986 (which had been the subject of the abortive chain-drive experiment), 160 (which received class 4A trucks in place of its original class 6A set) and 1370 (which was undergoing rebuilding at the time).

A set of regenerative control equipment had been developed in conjunction with the Municipal Tramways and Transport Association, which, in 1932, was in use on a Manchester car. At the request of T. E. Thomas, this equipment was transferred to London where it was installed into class E/1 car No. 779, and tried and tested in service for about four months. The car was placed on service 54, working between Victoria Station and Grove Park, a round journey of 22.62 miles, for which a running time of two hours was allocated. The total number of stops on one round trip was 138, averaging one stop every 290 yards, or 6.1 stops per mile.

It was stated that one of the reasons for the test was to study the action of compound motors running in series and parallel as against the more usual motors fitted into a standard car. After special tests, which were undertaken at night, the car was put into passenger service for a first period of about three weeks, where it became most noticeable that the number of times that the magnetic brake had to be applied was reduced by about 50%, and then only at the lower end of the speed scale. The rest of the stops were made using only the regenerative and dynamic features of the equipment, which resulted in the magnet shoes of No. 779 having a life of about 4½ times those used on a standard car.

It was also stated that, despite the fact that the motors transferred from Manchester were too small to give really satisfactory running under London conditions, the ability of the equipment to show a worthwhile saving in current used and in brake and rail wear was such that further tests with more substantial motors were thought to be worth consideration.

Resulting directly from this test, the Council decided to order equipments from several manufacturers, with the object of carrying out a comprehensive set of tests under all running conditions. By the time that the orders were ready to be placed, the LCC Tramways had passed into the hands of the LPTB. However, both Mr. Thomas

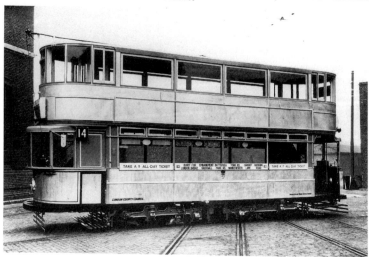

E/1 car No. 795 appeared in February 1932 with aluminium panelling on its sides; with the rest of the body painted in aluminium and grey; and fitted with vestibule screens. (Courtesy: L T Museum. U34205)

In May 1932, class M car No. 1726 was fitted with this unusual EMB Co. four wheel truck, together with vestibule screens, which it retained for the remainder of its existence. (LCC official view, A8832)

and Mr. G. F. Sinclair were retained by the new Board as General Manager, Tramways amd Tramways Rolling Stock Engineer respectively, and the experiment was continued, using cars Nos. 781 to 788, each fitted with equipment supplied by these manufacturers.

A further experiment was carried out early in 1933, when the Council equipped cars Nos. 1103 and 1104 with air brake equipment. After the formation of the LPTB, there were several other changes, but these will be dealt with at the appropriate time, when a history of that undertaking is published.

Car No. 835, experimentally fitted in May 1933 with a bow collector in place of the usual trolley pole, is seen in service on the line to Grove Park. (The late N. Elston)

The rather bulbous semi-screens fitted to No. 1539 (left) were not used on other cars. A pantograph was, however, treid out on No. 1172 (right). (Courtesy: [left] F. C. Carter collection: [right] L C C official view)

Experimental Features Applied To Some Cars

Car No.	Details	Date	
627	Painted orange	Apr	1926
	Painted red	May	1927
795	Aluminium panels. Screens	Feb	1932
820	Upholstered backrests, seats upper saloon	Oct	1931
835	Bow collector	May	1933
842	New type folding steps, side lifeguards	Apr	1921
843	"Ventura" air extractor vents	Jan	1928
844	Pantograph	May	1933
884	"Ventura" air extractor vents	Jan	1925
905, 907, 909, 910, 911, ***,	Fitted with collector skates for use on Bow Road		
	stud contact line	Jun	1908
962	"Numa" atmospheric bells	May	1926
978	Platform mirrors, for motormen use	Apr	1932
980	Peters' new type air extractor ventilators, top of corner pillars in quarter-light frames	no date	
984	- as 843 -	Jan	1925
1035	"Ashanco" air extractor ventilators (other cars later fitted)	Jan	1928
1056	Large service number stencil plates with access from upstairs canopy doors, reflected light destination screens	Jun	1926
1103	Fitted with air brake equipment		1932
1104	- do -		1932
1172	Improved destination indicator boxes, upholstered seats and back rests, upper saloon	Feb	1933
	fitted with pantograph	May	1933

Car No.	Details	Date
1214	Two special half-drop windows of "Rawlings" type, one in each saloon	no date
1235	Fitted with cushion or spring seats, lower saloon, Cushion seats upstairs, Four different types of adjustable windows, one in each corner of lower saloon, Upper deck seating reduced by two double seats to obtain better passenger circulation Large service number stencil plates	Dec 1926
1242	Improved type of motorman platform mirror	Jun 1927
1248	Experimental vestibule screens (see below)	Feb 1930
1270	Platform mirrors	Apr 1930
1272	Protective device for motorman (no details)	Sep 1930
1302	- as 1270 -	Apr 1930
1360	Bow collector	May 1933
1393	One-way air scoops in quarter lights, lower saloon	Jul 1928
1402	"Numa" air bells (second car to be dealt with)	Jul 1926
1506	Experimental vestibule screens (see below)	Feb 1930
1539	- do -	Feb 1930
1546	Patent ribbed panels	no date
1547	- as 1056 -	Jun 1926
1569	Rocker and end bottom quarter panels finished in vermilion red (as waist panels)	Feb 1927
1578	- as 1056 - (after damage) (overturned at Streatham, 10th October 1925)	Mar 1926
1620-1625	Painted with non-leaded paint	Jan 1912
1638	"Ventura" air extractor vents, top deck roof	Jan 1925
1658	- as 1056 -	Jun 1926
1688	- as 1056 -	Jun 1926
1712	Experimental re-arrangement of lighting (not Pullman)	Sep 1928
1715	Experimental English Electric Co. truck fitted	1933
1723	Experimental Brush Co. truck fitted, together with vestibule screens	Mar 1933
1726	Experimental EMB Co. truck fitted, together with vestibule screens	May 1932
1727	New seats upstairs. Interior painted	Dec 1931
1767	- as 1727 -	Dec 1932
1814	Trucks fitted with Hoffman roller bearings	no date
1817	Experimental Pullman car	Jun 1926
1851	Pullman standard car	Nov 1926
1898	Radial arm trucks fitted when new	1930
1931	Special livery for Subway opening, 7th January 1931	
1986	Experimental chain drive trucks fitted	1932
1989	Bucket seats, lower saloon	
120 (II)	- do -	
147 (II)	- do -	
168 (II)	- do -	

Experimental vestibule screens were placed on three cars of class E/1 during February 1930. No. 1248 was fitted with screens covering the width of the dashplates only; No. 1506 had vestibule screens completely protecting the platforms and staircases at either end (although each screen was different from the other); No. 1539 had about two-thirds of the dashplates covered. No. 1506 was the only successful example and, after extensive tests in service on both the northern and southern networks, became the model upon which the screening programme was based.

Non-Standard Equipments

Car No.	Supplier	Motor Details	Wheel Bearings
447	E E	DK 108/5H	Plain
511	B T-H	504 A	Plain
630	C P	Standard	Plain
781	G E C	WT 293 A	Plain
782	M V	114 CR	Plain
783	E E	304	Plain
784	C P	C 150 B	Plain
785	E E	301 A Reg. Field.	Plain
786	C P	C 150 B 5	Plain
787	G E C	WT 291 A	Plain
788	B T-H	509 S1	Plain
850	E E	DK 126 B	Plain
937	E E	? ?	Plain
1418	M V	114 DV	Plain
1441	M V	121 (special)	Plain

Other Special Work

1715	W	WH 220 (EE Special Single Truck)	Roller
1723	W	WH 220 (Brush Special Single Truck)	Roller
1726	W	WH 220 (EMB Special Single Truck)	Roller
1814	E E	31 C	Roller
1852	M V	105 (EMB Equal Wheel Bogie)	Roller
1853	M V	105 -do-	Roller
1964	E E	DK 126 A (Hoffman Bearings)	Roller

Note:-

EE: English Electric   B T-H: British Thomson-Houston
CP: Crompton Parkinson   G E C: General Electric Company
M V: Metropolitan Vickers   W: British Westinghouse

With regard to car No. 937, it was brought south in September 1918, and then transferred to Hammersmith. It was there that it lost its MSC License Plate to car No. 1426. No. 937 was recorded as being in the Central Repair Depot for six weeks in 1923, where it appears to have had a major rebuild. In April 1925 it was fitted with English Electric motors and controllers and sent to Clapham, where it remained until some time in 1934, when it was moved to New Cross.

Some work to cars shown above was carried out after 1st July 1933 by the London Passenger Transport Board.

Car Lighting

Until the Great War, tramcars showed one white light to the front which came from a lamp fitted into or on to the centre of each dash plate, and another from a small bullseye light fitted above the lower saloon bulkhead window. This light source was also used at the rear end by moving a red aspect over it, to form the rear lamp. During the war, the dash plate lamp, or "headlamp", was screened against the direct emission of light, but showed the fleet number of the car through a diffusing mask. Also as a wartime measure, taken as from 6th March 1916, two white sidelights were made compulsory, one of which was subsequently made to serve as a platform step light.

On 9th April 1919, the LCC was attempting to have this order rescinded and, at a meeting held between Messrs. Fell, Ireland and Mason of the LCC, together with Col. Pringle and Mr. Marwood of the Ministry of Transport Railway Department, they all decided that the restrictions were unnecessary and agreed to ask the Home Office, who had made the wartime order in the first place, to cancel it.

Col. Pringle reported to the Home Office that, in his opinion, the unique single lamp displayed by a tramcar was an advantage, as it indicated that the vehicle was railbound and had not the "freedom of movement" possessed by other street vehicles. The Home Office, however, disagreed and, on 30th September 1919, issued a further Order which stated that the two white lights must be retained and extended to tramway undertakings throughout Britain. This was opposed by almost all tramway managers, but nevertheless, on 17th February 1920, the "Lights on Vehicles Committee" of the Roads Department of the Ministry of Transport made a recommendation that tramcars be fitted in the same manner as other vehicles with more than two wheels. The Director General of Roads at the Ministry of Transport, Mr. J. S. Killick, stated on 21st April 1920 that tramcars would be expected to carry two white lights to the front, one on either side of the car and, if a central headlamp was also carried, it should not be more than seven inches in diameter. A red light should also be shown to the rear of the offside of each car.

As a result of this, or because of its implications, Mr. Fell decided that if an offside rear light was necessary, it may as well also do duty as one of the front lights (when the car was going in the opposite direction) and be used to illuminate a proposed service number plate, one of which could be fitted on either side of each car.

In July 1922, he suggested that eight cars be experimentally fitted up and stated that each one would probably cost about £2.10s, which sum would include the additional number plate stencils required for the circular routes. An estimate of £4,475 was given to fit 1,790 cars, but this did not include those from Leyton. Fell also said that the use of direct labour at the Central Repair Depot was the best way to deal with the manufacture of the number plate boxes and stencils. He further reported on 1st August that the eight cars "were being fitted up". Despite this, the Council instructed him to obtain tenders for the work, but out of seven firms approached, only two answered and, in his opinion, neither was satisfactory. He again recommended that direct labour be used to carry out the work.

Next, the representative of the Metropolitan Police, Supt. Bassom, on being consulted, said to the Rolling Stock Engineer on 7th December 1922 that "the Commissioner would not be likely to agree with any encroachment upon any further depth of the light than is permitted for the display of advertisements. The space allowed for advertisements is six inches from the cant rail. The depth of the plates used for 'end illuminated numbers' is 8½ inches"! This meant that, in effect, the LCC would be restricted to using plates of smaller size that those in use in the end windows of cars.

The Manager next recommended that one of the cars fitted up be made available so that he, with the Chairman and Vice-Chairman of the Council, together with a representative from the police could inspect it, "and do so as soon as possible". The outcome was that it was agreed that all 1,801 double deck cars in the fleet should be dealt with at an estimated cost of £4,627.10s.

With regard to the insistence that the work be carried out by direct labour, Fell reported on 1st February 1923 that facilities at Charlton for metal plate working were not adequate and recommended that tenders be invited for the supply of suitable fittings, but assembly be carried out by LCC labour. This time the total number of cars stated as being in need of fitting was 1,851 (including the remaining Leyton cars), at an estimated cost of £3,700 for the parts and £930 for their installation at the CRD.

The contract for the supply of 3,702 side service number indicator boxes with internal illumination, opaque glass side panels and a movable red aspect fitted at one end, together with 3,702 stencil plates was taken by Benjamin Electric Ltd. of Tottenham on 15th May 1923 in the sum of £2,746.10. 6d, plus an extra 1,988 plates for £99. 8s, making a total of £2,845.18. 6d. Some of the residue of the money estimate amounting to £930 was to go to fitting them by LCC staff. Deliveries commenced on 23rd August 1923 and in the first month 106 sets had been installed. The whole of the work was planned to take about one year and for this extra staff were taken into employment.

An experiment was carried out on 4th May 1923, when a modified set of "large end number plates" was put on display at Hampstead car shed, which would be expected to cost about £3.15s per car set, or a total of £6,755 if 1,081 cars were so fitted. However, no further action appears to have been taken at the time and, on 12th July, it was decided to abandon the experiment.

The next problem to be studied involved the level of interior lighting in the cars. this was brought about by the fact that the "1922" class E/1 cars came into service with the ceilings of both decks finished in white enamel instead of, as on all other cars, being of varnished natural wood finish. There was the realisation that this new arrangement improved the distribution of available light, which was also to be seen on many of the omnibuses of the time. So far as the 'buses were concerned, comment was made that the lighting level was more constant, whereas on the trams, the lights fluctuated with line voltage.

To improve matters, it was decided to paint all car ceilings on both decks with quick-drying white enamel, and as soon as the supply of 20-watt light bulbs ran out, to replace them with 30-watt ones. Any glass lamp shades were also to be removed and be replaced with "anti-glare" reflectors. By 26th September 1923, 1,550 out of 1,740 cars had been dealt with, and of the 190 remaining, 50 were to be dealt with in the following month when the cars were in for overhaul, the rest following on their visits to the works. By 16th January 1924, all had been completed.

Fog Lamps

A problem which beset the tramways, as indeed it did to all other forms of transport, was the incidence of fog during the winter months of each year. A normal damp mist, which, with the addition of tons of soot emanating from countless domestic and industrial chimneys could result in a fog which could bring visibility down to just a few feet and, on occasion, a few inches! In an attempt to deal with the problem of lack of vision in such conditions as this, a number of ideas were put forward from time to time, the most promising being the use of highly reflective chromium plated backplates behind high-wattage electric lamps. In March 1931, special fog lamps were ordered at a cost of £4,882.10s for 2,790 lamps (two per car) and the necessary switching equipment with which to control them.

The lamps were mounted on the right-hand side (off side) of the destination indicator boxes and were adjusted to direct a beam of light downwards at an angle of about 20° so that, in theory at least, the lamp beam would illuminate the surface of the road several feet in front of the car. It was also expected that the light beam would serve to warn other road users of the presence of a tramcar. The lamps, however, proved to be of limited use, as a thick fog blanketed all light, from whatever source.

The Tool Box

Every car in the fleet carried a tool chest, with the contents for use if required by the car crew while out on the road. The box, made of oak, contained a comprehensive set of equipment designed so that the user was able to deal with any minor emergency that might arise. Each box, which was secured by a seal, contained a contents card, which had to be marked up by the user in the event of the box being opened and any item used.

Contents

Item	No.	Description	Item	No.	Description
1	1	Feeder Pillar and Telephone Key	8		Ash Strips
			9	1	Adjustable Spanner
2	1	Lifting Jack	10	1	Chisel
3	1	2lb Hammer	11	1	Tin Disinfectant
4	1	Pair Hatch Lifters	12	1	Shackle
5	1	Screwdriver	13	1	Plough Lifting Rope
6	1	Pair Pliers	14		Tarred Yarn
7	1	Pair India Rubber Gloves	15		Waste Cotton
			16	1	Wood Block

Each box was clearly marked with the number of the car to which it had been allocated, and was stowed beneath one staircase. It was often used as a small table upon which to stand the conductor's ticket box and, of course, his tea can!

Chapter 48
Works Cars and Service Vehicles

In addition to the passenger rolling stock, there was a fleet of special-purpose vehicles used in connection with day-to-day operation and maintenance of the tramway system. Because of the special nature of the duties performed by most of these cars, they probably were not noticed much by the general public. The vehicles consisted of track watering tank cars and stores vans. The latter made regular daily journeys between the various tramway establishments, conveying the many items required to maintain the fleet of passenger cars and track sections in good condition. These vehicles were classified in accordance with the LCC practice of allocating a letter of the alphabet to each different type.

The First Watering Car

The original watering car, which was un-numbered and referred to as an "electric water tank", was put into service on 28th June 1904, but after just a few months in service, it became plain that one car was not sufficient for the volume of work required of it. In those days, the roads were invariably covered with a layer of coarse dust, much of which consisted of considerable amounts of dried ordure, dropped by the many horses which were used at that time as a means of traction.

Consideration has been given to the idea that this car may have been one of the two "locomotives" purchased for use at Greenwich Generating Station, but not, so far, put into service, and released temporarily for water car duties. These vehicles each consisted of a Brill 21E truck, upon which was a flat platform with a small body, driven and controlled with tramcar type equipments.

Alternatively, and more likely, it may have been an adaptation of a horse car body which had been fitted with electrical equipment and mounted on a Brill 21E truck in July 1903, to assess the possibility of running this type of car through from London to Kennington on the conduit system, and then being hauled on the cable line to Streatham.

The car in use had at least two rectangular-shaped tanks strapped to the open platform, and restrained by boards fitted to either side of the bodywork. The dashplates appear to be "home made", being higher than those in use on the class A cars, with which it was contemporary.

Class H Cars (Nos. 01-04)

On 16th May 1905, the decision was taken to purchase four new water tank cars. By Council agreement of 18th July, four cars, using standard tramway electrical equipments, were ordered from Messrs. Mountain & Gibson at a cost of £2,360. Each vehicle had a large capacity water tank within a box-shaped body 16 ft. 4 in. long, which was carried on a standard M & G 21E type four-wheeled truck. There

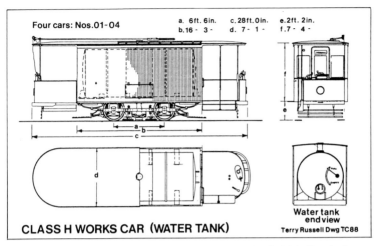

Four cars: Nos.01-04

a. 6ft. 6in. c. 28ft. 0in. e. 2ft. 2in.
b. 16 - 3 - d. 7 - 1 - f. 7 - 4 -

Water tank
end view

CLASS H WORKS CAR (WATER TANK)

Terry Russell Dwg TC88

were small open platforms at either end where the British Westinghouse 90M controllers were located and used to drive the Westinghouse type 200 motors.

Initially, the major part of the duty of these cars was, as has been mentioned, to keep the roads, and particularly the tram tracks well watered. In later years, with the incidence of the scourge of rail corrugation, attention was turned to keeping under control the roughness which developed on the running surfaces of the rails. Early in 1910, it was decided to modify the four water cars by fitting large carborundum blocks on either side of the trucks, which could be screwed down on to the rail surfaces and, with the aid of the water supply in the tanks, which was used as a lubricant, use these to rub away any uneven patches of corrugated metal. As there was insufficient room between the car wheels, track brake shoes and plough carriers for

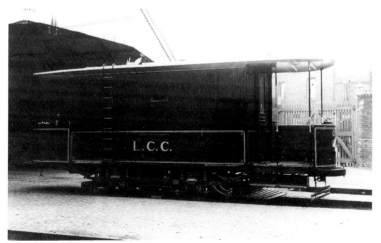

Water car No. 02 at Rye Lane depot in 1906, showing the ladder used to gain access to the water tank inlet. (L C C official view)

the rail grinding equipment to be suspended, it was decided to crank the carrier channels to allow more room, but this caused difficulties at ploughshifts. To overcome this, the plough carriers were relocated at the ends of the trucks. At the same time, it was thought that magnetic track brakes on these vehicles would not be necessary and they were removed. After these modifications had been carried out, one car, No. 01 was specially fitted with two trolley poles to enable it to be used on the Woolwich - Eltham double wire section.

Class J Cars (Nos. 05-06)

These two cars were the original stores carrying vehicles, built in much the same way as the water cars. Known as class J, the bodies, 16 ft. 4 in. long, were constructed by the LCC in 1908, and were placed on M & G Brill-type 21E trucks, with electrical equipment by British Westinghouse. The box bodies had centrally placed sliding doors on both sides, and were used to convey many general purpose items between the various car sheds, yards and depots.

Class K Cars (Nos. 07-010)
Class L Cars (Nos. 011-012)

With the continually expanding electrified system, the need was soon felt for more stores carrying vehicles, partly as a result of large quantities of mechanical and electrical components being required at the northern overhaul works at Holloway and Bow. On 8th December 1908, a contract was awarded to Messrs. Mountain & Gibson to supply four stores cars to be known as class K, which had 22 ft. long bodies, mounted on M & G Brill-type 21E trucks. Each car, like those of class J, had centrally placed sliding doors on each side of the body. The contract, at £3,230, was arranged to cover the cost of the four box vans, together with two open bodied cars, to be known as class L, and numbered 011 and 012. It was stipulated that all six cars were to be delivered early in 1909.

The open vans were unusual, as the 22 ft. long bodies were really no more than flat wagons, which had removable wooden side panels about

Stores carrying car No. 08 of class K, with ample room to display LCC Tramways advertisements. *(Greater London Photograph Library)*

3 ft. high. The end bulkheads, separating the van body from the driving platforms, were purely functional and gave no protection from the vagaries of the weather to either driver or guard.

One of the most unusual forms of electric four-wheeled truck used in Britain made its appearance in the construction of these two cars. They were built by Mountain & Gibson and incorporated Warner Radial Attachments, with the idea of giving the 9 ft. 6 in. wheelbase truck similar characteristics obtainable with a set of two normal four-wheeled bogies. Both cars at first had two trolley poles each, but before long, one was removed from each car. Heavy wheelsets, motors and similar items were carried by these two cars, whose sole occupation was to make daily journeys between the Central Repair Depot at Charlton and the car sheds and depots in both halves of the system.

Due to restrictions placed upon the operation of certain cars along Kingsland Road during the time that the side slot conduit was in use, several of the works cars bore signwritten plates stating that they were not to be worked between Stamford Hill and Shoreditch via Kingsland Road.

Class L/1 Cars (Nos. 013-014)

The next two stores (service) cars to be brought into use were box-bodied vehicles, whose Brill 21E trucks were originally used beneath class B passenger cars. During the Great War, several of the class B car bodies were sold to Sheffield and two of the trucks were used beneath two home-made wagon bodies, coupled as a two-car set. After several years languishing in the back of a depot, the set was brought out in 1924 to convey staff between the CRD and Camberwell Green during a strike of railwaymen. After this episode, the two vehicles were converted into rail grinders in 1925, complete with water tanks. The box bodies were built by the LCC, and fitted with Westinghouse T2C controllers and Westinghouse 220 motors. Weight of a complete car was given as 10 tons 10 cwts approximately.

Class L/2 Car (No. 015)

It became necessary in 1925 for the Council to put another stores car into service, in this case, to convey dry sand from the wharf to various car sheds. A class C car, No. 273 had its top deck removed and a new roof fitted over the single deck body. The internal fittings were removed from the lower saloon, and sliding doors fitted into the centre section on either side of the car body. One trolley pole was fitted, the base being fixed midway between the window pillars of one of the end sections of the body. The Westinghouse equipment was retained.

Miscellaneous Railed Vehicles

There were a number of pieces of equipment which were included in the early rolling stock lists, including some connected with track maintenance. These were:-

1903-04.	Electric conduit cleaning trollies,	2
1904-05.	Electric conduit cleaning trollies,	3
	Petrol driven rail grinder,	1
1905-06.	Electric conduit cleaning trollies,	3
	Petrol driven rail grinder,	1

By 1910, however, the electric conduit cleaning trollies were no longer included in the return; only the petrol driven rail grinder remained.

The Snowbrooms

By far the greatest input into the works car fleet came in 1926, when the first serious attempt was made to decide how to overcome a regular winter problem, whereby services, particularly those working on the conduit system, were disrupted on occasion by snowstorms. Until that time, attempts were made to clear the snow by fitting snow boards to some of the service cars, which was supposed to push the snow to one side. This was augmented by the use of horse-drawn snow ploughs, which proved to be insufficient to keep the tracks clear. Some local borough councils also used rock salt to disperse snow, but this caused damage to the conduit conductor tee-rails and their supporting insulators.

A large number of cars of classes B and C were either out of service or on the point of being taken out of passenger use and, early in 1926, the General Manager and Rolling Stock Engineer decided to experiment with a rotary snow broom, which was to be a reconstruction of a class B car.

A retractable broom mechanism was devised by the LCC, working in conjunction with the Kilmarnock Engineering Company, and designed in such a way to allow one to be fitted beneath each platform of a car. To enable this to be done, the body and platforms, together with the fenders, had to be raised nine inches, and this was achieved by inserting timber baulks between the truck and body and firmly bolting them together. Having raised the platforms, it was then necessary to provide fenders at the normal height, which was done by bolting on additional channel sections beneath the original ones, which, while eminently practical, gave the cars an unusual appearance.

The rotary brooms were fitted at an angle of about 15° out of square with the truck ends and were designed to sweep snow to the left-hand, or nearside of the car. The means of propulsion for the brooms came from the axles of the car when it was in motion. A toothed sprocket wheel was locked into place on each axle, each of which drove a chain very similar in appearance to an enlarged bicycle chain, at the outer end of which was a driven sprocket and gear wheel assembly, running freely on a splined shaft.

A north London snowbroom on the traverser at Holloway car shed. The vehicles were very little used. (Dr. H. Nicol. Courtesy: D. W. K. Jones)

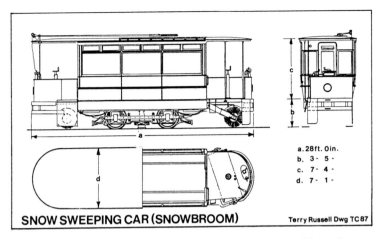

a. 28 ft. 0 in.
b. 3 - 5 -
c. 7 - 4 -
d. 7 - 1 -

SNOW SWEEPING CAR (SNOWBROOM)

Terry Russell Dwg TC 87

Two extended arms held the brush mechanism in position, the rear ends of which were bolted to specially shaped brackets fixed beneath the body, which also provided a pivotal point for the mechanism. The outer end of the assembly was normally held in the raised position, several inches above the road surface. When required for use, it could be lowered by means of a worm-wheel drive, operated by a handwheel mounted on a bracket on the platform, one at either end of the car. In whichever direction the car was travelling, the appropriate brush was made to turn by means of a platform-mounted lever which, when moved, engaged a second gear wheel into the primary one, which had the effect of turning the broom in the opposite direction to the primary source of motion, thereby sweeping the snow forward and to the left of the movement of the car.

Early in July 1926, the Rolling Stock Engineer suggested that 13 more of the class B cars could easily be adapted to work as snow sweepers at a probable cost of about £160 per car. Tenders were called for and on the 13th October, the contract was awarded to the Kilmarnock Engineering Company for 14 snow sweeping equipments (which included the original set) at £120 each. Additional preparatory work undertaken by the Council at the CRD was expected to cost about £40 per car. As part of the conversion of each car, the top deck cover and sides were removed, the floor forming the basis of the new roof for the single deck car. The former stairwells were boarded over and waterproof material applied to the new roof. To support the canopies, brackets were fitted to the off-sides where the stairs had previously been. Erection of the units was undertaken by the LCC at Charlton, but it is uncertain which cars, if any, were fitted at that time with trolley poles.

The first critical test came on Christmas Day and Boxing Day 1927, when a severe snowstorm swept across southern England. The brooms were put to work, keeping the tracks clear throughout the two days and nights, so allowing a reasonable car service to operate.

In January 1928 it was decided to convert another seven of the stored cars, and in this case, trolley poles, change-over switches and "long lead ploughs" were specified. The cost of converting these old passenger cars to snow sweepers was, as described in the Highways Committee minutes for 12th March 1929, approximately £172 each.

Table of Snowbrooms and Previous Class B Car Numbers

Broom	Car	Broom	Car	Broom	Car
016	150	023	141	030	101
017	153	024	189	031	163
018	195	025	125	032	102
019	165	026	183	033	194
020	182	027	149	034	169
021	168	028	120	035	144
022	106	029	134	036	132

Snowploughs

Early in 1931 the decision was taken to convert 18 of the disused class C cars into snowploughs, in the main for use on sections of track where there were overhead wires, although there were some which were not initially fitted with trolley poles. This move may have been made to concentrate, as far as possible, the snowbrooms on to the conduit sections, or to parts of the system where there was more likelihood of snow settling and drifting.

As each car was dealt with, the staircases and upper decks were removed and additional metal tubular uprights inserted to hold the canopies square. The lifeguards, safety trays and entry steps at each end of the car were next removed and replaced by planks of hardwood, mounted vertically, one fitted beneath the space left by the platform steps, the other at an angle of 45° from the front of the side-plank to a point beneath the end of the body on the nearside of the car. In later years a number of the cars went through a further conversion, when they received the standard snowbroom gear in place of the plough boards.

Table of Snowploughs and Previous Class C Car Numbers

Plough	Car	Plough	Car	Plough	Car
037	216	043	241	049	270
038	224	044	209	050	275
039	248	045	215	051	285
040	229	046	250	052	288
041	256	047	258	053	233
042	266	048	252	054	253

Snowplough No. 043, previously class C car No. 241, at Hampstead car shed. (D. W. K. Jones)

There were exceptions to the standard arrangement of removing upper decks from cars when using them for works purposes. Nos. 118 and 158 of class B were used for a time as snowploughs, as seen above, together with a class C car, No. 215, renumbered 045. (D. W. K. Jones)

CLASS & FLEET Nos.		TYPE	BODY	YEAR	BUILDER	TRUCKS TYPE & CLASS		MOTORS	CONT- ROLLERS
Exp H	— 01-04	Water Car Water Car	Open Box	1903 1905	LCC M & G	Brill 21E M & G 21E	2 2	— W 200	— W 90M
J	05-06	Stores Carrier	Box	1908	LCC	M & G 21E	2	W 200	W 90M
K	07-010	Stores Carrier	Box	1909	M & G	M & G 21E	2	DK 3A	W T2 A/C
L	011-012	Wheel Carrier	Open	1909	M & G	Warner Radial		DK 3A	W T2 A/C
L/1	013-014	Rail Grinder	Box	1925	LCC	Brill 21E	2	W 220	W T2 A/C
L/2	015	Sand Car	Box	1930	LCC	Brill 21E	2	W 220	W T2 A/C
—	016-036	Snowbroom		1926/7	LCC	Brill 21E	2	W 220	W T2 A/C
—	037-054	Snowplough		1930/1	LCC	Brill 21E	2	W 220	W T2 A/C

	WHEEL- BASE		WEIGHT			REF
Exp H	6 ft 6 in	—	10	15	1	a
J	6	6	8	11	2	
K	6	6	10	11	2	
L	9	0	10	8	3	
L/1	6	6				b
L/2	6	6				c
—	6	6				d
—	6	6				e

DK: Dick, Kerr & Co.
LCC: London County Council.
M & G: Mountain & Gibson.
W: Westinghouse Electric.

a. No detailed information available.
b. Cars originally of class L.
c. Originally class C car No. 273.
d. Converted from class B cars.
e. Converted from class C cars.

WORKS CARS.

The Road Service Vehicle Fleet

A fleet of horse drawn support road vehicles was used by various sections of the Tramways Department almost from the beginning of operations in 1899. Some of these were transferred from the London Tramways Company, but very soon, extra carts and wagons were brought into service. Soon after the first lines were electrified, the Highways Committee decided to recommend to the Council that the first two petrol driven motor lorries be purchased, and thereafter, the early motor lorry fleet was augmented with a number of steam driven lorries. In 1905, the first motor car was purchased for use by the Chief Officer and his senior staff, soon to be followed by several other motor cars. The following list gives as many details as are available of the original motor vehicle fleet, including all of the steam driven lorries.

Fleet No.	Reg'n No.	Maker	Maker No.	Date in Service	Cost £	Further Details
1	A 3651	Arrol Johnston		1904	388	Breakdown Lorry petrol, 3-ton, 12 h.p.
2	LC3922	-do-		1904)		Breakdown Lorry
3	LC4548	-do-		1905)		-do-
4 (?)	LC3923	-do-		1905)	1,211	-do-
				)		Flat platform
				)		Nos. 2, 3 & 4 were
				)		purchased from the
				)		Mo-Car Syndicate,
				)		August 1905.
5	LC1154	Wolseley		1905	*510	Landauette (sic) Personal use of the Chief Officer.
6	LC5995	Darracq		1906	250	10 h.p. motor car.
7	LC5996	-do-		1906	250	-do-
8	LN 522	-do-		1907	250	-do-
9	LN 523	-do-		1907	250	-do-
10	M 1476	Foden	1204	Mar 1907	470	Scrapped 1933 (LCC)
11	M 1477	-do-	1300	-do-	470	To H. Hooker, 1944
12	M 1498	-do-	1306	Apr 1907	470	To S.B.&D.Co. 1937
13	M 1499	-do-	1318	-do-	470	Scrapped 1933 (LCC)
14	M 1500	-do-	1330	May 1907	470	Scrapped 1937 (LPTB)

Note:- Nos. 10 to 14 all 5-ton capacity steam driven lorries.

Foden steam wagon No. 13, built in 1913, being loaded with coils of span wire in the CRD Stores. (*Greater London Photograph Library*)

Foden wagon No. 30 of 1914 vintage, used for conveying sand and ballast to track works sites. *(LCC official view)*

Fleet No.	Reg'n No.	Maker	Maker No.	Date in Service	Cost £	Further Details
15	No details					
16	A 7097	Panhard		1904	506	12 h.p. motor car.
17	No details					
18	No details					
19	LA9194	Enfield		1911	*475	Motor car.
20	LC8900	Argyll		1911	*350	Motor car.
21	No details					
22	D 8589			1912	*535	Motor lorry.
23	?			1912	*548	Motor lorry.
24	?			1912	*535	Motor lorry.
25	D 8906			1913	*535	Motor lorry.
						* Insurance values
26		A & O §		1914	973	To Army. August 1914
27		A & O §		1914		The two for £780
28		A & O §		1915		Price not known
29		A & O §		1915		Price not known
30PW	M 6919	Foden	4682	Oct 1914 ¶+		To S.B.&D.Co. 1937
31PW	M 6920	-do-	4848	Nov 1914 ¶+		Scrapped 1933 (LCC)
32PW	M 6921	-do-	4806	Dec 1914 ¶+		To D.&R.Monger 1938
33PW	M 6922	-do-	4852	Jan 1915 ¶+		To S.B.&D.Co. 1938
34PW	M 6923	-do-	4854	-do- ¶+		Scrapped 1938 (LPTB)
35PW	M 6924	-do-	4804	Feb 1915 ¶+		Scrapped 1938 (LPTB)
36PW	M 8759*	-do-	6426	1920		To S.B.&D.Co. 1937

§ Supplied by Allday & Onions. Fleet numbers subject to correction.
¶ All 5-ton capacity, steam driven. + Fitted with Herbert Morris jibs.
* Purchased secondhand 1919/20, ex-National Projectile Factory,Dudley.

37PW	FE3878	Clayton	T1053	Oct 1920	Scrapped by 1931
38PW	FE3879	-do-	T1040	-do-	Scrapped by 1932
39PW	FE3880	-do-	T1016	-do-	Scrapped by 1937
40PW	FE3925	-do-	T1039	Nov 1920	Scrapped by 1937
41PW	FE3926	-do-	T1037	-do-	Scrapped by 1937
42PW	FE3927	-do-	T1074	-do-	Scrapped by 1937

Carrying the fleet number 18, this Yorkshire transverse boiler wagon with a chain drive back axle, was used on conduit gully emptying duties, and survived until 1948. (W. J. Haynes)

Note:- Purchased from Clayton & Shuttleworth for £1,514 each.
All 5-ton capacity, steam driven.

7 cranes from J. W. Flowers at £279 each (Nos. 36 - 42).

17(2)	XX 780	Yorkshire	1510	May 1925	To S.B.&D.Co. 1939
18(2)	XX 781	-do-	1511	-do-	To Beverley Car Service 1948

Nos. 17(2) and 18(2) were steam driven gully wagons.
S.B.&D.Co. Steel Breaking & Dismantling Co. Chesterfield.

By 1932, other vehicles in use were:-

Tower wagons (petrol)	1	Lorries (petrol-electric)	1
Tower wagons (petrol-electric)	3	Mobile cranes (petrol-electric)	2
Tower wagons (electric)	2*	Cable trailers	2
Tower wagons (horse-drawn)	5		

* Note:- These two battery-electric tower wagons were what remained of
five which had been purchased between 1920 and 1925, the
first four supplied by Electricar/Edison Accumulators, in
service early in 1921, the last one by Electromobile/Edison
Accumulators and placed in service at the end of 1925. Cost
of the first four was £1,750 each, that of the last, £1,586.

One steam wagon in the 10 to 15 series, referred to as a "tractor"
by the LCC, was used during 1907-08 to haul horse cars to and from
Leytonstone Works when they went there for overhaul and repair.
Eleven horse drawn snow sweepers and four tower wagons were still
in use in 1911.

After the end of the Great War, the Council found it difficult to
bring the road vehicle fleet up to standard by purchase, and recourse
was made to hiring. In 1919 and 1920, £22,500 was spent on hiring
lorries for general use, and on motor cars and taxis for use by pay-
masters, etc. Four steam lorries were also on hire from Matthews
& Co. between 1st November 1920 and 30th April 1921 at a cost of
£3,200. During the next few years, as new and secondhand vehicles
were purchased, the necessity to hire became of less importance.

On 4th November 1920, the Council agreed to an experiment with a portable suction cleaner for removing debris from car floors at termini between journeys, but it was apparently a failure. Scrap tickets were to remain a problem. The provision of used ticket boxes was frowned upon by the police, who considered that they were unnecessary!

Tower Wagons

The need for the first tower wagons arose with the electrification on the overhead wire system of the lines in Woolwich, Hammersmith, Herne Hill and Norbury in 1908 and 1909. Horse drawn vehicles were used, consisting of flat wagons upon which were mounted retractable towers supplied by Messrs. Watlington, while the horses and drivers were hired from local contractors.

Three wagons were placed in service, later increased to four, the one for work in the Woolwich area with two horses supplied by John Murray; the two for Norwood and Streatham each with two horses, provided by Thomas Tilling, who also provided the single horse and driver for the wagon used at Hammersmith. At that time, three short sections of overhead wiring used on north side lines were attended to by Leyton UDC and West Ham Corporation. The agreements, which were renewed on 20th July 1915, stipulated that the overhead wires and fittings were to be examined weekly and maintained as necessary, with the LCC supplying all materials. Contracts were on an annual basis, with an additional hourly charge for call-out in the event of a breakdown.

A petrol-electric tower wagon of 1931. The script on the radiator reads "Thomas Tilling Ltd. London and Brighton". (G. L. Photo. Library)

At the beginning of 1915, the charge for the Hammersmith wagon was £184 per annum, with a call-out charge of 5/- per hour; that for Norwood, Norbury and Streatham, £287 p.a. with a call-out charge of 3/- per hour; while for Woolwich it was "about £200" p.a. with a call-out charge of 1/6d per hour. One year later these costs had risen to:-

Hammersmith:	£104 for 6 months; plus 3/- per hour call-out fee.
Norwood, Norbury and Streatham:	£166 for 6 months; plus 5/- per hour call-out fee.
Woolwich:	£115 for 6 months; plus 1/6d per hour call-out fee.

The use of horse drawn wagons remained until 1920, when they were augmented with the first of the electrically driven tower wagons to be put into service. By 1924, although there were five horse drawn tower wagons in stock, they were supplemented by five electric and one petrol-driven machines. The first of three Tilling-Stevens petrol-electric tower wagons was put into service in 1931. A photograph shows the vehicle, carrying the registration number XH 9257, in new condition, standing in the yard of the Central Repair Depot. By 1932, there were two electric, one petrol and three petrol-electric tower wagons in use.

Road Service Vehicle Garages

The earlier fleet of vehicles was distributed over the system and housed in many depots and yards. Prior to the war, with spare capacity becoming available at Rye Lane car shed, it was decided to concentrate some of the fleet at that depot. This was short-lived, however, as the vehicles had to be dispersed in 1914 when the War Department took over the premises. On 13th October 1914, authorisation had been given to provide covered accomodation at Poplar at a cost of £1,770 and at Kentish Town for £1,055, which between them would house eight motor vehicles, and this work was belatedly put in hand.

On 19th December 1919, after the return on Rye Lane shed to the LCC, the sum of £1,025 was allocated to pay for alterations to be made to the depot, with the intention of providing comprehensive works facilities for the road motor fleet. A number of the south side vehicles were also to be garaged there. The sum of £1,225 was also allocated for tools and plant, while the value of the vehicles was given as £27,600. Several in the fleet, however, were outstationed at Deptford Wharf and the Central Repair Depot. On the north side, Leven Road, Poplar permanent way depot in east London and also the permanent way depot at Leighton Park Road, Kentish Town were the two sites where most of the remainder were housed.

Special thanks must go to the members of the Road Locomotive Society, and in particular to Mr. J. H. Meredith for details shown above of the steam driven lorries used by the Council.

Chapter 49
Car Sheds and Depots

South London

As the company undertakings were taken into Council ownership, it became responsible for a large number of car depots and stables, sited in what may appear to have been a quite haphazard way. In fact, in respect of the company to which each building formerly belonged, most were built or acquired at convenient positions on that system.

In the early days of the programme for electrification it had been anticipated that the horse car depots, suitably modified, together with extensions to buildings and some new construction, would have been sufficient to house the anticipated car fleet. This forecast proved to be totally inadequate; by 1902, plans were being made for the purchase of a number of sites on which to build new, large car sheds. An agent, Mr. W. J. Hazel was employed to expedite land purchases.

During the years of company operation, no fewer than 59 depots, stables and works of various kinds were used to service the car fleets. Of these, 48 were used by the LCC for varying periods after purchase of the companies within the metropolitan area, 31 of these on the south side system, as listed below.

London Tramways Company.
 Clapham High Street
 Clapham "Plough"
 Streatham, Telford Avenue
 20 Brixton Road
 Kennington Cross (Balls Yard)
 Camberwell No. 1
 Camberwell No. 2
 Bowles Road, Old Kent Road
 Leo Street, Old Kent Road
 Queens Road, Peckham
 Penrose Street, Walworth
 Carter Street, Walworth
 Eastlake Road, L'boro Jcn
  (Horse Hospital)
 Rye Lane, Peckham
 Hoskins Street, Greenwich
 Marius Road, Balham
 County Wharf
 Deptford Wharf & Granary

Woolwich & South East London Trys Co.
 Lakedale Road, Plumstead
South Eastern Metropolitan Trys Co.
 Rushey Green, Catford
London, Deptford & Greenwich Trys Co.
 Evelyn Street, Deptford
London, Camberwell & Dulwich Twys Co.
 "King's Arms", East Dulwich Road
London Southern Tramways Co.
 Lansdowne Hill, West Norwood
 Stockwell Road, Depot No. 1
 Stockwell Road, Depot No. 2
South London Tramways Co.
 Jews Row, Wandsworth
 Clapham Junction
 Queens Road, Battersea
 Borough Road (disused)
 Gonsalva Road
 Battersea Wharf

A temporary horse car depot and stables, built by the LCC, was in use at Tunnel Avenue, Greenwich for a short time during the reconstruction of the tramway in Woolwich Road.

Permanent Car Sheds Used To House Electric Cars

South

Shed	Location	Nominal Capacity
Abbey Wood	Abbey Wood Road	25 (1910), later 86
Brixton Hill**	Brixton Hill	50 (approximately)
Camberwell	Camberwell New Road	64* (later 155, then 131)
Chiswick***	Chiswick High Road	
Clapham	High Street	176* (later 164)
Hammersmith	Great Queen Street	24* (later 59)
New Cross	New Cross Road	326*
Norwood	Norwood Road	74*
Streatham	29 Streatham Hill	68*
	31 Streatham Hill	49
Wandsworth	Jews Row	103*

   * Car capacity as at 31st March 1909.

  ** Brixton Hill car shed opened in 1924.

*** Chiswick car shed purchased by the LCC from LUT in 1922.

Note:- Where a reduced figure is shown as at Camberwell and at Clapham, the higher figure includes a number of single truck cars, while the lower figure is for all bogie cars.

Development of new permanent buildings for housing electric cars was the responsibility of the Architect's Department of the LCC, whose design team under the direction of Mr. W. E. Riley, F.R.I.B.A., chose what they called the "Roman Doric" style. The walls of all buildings were of yellow stock bricks, while internally in the early buildings there was a dado of glazed white brickwork 5 ft. 6 in. high. Entrance archways and other key points were built of Portland stone. Roofs were covered in blue Bangor slates with roof lights on the Helliwell system. Even though some variations on this theme were employed, the basic design was quite distinctive and was retained for the whole period of LCC control.

Temporary Car Sheds

Balham	Marius Road
Bowles Road	Old Kent Road
Deptford	Evelyn Street
Greenwich	Hoskins Street
Leo Street	Old Kent Road
Plumstead	Lakedale Road
Peckham	Peckham Road/Rye Lane

Penrose Street Works and Depot

The London Tramways Company had a comprehensive workshop which was situated at Penrose Street, Walworth, a side turning to the west of Walworth Road and not far from the "Elephant & Castle" public house and junction. After transfer to the LCC, the Council continued to maintain the works for several years, but due to the electrification of the system in south London, together with the re-arrangement of such services as car maintenance and repair, the works gradually lost its level of importance.

During 1906, it was decided that the installation should be closed down as from September. As there was ample accommodation for all repairs to be undertaken to horse cars and for many other engineering functions at the premises in Union Road, Leytonstone, much of the remaining work, together with the staff were transferred north of the river. This, in turn, allowed for the disposal of the Penrose Street premises, which were sub-let to the London Motor Omnibus Company for one year as from midsummer 1907 at a rent of £750, and then at a rent of £425 per annum for a further 36 years, which was the unexpired part of the lease held by the LCC. A premium of £5,500 was also to be paid by the omnibus company.

Clapham Depot and Car Shed

It was on the southern system that the first impact of electric traction was to be seen. Consideration had been given to providing accommodation for tramcars which would be used on a considerable mileage of new tramway, as well as on those lines to be subsequently reconstructed.

In LCC terminology there was a clear distinction between a depot and a car shed. The installations previously belonging to the horse tramway companies were generally referred to as depots (where cars and horses were housed in the same building) or as stables where only horses were kept. Specially constructed or reconstructed buildings intended to house only electric cars were termed car sheds. Despite this, however, in tramwayman's slang, the depot or car shed was almost always referred to as "the yard". The first such building to be attended to was the one at High Street, Clapham, where the horse car depot site was extended when the Council took an option on additional land, 28,132 square feet in area, which was purchased in 1901 for £5,018.

The first section of the new shed was built to accommodate 48 bogie cars. The entrance was in Clapham Park Road, where the properties acquired to make the entry were purchased for £1,300. Building work, including the installation of tracks and electrical equipment, was undertaken by the LCC Works Department at a cost of £30,000, while the car traverser was manufactured by Messrs. Dick, Kerr & Co. and cost £450. This section of the building while still incomplete was used to assemble the first of the new cars.

The High Street entrance to Clapham car shed was flanked by a grocery shop and the hairdressing saloons of J. Leslie, where a permanent wave for a lady could be obtained for 16/6d. (Courtesy: LTM U20062)

As soon as the first section became available, arrangements were made to demolish the remainder of the horse car depot and extend the electric car shed (known as No. 2 part). On 7th July 1903 the Council accepted the tender of Messrs. Kirk & Randall to do the work for £29,434, plus another £457. 9. 6d to construct a new entrance in High Street. Trackwork in the shed was installed by the Tramways Department at a cost of £3,500. The second section of the building was put into use progressively during the second half of 1904; by 31st March 1905, there were 81 cars housed there. Ultimate capacity was for 164 cars standing on 25 roads, served by two traversers. The Motor School was also established here, in which special facilities were provided to instruct trainee motormen in all aspects of the craft.

This shed was unusual in that it had two distinct entrance and exit routes. The "front" entrance was in High Street, and cars entered the shed by means of trailing points in both main line roads. These two tracks converged into a single line at the entrance, over which was a covered way with residential accommodation above. Once inside the premises, the tracks became double again and led to the traverser pit which was situated about one-third of the way into the building.

To the right-hand or south side of the shed were two entrance-exit roads which became a single line leading into Clapham Park Road, at the west end of which were the usual connections, northwards into High Street and south into The Pavement.

To enable cars to be driven under power on all roads, conductor tee-rails were provided throughout, placed as far to one side as possible to enable staff to move freely in the pits beneath the cars. To protect staff from injury from electric shock, teak casings surrounded the tee-rails, these being hinged to enable the car ploughs to be inspected and removed if required.

Balham Car Shed

At the same time as reconstruction work was being undertaken on the horse car depot at Clapham, it was decided that the depot at Marius Road, Balham should be temporarily converted to house some of the electric cars. On 22nd July 1902, a contract was entered into

This view of Balham car shed with its open-air traverser shows the rather basic method of construction employed. (LCC official view)

with Messrs. C. B. Roberts & Co. of Redhill to carry out this work at a cost of £2,140. In February 1903, the LCC made the necessary track alterations at a cost of £1,350. A traverser was supplied by Messrs. Dick, Kerr & Co. for £450 and installed outside the building on the front apron. This served the six storage roads, upon which a maximum of 36 cars could stand.

The shed was used as an overflow establishment for Clapham, but only until 28th August 1904 upon completion of stage two of the main building at Clapham. It was then held in reserve as a site which could be developed should the necessity arise. Part of it was later used as a dismantling depot for many of the surplus horse cars, while the remainder was used as a store.

Later Use

On 1st September 1915, the shed was re-opened to house trailer cars which were put on to the Merton-Embankment services, remaining in use and working from Marius Road until the withdrawal of the trailers on 18th November 1922, after which the shed was cleared and closed.

Camberwell Road; Rye Lane, Peckham; Bowles Road, Old Kent Road; Leo Street, Old Kent Road; Hoskins Street, Greenwich
Temporary Car Sheds

Concurrently with the work going on at Clapham and Balham, arrangements were being made to provide temporary accommodation for electric cars which were to work in south-east London. A Capital Vote of £7,100 was authorised for this purpose, of which £3,600 was allocated for architectural work. The remainder was for Tramways Department works, including track laying and the provision of electrical equipment for the "new" part of Rye Lane depot, additional car pits and lowering of floors where necessary to obtain sufficient height for the double deck open top cars to get safely in and out of the sheds. An allowance was also included for the erection of special overhead wire equipment at Rye Lane, Bowles Road, Leo Street and Hoskins Street depots, to enable cars to be moved under power.

Details of Works

Camberwell Road. Lower floor of shed and existing pit, and make additional pit.	£475		
Overhead work.	£250		
		£ 725	
Rye Lane (existing shed). Lower one track and make two additional pits.	£240		
Overhead work.	£475		
		£ 715	
Rye Lane (temporary shed). Lay rails,	£700		
Overhead work.	£475		
		£1,175	
Bowles Road. Lower floor of pit and make two extra pits.	£ 90		
Overhead work.	£300		
		£ 390	
Leo Street. Lowering of surfaces and forming new pavements and conduits.	£400		
		£ 400	
Greenwich. Make two extra pits.	£ 80		
Overhead work.	£200		
		£ 280	

Bowles Road, Old Kent Road;
Leo Street, Old Kent Road

Until a vast new car shed at "Fairlawn", New Cross was ready for occupation, it was necessary for these horse car depots to be retained. To serve their new purpose, certain alterations had to be made to the buildings. In each case, a conduit entry track was constructed from the street to a point outside the depot building in front of the track fan points. Here a pit was built with the track laid over it, and where the conduit tee-rails terminated, while the running rails were connected to the existing depot tracks. The ploughs of the cars coming into the shed were removed by a member of the staff working in the pit, after which the cars were provided with power from a special plug adaptor pushed into a suitable connector fitted beneath one canopy of each car.

In each depot, power for the plugs was collected from a pair of overhead wires electrically charged at 550 volts d.c., which were suspended by special insulated hangers running the length of the building. A small four-wheeled trolley, the grooved wheels on one side insulated from those on the other, was placed upon the wires. A long cable completed the assembly, and was terminated at the top end to collector brushes which rubbed against the wheels, while at the lower end it was fitted with a plug adaptor. It was similar in some respects to the Cedes Stoll system which was later developed for use with early trackless trolley vehicles.

The LCC Works Department undertook to alter Bowles Road and Leo Street depots, commencing work in January 1903, and it was expected that the alterations would take about six weeks to complete. The Tramways Department had already allocated £2,150 to modify the tracks at these two depots, together with those in the "old" part of Rye Lane and at Hoskins Street depots, while on 26th January 1904 the Department was authorised to spend another £150 on additional pits at Bowles Road and Leo Street. The depots remained in use until 20th and 28th May 1905 respectively.

It was decided by the Council on 1st May 1906 that Bowles Road shed would no longer be required for tramway purposes. The site, held under seven separate leases at a total cost of £467.8s per annum, was handed back to the freeholders, who were the Camberwell Charities as from 24th June 1906. Leo Street depot was retained for other purposes.

Hoskins Street, Greenwich

This small depot was on a riverside site which was eventually to be used as the nucleus of the area to be covered by the LCC Tramways Greenwich Generating Station. Due to problems which arose in the housing of the first electric cars, it became necessary to use this depot for a short time.

In common with the other temporary car sheds, alterations were made which included lowering the tracks into and inside the building, so that the open top, double deck cars which were to be used could gain entry and be stored there. Sufficient headroom was also required to allow for the erection of overhead wires upon which to install a trolley collector. The costs incurred in carrying out this work were included in the allocated sum, as has been described. The shed was brought into use in January 1904, remaining operative until 16th June 1905. After closure, the site was handed over to the contractors for redevelopment.

Rye Lane Peckham Depot

Of the temporary sheds, Rye Lane was to be exceptional as it had been decided to extend the car standing space considerably and to make this installation rather more "permanent" than the others. On 3rd February 1903 the Clyde Structural Iron Company of Glasgow obtained the contract to supply a new, temporary car shed structure at a cost of £1,228.17s. The foundation works were sub-let to Messrs. J & C Bowyer. The LCC installed the necessary trackwork, using old horse car rails lifted from sections of the Clapham to Tooting route when reconstruction of that line was undertaken. This work, together with the provision of overhead wiring and a plough access pit cost £1,675, and was carried out by labour within the Tramways Department. With regard to the existing horse car depot, two additional pits (making three in all) were provided at a further cost of £240. This section of the building was completed during the summer of 1903, in time to receive new cars for erection, which were to work on the next sections of electrified lines.

The Council next decided, in December 1903, to cover the open yard of the depot with a roof structure at a cost of £1,100, which was dealt with by the LCC Works Department. A pit had already been constructed along the front of the shed to accommodate a traverser. The result was a sizeable installation, capable of holding about 40 cars, standing on eight "main" and two subsidiary roads. Its first use as a running shed was to house some of the cars which were to work on the New Cross, Greenwich and Borough services. Access was by a trailing turnout installed into the "down" road in High Street, Peckham.

During the early period of electric car operation, and certainly until the end of 1906, there was considerable movement of cars from one depot to another; this was done to enable the cars used for new and extended services to be housed temporarily while new buildings were being constructed or old ones rebuilt, and also where extensive track reconstruction was taking place. The other sheds mainly concerned in these movements were Clapham, Streatham, Camberwell and New Cross. To give an example, on 28th May 1905, the cars used on the Camberwell to Vauxhall service were transferred from Clapham to Rye Lane shed. After several months, and once the new main sheds were substantially completed the cars were transferred away from Rye Lane to Camberwell.

As this site was so centrally placed, it was also used for works purposes for some time. A sand drying plant, among other items, was installed in October 1907. Considerable quantities of this commodity were required to fill the hoppers of the cars, and it had to be properly treated so that it did not clog in use. Sand was loaded into the drying machine hopper, which held 14 cwts. A worm gear conveyor placed the sand on to a circular spiral plate, which travelled over a coke fire, giving the sand a run of about 600 ft. (all within the 10 ft. x 3 ft. housing). The machine had a heating surface in the spiral of about 250 sq. ft. Dried sand was then passed into another storage bin with a capacity of 10 tons. The machine was driven by a 9 h.p. motor. Cost of drying was 4½d a ton.

Early motor cars and other road vehicles belonging to the LCC Tramways Department were usually housed at any convenient place, which did not allow for any proper facilities to be provided for either maintenance or overhaul. Resulting from this, the decision was taken to convert a part of the depot premises into a fully-equipped garage where much of the road fleet could be attended to.

It was not long after the establishment of the garage that the Great War started. The military authorities were then in need of various kinds of accommodation, which was met by request for the use of buildings and, later, by requisition. Rye Lane depot came into the first category when the local Territorial Army Commander "suggested" that part of the establishment be handed over "for the time being". It was not long before the whole site was taken over, remaining in the hands of the military for the remainder of the war and for some time after. Once the depot was handed back to the Council, the decision was taken to utilise it as a permanent way workshop and garage, but also as a place where miscellaneous types of work could be undertaken. As an example, several of the early trailer cars were dismantled there in 1921. Much of the road vehicle fleet was again garaged and serviced there after 1919, the necessary alterations to part of the building costing approximately £1,025 to effect, with an extra £1,225 for tools and plant.

In 1922, the shed was made ready to take on another role, when a section was prepared for use as an assembly works for the new cars of class E/1, Nos. 1727 to 1776. The traverser was restored to enable the assembled cars to be moved out of the building. Power for this function was supplied from the feeder serving the overhead electric crane, with a twin-wire trolley and flexible cable once again doing duty as the means of supplying current to the cars.

Once the last of the cars had been assembled, the depot was used as a general workshop for the electrical department, with facilities for making and repairing all kinds of miscellaneous items ranging from special illuminated signs such as:-

To L.C.C.
T R A M S
----------->

to the repair of mobile welding sets which were used by the permanent way department.

One of the specialised pieces of equipment to be manufactured and maintained by the staff at Rye Lane was known as a "paddle plough", which was used by the permanent way staff to collect power from the conduit tee-rails for energising welding equipment, lighting sets and the like. This item consisted of a shortened version of a plough shank, at the top of which was a handle which could be turned through 90°. Two extensible arms were fitted at the bottom of the shank, each of which carried an electrode. To obtain power from the conduit conductors, the whole assembly would be lowered through the slot at any point, then with the head of the plough resting on the slot rails, the handle would be turned, allowing the two electrodes to make contact with the tee-rails. Current would then flow through the plough cables fitted to the head of the plough to energise whatever equipment was being used at the time.

Evelyn Street, Deptford Depot

After conversion of the Deptford services to electric traction, the old depot and stables was declared surplus to requirements, but during early negotiations regarding disposal, it was used as a store. In May 1912, part of the stable accommodation was let to a local engineering firm, F. Francis & Son, for £90 a year on a short term tenancy. However, with the onset of the Great War, and the eventual use of trailer cars by the LCC, the depot was re-opened on 31st August 1916 to house some of these vehicles.

Trailer Shunting

An agreement was made with Thomas Tilling on 31st October 1916 for the use of two horses to haul trailers into and out from the depot at a cost of £145 per horse per year, which included forage, stabling and shoeing, all to be done on the depot site. This sum was reduced as from 1st April 1917 to £130 per horse per year, when the Council agreed to provide stable labour.

The introduction of mechanical towing of the trailers came in 1919. With the agreement of Deptford Borough Council, twin wire overhead was installed over the track from the street to the depot, which cost £700, and which was installed by the Tramways Department. However, the method used to haul the trailers in and out is still not known, but it is believed to have been either a specially adapted tramway vehicle or a motor lorry fitted with an electric motor and suitable controller.

The last trailers to be used on the LCCT worked on the services between Greenwich and London Bridge (70) and Greenwich and Waterloo Station (68) until 17th April 1924, and Evelyn Street depot was used to house these. Early in February 1925, with the withdrawal of trailers, the depot was used for dispersal of those bodies which were sold and then as a demolition site for the remainder, after which the building was disposed of.

Camberwell Car Sheds

The first section of the shed to house the early electric cars had been dealt with under the temporary arrangements made, when a part of the horse car depot was adapted for its new role. In February 1903, the Chief Officer suggested that the shed be used to house the cars serving the Camberwell district, and later, for those to Dulwich and Peckham Rye when the lines were constructed.

Camberwell shed was one of those to have two entrances. The one in Camberwell New Road, with the original head office of tramways at No. 303, next door, is seen in this view. (Courtesy: LTM U16010)

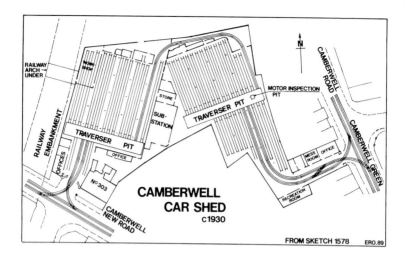

CAMBERWELL
CAR SHED
c1930

FROM SKETCH 1578   ERO.89

Authorisation had been given to build a new shed on ground which had been purchased in 1901, which lay between the South Eastern & Chatham Railway line, Camberwell New Road and Camberwell Green, after the plan to build a generating station on the site had been abandoned. To allow for the considerable building work to be carried out, it was decided on 5th December 1904 that cars which had been housed in the temporary premises for use on the Southwark to Camberwell and St. George's Church to Camberwell services should be moved away to Rye Lane shed. One week later, on 12th December, the cars for the Vauxhall to Camberwell and Westinster to Camberwell services were temporarily transferred to Clapham car shed.

It had cost £8,635. 2. 6d to obtain the freehold of the site, while total estimated costs for rebuilding the old depot and adding the new one, giving space for 61 cars were:-

Buildings,	£28,900
Tracks, etc.,	£ 2,000
Car Traverser,	£ 500

Total	£31,400

The first section cost £19,000 and was erected by the LCC Works Department, while the Tramways Department laid in the tracks at a cost of £3,190, both dealt with under contracts obtained on 17th May 1904. This part of the building was ready for use on 17th October 1905. A power sub-station was also provided during the course of this work.

A large extension to the shed was planned in 1913, building work being undertaken by Messrs. J. & C. Bowyer at a cost of £28,954, which included an extension to the sub-station. Completion of this part made the building unusual in that it consisted of two separate car sheds, joined at the back, and each with its traverser pit. The entrance to the westernmost building faced south on to Camberwell New Road, where the two entrance-exit tracks led away from the traverser pit and then crossed each other to join the street tracks at trailing points.

The entrance to the building on the east side, also with two tracks leading from the traverser pit out to Camberwell Road, fronted on to Camberwell Green and faced north-east. Both parts of the building complex were self-contained, but were connected together by one track, which started and ended at the traverser pits, winding its way through the the buildings in the process. Rails were laid by Tramways Department staff, and a second traverser costing £664 was supplied and installed by Brush/British Westinghouse. Work was completed in September 1914, and gave accommodation for an ultimate total of 155 cars, of which about half, at that time, were of the 4-wheeled type. This number was reduced to 131 bogie cars in later years. The allocation for July 1927 was 130 cars.

New Cross Car Shed

When the first electrified lines were opened in south-east London, the provision of a new, main car shed in the area was already being put in hand. It had already been decided that the ideal location for such an installation would be in New Cross Road, not far from New Cross Gate.

In 1901, the Council had decided, against much opposition, to use compulsory powers to purchase 7½ acres of land known as "Fairlawn" which belonged to the Haberdashers' Company ("The Master and Four Wardens of the Fraternity of the Art or Mystery of Haberdashers in the City of London"). The LCC included this proposed purchase in its 1902 Parliamentary Bill, but it was not allowed in the form presented. However, settlement for about four acres of land was reached by a compromise agreement made with the Haberdashers, which cost the LCC £11,500 plus £850 for legal fees and charges. Building costs for the car shed were expected to be about £152,000, which included the provision of a sub-station. Approval was given on 28th July 1903 for the contract for ground excavation works to be let to Messrs. J. & M. Patrick of London, at a cost of £6,541. This was followed on 24th November 1903 by the LCC Works Department contracting for the structure of the shed for £80,530, and the Tramways Department providing and laying the tracks, for which work the sum of £70,000 had been budgeted. Due to the importance of this car shed, both in size and in its position in the growing electric tramway network, structural details of this unusual building are described in some detail.

The workshops at New Cross car shed, c1906.   (LCC official view)

The site measured about 400 feet square and as originally seen was on an uphill slope from north to south, the north end being almost at road level, not far from the New Cross Gate road junction. The entrance to the site was to be about halfway along its width. An added complication to its development was that two sewers, the "Effra Branch" and the "High Level Main" ran from east to west beneath it, with the Effra Branch being quite close to the surface. To be able to accommodate these, the main floor of the building had to be formed sufficiently high so that no impediment would be placed in the line of the sewers or access to them, and also that inspection pits without obstructions could be provided for the use of tramcar maintenance staff.

The slope of the ground was at a gradient of about 1 in 45, the back of the site being about 14 feet above the front. The ground, fairly loose, had to be retained at the back by the construction of a concrete wall before any further work was done. Once completed, the base raft of concrete was laid across the ground, upon which all floor works were built. Tracks were supported on 14-inch brick piers and stanchions resting directly on the concrete base, except where the sewers ran beneath the site. At these places, tracks were placed on heavy steel girders laid on buttresses on either side of the sewers. It was also because of the existence of the sewers that the original plan for the shed to have two separate entrances was modified, resulting in the provision of a single entrance, consisting of a rather imposing Portland stone archway built in the "Roman-Doric" style. The roof structure, in nine bays, each of which had a span of 43 ft. 3 in., was of high tensile steel, the whole weighing about 1,700 tons. Blue Bangor slates and Helliwell's glazing provided the roof covering.

Stanchions and brick piers carried the car shed tracks at a height of 5 ft. above the base concrete raft and, allowing for space for the traverser pit and other sundry pieces of equipment such as washing bays, there was accommodation for 29 tracks on the north side of the traverser pit, each 140 ft. long, with another 32 tracks, each of a length of 175 ft. on the south side. This gave a total length of approximately 10,710 ft. (about two miles) on which 314 bogie cars, or 350 single truck cars could stand. This method of car shed construction was very expensive and, as pointed out by the LCC, was not an arrangement to be considered for general use.

Two tracks were laid in from the street, opening out to three once inside the entrance, and climbing at 1 in 45 for about 90 ft. into the body of the shed until floor level was reached just before the traverser pit. Two traversers by C. & A. Musker, with Westinghouse equipment, were used to bring cars to and from the exit roads and storage tracks. In view of the gradient of the entrance tracks, catch points were installed on each of the three tracks. As there was also considerable movement of road vehicles in and out of the depot area, the three tracks were fully paved. At the washing bays, all cars were washed daily, leathered off, brasswork polished, insides rubbed down and floors disinfected. A total of 95 men were employed in the running shed.

The first section of the shed was handed over to the operations department on 15th May 1905 with accommodation for 80 cars, to be followed during the next two days with accommodation for another 20. Final completion of the shed was scheduled for the early part of December 1905.

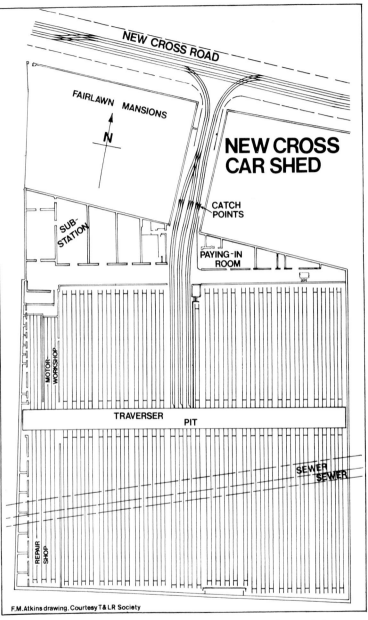

NEW CROSS ROAD

FAIRLAWN MANSIONS

N

**NEW CROSS
CAR SHED**

CATCH
POINTS

SUB-
STATION

PAYING-IN
ROOM

MOTOR-
WORKSHOP

TRAVERSER PIT

SEWER
SEWER

REPAIR
SHOP

F.M. Atkins drawing. Courtesy T & LR Society

The diagram shows the method used on the steeply graded access tracks to ensure that a runaway car would be derailed before reaching the main road. The line of the sewers can also be seen.

Until the new Central Repair Depot became available, part of the car shed space was earmarked for use as a repair works for the south side cars. Comprehensive mechanical and electrical repairs and repainting were undertaken in this part of the depot, and described in the technical press "as being of the highest quality". The great difficulty was that, within a comparatively short time, there was insufficient room available for the increasing amount of work waiting to be done, resulting in some of it being off-loaded to work areas in other sheds. The repair works remained in use until replaced by the opening, on 6th March 1909, of the first section of the Central Repair Depot. Part of the area vacated was returned for use as car standing space, with a section remaining as a workshop for on-site repairs. The total number of men employed in the works was 120.

In the erecting shop of the temporary repair depot there were four tracks beneath each bay of the roof, with the gangways between the tracks being sufficiently wide at 5 ft. 2½ in. to allow for safe working conditions, while at the places where the roof stanchions were sited, the gangways were 8 ft. 9½ in. wide. The working gangways themselves were formed of creosoted boards resting on joists, which in turn were supported by the brick piers which also carried the track rails.

The workshop was comprehensively fitted out with machinery, tools and plant sufficient to undertake any type of work required, including major damage repair. Quoted in the list of special machinery was a tyre turning lathe, a tyre boring machine, a hydraulic wheel press and a controller contact press. To enable car bodies to be lifted from their trucks, a 5-ton overhead gantry crane was installed, capable of running the whole length of the bay.

Streatham, Telford Avenue Car Shed

The next areas to be dealt with were Streatham and Wandsworth. Reconstruction of the lines in Streatham and Brixton was taking place during the spring of 1904. The cable-car shed at Streatham Hill, opposite Telford Avenue, was to be demolished and replaced with a completely new building to house 82 cars at an estimated cost of £35,000, and was to be carried out in two parts, due to the necessity of retaining one half of the building housing the temporary generating station, which was working in the old cable engine house. This was to remain until the first part of Greenwich Generating Station was available to take the load. The cars for the service to Streatham were being shedded as far away as Camberwell, Clapham and Rye Lane and, to provide much-needed car space for the expanding fleet, it was essential that at least half of the depot be made available as soon as possible.

A contract was awarded to the LCC Works Department on 1st November 1904 for the construction of the first part of the first building, at a cost of £16,180. Tracks were installed by the Tramways Department at a cost of approximately £3,100. Construction began early in 1905, with Messrs. Dorman, Long erecting the steelwork, and the building was completed by the end of the year. A traverser was supplied by Jessop & Appleby with electrical equipment by British Westinghouse for £674. The new shed was opened to traffic on 3rd February 1906, when the cars working on the Streatham to Westminster, Streatham to Blackfriars and Streatham to Borough services were moved in from Camberwell, with the night service cars on the Water Lane to Southwark route being transferred from Clapham.

The two sheds at Streatham, physically separated, were together more commonly known as "Telford Avenue". (Courtesy: LTM U16007)

On 26th May 1906 the temporary generating station was closed, its load transferred to Greenwich. The machinery was quickly dismantled, work then starting on the construction of the second part of the shed. Messrs. J. & C. Bowyer undertook this for £7,145, while paving and track work went to the LCC Works Department for £700. This section was completed in September 1907, providing accommodation for 68 cars, if 38 of these were single-truck 4-wheeled vehicles, or 59 bogie cars, on ten roads separated by the traverser pit.

In October 1910 it became necessary to consider extending the car shed yet again and an option was taken on the freehold of No. 31 Streatham Hill, the leasehold of which was already held by the Council. This was purchased on 21st February 1911 for £1,500. The LCC gave authority on 31st May. In a similar way to the problem which caused special construction methods to be adopted at New Cross car shed, the buildings at Telford Avenue had to be designed in such a way that freedom of access was given to a main water pipeline which bisected the site, this time from back to front. Due to the presence of the water main, it was necessary to design a separate building on the other side of the pipe and connect the two together by a footbridge. For operational purposes, the two buildings were classed as one shed, but physically were entirely separate.

The contract for building work was let to Messrs. Rowley Bros. of Tottenham in the sum of £12,997, with the Tramways Department laying the rails and providing ancillary services for £3,945. A traverser was supplied by Brush/British Westinghouse for £664 and sited about three-quarters of the way back from the entrance. Work was completed in February 1912, and there was accommodation for 49 bogie cars on six roads, including the entrance track. Access to the northern shed was by means of a single line from each of the street tracks, while the southern (new) shed was provided with a single trailing turnout from the "down" road of the main line. The total number of cars allocated to the Streatham sheds in July 1927, which included the satellite shed at Brixton Hill, was 138.

Jews Row, Wandsworth Car Shed

To allow for the expansion of electric services on a completely new line from Wandsworth to Tooting, as well as the reconstruction of horse tramways in the Wandsworth area, it was decided to build a new car shed on the site of the old horse car depot at Jews Row and on land next to it, which had been purchased under compulsory powers obtained in 1904. Properties purchased in 1904 and 1905 were Nos. 25, 27, 29, 31 and 33 Jews Row, at a total cost of £4,760.

Construction of the shed, which was in the usual "Roman-Doric" style, was large enough to house 103 cars, including some single-truck vehicles, standing on 16 roads. Building work was dealt with by the LCC Works Department, with trackwork by the Tramways Department, all at a cost of £34,000. Two traversers were supplied and installed by Jessop & Appleby Bros., with British Westinghouse equipment, for the total sum of £1,348. The installation was complete and available for use in August 1906. Access to and from the shed was by two tracks, which became one just outside the building, and led to the main line. In July 1927, there were 95 cars allocated to the shed.

Plumstead Depot

Narrow gauge horse cars worked between Plumstead, Woolwich and East Greenwich and, even before purchase, plans were being made by the LCC to electrify the section between Plumstead and Woolwich at the earliest opportunity, to be followed by new construction between Plumstead and Abbey Wood. It became obvious that temporary depot space would be needed for the electric cars, resulting in the decision being taken to convert part of the horse car depot at Lakedale Road, Plumstead to take double deck open top cars. It was not considered to be worthwhile to remodel the old depot to take roof-covered cars, as it was confidently expected that a new, large building at Abbey Wood would be ready for occupation by 1910, when top-covered cars would be put into service. Nevertheless, it was to cost the Council £2,040 to adapt the Plumstead building by providing several standard gauge tracks and the associated overhead wiring.

Horse cars and animals were transferred to temporary premises at Tunnel Avenue, East Greenwich in September 1907 in advance of the conversion work. Plumstead shed came into use again in April 1908 with the delivery of the first six of eight specially adapted class B electric cars, enabling a service to commence on 17th April. These were soon joined by the other two, together with four similarly reconstructed class D cars.

On 29th August 1910, Plumstead depot reverted to housing the few horse cars used on the shuttle service between Nile Street, Woolwich and the Dockyard, these being taken on a special standard-gauge flat wagon transporter to and from the narrow gauge horse car tracks, until, in November 1913, the last of the horse cars was taken off service. A detailed description of this interesting and unusual line is given in Volume I of this history.

Meantime, on 15th June 1910, part of the Plumstead premises was let for stable accommodation to Mackintosh Bros., a local firm of mineral water manufacturers, at an annual rent of £50. This was extended to cover additional stabling on 25th March 1912 for an extra £25 a year, the agreement to last until 24th June 1913.

On 6th August 1914, the building was handed over to the military authorities for use as a stables, reverting to LCC use at some time after the Great War. The approach track, together with its overhead wiring, until it was all disconnected from the main line about 1930, was used on rare occasions as a stand for an electric car which, for some reason or other, was unable to be taken to either Abbey Wood or New Cross, usually because of a breakdown. The site was eventually disposed of.

Abbey Wood Car Shed

The first moves were made early in 1905 to secure a site for a car shed for the authorised electric tramways between Eltham, Woolwich and Abbey Wood. As yet, the horse tramways worked by the Woolwich & South East London Tramways Company were still in private hands but, under the terms of an arbitration award, were due to become Council property as from midnight on 31st May/1st June 1905.

An agreement was signed on 23rd January 1906 to acquire property for £905 in Abbey Wood Road almost at the County boundary, which would provide for part of the land for the shed. The rest of the land required was expected to be the subject of compulsory purchase powers, an Act of Parliament to authorise this being obtained in 1906. This further acquisition would enlarge the site area to about 46,000 square feet at an extra cost of about £1,800. The plan was that the first part of the car shed to be built would hold 25 cars and the extension, when it came, would provide a further 61 car spaces.

On 16th February and 2nd March 1909, approval was given by the Council for the purchase of the remainder of the site for £2,700 and for the construction of the first part of the shed. Cost of the building was £10,644. 9. 2d, plus the cost of the trackwork, overhead wiring

This view of Abbey Wood car shed shows the unusual track layout. Access to the main line is to the right. *(Courtesy: LTM U19446)*

and electric lighting at an expected extra sum of £3,675. It was stated that the car shed was urgently required, as the temporary depot in use at Plumstead was totally inadequate for its purpose, and unsuitable for housing the top-covered double deck cars which had been ordered for the services.

A contract was let to Messrs. Kirk & Randall of Woolwich for the building work, while the rails were to be laid by the Council's own staff. Despite a problem encountered over the stabilisation of the rather treacherous sub-soil, the first section of the building was completed in February 1910, in time for delivery to and erection there of ten new class M cars for use on the Woolwich to Eltham service as from 23rd July 1910. Later, several bogie cars were assembled and stabled there to replace the open top cars which had been moved into Abbey Wood from Plumstead depot.

In July 1912, quotations were being invited for the construction of the extension to the shed. The successful tender was submitted by Messrs. Rowley Bros. at £16,981, while the Tramways Department were to lay the rails and provide fittings for £4,449. A traverser was supplied by the Brush Company. The extension was completed in October 1914, when a further 61 cars, which included a number of 4-wheeled class M cars, could be housed on 20 roads. The track layout at the entrance to the shed incorporated a reversing triangle for the stabling and turning of trailer cars which were in use from 1913 and during a large part of the Great War.

Although in theory a maximum of 86 cars could be housed, this number was never achieved. The area immediately behind the office block was declared to be unsuitable for car standing and was used as storage space for miscellaneous items such as spare wheelsets and electric motors. In July 1927, the allocation for the shed was 48 cars.

Norwood Car Shed

On 3rd November 1908, the Council accepted the tender of Charles Wall Ltd. for the erection of a new car shed in Norwood Road, West Norwood, about 200 yards north of the terminus, at a cost of £21,260. The freehold site, valued at £7,750 included a frontage of 200 feet length along the main road, upon which a fire brigade station was eventually built. The access tracks to the car shed, which had been built at the back of the site, were on the London side of the fire station.

The contract negotiated with Charles Wall allowed that company to sub-contract certain parts of the work to specialist firms. Granolithic work was entrusted to Messrs. Malcolm Macleod & Co; electric lighting to Messrs. Tredegar. This shed was equipped with overhead wires, the installation of these being carried out by the Tramways Department.

Accommodation was provided for 61 bogie cars on fifteen roads, with the traverser pit situated about one-third of the way into the storage area. The single traverser was supplied by Messrs. Mountain & Gibson as part of a bulk order for five, authorised on 2nd February 1909 at a total cost of £1,907. The completed shed was ready for occupation early in October 1909, but was never used to its maximum extent. In July 1927, only 46 cars were stabled there.

Hammersmith Car Shed

The first section of the isolated line from the top end of Scrubs Lane (Harrow Road) at Harlesden, southwards to Hammersmith and later Putney, work on which had commenced in 1907, was built and opened between Harlesden and Brook Green Road, Hammersmith on 30th May 1908. At the same time a lay-by, double track and double ended, was installed inside the entrance to the White City Exhibition site, which was the venue of the Franco-British Exhibition of that year. On 23rd January 1909 the section between Putney and Queen Street, Hammersmith was opened to traffic.

Early in 1905, the first moves were made to obtain a site for the eventual construction of a depot to house 57 cars, which was intended to be built in two parts. On 4th April, two properties at Nos. 243-245 Hammersmith Road were purchased for £9,000 freehold, the grounds of which backed on to Great Church Lane, which eventually became the way of entry to and exit from the new car shed when built.

The original intention was that following the construction of the first section of the building, it would be extended in later years to accommodate a further 25 cars. In fact, the figures of 57 and 82 cars were not to be realised as, due to subsequent changes in policy, the first section was constructed to hold 24 cars, the second part to take another 19 eventually, while the final extension, completed in August 1911 provided space for an extra 16 trams.

The LCC Works Department dealt with the construction of the building at a cost of £6,080 with extra temporary work at £530. Tracks and overhead wiring cost £1,125 and electric lighting added another £225 to the costs, both of these parts of the work being dealt with by the Tramways Department. Work commenced in October 1907 and was completed and ready for use in April 1908, in time to receive the 24 new class E/1 cars for assembly and testing prior to going into service on the line northwards to Scrubs Lane. A temporary sub-station was built at the same time.

Due to the stringent conditions laid down by the Public Carriage Office of the Metropolitan Police regarding overhaul and painting of cars, a repair works and paint shop was installed by the Tramways Department at a cost of £2,670, in lieu of the second portion of this part of the car shed. This was to remain in use from completion in 1909 until at least August 1915, when the isolated line was joined up at Wandsworth with the rest of the south side system. The space then reverted to its intended use as standing for up to 19 cars.

The final part of the building, to house 16 cars was built by Messrs. Charles Wall & Co., being ready for use in August 1911. This section of the building had cost £2,620, while trackwork and lighting was installed by the Tramways Department on a cost-of-work basis. Lastly, a traverser, costing £664 was supplied by the Brush Company, with electrical equipment by British Westinghouse. The traverser pit was situated at the front of the car shed, while access to and from the tramway at the north end of Fulham Palace Road was by a single line which became double just before its connection into the main lines. The allocation of cars to this and to Chiswick shed jointly in July 1927 was 70.

Chiswick Car Shed

When the London County Council took over the lines of the London United Tramways in the Hammersmith area on 2nd May 1922, the agreement also included the acquisition of part of the premises in Chiswick High Road, outside the County of London, which had been used by the company to house a number of their cars, but which was really surplus to their requirements. With more cars to be run by the LCC, mainly on service 26, together with a few on 89, it was decided to use the shed as an overflow establishment to Hammersmith.

It was an imposing structure, built in sections, some parts of it dating back to 1896. The "new" part of the building was constructed in 1899, with the intention of providing housing for the first of the new electric cars of the London United Tramways. The entrance roads opened out into an elongated track fan, and this in turn led to the five docking roads in the main part of the building which was on the western side, conspicuous by its arched roof and glazed half front. The second part of the building was equipped with six storage tracks, while a traverser, installed by the LUT and sited at the back of the shed, served the easternmost three tracks and also the four tracks in the old building, which became the main workshop for the maintenance and repair of the cars. A power generating station had been constructed in front of the eastern part of the car shed and which, by 1922, was only doing duty as a sub-station. This was retained by the company after the transfer of the remainder to the LCC.

It was revealed in 1925 that the tracks and parts of the foundations were in a very bad condition. The wooden sleepers under the running rails had almost totally rotted away, while the foundations beneath these had sunk to an alarming degree. Extra brick and concrete piers were constructed to provide a new foundation upon which to place the tracks.

During the course of the remedial work, it became clear that the tracks in the shed, together with those in the entrance yard outside, were all laid with old horse tramway rails and were, in the opinion of the Permanent Way Engineer, totally unsuited for carrying the heavy LCC cars, and would have to be renewed or "heavily repaired". In its last years under LCC control, the shed was used to house a number of out-of-service trams, some of which were awaiting disposal.

Brixton Hill Car Shed

After the cessation of hostilities in 1918, it became the policy of the Council to maintain, and possibly increase, the number of trailer cars which had been in use during the war. To this end it was decided to build a special trailer car shed in a central position and, as the largest users of trailers were by then on the services working from Clapham and Streatham car sheds, several sites were inspected in that locality. One, at No. 219 Brixton Hill, was considered to be the most suitable. The building on the site was known at that time as "Aspen House" and was already owned by the Council and in use by the Education Committee. Part of the grounds, being surplus to requirements, was transferred to the Tramways Department for development as the new "Streatham Trailer Car Shed".

A contract was signed on 8th September 1922 with the firm of L. H. & R. Roberts of Clapton, London for the construction of the new building at a cost of £16,050, plus £1,064 for a more substantial slate roof, instead of the original idea of an iron one. Trackwork was to be installed by the Tramways Department for a sum not to exceed £7,500, which included special work by Messrs. Hadfield. There was to be no conduit track in the building, as the trailers would be shunted in and out of the shed by some means not disclosed. The seven storage tracks, accommodating a total of about 50 cars, led out of the building via a track fan, which reduced the number of roads to one and, after passing through the entrance, divided into two, one track leading to the "down" main line, the other to the "up" line.

The building and its equipment was well on the way to completion, when there was a change of mind on the part of the Council as to the future use of trailer cars, resulting in the decision to use the new shed to house standard double deck electric cars. This necessitated the installation of overhead wires over the seven tracks and out of the building to the forecourt where twin ploughshifts were provided, one to each of the conduit tracks leading to the street.

Initially, there were no track bonds fitted, which precluded the use of single wire and earth return power collection. Instead, the twin wire system was installed, as used on the Woolwich-Eltham route, restricting access to cars fitted with two trolley poles and suitable changeover switches. Fortunately by then, a number of cars had been provided with two poles, including the new "1922 series" E/1 cars, some of which were drafted in to work from the new shed, renamed Brixton Hill Car Shed when it opened for business on 6th March 1924. In later years, with track bonding complete, the use of two poles became unnecessary.

This running shed was about a quarter of a mile away from, and to the north of Telford Avenue shed. For operational purposes however, it was worked as part of the Streatham complex and in conjunction with Telford Avenue, initially taking over part of services 16/18 and 22/24, with a total of 31 cars, but with many re-arrangements in later years.

Permanent Way Depots & Wharves

The largest of the main sites south of the Thames was at Deptford Wharf, Greenwich Road, on ground of about 61,000 sq. ft. in area and situated alongside Deptford Creek. The freehold of this was purchased by the Council in October 1906 for £12,500, together with another £8,220 which was spent on new buildings and plant. Special machinery, such as stone crushers, a planing machine and various cranes, was also provided. A further improvement was made to the premises during the summer of 1909, when the Deptford Creek embankment retaining wall was rebuilt by Messrs. Kirk & Randall at a cost of £3,675.

Another important depot was located at Battersea Wharf, alongside the Thames at the side of Battersea Park Road, which was purchased in July 1909 at a cost of £9,500 for the site and £3,385 for plant and buildings. It was here that for many years a considerable part of the dried sand used in the hoppers of the cars was processed and stored, and from where it was distributed. Eventually, in December 1928, the depot was closed.

Smaller installations were at Clarence Wharf, Albert Embankment, later closed; County Wharf, Belvedere Road, to the rear of County Hall, which was closed in 1928; Kennington Oval and Lupus Street, Pimlico, stone yards, later closed. Secondary establishments were situated at Leo Street, Old Kent Road which was closed in 1928 when the stores and materials were transferred to the C R D; Rye Lane, Peckham depot which, although mainly concerned in later years with road vehicle maintenance, had space allocated for the storage of various materials, and also for the assembly of special track work, etc.; and the Central Repair Depot itself.

Chapter 50
Car Sheds and Depots

North London

Dealing next with the depots and other installations on the system north of the Thames, out of a total of 30 owned by the North Metropolitan Tramways Company (including those of the late London Street Tramways Company), 23 were within the metropolitan area. Of those outside the LCC area, only the car works at Union Road, Leytonstone remained under the control of the Council for any length of time. Depots on the north side were:-

North Metropolitan Tramways Company.
Kingsland Granary
Poplar, Athol Street
Poplar, Blair Street
Canonbury, St. Paul's Road
Balls Pond, Woolgar Mews
Green Lanes
Grove Road
Woodville Road
Woodfield Road
Stamford Hill
Finsbury Park
Mare Street, Bohemia Place
Lea Bridge
Highgate
Metropolis Wharf, Kingsland
Bridge Wharf, Victoria Park
Union Road, Leytonstone *
Stratford Broadway *
Stratford, Martin Street *
Edmonton *
Romford Road No. 1 *
Romford Road No. 2 *
Barking Road *

London Street Tramways Company.
(operated by North Metropolitan Trys)
Junction Road
Cressy Road, Hampstead
Park Road, Hampstead
Warlters Road
Parkhurst Road
"Angel Yard", Islington
York Street (later Lorenzo Street)

Highgate Hill Tramways Company.
High Street, Highgate *

Harrow Road & Paddington Tramways Co.
(leased to MET Ltd.)
Trenmar Gardens ***

West Metropolitan Tramways Company.
(later London United Tramways, then
London United Electric Tramways)
High Road, Chiswick **
Acton *** .
Shepherds Bush ***
Richmond Road ***

* Outside LCC area, or not taken over by LCC.
** Purchased by LCC in 1922 with Hammersmith lines.
*** Outside LCC sphere of influence.

Permanent Car Sheds Used To House Electric Cars

North

Shed	Location	Nominal Capacity
Bow	Fairfield Road	54
Hackney	Bohemia Place	120
Hampstead	Cressy Road	157
Holloway	Pemberton Gardens	307 **
Poplar	Leven Road	92

| Stamford Hill | Rookwood Road | 131 |
| Leyton * | Lea Bridge Road | 60 |

* Taken over for operational purposes by the LCC in 1921.
** 307 if all bogie cars; up to 344 if some single truck cars.

Temporary Car Sheds
Kingsway Subway
Highbury   St. Paul's Road

Kingsway Subway Temporary Car Shed

The arrangements made to house the first of the single deck cars which were to work the Kingsway Subway services, had been the cause of some concern to the Council. Due to the restrictions placed upon it by the agreements made with the North Metropolitan Tramways Company at that time, the LCC found itself limited in its activities so far as reconstruction of its lines on the north side of the Thames was concerned.

However, an agreement was eventually reached with the company regarding reconstruction of the Theobalds Road line; the Council was proceeding with new sections of line in Rosebery Avenue and St. John Street, while plans were being made for further reconstruction as required. But there was no access to any of the proposed new car sheds, and even if there had been, none were yet built. It was decided to use the south end of the subway as a temporary depot, where car washing and regular maintenance could also be carried out.

For the time being, temporary tracks were laid beyond Aldwych Station, ending in a single stub in one of the tunnels beneath Aldwych. Pits were built at the end of the conduit tracks, which served both for inspection and for removing the car ploughs. The rails continued on from the pits to the storage space - but without the conduit rails. Beyond the pits, the whole area was paved with stone setts where, in one section, the cars were to be washed. Power to move the cars was obtained from a flexible cable, fitted with a plug end, which was inserted into a suitable socket on each car.

Highbury (Canonbury), St. Paul's Road Temporary Car Shed

After the opening of electric services from Aldwych Station to the "Angel" Islington, on 24th February 1906, the decision was taken to extend the line northwards as far as Highbury Corner, which would require the use of several more cars. The horse car depot at St. Paul's Road, Highbury was pressed into service to house the extra cars, a conduit track being laid from the depot to the main line. The existing horse car tracks inside the depot were used, with a plough removal pit provided at the entrance.

In a similar way to that used in the other temporary car sheds, the cars were moved around with the aid of a flexible cable and plug, power being fed from a trolley running along the top of two overhead wires. A special agreement had been made with Islington Borough Council regarding the use of these wires. Several cars were moved into the depot a few days before the opening of the extended service on 16th November 1906.

During this time of great activity, two further developments were taking place. The first was, that at long last, the Council had been able to obtain approval to extend the subway tracks southwards from Aldwych Station to the Victoria Embankment, which would mean that the temporary car storage space in the tunnel would have to go; the other development was that a new, very large permanent car shed at Holloway was under construction, together with an extension northwards of the conduit tracks from Highbury to Holloway and "Archway Tavern". Once completed, the cars for the subway service were moved out from both temporary locations to their new "home" at Holloway.

Holloway Car Shed

A site at Pemberton Gardens and Terrace, Holloway measuring 3⅝ acres in area, previously used by the Caledonian Football Club, was purchased from the Caledonian and Tufnell Park Syndicate on 12th December 1905 for £20,000 as the site for the erection of a car shed capable of accommodating over 300 cars. During the course of the purchase, it was suggested by the Midland Railway Company that an exchange of land be effected between the two in order to rectify and straighten the boundary line, and to make an improved means of access to the site. There was also a restriction on part of the site which prohibited the construction of buildings more than thirty feet in height, but this problem was overcome by negotiation.

Before, however, any building work could commence, it became necessary to arrange for a sewer to be diverted away from part of the site, which Islington Borough Council attended to for £150. Once this was done, the foundations for the buildings were laid by Messrs. Chas. Wall Ltd., who had obtained the contract for construction of the complete building for £83,885. Trackwork and paving cost another £6,250, lighting and other charges amounted to £5,850, while three traversers were supplied by Messrs. Heenan & Froude for £735 each.

The completed first section of the car shed was opened on 28th November 1907. The first of two entrance tracks was provided into the east side of the shed, along Pemberton Gardens from Holloway Road. On the completion of the second stage of the building, access from the west side, with a track along Monnery Road from Junction Road, was provided and first used in traffic on 30th November 1909.

This view, dated 30th June 1907, shows the progress being made in the construction of Holloway car shed. (Greater London Photograph Library)

The wheeldrop at Holloway car shed, showing the lifting gear and removeable rail sections. (Courtesy: LTM U12778)

For operational reasons, workings from the shed were divided into two sections, "west" and "east". A total of 26 storage roads was provided to the west of the traverser pit, with 22 on the east side, giving a stated capacity of 307 bogie or 344 single truck cars. On completion, this became the largest car shed on the north side and second largest on the system. Only New Cross was larger, both in area and capacity.

As the two parts of the system were isolated from one another at that time, apart from the Kinsgway Subway which could only accept single deck cars, arrangements had to be made for the renovation and repair of all double deck cars used on the northern system to take place in one of the car sheds in that area. It had been hoped that other routes connecting the two divisions would have been built, which in time would have solved the problem of transfers between the two, but this was not to be the case. No direct transfers would be possible for many years.

As a result, it was arranged that a section of Holloway shed would be set aside as an overhaul works in the same way that part of New Cross shed had been equipped. Cost of providing the workshops, which included the provision of heating and lighting plant, storage and staff accommodation, together with some alterations to the track layout was estimated to be £1,873. This work was carried out by the Tramways Department, beginning in the second half of 1908 and being made available for use in October 1909. Special stores cars were used to carry all the replacement items required to and from Holloway, which arrangement continued to apply for many years.

The first moves were made in November 1923 to re-arrange the overhaul works and paint shop. Due to the expected arrival of 28 more cars to serve the Amhurst Park line when completed, the decision was taken to remove the paint shop to Hampstead car shed. Work on this project was completed by the early summer of 1924.

It was in 1926 that an agreement with the Metropolitan Electric Tramways Ltd. was concluded with regard to the movement of LCC cars over the company's lines, to get them to and from the Central Repair Works at Charlton. Once implemented, this agreement remained in force until the new, deepened subway became available for use by double deck cars early in 1931. This finally allowed more space to be made available for stabling cars at Holloway, although a comprehensive workshop was still maintained to carry out all but the heaviest of repairs.

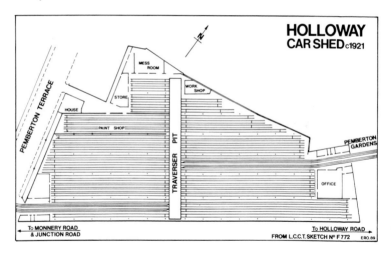

Poplar Car Shed

The first mention of a site for a car shed for electric tramcars in the Poplar district was in 1906 when the Council decided to revoke the leasing agreement with the North Metropolitan Tramways Company, taking on the operation itself and electrifying the lines on the conduit system as speedily as possible.

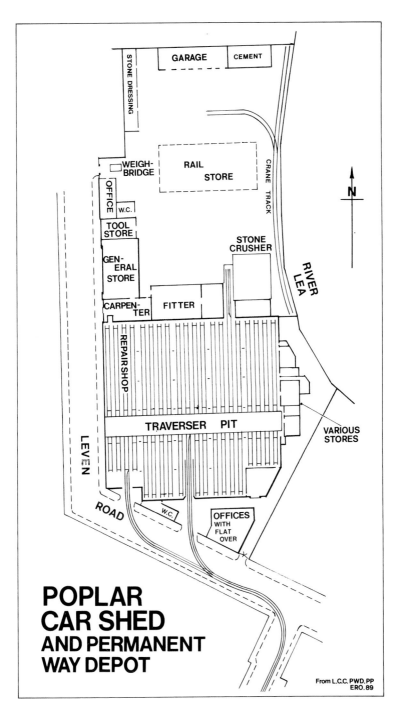

GARAGE CEMENT

STONE DRESSING

WEIGH-BRIDGE

RAIL STORE

CRANE TRACK

OFFICE

W.C.

TOOL STORE

GENERAL STORE

STONE CRUSHER

CARPENTER

FITTER

REPAIR SHOP

RIVER LEA

LEVEN

TRAVERSER PIT

VARIOUS STORES

ROAD

W.C.

OFFICES WITH FLAT OVER

N

POPLAR CAR SHED
AND PERMANENT WAY DEPOT

From L.C.C. PWD.PP
ERO.89

On 4th July 1905, a freehold site in Leven Road, Poplar, with a book value of £5,571. 1. 9d was transferred from the Education Department, while on 11th July arrangements were made to acquire additional property at a cost of £2,600 freehold, resulting in the purchase on 7th November of Nos. 122, 124 and 126 Leven Road for £972, and Nos. 191, 193 and 195 Abbott Road for £478 freehold. A lease attached to No. 193 Leven Road was purchased on 19th December for £332.10s., while the leaseholder of No. 191 successfully contested his claim for £300 in exchange for his right in the site, being also awarded a payment based on an interest rate of 5% on the capital sum whilst the case was pending. The tenants of the houses subject to the purchase were each given a small "disturbance" gratuity, ranging from one at £15, to most of the others at £1 each. The properties in Abbott Road were required to enable an access road to be constructed so that the car shed could be easily reached. The approach to the shed was from East India Dock Road, by a single line along Aberfeldy Street to the entrance road, where it diverged into two entry tracks to the car shed, and was constructed under powers obtained in the London County Council (Tramways & Improvements) Act, 1906.

The first section of the shed was built by Chas. Wall Ltd. at a contract price of £29,006 which had been agreed on 12th December 1905. The first part of the building was expected to be available by 22nd August 1906 to allow new cars of class E to be received from the builder, and as accommodation where they could be assembled and tested before services began about the end of October. The rest of the shed was to be available by 22nd October, with completion of all work in December. Installation of tracks and electric lighting was undertaken by the Tramways Department at a cost of £4,500. Chas. Wall was later asked to have the second part of the building available to the Council by 22nd September, in exchange for which the company would receive a bonus payment of £500, which was accepted and accomplished.

On 26th February 1907, it was agreed that a section of the car standing space be screened off to provide accommodation for a paint shop, in accordance with the regulation that all cars were to be re-painted annually. The area taken reduced standing space by four car lengths. The screens surrounding the paint shop were erected by W. Bain & Co. for £116.

The firm of Kirk & Randall Ltd. of Woolwich gained the contract to build the second section of the shed on November 1911 at a contract price of £14,325, which work completed the building. This provided space for a total of 96 cars, including the four in the paint shop. Two traversers were supplied by Messrs. Jessop & Appleby Bros. Ltd. for £674 each, including electrical equipment by British Westinghouse. These were sited about halfway along the length of the storage tracks, of which there were 18 to the front and 20 beyond the traverser pit.

After the closure of the paintshop following the transfer of this activity elsewhere, the standing space became available for more general use, and it is recorded that in July 1927 there were 90 cars shedded there.

A large area to the rear of the car shed was used to provide a permanent way depot. The site was conveniently placed alongside the River Lea, which allowed bulk deliveries and storage of items such as stone, sand, ballast, rails and other heavy conduit track materials. A stone crusher was also installed, which provided the aggregate used in concrete work.

Stamford Hill Car Shed

A site for a large car shed was purchased by private treaty on 23rd January 1906 at a freehold price of £4,000, when property in Rookwood Road, at the end of Egerton Road, Stamford Hill and just inside the County boundary, was conveyed to the Council.

To gain access to the proposed shed, the Council's cars would have to be driven over a short length of line owned and operated by the Metropolitan Electric Tramways Ltd., whose services in Middlesex terminated at Stamford Hill. In return for the company giving access rights to the Council, the LCC agreed to postpone the right of purchase in 1910 of a small part of the company's lines until 1930.

The building was constructed by Messrs. Holliday & Greenwood, and was of yellow stock bricks in the standard style adopted by the Council. A three-floor office block was placed between the two single-track entrances to the shed. The tracks, which divided from a single line laid along Egerton Road at the point where it crossed Rookwood Road, led to the traverser pit and the two traversers which, between them, served the 28 depot tracks on either side of the offices and to the rear of them. The traversers were supplied by Jessop & Appleby Ltd., with electrical equipment by British Westinghouse for £674 each, while tracks and lighting were installed by the Tramways Department. The front storage roads each accommodated two cars, the rear ones having room for three, making it possible for up to 140 cars to be housed. The first part of the building was completed early in February 1907, in time for the inauguration of services from Stamford Hill to Shoreditch on 7th February.

Total cost of the building was £112,000, and it was always used almost to capacity, to provide for the many services operating in the area. The July 1927 record shows that 122 cars were housed at Stamford Hill.

Hackney Car Shed

The horse car depot at Bohemia Place, Hackney was on a large and easily accessible site and, as it was suitably situated, it was decided in 1906 to construct a new car shed on the site to accommodate 120 electric cars. An estimated cost of £38,000 for the work was agreed to by the Council on 5th February 1907. The tender of Rowley Bros. of Tottenham in the sum of £24,078 was accepted on 26th March 1907 for a standard LCC Tramways style of building, with yellow brickwork, Portland stone top-work and grey slate roof. Other incidentals were expected to cost about £17,000, plus the cost of the trackwork, which was to be undertaken by the Tramways Department for a further £2,700. It was expected that the building would be ready for occupation in January 1909, but due to minor technical problems, it was to be 31st March before the building was finally handed over.

Two traversers had been ordered from Heenan & Froude in June 1907 for installation in this shed, but were transferred to Bow. Instead, in 1909, two machines were built and supplied by Messrs. Mountain & Gibson, which had originally been intended for use at the Central Repair Depot, Charlton.

Access into the shed from Mare Street was by two turnouts which converged into a single line running along Bohemia Place to the car shed entrance. Just inside the boundary wall, the line became double, remaining so all the way to the traverser pit. Five storage roads were sited to the left of the main tracks, and eight to the right, while there were fifteen roads on the other side of the traverser pit. A plough repair workshop was situated at the back of the building. There were normally over 100 cars stabled there, the figure for July 1927 being 115, which included several undergoing minor repair.

Bow Car Shed

A part of the site of the Grove Hall Asylum, Fairfield Road, Bow, two acres in extent, was specially purchased at a total price of £6,250 on which to construct a new car shed to accommodate an expected ultimate capacity of 151 cars. The tender of Messrs. Chas. Wall Ltd. to build the shed for £17,000, which cost was assessed on a schedule of prices basis, was accepted, with the proviso that the first section should be completed by 14th August 1908, in time to house the 52 cars required with which to run the first services. Trackwork and electric lighting was installed by the Tramways Department for £1,405, with two traversers being supplied by Heenan & Froude for £735 each.

It was at the incomplete Bow shed that the cars used on the ill-fated stud contact current collection system were housed. Studs to the design of Griffiths Bedell were laid into the depot area and on to one road for the purpose of testing the system. However, they were hardly ever used and were disconnected and left in the ground when the shed was wired by the Tramways Department for overhead trolley collection. Details of the G.B. system will be found in another chapter.

In October 1910, Messrs. Patman & Fotheringham agreed to build the second part of the car shed for £7,193, which extension would accommodate a further 36 cars. On 23rd May 1911, it was agreed that Messrs. Brecknell, Munro & Rogers would supply the overhead wire fittings for £76.18. 2d as part of single contract which also involved Hammersmith car shed. This part of the building was scheduled to be ready for use in June 1911, with a section of it to be used as a store. The third portion of the building, which would have accommodated the remainder of the expected fleet of 151 cars was never built.

The single track branch line in Fairfield Road opened out into two separate entry tracks, separated by the Night Inspectors' office and other miscellaneous accommodation. Eighteen storage tracks were sited in front of the traverser pit, which was situated about three-quarters of the way back from the entrances, with another seventeen tracks to the rear of it.

Due to the necessity to provide repair and overhaul facilities for cars on the northern system, until they could be brought south to the Central Repair Depot after 1926, a section of the shed was set aside for this purpose, with the result that the building was not used to the full as a running shed. However, even after 1926, when only a small section was used as a workshop, the remaining standing space for 79 bogie cars was never fully used. As an example, in July 1927, only 45 cars were housed there and, although this figure fluctuated from time to time, it rarely went beyond 54.

Hampstead Car Shed

In conjunction with the reconstruction of the tramways in the Hampstead and Tufnell Park areas, it was decided in 1913 to replace the horse car depot at Cressy Road with a new building which would have accommodation for 157 bogie cars. Access to the new shed was to be by a reconstructed track in Cressy Road from Fleet Road, while additional powers were sought to enable an access road to be built from Agincourt Road into Fleet Road and the depot. Cost of the work, including the construction of the approach roads and provision of tracks was estimated to be £52,594. Building work was undertaken by Messrs. Kerridge & Shaw to the usual LCC Tramways standard for £47,548. Trackwork and electrical wiring cost a further £6,200, causing the estimated figure to be exceeded by £1,154. Two car traversers were supplied by the Brush Company and the shed was brought into use in January 1914. At that time, it had been anticipated that a number of new tramway extensions would be built, justifying the use of the large, new shed. Due, in part, to the onset of the Great War, no new extensions were constructed.

Early in 1915, the building was taken over by the military, who used it as a garage for their vehicles and for other purposes. It remained in government hands until 1922, when finally it was returned to the LCC. After making a monetary claim against the War Office for dilapidations, the Council eventually received compensation for the damage sustained to the building.

In November 1923 it was decided to remove the north side paint shop from Holloway car shed, to release car standing space in that shed. As accommodation was available at Hampstead, the timber-framed, corrugated iron structure standing in Holloway shed was taken down and re-assembled at the new location, together with the install-ation of a hot-air drying plant. This work, which included the cost of additional equipment for the heating installation and all removal expenses, was provided for in an estimate of £2,800, and was undertaken by Tramways Department staff during the summer of 1924. The paint-shop remained in use until 1926, when arrangements were made to have all cars overhauled and repainted ·at the Central Repair Depot.

The traverser pit was situated about halfway between the entrance and the rear wall, with fourteen standing roads to the right of the two entrance tracks and two to the left of them, while eighteen were

Hampstead car shed under construction in 1913, showing the foundations for the running rails and traverser pit. (Greater London Photo. Library)

laid to the rear of the pit. Due to the fact that the Council was unable to make route extensions in the area, the car standing space was never used to anything like the extent provided for. In July 1927, after the painting department had been removed, only 60 service cars were shedded in this vast building, although some standing space was taken up with a number of out-of-service cars, particularly those of the ex-Leyton fleet.

Leyton Car Shed

The installation belonging to Leyton UDC Tramways in Lea Bridge Road was transferred to the LCC for operational purposes at the same time as the system of that undertaking in 1921. The car shed was built in similar style as many other medium-sized undertakings, with the nine docking roads accessed by means of a track-fan laid in the yard. A car works was also included in the complex, situated on the west side of the building. Access to this was from the westernmost depot road. In July 1927, 50 cars were housed there.

Until 1931 it remained in much the same condition as when it was in the hands of Leyton UDC, but then, prior to new cars of class E/3 being delivered, a traverser, supplied by Holt & Willetts was installed about halfway along the docking area, which gave greater flexibility in moving cars around the shed.

Car Shed Recreation Rooms

Fully equipped recreation rooms for the use of staff were provided at New Cross, Stamford Hill, Holloway, Poplar and Jews Row car sheds when the buildings were constructed. Eventually, all other depots were provided with similar accommodation, which included the provision of refreshment facilities, a rest area and a section where billiards and other table pastimes such as dominoes could be enjoyed by the staff in their off-duty hours. In some rooms, there was even a licensed bar.

In January 1909 the Council agreed to employ full-time stewards to keep the rooms tidy and in order, it being proposed that men "unfit for more trying or more responsible posts" should be offered these jobs at the rate of 28/- per week, which sum could be supplemented by a commission payment received from the sale of refreshments, etc.

Before long, organised Recreation and Sports Clubs were formed. During the winter months, it became usual for the staff to arrange concerts of various types, most of which could be attended by the families and friends of the staff. There were several "Minstrel Troupes" whose performances were in great demand, one of the first of these being formed by the staff at Holloway shed, with another soon to follow at Jews Row and rejoicing in the name of "The LCC (Wandsworth Depot) Minstrel Troupe". These musical groups performed regularly at social gatherings, and almost invariably at the Christmas parties held for the children of the members.

Other activities, such as cycling, cricket and football were indulged in by members of each recreation club, who displayed friendly rivalry to one another at many of these events.

Lastly, there were the Sick Clubs, formed and administered by members of each depot. These benevolent movements did much good work in helping to ease financial problems suffered by some members when they were unfortunate enough to be affected by illness or injury.

The North Side Car Works

So far as the northern system of the LCC Tramways was concerned, the original intention had been to utilise the works at Union Road, Leytonstone, which had been taken over with the North Metropolitan Tramways Company assets. The main disadvantage was that the works were outside the County and, in any event, would be expensive to adapt to allow for the heavy work involved in repairing electric cars (even though it was used for several years for the assembly of a number of new cars). Faced with this dilemma, the only practical solution was for the Council to resort to the use of running shed space in which to carry out repairs and renovations.

Fortunately, the new car shed built at Holloway had sufficient space to use for works purposes and, with the experience gained at New Cross in utilising shed space, similar arrangements were made, with the result that comprehensive facilities for the renovation and repair of cars were provided. On 9th February 1909, an allocation of £1,873 was made for the erection of paintshops at Holloway and at Hammersmith.

During the years that the northern system was separated from the south side, a continuous supply of overhauled and repaired car wheelsets and bogies, controllers, ploughs and other items, together with car body parts, were taken from the CRD to Holloway by special stores cars ("vans"), as well as returning the worn and damaged parts to Charlton via the shallow Kingsway Subway.

The demand for car shed space and repairing facilities increased at Holloway after the Great War, to such an extent that it became necessary to move the paintshop to Hampstead in May 1924, at a cost of £2,800, which was to complicate the programme for overhauling and repainting as required by the London Traffic Regulations. Smaller, subsidiary works were also set up at Bow and Poplar, where some repair and renovation also took place for several years.

Union Road, Leytonstone

The workshops at this installation were part of the undertaking of the North Metropolitan Tramways Company, who used the premises to maintain its car fleet, and to build new cars for its own use and for sale to other operators. It was taken over by the LCC with the rest of the company assets on 1st April 1906. In view of this addition to the LCC horse car fleet, it became necessary to consider centralising the work of maintenance and repair, instead of its being carried out in several establishments in different parts of London. An agreement was entered into with both the company and Leyton Urban District Council to allow the LCC to retain the tenancy of the works at a rent of £1,320 per annum for five years as from 1st April 1906.

Following this, it was decided to make the best possible use of the premises. With the phasing out of horse traction on the southern system, the Penrose Street Works at Walworth were closed in September 1906. Arrangements were made to transfer to Union Road the maintenance of what remained of the south side horse cars, and also to transfer the staff who were required to work on them.

About two years after the introduction of electric traction in south London, the Council decided to provide top covers for the 400 open top cars then in use. Some of these were constructed at Penrose Street works, but with its closure, the work was at first transferred to Rye

Lane depot. In May 1907, it was decided to make use of the resources at Union Road to manufacture the remainder of the parts required.

At this time of great activity, the Council arranged to construct 50 cars of class E/1 at the works, the description of which is given in the chapter dealing with this class of rolling stock. Those cars for use on the north side were, presumably, completed, while those for use on the southern system were most likely taken in sections, probably to Rye Lane depot and works, there to be assembled.

The lease on the premises expired on 31st March 1911 and the works closed down. Thereafter, all activities were transferred either to the Charlton Works or to one of the north side car sheds which had facilities for the overhaul and repair of cars.

Permanent Way Depots and Wharves

On the north side, within the boundaries of the County of London, the main wharves and permanent way depots which were inherited from the North Metropolitan Tramways were at Bridge Wharf, Victoria Park, leased until 1912, and Metropolis Wharf, Kingsland Road, leased until 1914, and both alongside the Regents Canal. These were replaced by a new wharf alongside Poplar car shed, and fronting on to the River Lea, and which was the largest establishment of its kind serving the LCC Tramways, at some 70,000 sq. ft. in area. Other sites were at Parkhurst Road, Holloway which was given up in 1912 in favour of the acquisition on 26th March 1912 of new freehold premises covering an area of 27,000 sq. ft. at Leighton Road, Kentish Town and costing £3,300; Holloway stoneyard, later disposed of and, after 1921, Leyton car shed yard. The premises at Deptford, Battersea, Old Kent Road, Poplar and Leyton each had a tramway siding installed to enable the stores cars to visit the premises as and when required.

With regard to properties which were leased to or owned by the North Metropolitan Tramways, a number of these were outside the County of London, but were required for the time being by the Council after it had taken over the company, to work certain services until other arrangements could be made. One such depot was at "Swan Yard", Stratford, upon which, as at 5th April 1906, a one-year lease was arranged at a cost of £3,100, with a three-month tenancy afterwards, if necessary. There was accommodation for 674 horses, but as the LCC only wanted to house 500 animals, an agreement was made to sub-let the remainder of the stabling area.

Car Traversers

A traverser, or transfer table, is a mechanical device used to move railed vehicles sideways across a track layout, usually within a depot, car shed or works. Traversers were installed in LCC Tramways car sheds to enable cars to be moved to or from any of the stabling tracks without the necessity for complex pointwork being incorporated into the track layouts of the sheds. Apart from the large area involved in employing a track fan at a depot entrance, as was used by many car shed and depot layouts where the overhead wire system was in use, it would have been extremely difficult, if not impossible in many cases, to design a comparable conduit layout, due to the presence of conduit slots and tee-rails and the necessity to support all the equipment on special gusset posts. There was also the problem of having a large number of electrical "gaps" in the layout, which could have resulted in cars continually getting "stuck on the dead" while negotiating these obstacles.

Supplied by C. & A. Musker, this traverser is working in Pit No. 1 at Camberwell car shed. *(LCC official view)*

Another consideration in favour of the use of traversers, was that it was not then essential for car sheds to be situated in prominent positions on roadsides, although some were. A number were sited behind other buildings, often shops or dwelling houses, with a single or double line of tracks leading from the road directly into the depot space. In several cases, the cars passed beneath entrance arches, over which purpose-built self-contained apartments were provided for the accommodation of a senior member of the car shed staff, usually the senior shed foreman.

The type of traverser used by the London County Council in the first installations was of girder construction. In each case, the machine ran in a specially constructed pit on two or, in the case of the early examples, three running rails. The two end carriages, constructed of rolled steel joists were connected together with steel plates, with the axle and countershaft bearings being bolted into the steel joists. The body of the traverser was formed of steel plate girders rivetted to the end carriages, and carried the steel plates to which the timber flooring panels, usually made from red deal, were attached. The side girders for supporting the floor and intermediate joists were of the "built-up lattice" type. To form the conduit slot on the traverser floor, two slot rails were bolted to the girders, making a slot one inch wide, the tops of the rails being level with the traverser floor. The ends of the track rails were flared to ensure that the wheels ran into the grooves.

The traverser pit or trough, constructed across the full width of the shed, was three feet lower than the tramway running rails, and the pit was just over 24 feet wide. The traverser ran on steel-tyred wheels which were fitted on to mild forged steel axles, along a pair of rails with a track gauge of 19 ft. 4½ in. In some cases there was an off-centre running rail as well to give stability to the structure. Powerful footbrakes were provided, operated by a pedal on the platform, the brake rigging so arranged that the traverser could be controlled and adjusted to within ¼-inch of the desired stopping place.

In car sheds where overhead wires were provided, the machines were usually of the "shallow" pattern, as there was no necessity to provide a sufficient depth wherein to install conduit gear. In these installations the traverser pit floors were about 15 inches lower than the depot floors.

There were two driving positions on a traverser as on a tramcar, with the driver working from the "front" end in whichever direction he was travelling. Power for the traverser motors was collected from conductor rails placed beneath the track in a conduit, or along the side walls of the running pit. The following table gives details of traversers initially ordered and shows the year of ordering, but not necessarily the year of installation. In several cases, traversers were installed in car sheds other than that for which they had been ordered. Costs in each case included electrical equipment, except for those supplied by Dick, Kerr & Co., and C. & A. Musker, which are recorded as being inclusive of motors, etc.

Table of Traverser Details

Car Shed		Year	Supplied by	Cost	
Balham	(1)	1903	Dick, Kerr & Co.	£450	
Clapham	(1)	1903	Dick, Kerr & Co.	£450	
	(2)	1904	C. & A. Musker	£485	
Rye Lane		1903			* (See note)
Camberwell	(1)	1904	C. & A. Musker	£485	
	(2)	1911	Brush Elec. Eng. Co.	£664	§ (See note)
New Cross	(1)	1905	C. & A. Musker	£485	
	(2)		C. & A. Musker	£485	
Streatham	(1)	1906	Jessop & Appleby	£674	
	(2)	1911	Brush Elec. Eng. Co.	£664	
Jews Row	(1)	1906	Jessop & Appleby	£674	
	(2)		Jessop & Appleby	£674	
Norwood	(1)	1909	Mountain & Gibson	£657	
Abbey Wood	(1)	1913	Brush Elec. Eng. Co.	£599	
Hammersmith	(1)	1911	Brush Elec. Eng. Co.	£664	
Brixton Hill			Not fitted		
Chiswick			No details		

* No details, but probably suppled by Dick, Kerr & Co.
§ Camberwell traverser No. 2 installed in 1914.

Poplar	(1)	1906	Jessop & Appleby	£674	
	(2)		Jessop & Appleby	£674	
Stamford Hill	(1)	1906	Jessop & Appleby	£674	
	(2)		Jessop & Appleby	£674	
Holloway	(1)	1907	Heenan & Froude	£735	
	(2)		Heenan & Froude	£735	
	(3)		Heenan & Froude	£735	
Bow	(1)	1907	Heenan & Froude	£735	
	(2)		Heenan & Froude	£735	
Hackney	(1)	1909	Mountain & Gibson	£657	
	(2)		Mountain & Gibson	£657	
Hampstead	(1)	1913	Brush Elec. Eng. Co.	£599	
	(2)		Brush Elec. Eng. Co.	£599	
Leyton	(1)	1931	Holt & Willetts	£700	
Central	(1)	1909	Appleby's Ltd.	£613 +	(See note)
Repair Depot	(2)	1909	Mountain & Gibson	£657	

+ One controller only.

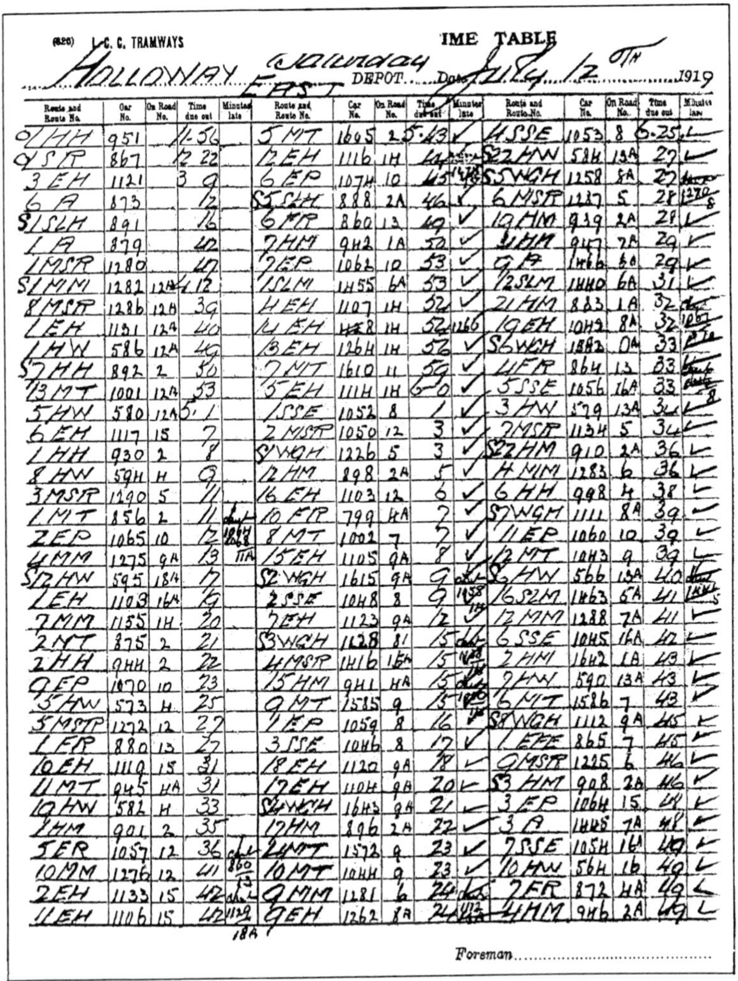

(820) L. C. C. TRAMWAYS — TIME TABLE

HOLLOWAY EAST DEPOT. Saturday Date July 12th 1919

Route and Route No.	Car No.	On Road No.	Time due out	Minutes late	Route and Route No.	Car No.	On Road No.	Time due out	Minutes late	Route and Route No.	Car No.	On Road No.	Time due out	Minutes late
0/HH	951		11-56		5MT	1605	2	5.43	✓	4SSE	1053	8	6.25	✓
9SR	867		12 22		12EH	1116	1H	44	[illegible]	S22HW	584	13A	27	✓
3EH	1121		3 9		6EP	1074	10	45	[illegible]	S5WGH	1258	8A	27	[illegible]
6A	873		12		S5SLH	888	2A	46	✓	6MSR	1237	5	28	1270 8
S1SLH	891		16		6MR	860	13	49	✓	19HM	939	2A	28	✓
1A	879		42		7HM	942	1A	52	✓	3HM	947	7A	29	✓
1MSR	1280		47		7EP	1062	10	53	✓	9A	1466	6A	29	✓
S1MM	1282	12A	4.12		1SLM	1455	6A	53	✓	12SLM	1440	6A	31	✓
8MSR	1286	12A	39		4EH	1107	1H	52	✓	21HM	883	1A	32	[illegible]
1EH	1131	12A	40		14EH	[illegible]	1H	52	1266	19EH	1049	8A	32	1067
1HW	586	12A	49		13EH	1264	1H	56	✓	S6WGH	1882	0A	33	[illegible]
S7HH	892	2	50		7MT	1610	11	59	✓	4FR	864	13	33	[illegible]
13MT	1001	12A	53		5EH	1114	1H	6-0	✓	5SSE	1056	16A	33	[illegible] 8
5HW	580	12A	5.1		1SSE	1052	8	1	✓	3HW	579	13A	34	✓
6EH	1117	15	7		2MSR	1050	12	3	✓	7MSR	1134	5	34	✓
1HH	930	2	8		S1WGH	1226	5	3	✓	S2HM	910	2A	36	✓
8HW	594	4	9		12HM	898	2A	5	✓	4MM	1283	6	36	✓
3MSR	1290	5	11		16EH	1103	12	6	✓	6HH	998	4	38	✓
1MT	856	2	11	[illegible]	10FR	799	4A	7	✓	S7WGM	1111	8A	39	✓
2EP	1065	10	12	1267 1268	8MT	1002	7	7	✓	11EP	1060	10	39	✓
4MM	1275	9A	13	11A	15EH	1105	9A	8	✓	12MT	1043	9	39	✓
S12HW	595	18A	17		S2WGH	1615	9A	9	[illegible]	S4HW	566	13A	40	[illegible]
1EH	1103	16A	19		2SSE	1048	8	9	1158 14	16SLM	1463	6A	41	[illegible] 5
7MM	1155	1H	20		7EH	1123	9A	12	✓	12MM	1288	7A	41	✓
2MT	875	2	21		S3WGH	1128	81	15	[illegible]	6SSE	1045	16A	42	✓
2HH	944	2	22		4MSR	1416	15A	15	[illegible]	2HM	1642	1A	43	✓
9EP	1070	10	23		15HM	941	4A	15	[illegible]	7HW	590	13A	43	✓
5HW	573	4	25		9MT	1585	9	15	[illegible]	6MT	1586	7	43	✓
5MSR	1272	12	27		1EP	1059	8	16	✓	S8WGH	1112	9A	45	✓
1FR	880	13	27		3SSE	1046	8	17	✓	1EFE	865	7	45	✓
10EH	1119	15	31		18EH	1120	9A	18	✓	9MSR	1225	6	46	✓
4MT	945	4A	31		17EH	1104	9A	20	✓	S3HM	908	2A	46	✓
19HW	582	4	33		S4WGH	1643	9A	21	✓	3EP	1064	15	48	✓
2HM	901	2	35		17HM	896	2A	22	✓	3A	1445	7A	48	✓
5FR	1057	12	36	[illegible]	4MT	1572	9	23	✓	7SSE	1054	16A	49	✓
10MM	1276	12	41	860 13	10MT	1044	9	23	✓	10HW	564	16	49	✓
2EH	1133	15	42	[illegible]	9MM	1281	6	24	[illegible]	7FR	872	4A	49	✓
11EH	1106	15	42	1129 18A	9EH	1262	8A	24	1113	4MM	946	2A	49	✓

Foreman..

A WORKSHEET OF THE EARLY TURN TRAVERSERMAN ON 12th JULY 1919

Motors and controllers were of standard design, and apart from the equipments for those supplied by Dick, Kerr & Co. for use at Balham and Clapham sheds, the remainder came from British Westinghouse. All motors and controllers were interchangeable with stock tramcar items, and in the case of the Westinghouse equipment, use was made of type 200 motors in the first instance, later upgraded to type 220, while controllers were of type 90M. At the time of the motor and controller replacement programme which was undertaken in 1924, the opportunity was taken to remove any of the old 90M controllers which remained in service on the traversers and replace them with type T2A or T2C.

Two traversers were installed into each of the larger sheds (three at Holloway in the first instance) at the insistence of A. L. C. Fell, who commented that if only one machine was available for use, there would always be a possibility that, should it break down, it would be difficult, if not impossible, to move cars in or out of the shed. In such a case, the ensuing chaos could bring services in some parts to a halt, and this could not be tolerated.

Over the years, several modifications were made to the existing equipments, while additional traversers were installed at the Central Repair Depot. Due to the increasingly heavy loads which the machines were called upon to bear, it was inevitable that there should be several structural failures, mainly on the original machines and most likely caused by metal fatigue in the girders. On 21st July 1931, five new traversers were ordered from Messrs. Holt & Willetts at a cost of £2,525, to replace worn-out equipment at New Cross (2), Camberwell, Clapham and Streatham.

Car Washing Plants

It had always been the policy of the LCC to wash cars daily, a large staff being kept fully occupied in each car shed. Traditional methods of washing were employed, all work being done by hand. To enable the upper parts of a car to be attended to, each shed was supplied with a number of wooden tower trolleys, which could be moved along the walkways situated between the depot tracks, and from which the staff could work at various levels, as required.

Early in 1925, the Rolling Stock Engineer, W. E. Ireland, devised a system of washing which was considered to be a much-needed improvement over the old method. It was also stated that the annual savings expected with the use of machines instead of employing a large number of men would be approximately £70,000.

Experiments were carried out between May 1925 and April 1926 with a two-unit washing plant, which had been installed in Norwood car shed. The pilot plant cost about £200 and was constructed and erected by the LCC, the expenditure being covered on a maintenance account.

Satisfied with the results of the experiment, authority was sought by J. K. Bruce in April 1926 to arrange to have a four-unit washing plant installed at Holloway car shed. Approval was given on 18th May 1926 for expenditure amounting to £600 for the project, but this time the plant was to be supplied and installed by Messrs. Brecknell, Munro & Rogers. It was completed and ready for inspection by the Highways Committee on 1st March 1927.

Each washing plant unit consisted of a moveable overhead gantry driven by electric motors which, through clutch assemblies, transmitted their power to driving shafts, counter shafts and reduction gears. High pressure water jets were sprayed on to the sides and ends of a car as it stood in the washing bay, the whole process being under the control of one operator.

The machine was of tubular construction, from each side of which was suspended a vertical spray pipe, which was traversed on runways for the length of the car being washed. The spray pipes were automatically swivelled to an angle for washing the ends of the vehicle as required. A small electric motor was used to traverse the machine, mounted in the roof of the car shed, together with suitable reduction gear, which was driven by means of a roller chain to a countershaft and link-belt chain to the machine. If machines were required in pairs,

An outdoor car washer was installed at Hammersmith shed. Car No. 460 of class E is being attended to. ("Passenger Transport", R. S. Pilcher. Courtesy: J. H. Price)

A revised washing method employing men wielding high pressure hoses in use at Holloway shed in 1932. (Courtesy: Tramway Museum Society)

friction clutches and automatic brakes were fitted to the countershaft, but if a single machine only was required, traversing control would be direct from the motor. Traversing speed was approximately 36 feet per minute.

Water supply was taken from the mains if the pressure was not less than about 40 lbs/sq. in. If less than this it could be increased by means of an electrically driven centrifugal pump. A rubber hose provided the connection between the supply and machine, and this was carried on a specially designed suspension gear in the roof of the car shed. All control gear, such as valves, switches, clutches, etc. was mounted on a platform, either in the roof or on the floor of the shed as required.

While the machine was in course of erection at Holloway, Mr. Bruce recommended that 30 units be installed at the other car sheds, including Chiswick, Leyton and Brixton Hill. This resulted in the maintenance estimate being cancelled, and the £600 added to a capital estimate of £13,750, of which £11,870 was for the manufacture, supply and delivery of the equipments and £1,880 for their installation, which was part of a sum authorised on a proposal, not carried into effect, to provide new high-power motor equipment to sixty class E/1 cars working on the north side system.

An offer from Brecknell, Munro & Rogers to supply, erect and maintain eleven machines for £4,031.10s was accepted by the Council and an order given to the General Manager on 22nd April 1927 to proceed. Brecknell tendered and gained the contract for a further ten units in July 1927. Cost of these was £4,720. 5s. The balance of the capital sum was applied to only eight of the other nine units, as it was considered that Brixton Hill shed did not need one, as it was only a short distance away from the Streatham sheds.

Steelwork for the gantries, etc. came from several specialist firms, including Redpath, Brown & Co. Ltd. and Higgs & Hill Ltd. Pipework, pumps and valves were supplied by Barrett & Wright Ltd. The washing machines were located and brought into service as shown:-

Holloway	Nov 1926	Camberwell I	11 Nov 1927
Streatham I	1 Sep 1927	Camberwell II	11 Nov 1927
Streatham II	5 Sep 1927	Jews Row	18 Nov 1927
Clapham I	12 Sep 1927	Hampstead	22 Nov 1927
Clapham II	12 Sep 1927	Bow	30 Nov 1927
Stamford Hill	26 Sep 1927	Abbey Wood	10 Dec 1927
New Cross	10 Oct 1927	Hammersmith	20 Dec 1927
Hackney	24 Oct 1927	Leyton	10 Jan 1928
Poplar	24 Oct 1927	Chiswick	23 Jan 1928
Norwood	2 Nov 1927	(This replaced the pilot plant)	

Brixton Hill was not equipped.
By March 1928, all work had been completed.

On 14th December 1927 it was stated that additional work on the installation of the machines was required. It was neccesary to provide extra guards to protect the overhead wires at Norwood car shed from the possibility of contact with trailing parts of the equipment, and also to provide an additional guard to restrain the driving chain in the event of it breaking. This required the provision of safety guards at all car sheds where overhead wires were in use. At another meeting of the Highways Committee on 26th January 1928, expenditure of another £350 was agreed to, so that the overhead wiring could be modified, to guard against the possibility of staff suffering electric shock. All this work was carried out by LCC labour.

Staff Problems

It had been estimated that about £70,000 could be "saved" annually by using the new equipment, instead of employing a large number of men to do the job. This policy when carried into effect, however, was to be the cause of a considerable backlash.

Until the beginning of 1928, the dismissals of washing staff, although accompanied by considerable bad feeling, went ahead as the machines were brought into service. In March 1928, however, a furore arose over the dismissal of seven men from Leyton shed, which, although worked as part of the LCC system, was still nominally owned by Leyton UDC. J.K. Bruce justified the use of the machines on the grounds of economy and efficiency, and although this approach could not be challenged, it came to be seen that a grave injustice had taken place. Accusations were levelled at Bruce of being thoughtless (although he was considered to be a well-meaning man), and it was stressed that there had been ample opportunity to find other work for these people, as it had taken a considerable time to install the machines.

The Council then made special arrangements to re-employ as many of the men as possible. By May 1928, 107 had been re-engaged in the Tramways Department, some of these to deal with the excess of water which tended to collect on the car platforms after being washed. Nine others were employed elsewhere. A special unit was then set up to attempt to help the others to find suitable work. In all, by the end of May, 232 men had been re-employed in other Council departments, while 18 had found employment elsewhere.

Subsequent Arrangements

The use of the machines appeared to have been a "mixed blessing" to the Council, most likely because there was no easy way of removing stubborn patches of dirt and grease from the lower levels of the body sides. In December 1929, Mr. Ireland, the Rolling Stock Engineer, was conducting experiments with a car brushing machine, to be used in conjunction with the washing machine, in an effort to overcome the problem.

By 1931, however, a partial reversion had been made to a more traditional approach to washing the cars, with the use of high pressure hoses to which long-handled brushes were fitted, and used in conjunction with the washing machines. Two of these, one on either side of the car body and each wielded by one man, were used to spray, wash and scrub the bodywork clean.

Chapter 51
Routes and Services

North, pre-1913

Upon the takeover of the North Metropolitan Tramways, 5,571 horses, valued at £21.14s each, together with 533 horse cars at £78 each were added to LCC assets. In all, these vehicles and horses between them worked 26 services, covering virtually the whole of the metropolis north of the Thames, except for the areas where the Harrow Road & Paddington Tramways, the London United Tramways, the Lea Bridge, Leyton & Walthamstow Tramways and the Highgate Hill Tramways operated. The following table gives details of the services worked in 1906, and also shows in parentheses the numbers given to many of the replacement electric car services in 1912, or to the nearest equivalent service working within the LCC area.

(1) Euston Road - Hampstead	(45) Moorgate - Stamford Hill
(3) Holborn - Hampstead	(47) London Docks - Stamford Hill
(5) Moorgate - Hampstead	(49) Worship Street - Stamford Hill
(7) Holborn - Swains Lane (Parliament Hill Fields)	(51) Bloomsbury - Lower Clapton via Hackney Road
(9) Moorgate - "Archway Tavern" via Upper Street	(53) Aldgate - Stamford Hill
(13) Aldersgate - "Archway Tavern"	(61) Aldgate - Bow - (Stratford)
(17) Farringdon - "Archway Tavern"	(65) Bloomsbury - Poplar
(19) Euston - "Archway Tavern"	(67) Aldgate - Poplar
(21) Holborn - Finsbury Park	(71) West India Docks - South Hackney
(25) Moorgate - Finsbury Park	(73) Moorgate - "Archway Tavern" via Liverpool Road
(27) Euston - Finsbury Park	
(37) Aldersgate - Manor House	(75) Moorgate - Finsbury Park via New North Road
(41) Moorgate - Manor House	
(43) Holborn - Stamford Hill	(77) Aldersgate - Hackney

While massive reconstruction works were going on all over the north side system during the years from 1906 to 1913, particularly where junction layouts were being dealt with, many unusual routings were employed to get horse cars in to the central London termini. As an example, the services between "Archway Tavern" and Holborn were worked for a time in two parts when junction reconstruction was being carried out at the "Angel", Islington. The cars were diverted via the Liverpool Road line when the bridge at Highbury was being rebuilt in 1907, while services between Finsbury Park and Holborn via Camden Road and between Finsbury Park and Aldersgate were worked in two sections, then diverted via Liverpool Road for a time, then again run on their original routes. The upheaval was enormous, while variations in routes were complex.

When additional work was being undertaken at the junction layout at Holborn Hall between 16th September and 9th October 1907, the car services using the lower part of Gray's Inn Road were suspended. In the same way, when reconstruction was taking place on stretches of line in the Camden Town and Kentish Town districts, services were re-routed over adjacent tracks. In one case, cars were worked over a section of line in Kentish Town Road where a regular service did not run, except for the statutory cars which had to be operated at least once every three months in order to maintain the rights of the Council. In this connection, this little-used line was to see such a working on 5th September 1910 when a horse car worked over it, carrying two fares at ½d and four at 1d, the passengers most likely being members of the LCCT staff. This journey was also possibly the final run before abandonment.

The first electrification project to be undertaken on the north side was when the Metropolitan Electric Tramways Ltd. built a new line southwards from East Finchley and came to an agreement with the LCC to enable the company to extend beyond the Middlesex boundary at Highgate Archway into London, to terminate at the foot of Archway Road. This line, constructed on the overhead wire arrangement, opened to traffic on 22nd December 1905. As the LCC was committed at that time to conduit working, it was to be several years before a connection was made with the MET line and through services worked.

This was followed on 24th February 1906 by the opening to public services of the novel Kingsway Subway between Aldwych, at a station in the subway, to the "Angel", Islington, over tracks in Theobalds Road which had been completely reconstructed in advance of the fore-closure of the North Metropolitan Tramways Company lease, and over new tracks in Rosebery Avenue and St. John Street.

Class F car, No. 554, working on line between Aldwych and "Angel" Islington, and seen in Rosebery Avenue in company with various forms of horse-drawn transport and an early motor car. (Commercial view)

Following this part of the electrification programme, work was carried out in more or less an east to west direction, beginning with the Poplar and Bow divisions, but with some other sections being dealt with at the same time. In order that progress can be followed in a chronological manner, the description of the introduction of electric car services is given in this way.

THE POPLAR AND BOW SECTIONS

The Poplar Line

After great upheaval and the eventual reconstruction of the lines in Commercial Road and East India Dock Road, the section of electric conduit-worked tramway between Poplar, Aberfeldy Street and White-chapel, Gardiners Corner (65/67) opened to traffic on 15th December 1906, using new cars of class E, which were housed in the newly built car shed at Leven Road, Poplar.

Work had commenced on 24th May 1906 when the first section of road between Poplar and Kirby Street, a distance of about a half-mile was closed to car traffic. It was re-opened to horse cars on 4th August and, in the meantime, the horses and cars had to be moved out of Poplar depot while it was cut off from the rest of the line. This kind of "putting and taking" was to become almost routine as the various sections of track were dealt with.

Similarly, considerable work had been going on for several months on the remainder of the route. Between High Street, Whitechapel and Bloomsbury construction was made more difficult by the installation of eight complicated junction layouts. At last, on 16th January 1907, electric cars were extended over the new work, providing a through service between Poplar and Bloomsbury (65). However, the short working service on the Commercial Road line between Whitechapel and Poplar was maintained and, when the line to Aldgate opened to traffic on 29th March 1907, it was extended to the new terminus. On 9th July 1908, a weekday rush hours service (65EX) began working between the northern entrance to Blackwall Tunnel and Smithfield.

Gardiners Corner in 1909, with a horse car on the Bow Road service passing in front of a class E car bound for Poplar. (LCC official view)

Through Working Services via Poplar

So far as this route was concerned, it continued to work only as far as the County boundary for several more years. Although LCC cars were unable to work any further east for the time being, arrangements were made with Poplar Borough Council and West Ham Corporation

Tramways to begin a service on 6th November 1908 on the isolated eastern section of East India Dock Road where overhead wires had been installed, then on a route via Canning Town to Wanstead Flats. East Ham Corporation Tramways also ran cars from East India Dock Road to Barking.

At last, early in December 1912, a connection was made with the West Ham Tramways at Canning Town, a ploughshift being installed just west of Iron Bridge. Cars of four undertakings, the LCC, West Ham, East Ham and Barking, were then able to take part in joint services, which began on 20th December 1912. These worked between Aldgate and Canning Town (67) daily, and between Aldgate, Barking Broadway and Loxford Bridge (69) daily.

The Bow Road Line

It has been described in another chapter how an attempt was made to provide an electrically worked line along part of Whitechapel Road and Bow Road, using the "stud contact" system. It had been intended that about 25 cars would be required to provide a service between Bow Bridge and Aldgate and, in the first instance, three were fitted up with collecting gear and put to work on the experimental line on 25th June 1908, while the existing horse car service was reduced by three cars. The electric car service, using this method of power collection was an almost total failure, resulting in the cars being withdrawn from service on 17th July.

A full horse car service was re-introduced the next day and, as the line was subjected to a second reconstruction, this time to the normal conduit system for a part of it and the overhead wire method for the remainder, the horses and their cars were worked in sections as the demands of the engineers would allow. At last, on 31st July 1909, electric cars again took over, operating the complete service between Bow Bridge and Aldgate (61).

Through Working Services via Bow Bridge

The first agreement regarding through running services was made and put into operation on 11th May 1910, when the LCC, West Ham Corporation, East Ham Corporation and Leyton UDC Tramways began joint operations between Aldgate, Bow, Stratford and Leytonstone "Green Man" (61) and between Aldgate, Stratford, Manor Park and Ilford (63). A number of trial runs and clearance tests had been carried out during November and December 1909 and in April 1910. Due mainly to the cars of the smaller municipal undertakings being higher than the LCC cars, they were unable to pass safely beneath the railway bridge crossing over Bow Road until alterations were made to the track and overhead wiring. Once the problems had been overcome, cars of West Ham, East Ham and Leyton, many of them of the 4-wheel type, could be seen at Aldgate, while the large bogie cars of the LCC ventured out of London for the first time.

The agreement, concluded in January 1910, authorised each authority to:-
1. Retain its own receipts.
2. Pay its own expenses.
3. Provide free power to the other authorities.
4. Run a number of cars according to the mileage in its own area.
5. Due to the higher expenses incurred by the LCC in running heavy cars, the Council to be allowed to operate 5% more than its share.

6. All cars to run right through.
7. Each authority to:-
   (a). Maintain its own rates of pay and conditions of service.
   (b). Supply its own tickets.
   (c). Use ploughs supplied by the LCC.

Seven LCC cars were used at first, in company with West Ham and Leyton cars, working to the "Green Man" on Mondays to Fridays and Saturday mornings, and being extended to Epping Forest, "Rising Sun" via Whipps Cross on Saturday afternoons and all day on Sundays. At the same time, a supplementary service of eleven cars continued to work between Aldgate and Bow Bridge. On 25th May, however, the short workings were discontinued, and instead, fifteen cars worked on the through service, with every third one running to Whipps Cross. This extension was the forerunner of a regular summer weekend arrangement which was agreed to in December 1911. During 1912, certain cars were extended from "Green Man" to "Baker s Arms", while on Saturday afternoons as from 24th May, part of the service was diverted at Whipps Cross to work to Epping Forest "Rising Sun". The next day, the rest of the service was extended to Whipps Cross.

On the service to Ilford (63), eight LCC cars were put on, but on 25th May 1910, this number was increased to fifteen. Apart from changes made from time to time in the number of cars allocated to the service, it remained very stable in its working between Aldgate and Ilford Broadway. On the short section within the area of Ilford UDC, the LCC, West Ham and East Ham cars were each charged 6d per car mile for the privilege of working along Ilford Hill.

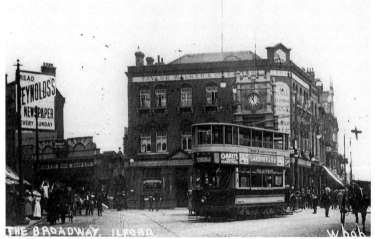

Standing at the Ilford Broadway terminus, E/1 car No. 1345 is being made ready for the return journey to Aldgate.   *(Commercial view)*

The Victoria Park Line

This cross-country line, working between West India Docks and Hackney was not electrified until 1921, and although the service was allocated the number 71 in 1912, this was not carried on the horse drawn cars.

The Stamford Hill Section via Kingsland Road

At the same time as the Poplar route was being reconstructed, considerable road work was being carried out on the long straight line between Shoreditch and Stamford Hill via Kingsland Road and Stoke Newington. It will be recalled that it was along Kingsland Road that an experimental side-slot conduit line was laid, which required the use of cars equipped with specially adapted plough carriers to enable them to work satisfactorily over both the side slot line and the normal centre slot sections.

Between 14th May 1906 and 5th February 1907, the horse car services were interrupted a number of times while reconstruction work was being carried out. Finally, on 6th February 1907, the first electric cars made their appearance on this route, working from the Stamford Hill car shed and providing a service between Stamford Hill and Shoreditch Church (45). An all-night service between the same two terminal points commenced on 11th February, working to a headway of 25 minutes.

The new electric cars had only been running for about four weeks when, on 7th March, a massive electrical breakdown at both Mildmay Park and Shoreditch sub-stations brought the whole service to a halt. It was decided to withdraw the electric cars and replace them with horse cars, with eleven being provided. Later the same day, however, six electric cars were able to operate, but the full electric service was not able to run until the morning of 10th. During the next two years, more power problems were to affect the system, but in these cases were mainly due to insufficient generating capacity being available at times.

Meanwhile, reconstruction work had been completed on several sections of line south of Shoreditch Church, and, after inspections had been carried out, these were made available to the electric cars. On 29th March 1907, the original service (45) was extended to Moorgate Street via Old Street and the lower end of City Road. At the same time, two new services were introduced, working between Stamford Hill and Holborn via Old Street, Clerkenwell Road and Gray's Inn Road (lower) (43) and Stamford Hill and London Docks via Shoreditch High Street, Commercial Street and Leman Street (47).

Class E car No. 705, working on the service to London Docks, stands at Stamford Hill terminus. (Commercial view. Courtesy: A. D. Packer)

Two weeks later, on 9th April, a fourth service was added to the group, when electric cars began to work on weekdays only between Stamford Hill, Shoreditch High Street and a point in Norton Folgate just north of the boundary with the City of London (49). With the introduction of this, no further changes were made within the group until after numbering was introduced.

A double junction and stub-end lay-by was provided at Cazenove Road, situated at the north end of High Street, Stoke Newington, which replaced a similar horse car terminal point. Just over half a mile to the south of the Stamford Hill terminus, it was opened in November 1911, and allowed for short working cars to stand clear of the main road tracks.

The Cambridge Heath, Hackney & Lea Bridge Section

Bloomsbury - Shoreditch - Cambridge Heath - Hackney - Stamford Hill or Leyton

Upon the opening of Hackney Road to electric cars on 18th May 1907, a daily service was instituted between Bloomsbury and Cambridge Heath (51/1). As reconstruction proceeded, the service was extended, firstly to Hackney via Mare Street on 31st July 1909 and then on to Stamford Hill via Clapton Common on 23rd September 1909. A short service of cars working in rush hours between Bloomsbury and Hackney augmented the main daily service and, on 11th December 1911, these were extended to work along Lea Bridge Road to Leyton "Bakers Arms" as a full daily service (55/2).

King's Cross - Cambridge Heath - (Hackney - Stamford Hill)

A rather unusual service of electric cars was introduced on 28th May 1909 between King's Cross and Cambridge Heath, working by way of King's Cross Road, Farringdon Road, Clerkenwell Road, Old Street and Hackney Road (55/1). After about three months, and quite possibly to avoid congestion at the eastern end of Old Street where there were two sections of single track, the eastbound service was re-routed via Great Eastern Street and High Street, Shoreditch on 24th September 1909. It was extended on 27th September to Stamford Hill via Hackney. This working, however, was to be short-lived, as it was completely withdrawn on 6th January 1910, being replaced by a service between Stamford Hill and Aldgate via Hackney, Cambridge Heath and Whitechapel (53), when the lower part of Cambridge Heath Road was opened to electric cars. The service was revised on 30th May 1910, when some of the twenty cars working out from Aldgate were turned at Hackney on weekday mornings.

Moorgate - Cambridge Heath - Lower Clapton - (Leyton)

Another service to be introduced on 6th January 1910 was between Moorgate Street and Lower Clapton via Hackney Road, Cambridge Heath and Mare Street (57). When the lines of the LCC and Leyton UDC Tramways were connected up at Lea Bridge Road and a plough-shift installed, it allowed, as from 1st July 1910, this service to be extended to Leyton "Bakers Arms" and Epping Forest "Rising Sun" on a daily basis (57). It was also supplemented as from 31st July with a service of twelve cars working between Norton Folgate and "Rising Sun" on Sundays only (57EX). On 30th September, however, the weekday service was curtailed at Whipps Cross.

Aldgate - Mile End Gate - Cambridge Heath - Hackney - Leyton

Another new service to be introduced on 1st July 1910, and joint with Leyton, was from Aldgate via Whitechapel Road, Cambridge Heath, Hackney and Lea Bridge Road to "Bakers Arms" during weekday rush hours, extended to "Rising Sun" all day on Saturdays and Sundays (59/1). As from 29th September 1910, however, the outer terminus became Whipps Cross for the Saturday and late Sunday evening service. The same pattern was repeated in 1911, but on 8th December, the outer end was cut back to "Bakers Arms", the service then becoming daily as from 11th. At the same time, the Moorgate Street and "Bakers Arms" service (57) was reduced to work in rush hours only on weekdays, although it continued to run on Sundays for a little longer.

Consolidation of Services

On 7th April 1912, the Sunday service working between Leyton "Bakers Arms" and Norton Folgate (57EX) was diverted at Shoreditch to run to Bloomsbury. This was followed on 5th May with the Sunday cars to Moorgate Street (57) also being re-routed to Bloomsbury (55/2). In common with most other services working to "Bakers Arms" and Whipps Cross, cars were extended to Epping Forest "Rising Sun" during the summer season of each year, usually between May and the end of September.

Next, on 2nd November 1912, services working between Bloomsbury and Stamford Hill (51/1) and between Aldgate and "Bakers Arms" (59/1) were withdrawn, and additional cars were provided on the Aldgate and Stamford Hill (53) and the Bloomsbury and "Bakers Arms" (55/2) services to compensate.

Islington, Highbury and Holloway Section

via The "Angel"

The complexity of tramcar services working to different parts of north London via the "Angel", Islington and, in 1906 all horse drawn, meant that on conversion to electric working there would inevitably be considerable disruption, caused by the division of services or diversion of cars away from the reconstruction sites, to maintain, as far as possible, a continuous service to the public.

The attitude of the London General Omnibus Company to tramway electrification was also making itself felt, and their management appeared to be trying assiduously to cash in on the work by starting up fresh services to cover almost all roads anywhere near those where reconstruction was taking place. This was probably done with the idea of attracting tramway passengers away from the cars - and keeping them once they had been drawn away. To this end, Fell insisted that, so far as possible, services should be kept in operation, even though it was known that the cost would be high and operation difficult.

The first new work was the extension of the Kingsway Subway services (33/35) northward from the "Angel" to Highbury Corner, which opened along High Street and Upper Street on 16th November 1906. At the same time, the horse car depot at Highbury Corner, known as "Canonbury", which had been adapted to hold some of the single deck electric subway cars, was brought into use.

On 16th January 1907, the same day as the line along Clerkenwell Road to Bloomsbury was opened to electric cars, the short length of Gray's Inn Road from Holborn Hall to the terminus was brought

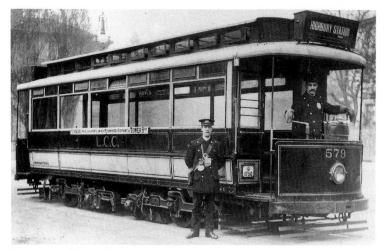

The crew of No. 579 stand ready to take their car into service between Highbury and Tower Bridge. (LCC official view. Courtesy: A. D. Packer)

into use. A daily service of cars was provided between Holborn, the "Angel" and Highbury Station (15), but six months later, on 15th June 1907, it was withdrawn. However, after the opening of the Highbury Bridge, the service was reinstated between Holborn and Highbury, and extended to "Archway Tavern" (15) on a daily basis.

On completion of work in City Road between Old Street and the "Angel" and along Pentonville Road to King's Cross, an electric car service was inititated on 29th July 1907 between Moorgate Street and King's Cross (5). A four-minute service was provided, requiring the use of nine cars, these being supplied from Poplar car shed. At the same time, another service was started, working between Moorgate Street and Highbury Corner (9), for which ten cars provided a four-minute service, these also coming from Poplar. On 28th November 1907, roadwork being complete between the north side of the road bridge at Highbury and the "Archway Tavern", three double deck cars working out of Holloway car shed provided a shuttle service (9) between these two points. The number of cars in use was increased to six on 2nd December, once more vehicles became available.

Following reconstruction work in Goswell Road, electric cars began running between Aldersgate and Highbury on 27th November 1907 (13). In this case, several of the single deck subway cars were used for the time being, until access could be obtained to the new car shed at Holloway.

At last, on 18th December 1907, Highbury Bridge, carrying the road over the railway line, was opened. In the evening of 17th, ten of the cars provided by Poplar car shed and working on the temporary services were run into Holloway shed, together with those in use along the Holloway Road, and the subway cars stabled at Canonbury. On the following morning, a through service was worked between "Archway Tavern" and Moorgate Street (9), and Aldersgate (13).

An extension was made southwards through the new section of the Kingsway Subway and out on to the Victoria Embankment on 11th April 1908, and two new services were provided.

Subway car No. 571 being turned at Highbury, to return to Kennington. No. 865 is bound for Highgate. (Commercial view. Courtesy: J. B. Gent)

(a) Highbury Station, "Angel", Bloomsbury, Subway, Westminster, "Elephant", Tower Bridge (33).
(b) Highbury Station, Subway, Westminster, Kennington Gate (35).
Both these were worked as daily services. However, on 28th January 1909, the Kennington service was diverted to run via Vauxhall, Nine Elms Lane and Queens Road to Lavender Hill, Battersea.

The next electric services which went via the "Angel" were those between Finsbury Park and Smithfield via Holloway Road and St. John Street (23) daily, and Finsbury Park and Moorgate Street via Holloway Road and City Road (25) daily, which commenced working on 9th July 1908. There were also early morning cars to Holborn via Rosebery Avenue and to Aldersgate via Goswell Road. On 7th December, however, three of the early cars to Aldersgate were diverted to Smithfield (23), together with two early cars on the Aldersgate service (13/1) to cater for meat market workers.

On the opening of Essex Road to electric cars on 31st July 1909, more changes were to be seen. The subway cars working between Lavender Hill and Highbury were diverted at Agricultural Hall to run along Essex Road as far as St. Paul's Road (35A), while a new daily service between Aldersgate and St. Paul's Road via Goswell Road and "Angel" (37) was started. This was followed on 11th October 1909 by another new service of double deck cars between Southampton Row and St. Paul's Road via Rosebery Avenue (39).

Next, on 2nd December 1909, the Lavender Hill and St. Paul's Road service (35A) was cut back to "Angel", while another new, but short-lived service made its appearance, working between Southampton Row and Hop Exchange via the subway and Blackfriars, but this had again been withdrawn by 23rd January 1910.

On 10th May 1910, the southern end of the subway service was withdrawn between Vauxhall and Lavender Hill. Eighteen months later, on 12th November 1911, Sunday workings on the St. Paul's Road and Aldersgate (37) service were withdrawn, while on 4th February 1912, the Bloomsbury service was reduced to the status of rush hours only on Mondays-Fridays, early mornings and p.m. on Saturdays and after 6 p.m. on Sundays. During suspension hours, the subway cars working between Vauxhall and "Angel" were extended to cover. Later that year, a full daily service was restored between Bloomsbury and St. Paul's Road (35/51), while the final change made before numbering came on 26th May 1912 when the Aldersgate and Highbury service (13) was extended to "Archway Tavern" on Sundays.

The line between "Archway Tavern" and Highgate Village, Southwood Lane, which traversed the very steep Highgate Hill and was once the centre of operations of the narrow gauge cable tramway, re-opened for use by electric cars on 25th March 1910. In the first instance, a shuttle service was worked up and down the hill, which arrangements were maintained until 12th December 1910, when the cars working between Moorgate Street and "Archway Tavern" were extended up the hill to provide the villagers with a through service to London (9). In conjunction with this, a subsidiary service was also provided, working between Moorgate and "Archway Tavern" via "Angel" on weekdays only. The special cars of class M were used for these services.

One new line of route, although not directly concerned with, or passing by the "Angel", merits mention at this stage. On 15th August, 1908, the newly electrified line in Caledonian Road between Holloway Road and Pentonville Road, King's Cross, 1 ml. 1,484 yds. in length, was the recipient of new services between Finsbury Park and King's Cross Station (21) and between "Archway Tavern" and King's Cross (17). It was to prove to be a very strategic link, directly connecting the termini at Holborn and Farringdon with Upper Holloway and by-passing the busy "Angel" Islington complex.

The line from Highbury Corner to Old Street via New North Road (75) was still worked with horse cars when service numbers were introduced, and was not electrified until June 1914. There was, however, one line in the division which was never to be electrified and that was the one along Liverpool Road, Islington. It had been intended that this should be reconstructed, and junction layouts had been installed at both ends of the road. However, once Holloway Road and Upper Street had been converted, the Council came to the conclusion that a line running parallel with those roads would not be economically viable and, in July 1913, the decision was taken to abandon the route. The last horse cars ran on 12th July.

The Canonbury, Dalston & Manor House Lines

This sector of the northern tramways retained its horse drawn cars for longer than most of the others. The first section to be reconstructed, along Green Lanes and Mildmay Park from Manor House to Dalston Junction (41) saw electric cars shuttling up and down for the first time on 3rd August 1912. On 26th November 1912, electric cars were extended over the junction with Balls Pond Road, working through Southgate Road and a newly built line in Baring Street as far as the New North Road, which was to become its terminus for almost the next year and a half, while horse cars still provided a connection southwards to Moorgate Street and north to Highbury.

As the junction work and tracks in the eastern half of Balls Pond Road were now available for electric cars, those serving Essex Road were extended to Manor House as from 26th November 1912. As service numbers were introduced about this time, these two became 37 between Aldersgate and Manor House, with 51 between Bloomsbury and Manor House.

The Camden Town & Hampstead Section

This part of the network consisted of much of the track mileage of the former London Street Tramways Company, and although connected to the Holloway Road "spine" in several places, was a more or less self-contained section of the LCC Tramways in 1906. However, part of the section was opened to electric cars on 29th July 1907, when a service, with cars every four minutes began working between Moorgate and King's Cross via Pentonville Road (5), and on 5th December 1907, when five electric cars began to work between Holborn and King's Cross via Gray's Inn Road (21).

In November and December 1908, several re-arrangements were made to the horse car services in the Camden Town and Kentish Town districts, to allow for reconstruction of the tramway. In conjunction with this, the tracks in the southern part of Kentish Town Road, which had not had a regular service worked upon them for some time, were brought into use as a diversionary route.

The first section to be re-opened was between "Nag's Head" and Camden Town Station (27). Next, the remainder of the line southward, through Camden Road, High Street and Hampstead Road was brought into use on 28th May, when the car service was extended from Camden Town Station to Euston Road (27). At the same time, a new "cut off" line was opened through Swinton Street, King's Cross, its purpose being to ease congestion in Pentonville Road and King's Cross Road.

The ⅝-mile length of conduit line from King's Cross, along Pancras Road and Crowndale Road opened on 22nd July 1909 and the Moorgate service (5) extended along it. This was followed on 10th September by the opening of the short section between Hampstead terminus and Great College Street via Prince of Wales Road (3) with a shuttle service of cars. Four days later, on 14th September, the Great College Street line opened, allowing a through service to be run between Euston Road and Hampstead via High Street, Camden Town and Prince of Wales Road (1/1) and between Holborn and Hampstead (3).

E/1 car No. 1059, working between Finsbury Park and Camden Town, crossing the "Nag's Head" junction into Parkhurst Road. The motorman seems to be wary of the taxi's movements. (Courtesy: A. D. Packer)

On 30th November, great changes were made when the remainder of the lines in the north end of High Street, Chalk Farm Road, the top end of Kentish Town Road, Fortess Road and Junction Road were opened to electric cars. The services then provided were:-

Hampstead - Euston Road via Chalk Farm Road (1/2)

Highgate - Euston Road via Junction Road (19)

Holborn - King's Cross, extended to Kentish Town Station (7)

Holborn - Hampstead via King's Cross, Great College Street and Prince of Wales Road (3)

Moorgate - Prince of Wales Road, "Mother Shipton" (5)
(On 25th March 1910, this service was extended to Hampstead) (5).

One year later, on 20th May 1911, the Highgate Road line to Swains Lane opened and the Holborn and Kentish Town Station service (7) was extended to its new terminus, known as Parliament Hill Fields.

The last and very important connection was completed on 1st July 1912, when the new tracks across the bridge over the Metropolitan District Railway lines at King's Cross were finally opened for service. This gave a direct connection between the tracks in Caledonian Road with those in Gray's Inn Road and King's Cross Road, and dispensed with a complex crossing arrangement. In conjunction with this, and the use of the diversionary line in Swinton Street, direct services were possible between "Archway Tavern", Caledonian Road, King's Cross and Farringdon (17), and between Finsbury Park, Caledonian Road, King's Cross and Holborn (21).

Through Service with MET

A comprehensive agreement was formulated between the Council and MET Ltd. for the joint working of cars over the lines of both undertakings, and first took effect as from 1st August 1912. A conduit ploughshift had been installed in Seven Sisters Road opposite Blackstock Road, and the line between Finsbury Park and Manor House taken into LCC ownership in readiness for the operation of through cars. The first services were worked between Euston Road and Palmers Green via Camden Town, Manor House and Green Lanes (31) and between Euston Road and Enfield (29). All subsequent re-arrangements are dealt with in the chapters dealing with numbered services.

Chapter 52
Routes and Services

North, 1913–1933

Numbering of Car Services

During the autumn of 1912, cars began to appear with numbers denoting which services they were working on. The following table gives the complete list of numbered services on the northern division as presented in the Map & Guide for December 1912.

1 Hampstead (South End Green), Chalk Farm Road, Camden Town, Euston Road.

3 Hampstead (South End Green), Prince of Wales Road, Great College Street, King's Cross, Gray's Inn Road, Holborn.

5 Hampstead (South End Green), Chalk Farm Road, Camden Town, Crowndale Road, King's Cross, "Angel", City Road, Moorgate Street.

7 Parliament Hill Fields (Swains Lane), Kentish Town, Great College Street, King's Cross, Gray's Inn Road, Holborn.

9 Highgate Village, "Archway Tavern", Holloway Road, Upper Street, "Angel", City Road, Moorgate Street.

11 "Archway Tavern", Holloway Road, Upper Street, "Angel", City Road, Moorgate Street.

13 "Archway Tavern", Holloway Road, Upper Street, "Angel", Goswell Road, Aldersgate.

15 "Archway Tavern", Holloway Road, Upper Street, "Angel", Rosebery Avenue, Holborn.

17 "Archway Tavern", Holloway Road, Caledonian Road, King's Cross, King's Cross Road (northbound), Swinton Street (southbound), Farringdon Road, Farringdon Street Station.

19 "Archway Tavern", Kentish Town, Camden Town, Euston Road.

21 Finsbury Park, Seven Sisters Road, Caledonian Road, King's Cross, Gray's Inn Road, Holborn.

23 Finsbury Park, Seven Sisters Road, Holloway Road, Upper Street, "Angel", St. John Street, Smithfield.

25 Finsbury Park, Seven Sisters Road, Holloway Road, Upper Street, "Angel", City Road, Moorgate Street.

27 Finsbury Park, Seven Sisters Road, Camden Road, Camden Town, Euston Road. (Monday – Saturday rush hours; Sundays after 1 p.m.).

29 Enfield, Palmers Green, Wood Green, Manor House, Finsbury Park, Seven Sisters Road, Camden Road, Camden Town, Euston Road.

31 Palmers Green, Wood Green, Manor House, Finsbury Park, Seven Sisters Road, Camden Road, Camden Town, Euston Road. (Mondays – Saturdays only).

33 Highbury, "Angel", Bloomsbury, Kingsway Subway, Westminster, "Elephant & Castle", Tower Bridge Road.

35 "Angel", Bloomsbury, Kingsway Subway, Westminster, Vauxhall, Battersea Park Road, Falcon Road, Clapham Junction. (On Sundays, extended from "Angel" via Essex Road to Mildmay Park, St. Paul's Road).

37 Manor House, Green Lanes, Essex Road, "Angel", Goswell Road, Aldersgate.

39 Mildmay Park (St. Paul's Road), Essex Road, "Angel", Rosebery Avenue, Bloomsbury.
   (Monday - Saturday rush hours only).

41 Manor House, Green Lanes, Southgate Road, New North Road (Baring Street).

43 Stamford Hill, Stoke Newington, Dalston Junction, Kingsland Road, Shoreditch, Old Street, Holborn.

45 Stamford Hill, Stoke Newington, Dalston Junction, Kingsland Road, Shoreditch, Old Street, Moorgate Street.

47 Stamford Hill, Stoke Newington, Dalston Junction, Kingsland Road, Shoreditch, Commercial Street, London Docks.

49 Stamford Hill, Stoke Newington, Dalston Junction, Kingsland Road, Shoreditch, Norton Folgate.
   (Monday - Saturday only, but not after 9 p.m.).

51 Manor House, Green Lanes, Essex Road, "Angel", Rosebery Avenue, Bloomsbury.

53 Clapton Common (Stamford Hill), Hackney, Cambridge Heath, Whitechapel, Aldgate.

55 Leyton "Bakers Arms", Lea Bridge Road, Hackney, Hackney Road, Shoreditch, Old Street, Bloomsbury.
   (Extended on Sundays from "Bakers Arms" via Whipps Cross to Epping Forest "Rising Sun").

57 Leyton "Bakers Arms", Lea Bridge Road, Hackney, Hackney Road, Shoreditch, Old Street, Moorgate Street.
   (Monday - Saturday rush hours only).

61 Whipps Cross, Leytonstone, Stratford, Bow Bridge, Mile End Road, Whitechapel, Aldgate.
   (Extended Monday - Saturday from Whipps Cross to "Bakers Arms" Leyton).

63 Ilford Broadway, Manor Park, Stratford, Bow Bridge, Mile End Road, Whitechapel, Aldgate.

65 Poplar, East India Dock Road, Commercial Road, Commercial Street, Old Street, Bloomsbury.

67 Canning Town Fire Station, Poplar, East India Dock Road, Commercial Road, Aldgate.

69 Barking (Loxford Bridge), East Ham, Barking Road, Canning Town, Poplar, East India Dock Road, Commercial Road, Aldgate.

71 Victoria Park (South Hackney), Grove Road, Burdett Road, West India Docks.
   (Horse car service).

73 Liverpool Road service between Holloway Road and Upper Street.
   (Horse car service).

75 Highbury Station, New North Road, Moorgate Street.
   (Horse car service - restricted due to electrification).

Night Services

Stamford Hill, Stoke Newington, Dalston Junction, Kingsland Road, Old Street, Holborn.
Poplar, East India Dock Road, Commercial Road, Commercial Street, Old Street, Bloomsbury.
"Archway Tavern", Holloway Road, Upper Street, "Angel", Rosebery Avenue, Bloomsbury.
Bow Bridge, Mile End, Whitechapel, Aldgate.
Hampstead (South End Green), Prince of Wales Road, Great College Street, King's Cross, Gray's Inn Road, Holborn.
These services did not operate on Saturday nights/Sunday mornings.

The Network, 1913 – 1933

With the introduction of service numbering, odd numbers, beginning with 1 were allocated to services working north of the Thames. In direct contrast to the way in which numbers were issued on the south side services, a logical scheme was adopted, with the westernmost electric car services working from Hampstead shed receiving the lowest, from 1 to 5, and those in the east, working from Poplar shed being given the highest, from 65 to 69. The three horse car services which remained were given the numbers 71, 73 and 75. After these numbers had been allocated, and as the electrification programme continued, together with other changes which were made, including the provision of additional services, the highest numbers, out of sequence with the original arrangements, were used or re-issued as required. In the following section, the routes and services are described in number order, wherever possible working from west to east.

Hampstead Group

On 1st December 1912, there were three tram services working to Hampstead (South End Green). Operated at that time by Holloway car shed, they were:-
1. Euston Road via Chalk Farm Road and Camden Town;
3. Holborn via Prince of Wales Road and King's Cross;
5. Moorgate via Chalk Farm, Camden Road and "Angel".

In January 1914, the cars used on these services were transferred to the new shed which had been opened at Hampstead, but service number 1 was not to be maintained for much longer, while the new shed was eventually to be used for purposes very different from those intended by the LCC.

The increasing pressure on manpower caused by the Great War was no doubt a strong factor in the withdrawal of service 1 as from 22nd June 1915. Passengers wishing to travel between Hampstead and Euston Road were afforded transfer facilities, changing at Camden High Street

Two class M cars at Highgate Village, dressed for working on service 5, which normally ran between Hampstead and Moorgate.   *(LCCT view)*

between cars on service 3 and those on 19, 27 or 29. However, a remnant of service 1 remained in post-war years, when a special Bank Holiday service was worked between Euston Road and Hampstead to take passengers to and from the holiday funfairs which were held on the Heath. Operated by Holloway car shed, this special service used "EX" number stencil plates, and lasted until the Hampstead routes were converted to trolleybus operation by the L P T B in 1938.

Services 3 and 5 remained unchanged throughout the whole period under review, but were worked again from Holloway shed from 9th January 1916 until 13th May 1920 whilst Hampstead shed was under requisition by the War Office, for use as a military garage and store.

Parliament Hill Fields

At the commencement of numbering, only one service was working to this terminus, and was:-

7. Holborn via Kentish Town, King's Cross and Gray's Inn Road. Later services were:-

73. Euston Road via Kentish Town and Camden Town.
15. Moorgate via Kentish Town, King's Cross and "Angel".
25. Euston Road via Kentish Town and Camden Town.

With cars initially provided by Holloway car shed, service 7 was to remain as the only one to serve this terminus until, on 2nd February 1914, it was joined by a new Monday to Saturday rush hours service 73 to Euston Road via Kentish Town and Camden Town. By this time, the cars had been transferred to Hampstead shed. Service 73, however, was an early wartime casualty, being withdrawn on 1st December 1914, leaving the 7 to deal with the traffic. Operation of service 7 was again transferred to Holloway on 25th November 1915, when the first part of Hampstead car shed was handed over to the War Department. Available evidence indicates that Holloway retained responsibility for service 7 until after the end of LCC control.

Another eight years were to elapse before a second service was again worked to Parliament Hill Fields. On 9th July 1924, cars displaying the number 15 began working to Moorgate via King's Cross,

Passengers board class E car No. 637 on service 7 at Parliament Hill Fields. The car is scheduled to return to Holborn. (Commercial view)

Pentonville Road, "Angel" and City Road. It is likely that the number of cars on services 5 and 7 were slightly reduced, although the total level of service offered was greater on all sections of route.

A further attempt was made in 1928 to attract new traffic by the re-introduction of a service to Euston Road. Numbered 25, it began working on a daily basis on 24th May, and, to compensate, reductions were made in the number of cars working on services 7 and 15. From 25th May 1931 it was withdrawn on Sundays and reduced to rush hour operation during the rest of the week. However, from 27th June, the Saturday service was partially restored, when cars worked all day until about 7 p.m. The final change under LCC control saw the Saturday evening service restored until 10 p.m. from 1st October 1932.

Highgate Archway Group

At the end of 1912, there were six services working from the large car shed at Pemberton Gardens, Upper Holloway, being:-
9. Highgate Village and Moorgate Street.
11. "Archway Tavern" and Moorgate Street.
13. "Archway Tavern" and Aldersgate Street.
15. "Archway Tavern" and Holborn.
17. "Archway Tavern" and Farringdon Street Station.
19. "Archway Tavern" and Euston Road.
These were later joined by two more:-
69. "Archway Tavern" and Euston Road.
71. "Archway Tavern" and Moorgate.

Service 9 operated daily between Highgate Village and Moorgate via Holloway Road, "Angel" and City Road. During weekday rush hours, short working cars, numbered 11, ran between "Archway Tavern" and Moorgate. Use of this number ceased on 25th June 1914 when it was used for the new electric car service to run via New North Road.

On 24th September 1914, service 9 became subject to the through running agreement between the LCC and the Metropolitan Electric Tramways, when it was diverted at "Archway Tavern" to run via East Finchley, North Finchley and Whetstone to Barnet. MET service 38, working between "Archway Tavern" and Barnet was withdrawn from this date, and cars of both undertakings worked on service 9, those of the LCC being of class E/1. On the same day, as is described below, LCC service 19 was extended from "Archway Tavern" to North Finchley "Tally Ho!", replacing MET service 36, which had been a short working of MET 38. After a short time, these were revised when service 9 was withdrawn between North Finchley and Barnet, while service 19 was extended in its place. For the remainder of the war period, the LCC retained sole responsibility for the operation of service 9, working from Holloway car shed.

The next change came on 22nd May 1920, when the 9 was again extended to Barnet, but this time on Sundays for the summer season, and this was repeated every year up to and including 1927, usually from the middle of May until mid-October, although in 1926 it was not until 24th July that the extension was made. This may well have been an attempt to recoup losses incurred during the General Strike of that year. A Saturday extension to Barnet after 2 p.m. was also introduced in the summer of 1922, but in the following years up to 1927, a similar extension commenced at the earlier hour of 11.30 a.m.

A three-day fair, held annually at Barnet, usually began on 4th September (or 5th if the 4th fell on a Sunday) and to help cope with

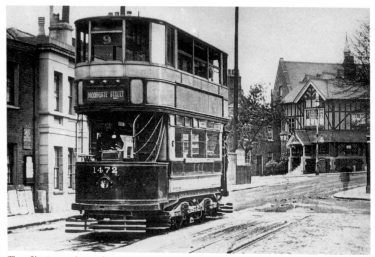

The first number given to the Highgate Village service was 9, as carried by car 1472, working to Moorgate via "Angel". (*LCC official view*)

the extra crowds, service 9 (in company with others) was extended to Barnet for that period every year from 1920 onwards.

With the opening of the Canonbury Road and New North Road tramway to electric traction on 25th June 1914, service 11 became a daily working between Moorgate and "Archway Tavern" via New North Road, Highbury Corner and Holloway Road. On Mondays to Fridays between 9 a.m. and 4 p.m., Saturdays between 9 a.m. and 12 noon and all day on Sundays, cars on service 11 were extended up Highgate Hill to Highgate Village, being supplementary to service 9. Upon the diversion of service 9 to Barnet as from 25th September 1914, the 11 was extended daily to provide the main service to Highgate Village, which was destined to be its northern terminus for the remainder of its existence. During 1931 the class M cars were replaced by new, larger capacity cars of class HR/2, resulting, from 12th November, in the number of cars required to provide the Monday to Saturday service being reduced from 22 to 19, and the service interval increased from 3 to 3½ minutes.

The attractions of Highgate Village and the adjoining Hampstead Heath provided a lucrative source of Sunday traffic for the Highgate Hill tramway. On 27th May 1928, an extra Sunday service was provided between Highbury Station and Highgate Village under the number 11EX. This, however, only lasted for two weeks, as from 10th June, it was replaced by an extra service with the number 17EX, details of which are given below.

On 1st December 1912, service number 13 ran from "Archway Tavern" to Aldersgate via Holloway Road, "Angel" and Goswell Road. At this time it was a daily service, and from July until November 1913 was extended to Highgate Village on Sundays, using cars of class M not required for service 11. Sunday working ceased from 1st January 1922, as it was considered that sufficient alternative facilities existed for passengers, by changing at the "Angel" between services 9 and 35 (to and from "Archway") and service 77 (Aldersgate).

Class M car No. 1449 on service 11, passing Finsbury Square on its way to Moorgate Street.   (Commercial view. Courtesy: A. D. Packer)

Weekday workings remained virtually unchanged until 8th May 1930, when the Monday to Friday service was restricted to busy hours only. Double deck cars had been introduced on service 35 in January 1930 (when Kingsway Subway was closed for reconstruction) and its additional capacity was possibly a factor in considering economies on service 13. The re-opening of Kingsway Subway on 15th January 1931 resulted in extensive changes being made to services working in north London, and as part of this, the number of cars working on service 13 was reduced from ten to eight, as a more frequent service was offered on the 35 along Holloway Road. A further reduction came on 3rd October 1931, when the 13 was restricted on Saturdays to working in rush hours only.

The service working between "Archway Tavern" and Holborn on weekdays only was given the number 15. From 20th April 1915, it was reduced to working during rush hours only, as regular weekday workings between the "Angel" and Holborn were provided by service 75. The 15 had been withdrawn by October 1915, and the number remained dormant until July 1924, when it was brought into use once again for the new service working between Moorgate and Parliament Hill Fields, as mentioned earlier.

Service 17 was one of the few working from Holloway car shed which did not change in the twenty years between 1913 and 1933. It was routed through Holloway Road, Caledonian Road, King's Cross Road and Farringdon Road, and suffered very little from omnibus competition. A temporary alteration took place in 1915 when, following an air raid over the City on 8th September, Farringdon Road was closed until 2nd October, during which time cars were reversed at Clerkenwell Road. After the war, the well-known Caledonian Market drew large crowds every Friday, resulting in the busy hours service being operated throughout that day from 26th October 1923 until 8th May 1930, when the standard Monday to Thursday service was applied on Mondays to Fridays.

Car No. 537 in red livery, on service 15, travelling northwards to Parliament Hill Fields. *(Commercial view)*

On 10th June 1928, a new Sunday extra service with the number 17EX began working between King's Cross and Highgate Village via the route of the 17 to "Archway Tavern". This special service had been run between Highbury Station and Highgate Village on 27th May and 3rd June 1928 under the number 11EX. At the end of the 1928 summer season, the "EX" cars were brought into the main Sunday schedule for the 17, when the Sunday service was extended on 14th October from "Archway Tavern" to Highgate Village. Finally, this Sunday extension was withdrawn from 22nd May 1932, by which time the new class HR/2 cars had entered service, and for a few months, these cars may have worked on the Sunday 17.

Service 19, last of the Highgate Group, was at first a comparatively short one, working from "Archway Tavern" to Euston Road via Kentish Town and Camden Town. On 24th September 1914, together with LCC 9 it became part of a through-running service worked with the MET and extended to North Finchley, "Tally Ho!". From 1st December 1914, service 19 was extended from "Tally Ho!" to Barnet, replacing cars on the 9. Given the difficult operating conditions of wartime, the service to Barnet may well have suffered with the cars on the 9 having to make their way through from Moorgate, while the shorter route from Euston Road on service 19 might have offered greater reliability.

With the Barnet extension, the MET became solely responsible for service 19, whilst the LCC ran service 9. Due to war conditions, the MET experienced difficulties in maintaining the required number of conduit-equipped cars, and to ease the problem, service 19 was withdrawn between "Tally Ho!" and Barnet from 26th February 1917. Additional cars between "Archway Tavern" and East Finchley were provided by extending service 69 northwards from "Archway Tavern". The 19 returned to Barnet from 2nd September 1918, by which time the MET had been able to have more cars equipped for conduit working. In the interim, the company had re-introduced its service 38 between North Finchley and Barnet.

The MET retained control of service 19 until the LPTB took over all tram services on 1st July 1933. However, from 29th October 1931, the LCC provided two cars on Mondays to Saturdays, the Saturday quota being increased to five from 5th May 1932, then again being reduced to three from 28th January 1933. These workings were possibly arranged for mileage balancing purposes.

Two cars were also provided by the LCC to work on service 19EX between "Archway Tavern" and Euston Road in rush hours on Mondays to Saturdays as from 29th October 1931. As service 69 was withdrawn from the same date, the cars were probably put on to cover for the reduction in that service. The workings on 19EX were extended to "Tally Ho!" on Mondays to Fridays from 20th June, and on Saturdays from 22nd October 1932.

Reverting to 1914, it was found necessary to operate more cars between Euston Road and "Archway Tavern", and in October or November, a daily service appeared bearing the number 69. This was done in order that the LCC would not violate the through running agreement by working the extra mileage under the number 19. By January 1916, however, service 69 had been withdrawn on Sundays. A year later, the MET was having trouble with rolling stock, and on 26th February 1917 the 69 was extended to Fortis Green Road during rush hours on weekdays, although the slack hours service still terminated at "Archway Tavern". A further rush hours extension took place on 26th November 1919, when the new terminus became "Tally Ho!", whilst during the period of the Barnet Fair in September of each year, it was extended to Station Road, Barnet.

From 28th May 1928, slack hour workings were withdrawn, leaving the 69 to run between Euston Road and "Tally Ho!" in rush hours only, although between Kentish Town and Euston Road the loss was balanced by a new service to and from Parliament Hill Fields, numbered 25. On 11th October, service 69 was withdrawn between East Finchley and North Finchley, but again returning to "Tally Ho!" North Finchley on 12th August 1929, but still only in rush hours.

The next change came on 8th May 1930, when it was diverted at Mornington Crescent to run to Farringdon Street Station via Pancras Road and King's Cross, offering an additional service along King's Cross and Farringdon Roads. It was also made a daily service, working during the midday period on Mondays to Fridays and outside rush hours on Saturdays between "Archway Tavern" and Farringdon Street. This, however, only lasted for about eighteen months, being withdrawn from 29th October 1931, with a compensating improvement to the frequencies of parallel services 9 and 19, as well as extra cars on 19EX. The number 69 was not used by the LCC again.

The last service to be mentioned in this section only operated for about two months in October and November 1914. Numbered 71, it worked between "Archway Tavern" and Moorgate via "Angel", and appears to have been a way for the LCC to operate extra cars on service 9 without violating the joint agreement. However, this was amended from 1st December 1914 when service 9 was cut back from Barnet to North Finchley, and possibly the extra cars required over the southern end of the route were brought into the arrangement, as service 71 did not appear on the January 1915 map and guide.

Finsbury Park Group

In December 1912, six services were worked to Finsbury Park via Seven Sisters Road, with two more added shortly afterwards. The original ones were:-
21. Finsbury Park and Holborn.
23. Finsbury Park and Smithfield.

25. Finsbury Park and Moorgate Street.
27. Finsbury Park and Euston Road.
29. Enfield and Euston Road.
31. Palmers Green and Euston Road.
Later additions were:-
59. Edmonton and Holborn.
79. Waltham Cross and Smithfield.
Services 29 and 31, later joined by 59 and 79, were all worked jointly with the Metropolitan Electric Tramways.

Service 21 ran daily from Holborn via King's Cross and Caledonian Road. On 1st March 1913, an extension of the through running agreement with the MET came into force, when alternate weekday cars on the service were extended to Edmonton Town Hall via Manor House, Seven Sisters and Tottenham, although cars on the extended service carried the number 59. On Sundays, the entire service was extended and use of the number 21 ceased on this day. Further variations to service 59 are detailed below.

As from 23rd November 1913, the service 21 cars which normally terminated at Finsbury Park, were extended to Woodhouse Road, North Finchley via Manor House, Wood Green and New Southgate. This extension also came within the terms of the through running agreement, and the LCC number 21 was used. The MET service 34, which had been running between Finsbury Park and North Finchley, continued to run but was halved in frequency. Both the LCC and MET provided cars for the 21, which once again became a daily service.

As mentioned earlier, the MET had difficulty in providing suitable rolling stock for working on LCC conduit sections during the Great War years, notably from 1916 onwards. Consequently, from 3rd May 1917, service 21 was confined to the LCC area, working as far as Manor House, whilst the MET worked a service between Finsbury Park and North Finchley, again using the number 34. Possibly due to traffic pressures, the LCC service was extended to Wood Green Junction during rush hours on Mondays to Saturdays and on Saturday afternoons and evenings as from 10th November 1917, but was withdrawn on Sundays.

Things remained like this until 27th October 1920, when the service again became daily, and worked between Holborn and Woodhouse Road, North Finchley. On 24th September 1923 it was extended a few yards to "Tally Ho!" Corner. During the three day period of the Barnet Fair each year, it was usually extended to Station Road, Barnet in the afternoons and evenings. Although running over MET metals was resumed in October 1920, the LCC remained in sole charge of the service, whilst the MET undertook the operation of service 29. However, records show that between three and five MET cars were worked daily on the 21 between 20th May 1925 and 13th July 1926. Several MET cars were allocated to the service from 8th May 1930, while from 29th January 1931, the MET took control of the 21, with service 29 becoming the responsibility of the LCC. It is probable that these variations were introduced to balance the agreed working mileages.

Service 23 worked daily between Smithfield Market and Finsbury Park via the "Angel" and Seven Sisters Road. As a further part of the through running agreement, some cars on service 23 were extended from Finsbury Park to Waltham Cross via Manor House, Tottenham and Ponders End as from 23rd June 1913, replacing part of MET service 24, which had worked north of Finsbury Park. The new through service was numbered 79 and cars were provided by both authorities. Curiously, both the LCC and MET retained parts of their former services. By

October 1914, service 23 had been withdrawn, while the MET withdrew their service 24 at about the same time. However, short working cars continued to turn at Finsbury Park from both directions, all under the number 79. The number 23 was not used again by the LCC.

The service numbered 25 had two periods of working in the Finsbury Park area, together with one in the Hampstead and Parliament Hill Fields group in later years. In December 1912 it was running as a daily service between Finsbury Park and Moorgate via Seven Sisters Road, Holloway Road and "Angel", being withdrawn in the spring of 1915. LCC records state that this withdrawal took place during March or April 1915, although the service was still advertised in the July 1915 issue of the map and guide. Alternative facilities were offered by the faster service 11 which travelled via New North Road.

The second appearance of the number 25 was on 29th March 1922, when a service was introduced which worked between Euston Road and New Southgate during weekday rush hours. It is possible that the journeys utilised short working cars on services 21 (northwards) and 27 (southwards). The service was extended to Barnet after 3 p.m. on Fair Days during September 1922, in common with services 9 and 21. After nearly twelve months of operation, it was withdrawn at the end of the schedule on 13th February 1923, being replaced on 14th by increases in the numbers of cars on services 21, 27, 29 and 31. Lastly, it again appeared on 24th May 1928 as mentioned in the section dealing with the Parliament Hill Fields group.

Referring now to service 27, at the time of numbering it was only working during weekday rush hours and on Sunday evenings between Euston Road and Finsbury Park via Camden Town and Camden Road. On the introduction of the through running agreement, it was extended on 1st March 1913 from Finsbury Park to Seven Sisters Corner on Saturday afternoons and evenings and on Sunday evenings. On 13th September 1913, the Monday to Saturday rush hour service was extended to Tottenham (Snells Park), with the Sunday service running to Seven Sisters Corner only. By January 1914, the Sunday service had been reduced to evenings only, starting at 6 p.m. In October of that year, service 27 began to work to Seven Sisters Corner all day on weekdays, and on Sundays from 6 p.m., while the Snells Park workings were withdrawn. Restrictions imposed by the war resulted in the Monday to Saturday service finishing at 8.30 p.m., while on Sundays the service only worked between 4 p.m. and 10 p.m.

The 1919 edition of the map and guide shows service 27 as starting at 11.30 a.m. on Sundays, an alteration which may have taken place when it was extended to Edmonton Town Hall from 12th May 1918. A Monday to Saturday rush hours and Saturday afternoons and evenings extension to Edmonton was introduced from 26th November 1919, with a supplementary service being added (again during rush hours) between Tottenham Court Road and Seven Sisters Corner. These were extended to Bruce Grove from 14th April 1920. A daily Monday to Friday service began working to Edmonton Town Hall on 25th August 1920, although there may have been a limited service over the section since 26th November 1919, when MET cars from Edmonton depot began working on the service for the first time.

With the withdrawal of service 25 on 13th February 1923, the 27 was extended to Edmonton all day, and the Bruce Grove rush hour extras were extended to Snells Park, using the number 27A. However, on 1st April 1924, the new tramway along Amhurst Park was opened and service 53 was extended from Stamford Hill to Euston Road via

Finsbury Park. Because of the extra cars running between Seven Sisters Road and Euston, service 27A was withdrawn.

On 9th July 1924, new schedules were introduced at several car sheds in north London, resulting in nine workings on 27 being transferred from the LCC to the MET. The Sunday service was withdrawn after 7th October 1928, but extra cars were provided on 59 instead. During the remainder of the period under review, the 27 was worked by both LCC and MET cars on weekdays only, although from 10th October 1931 the Saturday evening service was withdrawn.

The last two numbers to be allocated to original services working within the Finsbury Park group were 29 and 31. These had the distinction of being the first LCC services to work in the MET area. What became 29 began working between Euston Road and Enfield on 1st August 1912 and soon after, short workings to Aldermans Hill appeared. When numbering was introduced, the Enfield cars became 29, with 31 being allocated to the Monday to Saturday workings to Aldermans Hill. As the nature of short workings tended to be on an "as required" basis, the hours of operation of service 31 fluctuated. From February 1913, the 31 was working on a daily basis, but by October 1914, the service between rush hours on Monday to Saturday had been withdrawn. However, it was maintained throughout the evenings, the last cars leaving the termini at about 11.30 p.m. The map and guide for October 1915 showed that the 31 was running all day, but with the publication of the 1919 map, no Sunday service was advertised. Throughout this time the 29 remained as a daily working.

On 26th November 1919, the MET assumed operation of service 31, but this was not to last. On 2nd June 1920, it was again taken over by the LCC, with the MET working service 59. Further exchanges took place on 27th October when the MET took over the major share of the 29, with the LCC having total control of service 21, while, on 9th February 1921, operation of the 31 again passed to the MET.

As the built-up area spread northwards towards Enfield, the short working cars to Aldermans Hill were extended to Winchmore Hill, "Green Dragon" on 24th May 1922, retaining the number 31, but on 14th May 1923, all short journey cars were worked under the number 29, and the number 31 fell into disuse until the Kingsway Subway was re-opened in 1931 and the number allocated to a new service. By June 1924, the MET were operating service 29 in its entirety, but as mentioned in the section dealing with service 21, the major share of the 29 passed back to the LCC from 29th January 1931. From then on, the numbers of cars provided, varied between the two operators as this extract from LCC records shows:-

Number of cars by operator - service 29

Date	Mon - Fri		Saturday		Sunday	
	LCC	MET	LCC	MET	LCC	MET
18.12.1929	--	31	--	31	--	19
29.01.1931	29	2	29	2	18	1
05.03.1931	25	6	25	2	18	1
06.08.1931	27	4	27	4	19	--
17.03.1932	26	5	26	5	19	--
24.04.1932	26	5	26	5	25	3
08.05.1932	26	5	26	5	25	3*
27.10.1932	23	8	23	8	23	5
07.12.1932	23	15	23	8**	23	5
26.01.1933	19	19	19	12**	19	9
01.06.1933	19	12§	19	12**	19	9§§

Enfield Town terminus in the early 1920s, with E/1 car No. 1052 on LCC service 29, ready to return to Euston. (Commercial. C. A. Hodge)

Notes:-   * Plus 13 MET cars on service 29EX
          ** Plus 7 EX cars in MET area
           § Plus 12 EX cars
          §§ Plus 10 EX cars

There was a regular "reckoning up" between the accountants of each operator. Having decided "who owed what to whom", the timetable was arranged to balance the mileage. This re-arrangement between the LCC and MET was not unique to service 29, as all joint services were subject to this process, and it is likely that only the very keen observer would have noticed the changes taking place on any one route.

Other services were introduced in the Finsbury Park area as the LCC carried out improvements to traffic patterns. The first of these was a new one numbered 39, making a re-appearance following a period of operation between Newington Green and Bloomsbury, which ceased on 6th March 1914. When the Canonbury Road tramway was re-opened for electric traction on 25th June 1914, a new service with this number was provided during Monday to Saturday busy hours between Finsbury Park and Moorgate via Holloway Road and Canonbury Road. Its subsequent date of withdrawal is not recorded, but by November 1914, it had gone.

The number returned to the Finsbury Park area on 12th December 1921 on a new through rushhour service between Aldersgate and Bruce Grove via "Angel", Holloway Road, Finsbury Park, Wood Green and Lordship Lane. On 29th March 1922, the service became an all day one on weekdays until 9th July 1924, when it was withdrawn, being replaced over its entire length by an extension of service 71 from Wood Green. Less than nine months later, on 4th March 1925, service 39 was re-instated between the same two points, the 71 being again curtailed at Wood Green. It remained unaltered until 5th March 1931, when it was finally withdrawn. It was again replaced by an extension of service 71 from Wood Green to Aldersgate.

Service 53, which worked between Aldgate and Stamford Hill was extended to Euston Road on 1st April 1924 via Amhurst Park, Manor

House and Finsbury Park. Service 71, already mentioned above in connection with service 39, made a brief appearance in the Finsbury Park area during 1924 and a more permanent one after March 1931. Services 53 and 71 are dealt with in the Hackney section.

The remaining services to be considered in this section are those numbered 59 and 79, the first of which was introduced on 1st March 1913 in conjunction with the through running agreement. This really was an extension from Finsbury Park to Tottenham of alternate cars on service 21. It is likely that some short working cars on MET service 24 (which worked between Finsbury Park and Waltham Cross) were also withdrawn on the introduction of the 59. For a short period in 1921, it was extended to Enfield Wash (Southbury Road) on Saturdays until 3 p.m. As these extensions were not shown on the LCC Tramways maps and guides issued during 1922, it is concluded that service 59 was withdrawn north of Edmonton Town Hall during the winter of 1921/22.

Service 79, introduced between Smithfield and Waltham Cross on 23rd June 1913, linked up cars working on LCC service 23 from the south with those on MET service 24 north of Finsbury Park. Both undertakings provided cars for both services, although each retained control of short working cars on either side of the boundary at Finsbury Park Station, using the original numbers. During the early months of the Great War, use of separate numbers was discontinued, although the short services continued to work under the number 79. When the LCC extended service 49 northwards from Stamford Hill on 7th June 1920, the MET took over conplete operation of services 59 and 79. The 59, however, returned to the LCC on 27th October 1920, but by 1924 it was once again under MET control.

Apart from changes of operator, services 59 and 79 remained unaltered until 24th April 1932, when the 79 was diverted on Sundays at Ponders End to run along Southbury Road to Enfield Town, which left Waltham Cross without a tram service on that day. No further changes were introduced before the LPTB assumed control on 1st July 1933.

The Kingsway Subway Group

In Volume I of this history, the services using Kingsway Subway and those affected by them were discussed from the point of view of southern system operation. Administered mainly from the Northern Divisional Office, the Kingsway Subway group are discussed in this volume from the northern system point of view. Certain clarifications of detail which have emerged since the publication of Volume I have also been included.

The numbers 33 and 35 were given to the single deck cars working daily through the subway and via Westminster Bridge. The former was working between Highbury Station and Tower Bridge, with the latter running between the "Angel" and Clapham Junction via Battersea Park Road. On Sundays, service 35 was extended from the "Angel" via Essex Road to St. Paul's Road, Mildmay Park.

On 28th October 1913, with the introduction of a new service numbered 86 between Clapham Junction and Waterloo Bridge, and worked by double deck cars, service 35 was withdrawn, being covered by extra cars on service 33 between Westminster Station and Southampton Row. Strengthening of the services north of the subway was provided by extra cars on services 39 and 51, which ran over the same roads as the 33 and erstwhile 35 as far as the "Angel".

The southern terminus of service 35 was at St. George's Road, near the "Elephant & Castle". (The late G. N. Sutherland. Courtesy: P. J. Davis)

The single deck cars may well have proved to have been inadequate for the traffic on offer, and these changes permitted the use of more double deck cars over the unrestricted sections of line on either side of the subway, with passengers able to obtain transfer tickets for journeys which now required a change of car. The withdrawal of service 35 was short-lived, however. On 6th March 1914 it re-appeared, as a weekday and Sunday evening service between the "Angel" and Westminster Bridge.

By October 1915, service 33 had been withdrawn and 35 extended to Highbury Station on a daily basis. No further changes were made until 24th October 1921, when 35 was extended from Highbury Station to Highgate "Archway Tavern". From the same day, additional cars were provided during busy hours between Westminster and Highbury, and from 14th November these received the number 33. Both were extended over Westminster Bridge to County Hall from 24th July 1922, where they reversed on a crossover at Stangate. Following the install-ation of a new crossover at the end of St. George's Road near Newington Butts, the service was extended to the "Elephant & Castle" via St. George's Road on 27th June 1924.

No more changes were made until 16th January 1930 when, to release some of the single deck cars for "reconstruction" as double deckers, service 35 was suspended. This reduced the Monday to Friday requirement of subway cars from 37 to 24. On 2nd February, the subway was closed for reconstruction, which took place after the morning rush hour, possibly with the intention of transferring what remained of the cars to a south side car shed or the Central Repair Depot. Service 33 was withdrawn, while 35 was re-introduced between Bloomsbury and "Archway Tavern", using double deck cars, some of which consisted of new bodies mounted on the trucks of the old single deck cars.

During the eleven months that the subway was closed, special replacement omnibus services were provided by the L G O C on behalf of the Council. From 3rd February 1930, service 175 was introduced, working daily between Islington and Victoria Embankment via Rosebery

Avenue and Kingsway. Operated from Nunhead and Tottenham garages, covered-top type NS buses were used, running every 3 to 5 minutes on weekdays, with a 6 minute service on Sundays. Working between Kingsway and the Embankment by way of the Strand and Northumberland Avenue, they returned via Norfolk Street. On 23rd March, the Sunday service was withdrawn. From 14th May, the headway on service 175 was widened to a bus every 6 minutes, although during Monday to Saturday busy hours an additional bus service was introduced between Islington and Waterloo Station via Kingsway and Waterloo Bridge. Numbered 161, it was also operated by covered-top type NS buses from Nunhead and Tottenham garages on a 12 minute headway. Both bus services were withdrawn after 14th January 1931.

The enlarged subway opened on 15th January 1931 and two new services, numbered 31 and 33, joined the 35 in providing facilities through it. Service 31 was totally new, working between Hackney Station and Wandsworth on weekdays, but extended on Saturday afternoons and evenings to Tooting Junction. On Sundays it ran between Leyton Station (LMS) and Westminster Station via Lea Bridge Road to Hackney and then over its normal weekday route, which, incidentally, replaced service 55 on that day. The Sunday service was altered from 19th April, when it was extended from Westminster Station to Tooting Junction via Wandsworth, but was withdrawn between Hackney and Leyton Station. At the end of the summer season on 4th October 1931, the Sunday service worked between Wandsworth and Leyton "Bakers Arms".

The summer Sunday service in 1932 followed the pattern set the year before when, from 8th May until 25th September, the service worked between Hackney Station and Tooting Junction. After this date, it reverted to working between "Bakers Arms" and Wandsworth. The last month of LCC control in 1933 saw service 31 again extended to Tooting from 4th June. This time, however, the service to "Bakers Arms" was retained, giving a run of over 16 miles. The above notes clarify the early workings of the service, and correct an error in the text of Volume I.

Experimental car No. 1 awaits the passage of two cars on service 77, before crossing the "Angel" junction, bound for Kingsway Subway and south London. (Late G. N. Sutherden. Courtesy: Tramway Museum Soc'y)

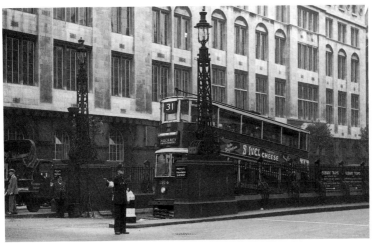

Car No. 1914, standing at the top of the subway ramp, ready to move forward into Theobalds Road. *(Courtesy: L. T. Museum. U12827)*

The second of the new subway services, numbered 33, worked during weekday rush hours, following the same route between Highbury and Westminster as it had done prior to the subway closure. South of Westminster, it was extended to Brixton, Water Lane via Kennington Road, with some journeys further extended to Telford Avenue and Streatham Library. Some cars were provided by Holloway shed as before and, additionally, others were from Streatham.

This arrangement did not last for very long. From 14th May the service was diverted at Brixton to work to West Norwood via Effra Road. At the same time, it became a regular daily working, while the Streatham allocation of cars was replaced by one from Norwood. The diversion to Norwood covered the same route as service 76 (Victoria Embankment and West Norwood via Westminster), which was withdrawn. Another change at the northern end took place on 8th October, when it was diverted at Islington Green to run to Manor House via Essex Road and Green Lanes, instead of to Highbury Station. This change resulted in the withdrawal of service 37 (Aldersgate and Manor House) and the diversion of service 51 to run from Aldersgate instead of Bloomsbury.

Service 35, the last of the three, had been running between Highgate and Bloomsbury while the subway was closed. It was extended to New Cross via Kennington, and with this extension, additional cars were provided by Streatham shed. On 14th May 1931, the Streatham cars were transferred to Camberwell, and the service was extended to Brockley Rise, Cranston Road. It was further extended to Valeswood Road, Downham on 30th August, with a Saturday evening extension to the same place as from 10th October. However, on 5th March 1932, the service was terminated once again at Brockley Rise, but on 30th June it was extended daily to Forest Hill, being re-routed to run via Walworth Road instead of by way of Kennington. This transposed the workings of 35 and 72 between Lambeth North and Camberwell, while the 72 was displaced between New Cross and Forest Hill by its diversion to Woolwich, as described in Volume I. The final change was made on 1st June by the addition of extra Monday to Friday midday workings between Highbury and "Elephant & Castle", bearing the number 35A.

The Manor House and Green Lanes Group

This small group consisted of four services.

37. Manor House and Aldersgate via Essex Road and "Angel".
39. Newington Green and Bloomsbury via Essex Road and "Angel".
41. Manor House and New North Road via Newington Green and Southgate Road.
51. Manor House and Bloomsbury via Essex Road and "Angel".

The service numbered 37 worked on weekdays only and at no time during its LCC existence changed its terminal points, although on 9th April 1914 it was relegated from working throughout the day to the status of a rush hours only service. It is recorded that on 2nd June 1920, Holloway took over the workings of the 37 from Hackney, which then remained unaltered until its withdrawal after 7th October 1931, when it was replaced by service 51, details of which are given below.

Service 39 only operated during rush hours and evenings on Mondays to Saturdays and was a short working of service 51. It was withdrawn on 6th March 1914, and possibly these journeys were incorporated into those of the 51. The number was next used in June 1914 for the short lived service of cars which was run between Moorgate and Finsbury Park via Canonbury Road, dealt with in the Finsbury Park group.

In December 1912, the number 41 was allocated to the service working between Manor House and the junction of Baring Street and New North Road. This had been extended from Mildmay Park on 26th November 1912, when the tracks in Southgate Road and Baring Street were opened for electric operation. At that time, the service could not reach a London terminus as horse cars were still running along New North Road and East Road to Moorgate, working alongside electric cars between the junction of East Road with City Road at Dawson's Corner, and the terminus. New North Road and East Road opened for electric traction on 25th June 1914, and service 41 was extended to Moorgate by way of Dawson's Corner.

Car No. 1046 of class E/1 on service 41, approaching Newington Green on a journey to Moorgate. The recently overhauled and repainted car still retains its original indicator signal lights. (Courtesy: J. H. Meredith)

Fourteen years were to elapse before any further changes were made. From 29th November 1928, the 41 was extended northwards to Wood Green Junction (where the Underground station now stands), giving a six minute service during rush hours and eight at all other times on Mondays to Fridays and until 2 p.m. on Saturdays. During busy hours the 41 headed even further north to Aldermans Hill, Palmers Green, providing an extra service to that area. The extension was made as part of the joint through running agreement, although the LCC retained responsibility for the operation of the service. From 6th June 1929, additional cars were worked north of Manor House to cater for the crowds attending dog racing at Harringay Stadium.

From 29th January 1931, services working along the Green Lanes corridor were revised, and the 41 was withdrawn between Manor House and Wood Green outside Monday to Friday busy hours and between them on Saturdays. The busy hour service was further extended to Winchmore Hill from 17th March 1932, still worked entirely by LCC cars. This was to be its final form when under LCC control.

A service 41EX was operated (using "EX" number plates) from 28th November 1928 between Manor House and Aldersgate during Monday to Saturday busy hours. The route was exactly that followed by the 37, and after October 1931, the 51. It remained in this form into the London Transport era.

The use of the number 51 in this group is out of numerical sequence, but is thought to have been allocated originally to the Bloomsbury and Stamford Hill via Hackney service, which was withdrawn in November 1912, and was subsequently used on a service between Bloomsbury and Manor House via Essex Road and Green Lanes. It was extended over MET metals from Manor House to Muswell Hill via Green Lanes and Hornsey High Street from 16th August 1914, with cars provided by both the LCC and MET. This extension replaced MET service 28 which had been working between Finsbury Park and Muswell Hill. Due to a shortage of suitable rolling stock during the Great War, service 51 was divided into two sections from 1st May 1916, each part terminating at Manor House, with both undertakings using the same number for their respective halves.

On its southern section there were alternative services working over its entire length, and from 15th February 1917, the Monday to Friday workings were confined to busy hours, although weekend operations remained unaltered. Through passengers on Mondays to Fridays were afforded transfer facilities, changing between cars on services 41 and 81 at Balls Pond Road. The LCC next withdrew the Sunday cars on service 51 as from 23rd September 1917, running extra cars on the 41 instead.

As conditions improved after the end of the war, service 51 began working all day on Mondays to Saturdays from 3rd March 1919. This was followed on 7th July 1920 by its restoration as a daily through running service between Muswell Hill and Bloomsbury. Operation also became the sole responsibility of the MET, who had equipped some of its four-wheel open top type D cars for working on the conduit system. The late A. W. McCall recalled that "these made a strange sight as they threaded their way very sedately amongst the single-deck subway cars and the more modern class E and E/1 cars of the LCC". These continued to provide the regular service on the 51 until they were displaced in 1931 by covered top cars, themselves made redundant by the new "Feltham" type cars.

However, during 1928 the service was made the subject of economy measures when, on 2nd May, it was completely withdrawn on Sundays and between Manor House and Bloomsbury outside weekday busy hours. Loss of the through link between Islington and Green Lanes was clearly unpopular, as the non-busy hours service was restored to Bloomsbury from 28th November, although there was still no Sunday service.

The last change to be made before the end of LCC control came on 8th October 1931, when subway service 33 was diverted at Islington Green to work to Manor House via Essex Road and Green Lanes, instead of to Highbury Station. As this provided a direct link between Manor House and Bloomsbury, the 51 was re-routed at "Angel" Islington to Aldersgate via Goswell Road, completely replacing service 37 which was withdrawn. The 37 had been working only during rush hours, whereas the cars on the 51 now worked all day.

The Kingsland Road Group

The four services working in the Stamford Hill area when numbering was introduced were:-

43. Stamford Hill and Holborn via Kingsland Road.
45. Stamford Hill and Moorgate via Kingsland Road.
47. Stamford Hill and London Docks via Kingsland Road.
49. Stamford Hill and Norton Folgate via Kingsland Road.

Two later services were:-

75. Stamford Hill and Holborn via Essex Road.
83. Stamford Hill and Moorgate via Southgate Road.

The side slot conduit system in use along part of Kingsland Road lasted longer than planned, thereby restricting expansion of the services along that road for many years.

Regular service on the 43 was via Shoreditch and Clerkenwell Road and remained unaltered from 1912 until 8th March 1931. From that day, Sunday cars travelling towards Stamford Hill were re-routed via Great Eastern Street and High Street, Shoreditch, instead of running via Old Street. This was the only change made in LCC days.

As with other LCC services, use of a number was not necessarily confined to regular operations between termini. In the case of service 43, it is recorded that there were Monday to Saturday p.m. busy hour "EX" journeys to and from Smithfield, which left the normal route in Clerkenwell Road. The dates of operation are not known, but records show that from 21st January 1932, three "EX" cars were incorporated into the regular Monday to Friday schedule, whilst the Saturday service appears to have been augmented from 11th March 1933. A morning busy hours service to Smithfield was also provided by "EX" cars on service 49.

Service 45 was at first a daily working between Stamford Hill and Moorgate via Old Street and City Road, but from 7th December 1915 was withdrawn after 9 p.m. on weekdays, whilst on Sundays it was confined to afternoon and evening working. Early in 1916, the Sunday service was withdrawn. By the time that the map and guide for spring 1918 was issued, service 45 was not working after about 7.30 p.m. on Mondays to Fridays or after about 4.30 p.m. on Saturdays. From 5th August 1924, Saturday workings were further reduced, the last cars running from Moorgate at about 3 p.m. The service was finally withdrawn after 27th May 1931, a part replacement being effected by working two additional "EX" cars on service 49.

Like the 43, service 47 led a largely unaltered existence, working between Stamford Hill and London Docks. The only change worthy of

Stamford Hill & Kingsland Road Routes
GOOD FRIDAY, 1917

From	To	First Cars	Last Cars
STAMFORD HILL —	HOLBORN	4.23, 5.0, 5.10, 5.22 5.35, 5.47, 6.10, 6.21	12.0, 12.15 12.40
,, —	LONDON DOCKS	8.40, 8.52, 9.4	11.47
,, —	LIVERPOOL ST. STN.	6.50, 7.0, 7.10	11.32
HOLBORN —	STAMFORD HILL	4.59, 5.36, 5.46, 5.58 6.11, 6.23, 6.45, 6.57	12.36, 12.52 1.17
LONDON DOCKS —	,,	9.10, 9.22, 9.34	12.23
LIVERPOOL ST. STN. —	,,	7.16, 7.26	12.0

EASTER MONDAY, 1917

From	To	First Cars	Last Cars
STAMFORD HILL —	HOLBORN	4.23, 5.10, 5.35 6.21, 6.45, 7.40	12.0, 12.15 12.40
,, —	LONDON DOCKS	7.22, 7.34, 7.46, 7.58	11.42
,, —	LIVERPOOL ST. STN.	6.30, 6.40, 6.50, 7.8, 7.16	11.48
HOLBORN —	STAMFORD HILL	4.59, 5.46, 6.12 6.57, 7.21	12.35, 12.52 1.17
LONDON DOCKS —	,,	7.54, 8.6, 8.18, 8.30	12.13
LIVERPOOL ST. STN. —	,,	6.56, 7.16, 7.26	12.14

ALL NIGHT SERVICES WILL RUN AS USUAL

62 Finsbury Pavement, E.C. 2   A. L. C. FELL, General Manager

note, occurred in 1929 when, between 7th August and 3rd October, the reconstruction of the track layout in High Street, Whitechapel caused the service to be reversed in Commercial Street, leaving Leman Street unserved for the duration of the works.

In December 1912, service 49 worked only on Monday to Saturday busy hours between between Stamford Hill and Norton Folgate (which is the stretch of road linking High Street Shoreditch with Bishopsgate). The LCC had obtained powers to extend the tramway along Bishopsgate, to terminate close by Liverpool Street Station, in the process crossing the boundary into the City of London. The new line opened on 20th March 1913 and the 49 was extended to the new terminus, at the same time being upgraded to a full daily service. It is possible that there was a slight reduction in the number of cars on services 43, 45 and 47 to compensate for this.

It was necessary at Stamford Hill for LCC cars to obtain access to and from the car shed and terminus by running over a short section of MET track. However, at this time, there was no ploughshift, as it had been decided that for the time being at least, there would be no through working by either party. This would have to wait until the side slot conduit section in Kingsland Road had been converted to the normal centre slot system, so that MET cars, should they be used, could be fitted with the standard plough carriers. In the event, nothing was done until nearly two years after the end of the Great War.

On 2nd June 1920, after many of the LCC cars had been fitted with trolley poles, and a ploughshift installed north of Stamford Hill junction, cars working on service 49 were extended to Edmonton Town Hall daily and further north to Waltham Cross during the afternoons and evenings of Saturdays and Sundays. On 24th May 1922, the Monday to Saturday rush hour service was also extended to Waltham Cross. The Kingsland Road side slot track was eventually replaced with the normal centre slot system in 1922, but the MET did not take part in working the service.

On 27th June 1923, the 49 was extended to Waltham Cross as a daily working. This, however, was not to last for long, as from 12th March 1924 it was withdrawn during Monday to Saturday rush hours between Ponders End (Southbury Road) and Waltham Cross, and outside these hours between Edmonton Town Hall and Waltham Cross. At weekends, the service continued to operate to Waltham Cross during the afternoons and evenings, until, from 5th October 1924, the northern terminus once again became Edmonton Town Hall.

The Sunday afternoon and evening extension to Waltham Cross was repeated in 1925, from 24th May until 11th October. In 1926, the summer season, so far as the LCC was concerned, lasted from 31st July until 17th October, when the extension was made on Saturdays and Sunday afternoons and evenings, while in 1927, it was from 14th May until 8th October. This arrangement, however, was not repeated again until after 1933 with the coming of the LPTB.

After October 1927, service 49 worked daily between Liverpool Street Station and Edmonton Town Hall, with the addition of a Monday to Friday rush hours extension to Ponders End. From 5th March 1931, the Ponders End service was extended along Southbury Road to the end of the line at Enfield, whilst on Saturdays, this extension worked throughout the day. One small change took place before the LCC relinquished control, when, from 24th April 1932, service 49 was withdrawn on Sundays between Bruce Grove, Tottenham and Edmonton Town Hall.

Extra cars were provided along Kingsland Road at busy times, usually displaying the service indication "EX". For administrative purposes these were usually regarded as being part of service 49, and shown on working documents as "49EX". The working of "EX" cars was not unique to the Kingsland Road route, but the reader may be interested to see how they were dealt with in this case. The researched records date from 26th January 1925, and show that four cars were provided during busy hours on Mondays to Fridays. Four "EX" cars were also operated on Saturdays but were kept out all day, no doubt offering assistance to the regular cars in moving shoppers to and from the various markets along the Kingsland Road and Stoke Newington Road corridor. The Monday to Friday extra cars were reduced to three from 26th April 1926, then suffered a summer suspension from 3rd August to 1st September 1927 (which also included the Saturday cars), and were completely withdrawn from 25th October 1928.

Four Monday to Friday "EX" cars re-appeared from 29th May 1930, working between Smithfield and Dalston Junction. A week later, on 6th June, these were reversed alternately at Downham Road or

Class E/1 car No. 796, bound for Liverpool Street, stands at the stop outside the Majestic Cinema and almost opposite Stoke Newington Police Station. (Commercial view)

Amhurst Road during the morning busy hours. A further two Monday to Friday cars were added on 28th May 1931, whilst from 29th October, additional morning journeys were provided to Smithfield on Mondays to Saturdays. The evening busy hour and Saturday midday link between Smithfield and the Kingsland Road was provided by "EX" cars working under service 43, and were used to fill the gaps in the regular workings (caused by incidents and failures) as well as relieving "pressure points" on any of the Kingsland Road services.

When dealing in Volume I with car services provided on the south side of the system, mention was made (page 410) of the noticeably slower average speeds of cars on services 68 and 70. This was ascribed to the volume of slow moving traffic to and from the docks between London Bridge and Deptford. Even slower average speeds were recorded for service 47, as shown in this table which was compiled on 26th January 1925.

Service	A.M. busy	Midday	P.M. busy
43	9.18	8.41	8.65
45	9.47	8.79	8.79
47	8.87	8.33	8.33
49	9.43	9.67	9.43

(all speeds shown in miles per hour)

It is possible that congestion at the Spitalfields vegetable market in Commercial Street and the docks traffic in Leman Street contributed to the slower running on the 47. On services 43 and 45 the single track sections through Old Street and at its junction with Kingsland Road, were also factors in slow running.

Following the reconstruction of the Graham Road and Balls Pond Road tramway for electric working, a new junction was laid in at Dalston Junction. This permitted the operation of electric cars from the Stamford Hill direction towards Essex Road and Islington, and was opened on 25th June 1914. Two new services were introduced using this connection and these carried the numbers 75 and 83.

The number 75 had previously been used for a horse car service running between Highbury Station and Moorgate via New North Road, which was withdrawn on 23rd June 1913 to enable electrification to take place. The new electric car service 75 was introduced between Stamford Hill and Holborn via Essex Road, the "Angel" and Rosebery Avenue on 25th June 1914, at first worked during Monday to Saturday busy hours, but becoming an all day service on weekdays from 20th April 1915. This compensated for the withdrawal of service 15 outside busy hours. Service 75 was subjected to no major changes during the remaining 18 years of LCC control, and only one minor one, when, from October 1931, later cars were provided on Saturdays.

The second new service, numbered 83, was also introduced on 25th June 1914, and provided a direct link between Moorgate and Stamford Hill via Kingsland Road, Southgate Road and City Road. Like the 75, it worked only during busy hours on Mondays to Saturdays, continuing in this way for a number of years. On 9th July 1923, however, it was improved to work during the midday period, although the last car still left Moorgate terminus at about 8 p.m. With the issue of the November 1931 map and guide, service 83 is shown as working throughout Saturday evenings, with the last car leaving Moorgate just before midnight. It is possible that this change to the 83 was effected from 10th October, when cars on service 41 were reduced in number on Saturday evenings. By November 1932, evening workings had been introduced on Mondays to Fridays, making the 83 an all-day weekday service.

The Hackney Group

Prior to 2nd November 1912 five services were working via Hackney. These were:-

Stamford Hill (Clapton Common) and Aldgate via Clapton, Hackney, Cambridge Heath and Whitechapel.

Stamford Hill (Clapton Common) and Bloomsbury via Clapton, Hackney, Cambridge Heath and Shoreditch.

Leyton "Bakers Arms" and Bloomsbury via Hackney, Cambridge Heath and Shoreditch.
(From Epping Forest "Rising Sun" on Sundays).

Leyton "Bakers Arms" and Moorgate via Hackney, Cambridge Heath, and Shoreditch.

Leyton "Bakers Arms" and Aldgate via Hackney, Cambridge Heath and Whitechapel.

On 2nd November, the LCC carried out a re-organisation of services in the area; two were withdrawn (Stamford Hill & Bloomsbury and Leyton & Aldgate), being replaced by more frequent services over the other routes. This might have been carried out in conjunction with the through running arrangements made for working across Bow Bridge, which began about the same time. In December 1912, the three remaining services were given these numbers:-

53. Stamford Hill (Clapton Common) and Aldgate.
55. Leyton "Bakers Arms" and Bloomsbury.
(From Epping Forest "Rising Sun" on Sundays).
57. Leyton "Bakers Arms" and Moorgate.

The absence of numbers 51 and 59 suggests that these were intended for the two withdrawn services, a fact which has been the subject of speculation for many years. It would have been logical for the two Stamford Hill services to be numbered 51 and 53, with those via Lea Bridge Road receiving 55, 57 and 59, and would have fitted in with the general pattern of numbering. There is evidence to indicate that service numbers were placed on many of the cars from September 1912, in which case use of the numbers 51 and 59 may well have taken place, although this cannot be substantiated.

The destination indicators of cars on service 53 showed "Clapton Common", but they actually terminated a few yards short of Stamford Hill cross-roads. Service 53 remained unaltered for nearly twelve years, until it was extended with the opening of the new tramway along Amhurst Park on 1st April 1924. This should have taken place on 23rd March, but due to a strike of tramwaymen, it had to be postponed. The new extension of the service brought it into Euston Road via Amhurst Park, Manor House, Finsbury Park and Camden Town, giving it the distinction of having its terminal points both in central London and about three miles apart! With this extension, services along the Camden and Seven Sisters Roads were revised from the same date and the busy hour cars which had worked on service 27A between Euston Road and Seven Sisters Corner were withdrawn.

Cars on service 53 had been provided by Hackney and Stamford Hill sheds for many years, although the numbers varied between the two from time to time in order to balance car allocations. This became more important as services working along the Kingsland Road increased. Provision could then be made to transfer some workings of the 53 to Hackney when necessary. In turn, workings on certain other services were moved to Holloway. An example of this is to be seen when, on 2nd August 1920, the Stamford Hill allocation was taken up by Hackney, but, on the opening of the Amhurst Park line, it appears that Stamford Hill shed once again took up a share of the duties. However, after 3rd May 1928, both Hackney and Stamford Hill lost their workings of the service to Holloway.

During the closure of the Gardiners Corner junction layout between August and October 1929, service 53 cars were reversed at St. Mary's Church in High Street, Whitechapel. After its return to Aldgate, the service remained unaltered, becoming a well-used link across north east London. Even to this day a busy bus service numbered 253, after its predecessor, trolleybus service 653, still operates the curious "horse shoe" shaped route between Aldgate and Mornington Crescent.

On 1st December 1912, service 55 was one of the early examples of through running to be seen in the London area, having begun operation on 11th December 1911. Although working daily between Bloomsbury and Leyton "Bakers Arms", there was a Sunday extension to Epping Forest "Rising Sun". This was possibly intended to offer a day out to residents of the north-east and east London suburbs at a time when even a one week holiday with pay was an unattainable dream for many people. Information taken from several issues of the LCC Tramways map and guide, indicates that the "Rising Sun" extension was an all year round working, although by the time that the guide for 1915 was issued, the extension had been withdrawn. It was transferred to service 81, which had reached the "Bakers Arms" in January 1915 and was extended to the "Rising Sun" during the spring of that year.

From 18th October 1916, services 55 and 57 were suspended along Lea Bridge Road after 11 p.m. as a precaution against damage from air raids, following a number of such incidents perpetrated by the German Air Force. Normal last cars were restored at the end of the war, although the date is not recorded.

Sunday workings to the "Rising Sun" were resumed in the summer seasons from 1921 onwards, operating in this and subsequent years

The Manor House tram shelters seen in February 1933, with E/1 car No. 1607 at the stop.   *(Courtesy: London Transport Museum)*

as follows (all dates inclusive):-

1921	24th July until	30th October;
1922	Spring* until	10th September;
1923	Spring* until	14th October;
1924	20th April until	28th September;
1925	24th May until	4th October;
1926	31st July until	17th October;
1927	8th May until	30th October;
1928	6th May until	7th October.

Note: * These dates have not been ascertained.

The daily pattern changed from 11th October 1928, when service 55 was extended from "Bakers Arms", along Leyton High Road to Leyton Station (LMS). When the summer Sunday schedule was introduced on 19th May 1929, alternate cars were diverted at the "Bakers Arms" to run all day to the "Rising Sun", while other cars to Leyton Station were further extended during the afternoons to Wanstead Flats. This lasted until after 29th September, when winter Sunday schedules were re-introduced. From 29th June 1929, cars were extended from Leyton Station (LMS) to Wanstead Flats after 2.30 p.m. on Saturdays, and this arrangement remained in force throughout the following winter, but with extended workings commencing at about 11.30 a.m. from 1st February 1930. On Sundays, between 22nd May and 12th October 1930, alternate cars worked to either "Rising Sun" (all day) or Leyton Station (LMS) (mornings) and Wanstead Flats (afternoons).

With the opening of the reconstructed Kingsway Subway on 15th January 1931, subway service 31 worked between Wandsworth and Hackney on weekdays, but on Sundays worked between Westminster Station and Leyton Station (LMS), which exactly duplicated the route of service 55, which was withdrawn on that day. On 19th April 1931, summer timetables were again introduced, and service 31 was curtailed at Hackney on Sundays, with service 55 appearing between Bloomsbury and the "Rising Sun" (all day), or Wanstead Flats (during afternoons and evenings), as in 1930. The Monday to Saturday service was also altered, being extended along Leyton High Road from the LMS station to the LNER station. Sunday workings on service 55 ceased from 4th October 1931, when service 31 was again extended, this time to the "Bakers Arms". The 55 returned to the road on Sundays between 8th May and 18th September 1923. The summer Sunday workings from 4th June 1933 were, however, slightly amended, as service 31 was not cut back to Hackney and the 55 only operated during afternoons and evenings to Wanstead Flats, with the "Rising Sun" journeys being left to service 81. Throughout the years, it is understood that service 55 was always worked by LCC cars, with the Leyton UDC Tramways contribution under the through running agreement being an allocation on service 57, as well as on services 61 and 81, described below.

Service 57 was, at the end of 1912, a Monday to Saturday rush hour working between "Bakers Arms" and Moorgate via Lea Bridge Road, Clapton and Hackney Road and was entirely worked by cars of the Leyton UDC Tramways. It is said that Leyton were not very happy with this arrangement, pressing the LCC to begin a service to Liverpool Street Station to counteract the introduction of an omnibus service numbered 35, which at that time worked between Walthamstow and "Elephant & Castle". The opening of the short line from Norton Folgate to Liverpool Street Station (in Bishopsgate) on 20th March 1913 saw Leyton's wish fulfilled, when the 57 was diverted at Shoreditch Church to run to the new terminus as a daily service. However, on 13th April, an extension was also made at the other end of the line, when the cars were scheduled to run to Epping Forest "Rising Sun" between 11.30 a.m. and 6.30 p.m. daily, followed on 27th April with an extended service right through the evenings until the end of the service for the day.

From 1st October 1913, operation to "Rising Sun" was confined to Saturdays and Sundays for some weeks, so as to allow Leyton UDC to relay the tracks between "Bakers Arms" and Fraser Road, Leyton. The Saturday extension, however, was withdrawn from 30th October 1913, leaving the "Rising Sun" service to be worked on Sundays only, which continued until some time after April 1916, when it most likely fell

Walthamstow car No. 64, seen at Bell Corner, on its way to Chingford Mount on the through service from Liverpool Street. (Courtesy: T.M.S.)

victim to the pressures of the Great War. As already mentioned in the section dealing with service 55, after 18th October 1916, cars were not worked along Lea Bridge Road beyond Kenninghall Road later than 11 p.m.

By 1918, service 57 was still working between Liverpool Street Station and the "Bakers Arms" "in conjunction with the Leyton Urban District Council". As already mentioned in the section dealing with the Finsbury Park group, joint running services were subject to operational changes brought about by the necessity to balance mileages worked. Records show that from 25th March 1920, the 57 was worked entirely by Leyton, but the same records indicate that, during November, two LCC cars were worked daily for "mileage purposes". This activity became unnecessary from 1st July 1921, when the LCC took over the management of the Leyton Tramways.

The Sunday extension from "Bakers Arms" to "Rising Sun" returned for the summers of 1920 and 1921. Journeys to the "Rising Sun" were also provided during the midday fare period on Mondays to Fridays as from 2nd August 1921, but from 20th September, these extended runs were withdrawn, to be followed by the withdrawal of the Sunday extension from 6th November. Thereafter, Sunday extensions were:-
                Summer 1922, from spring* until 1st October;
                        1923, from spring* until 14th October;
                        1924, from 20th April until 28th October;
                        1925, from 24th May until 4th October.
Note: * These dates have not been ascertained.

Through running arrangements with Walthamstow Corporation Light Railways were introduced in May 1925, although at first it was confined to the ex-Leyton services 7 and 8, now worked by the LCC. By this time, LGOC buses (and those of other companies) were competing with trams throughout London and, in an effort to "fight back", negotiations were entered into between Walthamstow Corporation, Leyton UDC and the LCC. One result was to arrange a direct service between Chingford Mount and central London, to compete in part with bus service 38, which ran to Victoria. Car service 57 was to provide this facility, albeit serving the City rather than the West End, as bus 38 did. The new service may also have abstracted traffic from the L&NE Railway line between Chingford, Walthamstow and Liverpool Street. Service 57 was extended from "Bakers Arms" to Chingford Mount by way of Hoe Street, on 24th January 1926.

This extension replaced Leyton service 8 between "Bakers Arms" and Chingford Mount. At first, service 57 was operated entirely with LCC cars, but Walthamstow subsequently obtained a fleet of cars similar in many ways to the LCC E/1s, but with greatly improved bodywork and motors, the first of these coming into service on 6th November 1927, and with the full quota running as from 16th January 1928. As the Walthamstow cars were delivered, schedules were changed to accommodate the new arrivals as shown here:-

Date	Car Shed	Mon-Fri	Saturday	Sunday
7th November 1927	Leyton	17	13	10
	Hackney	11	13	4
	Walthamstow	5	5	4
16th January 1928	Leyton	17	13	4
	Hackney	6	6	4
	Walthamstow	10	10	4
3rd May 1928	Leyton	23	19	13
	Walthamstow	10	10	8

No major changes are recorded for service 57 after the extension to Chingford Mount, although there were minor adjustments to the allocations to conform with the mileage balancing arrangements.

Later Services

The following services were initiated after the introduction of numbering.

     71. West India Docks and Hackney, Mare Street.
     77. Dalston Junction and Hackney Station.
     81. Bloomsbury and Hackney Station.

The horse car service working between South Hackney (Cassland Road) and West India Docks via Grove Road and Burdett Road was allocated the number 71, although the cars did not carry it. It was operated from a depot in Grove Road, Mile End, but on 11th August 1914 the service was discontinued owing to the War Department having impressed a large number of the Council's horses. As mentioned elsewhere, it had been planned to electrify the line, but due to the war, those along Grove Road and Burdett Road remained closed.

Cars on service 71 worked between Aldgate and Wood Green. Here, E/1 car No. 854, is crossing Clapton Common. (Commercial view)

Meanwhile, the number 71 had been used for a short-lived service working along Holloway Road in the autumn of 1914, but was eventually thrown spare, remaining so until after the end of the war. Work on the electrification of the Grove Road and Burdett Road lines, using the overhead wire system, eventually began during 1920, with a short extension being laid into Well Street, and upon the inauguration of an electric car service on 28th July 1921, the number 71 was again used.

On 1st December, a ploughshift was installed at the west end of Well Street, and a connection made with the tracks in Mare Street, allowing a through service of cars to operate to Hackney and beyond. (There was another ploughshift at the south end of Burdett Road, with a connection into East India Dock Road, to allow access for cars from and to Poplar car shed). On the same day, service 71 was withdrawn, being replaced by an extension of service 77.

Car No. 642 stops at the junction of Grove Road with Mile End Road,
on the way to West India Docks. *(Courtesy: LTM U14267)*

The opening of the Amhurst Park tramway resulted in further through running possibilities on to MET metals, and part of service 53 which had terminated at "Clapton Common" was extended to Wood Green via Tottenham and Lordship Lane. As the number 53 had been used for the extension to Euston Road, the Wood Green service was given the number 71. Just over three months later, on 9th July 1924, it was extended from Wood Green to Aldersgate via Green Lanes, Finsbury Park, Holloway Road and "Angel" on Mondays to Saturdays, replacing service 39, which was withdrawn. This lengthy working may well have caused operating difficulties, and less than nine months later, on 4th March 1925, service 71 was withdrawn between Bruce Grove and Aldersgate and service 39 was re-introduced. From 16th January 1928, an extension from Bruce Grove to Wood Green operated during Monday to Saturday busy hours as well as on Sundays.

In the November 1928 issue of the LCC Tramways map and guide, service 71 is shown as working to Wood Green all day on Saturdays until past midnight. As on service 53, the 71 was curtailed at St. Mary's Church, Whitechapel during track reconstruction works between 7th August and 3rd October 1929. From 5th March 1931, the service was again extended from Wood Green to Aldersgate on weekdays in place of 39, which was finally withdrawn. This was the last change to be made in LCC days. Operation of service 71 had generally been with cars from Stamford Hill and Hackney sheds, but it is possible that, when extended to replace service 39, the 71 would have been given some workings from Holloway.

Service 77 began on 20th March 1913 as an electrically worked shuttle service between Dalston Lane (Mayfield Road) and Hackney Station via Graham Road, at a fare of ½d. From 26th July, cars were extended a short distance at Dalston to Balls Pond Road. When the electrified line in Balls Pond Road was opened on 6th March 1914, service 77 was extended from Dalston Junction to Aldersgate via Essex Road and "Angel". During March 1915, the service was extended 'round the corner' in Hackney from Graham Road to Kenninghall Road, Lower Clapton. By the time that the map and guide for October 1915 had been issued, the Kenninghall Road extension had been withdrawn, as had both the Monday to Saturday evening and all-day Sunday services.

From 1st December 1921, the 77 was extended from Graham Road via Mare Street to Well Street, and then over the route of service 71 to West India Docks. It is also possible that this date saw the restoration of the evening and Sunday services to the 77, and it now worked all day every day between Aldersgate and West India Docks. Although cars were initially provided by Hackney shed, part of service 77 was transferred to Poplar as from 1st December 1921, but returned to Hackney from 3rd May 1928.

Service 81, with cars working from Hackney shed, first appeared on 6th March 1914. When the Balls Pond Road line was opened for electric traction, the service began working between Bloomsbury and Hackney Station via Essex Road and Graham Road. Although a single line curve was laid in between the "up" track in Graham Road and the "up" track in Mare Street, it was only used for depot workings. This was replaced by a double track junction which opened on 11th January 1915, enabling the service to be extended to Leyton "Bakers Arms" via Lea Bridge Road. In April of the same year it was further extended to Epping Forest "Rising Sun" on Sundays, but this extension had been withdrawn by the time that the April 1916 issue of the map and guide was published. The next mention of the service working to "Rising Sun" was on Saturday afternoons and evenings from 15th May 1920, to be followed by Sunday journeys in July. However, in this case, this extension continued to work throughout the 1920-21 winter.

On 11th July 1921, after the LCC had taken over the workings of the Leyton system, the 81 began working between Bloomsbury and Whipps Cross on a daily basis. On Mondays to Saturdays after 9 a.m. and all day on Sundays the service was extended to "Rising Sun".

Early in 1931, the Leyton and Walthamstow tracks were connected at the "Rising Sun" and, from 5th March, service 81 was extended to Woodford, "Napier Arms" as a full daily service, remaining unchanged from then on.

After the re-opening of the Kingsway Subway, the Council was continually looking into ways and means of making improvements in the services connecting north and south London. On 10th November 1931, the Highways Committee was asked to consider extending service 81 to a terminus in south London. However, as only 30 cars per hour were allowed through the subway in each direction, and all available paths were taken up by existing services, any increase in workings on the 81 would be at the expense of the others. The suggestion was not taken up.

The Bow Road Group of Services

When numbering was introduced these services were working along the Bow Road:-

61. Aldgate and Whipps Cross, via Bow Road, Stratford and Leytonstone. Extended on Mondays to Saturdays to Leyton "Bakers Arms".

63. Aldgate and Ilford Broadway, via Bow Road, Stratford and Manor Park.

Leyton E/3 car, No. 193, displaying "Bakers Arms" as its destination, ready to leave Aldgate for Leyton via Stratford on service 61. This car was one that was fitted with truck side covers. (Unknown)

From 3rd May 1913, service 61 was diverted at Whipps Cross to run to Epping Forest "Rising Sun" on Saturdays after 12.30 p.m. and all day on Sundays. By the time that the December 1913 issue of the map and guide had been published, there was no mention of a Saturday service. It apparently continued to work through to "Rising Sun" on Sundays throughout the war.

The effects of the Great War brought about the closure of several inner area stations on the Great Eastern Railway. Facilities for those passengers displaced from Coburn Road and Grove Road stations were provided for by extra cars being run on services 61 and 63 between Bow Bridge and Aldgate as from 22nd May 1916. Also, as a result of the policy of the local authorities with regard to air raid precautions, services in the Leyton area were suspended after 11 p.m. from 23rd October 1916. They were restored when conditions allowed.

In post-war years, service 61 normally ran between Aldgate and "Bakers Arms", although in summer months there were Sunday workings to "Rising Sun". To cope with the extra passenger traffic generated in the weeks before Christmas 1924, Saturday services were worked on Mondays to Fridays between 8th and 24th December. During the summers of 1925 to 1927, alternate cars on Sundays ran to "Bakers Arms" and "Rising Sun", but this finally ceased in October 1927, when all cars on the 61 thereafter worked between Aldgate and "Bakers Arms" daily.

Service 63 remained basically unaltered, with cars plying between Aldgate and Ilford Broadway, although several changes of a temporary nature were made from time to time, as these examples show.
1. From 4th July 1919 until 9th January 1920, cars were turned at Manor Park Broadway, while East Ham Corporation were relaying their tracks.
2. There was a national strike of coal miners in 1921, and, to economise on fuel consumption, tram services were reduced between 28th April

Operation of service 63 was shared between the LCC, East Ham and West Ham Corporations. East Ham car No. 56, seen here, illustrates its similarity with the LCC class E/1 cars. (Courtesy: R. Elliott)

and 5th July, with further reductions imposed between 8th May and 29th May, when LCC cars on services 61 and 63 were curtailed at Bow Bridge before 5.30 a.m. and after 10 p.m. on Mondays to Saturdays. On Sundays the curtailment was more severe, with cars not crossing Bow Bridge until after 1.30 p.m.

3. As with service 61, Saturday services were worked on Mondays to Fridays between 8th and 24th December 1924.

4. In common with other services which crossed the junction layout at Whitechapel, cars on services 61 and 63 were reversed at St. Mary's Church between 7th August and 3rd October 1929, during the period that the tracks were being re-arranged.

The Commercial Road and Poplar Group

According to the December 1912 issue of the LCC Tramways map and guide, three services were in operation along Commercial Road:

    65. Bloomsbury and Poplar.
    67. Aldgate and East Ham Town Hall.
    69. Aldgate and Barking (Loxford Bridge).

Through running services between the LCC, West Ham and East Ham Corporations and Barking Town UDC Light Railways actually began on 20th December 1912. So far as can be ascertained, the LCC exclusively worked services 65 and 67 at that time, whilst the 69 was jointly worked by all four authorities.

Service 65 was not included in the joint agreement, although by December 1913, it had been extended across the Iron Bridge to Canning Town Fire Station. As part of the reorganisation consequent upon the withdrawal of service 69 from 1st June 1914, the 65 was extended during Monday to Saturday busy hours to Green Street, Barking Road. The next change came on 22nd November 1915, when the weekday ordinary service was curtailed to run only between Bloomsbury and

The motorman of this early morning car working on service 65, prepares to bring his charge across the crossover alongside East India Docks. (Courtesy: Central Photos)

Poplar, the rush hour service still working to Green Street and the Sunday service to Canning Town Fire Station.

A rush hour extension to East Ham Town Hall was introduced from 9th March 1925, while, from 16th October 1926, this also operated on Saturday afternoons. The Saturday afternoon extension ceased from 11th October 1928, after which the service remained unchanged during the rest of the time it was worked by the Council. With regard to the provision of cars, until 3rd May 1928, they came from both Bow and Poplar sheds, but after this date, all cars came from Poplar.

When numbered, the 67 worked a daily service, but on 13th January 1913 it was withdrawn on Sundays. On 1st June 1914 it was extended to Barking Broadway to replace service 69, and a Sunday service was also introduced. The 67 then remained in this form for the rest of its existence. However, both the 65 and 67 were affected by two temporary alterations. The first was when the 1921 miners' strike caused LCC cars to be curtailed at Iron Bridge after 10 p.m. daily, before 5.30 a.m. on Mondays to Saturdays and before 1.30 p.m. on Sundays. This lasted from 8th to 25th May.

The second alteration resulted from the reconstruction of the track layout at Gardiners Corner in 1929, when cars on both services which were approaching Aldgate from the east were reversed short of the roadworks, while service 65 cars coming from Bloomsbury were turned back in Commercial Street. By this time, service 67 was being worked jointly with East Ham and West Ham Corporations, with Poplar car shed providing the LCC share. Cars proceeding to the western arm of the 65 service during the road works, would have had a circuitous journey, possibly by way of Hackney Road.

Operation of service 69 along the Commercial Road did not last long. Barking Urban District Council was a reluctant tramway operator and was continually trying to find someone willing enough to work its tramways on its behalf. Eventually, from 1st June 1914, Ilford agreed to work the line from Loxford Bridge to Barking Broadway as part of its local service. This resulted in service 69 being withdrawn at the end of the schedule on 31st May. On the following day, service 67 was extended to cover the route to Barking Broadway, as recorded above.

Leyton Local Services

    7. "Bakers Arms", Leyton High Road, "Thatched House", Stratford, Plaistow, Balaam Street, Freemasons Road, V. & A. Docks.

    8. "Bakers Arms", Leyton High Road, "Thatched House", Wanstead Flats, Forest Gate, Plaistow, Balaam Street, Freemasons Road, V. & A. Docks.

These two services were worked jointly between Leyton and West Ham, in which the LCC took an interest in the Leyton area as from 1st July 1921. A working agreement was made with Walthamstow UDC Light Railways in 1925 and, from 31st May, both services were extended to Chingford Mount, although service 8 did not run north of "Bakers Arms" between 9.40 a.m. and 4.20 p.m. on Mondays to Fridays. As part of the regular dialogue between the LCC and its partners in the joint operation, it was mentioned in 1925 that there were insufficient four wheeled cars owned by Leyton to work on both services 7 and 8. It was agreed that LCC cars would operate service 61 completely, displacing West Ham cars to enable them to work additional mileage on services 63, (L)7 and (L)8. When the 57 was diverted to Chingford on 24th January 1926, service 8 was again curtailed at "Bakers Arms", at which terminus it remained until after the LPTB was formed in July 1933. By August 1931, service (L)7 was operated entirely by Leyton and (L)8 by West Ham cars.

Class M car No. 1440, one of the batch originally allocated to the Highgate Hill service, seen in 1933 at Walthamstow, at work on the long suburban service between Victoria & Albert Docks and Chingford Mount.

(Courtesy: M. J. O'Connor)

List of Car Services as at 30th June 1933.
All services operated daily, unless otherwise shown.

3 Hampstead (South End Green), Prince of Wales Road, Great College Street, King's Cross, Gray's Inn Road, Holborn.

5 Hampstead (South End Green), Chalk Farm Road, Camden Town, Crowndale Road, King's Cross, "Angel", City Road, Moorgate.

7 Parliament Hill Fields, Kentish Town, Great College Street, King's Cross, Gray's Inn Road, Holborn.

9 North Finchley "Tally Ho!", East Finchley, "Archway Tavern", Holloway Road, Upper Street, "Angel", City Road, Moorgate.

11 Highgate Village, Holloway Road, Highbury, New North Road, City Road, Moorgate.

13 "Archway Tavern", Holloway Road, Upper Street, "Angel", Goswell Road, Aldersgate.
   (Monday to Saturday rush hours only).

15 Parliament Hill Fields, Kentish Town, Great College Street, King's Cross, "Angel", City Road, Moorgate.

17 "Archway Tavern", Holloway Road, Caledonian Road, King's Cross, Farringdon Road, Farringdon Street Station.
   (Northbound cars travelled via King's Cross Road,
      southbound via Swinton Street).

19 Barnet, Whetstone, North Finchley "Tally Ho!", East Finchley, "Archway Tavern", Kentish Town, Camden Town, Euston Road.

21 North Finchley "Tally Ho!", New Southgate, Wood Green, Harringay, Manor House, Finsbury Park, Caledonian Road, King's Cross, Gray's Inn Road, Holborn.

25 Parliament Hill Fields, Kentish Town, Camden Town, Euston Road.
   (Monday to Saturday rush hours and Saturday p.m.).

27 Edmonton Town Hall, Tottenham, Seven Sisters Corner, Manor House, Finsbury Park, Camden Town, Euston Road.

29 Enfield, Palmers Green, Wood Green, Harringay, Manor House, Finsbury Park, Camden Town, Euston Road.

31 Hackney Station, Hackney Road, Shoreditch, Bloomsbury, Kingsway Subway, Victoria Embankment, Westminster, Vauxhall, Battersea Park Road, Wandsworth.
   (Extended on Sundays from Hackney to Leyton "Bakers Arms", and from Wandsworth to Tooting Junction).

33 Manor House, Green Lanes, Essex Road, "Angel", Bloomsbury, Kingsway Subway, Victoria Embankment, Westminster, Kennington, Brixton, Effra Road, Herne Hill, West Norwood.

35 "Archway Tavern", Holloway Road, "Angel", Bloomsbury, Kingsway Subway, Victoria Embankment, Westminster, "Elephant & Castle", Walworth Road, Camberwell, New Cross, Brockley, Crofton Park, Brockley Rise, Forest Hill Station.
   (Between "Elephant" and Westminster, "up" cars via St. George's Road, "down" cars via St. George's Circus and London Road).

35 Highbury Station, then as 35 to "Elephant".
 A (Monday to Friday midday hours only).
   ("up" and "down" cars via St. George's Road in both directions between Westminster and "Elephant").

41 Manor House, Green Lanes, Southgate Road, New North Road, City Road, Moorgate.
   (During Monday to Saturday rush hours extended from Manor House to Wood Green and Winchmore Hill).

43 Stamford Hill, Stoke Newington, Dalston Junction, Kingsland Road, Shoreditch, Old Street, Holborn.

47 Stamford Hill, Stoke Newington, Dalston Junction, Kingsland Road, Shoreditch, Commercial Street, Leman Street, London Docks.

49 Tottenham (Bruce Grove), Stamford Hill, Stoke Newington, Dalston Junction, Kingsland Road, Shoreditch, Liverpool Street Station.
(Extended Monday to Saturday from Tottenham to Edmonton, and further extended in rush hours to Ponders End and Enfield).

51 Muswell Hill, Harringay, Manor House, Green Lanes, Essex Road, "Angel", Goswell Road, Aldersgate.
(Monday to Saturday only).

53 Euston Road, Camden Town, Camden Road, Finsbury Park, Manor House, Amhurst Park, Stamford Hill, Clapton Common, Hackney, Cambridge Heath, Whitechapel, Aldgate.

55 Leyton Station (LNER), "Bakers Arms", Lea Bridge Road, Hackney, Cambridge Heath, Shoreditch, Old Street, Bloomsbury.
(Monday to Saturday and on summer Sundays after 12.30 p.m. Also extended on summer Sundays from Leyton Station (LNER) to Wanstead Flats).

57 Chingford Mount, Walthamstow, "Bakers Arms", Lea Bridge Road, Hackney, Cambridge Heath, Shoreditch, Liverpool Street Station.

59 Edmonton, Tottenham, Manor House, Finsbury Park, Caledonian Road, King's Cross, Gray's Inn Road, Holborn.

61 Leyton "Bakers Arms", Whipps Cross, Leytonstone, Stratford, Bow Bridge, Mile End, Whitechapel, Aldgate.

63 Ilford Broadway, Manor Park, Stratford, Bow Bridge, Mile End, Whitechapel, Aldgate.

65 Poplar (Blackwall Tunnel), East India Dock Road, Commercial Road, Commercial Street, Old Street, Bloomsbury.
(Extended on Sundays from Poplar to Canning Town).

67 Barking Broadway, East Ham, Canning Town, Poplar, East India Dock Road, Commercial Road, Aldgate.

71 Aldgate, Whitechapel, Cambridge Heath, Hackney, Clapton Common, Stamford Hill, Tottenham, Wood Green.
(Extended Monday to Saturday from Wood Green to Harringay, Manor House, Finsbury Park, Holloway Road, "Angel", Goswell Road, Aldersgate).

75 Stamford Hill, Stoke Newington, Dalston Junction, Essex Road, "Angel", Rosebery Avenue, Holborn.
(Monday to Saturday only).

77 West India Docks, Burdett Road, Grove Road, Well Street, Hackney, Dalston Junction, Essex Road, "Angel", Goswell Road, Aldersgate.

79 Waltham Cross, Freezy Water, Ponders End, Edmonton, Tottenham, Manor House, Finsbury Park, Holloway Road, Upper Street, "Angel", St. John Street, Smithfield.
(Monday to Saturday only).
(Sunday: Enfield, Southbury Road, Ponders End, then as above to Smithfield).

81 Woodford "Napier Arms", Epping Forest "Rising Sun", Whipps Cross, "Bakers Arms", Lea Bridge Road, Hackney, Dalston Junction, Essex Road, "Angel", Rosebery Avenue, Bloomsbury.

83 Stamford Hill, Stoke Newington, Dalston Junction, Southgate Road, New North Road, City Road, Moorgate.
(Monday to Friday until 7.30 p.m. and all day Saturday).

(L)7 Chingford Mount, Walthamstow, "Bakers Arms", Leyton High Road, Stratford, Plaistow, Balaam Street, V. & A. Docks.

(L)8 Leyton "Bakers Arms", Leyton High Road, Cann Hall Road, Wanstead Flats, Forest Gate, Plaistow, V. & A. Docks.

Extra services, such as those that ran only on Bank Holidays, and usually denoted by the indication "EX", were not normally shown on the maps and guides which were issued to the public, and are therefore not included in this table.

Service unceasing is rendered by L.C.C. Tramways, which work for **24 Hours per Day** and provide the widest facilities

TRAVEL QUICKLY READ IN COMFORT

Under Cover all the Way

L.C.C. TRAMWAYS HAVE BEEN CHARGED WITH £813,000 FOR **STREET IMPROVEMENTS** *Travel by Tram at all Times*	**LONDON'S TRAMWAYS** HAVE AN AVERAGE SPEED OF **9¾ MILES PER HOUR** (Including Stops) THE HIGHEST IN THE KINGDOM *Travel by Tram at all Times*

The Council regularly brought its tramcar services to the notice of the public by means of advertisements, many of which were in their own publications. A selection of these is displayed above.

Night Services

In the same way that night services were introduced on the system south of the Thames, it was decided that this facility should be given to the people living and working in the northern area. Negotiations were entered into with the North Metropolitan Tramways, resulting in the following services being introduced.

Stamford Hill, Stoke Newington, Kingsland Road, Old Street, Holborn.
Poplar, Commercial Road, Commercial Street, Bloomsbury.
Holloway, Caledonian Road, King's Cross, Holborn.
Bow Bridge, Mile End, Whitechapel, Aldgate.
Hampstead, Prince of Wales Road, Great College Street, King's Cross, Gray's Inn Road, Holborn.

With electrification, a similar pattern of services continued, except that the service from Holloway was diverted to run via the "Angel" and Rosebery Avenue to Bloomsbury. Cars ran at about 30-minute intervals on all lines, but none carried service numbers.

The only other change of note was the withdrawal of the Bow Bridge and Aldgate service during the Great War, reported as being due to lack of patronage. Although a "night service" was not restored to this route, nocturnal passengers were catered for by the provision of very late and very early cars working on the normal day services.

Night Services in 1933

Stamford Hill, Stoke Newington, Dalston Junction, Kingsland Road, Old Street, Holborn.
Poplar, East India Dock Road, Commercial Road, Commercial Street, Old Street, Bloomsbury.
"Archway Tavern", Holloway Road, Upper Street, "Angel", Rosebery Avenue, Bloomsbury.
Hampstead (South End Green), Prince of Wales Road, Great College Street, King's Cross, Gray's Inn Road, Holborn.
These services did not operate on Saturday nights/Sunday mornings.

Certain day services had late night and early morning journeys throughout the week, which could be considered as providing almost an all-night service. On Saturday nights/Sunday mornings when the official all-night cars did not operate, late and early cars (displaying service numbers) worked on daytime schedules. An example of this was the service 3 car which worked from Hampstead car shed (Cressy Road) at 1.15 a.m. to "Angel" via King's Cross and Pentonville Road, returning to Hampstead at 1.40 a.m. This journey was more appropriate to service 5.

1.30 p.m. The car roof separated from the upper saloon.

2.00 p.m. A view of the underside of the stricken tramcar.

2.30 p.m. The car roof after being loaded on to a lorry.

Car No. 1370 overturned in Harleyford Road, Kennington, early in the morning of 3rd June 1933. Removal was carried out during the later part of the day. *(Courtesy: Tramway Museum Society)*

3.15 p.m. The car, upright, being prepared for jacking up.

4.30 p.m. The re-trucked car about to be towed to the track.

4.45 p.m. No. 1370 being towed away by E/1 car No. 795.

The removal process involved the use of breakdown gangs and their road vehicles, as can be seen in the view showing the car roof placed upon a lorry for removal from the site.

Chapter 53
Managers and Staff

The Chief Officers of Tramways

Alfred Baker

Born at Nottingham on 18th August 1861, Alfred Baker, on leaving school started work with the Nottingham & District Tramways Company as a horse tramcar conductor. Rising through the company ranks, he eventually became its Manager in 1895. The Corporation took over in 1897 and Baker remained in office, supervising the arrangements for the conversion of the system to electric traction. However, he did not remain at Nottingham long enough to witness the opening of the first electric section.

In 1898, the London County Council decided to appoint a Chief Officer of Tramways to oversee the transfer of the London Tramways Company to the Council, and afterwards to manage the new undertaking. In December, Baker accepted the post and, as a first step was appointed manager of the London Tramways Company, so as to be able to hand it over to the LCC at midnight on 31st December 1898 and, at the same time, accept it on behalf of the Council as the London County Council (Southern) Tramways.

He officially became Chief Officer of the LCC Tramways at an initial salary of £1,000 per annum, shortly after the transfer of the company to the Council. He then had the responsibility, together with Dr. A. B. Kennedy, of arranging for the electrification of the first sections of the system. The slot conduit system was the only one, at that time, that the Council intended to use, and it became the only one that many of the local authorities would accept.

Baker, however, became disillusioned by the many obstructions placed in his path, resulting from the peculiar two-tier system of local government which prevailed in the metropolis. He often found himself at odds with representatives of the local Borough Councils and, perhaps, just as important, with the chief and senior officers of the Metropolitan Police. This resulted in his decision to leave the capital and seek his place in transport elsewhere. In July 1903, he accepted the post of General Manager of Birmingham Corporation Tramways. He finally left London for Birmingham on 1st October 1903, and was succeeded by Aubrey Llewellyn Coventry Fell.

Aubrey Llewellyn Coventry Fell

The fifth son of S. G. Fell, J.P. of Ickham Hall near Canterbury, Kent, Aubrey Llewellyn Coventry Fell was born at Llangollen on 8th July 1869. His subsequent scholarly interests were to lead him to take up electrical engineering as a career.

His first important appointment was with the British Thomson-Houston Company, where he helped with the electrification of the tramways of Cork. This was followed in 1897 by his appointment as Electrical Engineer to Sheffield Corporation Tramways, in which city he was responsible for the conversion to electric traction of several of the routes. He became General Manager of the undertaking in 1900, but after only three years he accepted the position of Chief Officer to the LCC Tramways in place of Alfred Baker. His move to London took place on 7th December 1903, just over six months after the opening of the first conduit-worked line. He took over the responsibility for the electrification of the remainder of the system, much of it using conduit track, but with also a substantial part of it using the overhead wire method.

Like Baker before him, he had to contend with the ever-present political battles that were being fought over the electrification of the undertaking and of its desire to make considerable extensions to it. He was also to be involved in constant argument with the Commissioner of Police and his staff.

In 1905, he made his first of several visits to the United States of America to study tramway operation there, and to see at first hand how the authorities coped with the conduit system, particularly where change-over arrangements were made with regard to working between the conduit and overhead wire systems. The result was the "plough-shift" arrangement, which was unique to London. He also studied various other aspects of tramway operation, upon which he presented reports to the Council, including one on braking systems and another on rail corrugation.

With his design team, he was instrumental in bringing a new era to tramcar construction, of which the legendary LCC class E bogie car and the improved class E/1 car were the outcome. In all, over 1,000 of these were built for service in the capital, together with 100 of class M, which was a four-wheeled version of the E/1.

He became the President of the Municipal Tramways Association in 1909, in which institute he played an active part for many years, and he was also a member of the Institutes of Civil, Electrical and Mechanical Engineers, the Tramways & Light Railways Association and the Institute of Transport.

His most difficult period was during the Great War. Probably the worst phase was in 1915, when he became almost isolated in his attitude towards his staff during the disastrous strike of that year. It was this that led to many people deploring his actions as an "unofficial conscription officer" when he refused to reinstate many men of military age after the strike was over. This was followed by a serious illness in 1916, which kept him away from duty for the greater part of a year. Despite these reverses, he did much good work during those fateful years, for which he received recognition by the award of the C.B.E. in 1920.

After the end of the war, he was almost constantly engaged in fighting off the worst aspects of the "omnibus war" which developed. This, and the long, gruelling period when he was attempting to gain more recognition for the tramway, both in terms of expansion and in its statutory right to be there, left him in poor physical condition as described in a respected journal of the time, "The Tramway and Railway World". "... Owing to local circumstances, Mr. Fell has had probably a more onerous task than most tramway managers. Only those intimately acquainted with the conditions under which the work of the

Alfred Baker

Aubrey Llewellyn Coventry Fell

Joshua Kidd Bruce

Theodore Eastaway Thomas

Council's tramway department is carried out can have any idea of the great difficulties that confront the management, in attempting to develop the undertaking on sound business principles. The task is, indeed, all but insuperable, and it is surprising that in the face of great obstacles, so large a measure of success has been achieved. ..."

Towards the end of 1924, he underwent an examination by the Council's medical adviser, who decided that he was no longer fit to carry out his arduous duties. He was granted a pension of £974 a year, plus a fee of £250 for his retention for one year in a consultative capacity. He formally retired on 31st December 1924. In retirement, he lived for a number of years at Ripple Lodge, near Dover. He died on 4th October 1948, aged 79 years.

Joshua Kidd Bruce

Born in 1872 at Strathmore, Scotland, Joshua Kidd Bruce trained as a veterinary surgeon and eventually became Veterinary Officer to the London Tramways Company during the 1890s, where he was also charged with the management of the depots and stables of the company. Upon the company being taken over by the London County Council in 1899, he continued to deal with veterinary matters on behalf of the Council. In June 1903, the Traffic Manager, Mr. Scott, was taken seriously ill and was medically retired. Bruce took over the responsibility for this duty in addition to his own. After the North Metropolitan Tramways Company was absorbed into the LCC Tramways in 1906, Bruce was given authority to deal with traffic matters over the whole network, finally becoming Traffic Manager in 1910.

During the Great War, he became chief assistant to A. L. C. Fell, during which time he took on the job of managing the undertaking completely while Fell was away ill. At this time also, he was appointed to the position of Deputy Chief Officer of Tramways. On 1st January 1925 he became Acting General Manager on the retirement of Fell, while on 21st July 1925 he accepted the appointment to the post of General Manager of Tramways at a salary of £2,000 p.a. In 1926 he became a member of the Council of the Institute of Transport.

It was Bruce who brought the undertaking up to date. Almost as soon as he took over from Fell he introduced far-reaching changes, the most important of which was to deal with the modernisation of the rolling stock. The "pullmanisation" programme was his masterpiece, and was to change the image of the undertaking completely. Sadly, like his predecessor, he became the victim of ill-health, having to retire in June 1930. He was succeeded by T. E. Thomas. Regrettably, Bruce died on 23rd September 1931, aged 59 years.

Theodore Eastaway Thomas

Born on 9th February 1882 in south London, Theodore Eastaway Thomas, the son of Philip Henry Thomas was educated at Battersea Grammar School. He joined the London United Tramways in 1899, in the drawing office of the District Engineer, where he became concerned with the electrification of the system. He became a District Engineer in 1902 at the early age of 20 years; in 1909 he accepted the post of Commercial Superintendent, while in later years he was promoted to the post of Assistant to the Commercial Manager.

He moved to the London County Council Tramways on 19th June 1917, when he accepted the position of Development Superintendent. Not long afterwards he became a founder member of the Institute of

Transport. In 1925, with the promotion of J.K.Bruce from Traffic Manager to the post of General Manager of Tramways, Thomas was appointed Traffic Manager in his place, a position he held until the retirement of Bruce. On 1st July 1930, he was appointed General Manager of Tramways.

The improvements which Bruce had instituted, continued to be implemented by Thomas, together with the introduction of a completely new concept in tramcar design, of which "Bluebird", the new No.1, was to be the only example. One year after its introduction in 1932, the LCC Tramways became part of the undertaking of the London Passenger Transport Board. T.E.Thomas became General Manager, Tramways (South & East) but, after about six months, became General Manager (Trams & Trolleybuses) for the whole of the system.

After being awarded the C.B.E. in July 1941, he continued to work for London Transport in various capacities until his retirement on 20th October 1945. He subsequently became a director of the Lancashire United Omnibus Company and also the associated South Lancashire trolleybus undertaking. He was knighted in the New Year's Honours List in January 1946. Sir Theodore Eastaway Thomas, C.B.E. died at Brighton on 3rd July 1951, aged 69 years.

STAFF & PAY, 1899 - 1918

Following the takeover of the London Tramways Company, staff conditions, salaries and wages were immediately slightly improved. For those who were "in the ranks" (for this undertaking was to be seen in quasi-military style), the increase in wages was the most welcome of the improvements, with the outlawing of the pernicious system of fines, which were levied for almost all misdemeanours, coming a close second. Given that a particular member of the staff was hard-working, honourable and suitably subservient, there was a fair chance that he would retain his position, despite the then general "hire and fire" philosophy which prevailed. Senior members of the management were, however, in a totally different category. For what was accepted as a good salary, and a reasonable tenure of office to go with it, these people were expected to give their whole time and attention to the undertaking, almost to the exclusion of all else. Details of senior staff and the salaries that they commanded upon takeover are given in Volume I, page 142.

Things had just settled down when the Superintendent of Conductors, Miss E. Penman, died on 1st August 1899 after a short illness. Apart from the natural shock of this event, the Council was in something of a quandary regarding her replacement, which led to a reorganisation of the management structure. It was quite unusual for a woman to be in such a senior position in industry at that time, the more so as Miss Penman had virtual control of all the male conductors.

The Traffic Manager, Mr. W. Scott was given the responsibility for the employment of conductors and Mr. J. Terry, the Chief Traffic Inspector was given the position and title of Traffic Superintendent and transferred to work as assistant to Mr. Scott at a salary of £160 per annum. The Principal Assistant of Women Checkers, Miss E. Hodge, was promoted to become Superintendent of Women Checkers at a salary of £150 per annum, and given rent-free rooms at Head Office, No. 303 Camberwell New Road. No allowance, however, was given towards the cost of lighting and coal for heating.

Into The Twentieth Century

There were considerable discrepancies in the levels of wages and salaries paid to the lower grades of staff and employees by the various tramway companies and which the LCC was pledged to eradicate at the earliest opportunity. In 1901, the Council published the following table, giving rates of pay for most grades.

Grade	Weekly Pay	Days per Week	Hours per Week
Driver	28/6 to 37/6	6	60
Conductor	28/6 to 37/6	6	60
Stableman	26/-	6	60
Washer	25/- to 30/-	6	60
Farrier	39/- to 43/6	6	54
Track Cleaner	25/-	6	60
Pointsman	18/- to 24/-	6	60
Trace Boy	14/- to 18/-	6	60
Ticket Inspector	42/-	6	60
Regulator	42/-	6	60
Night Inspector	42/-	6	60
Foreman	42/- to 64/6	7	70
Depot Foreman	42/-	7	70

Note: The six day week as opposed to one of seven days amounted to one day off without pay. This was later rectified.

This table was, in the main, something of a compromise. The problem associated with pay continued to exercise the minds of LCC management for several years. In March 1903 the pay scales were again reviewed and some small amendments made.

The next change came as a result of the electrification programme. In October 1902, the Council arranged to begin training 250 horse car drivers to become electric car motormen. In the first place, two qualified instructors, who were each paid £4 per week, had the job of training the men. The trainee drivers were paid the normal rate while they were learning to handle the electric cars. The pay, however, remained at the maximum of 37/6d per week after training, for six days work a week, each of ten hours' duty. With regard to other daily paid staff, there were some small improvements in certain of the grades, which appeared to be a levelling up of rates as more company tramways were taken over by the Council.

Having commenced electric car services, and being anxious to present a business image to the public, the Council arranged for extra car washers to be employed, to ensure that every car would be properly washed down, swept out and all brass polished daily. So that "extra care" would be taken in the work, the pay structure was improved to encourage "better workmanship". From 5th June 1903, Superintendents of Car Washers received between 38/- and 50/- per week, Foremen between 30/- and 35/- per week, and Washers between 25/- and 30/- per week.

The women checkers, whose duties were to deal with the bulk issue of tickets to the boxes used by conductors, attend to the returns from the ticket boxes after use, check waybills and deal with all other incidental matters associated with the handling of tickets, had their pay improved as from 3rd May 1904 from the old (1899) rate of 15/- to 30/- per week, to a new (1904) rate of between 15/- and 40/- per week. A duty which they "lost", involved the collection of fare takings from conductors. In the years preceding LCC operation, and in the first years of Council control, money was collected from conductors at the end of each journey by women checkers who were stationed in special offices sited near to the terminal points of each route.

The Bronze Coin Distributor

The duties of this officer involved the collection, distribution, storage and banking of the huge number of pennies and halfpennies then circulating on the tramways. In April 1904, it was becoming very difficult for him to carry out his task properly, as the Tramways Department was totally unable to dispose of much of the money, which amounted to £2,170 in pennies and £1,920 in halfpennies, all of which was stored in the office at Camberwell. The banks would not accept them without payment, and this the Council would not tolerate. By December, the distributor was supplying large quantities of the coins to many department stores and public houses.

After communicating with the Royal Mint, the Tramways Manager was assured that supplies of copper coin would be withheld in London for a while, and applicants would be advised to contact the Tramways Department. A further suggestion from the Mint, not taken up, was that the Department should arrange to supply "out of town" applicants at the Council's expense!

Human Problems

With the closure of the Kennington to Streatham cable line in April 1904 for reconstruction, 57 drivers, 59 conductors and 12 car washers were temporarily put out of work. Of these, 52 drivers and 58 conductors were sent to other depots, while the last of the conductors was discharged for "neglect of duty". With regard to the remaining five drivers, two went on two months' leave, while the other three, as "recently recruited hands", were discharged. Ten drivers and six conductors from other depots, recently employed, were discharged, with one day's pay in lieu of notice.

The washers were dealt with in the same way, and in all cases the most recently employed at the other depots had to "stand down" as spare men for the time being. With regard to regulators, the most recently promoted "were sent back to their cars". With the re-opening of the line with electric cars, it was expected that re-deployment would once again put the staff position right.

Another problem arose in October 1904, when the Chief Officer made a statement that all electric car motormen must have their eyes tested for good vision, and also have a general health check. This, as may be imagined, caused an uproar, and the men at Clapham and New Cross sheds refused to co-operate, many fearing that, if they failed either test, they would be put out of work.

After considerable negotiation, an agreement was reached, whereby any man who did not pass the eye test would be offered work as a conductor, provided that his health was otherwise reasonable, while the rest would be offered alternative work. A report made on 1st May 1905 shows that of 340 motormen who took the eyesight test, 40 failed. Of this number, 28 were accepted for work as conductors, one as a van man, one as a car washer, four as assistant regulators and two as pointsmen. The other two resigned. The practice of attempting to find alternative employment for those who failed the eye test "was to continue".

Further Changes to Staff

The next large increase in staffing came with the construction and commissioning of power generating plant, temporary and permanent, together with the takeover of the North Metropolitan Tramways, largest of the erstwhile company systems. The bulk of this occurred in 1906, and increased the number of staff employed to double its size almost overnight. All staff, with the exception of the Managing Director, Consulting Engineer, and Veterinary Surgeon to the Company and a few others, were taken into LCC employment.

Other staff transferred from the North Metropolitan Company, such as horsekeepers, track cleaners, car washers, pole turners and granary labourers had worked a seven-day week for the company. Under LCC rules, a six-day week was in force, but it was agreed that these men should receive the same pay for six days' work with the LCC as they did for seven with the company.

With the gradual decline in the use of horses, the large staff who had been employed in maintaining and making horse harness and other leather goods associated with them, were gradually being worked out of a job. The same applied to men who worked in the stables as horse-keepers and grooms. However, the Chief Officer, mindful of this problem after the difficulties encountered with the temporary closure of the Streatham cable line, went to great pains to ensure that work was found in other parts of the undertaking for those who sought it, in whatever capacity. In the case of the closure of Penrose Street works, all work on horse cars and leather work was then concentrated at Union Road, Leytonstone works, to which place several of the more senior members of the staff were transferred.

In December 1906, a change was made in the rates of pay of motor-men, drivers and conductors. In general, the old company rates had been from 4/9d a day on entry to the service, then six months at 5/3d, six months at 5/9d, after which 6/3d were payable. This scale was replaced with one which involved the motormen in passing two tests. On entry to motorman grade, 5/- a day was payable for six months, then 5/3d for the next six months, after which a test had to be taken to gain entry to the next grade. This was then paid at the rate of 5/9d for six months, 6/3d for another six months, and then, after a further test, 6/6d a day. An exception was made for motormen already in post, who did not have the need to pass the preliminary examination.

At the same time, it was recognised that motormen who drove electric cars on the hilly route between Camberwell and Dulwich were worthy of a supplement to their pay, in return for the responsibility they shouldered in controlling their cars on this steeply graded line. For the first twelve months of duty on the line, an extra 2d a day was paid and a "special service" badge issued; after twelve months' duty, an extra 2d a day and a second badge was awarded, while after 24 months on the route, another 2d a day and a third badge was given.

Each conductor and motorman had to be licensed by the Metro-politan Police, and each license cost 5/-; conductors who were required to drive had therefore to pay 10/- for two licenses. This was thought by some senior members of the tramways departments in the metropolis to be unfair and unnecessary. In June 1910, William Murray, Manager of Walthamstow Light Railways successfully persuaded the police to issue composite licenses to these men at a single fee of 5/-.

The work load which J. K. Bruce was called upon to carry was again increased early in 1909, when the Horse Superintendent, Capt.

Ford became ill. Mr. Bruce, while undertaking the duty of Traffic Manager, was nevertheless still involved with horsing arrangements to some degree. As he was a qualified veterinary surgeon, his skills were still in demand. According to a minute written by Mr. Fell, "Bruce, as Veterinary Surgeon to the Tramways Department, had done excellent work".

The Clapham Motor School

With the realisation that special training would be required to acquaint men in the art of driving the new electric cars, arrangements were made to set up a motor school. Initially situated at Camberwell car shed, it was moved to Clapham in August 1906, where the new school was provided with comprehensive facilities for the thorough training of all LCC Tramways motormen, remaining there for virtually the whole period of tramway operation in London.

Once accepted for training, the candidate reported to the school for a four-week course of instruction. A number of lectures, including one on electrical safety, prepared him for tests of knowledge on the working of an electric car. The lectures were backed up by practical demonstrations on how to handle the various types of controller in use, together with operational work on a skeleton four-wheeled car, which consisted of a Brill 21E motorised truck, upon which was mounted a sectionalised body, complete with all cables, switches, lighting and a controller unit at one end.

After initial instruction, each trainee went out with an instructor and shown how to handle a car on the road and, if satisfactory, was then allocated a place with an experienced motorman on a service car, with whom he stayed for about three weeks. Following this, and if successful in passing several other tests, he was finally authorised to drive a tramcar in public service, and was then issued with a license to drive, which was dealt with by the Metropolitan Police. He then was allocated to a car shed but before taking up duty, drove a special car over the whole north or south side network, accompanied by an instructor, in order to "learn the road".

Trainee motormen at the Motor School, Clapham. (*Courtesy: T.M.S.*)

Practical driving instruction at the Motor School was given on a working model of a tramcar. (Greater London Photograph Library)

In the years before the Great War, the time spent in the motor school was not paid for by the Council. However, in later years, any time spent on training was considered to be official duty and attracted payment, at first at half rate, but subsequently at the normal basic wage.

The Great War

It has been mentioned in Volume I how the Great War caused many problems to staff on all parts of the system. As the period between 1914 and 1918 was such an important and difficult one, the following additional notes will, it is hoped, give a greater insight into the day-to-day working of the undertaking during that time.

Upon the outbreak of the war, a large number of men, both army and navy reservists and volunteers, joined the military services. By mid-September, 214 motormen, 161 conductors and 432 other grades, 807 in all, had gone. They were all awarded half pay while with the services. By mid-October, 1,294 had answered the call to the colours, which was roughly 10% of the total staff. In an effort to ease the situation on the cars, "assistant conductors", who were boys between the ages of 16 and 19, were employed, but this did not last for very long. On 10th November 1914, the Council resolved to pay all "officials and employees" who were serving with H.M. Forces full civil pay less service pay and separation allowances. A special vote of £36,700 was made for the purpose.

LCC Regulations at that time made provision for motormen and conductors, when learning their jobs, to receive half pay. As a result of the large numbers of staff joining the military services, conductors were asked if they would consider becoming motormen, with car shed and other staff being offered conductor duties. In order that those who volunteered would not suffer financially, it was agreed that they should be paid at ordinary rates while learning.

In those hard days, discipline in the Department was itself quite militaristic in outlook. When war came, it appeared to become even more so. With the depleted ranks of conductors and motormen being left to carry on as best they could, it became obvious that they were not to be allowed to do "normal" duties, or take "normal" leave of absence without considerable problems arising. An early example of the official attitude was to be seen on 19th December 1914, when a notice referring to Christmas Leave was posted in the car sheds. A summary of the content will indicate how strongly the management were to deal with the matter. "In view of numbers called up or enlisting, it will not be possible to grant Christmas Leave to the extent in previous years. Employees absent without leave render themselves liable to instant dismissal". This was followed on 27th February 1915 with "No applications for leave extending over the Easter Holiday will be considered ..."

There was a stream of exhortations to motormen and conductors regarding the lighting restrictions applicable on cars, and how to drive the cars without causing electrical flashing on the overhead wire and in the conduits. They were instructed to observe the very strict speed limit of six miles per hour which had been set during "aircraft activity", with the threat of dire penalties for any detected breach of Defence of the Realm Regulations.

The 1915 Strike

It all started as a result of an agreement made by the Traffic Conciliation Board on 26th June 1914 and 30th July 1914, which stated that "no decision made should be re-opened for twelve months", and particularly referred to agreements made with regard to pay rates. On 22nd February 1915, less than twelve months since the previous pay review, the trades unions asked for a 15% increase in wages resulting from large rises in the cost of living index due to war conditions.

In an effort towards conciliation, the Council offered 10% on certain conditions, with a rate of 30/- a week being the dividing line between those who got the 10% and those who did not. Other concessions offered were:-

A guaranteed minimum of 30/- a week for spare men on 5/- a day to be based on six days;

A spare man called in on the seventh day in the pay week to receive an additional payment for that day or to be paid 1/- for showing up in the event of work not being allotted.

The existing temporary arrangement under which crews were paid 6d per day for training other men to be continued.

Resulting from the apparently negative attitude of the LCC, a protest meeting was held on 12th May at 11.30 p.m. at the Gaiety Theatre, Brixton Road, where, among other things, unkind comments were made about the Council. Two days later, some early turn New Cross men refused to take out cars. Mr. Fell asked them to take out "the Woolwich service cars". Again, the answer, according to Fell, was "no". The Woolwich service, however, was reputedly kept working. It was reported in some sections of the Press that the men had offered to keep the Woolwich service going, but Fell disputed this.

The general grievance flared into a dispute regarding the long hours worked by car crews, together with the original one over pay. Some Streatham men then joined in with those from New Cross, which resulted - at that time - in about one-third of the south side cars being at a standstill. Fell retaliated by saying that "any employee who fails to report for duty at the appointed time on Saturday 15th May 1915 will be considered as having left the service". Meanwhile, the Chairman of the LCC Mr. (later Sir) Cyril Jackson met the leader of the Union, Mr. Watson, offering arbitration on all points, but maintaining that the date of 29th June was the earliest that it could be brought to the Tramways Committee for consideration. The men rejected this and voted for an all-out strike.

On Sunday 16th May, only a very sparse service was running into Woolwich, which was, in the main, being crewed by Regulators and Inspectors. Resulting from the strike, Fell had a notice posted on Saturday 22nd May stating "that all men on strike who are eligible for military or naval service are instructed to forthwith return their uniforms and badges to the tramway depots". This was followed on Wednesday 26th May by a statement " ... no man who is eligible for H.M. Forces is to be allowed to resume work on the tramways", which resulted in Fell, together with the Chairman of the Council, being accused of being, or of acting as conscription officers, when, in fact, there was no conscription of personnel at the time.

Nevertheless, an arbitrator was appointed, whose award was announced on 4th June. A war bonus of 3/- a week or 6d a day was to be given to the Electrical Section staff earning up to 40/- a week, and extended to the Traffic Section staff for the duration of the war, "provided that it did not last for more than three years"! The new agreement was to take effect as from 22nd July. On Sunday 5th June, the strike was over. On 6th July, the whole matter was referred to the Traffic Conciliation Board for ratification.

Resulting from the edict of the Chief Officer, 184 conductors and 194 motormen were dismissed the service, and those of military age were not taken back either, while 117 conductors and 68 motormen were reinstated. Those members of the various staffs who remained "loyal" to the Tramways Department were rewarded. Inspectors and regulators who worked as conductors or motormen each received £3, while motormen and conductors who worked normally each received £2. Clerical staff who acted in any capacity each received normal rates of pay, plus the pay of either conductor or motorman for the number of days this class of work was carried out.

Due to the shortage of conductors and motormen experienced as the direct result of the outcome of the strike, applications were invited from other staff in the Tramways Department to take up driving and conducting, but only for staff over the age of 38 years. However, by the end of December 1915, there appeared to be a more wary approach to recruitment, as a compulsory call-up was announced. The Chief Officer was keen to point out that if anyone received call-up papers who was "officially badged", whose name was starred in the National Service Register for munitions work, or who was engaged in a reserved occupation, he should advise the Chief Officer in person, presumably so that the call-up might be deferred or cancelled. In August 1916, he asked that conductors who would not be called up for military service should perform a "patriotic action" by coming forward to act as motormen for the rest of the war. For any who did, the costs incurred in taking the medical examination and in obtaining a composite license would be borne by the Council.

Women Conductors

By the winter of 1915, it had at last been realised that, to maintain services to anything like the standard required by the wartime situation that had developed, platform staff would have to be recruited from other sources. This could only mean that the ladies would be called upon to fill many of the vacancies. There had been considerable discussion whether the fair sex would be allowed to drive the cars, but the Metropolitan Police, among other, would have none of it! However, under pressure from many sources, all parties agreed that women would be encouraged to take up many of the vacancies in the ranks of the conductors. Initially, it was suggested that women should be paid at the rate of 5/- a day plus increments, plus an extra 6d a day or 3/- a week, and to be issued with uniform clothing. At first, it was thought that the women would be allowed to share duties and the pay that went with it, but at the meeting of the Council on 23rd November 1915, this idea was rejected. Women employed as conductors would be expected to carry out complete duties in the same way as the men.

On 21st March 1916, another dimension was added to the interesting question of the employment of women in the Tramways Department. In a document headed "The Employment of Married Women", it re-iterated the statement made on 23rd November 1915, "that women be employed during the war and for so long after as necessary", but then added a rider "and married women be employed at the Central Repair Depot"! The first barrier, the employment of unmarried ladies and widows at Charlton, had been broken down some time earlier, when it was "discovered" that women were more adept than the men were at doing certain types of work, such as armature coil winding, being employed on duties such as this. Now the second hurdle had been overcome, but at that time only for the duration of the war.

Wartime Fashions

It was the custom at that time for ladies to wear rather ornate and sometimes large hats. It seems that it was somewhat difficult to keep these things on, and so an item known as a hatpin was frequently used to hold the hat in place. Hatpins came in all sizes, some of them about ten inches long. One end would be decorated with a small piece of real or imitation semi-precious stone, while the other end was usually as sharp as a large darning needle. As the unprotected end of a hatpin could cause quite severe injury to anyone who came into

A wartime conductress dressed in the rather drab uniform which was issued to them, and wearing ankle height boots to protect her from knocks and bumps.
(LCC official view)

contact with it, the Council displayed notices in the cars spelling out the potential dangers, at the same time appealing to women not to wear pins with unprotected points.

By the summer of 1916, considerable numbers of women were being employed as conductors. The type of headgear issued to them was rather in the style of a "panama" hat and, presumably required the use of a hatpin to keep it in place. Possibly due to the likelihood of having claims made against the Council by passengers alleging personal injury or damage to clothing by one of these pins, the Chief Officer, on 8th June 1916, issued an instruction to all lady conductors that they should wear short hatpins or protect the points of longer ones if worn.

Even during the dark days of war, the ladies were likely to keep one eye on fashionable habits, resulting on 22nd June 1917 in a Notice being displayed in all depots and car sheds. This time it referred to the growing practice of the adornment of uniform jackets with items not provided by the Tramways Department, and was worded as follows:-

"Notice to Women Conductors:
It has been observed that lace and other fancy collars are being worn over the uniform provided. The uniform must be worn exactly as supplied".

The uniform issue consisted of a long linen jacket and an equally long, rather shapeless ankle length skirt. It is not surprising that the wearers attempted from time to time to brighten up their rather drab and dismal clothing.

Women and Driving

With regard to the employment of women as tram and omnibus drivers, this had finally been allowed in many parts of Britain, but not in London. In April 1916, however, the South Metropolitan Tramways Company proposed that women be employed in that capacity, and it was this that brought forth a storm of protest from drivers and conductors (including some of the women conductors) of the South Metropolitan, which culminated in a short strike and, naturally, brought to the surface several other bones of contention.

The Tramway Workers Union became involved, taking a deputation and apparently made the statement "that it was highly dangerous to put women on the front platforms of tramcars. Women would have difficulty with hand brakes. If they went as drivers, the position of the men must be protected for their jobs after the war. Men should also be paid more ...". The Commissioner of Police did not consider it to be such a good idea, either. And so the war of words rumbled on.

The Conference on The Employment of Women on Tramways in the London Area took place on 16th February 1917. In the comments made by Mr. Dalrymple, whose undertaking did employ women drivers, it was stated that, although they could drive the vehicles and use the magnetic brakes satisfactorily, it was extremely difficult to recruit the right type of woman for the job. His experience was that, should a woman driver have the slightest accident, she would "go to pieces" and "it was difficult to persuade her to return to work". He also said that munitions work paid so much better that many would not stay on the trams.

The General Secretary of the Union said that there was no need to employ women as drivers. There were plenty of men over military age who were able and willing to do the work, but he admitted that, like the women, many men went into munitions work. He then made the comment that there would be every liklihood of an all-out strike of tram, 'bus and taxi men if the Ministry of Munitions or the Board of Trade authorised the employment of women as drivers in London. They were never so employed.

The 1917 Reorganisation

The management arrangements in the Tramways Department as they were set up in 1899 had hardly been altered since that time and, with the great size that the undertaking had grown to, the Council came to the conclusion in 1917 that the time was right for a complete review of duties and responsibilities. It was proposed that the structure should be replaced by one in which the Chief Officer would have direct control of five Branches, with each Branch having a number of Sections. The intended arrangement was:-

Traffic (Manager)
  Development: Operations:
Rolling Stock (Engineer)
  Rolling Stock: Repair Depot:
Electrical (Engineer)
  Power Station: Distribution (S):   Distribution (N):
Permanent Way (Engineer)
  P.W. South   P.W. North: Building:
General (Chief Clerk)
  Clerical: Accounts: Stores: Ticket Checking: Claims: Printing:

Car sheds, which were to be put under the control of the Permanent Way Branch, were to be classified as "A", "B" or "C", depending upon "the approximate weekly car services" provided by the shed. The only three to receive the "A" category were Clapham, Holloway and New Cross, each with over 900 "services". Those marked "B" were between 450 and 900, while those in class "C" were below 450. This classification also determined the rates of pay of the supervisory staff at the sheds. In a similar manner, the permanent way depots at Belvedere Road, Poplar and Deptford were classed as "A", those at Battersea and Leighton Road were "B" and Holloway was "C".

The effects of this reorganisation were expected to be far reaching, with changes throughout the undertaking, right down to the supervisory grades in every department. Due to the awful problems associated with the war, it was decided that implementation of the scheme, with a few exceptions, could not be attempted until after the end of hostilities. Nevertheless, preparations for change were made during the next two years as any opportunity presented itself, until, in July 1919, the main sections of the plan were brought into effect.

STAFF & PAY, 1919 - 1933

Armistice and Pay Changes

The Armistice took effect as from 11th November 1918, to the great relief of all. On 18th November, all operational staff were granted one day's extra pay as "thanksgiving" for all their hard work and loyalty to the Council. This was followed by all cars being returned to their sheds by 4 p.m. on Christmas Day, so allowing almost all staff to be with their families for the remainder of this day.

It was during 1919 that the first of many changes were made to the pay and conditions of the various members of the staff. With effect from 27th March, the 8-hour day, 48-hour working week was introduced for traffic grades, who were also to be paid "time and a half" for work on Easter Monday, Whitsun Monday, August Bank Holiday and Boxing Day. Other penalty rates were "time and a quarter" for the first two hours of overtime, with "time and a half" for all hours over this. Six days' annual holiday were to be granted after 12 months' continuous service, with an extra two days for the year 1920. The first steps were also taken in terminating the employment of women conductors, when, in October, the ladies were thanked for their services and, over a period of several months, were relieved of their jobs.

Instead of pay increases being made to all staff during the war period (except for normal incremental payments), a "temporary cost of living war wage" or bonus was added to the pre-war wage or salary of each member of the staff. By the end of 1918 this payment amounted to almost as much as the basic wage, but declined to about 50% of it by 1924, due to post-war wage increases. It was finally absorbed into and became part of the wage or salary in June 1930, when it stood at about 60% of the basic rate. During the years, this had been complicated by a reduction in various rates of pay, when the "cost of living" was supposedly being reduced, a situation which was hotly contested by the representatives of the various staff associations.

The General Strike of 1926

A "State of Emergency" was declared by Royal Proclamation on 1st May 1926 when a General Strike was declared by the several trades unions representing transport and other workers, in support of the coal miners, who were in dispute with their empoyers for better pay and conditions. At midnight on Monday 3rd May, all car services ceased. Pickets were posted at all car sheds and depots, works and sub-stations.

In an effort to combat the effects of the strike, the Council decided to enrol volunteers to operate some sort of service, and on Tuesday and Wednesday 4th and 5th May a number of persons offered their services. So far as motormen and conductors were concerned, this meant that the volunteers had to be trained in the best way that could be arranged, and this could only be inside the car sheds. It also meant that the volunteers would be incarcerated within the confines of the buildings for as long as necessary.

On the afternoon of 5th May at just after 4 p.m. an attempt was made, under police protection, to run twelve cars from Camberwell car shed, to provide a service from there to New Scotland Yard on Victoria Embankment. As the cars were driven out, they were attacked by a hostile crowd, resulting in several volunteers being injured and the windows of ten cars smashed. Four crews successfully got their charges to the Embankment - and then made at all speed again for the safety of the car shed. The police made a number of arrests during this skirmish, resulting in about 40 men being convicted and fined or imprisoned for various offences.

The strike was called off by the T U C shortly after midday on Wednesday 12th May 1926. Before any cars could be run, the tracks had to be cleared of obstructions, mainly steel bolts and other metal objects which had been knocked into the conduit slots. The north side work proceeded satisfactorily, but at New Cross and Clapham on

A group of volunteers take out class E car No. 501 from New Cross car shed during the General Strike, with the hope of providing a service. They were not very successful. *(Photographer unknown)*

the south side, hostile crowds gathered round the track-clearing parties and the police decided that these men should not be subjected to abuse, and instructed them to stop work. On the following day there were still no cars at work in south London, although on the north side, a few cars worked by volunteers and several members of the staff who did not join in the strike, were to be seen on the Hampstead and King's Cross service, while some from Hammersmith shed worked between Harlesden and Putney.

At 5.30 p.m. on 13th May, the first of two agreements was made between the Council and the unions, with the second being announced at 1.30 a.m. on Friday 14th. So far as the Tramways Department was concerned, they agreed to reinstate all men who had been on strike, but not necessarily in their former grades. Other conditions laid down were that any volunteer who chose to remain in the service was not to be "interfered with" in any way; that all car services were to commence as soon as possible; that there was to be no alteration to either wages paid or conditions of service; that staff who did not take part in the strike were to be granted extra leave. Normal services were resumed during the weekend of 14th-16th May.

Into the Thirties

By 1930, the War Bonus Scheme was gradually being replaced by a more up-to-date arrangement. On 16th May, after discussions with the National Foremen's Association, the General Manager proposed that the pay of minor officials, which included those in the grades of foremen, inspectors and regulators, should be consolidated by including the bonus in the basic figure. In some cases, the pay ceiling was to be improved so that the recipient on the minimum of the scale should receive more than the highest paid member of the staff working under his or her control. The scheme was introduced on 1st July 1930.

Staff Employed

It has been said that the LCC Tramways was not only a public transport operator, but a more or less complete industrial undertaking in its own right. The following table, showing the numbers of staff employed to a total of 13,552 as at the week ended 25th June 1930 will bear out this statement. Although there were variations from time to time, the figures will give sufficient indication of the sheer size of the Department, which was maintained in much the same form until it was handed over to the London Passenger Transport Board, although by then the number of persons employed had decreased to about 13,000.

Traffic Branch

Superintendents, Inspectors, Regulators and Day Clerks	660
Motormen	3,552
Conductors	3,592
Plough Shifters, Gatemen, Stop Sign Washers, etc.	77
Pointsmen	281
Recreation Room Stewards	32
Charge Hands (Breakdowns)	5
Breakdown Hands	40
Punch Repairers	24

	8,263

Electrical Branch
Greenwich Power Station
Relief Charge Engineers, Foremen and Assistants   11
Power Station Staff
Switchboard Attendants, Boiler Cleaners
  Ash Hopper and Ash Conveyor Men, Cleaners,
  Greasers, Stokers, etc.   282
Storekeepers and Depot Clerks   5
Sub-stations
Charge Engineers and Assistant Sub-station Attendants   202
Testing Engineer, Depot Clerks, etc.   4
Electrical Fitters and Mates, Meter Repairer,
  Telephone Operator   25
Electrical Equipment, Line and Cables
Foremen and Assistants, Storekeepers   10
Cable Hands, etc.   276
Depot Wiring
Foremen   1
Electricians and Mates, etc.   22

            838

Rolling Stock Branch
Central Car Repair Depot and Works
Foremen, Inspectors and Chargehands   38
Clerks and Storekeepers   18
Armature Winders, Electricians and Mates   121
Fitters, Turners, Millwrights and Blacksmiths   178
Bodymakers, Coach Painters, Sawyers, etc.   261
Hammermen, Plough Repairers, Drillers, etc.   135
Labourers (male)   180
Labourers (female)   22
Apprentices and Youths   117
Constables, Shop and Yard Cleaners   10
Recreation Steward   1
Lorry Drivers and Assistants   14
Central Stores Staff   32

Car Sheds
Foremen, Chargehands and Inspectors   49
Clerks and Storekeepers   39
Lorry Drivers, Assistants and Chauffeurs   21
Bodymakers and Coach Painters   38
Fitters, Electricians and Mates   79
General Employees, Car Sheds,
  Brakesmen and Mates, Truckmen, Labourers,
  Shunters, Traversermen, etc.   875
Car Washers   666

            2,894

Permanent Way Branch
Gangs
Foremen, Assistants and Inspectors   24
Gangers   41
Watchmen   98
Labourers   371
Paviours, Platelayers, Hammermen, etc.   260
Youths   13
Point Adjusters and Assistants   133

Permanent Way Wharves

Foremen, Assistants and Chargehands	8
Clerks and Storekeepers	13
Lorry Drivers and Assistants	36
Labourers, etc.	62
Fitters, Turners, Blacksmiths, etc.	31
Sundry Wharf Employees, Hammermen, Drillers, Platelayers, etc.	54

Conduit Cleaners

Foremen	2
Conduit Cleaners, etc.	88

Buildings

Foremen and Fire Inspector	3
Carpenters, Bricklayers, etc.	92
Labourers, etc.	91

	1,420

General Branch

Printing Employees (male)	33
Printing Employees (female)	34
Claims Assessors	3
Ticket Porters and Lorry Drivers	31
Charwomen	29
Telephone Operators	3
Advertisement Inspector	1
Chargehand, Ticket Boxes	1
Watchmen	2

	137
	=======
Grand total	13,552
	=======

Finally, senior staff in post at the time of the handover in 1933 were:-

General Manager,	T. E. Thomas
Commercial Manager,	G. H. Brooks
Development Superintendent,	F. Scothorne
Accountant,	F. J. Geary
Printing Shop Superintendent,	J. C. Allsop
Superintendent of Women Checkers,	Miss L. Thomson
Punch Shop Superintendent,	G. Gibson
Electrical Engineer,	J. H. Parker
Power Station Engineer,	J. J. McGregor
Distribution Engineer,	T. L. Horn
Generation Engineer,	M. F. Allsop
Combustion Engineers,	S. C. Tranter
	T. W. Hudson
Rolling Stock Engineer,	G. F. Sinclair
Permanent Way Engineer,	F. Croom Johnson
Northern Divisional Engineer,	A. S. Young
Southern Divisional Engineer,	R. E. S. Mackintyre
Traffic Operations Superintendent,	S. R. Geary
Divisional Traffic Superintendents,	F. Schofield
	T. J. Tilston
Motor School Superintendent,	E. T. Bancroft
Claims Superintendent,	T. R. Ierland

Staff Uniforms

The London Tramways Company, the North Metropolitan Tramways Company and the London Street Tramways Company provided their conductors with dark blue serge jackets and peaked "pillbox" caps. In Victorian and Edwardian times, family doctors distributed pills in small, round cardboard boxes and this shape, considerably enlarged and with the addition of a peak, was used as the basis for the "pillbox" cap. Usually, the caps were adorned with some kind of brass badge, showing the company name or its initials, and sometimes the staff number of the conductor as well.

Drivers of horse cars only received bowler hats, often, but not necessarily, brown in colour, but were expected to equip themselves with the rest of their clothing, including a heavy overcoat and stout boots. It was also quite usual for the men to wear long leather aprons, to protect themselves from the dirt thrown up by the horses. When the London County Council took over the various companies, it was decided that, during the period that the horse cars continued to operate, these arrangements would remain, but the drivers were to be issued with proper uniform overcoats. This gesture was to cost the Council approximately £1,600.

By the time that electrification took place, the issue of uniforms to platform staff on tramways throughout the country was becoming quite usual. The LCC, partly following this trend, issued conductors and motormen with quite heavy, navy blue serge double-breasted jackets of considerable length. Two rows of brass buttons, every one of which was embossed with the letters "LCC" in upper case script, were sown on to the jacket front. This style of jacket was topped with either a "bandmaster" cap, which was a "softer" version of the pillbox type, or one of more modern "military" style. A suitable badge completed the issue. Uniform trousers were not provided free, but had to be purchased, this arrangement continuing until 1922, when finally this article of clothing was added to the list in exchange for jackets and caps having to last two years instead of one! Only motormen, however, were ever issued with greatcoats and parramatta stormcoats; conductors had to make do with heavy duty jackets during the winter months, with one made from a lighter material for summer wear. Both jacket and trousers were embellished with thin red piping. Contracts were raised with specialist clothing suppliers, one of the first being Messrs. C. J. Webb & Co., who held the contract for several years. Others included Messrs. Lotery & Co. and Messrs. Cantor & Co., who provided clothing in post-war years.

The uniform provided for each woman conductor during the Great War consisted of a rather shapeless navy blue ankle-length linen skirt, together with a hip-length jacket complete with patch pockets, and a "panama" style hat.

After the war, the style of uniform issued to the men underwent a subtle change, no doubt due to the military influence that had been prominent for so many years. Caps became more "military" in shape, while jackets showed a rather severe, if more practical cut. Conductors and motormen provided their own footwear, and it was usual for them to wear quite substantial boots or shoes, more usually the latter. In conjunction with the boots, many men wore knee-length leather leggings over their trousers, to assist in keeping themselves warm in the fickle British climate, working as they were on open ended cars, and also to give them a measure of protection against knocks and bumps while going about their duties.

Conductor

Motorman

Inspector

Cap badges issued to the various grades of traffic staff during the during the period immediately following the Great War.

Cap badges for motormen were of the "skeleton" style, made of brass and bearing the legend   L C C
                                                                     T
                                   MOTORMAN
within an oval-shaped border. Conductors' badges were quite different, merely showing the letters L C C T in upper case script, and surrounded by a supporter of wreathed laurel leaves.

Two other items, gauntlet gloves and eye goggles would have been seen adorning motormen standing at the controls of open-ended cars. In LCC days, neither of these items were issued to the men - they had to be purchased. In fact, regarding the use of goggles, this practice was frowned upon for a number of years, although it was tolerated. Both the management and the Metropolitan Police were of the opinion that the use of goggles might possibly impair the vision of drivers, rather than improve it. But this could not really be proved, hence the tolerance. However, in 1921, a change of heart resulted in the authorisation of the use of goggles of an "approved" type, but still having to be purchased by the user.

There was one other small item which could often be seen in use on the front platform. Constant use of the brass handbrake handle caused it to impart a blue "polished" appearance to the palm of the right hand of the motorman, unless he was wearing gloves, in which case the glove palm became "polished" instead. In warmer weather, an old sock would often be seen, draped over the handbrake staff, giving protection to the hand of the man and, at the same time, ensuring that the handle remained brightly polished!

With electrification, the duties of pointsmen, plough shifters and general track maintenance men came into prominence, and these people too, expected to be provided with some kind of uniform clothing. Until 1922, they were issued with secondhand items, but following representations to the management regarding this practice, they too received a set of new clothing every two years and a new cap every twelve months.

903

*Left: The crew of car No. 1094 pose for the camera at Gresham Road,
Brixton, terminus.   Both men wear military style caps and heavyweight
jackets.*
*Right: Uniform for supervisory grades was of rather better quality
than was provided to car crews.   (Courtesy: A. D. Packer)*

Uniforms for supervisory staff were quite different. For several
years after 1903, district inspectors, inspectors and regulators wore
long, fully-frocked tail coats, embellished with suitable buttons, while
the headgear consisted of a top hat with the badge of office displayed
just above the brim. Gradually, however, the style changed; the frock
coat proved to be a nuisance, as indeed, was the top hat. By 1909,
the uniform had standardised on a severely cut jacket, suitable trousers
and a "bandmaster" type cap adorned with a "gold thread" badge.
District inspectors displayed their badges of office by having the peaks
of their caps suitably "dressed" with cotton braid. In the same way
that the uniforms of platform staff were influenced by the Great
War, those of the supervisors also changed. The jacket, still made
from heavy serge, displayed the letters "LCC" in "gold thread" on
each lapel, while black uniform buttons were used. The "bandmaster"
cap was replaced with one of a new style in July 1920, which appeared
to be a "softer" version of the military pattern. The cloth badge,
however, lasted a little longer, but was eventually replaced with a
silvered button badge bearing the name of the rank of the wearer,
"INSPECTOR" or "REGULATOR". The badge of a district inspector was
gilded, while the peak of the cap was braided. All these people were
also issued with heavy duty overcoats and parramatta raincoats.

Tea Cans

This most important item was carried by most tramwaymen. Most of the duties performed did not allow of a meal break. This meant that car crews had to make do with what they could get while on the move. To most, sandwiches were the usual means of obtaining sustenance, which were eaten during a journey, and which were washed down with copious quantities of hot, strong tea, which was dispensed from enamelled metal containers, which came in any one of a number of colours from white to dark blue. Each can was made in two parts. The body held about one pint of fluid, while the lid was shaped in such a way that it also did duty as a cup, even having a small handle fixed to one side of it. There was also a collapsible carrying handle fitted to the body of the can.

In earlier days, it was quite common for members of the families of the men - usually one of the boys, if they had any - to take meals and tea to meet the men at appointed places along the routes at certain times, and there to hand over the refreshments. In later years it was more usual for the car crews to purchase the tea from any one of many "Dining Rooms", of which there were a considerable number in the capital. The usual drill was for the motorman to stop his car adjacent to one of these establishments, while the conductor made for it at all speed, had the cans filled with piping hot tea and then went back to his car to continue on the journey. As it was all done "officially", it was in the interests of the proprietor of the shop to give preferential service to tramwaymen, which he almost always did.

The LCC Tramwaymens' Brotherhood

The Parish Church of St. Mark, Kennington, stands in ground which, during the tramway era, had the line to Clapham passing to the west of it, the line to Brixton to the east, and the line between Vauxhall and Camberwell on its north side.

The LCC Tramways Bandsmen at the head of a procession in Clapham, returning from the funeral of a colleague. *(The late S. V. Kempson)*

905

During the early years of the twentieth century, a Brotherhood of Tramwaymen was formed by the Vicar. With electrification of the tramways and the large increase in the numbers of men employed, the Brotherhood prospered, to such an extent that St. Mark's Tramway Hall was dedicated to the membership for their use. Church Parades were organised, including a mammoth Annual Parade, to which all L C C tramwaymen in uniform were invited if they could be spared from duty, with an important element in the Parade being the presence of the L C C Tramways Band.

With the onset of the Great War, the Brotherhood pledged to take care of the families of men who had gone away to the armed forces, while its social and religious activities were maintained, including the Parades. With the employment of women conductors, a place was found for them in the organisation, an example of which is to be seen on the occasion of the 14th Annual Parade, held on Sunday 4th February 1917. The men were welcomed by the Vicar, the Rev. Dr. Darlington, while the lady conductors were entertained to tea by Mrs. Darlington.

The Brotherhood continued to be active after the war, and by then had opened its doors to omnibusmen, taxi drivers and tube railway employees. It remained part of the L C C Tramways "family" until the formation of the L P T B.

Record of War Service and War Memorials

On 9th November 1920, the Council decided to present a "Record of War Service" to each member of the staff who had served in the armed forces in the Great War, or to the next-of-kin of those who had died on active service. The Record consisted of a bound book which included a short history of the war, together with brief particulars of the service undertaken by each member, and the conditions obtaining to those who lost their lives. Members of all departments within the London County Council who served in any capacity are mentioned, and of these, the names of 3,487 tramwaymen are recorded, of whom 328 did not survive the war. As a further mark of respect to those who lost their lives, special War Memorials were set up in tramway car sheds, naming those who did not return.

Chapter 54
Fares and Tickets

Early Fares Policy

The arrangements adopted by the tramway companies for working out the scales of fares to be charged, while basically adhering to the one penny per mile standard, nevertheless tended to apply their rules in a rather flexible manner. Within the metropolitan area, all but one undertaking had a minimum fare of 1d for all passengers, whether adults or children, in addition to which many charged a premium fare on Sundays. The London Tramways Company, however, had introduced halfpenny fares during the last decade of the eighteenth century which applied to journeys of a nominal half mile length. A fare of 1½d was also available for those wishing to travel a little further than the penny fare would allow. This proved to be a popular move.

With the formation of the London County Council, one of its stated aims was that, when control of the tramways passed to it, fares would be standardised on all services, with a minimum fare of ½d for journeys of up to about one mile, then 1d for two miles, 1½d for three, and so on up to a maximum of 4d for the longest journeys. One effect of this policy was expected to be a considerable increase in the load placed upon those who produced the tickets for use with the new fares structure.

Once the principle of halfpenny fares had been established, it was introduced over the system as the opportunity arose, but it took several years to fully implement. In almost all cases, this also meant that, for the first twelve months or so after LCC ownership, there would be the expectation of some financial loss, but as patronage increased, this would only remain as a short term problem.

The first real effect was to be seen with the electrification of the London and Tooting services in May 1903, when fares were considerably readjusted and a fresh set of tickets issued. By this time also, several of the smaller south side companies were being taken over, and their fares were being altered to conform with the new policy.

The next big step was taken in 1906, when the North Metropolitan Tramways Company services passed to the LCC, and the fares structure was rearranged to match that in use on the south London services. Initially, the range covered fares up to 4d, but by 1914, with the introduction of through electric car services into Middlesex, this had been extended to cover fares up to 5d.

The tramways were bound by statute to carry workmen to and from their places of employment at special rates of fare. One of the conditions imposed by the companies and the Council was that the early journeys should be completed by 8 a.m. How this affected the services provided by the Council is described in the section dealing with pre-war two journey tickets.

Fares for Children

Considerable pressure had been exerted several times in attempts to obtain reduced fares for children, but none had been successful, except for the issue of such tickets on behalf of handicapped children attending special schools. On 1st July 1914, the Metropolitan Electric Tramways introduced reduced fares for children aged between 5 and 12 years. This caused the LCC to reconsider its position, resulting in the facility being introduced for children up to the age of 14 years, on Saturdays, Sundays and Bank Holidays as from 29th July 1914. The farescale was ½d for ½d and 1d adult single fares; 1d for 1½d and 2d; 1½d for 2½d and 3d. The issue was introduced on a daily basis on 1st July 1915, when it applied to both single and transfer fares.

The Great War and Fares Policy

The fares structure in 1914 was, in general, still quite simple in format, with a single stage or section arrangement in use. Attempts had been made to introduce overlapping stages on some services, but this was not consistently applied. The first year of the war did little to alter this, and the structure remained reasonably stable until the end of 1915. By then, however, the demands of war began to cause some difficulty in the provision of car services, while restrictions on the use of transfer and return tickets were imposed, and were to continue for the next four years. It had also been policy to charge workman fares on the all-night cars, but this facility was withdrawn as from 1st January 1916.

Wartime Fare Increases

On 27th May 1917, the first of the wartime fare increases was imposed, when the Council authorised the suspension of the ½d adult single fare and all ordinary return fares. This was followed as from 3rd October by restricting the use of workman return tickets. Until that date, it had again become the practice to allow passengers to use the return facility in a rather liberal manner and not necessarily over the sections for which the ticket was issued on the first journey. Staff were instructed that this was no longer to be allowed; that the passengers must only travel over the sections for which tickets were issued in the first place. Most transfer fares were also suspended, with the exception of those to points where no direct service was available.

The Highways Committee issued a draft report on 25th April 1918, recommending further alterations and suspension of facilities, which were introduced on 7th May. In the case of ordinary fares, the length of each section was reduced to 0.6 mile, with three sections for 1d, 6 for 2d, 9 for 3d and all above that for 4d. Odd halfpenny fares were suspended, as also were those ordinary transfer fares remaining, together with ordinary child fares. Workman fares were revised, giving 4 sections on one car for 1d single, and 2d with transfer for any over this number; 2d return for 4 sections with the return journey to be made over the same sections, and 3d return with transfer for any more than 4 sections.

Post War Fares Policy

At the end of 1918, the Council made a survey of the financial situation as it affected tramway fares, and the way in which revisions already made and those proposed would affect it. Following this, an agreement was made with the Trades Unions on 20th March 1919, regarding the introduction of a 48 - hour working week, which would probably cost an additional £36,000 in a full year. This caused the Council to look again in some detail at the whole financial situation as it had developed since 1914, and to ways and means of improving it. Increases in working expenses during the war years were:-

YEAR	CAR MILES	WORKING EXPENSES	CAR MILE
1913/14	59,209,289	£1,585,251	6.50d
1914/15	58,978,792	£1,684,243	6.89d
1915/16	47,879,675	£1,683,660	8.44d
1916/17	49,478,973	£1,817,693	8.82d
1917/18	49,189,866	£2,128,685	10.38d
1918/19	48,052,801	£2,811,465	14.04d
1919/20 (est)	53,000,000	£3,521,925	15.94d
(actual)	53,156,060	£3,680,899	16.62d

The purpose of the proposed increase in mileage for 1919 was in part intended to combat threatened motor omnibus competition. Also, with the introduction of a cheap midday fare (which did not materialise at that time) the Council would, it was hoped, make ends meet.

Following the Highways Committee recommendations of 15th April 1919, fare changes were introduced on south side services on 27th; on north side services at Holloway car shed (except for services 41 and 51) on 11th May; on services 41 and 51 at Holloway, and at Stamford Hill and Hackney car sheds on 18th May; at Bow and Poplar car sheds on 25th May, and provided for each 1d journey to be reduced from 1.8 miles to 1.5, made up of two sections of 0.75 mile; the 2d fare to cover 4 sections; 3d for 6 sections; 4d for 8 and over. Workman single fares to be discontinued, and return fares to be 2d for a journey of 2 miles each way, no transfer; 3d for 3 miles, no transfer; 4d for 4 miles, no transfer; 5d for over 4 miles, with transfer.

Opposition had been voiced to the suspension of child fares, and efforts continued to be made to get the ½d fare restored. The Council refused, but did agree to introduce a child fare of 1d for an adult fare of 2d; then 2d for an adult fare of 3d or 4d; and 3d for any adult fare over 4d. These were applied as from 1st July 1919. But even after this, argument continued over losses incurred, particularly with regard to workman fares, which were said to be "now" losing £105,000 a year, while the all-night service cars were losing about £2,600.

It was decided in December 1919 that fares would have to be raised yet again, but it was not until 19th April 1920 that changes were made on south side services and 10th May in the north. While the length of a section would reduce to 0.6 mile, only two were given for each penny unit, with the introduction of a 5d maximum single fare for more than 8 sections. The 3d and 5d workman return fares were abolished. However, an effort was made to attract more off-peak riders with the introduction of a maximum fare of 2d for a single journey on all cars timed to arrive at central London termini between 10.30 a.m. and 4.30 p.m. and on all cars timed to leave the central termini between 10 a.m. and 4 p.m. on Mondays to Fridays.

Immediately following these increases, another report compiled during May and June recommended that consideration should again be given to increasing fares, reducing section length, or imposing a combination of both. This time, however, use of a Statutory Order, dated 17th August 1920, was resorted to, resulting in the following rearrangements, which came into effect on 26th September 1920. The ordinary 1d single fare to be for one section of 0.6 mile; then

1½d for 2 sections; 2d for 3; 3d for 5; 4d for 8; 5d for 12; and 6d for more than 12, with a transfer if required. Workman fares, 2d return for 3 sections; 4d for 6; with 6d over 6, with transfer if required. Workman single fares were abolished (suspended in May 1919), while child fares were to be 1d single for 3 sections; 2d for 8; 3d for over 8. The maximum midday single fare of 2d, with 3 sections for 1d was to be retained.

Following this severe increase, there was a loss of passengers which persisted for the rest of the year. By the middle of 1921, the Council was forced to reconsider its fares policy once more, to try to win back more short journey riders, introducing the following revisions on 1st December. The standard single section remained at 0.6 mile, with 2 sections for 1d, 4 for 2d, 6 for 3d, 8 for 4d, 12 for 5d, and over 12 for 6d, while each stage would overlap the next by one section. The 2d midday fare was extended to cover the Leyton and West Ham areas, while 2d and higher fares effective between Blackfriars and Westminster via Victoria Embankment were extended to cover an extra farestage on the circular services.

On 1st January 1923, workman fares were again revised to give for 2d a return journey of 4 sections each way, but no transfer; 4d for 8 sections, no transfer; 6d for over 8 sections, with transfer if required. The 1d ordinary single midday fare remained at 3 sections, with 2d for any over this on any one car.

Child fares were reduced as from 26th June 1923, with the 1d fare covering any distance on any one car during the midday period, and a maximum of 2d at all other times. The Leyton area was to be included in this arrangement. West Ham, however, had withdrawn from the cheap fares agreement as from 1st January 1923.

Despite these rearrangements, financial problems remained, and the Council decided, on 22nd November 1923, to try a different approach by reducing certain fares as from 1st January 1924, mainly by introducing return fares at a discount on single fare rates and by limiting the maximum single fare payable within the County of London to 5d. The new fare structure became:-

1d single,	2 sections.
2d single, 3d return;	4 sections.
3d single, 5d return;	6 sections, with transfer.
4d single, 6d return;	8 sections, with transfer.
5d single, 8d return;	over 8 sections, with transfer.

Workman fares were to be 2d return for 4 sections; 4d for 8; 5d for 12; and 6d for any over 12, with the 4d, 5d and 6d offering transfers. All were retained for the remainder of the time that the Council operated the tramways.

In February 1924, return tickets to central London were made available for return from any central terminus, so long as the original fare was not less than that applying at the point from which the return journey was made. The maximum fare ordinary return and workman return tickets which had been issued for a first, direct journey, were also made available for a transfer on the return journey. This was followed on 9th December by allowing transfers on return journeys where the ordinary return fare was 6d and workman return was 4d, and where tickets were issued for a direct first journey.

Through Workings to Hampton Court and Mitcham Cricket Green

LCC cars on services 2 and 4 began to work through to Hampton Court via Wimbledon and Kingston on Saturday afternoons and Sundays beginning in May 1926, while service 8 was extended to Mitcham, Cricket Green as from 1st September. Special sections on the backs of the normal tickets were used in conjunction with these services, and the stages between Wimbledon and Hampton Court and between Tooting Junction and Cricket Green, together with transfer at Hampton Court for "Karsino" and at Mitcham Fair Green for "Blue House" were printed, complete with stage numbers which had been allocated by the LCC. These were in ascending order and at variance with those of the London United Tramways and South Metropolitan Electric Tramways companies. The division of fares taken was worked out on a mileage basis after deducting running costs. Due to trolleybuses replacing the LUT cars on 2nd September 1931, the LCC cars did not work beyond Wimbledon after this date.

London and Croydon Through Services

The tracks of the LCC and Croydon Corporation Tramways were joined at Norbury in February 1926, and through daily services began on 7th, worked by both undertakings. New tickets were issued, the LCC set being an extension of the issue used as far as Norbury.

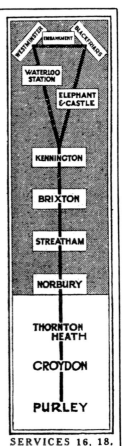

CROYDON AND
Victoria Embankment

Through Service by Tramway

THE connecting-up of adjacent tramway systems in Greater London is of advantage to the public. A through service means a better and cheaper one.

By arrangement with Croydon Corporation a through service of London County Council tramcars now runs between Purley, Croydon and Victoria Embankment via both Westminster & Blackfriars Bridges.

Cars will run every 3 minutes alternately via Westminster Bridge and Blackfriars Bridge.

There is no longer any occasion to change at Norbury and re-book. The tramcars on this route have the most up-to-date equipment. The running time between, say, West Croydon and Westminster is 52 minutes and the ordinary fare 8d.

The diagram shows important districts now served by through tramcars for the first time. Town, suburb and country are to be found on this service, which is the longest in or around London.

L.C.C. TRAMS

WESTMINSTER · EMBANKMENT · BLACKFRIARS

WATERLOO STATION

ELEPHANT & CASTLE

KENNINGTON

BRIXTON

STREATHAM

NORBURY

THORNTON HEATH

CROYDON

PURLEY

SERVICES 16, 18.

911

Tickets issued by Croydon, however, while conforming in the main to LCC practice, were quite distinctive in appearance, with slightly richer colour tints. Printed by the Bell Punch Company, they carried the title "Croydon Corporation & LCC Tramways", and were without fare stage numbers.

The Shilling All-Day

An experimental facility introduced on Saturday, 3rd January 1925 was a daily ticket available for unlimited travel anywhere on the system on the day of issue, and known as the "1/- All-day". It was intended for use on Saturdays and Sundays only and was a great success, so much so that on 21st July the experiment was extended to become a regular daily issue. The area of availability covered the tramways within the County of London (with a couple of exceptions), Leyton, and between Merton and Wimbledon. As an indication of its popularity, 44,652 were sold in the four weekends ending 14th June 1925.

The original instructions regarding the use of the ticket included the rule that they had to be shown to and cancelled by the conductor on each car boarded. This meant that a ticket that was well used had very little space left for cancelling towards the end of the day, and resulted in many conductors just checking the ticket visually.

Availability was extended on 1st December 1926 to the through working services in West Ham, East Ham and Walthamstow, and on 1st June 1927 to local services within those areas. A further extension was inaugurated in 1928, allowing the holder to travel on LUT cars in the Hammersmith area as far as County boundary points. Lastly, on 1st June 1932, the area of availability was again extended to cover the Croydon Corporation Tramways network.

Subsequent Improvements and Additional Facilities

Transfer facilities were further extended on 23rd February 1926, to allow 4d and 6d workman return and 5d, 6d and 8d ordinary return ticket holders on all services to travel, subject to the name of an alternative destination being printed on the ticket, to or from such point, provided that it was within the fare value of the ticket. Return tickets issued in respect of direct services worked during rush hours or weekdays only, were also made available for use with transfers when direct services were not in operation.

More additions were made in 1927. The "Board The First Car" transfer facility was restored in conjunction with the 2d midday fare issue and the corresponding 1d child fare on Mondays to Fridays, and was further extended on 1st June to the 5d ordinary single adult and 2d child single fares. A 6d all-day ticket for children was put on daily issue for a four month period from June to September, with conditions similar to those applying to the 1/- adult fare. This was again issued daily from 1st April to 30th September 1928, 1919 and 1930, with an extended issue on Saturdays and Sundays during October of each year. The final bonus came on 20th June, when 2d midday tickets were issued on cars leaving central London termini between 9.30 a.m. (previously 10 a.m.) and 4 p.m., and on cars timed to arrive at central termini between 10.30 a.m. and 5 p.m. (previously 4.30 p.m.)

A 4d ticket for scholars up to 16 years of age was issued as an experiment during the autumn term of 1930. The facility was made permanent on 16th December, with the 6d all-day ticket on issue for children under 14 years when the 4d ticket was not available. The two

1/- ALL DAY TICKETS

are issued on Saturdays and Sundays, entitling the holder to travel on the L.C.C. Tramways at all times and by all services on the day of issue.

The area covered by these tickets consists of 164 miles of tramway located as follows:—

THE COUNTY OF LONDON
(excepting West of Hammersmith Broadway, and between Manor House & Amhurst Park)

LEYTON

WIMBLEDON (L.C.C. Services only)

North of the Thames the boundaries are

Hammersmith Broadway	Leyton
Scrubs Lane (Harrow Road)	Epping Forest (Rising Sun)
Hampstead	Thatched House (To or from Leyton)
Highgate Village	Wanstead Flats (From Leyton)
Highgate Archway	
Manor House (Finsbury Park)	Bow Bridge
Stamford Hill	Canning Town (Fire Station)

The possibilities are enormous. On Saturdays the purchaser of a 1/- ticket can travel to and from business in the morning, park or playing field in the afternoon, and theatre or cinema, dinner or dance, in the evening.

On Sundays friends living at a distance may be visited with the knowledge that the outlay on fares is limited to 1/-

The holder of a 1/- ticket can travel as often as desired and change cars anywhere.

Cheap Midday Tickets

2d ALL THE WAY
1d FOR THREE SECTIONS

are issued on L.C.C. Tramways

IN THE COUNTY OF LONDON
(excepting West of Hammersmith Broadway and between Manor House and Amhurst Park)

LEYTON

WIMBLEDON

FROM MONDAY TO FRIDAY
(excepting Christmas Day, Good Friday and Public Holidays)

Midday Tickets are issued on cars timed
to leave Central London Termini between
10 a.m. and 4 p.m. and
to arrive at Central London Termini between
10.30 a.m. and 4.30 p.m.

LONGEST DISTANCE FOR 2d—

Victoria Embankment to Abbey Wood 13½ miles

Average distance for 1d about 2 miles

In the same period the
MIDDAY FARE FOR A CHILD UNDER 14
is
1d ALL THE WAY

Cheap Return Tickets

for ordinary passengers
are issued on L.C.C. Tramways
EVERY DAY

IN THE COUNTY OF LONDON
(excepting West of Hammersmith Broadway and between Manor House and Amhurst Park)

LEYTON — WIMBLEDON

WEST HAM — EAST HAM

Return journey		Single journey	Average miles
5d	for	3d	7½
6d	„	4d	10
8d	„	5d	18¼
9d	„	5½d	On East Ham and
		6d	West Ham Routes

On six journeys to and from Central London a Suburban resident may save as much as 1/- a week by taking Return Tickets on the Tramway.

TRANSFER FACILITIES

8d Transfer Return Tickets are issued between all Suburban and Central London points not provided with a direct service.

Choice of Return Routes

A Cheap Return Ticket issued to a Central London terminus is available for return as follows:—

5d or 6d	*Direct from any Central London terminus (or corresponding fare point) to the point from which the ticket was issued, provided that the fare for the alternative route is no greater.*
6d	*As transfer over the same route as for the outward journey made direct (provided that the change point specified is observed). This facility applies only to services where the maximum ordinary return fare is 6d.*
8d	*Direct from any Central London terminus;* *As transfer over the same route as for the outward journey made direct (provided that the change point specified is observed).*

In addition, a return ticket issued for a direct journey or as a transfer can be used for return
Direct or as transfer from any other Central London terminus.

The above facilities apply equally to return journeys TO Central London termini. In no case, however, may the Suburban point be varied. Where the fare for an alternative route on a return journey is greater than that on the outward journey, excess fare is payable.

Jan-July 1925

values were printed on one ticket, the 4d green on one side, the 6d yellow on the other. The pupil ticket could be used for unlimited travel between 7.30 a.m. and 5.30 p.m. on Mondays to Fridays during school term, but in 1932 the time limit was extended to 6 p.m.

A 2d all-the-way Sunday fare was introduced during the beginning of August and the end of October 1930, with a corresponding 1d fare for children, and was quite a success. The fare was again introduced from 19th April to 27th September 1931, but this time was pronounced a qualified success, much dependent on the weather. In 1932, between 17th April and 25th September, a modified cheap Sunday fare was introduced, with the issue of a 3d all-the-way single ticket and a corresponding 5d Cheap Sunday Return. The child ticket was priced at 1d all-the-way (as in previous years) and all these values carried transfer facilities.

A rather unusual arrangement was made during the summer season of 1931, when the Council negotiated for passengers of steam pleasure boats travelling between London and Greenwich to make the return journey by tram. There must have been a sense of nostalgia in this, repeating as it did the efforts of the Council to popularies this form of travel in 1905-06. This time, however, the boats were operated by one of the companies which had plied the Thames for many years.

The last bargain fare introduced by the LCC Tramways became available as from 26th April 1932 when a 6d Evening Tourist ticket was issued, available from 6 p.m. until sometime after midnight with the closure of the day's services. The first experimental period was for six months, but was extended at the end of October for a further six months. In April 1933, it was extended yet again for an unspecified period. The area covered was the same as for the 1/- all-day ticket, including, as from 1st June 1932, the tramways of Croydon Corporation.

Through Bookings with the Underground Group - After 1918

So far as the activities of the combine-owned tramways were concerned, there was always an element of co-operation and through running, mainly in conjunction with the Metropolitan Electric Tramways. Transfer tickets issued for "tram/bus" or "bus-tram" travel, however, were almost non-existent, so it was considered as something of a breakthrough when the LGOC offered this facility in conjunction with the LCC tramcars for passengers travelling via Victoria. This was introduced in December 1920 on omnibus services working from Sloane Square, Bond Street (Piccadilly), Mount Street (Park Lane) and Westminster (Bridge Street) to Vauxhall, at a fare of 1d. On 16th February 1921, fares at 2d, 3d, 4d and 5d were added to the list, and an additional 1½d stage introduced. The scheme was again extended in July 1921 when through bookings were made available via Moorgate, Southwark Bridge, Gray's Inn Road, Euston Road and via Charing Cross. All, however, were withdrawn on 31st October 1922 due, it was said, to lack of patronage.

In later years some through bookings were able to be made with the Underground Railways, in particular at Hammersmith in conjunction with the Metropolitan District Railway, but these were of fairly limited scope.

Luggage Tickets and Fare

One of the first special tickets with a value of 2d was issued by the Council in 1906, soon after the services of the North Metropolitan

Tramways Company were taken over. The ticket seen, numbered C 8500 and coloured purple, and stating "Passengers Luggage Ticket", was issued on the Hampstead and Euston Road service. An explanation giving the reason for its issue, states that it was the policy of the Council to charge for this facility as against what had been common in company days, when it was customary for luggage to be carried "free", the passenger "tipping" the driver for this service on leaving the car.

From its introduction, the "fare" (if it can be called that) for luggage, consisting of any bag, parcel or package which could not be conveniently taken by the passenger into the car, was carried on the front platform and was always 2d for any journey of any distance on any one car. In the early days it was catered for by a special ticket issue as stated above, or by a section printed at the bottom of the ordinary 2d single tickets.

With the rearrangement of fares after the war, a more positive measure of security to passengers and their luggage was devised. A special standard colour 2d ticket was designed, showing the conditions of issue and the stage points "up" and "down", into one of which the punch hole was directed by the conductor on issue to the passenger. Behind each ticket in the pack and bearing the same serial number was a gummed counterfoil stating on its face "The Motorman must attach this LABEL to the LUGGAGE. The Luggage must not be returned to passenger unless a ticket with the same number is given up". On issue the gummed label was usually fixed to the luggage by the conductor, while at the alighting point the passenger handed the luggage ticket to the motorman, receiving the luggage in exchange.

For the whole of the time that the LCC was the tramway authority, this fare never changed in any way. Even after 1933, it remained the only fare that was never increased during the whole of the existence of tramways in London.

Fare Tokens

It was common practice to offer fare tokens to the public, usually at a discount price for fixed quantities, and also to issue them to personnel in various departments of the undertaking and, in the case of municipalities, to other departments, where members of the staff, or visitors, would have to travel by tram to and from these places. The LCC was no exception to this method of payment for travel, and issued tokens made of plastic material and of a size approximately the same as an imperial halfpenny. Two values were issued, that for one halfpenny being coloured black and having the value "½d" embossed on one side, with the 1889 oval-shaped emblem of the Council on the other. Tokens of this value also had three equally spaced small holes drilled triangularly through them. The token with a face value of one penny was coloured red or brown, depending upon the issue and the manufacturer, and were without the small holes.

It was reported to the Council on 11th June 1907 that the use of tokens had declined since their introduction on 25th October 1904, but after consideration it was decided to continue with their use. However, after the end of the Great War, the practice of selling them to members of the public had been discontinued, but they were still retained for use within the Tramways Department, and for issue to other LCC Departments, in particular, those where the welfare of children was concerned.

LCC Tramways
Fare Tokens

½D black, 1D red

THE TICKETING SYSTEM OF THE LCC TRAMWAYS

The London County Council Tramways inherited a rather complex ticketing organisation. After 1896, the North Metropolitan Tramways Company operated services in north London as lessees of the Council. Tickets were supplied by the Bell Punch and Printing Company Ltd. as they had been for many years, and purchased at between 3¾d and 6d a thousand according to length. Ticket punches were hired at a rental of 15/- per punch a year.

All but one of the other companies operating in the metropolitan area also hired ticket punches and purchased tickets. The exception, the London Tramways Company, had printed its own supply of tickets in a printing works at 301-3 Camberwell New Road since 1892 under the superintendence of Mr. J. S. Ashley. He was also responsible for the manufacture of ticket punches in premises at the company workshop at Penrose Street, Walworth. When taken into LCC ownership on 1st January 1899, the ticket printing and punch works were retained. Only the headings on the tickets were altered to signify the new owner.

From its inception on 1st January 1899 to its demise on 30th June 1933, the London County Council Tramways sold just over 17,400 million tickets of a total weight, at two million to one ton, of about 9,000 tons which, including the use of return and day tickets, covered over 20,000 million passenger journeys. Only a small part of this vast number of tickets was bought in from outside suppliers. Taking a random selection of four unrelated years, the approximate output from the ticket works was just over 117 million in 1899; 550 million in 1913-4; 713 million in 1928-9; and 677 million in 1932-3.

Two new machines were purchased on 20th December 1904 to assist in producing the continually-rising numbers of tickets required, while another ticket printing and rotary cutting machine was obtained on 18th March 1906 for £950. It was then stated that the acquisition of more company systems, together with Council takeover of the north side tramways (with the exception of the Highgate Hill line) would make it necessary to increase production, already 200 million a year, to 300 million "in the near future". This proved to be an under-estimate, as the introduction of ½d fares on services taken over since 1902 had increased patronage to such an extent that the enormous quantity of 314 million had been reached by the end of the 1906 financial year.

On 28th July 1909, authorisation was given to purchase one rotary printing machine at a cost of £985, together with one guillotine and two stitching machines for another £500, to cope with the continuing increase in ticket requirements.

The First Move of the Ticket Works

During October and November 1910, the ticket works was to suffer something of an upheaval. In common with the removal of much of the Tramways Department Head Office away from Camberwell, the ticket printing workshop and checking sections were moved into part of the building complex at 21-23 Belvedere Road, Lambeth, which was at the back of the new County Hall then under construction, and where they were to remain for the next twelve years.

The Second Move

With the resumption after the war of the development of and the extension to County Hall, it became necessary to vacate the buildings occupied by the ticket printing and checking sections. Together with other departments, they were moved during February 1923 into premises located on Victoria Embankment, which had been formerly used by the Education Department. After considerable rebuilding work had been completed at Belvedere Road, both to the main building and the garage premises to the rear of it, the 200 staff of the ticket checking section and the 100 or so of the printing works moved back in July 1923.

Due in part to the consequences of the move, the printing section was only able to undertake the minimum amount of work, with recourse being made to "short-time" working. However, as the department once more began to undertake general work for other departments of the LCC, this expedient was not in force for very long. To cope with this build-up, another rotary press was obtained from Messrs. Stokes & Smith in October 1923 for £750. The extra intake of work was to be shortlived, as the decision was taken in March 1924 to run down the general printing capacity of the works and concentrated solely on tickets and subjects allied to tickets, such as waybills, etc.

Ticket production had reached about 680 million a year, and to increase output and replace and augment the older plant, the Council agreed on 20th January 1925 to the development of a new rotary ticket printing machine. The two still in service had been designed by Mr. Ashley and built to Council specification. Ashley had been with the LCC since 1899 and was due to retire on 31st October 1925 on his 65th birthday. Because of his involvement with the development of the new machine, he agreed to remain in the service for another year. The new press was built by David Carlan & Sons Ltd. for £3,745, and put into service early in 1927, several months later than expected. By this time, ticket output had soared to a little over 700 million annually.

The Effra Road Works

Due to delay in commissioning the machine, the Superintendent was asked to stay in post for yet another year, but even this was not to be the end for him. The Council decided in 1926 to move the ticketing sections away from Belvedere Road. Ticket stock would have to be built up prior to the move, and this, and the actual removal meant that the services of Ashley would still be desirable. He agreed to stay until 31st October 1928 to supervise the complete removal.

Suitable premises became available early in 1927 at 51-53 Effra Road, Brixton, which, together with two houses within the freehold had formerly been used by Messrs. Rowntree Ltd., chocolate factors. On 26th July, it was agreed to acquire the site for £16,000 and then spend £17,040 in adapting the building for its new use. The area consisted of a total of 38,000 square feet of land of which 7,500 square feet could not be built upon, owing to restrictions imposed by the "Rush Common Inclosure Act" of c1810, which prohibited building on certain parts of the land that was once "waste" or common ground. In the case of this property, the frontage, together with the others on the east side of Effra Road, was affected by this Act.

At the Dalberg Road end of the site, in rear (east) of Effra Road, a motor garage, which was approached by an entry beneath No. 24A Dalberg Road, was included in the purchase. So as to secure all rights on the property, No. 24A was also purchased. A building extension was planned to go over the area used as garages, while the houses were to be remodelled as staff accommodation.

Removal was carried out during the summer of 1928. Ticket and paper stocks were moved into the new premises by the Tramways Department, for which £217 had been allocated, while machinery was transferred during the weekend of 11th-12th August by Messrs. Usher, Walker & Co. for £1,230. At the same time, some obsolete machines were discarded and new ones installed, while improvements were carried out to other machines still in use. Conversion of ticket checking work from the old handling method to the conveyor table system commenced on 28th August. The timetable was:-

1928.	12th August.	Ticket printing plant moved to Effra Road.
	23rd August.	Conveyor ticket checking system Table "A" used for training women checkers.
	28th August.	Ticket output commenced for Camberwell car shed. Waybills sent to night inspectors instead of being placed in boxes.
	8th September.	Furniture, etc. for the ticket section moved from Belvedere Road to Effra Road.
	10th September.	Full staff of women checkers at Effra Road.
	15th September.	Conveyor table "B" put into use.
	22nd September.	Conveyor table "C" (Saturday work) in use.
	23rd September.	All work transferred to moving tables.
	13th December.	All ticket staff at Effra Road.
1929.	3rd January.	Ticket checking Comptometers in use.
	2nd February.	Fibre ticket boxes for issue to conductors in use in place of tin boxes.

J. S. Ashley retired on 31st October 1928, aged 68 years. At his retirement function, special mention was made of his long and faithful service to the LCC Tramways and, as a mark of its appreciation, the Council granted him an extra sum of £24.13s a year over and above his retirement pension of £183 a year, together with a once-for-all gratuity of £471. He was also retained as a consultant for six months as from 1st November 1928 at a fee of £242. In a tribute to him, it was stated that, mainly due to his efforts, the Council was able to produce the vast quantities of tickets required at a less cost than any other ticket producing undertaking anywhere else in Britain.

In November 1928 the printing works once again had its activities expanded after several years of dealing only with tickets and allied

Stacks of tickets awaiting finishing and trimming at the Effra Road ticket works.   *(Greater London Photograph Library)*

Ticket checking staff at Effra Road ticket works, making up conductors' ticket boxes.   *(Greater London Photograph Library)*

work, when such items as folders, posters and departmental forms were produced. To deal with this extra output, a vertical jobbing press was obtained from the Miehle Printing Press & Manufacturing Co. Ltd. for £850. At the same time, one of the existing rotary ticket printing machines which had been moved from Belvedere Road was modified and updated by Carlan & Sons for £600. Final additions were made in April 1929, when an "Adrema" printing machine was purchased for £350, and in May 1930 when another "Miehle" jobbing press was ordered at a cost of £1,423, and a "Cundall" folding machine obtained for £616.10s. The last two pieces of equipment were acquired to enable the Council to print and fold its own maps and guides.

"Ticket Middles"

The Council, following the pattern set by the London Tramways Company, purchased card for the manufacture of tickets on an annual contract basis from an Agent. The material used was a coarse thin card known as "pulp" or "ticket middles", supplied in white and in tints of specified colours depending on fare values. Colours used were:- ½d, salmon; 1d, white; 1½d, apple green; 2d, pink; 3d, blue; 4d, magenta.

The lengths of card, up to a half-mile long, were wound on to reels for delivery to the ticket works, where they were slit into sections, four tickets in width. The required information was then printed on to one side of the paper and, if it was not needed for further text, an advertisement on the other. The strip was then slit into single ticket widths and cut into shorter lengths for numbering and making the final cut into ticket lengths, one hundred strips at a time. Packs were then divided into two of fifty tickets each, stapled and stacked ready for the attention of the ticket checking staff.

After several suppliers in turn had provided the material, the supply for 1909 was purchased from a Swedish company, through their Agent, R. L. Lundgren, for £10 per ton (less 5%) for white pulp and £11 for coloured. A total of 200 tons was purchased for the year which cost approximately £2,100, resulting in a figure of 2.8d per thousand tickets produced.

The North Metropolitan Tramways used tickets of different colours for the various fare values from those in use on the LCC tramways south of the Thames. On takeover of the north side services by the LCC in 1906, the arrangements were allowed to stand for the time being. Tickets were supplied by the Bell Punch Company and the colours in use were:-
Single: ½d, salmon; 1d, blue; 1½d, green; 2d, white; 2½d, light brown;
3d, pink; 3½d, lilac; 4d, yellow; 4½d, deep brown; 5d, grey/green
Return: 2d, pink; 3d, red.
Workman: d single, primrose; 1d return, orange.

As the tickets supplied by the Council were cheaper than those purchased from Bell Punch, it was decided that when the contract with the company expired on 24th June 1910, it would not be renewed. All tickets for the whole system would then be produced at Camberwell, which would also allow for the ticket styles and colours to be made standard. This took place on the following dates in 1911.
28th March: New pattern tickets with numbered sections introduced on the northern tramways.
1st July: 3d return tickets, colour changed from red to blue.
3rd July: 1d, 2d and 3d single tickets (except for those used on through running services and Poplar routes) had colours altered to match those used on the southern section.
4th October: Rearrangement of fare stage numbers on various routes on the northern section.
By 1914, the colours generally in use were:-
½d, salmon; 1d, white; 1½d, light green; 2d, pink; 2½d, buff; 3d, blue; 3½d, violet; 4d, yellow; 5d, brown (added later).

The Pulp Contract and the Great War

The contract for pulp went to another supplier in 1911 for a slightly reduced price but reverted to Lundgren in 1912, where it stayed for several more years. Soon after the outbreak of the Great War, it became difficult to obtain supplies from Sweden, involving the Council in much extra work in arranging for the purchase of material from other sources. By the end of 1914 the cost of pulp, including the imposition of war-risk insurance, had risen by about 72% but, by making use of multi-contractural purchaseing, extra stocks were laid in which, it was hoped, would help to offset any future shortfall. The intake for 1915 therefore, was for much more pulp than would be required for that year, with 215 tons of white and 300 tons of colours bought in.

Wartime restrictions grew even more onerous in 1916, and the supply problem was acute, it being a case of obtaining anything that was available and making the best of it. At first, tickets appeared in non-standard colours, the LCC resorting to overprinting the fare values in different coloured inks in order to make it clear just what the ticket values were. By 1917, however, even this expedient was found to be most difficult to maintain, and it was then that tickets made from white card pulp began to appear with coloured inked stripes along the front and back edges and, in some instances, with the fare values shown as overprints.

This enabled the Council to revert (almost) to standard colouring for ticket values, but using ink instead of tinted paper. So long as the background colour of the pulp was more or less consistent, at any one of a varying number of shades from pure white to something looking almost like light grey, it did not matter very much. And so it was, that almost accidentally, the foundations were laid for what was to become a distinctive set of tickets which developed after the end of the war. As an example of the new arrangements, the range of tickets provided as from June 1917 for service 54, Victoria Station to Southend Village via Lewisham and Catford, showed that all were of white card with coloured inked stripes printed thereon, these being:-

Ordinary single:		Child single:
1d, white	3d, blue	½d, yellow
1½d, apple green	4d, green	1d, white
2d, purple / pink	5d, brown	1½d, apple green
2½d, mauve	6d, primrose yellow	
	Workman 1d single, white	
	Workman 2d return, salmon	

Post War Improvements

After the end of the war, the Council decided to use the resources of its Stores Department to make bulk purchases of pulp, the Tramways Department in turn purchasing it from Stores. Gradually, after 1919, the quality of the paper used was improved until it was probably the best that could be obtained for the economical production of tickets. During the early 1920s, efforts were made to build up a considerable stock of ticket middles, with a nominal 125 tons being retained in stock at all times.

Except for special issues, for which separate arrangements were made, ticket pulp was white, with all distinctive markings on single tickets, such as fare values, as coloured overprints, and fare colours as inked stripes along the edges of the tickets. Workman returns, ordinary returns and later, all-day and evening tickets, although printed on white card, continued to show the fare value in black within the text matter, duplicated on some of the ordinary returns as overprints, and all had the standard coloured edges for the fare values. Workman returns were made conspicuous by having a coloured stripe, either red, green or blue, printed diagonally across the front of each ticket from top right to bottom left.

Rolls of ticket middles being cut into reels four tickets in width, ready for printing. *(Greater London Photograph Library)*

This method of production continued throughout the 1920s and early 1930s, until the LCC relinquished control of the tramways to the LPTB. During this period, the range was constantly added to as new facilities were made available. In fact, London Transport used the system intact for all tram, and later, trolleybus services for several more years before making any alterations. The colours used were:- ½d, violet; 1d, white; 1½d, orange; 2d, purple-pink; 2½d, chocolate brown; 3d, blue, 3½d, dull purple (SP); 4d, green; 4½d, "creamy salmon" (SP); 5d, grey-brown; 5½d, sepia (SP); 6d, primrose; 6½d, oxford blue (SP); 7d, bright pink; 7½d, pink, blue hatch (SP); 8d, slate grey; 9d, deep blue; 10d, deep crimson (R); 11d, rose pink (R); 1/-, purple, red hatching; 1s/1d, green, red hatching (R).

Notes: (SP) - Special Purposes, east London and outside LCC area.
    (R) - Restricted use only.

Many of the odd halfpenny values were only used on "traffic audit" days, when only one ticket was issued for each passenger journey. Those used for this purpose were of the numbered stage variety, often known as "deaf and dumb", as they did not show any stage names and were therefore available for use anywhere on the system. The audit was confined to passengers boarding cars in the LCC area, but tickets such as 3d child and 3d cheap midday were also included to allow for overlaps into areas beyond the LCC boundary.

Ticket Reference Numbers

To assist ticket processing staff in identifying information required for printing on the large numbers of different tickets, a simple system of references was used. This evolved into a series of numbers and letters, each number identifying a service or group of services, with the suffix letter used to show each printing modification made.

The earliest printing codes appear to have been similar to those used on tickets of the North Metropolitan Tramways Company. The codes do not seem to have followed any set pattern. A few examples are:- The Kingsland Road services, 1d blue, 7A, 7B, etc. (1906-8).

Stamford Hill & Aldgate via Hackney, 1d blue, 13A, etc. (1908).

Bow & Aldgate, 1d blue, 14A, etc. (1908).

On the southern section, code numbers seem to have been adopted by the LCC after about 1908, when a rather complex if irregular series was brought into use. In some cases there were up to five numbers on one ticket. Two examples are:-

Plumstead and Waterloo Station via Old Kent Road, 1d white, double transfer, 1-o, (1911-2).

Clapham or Streatham and London termini,
3½d violet, 9, 10, 28, 29, 32. (1911-2).

With the introduction of service numbering in 1912, the earliest tickets had these numbers applied as their codes in conjunction with a suffix letter denoting the printing order, as seen here:-

Service 11, code 11a, b, etc.

Service 21, code 21a, b, etc.

Services 46/48/54, code 46/48/54a, b, etc.

Service 8, code 8a, b, etc., letters in either upper or lower case.

It is likely that the first wartime changes of code came in 1916 or 1917. Again, there did not seem to be any set pattern applied, although service numbers were, by then, being printed in bold type. A few examples are:-

Service 9, code 89a, etc.   Services 48/54, code 142a, etc.

Service 11, code 91a, etc.   Services 74/80, code 37a, etc.

Service 40, code 52a, etc.   Service 75, code 32a, etc.

Standardisation appears to have taken place in 1919 or 1920, when what later came to be known as the "Effra Road" coding system was brought into use (although the printing section was not moved to Effra Road until 1927). Reference numbers were issued in service-number order, beginning with the even numbered services on the southern system and followed consecutively by the odd numbered services on the north side. Where two or more services used a common routing or were combined in other ways, such as by ticketing common to them, the reference number of the lowest service number was usually used, although there were a few exceptions. The suffix letter, usually printed in the upper case, continued to show the order of printing.

Information given by the late W. H. Bett, in his Paper published jointly by the Light Railway Transit Association and the Transport Ticket Society in 1951, shows that a very clear pattern emerged with the use of this system of identification, and he included "formulae" used for working out which service number(s) received which reference number. Firstly, for south side services, the number "1" was allocated to services 2 and 4; service 6 received reference 2; service 8, ref. 3; service 10, ref. 4; service 12, ref. 5; service 14, ref. 6; services 16 and 18, ref. 7; service 20, ref. 8. From then on, use of "formula 1" will give the correct reference number.

$$Ref = \frac{Service}{2} \text{ minus } 2$$

With regard to north side services, after allocating the number 40 to service 1, "formula 2" holds good.

$$Ref = \frac{Service \text{ minus } 1}{2} \text{ plus } 40$$

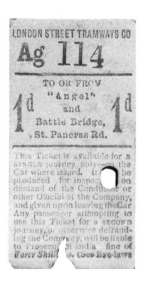

London Street Tramways Co.
Fb 0614: 1d single, white (grey with age), issued on the Caledonian Road
service after 1878. Ua 2537: 3d single, pink with blue overprint, issued
c 1885.   Fa 8046: 1d single, white with red overprint, issued c 1885.
Ag 114: 1d single, white, printed by T. J. Whiting, and used on the
Pentonville Road line c 1878.

Highgate Hill Cable Tramway.
R 9555: 2d single, uphill fare, purple, issued by the first company.
I 0095: 1d single, white, for use either up or downhill, issued by a
later company.

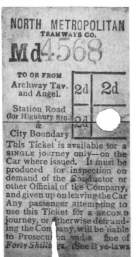

North Metropolitan Tramways Co.
Md 4568: 2d single, white, printed by T. J. Whiting, issued in the early
years of the company.   F 4041: 1½d single, green ticket printed by the
Bell Punch Company.   Bf 1161: 1d single, blue, used on the "Archway
Tavern" and "Angel" service.   Aj 2660: 2d single, white, issued on
"Archway Tavern" to City via "Angel" service.   6737 Ys: 2d single,
white, printed by T. J. Whiting, issued prior to 1879.   Dh 6209: A buff
coloured exchange ticket, issued on production by the passenger of a
two-journey ticket.

There were additional codes which were used for certain issues, including Ref. 88, used to identify information printed on local Leyton service 7, and on some 2d adult and 1d child midday tickets until about 1927; Ref. 89, applied to material printed on Leyton service 8; and Ref. 40 used to identify material displayed on 4d ordinary maximum fare tickets and the corresponding 2d child tickets which carried no transfers.

A further distinction concerns certain New Cross/Abbey Wood issues, of which the 5d single is one. In later LCC days, this bore the upper case letter A as the code, followed by a lower case suffix letter to denote the printing order (e.g. A-c). This arrangements continued to be used by the LPTB for some time after 1933.

So far as the allocation of suffix letters was concerned, each change in text matter on the front of the ticket received the next unused letter of the alphabet, while any printed matter on the backs received the symbol "Rev" in addition to reference numbers and letters. The numbers matched those on the faces, but the letters could reflect a difference in the number of times that the material had been altered. As an example, a ticket for services 68 & 70, reference 32, may show "32D" on the face, with "Rev" "32C" on the back.

Car Service Numbers on Tickets

After car services were numbered in 1912, these were printed in the tickets in characters of much the same size as the rest of the text matter. With the introduction of the 1917 fare changes, the opportunity was taken to give more prominence to this aspect of ticket information. On each of the subsequent fare and farestage alterations, this was accentuated, until by 1922-23, they had become an important part of the display matter.

Numbering of Fare Stages and Sections

Despite the introduction of stage and section numbers on northern system tickets in March 1911, their use on the south side does not seem to have been made in any consistent way. It appears that numbers were applied only when the metal printing plates were renewed for any reason. In general, each service had its own numbering scheme, the central London terminus usually, but not necessarily, being allocated Stage 1, then each stage numbered in ascending order towards the suburban terminus.

In some cases, depending on the service operated, arrangements were made so that at important traffic points, such as "Angel" Islington or "Elephant & Castle", a common number might be used. This could, and did, mean that one or two stages may have been left unnumbered, or that more than one stage would receive the same number.

Ticket Serial Letters & Numbers

The serial letters (e.g. Ff) printed at the same time as the rest of the information, appeared at the top left-hand side of the tickets with the serial numbers following. The first symbol consisted of a capital letter in the series A to Y. The second, when used, was printed either in the lower case, or as a reduced version of the upper, and utilised the whole alphabet. The letters were followed by a four-figure number, which was printed separately at a later stage of production. Each series began with 0000 and ended with 9999. Every value of ticket was printed throughout the range, and consisted of 6,750,000 tickets for each group of services, made up of 25 sets from "A" to "Y", with the sub-sets having 27 blocks of 10,000 each, from "blank", then from "a" to "z". A complete set was:-

A 0000 to A 9999 through to   Y 0000 to Y 9999
Aa 0000 to Aa 9999 through to   Az 0000 to Az 9999
Ba 0000 to Ba 9999 and so on to Yz 0000 to Yz 9999

Single Journey Tickets

The tickets of the London Tramways Company were of the fully geographical style, with details of each journey allowed for the fare paid printed in each punch space. "Down" stages were to the left-hand side and "up" stages (printed the other way up) to the right. After 1st January 1899 the style was retained and, at first, only the company title was replaced by LONDON COUNTY COUNCIL TRAMS, printed centrally in the space between the stage names. Soon, however, the Council simplified the way in which the information was presented, by replacing the full journey descriptions with single fare stages, with conductors then punching each ticket at the destination point for which the passenger had paid fare.

Two Journey & Return Tickets

The first recorded issues of two-journey tickets were those made to "artisans and daily labourers", almost from the beginning of tramway operation. For a payment of either ½d, 1d or 2d, "workmen" were allowed to travel on weekdays on special cars for up to the whole length of the route, both in the morning and at night. This arrangement was modified over the years to enable workmen to travel on ordinary service cars, provided that the first journeys were completed before 8 a.m., and it was this system that was inherited by the LCC.

As from 1st January 1901 the first change was made. From this date, a workman was issued with a two-journey ticket for a fare of 1d, which entitled him to make his first journey of the day. On the return trip, which could be made at any time, on any car, on any route, the passenger handed the two-journey ticket to the conductor together with 1d and received another ticket entitling him to travel to his destination. This rather generous provision was, once the system got to be "known", subject to considerable abuse as it seems that it soon became a popular way of getting "cheap" rides.

The General Manager reported that in the year ended 31st March 1902, 2,465,389 two-journey tickets had been issued, but only 1,992,223 had been given up for a return journey, leaving a balance of 473,166 rides still to be taken. But as about 8,000 were used over the Easter weekend and most of them for 3d journeys, he had decided that, instead of being used by genuine workmen to and from their places of work, the tickets were taken so that wives and families might have a cheap ride on Sundays and Holidays. He then proposed that the tickets should no longer be available for use at these times and, while the Council agreed, it was pointed out that the outstanding tickets could not legally be refused for travel. The practice would cease with the issue of new tickets after the rules had been changed.

The new arrangements were introduced on 9th May 1904, with both journeys having to be taken on the day of issue of a ticket. The rules, however, still allowed for the diminishing number of tickets of the old type to be honoured when presented. From then on, until at last the LCC declared that no more would be accepted, they were presented

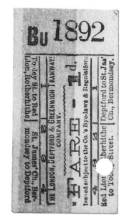

London, Deptford & Greenwich Tramways Co.
Vu 7983: 1d single, green, with "tear-off" corners to validate the
ticket for the journey paid for. Bd 0834: 1d single, white, for restricted
use on the main line.   Bu 1892: 1d single, red and white, issued on
the Tooley Street line.

South Eastern Metropolitan Tramways Co.
JL 5541: 1d single, white.   0995: A free pass, coloured brown, which
was issued to passengers holding season tickets. Printed by T. J. Whiting.
Woolwich & South East London Tramways Co.
K 9229: 3d single through fare, colour light blue, printer, T. J. Whiting.

South London Tramways Co.
Ca 8715: 1d single, white, printed by Whiting, used on Wandsworth and Westminster service via "Princes Head".   Kb 8345: 2d single, pink, printer, Bell Punch Co. and used on the Wandsworth and Borough via "Princes Head" service.   Ed 3303: 1d single, omnibus service ticket, colour white, printed by Whiting.   Ta 3648: 3d single, "deaf and dumb" issue, colour blue, supplied by Bell Punch Co.

London Southern Tramways Co.
Do 2285: 1d single, white "universal" issue, probably the last series to be issued by the company.   W 4559: 2d single "universal", magenta, printed by Bell Punch.

929

at the rate of about 3,000 a month, many of them used by persons of reputed "superior class", to whom they were never originally issued!

The new tickets were printed with month and year of issue shown in the text and with the days of the month printed round three sides of each ticket for punching in the correct place by the conductor. It was pointed out that it was not transferable to another person; was available for return only on the day of issue and only upon the service on which it was issued for the first journey; and was only valid for a second journey if these conditions were met.

London County Council steamboat services commenced in 1905, and return tickets were issued, being similar in style to the "Edmondson" tickets in use on the railways. The first series involved travel between Westminster and Greenwich by boat, returning to Westminster by boat, or by tram, or vice-versa, and available from 17th June for a return fare of 5d. The facility was extended on 17th August for journeys between London and Wandsworth and subsequently further extended to other services where there was an easy interchange between boat and tram. It was a facility that was to be short-lived as, by the end of 1907, the steamboat service was withdrawn, never to return.

A limited number of ordinary return fares were introduced on 1st June 1906 on the northern system. Services working between "Archway Tavern" & Euston Road, and between Hampstead & Euston Road were the first to provide this facility at a fare of 2d single, 3d return. In 1909 it was extended to services operating between Finsbury Park and central London termini. On the southern system, the only ordinary return ticket facilities provided at that time (apart from the tram/boat tickets) were on the horse car services between Wandsworth & Hop Exchange, 6d; Wandsworth & Westminster, 4½d; Battersea Park & London Bridge 4d; or to Westminster, 2½d, which were introduced on 28th November 1905 and were retained when the services were electrified. It was not until 10th July 1912 that the more general introduction of return fares was implemented, and from then on, a considerable number were introduced, with a maximum fare of 3d single, 5d return.

Transfer Tickets and Fares

Transfer tickets appear to have been first issued on the southern services on 26th January 1901 when passengers on the all-night horse cars working between Blackfriars & Clapham and Westminster & Brixton were allowed to change cars at Kennington. The next known issue was in October 1903, when the ill-fated conduit electric to cable service between London and Streatham was hastily withdrawn after a life of only about six weeks, and the lightweight ex-horse cars brought back into service between Kennington and Streatham, with the passengers changing cars at Kennington. In both cases, the tickets received by passengers on the first car, which showed a transfer section, were, on presentation to the conductor on the second car, torn into two, the bottom portion being returned to the passenger.

As from 26th May 1906, transfers were issued on services working between East Hill, Wandsworth & Borough, Latchmere Road & Hop Exchange; Camberwell Green & Victoria. In each case the transfer point was at Vauxhall.

On the northern system, transfer tickets were in use on the newly-electrified subway line which initially worked only between "The Angel" Islington and Aldwych. Passengers were carried through to Bloomsbury from outlying areas by changing cars at various points. The facility was extended on 6th December 1908 when the subway services were extended beyond Aldwych to points south of the Thames.

There is one known case of double transfer tickets being issued as from April 1912. On the long route between London, Woolwich and Abbey Wood, service were worked in three parts; London to Chapel Street, Woolwich by electric cars; onwards to Woolwich, Nile Street by horse cars; then on to Abbey Wood by electric cars. On 1d fares, one transfer could be effected, while, for 1½d and above, two transfers, from electric, to horse, to electric cars were allowed. A 1d double transfer workman single ticket was also on issue. This arrangement continued until the horse tramway was closed for reconstruction in November 1913.

LCC and Croydon Corporation Through Bookings

A comprehensive arrangement was made as from 31st July 1909 between the LCC and Croydon Corporation, applicable to the London, Norbury and Croydon route. This involved through bookings between the two systems, where passengers transferred between cars at Norbury, and catered for a journey made from any stage point on either section of line to any point on the other. The maximum fare between John Carpenter Street and Purley was 7d, of which the LCC share was 4d. Each undertaking paid its own working expenses.

To enable the share of each fare to be correctly apportioned, special two-part tickets were printed in black on white paper. These were double the width and half the thickness of a normal ticket. Each pair of tickets had a central perforation vertically between the two and was folded along it. The tickets had the fare stages printed in descending order from central London termini together with the fare applicable to one stage before the County boundary. Beneath the thin black dividing line, the stages beyond the London County boundary to Purley were printed, together with the fare which was to be credited to Croydon Corporation. On issue, the conductor punched the folded ticket at the stage at which the passenger boarded the car, which would also indicate the fare payable as far as the County boundary, and at the stage in the other area to which the passenger wished to travel, which would also show the fare payable for that section. The ticket was then torn in two, the half retained by the conductor being paid in for accounting purposes. On the second car the passenger handed the ticket to the conductor, who issued an exchange ticket valid for the remainder of the journey.

The scheme was very successful as the following extract from the accounts show. During the twelve months from 31st July 1909 the sum due to the LCC was £8,948. 7. 1d, while Croydon was credited with £4,187.15. 5d. Eventually, however, this scheme was replaced by the issue of ordinary transfer tickets.

The LCC, West Ham and Leyton

Another advance was made with the introduction of through and joint running of car services over county boundaries, but not necessarily making use of through tickets. However, such tickets appear to have been available with the agreement made between the LCC and West Ham Corporation when, as from 26th January 1909 the services between Aldgate and Stratford via Bow Bridge were jointly worked, with takings being divided on a mileage basis. In later years, further agreements

London Tramways Company.

Opposite page. 9342: An early 1d single, white, used on the Greenwich service.   1083: 2d single, maganta, used on the Greenwich service. 2503: 3d blue with red overprint, "high fare" ticket, issued on the cable line.   3009: ½d single, colour salmon, used on the Greenwich service.   3165: 1d single, white with red overprinted serial letters. 7114: ½d single, red with blue overprint.   So 9143: LCC ½d ticket covering the same services as LTC ticket 7114.

London County Council Tramways.

Above.   Yb 7815: 1½d single, light green, supplied by Bell Punch Co. Hb 6922: 2d single, white, with luggage section. Printed by Bell Punch. B 0620: 3½d single, lilac, issued on the short-lived Hammersmith and Edgware Road service in 1911. Lw 8049: "Universal" exchange ticket, colour buff.   Ba 5724: Pre-1914 northern area luggage ticket, mauve. Ka 4023: 2d single, white, used on early subway services.

were made with Leyton, East Ham and Walthamstow, and covered all services crossing the various boundaries.

The Metropolitan Electric Tramways

Probably the best known through running agreements entered into by the Council, were those made with the MET Ltd. on services using Seven Sisters Road or via Holloway and "Archway Tavern". The first was from Euston Road to Enfield via Finsbury Park, which began on 30th April 1912. In this case, and others subsequently instituted, the fare structure was mainly at the rate of ½d a mile in the LCC area, slightly more in Middlesex. Fare income on through services was divided according to the track length of each authority for the route or routes concerned. No transfers to omnibus or underground trains were to be permitted without the consent of the LCC.

Tram, Tube and Omnibus Transfers

A complete departure from what was considered normal (so far as the LCC was concerned) in the issue of transfer tickets was embarked upon on 1st December 1914. The LCC Tramways, the Metropolitan Electric Tramways, the London Electric Railways and the London General Omnibus Company, provided a new facility for people travelling by tube railway to or from certain stations in central London and changing to or from tram or 'bus at Highgate "Archway Tavern". At the transfer point, they were able to continue their journeys to or from Highgate, Fortis Green or North Finchley.

Upon reconsideration of the agreement on 10th June 1915, LCC support was withdrawn from the scheme. However, on 18th July 1916, the Council stated that "through tickets on issue on the Central London and London Electric Railways to 'The Winchester' and Fortis Green Road, enable the holders to travel to those parts by 'bus. It is now arranged that these be available by 'bus or tram". This reinstatement was not to last for long, being finally withdrawn in October 1917.

The LCC Agreement with Bexley UDC Tramways

This agreement, while of limited scope, paved the way for the operation of a very long through service. On 1st July 1914, it was agreed to introduce through bookings between the Waterloo Bridge terminus of LCC services 38 and 40 and Bexleyheath Market Place on the Bexley UDC Tramways, passengers changing cars at Plumstead, Wickham Lane, at a transfer return fare of 8d and a distance each way of 15 miles 486 yards. In conjunction with the transfer fare, service 38 cars were extended to Bexleyheath on Saturday afternoons and Sundays as from 11th July. On 2nd October, the issue of a transfer return for a fare of 9d became available between London and Barnehurst (Northumberland Heath), a distance of 16 miles 1,320 yards each way.

By mid-1915 the through running agreement on Saturday afternoons and Sundays was discontinued, the last through service running on the weekend of 5th/6th June. The issue of transfer tickets continued, however, only until 1st March 1917, when they were finally withdrawn, due to the pressures of wartime.

"Board The First Car"

The final pre-war facility offered was referred to as "Board The First Car". This meant, for some journeys, a passenger could get on to the first car to come along and transfer at a convenient point to another car to complete the journey, whether on the same line of route or not.

TICKET PUNCHES AND CANCELLERS

The Ticket Punch Department and Mr. George Gibson

The ticket punch works of the LCC Tramways, which had been inherited from the London Tramways Company, was situated at the car repair works at Penrose Street, Walworth, with a subsidiary repair workshop at 303 Camberwell New Road. The type of machine in use was a hand-held trigger-operated registering box punch made of brass, of an approximate size of 4 in. x 3½ in. x 1 in. The rights relating to the manufacture of this type of ticket punch were assigned to the London Tramways Company in exchange for a royalty payment of 6/- to the inventor for every punch made. This right was transferred to the LCC Tramways who continued to pay the 6/- fee.

In May 1906 the Council employed Mr. George Gibson, whose task it became to see that the whole of the punch stock was kept in good repair, and to be responsible for the manufacture of new punches as and when required. From records researched, there are indications that the patent rights for the punches made and used by the LCCT belonged to Gibson. At the beginning of the Great War, he made a voluntary agreement with the Council, whereby his invention of a cancelling machine could be used by the LCC without royalty payment to him. Machines of this type were eventually used by all conductors on the LCC Tramways. His patents, of great benefit to the Council (admitted in a Minute) were, in 1923, applied to 1,500 ticket punches and 1,700 cancelling machines out of a grand total of 6,050 in use.

On 23rd January 1923 he was promoted to the permanent staff and re-designated "Punch Shop Superintendent", with a suitable increase in salary to go with his new status. Gibson retained his position upon the formation of the London Passenger Transport Board in 1933.

The Trigger Operated Box Punch

This machine, made of brass, was suspended by a chain which was sometimes fixed at the other end to the conductor's cash bag, or to a suitable anchor point on the bag strap. Some conductors, however, preferred to hang the machine, on its chain, around the neck. These machines were only used on the south side tramways.

In common with the policy developed to deal with the expected increase in ticket output as the tramway network was enlarged, and due to the LTC only making enough punches for its needs towards the end of its tenure, the works was made ready to manufacture additional new punches at a cost of approximately 42/- per punch, of which 6/- was royalty payment. An additional 3/- per punch a year was allowed for maintenance purposes. Between 1st January 1899 and 24th July 1900 the Council had already had 300 machines built at a total cost of £630, and made a decision to build another 500 costing £1,050, so that as more undertakings fell to the LCC, the punches in use could be replaced by its own.

The manufacture of another 500 machines was authorised on 28th November 1905, and cost of these included £50 for special tools and

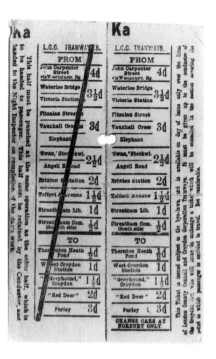

London County Council Tramways

Above.   Ka ----: Universal fare duplex ticket, colour buff, issued on LCC/CCT services.   The part with the black line was retained by the conductor.   3136: Light green colour return half of 5d LCC steamboat service ticket.   Z 2433: Exchange steamboat/tram ticket, colour brown.

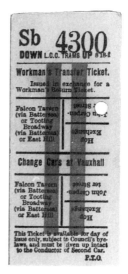

Opposite. L 3547: *1d single with double transfer, colour white, used on Greenwich-Woolwich service, c 1912.* L 6952: *1d workman single, white, with double transfer, Greenwich-Woolwich service, c 1912. Ra 5236: 1d workman single with transfer, subway service, colour white.*

Above. J 8215: *Limited journey exchange ticket for use with transfer. E 1729: Workman return exchange ticket, colour mauve with red bar. Sb 4300: Workman return transfer exchange issue, mauve with red bars. I 8254: 1d workman exchange with transfer stub, issued on payment of 1d and surrender of original ticket. D 2171: 2d workman return, dated for 8th June 1904. Colour salmon with red overprint. B 6305: 3d fixed value return exchange ticket, colour buff with red overprint*

£150 royalty. After the completion of this batch, on which £1,025 was expended, the workshop was moved from Penrose Street to Camberwell New Road in readiness for the disposal of the Walworth premises. Another 500 punches were built in November 1906, but this time the casings were made from "nickel silver" instead of brass. Cost was estimated to be £1,000, which did not include any royalty payment, as Mr. Gibson was now the overseer of the workshop.

On 1st April 1906, the North Metropolitan Tramways Company lease on the northern system was terminated by the Council. The company had been using Bell Punch Company ticket punches, supplied under a hiring agreement, at 15/- per punch a year, including repairs. It was not expected that this contract, due to expire on 24th June 1910 would be renewed, as the Council had decided to assemble 2,000 punches in its own works for use on the northern system, together with an extra 500 for use on the south side. It had been anticipated at the time that royalty payment would need to be made, an inclusive sum of £4,800 being considered to be sufficient to finance this arrangement.

Early in 1909, however, an offer was received from Bell Punch stating that it was willing to continue to supply the punches required for the northern system, at the rate of 10/- per punch a year for a period of five years as from 1st January. The company would also allow a rebate of 5/- per punch a year for the six months ending on 31st December 1908, on all machines under the old contract. It would also accept liability for repairs, and stated its willingness to supply the additional 500 required at the new rate.

The Council estimated that the cost for five years under these terms would be £4,394, while £4,252 would be required if the 2,000 machines were made up in its own workshops. Conversely, if the manufacture by the Tramways Department was to be deferred by five years, the royalty payment of 6/- per punch would no longer have to be paid. Thus, with the possibility of an improved punch being available, the Council accepted the offer, the two sides coming to terms on 30th March 1909.

The punch works were once again moved in October 1910, this time to premises at the rear of 23 Belvedere Road, Lambeth. This move was made to enable more space to be made available for the workshop, and allow for an extension to be made to Camberwell car shed.

The five year agreement with the Bell Punch Company was due to expire on 31st December 1913, but on 30th July it was agreed that it be extended on a "six months' notice by either side" basis, to expire on 30th June 1914 or on 30th June of any subsequent year. With this in mind, the Council, on 3rd March 1915 decided to invite tenders for the purchase of 2,500 ticket punches. On 27th April, however, Mr. Gibson informed his employer that he had invented a new type of registering punch, and the decision was made, with his agreement, that the new design could be used without royalty payment.

Meantime, Bell Punch sought a further agreement with the LCC. This resulted in the Council agreeing to purchase the existing machines on a six-year hiring arrangement at an estimated cost of £5,393, and the company would continue to service them during that period. In October 1915, 2,445 ticket punches passed into Council hands. The north side conductors, therefore continued to use strap-mounted Bell Punch machines, which made a circular hole within the ticket, together with "Gibson" cancelling machines (which are described elsewhere), while on the south side, Gibson cancelling machines were used, but hand-held box-type trigger ticket punches, which made a "half-moon"

Left: An original LCC hand-held ticket punch, used on south London
services until about 1930. *(Courtesy: D. Jones)*

Right: A Bell Punch Company machine used on north London services
until about 1930. *(Courtesy: A. D. Packer)*

shaped hole on the side of the ticket, were still in general service.

With the return of peaceful conditions and the subsequent increase
in staff, more cars could be run, which in turn meant that more ticket
punches would be required. Many of the existing machines, some
almost 20 years old, were also in a very worn condition and would
soon have to be replaced. The decision was taken on 29th July 1919
for 500 punches of the type designed by Gibson to be assembled in the
Council's workshop from specially made parts, at an estimated cost of
£1,000. The additional tools and equipment required were purchased for
£119 and which, on completion of the work, would be available for
further assembly processes as and when required, and would also be of
use in the maintenance and repair of the new punches.

On 27th July 1920, tenders were invited for the supply of parts for
another 300 machines at an estimated cost of £750. However, delay
had been experienced in obtaining the items for the first consignment,
with the result that, on 8th November 1921 the decision was taken to
amalgamate the two estimates, the work then being carried out as a
continuous programme. The "A"-type punch, which made a circular
hole within the ticket, had arrived!

Leyton Urban District Council Tramways were taken over for
operational purposes by the LCC on 1st April 1921. The Bell Punch
machines in use remained in use until 31st March 1922, when these
were replaced by Council stock. At the same time, an order was
issued to the workshop to build another 250 "A" punches. Over the next
five years another 550 were assembled, being used as required alongside
the original LTC/LCC and Bell machines.

By 1927, with the new County Hall extension building programme
impinging upon the site of the punch works, the decision was taken
to remove the whole of the works to new premises once again. A
suitable site was eventually found behind the tramways sub-station in
Stockwell Road, Brixton, and a new building erected. On completion,
the punch repair works staff moved in on 27th August 1928.

Above. QQ 0420: 2½d single, white with purple stripes, with exchange portion for transfer to Underground Railway. Hp 0484: 2d single, pink stripes, with luggage section, early wartime. Fa 0080: 4d workman return, New Cross issue, early wartime. N 424: Yellow 1d value coupon issued to special constables during the early years of the Great War. K 7251: ½d child single with transfer, issued 1914-5, colour salmon with red overprint. T 1337: 8d return with transfer, between London and Bexleyheath, 1914-7. Grey/white with blue stripes.

Opposite. S 2683: 2d standard post-war single, "purple-pink" stripes, used on the through London, Wimbledon and Hampton Court services, 1926-31. Front and back of ticket shown. Bi 5566. 5d ordinary single with transfer sections. Brown stripes with red overprint.

Above. 4d single, green with red overprint. Poplar car shed issue,
late 1920s. D 9681: 1d ordinary single, white with red overprint.
Pq 9675: 1d ordinary single, white with green overprint.
All tickets shown on these pages printed by LCC.

The General Manager advised the Council on 24th November 1927 that, in his view, consideration should be given to re-equipping all conductors with new ticket punches. He said that the remaining trigger-type box punches together with the Bell punches, of which there was a combined total of 5,500, were all over 20 years old, badly worn and costly to maintain. In contrast, the 1,660 "A"-type punches in use since 1919 had proved to be very reliable. He recommended that 6,000 more of these be built, which would be sufficient to replace all the old machines, and also provide enough spares to meet requirements at times of pressure. Total cost was expected to be about £11,000, with a write-off value of £2,850 included for the old machines.

A progress report dated 17th December 1929 showed that in 1923 there were 6,050 ticket punches and 1,700 cancelling machines in use, while in 1928, 7,900 punches and 2,100 cancellers were in stock and new machines were still being manufactured. It also stated that the duties of the superintendent now included responsibility for the repair of recording clocks, small machines and instruments, as well as for the design and preparation of patterns, jigs and templates for special tools in use in the workshop.

Ticket Cancelling Machines

The usual method of ticket cancellation in use on tramways in the metropolitan area when transfer and return tickets were first issued, was that on the second car:-
a) a small piece of the ticket would be cut out with the aid of a pair of hand nippers, or
b) a ticket stub, usually at the bottom of the ticket and printed with the serial number of the issued ticket, would be torn from the presented ticket by the conductor, or
c) the conductor would collect the presented ticket as cash, issuing a special "exchange" ticket valid for the remainder of the journey, and punched in the usual way by the registering punch.

With the issue of return journey tickets by the North Metropolitan Tramways Company, the use of exchange tickets for the second journey became commonplace, this method being retained by the LCC upon the takeover of the company in 1906. When transfer tickets were brought into use on the southern system, it became policy for the conductor to tear a piece from the ticket when the second part of the journey was made. Some of the early transfers were introduced as the direct result of electrification of sections of track and were quite temporary. It became essential, therefore, for the transfer system to be made as simple as possible, it being considered that the issue of exchange tickets on such a large scale would be too costly.

With the general introduction of transfer tickets and, later, return tickets which were also transfers in both directions, a rather complex ticket issuing and accounting arrangement became necessary to satisfy the LCC regulations as they stood at the time. This was foreseen by Mr. Gibson who, in January 1911, designed and built a small machine which could be used as a non-registering cancelling apparatus for tickets. He reasoned that by using his machine, a considerable saving in conductors' time and effort would result, together with economies in the issue of exchange tickets.

The machine consisted of a metal box about 3 in. x 2 in. x 2 in. in size, strap-mounted and usually fixed to the upper part of the cash bag strap. By means of a lever projecting from the front of the device the conductor could, by pressing this inwards, move a small wedge-shaped knife fitted inside the box and so cut a piece out of the inserted ticket. At the same time, the machine number was printed to the right of the notch, while the car service journey number, printed to the left of it, could be changed as necessary by the conductor.

Several improvements were subsequently made and incorporated into the design, so that the manufacture of parts for 1,500 machines, to be assembled by the Tramways Department, could go ahead. Cost was £900 for this batch, with a further £120 allowed for 200 more which were ordered in February 1915. Manufacture took a considerable time and meanwhile the issue of exchange tickets, or of tearing pieces from tickets continued until just after the outbreak of the 1914 war. The machines first went into service on the northern system, to be followed on the south side in the early months of 1915. It had been estimated that about £1,500 would be saved annually in connection with ticket printing and checking once all conductors were provided with these machines.

Their use in the early days caused some problems as, due to rather onerous regulations which had been introduced with regard to the method of working coupled with the novelty of them, it was inevitable that there should be some misuse of the cancellers. When first issued, a notice was cirulated to all conductors stating:- "5th December 1914. Cancelling machines. The machine for cancelling return and transfer tickets is in operation on certain routes on the northern section of the tramways. Conductors who are not provided with these machines must issue exchange tickets in exchange for transfer (or) return tickets cancelled above the double line with the machine when presented at the change point for the continuation of the journey".

This was followed at regular intervals by various instructions and exhortations being published, including the following:-
"22nd March 1915. Cancelling machines. In several cases recently it has been impossible to trace the conductors who cancelled tickets with cancelling machines, owing to the figures being illegible. The pads of each machine must be kept well inked and each machine must be tested before being issued.
"18th May 1916. The attention of conductors is called to the following notice ... 'At the end of each journey the conductor must alter the journey number on the machine to correspond with the journey number on the time board. Any conductor neglecting to carry out this instruction will be sharply dealt with'.
"12th April 1917. Care of cancelling machines in depots. These are to be strictly observed. Each machine is to be dealt with by inking twice a week, oiling regularly and cleaning properly. The following articles are to be held on hand at depots:-
1. Ink. 2. Oil. 3. Wire brush. 4. Testing strips. 5. Screwdriver.
6. Small screws for replacement. 7. Conductors' Instruction Cards.
All above are available from the Punch Repairing Shop, 23 Belvedere Road. All defective machines are to be returned to the Shop ...".

Despite the almost constant barrage of instructions and veiled threats issued with regard to the use and "abuse" of these machines, it seems that no great notice was taken and, on hindsight, it is probably true to say that it did not really matter whether the cancelled ticket showed a journey number or that the ink was smudged. It will be appreciated that conductors were, at that time, working under great difficulties, with constant capacity loads and, at night, with restricted car lighting. The General Manager, however, seems to have eventually given up the struggle, as many other improtant matters required his attention.

Above: Bf 2835: 6d ordinary return with transfer, primrose yellow with red date overprint. Pv 0908: 3d ordinary single, blue with red overprint, with special facility for "marrying" with 5d single to make 8d return fare. Qc 1744: 8d ordinary return with transfer, showing days of week instead of fixed date. Colour grey with red overprint.

Opposite. R 3843: 2d fixed date workman return, purple-pink with faint overprint 'JUN 17'. Ui 0846: 4d workman return, green with red diagonal line. The back of the ticket shows a religious tract issued by The Salvation Army. YA 0308: 6d ordinary return, primrose yellow with red dated overprint 'APR 7'. The skeleton letter R is in black. Sb 8287: 5d return, cheap Sunday all-the-way fare with transfer. Colour light brown. Issued in 1932. Vd 0161: 1d child all-the-way cheap fare with transfer. The red overprint showing the "lozenges" denotes a cheap midday fare value.

R 3843
56B L.C.C. Trams
33-35 | Waterloo Br. 2 (Savoy St.)
2d Work. | Westminstr Station 3
| York Rd or Christchch 4
1 Southampton Row | Fitzalan Street 5
2 Farringdon Road (Rosebery Avenue) | Kennington Gate 6
3 Angel | Camberwell Green 7
4 Essex Street (Upper St) | Town Hall Camberwell 8
5 Highbury Station | Rye Lane 9
6 Nags Head | Queens Rd. Stn. 10
7 Holloway Station, M.R. | New X Gate 11
8 Archway Tavern | Malpas Rd. (Lewisham High Rd) 12
12 Norwood | Brockley Cross 13
11 Tulse Hill | Crofton Pk. Stn. 14
10 Croxted Road | Cranston Road 16
9 Dalberg Road | Angel Road 7
8 Brixton Stn. Acre Ln. or Stockwell Rd.

This ticket is issued subject to the Council's by-laws, must be shown or given upon demand, and is only available for a return journey on day of issue. Not transferable.

YA 0308
78A L.C.C. TRAMWAYS
For alternative return journeys only
Change at Holborn Hall
Farringdon Road | Kings Cross
Midway Park | Nags Head
Change at ANGEL
Manor House & Aldersgate, Smithfield or Waterloo Br. | 77 S | Camden Hill and Aldersgate, Smithfield or Kings Cross
H Aldersgate or Smithfld | Mansell Road and Aldersgate, Smithfield
P Filds and Aldersgate, Smithfield
Charing Cross HACKNEY STATION | Passenger Road (Bacton) and West Ind's Docks
Change at DALSTON JUNCTION | Cannon Road, Blackstock, Islington
C East Rd Stn. and Aldersgate | W End Rd and
M West Rd Stn & Percival Street | B and
* Alternative Return Route provided to suburban points if not varied 10

Tickets is issued subject... must be shown or given... available for a return journey... only for the suburban point to or from issued. See over.

Ui 0846
60F L.C.C. Tramways
Service 81
Workman's Return
Kennington Road and Westbury Road or 'The' Hackney Road or Dean Road | D | St. Paul's Road and
Barkhouse Road and Farringdon Road | Bakers Arms | 4

This ticket is issued subject to the Council's by-laws, and is only available for a return journey on day of issue, and only between the points for which it is issued. Not transferable.

THE SALVATION ARMY
Proclaims that
Read "THE WAR CRY"
General Booth

Sin will destroy, Christ will save.
Love will redeem.
London, E.C.4

Sb 8287
5E L.C.C. Tramways
CHEAP SUNDAY
5d Ret.

Change at A (see back)	LONDON TERM. or Southampton Row	7-14-21-28-4-11 Sept. Aug.
SUBURBAN TERM. L.C.C. Area (See back)		7-14-21-28-4-11 Sept.
Change at B (see back)	LONDON TERMINUS or Southampton Row	7-14-21-28-4-11 Sept. Aug.
SUBURBAN TERMINUS L.C.C. area (See back)		7-14-21-28-4-11 Sept.
Ser. 12 14 26 28 30 32	LONDON TERMINUS (not beyond Young's Corner)	7-14-21-28-4-11 Sept. Aug.
SUBURBAN TERMINUS (not beyond Beech Ln Harrow Rd)		7-14-21-28-4-11 Sept.

Vd 0161
450 L.C.C. Tramways

SUBURBAN TERMINUS	CHEAP FARE
but only The Winchester Manor House feis Finsbury Pk or Mildmay Pk, Stamford Hill Lewisbarst Pk, Rising Sun or Blackwall Tunnel	11 17 27 See over for conditions of issue
CHANGE AT	LONDON TERMINUS or County Hall
A Archway Tavern	Change at Archway Tav.
C Camden Town	Camden Town
H Highbury Station	Highbury Station
K Kings Cross	Kings Cross
N Nags Head	Nags Head
O Old Street (City Road)	Old St. (City Road) or Gardiner's Cnr or County Hall
B Rosebery Av. Farringdon	Rosebery Av. Farringdon

(centre triangle) D CH BD

Highgate Village	LONDON TERMINUS
E Edmonton Town Hall	Camden Tn Sn Und. or N.L.R.
A Angel Bridge	Bracknock Road
Northumberland Park	Nags Head, Holloway
Lordship Ln. Tottenham	Holloway Stn., M.R.
Bruce Grove Station	Finsb'y Pk or Archway
West Gn. Rd. Tottenham	Manor House
St Anns Rd Station	Amhurst Park

945

Post War Progress

The machines designed by Mr. Gibson continued to be used by conductors on all services. By 1929, the machine was further developed in an effort to dispense with the inked pad and other paraphernalia associated with it. In the new model, the machine number was cut into the ticket by a series of thin circular blades passing through it in the same way that was usual with the normal registering punch, but still retaining the wedge-shaped notch cut from the side of the ticket. (The Bell Punch Company had first introduced a machine of this type, but showing differences in detail, in 1922-23). Thus, the perforated cancelling mark, without a journey number, came into use on the LCC Tramways in February 1929.

∧ x x x

During the remainder of the time that the tramways were under Council control, development of the machine continued with, in the spring of 1931, the ultimate in design; a cancelling machine that:-
a) cut a small hole in the ticket, beneath which was the machine serial number, or
b) cut a small hole in the ticket, over which was an upper case letter, and beneath it, the machine serial number.

<pre>
        type (a)   o   type (b)   x
                 x x x   o
                                           x x x
</pre>

The Ticket Checking Section

This department was an important part of the establishment and was closely associated with the printing department. In LTC days, part of its function was the actual printing and numbering of new tickets as well as dealing with the returns. The section was staffed exclusively by women, with a senior woman officer in charge of the group. At the time of the acquisition of the company by the LCC, the checking staff superintendent, Miss E. Penman, controlled 58 women clerks who dealt with all ticket and cash transactions resulting therefrom. She died in the summer of 1899. Miss E. Hodge, the deputy to Miss Penman was promoted to the position of superintendent.

There were a number of strategically placed traffic cash offices where conductors were instructed to pay in the takings for each journey made, and these were staffed by women of the ticket checking section. Receipts were issued to conductors in exchange for the money paid in which, in conjunction with waybills and serial numbers of tickets, gave a complete record of the day's work. All cash offices were open from 8.30 a.m. to 11 p.m., seven days a week, with staff working shift duties to cover the period. Each member of the staff had one day off duty in seven.

In the ticket checking section at Head Office, bulk ticket stocks for the day in advance of that being worked were requisitioned by the superintendent and recorded in a "day book", afterwards being posted into a stock book for recording their distribution. Sufficient tickets of each value required for every duty, with an estimated number of extras, were packed in a metal box together with a registering ticket punch and a waybill, plus 3s/6d in small change for use as a "float" for each conductor. The boxes were then stacked into carrying cases which, when full, were locked prior to being conveyed to each depot. The night inspectors, after taking charge of their consignments, were able to unlock the chests and hand out the boxes to conductors as required.

One of many changes made by the LCC was that all checking staff, from the superintendent to the youngest and most junior member was assessed for seniority, sense of responsibility and level of loyalty and insured by the Council accordingly, in sums varying from £1,000 for the superintendent to £100 each for the lowest grade of checker. This was intended to indemnify the employer and employed in a number of ways, not least to give cover to each lady in case she was robbed while on duty! The second change was that, in the opinion of the Highways Committee of the Council, the women were worth more than they were receiving from the company, resulting in pay increases from 13th November 1900. The old rate of between 9/- and 14/- a week was replaced by a rate of between 10/- and 20/-. Supervisors were to receive an extra 2s/6d a week.

Arrangements made by the North Metropolitan Tramways Company for the distribution and checking of tickets were very similar to those employed on the southern system. It remained intact for several more years, until the Council moved the southern ticket printing and checking section to premises at 23 Belvedere Road, Lambeth in 1910. Subsequently, the work became more contralised and the practice of handing in takings at cash offices gradually gave way to conductors instead paying in all money on completion of duty at special offices set up in the car sheds, while the checkers concentrated on dealing with ticket supply and returns.

Pay reviews were undertaken from time to time, with modest increases being granted in 1904 and 1906. It was again decided in 1912 that, due to the increased workload and more complex operations involved, the staff should receive increased rates of pay. These were:-

       Junior Female Employees, 10/- to 18/-
       Senior Female Employees, 19/- to 24/-
       Forewomen,   30/- to 35/- a week.

Supervisors and above were to receive between 40/- and 60/- a week according to rank, while all were to be subject to a system of annual increments, to take effect as from 2nd May. Post war conditions saw the level of pay increased from time to time, in accordance with an agreed scale for people in all sections of the Tramways Department.

The greatest change of all came when the department moved from Belvedere Road to Effra Road, Brixton. As described elsewhere, the whole method of ticket checking and issue was brought up to date, and over the remaining years of Council control, this section was to attain increasing importance as the numbers of tickets issued reached enormous levels, requiring the attention of a greatly expanded staff.

Cash Bags

Conductors' cash bags, made of leather, were manufactured by the craftsmen of the Tramways Department. This was another ancillary service which came into LCC ownership from the London Tramways Company and the North Metropolitan Tramways. In horse car days, the leather workshops would have been a very important part of the undertaking, producing all kinds of leather goods.

The type of bag used was quite distinctive in appearance, rather bulky and with a large top flap which could be closed when the bag was not in use. It cost the Tramways Department 5s/9d to produce a cash bag in the years before the Great War. It also became usual for conductors to use the bags as receptacles for the hand-held ticket punches when not actually being used.

Above. Xe 0000: *4d pupil ride-at-will ticket, issued on schooldays only. Green stripes on white ticket. A 6d child all-day value was printed on the back of the 4d pupil ticket, with primrose yellow edges. Issued on Saturdays, Sundays and school holidays. Ug 2631: 6d evening tourist, with red stripes over yellow edges, and the skeleton letter T overprinted in red on yellow.*

Opposite. Y 0052: *The first issue of the 1/- all-day, colours yellow in the centre section and orange/pink stripes on edges on white paper, with the overprint in light red. The original issue was on Saturdays and Sundays only. Tv 1201: The standard 1/- all-day, with blue central section and red diagonal stripes on edges. An availability diagram was printed on the backs of the tickets. Jk 7284: 2d cheap midday all-the-way fare, with red stripes and the overprint showing the midday identification, a line of "lozenges" behind the fare value. The fare also had a transfer facility. Mv 4728: An alternative 2d midday fare ticket, but without transfer facility, and available to any one of a number of suburban termini. Gh 9229: 1d single midday fare, giving three sections for the fare paid. Coloured white with red overprint.*

948

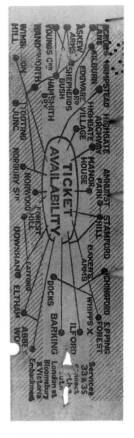

On the north side system, numbered cash bags, punch straps and punch plates (which second and third items were not initially used on the south side) were issued to all conductors, in accordance with the general regulations applying to all staff.

Whistles

All conductors were supplied with whistles. One of the suppliers was J. Hudson & Co. of Birmingham, whose product was known as "Hudson's Patent Inimitable Glasgow Thunderer", shortened to "The Thunderer", while in later years many whistles carried the impressive inscription "The Acme Thunderer". All were also stamped "LCCT".

In the days of the horse cars, whistles were also carried by drivers, who, by this means were able to signal their presence to other road users who were running their vehicles on the tram tracks. Electric cars were fitted with foot operated warning bells for use by motormen, making whistles unnecessary.

The whistle was usually carried on a long chain slung around the neck, or on a shorter one fastened into a suitable buttonhole in the jacket lapel. It was an important part of a conductor's kit. When he was on the top deck of a car, a whistle signal would be given as there were no signal bells available, and the motorman would know by the whistle that the conductor was "outside" and act according to certain rules applying to this situation. Whistles were also used for many other purposes, notably by inspectors and regulators, who were in control of ticket checking and car timings.

Ticket Racks

Until 1922, it was obligatory for conductors to purchase their own ticket racks. These were made in varying lengths, the most common being from 6 to 8 containers on each side of the rack. Each container consisted of a spring-operated retaining bar or clip (rather like a mousetrap mechanism), which held a pack of tickets in place in the rack. Subsequently, the Council agreed to pay an allowance of 3/- to all new conductors in acknowledgement of the fact that this item was purely for tramway use. It was stipulated that conductors should maintain the racks in good condition. The allowance was soon to be the cause of some discontent, which resulted in all conductors receiving the payment. By 1933, on the formation of the LPTB, the practice of conductors having to purchase this item had ceased, but it is not known exactly when this occurred.

Staff Passes

Authority was given on 25th October 1904 for passes to be issued to certain grades of staff who had to travel while on duty, and consisted of a card bearing a photograph of the user. It was renewable annually and had to be authorised by the Chief Officer of Tramways. Uniformed staff were able to travel to and from duty without charge.

Also in use were enamelled iron wrist badges, or "duty passes", oval in shape, with black lettering on a white background, which showed the legend: **London County Council Tramways**
No. ***
These were issued to permanent way and other outdoor non-uniformed staff, to allow them to go about their duties in connection with the tramway system.

Chapter 55
Miscellanea

Advertisements on Cars

It had always been the tradition that horse drawn tramcars and omnibuses carried advertisements, both within the vehicles and on the outsides. This source of revenue was considered by tramway companies to be, in some measure, the way in which the cost of the annual renovation of the cars was financed.

When the first electric cars were put into service, considerable thought was given to this matter. There was opposition from some members of the LCC in the first place to what was considered to be "disfigurement" of the tramcars; any attempt to place advertisements being resisted. This attitude was over-ruled however, as it was soon realised that, in the same way that it applied to the horse cars, the revenue received from advertising, particularly on the outsides of the cars, would be a useful contribution towards the cost of the annual repaint. The only constraint put upon the Tramways Department by the Highways Committee in February 1903 was that any advertising taken must be dealt with very carefully and "must be seen to be in good taste". Religious writings were always acceptable, and there was even a body, "The London Tramcar & Omnibus Scripture Text Mission" who made good use of the transparent "glacier" panel advertisements which fitted into the ventilator lights. On the other hand, it was stressed that no company dealing with alcohol in any form would be allowed access to the Council's cars. This ban, however, was eventually lifted.

For many years, Messrs. R. Frost Smith had been the contractor employed by the North Metropolitan Tramways Company for obtaining advertising matter for display on the company cars. When the Council became involved in the management of this source of income, it decided to put the agency work out to tender, which resulted in Frost Smith losing the contract to Messrs. Courtenay. Subsequently, other contractors became involved in the presentation of advertising matter, among them such well-known names as W. H. Smith & Son, Messrs. Sells, and Frank Mason & Co. Ltd.

Unlike the standards obtaining on the horse cars, the LCC were much more concerned about where such advertisements should appear on the electric cars. This resulted in a list being drawn up of sites and sizes to be strictly adhered to. On open-top bogie cars, side boards could be fixed to the decency panels above the car bodies, but were not to exceed 21 ft. 1 in. in length and 1 ft. 10½ in. in depth. Curved end boards were also permitted on either side of the car at each end, but were not to be more than 4 ft. 6 in. long. The dimensions quoted for panels placed on the outsides of single truck cars were a maximum of 16 ft. long, by 1 ft. 10½ in. deep.

With regard to advertisements to be seen by passengers seated inside the cars, this was at first restricted to coloured glass panels of "approved tints" and known as "advertising glaciers", which were made to fit into the frames of the ventilator lights on either side of a car. Each glacier space was rented to the advertiser for £1 per annum. Cost of preparing the advertising matter was to be borne by the LCC, except for printed cards, bills or glaciers, or for writing in gold, or for illustrations, where the advertiser would be expected to provide the material.

Early in 1905, encouraged by the success of this enterprise, the Council agreed to allow the use of enamelled metal finger plates which carried advertisements, to be fixed to the lower saloon door frames above and below the commode handles. Two standard lengths, 10 in. or 12 in. were authorised, in each case of a width of 3½ in., which was to cost the advertiser 8/- per car per annum.

With the standardisation obtained by the use of top-covered cars of classes E and E/1, together with the enclosure of the open top decks of the older cars, a new set of advertising panel lengths was published in conjunction with the use of enamelled iron plates. All new tenders called for plates in the following sizes:-

20 ft. 11 in. x 1 ft. 10½ in. Whole straight sides, bogie cars, £20 p.a.
16 ft.   x 1 ft. 10½ in. Whole straight sides, small cars, £16 p.a.
 5 ft. 1 in. x 1 ft. 10½ in. Corner plates, bogie cars, £5 p.a.
 4 ft. 10 in. x 1 ft. 10½ in. Corner plates, small cars, £5 p.a.

A new opportunity arose early in 1913 to obtain more revenue from advertising, when stencil service number plates were installed in all cars. The back-plate reflectors to these were soon used to carry advertisements, employing the same principle as was used with the number plates, with glass bead "spheres" being mounted in holes drilled in the plates. The Home & Colonial Stores took a block booking which allowed one advertisement bearing the name of the company to be displayed in all 1,675 cars in the fleet at a cost of 12/3d per car per year. At night, the notices must have looked very effective to passengers travelling on the upper decks and, no doubt, convinced some of them that they should use the goods and services provided by this company.

The Great War appeared to have had little effect on advertising, except that the severe restrictions placed upon lighting in the cars was the cause of the eventual demise of the glass-bead advertisements on the upper decks. The loss of these was in some measure made good by the use of the two side panels of the dashplates nearest to the body sides, upon which to paste printed paper advertisements.

New efforts were made after the war to obtain suitable material for display. One such contract, of interest to east London inhabitants, was for the display on 200 cars working in that area of ventilator "transparency" (formerly "glacier") panels of an advertisement for "wines from the Holy Land", for three years at a cost of £90 per annum. This was followed in May 1922 with advertisements on 100 window spaces at a cost of £150 per annum for three years, in English and Yiddish, for "Palwin" wines, brandies and liqueurs. Other products, such as "Pear's Soap", "Sanatogen", and "Hall's Tonic Wine", to name but a few, together with a number of religious notices were on display. These were augmented by the use of transparencies stuck on to the glass of the main windows, just below the cant rails, which had the advantage of being able to accommodate two oblong notices, with an oval shaped one in between, in each window space.

Inside every car were two glazed bulkhead panels, one at either end. One of these contained the faretable for the service that the car was being worked on at the time; the other carried advertising material, much of it concerning the Tramways Department. In February 1922, however, an agreement was made with the Education Department to allow the display of drawings and pictures which had been designed by the students of the LCC Central School of Arts and Crafts. There was a series of 12 posters, each one dealing with a different aspect of London life, and 2,000 copies were printed of every one for eventual display in the cars. The cost of this to the Education Department was £650. One of the most popular of these colourful notices showed a large multi-hued parrot, while another depicted a "domestic" scene in the monkey house, with the text matter in both cases urging the public to visit London Zoo, and recommending that they travel to and from it by LCC Tramways.

With regard to displays on the main external side panels, which by this time had come to be known as "whole sides", many large and well-known companies placed long term contracts for fixing enamelled iron plates bearing their advertisements to hundreds of cars. The newspaper industry was well represented in this field, the "Daily Mail" being one of the foremost. On the curved end panels, one could always see an advertisement on almost every car extolling the virtues of "Oakey's Wellington Knife Polish", while another urged people to use "Hudson's Soap".

An M class car, standing at Eltham Church, "dressed overall" with metal panel advertisements on the upper deck side panels, together with a full set of ventilator transparency advertisements. (LCC official view)

Advertisements on Tickets

In a similar way to that adopted with advertising on the cars, the Council was concerned that printed matter, particularly on the backs of tickets, did not offend any section of the community. At first, no advertisements for alcoholic drinks would be countenanced, but this restriction was eventually lifted, provided that due regard to advertising

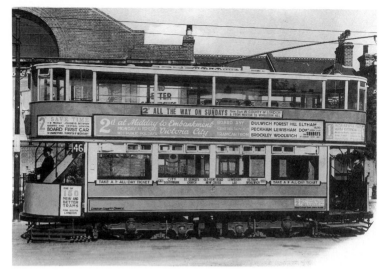

A new class E/3 car with a complete set of paper notices extolling the fares policy of the LCC Tramways. (Courtesy: L T Museum, 16514)

ethics was maintained. Even so, ticket advertising was still a minority activity so far as the LCC was concerned, more especially in the years after the Great War. Usually, there was so much essential information printed on both sides of tickets, that only a small proportion of the output was available for public use.

Handbills and Notices

Entertainments offered in London parks in summer time included performances by various bands of music, drawn from all over the region. These were publicised by the issue of small folded cards, distributed free to the public, and which included details of all tram services which went anywhere near the parks concerned. Similar cards were issued from time to time with regard to cricket and football matches played in London.

During the last years of the 1920s, the Tramways Department began an annual summer issue of "The London Holiday-Maker", which was a newspaper-type publication, issued free to all who asked for it. It contained tips and hints for people who wished to see the sights of London from a tramcar, and it also told them how to get to many places of interest in the LCC area. The final issue of this paper was made just a few weeks before the LPTB took over the tramways of London.

Fixed Site Advertising

In order to give maximum publicity to tramway services, particularly after the end of the Great War, the Council arranged to erect fixed signs at strategic positions throughout the whole of central London. These gave details of all service numbers and the destinations served. Many were illuminated by gas lamps which were installed inside the double sided signs. All were quite specific in the information imparted to the public.

Billboard advertising was used to bring LCC Tramways services to the notice of the public. (N. D. W. Elston. Courtesy: G. E. Baddeley)

Other important sites, such as the large tramway shelters which had been erected at busy points, were adequately provided with publicity material, with several even having illustrated track maps, whereby intending passengers could, by pressing the requisite button, find out the service number of the car required, together with the route it would take to its destination.

Maps and Guides

The first Official Tramways Guide was published for the London County Council by Odhams and Southwood & Smith & Co. Ltd. in May 1908, when the Highways Committee recommended that such a publication be made available to the people of London as a service to the travelling public and the Council's tramway system. It consisted of a booklet containing 132 pages of information, together with 20 pages of advertising matter, and was sold at a price of one penny. The first 54 pages of the guide described places of interest in London and how to get to them by tram, while the second part of the booklet gave a description of routes, services and fares. The term "route" was used to describe each sector of the track mileage in turn, upon which was superimposed a number of services or parts of services.

A similar publication was produced in much the same form for the year 1909, and sold at one penny. However, in 1911, a "Coronation Issue" was specially produced for the Council, this time by Advertising Concessions (Parent) Co. Ltd., which contained 200 pages of text and advertising, together with a track map, again showing numbered "routes" as before.

Meanwhile, reverting to 1909, the Council decided to publish a "6d map", showing all relevant details of the lines of the undertaking, and agreed with Messrs. G. W. Bacon on 16th February that they should produce it. The first batch was printed in 1910, but appeared to be something of a failure, as large stocks were left unsold. The result was that Bacon was released from the contract without penalty.

In much the same way, the Council decided that the 1911 Guide, admirable as it was, proved to be far too expensive for continuing publication. Instead, the decision was taken in June 1912 that, as the car services were about to be numbered, a more practical arrangement would be to issue a map and guide free to the public, printed on a single sheet of heavy paper.

The printing section of the Tramways Department was nominated to undertake the task, and for this a special folding machine was purchased for £99 from A. Edler & Co. of Old Street, London. A further £175 was spent on providing tin boxes in all cars, in which the free maps would be placed for issue to passengers. The first issue of the new map appeared in December 1912, with updated versions following as required.

After printing and issuing the maps for about 18 months, the Council came to the conclusion that it would be better to have the work done by a commercial printer and, in June 1914, commissioned Messrs. Johnson, Riddle & Co. to do it. The first contract was carried out at the rate of 8/6d per thousand, but the company indicated that, due to the war, the cost would have to go up. Several issues appeared during the next two years, but in May 1916, it was decided that no more would be printed until more favourable circumstances prevailed.

In the spring of 1918, Fell made the suggestion that, as there was a considerable quantity of suitable paper still in store for producing maps and guides, and due to the large numbers of British and Colonial servicemen on leave in and around London, it would be a worthwhile exercise to publish a guide for the benefit of the public. It was the only one to be issued in that year.

At last, in 1919, it was possible for arrangements to be made to publish the first post-war issue of the map and guide. Format was very similar to that used previously. This issue was also incorporated into the "Bus, Tube & Tram Guide to London", published in June 1920 by the "Evening News". Bus and Underground maps, however, were not included.

The next issue appeared in May 1921, to be followed at nominal six-monthly intervals thereafter, and were printed by Waterlow & Sons. By November 1923, the print order had reached 250,000 an issue, with an added 3,300 of special wall maps for use in public libraries, schools and other places where it was felt that they were required. Average cost of each issue of folded maps was between £550 and £600, while the wall maps added about £250 to each bill. With the November 1928 issue, printing reverted to the Tramways Department print room which, by then, had been transferred to new premises at Effra Road, Brixton. Thereafter, all issues came from the same source.

In 1924, the firm of Ed. J. Burrow & Co. Ltd. issued two comprehensive guide books, entitled "Round & About London By Tram", each of which sold for 6d. Volume I dealt with the districts north of the Thames, while Volume II covered the area south of the river, but included the Victoria Embankment. Each book consisted of about 232 pages, including advertising, and both issues included an official LCC Tramways Map & Guide, which was pasted into the inside of the back cover. Such was the popularity of these books, that both were re-issued in 1929.

Stopping Places & Stop Signs

When a tramway was inspected by the Board of Trade (later the Ministry of Transport) Inspecting Officer, he made recommendations regarding the imposition of compulsory stops which had to be made at certain places along the line of route. At all these places, the Council installed "stop signs" to inform motormen and intending passengers

*Left: One of the large number of ornamental post-mounted request
stop signs used on the LCC Tramways.*
*Right: A more traditional flag shaped sign, denoting a compulsory
stopping place.   (From LCC views)*

that "all cars stopped here". Several years later, it was decided that
"request stops" should be sited at suitable places between the main
stops. On 23rd June 1908, the Council resolved to apply to Parliament
for powers to allow the establishment of stops "in such positions as
may be thought fit".

This resulted in the Council being able to place stop signs on posts
in suitable places on the pavements, for which a small annual rate was
charged for each one the local authorities concerned.   Both signs
and posts were supplied and fixed by the LCC, who maintained a
staff to deal with them.   It was not within the power of the LCC
however, to fix stop signs to lamp posts and other articles of street
furniture.   On 19th July 1910, it was resolved that, as it would be
advanatgeous to be able to do this, and as the police already had such
powers, the Council would seek similar authority in its Tramways &
Improvements Bill for 1911.   Arising from this, it fell to the LCC to
fit and remove lamp posts at its own expense when wishing to use
the facility.   Examples of the costs involved when LCC-owned posts
were used are:- Nine Elms Lane to East Hill, Wandsworth, £67.15. 4d.
            Camden Town to Hampstead, £51.18.11d.
            Brixton to Herne Hill and Wandsworth to Putney, £21.

Several styles of sign were developed.   The compulsory stop was
indicated by the use of a white enamelled plate displaying the legend
ALL CARS
STOP
HERE

"ALL CARS" and "HERE" were in red enamel, with the word "STOP" being in blue on a white background. Request stops were distinguished by the use of red plates, the words "CARS" and "HERE IF REQUIRED" being in white, while the word "STOP" was in blue on a white oblong background.
CARS
STOP
HERE IF REQUIRED

The plates were made in several shapes. The first were oblong in form and double sided, either being suspended from brackets which were fixed to posts, or else being fitted round posts, with a face on either side of it. A variation on this theme, using a post-mounted sign was to be seen in the large numbers shaped rather like a "clover leaf" and enclosed in an ornate cast-iron frame, and used for both the compulsory and request types.

In certain places, the cars were compulsorily brought to a halt, but the stops were not allowed to be used by passengers. These were clearly marked "NOT FOR PASSENGERS" with white oblong "strip" signs, upon which the words were displayed in red, and being mounted horizontally across the centre of the stop sign plate.

Fare stage numbering was introduced gradually after 1913, spreading over a number of years before being fully implemented. Eventually, during the early months of 1926, a new and very distinctive type of sign made its appearance at "fare stage points", bearing the legend
LCC TRAMWAYS
FARE STAGE
ALL CARS
STOP
HERE
The plate had equally spaced enamelled sections in deep yellow and brown, the lettering being in brown and deep yellow. It was oblong in shape and mounted in a cast-iron frame.

At certain important points, such as central London termini and some exceptionally busy traffic points, as well as at hazardous or potentially dangerous places, illuminated signs were used. The lettering was as for compulsory stops, with each sign being made up of two glass panels, painted black on the inside, with clear or white opaque lettering, placed back to back in a frame, in which they stood about six inches apart at the top and three inches at the bottom. At night they were liiuminated from the inside by incandescent gas mantles.

Special illuminated signs of another type were to be seen at busy traffic points where information was given to intending passengers of all car services working from those stops. Signs of an unusual pattern were also to be seen outside car sheds at the entrance-exit points, where pedestrians were exhorted to "Beware, Cars Crossing". The illuminated faces of these were circular in shape, and were usually fixed on top of ten-feet high metal posts.

Passenger "Weather" Shelters

Another facility offered was the provision of "weather shelters" at many important points on the system, including most of the termini, and at busy car-changing points such as Westminster and New Cross Gate. Many were built of English Oak, the Westminster one being built in 1909 by Messrs. Elliotts Moulding & Joinery Co. for £185, which included glazed sides and frames for information posters. In the case of the shelter at New Cross Gate, this was also built in 1909 by the St. Pancras Iron Works Ltd. for £305, which included "incidentals".

The passenger waiting shelter at Stamford Hill was sited by the end of the lay-by track. It was fitted up with notices advising intending passengers of the services provided. (Courtesy: L T Museum, U 12746)

Queues

No regulations were framed until 1912 to deal with the control of intending passengers at stopping places. In most cases, it was "every man (or woman) for him (her) self", with often, great throngs of people fighting to get on to the cars. In June 1912, the Council decided to seek authority from Parliament to make and enforce a bye-law to compel six or more persons waiting for tramcars to form themselves into orderly lines, or queues, standing two abreast. Also included was a provision for queues to be controlled by officials of the Tramways Department. Despite the objection of the police to this, the Select Committee authorised the LCC to make such a bye-law and apply it. It does not, however, appear to have been regularly enforced, even during the Great War when the system was under the greatest pressure.

There were also several places where specially constructed "pens" or queues were placed, where the persons waiting for cars were obliged to stand, under cover, in orderly lines. Probably the best known was the series of structures at Blackfriars, where huge crowds gathered at peak times to travel on their homeward journeys from their workplaces.

Carriage of Dogs

It had never been the policy of the tramway companies to allow dogs to be carried on the horse cars, despite representations which were made by dog owners from time to time. This restriction was upheld by the LCC and maintained into the first years of electric car operation. After many more complaints made over a period of several years, the Council, in 1911, gave way and allowed dogs to be carried, but only at the discretion of conductors and under strict control by the passengers concerned. No fare was payable for any animal, but all dogs had to be taken to the upper decks of the cars.

London County Council Steamboats

The River Thames was always important for travel; in fact, from the founding of London until about 1840 it was the only effective highway through and near the capital. The railways changed all that in the space of a few years, making the river more or less redundant for the passage of regular travellers, although "trippers" and leisure seekers were still very much catered for.

When the LCC took control of the metropolis, involvement in the provision of public transport was sought by that body, mainly in street tramways but with the possibility also of making use of the river for journeys between Greenwich and Millwall in the east, the City and Westminster, and westwards to and from Chelsea and Putney. It was even considered that Hammersmith in the west and Woolwich in the east could be included.

The Progressive Party took up the challenge in 1903, at the same time as the first electrification project for tramways was under way, deciding that a comprehensive service should be provided. Armed with the Thames River Steamboat Service Act, 1904, the Council set about making the dream a reality. Thirty purpose-built boats were purchased at between £5,950 and £6,500 each; crews were recruited and put under the charge of Capt. A. R. Owen, who, as manager, was responsible to the Rivers Committee for all aspects of the proposed services. A large number of piers were purchased, seventeen from the Thames Conservancy Board, six from the Thames Steamboat Company (1897) Ltd., the Greenwich Pier from the Greenwich Pier Company and the Charing Cross Pier from the South Eastern & Chatham Railway. Other properties and two coal hulks were also taken over. The cost incurred in setting up this service was £28,000 in addition to that of the boats.

The steamboats were named after distinguished persons of the day "more particularly connected with the River Thames or by reason of their work in connection therewith". Those so honoured were:- King Alfred, Fitz Ailwin, Alleyn, Boydell, Brunel, Carlyle, Caxton, Chaucer, Colechurch, Francis Drake, Gibbon, Earl Godwin, Gresham, Edmund Ironside, Ben Jonson, Charles Lamb, Marlowe, Thomas More, Morris, Olaf, Pepys, Purcell, Raleigh, Rennie, Shakespeare, Sloane, Turner, Vanbrugh, Whittington, Christopher Wren.

From 17th June 1905, when the service was inaugurated by HRH The Prince of Wales, who travelled to Greenwich by boat and returned to Westminster by tram, steamboats were run at regular 15-minute intervals throughout each day of that summer. Boats called at all piers between Hammersmith and Greenwich, with special extra early boats for workmen, and additional "express" boats in the mornings and evenings. After a few days, the service was divided at Westminster, but several weeks later, a divided service was also worked between Greenwich and Chelsea (Cadogan Pier). One of the reasons given for this change was that, due to certain heavy tidal flows, better time-keeping could result by working the service in this way.

Coupled with the steamboat service, special return tickets were issued, allowing the holders to travel by tram on the second journey to either Greenwich or Westminster, which arrangement was soon extended to cover the Charing Cross, Temple, Waterloo and Blackfriars Piers. Later still in the summer of 1905, other tramway services calling near to other piers were brought into the scheme at return fares from 2½d to 6d. For the 13 weeks to 16th September, 2,763,123 passengers were carried, of which 155,286 used the trams for the return journeys. £21,718 went to the Steamboat Account.

As expected, traffic was less from the end of the autumn, but it was anticipated that the numbers of passengers would rise again in the spring of 1906 and, as an insurance, reduced services were run during the winter of 1905. Even with this service at very low fares, several of the private boat undertakings, threatened by the new venture, cut their fares to ridiculously low levels, an example being a journey from Greenwich to Westminster, or vice versa, for as little as 1½d.

The summer service in 1906 was not so well patronised as in the previous year, and it was decided that as a loss was incurred on the 1905-06 winter service, the boats would be withdrawn during the coming winter. In December 1906, the service was transferred to the Highways Committee, with the intention of integrating it into "part of the general traffic service of London". One of the effects to be seen was that the annual overhaul of the boats was to be placed upon the shoulders of the Tramways Manager!

A summer-months-only service was arranged for 1907, the return fare between London and Greenwich being 7d, with a similar fare to Putney. Service ceased as from 1st November 1907 for the winter, and all boats were laid up in the Surrey Commercial Docks. They were never used again! Despite efforts which were made over several years to sell off the boats, some remained to be broken up where they lay. It is recorded that by the beginning of July 1909, eight boats had been disposed of at the following prices:-

Alleyn	£705	Colechurch	£500
Ben Jonson	£500	Olaf	£500
Brunel	£500	Turner	£500
Carlyle	£705	Whittington	£500

This excursion into water transport, admirable though the principle may have been, cost the ratepayers of London £137,083. 1.10d in losses for operating the services, in addition to the capital costs. It also cost the Progressives their prestige and more particularly, the majority which they held in the Council for some time to come afterwards.

LCC steamboats plied the Thames to Greenwich, and here, two of the vessels are moored at that pier. (Courtesy: F. L. Dix)

Financial Arrangements

The founding of the LCC Tramways was an enormous step for the Council to take, knowing as it did that the sums to be expended in buying-in all the tramway companies within the County, together with electrification costs after they were purchased, would total several million pounds.

Under the terms of the Local Government Act, 1888, the Council was empowered to raise money to finance loans to the 28 Metropolitan Boroughs; for funding all departments of the County Council; and for carrying out a number of major projects including the purchase of the tramway companies and electrification of the network. The methods used were that, in the first place, a Money Bill had to be promoted each year and, depending upon the attitude of Parliament, the Bill would be enacted, usually with some of the content withdrawn. Following this, the County Council made preparations for:-

(a) the creation and issue of Consolidated Stock;
(b) arranging for access to the Consolidated Loans Fund;
(c) acting otherwise in accordance with the provisions of the Act(s) regulating the raising of money for capital purposes;
(d) grants from central government:

It was usual for Bonds to be issued in conjunction with the Consolidated Loans Fund. The London County Consolidated Stock was, at that time, usually issued at 3%.

County Council income came mainly in the form of a proportion of an Annual Rate which was levied upon all property owners and householders, and which was collected on behalf of the Council by the local authorities in each of the 28 boroughs. However, so far as the Tramways Department was concerned, it was expected that the undertaking would eventually make substantial operating surpluses, making it self-sufficient, but with the guarantee that in the event of a shortfall of income, the County could call upon the ratepayers to make good any deficiency.

The first big expense was the purchase of the lines and buildings of the London Street Tramways and North Metropolitan Tramways companies in 1895 and 1896, followed in 1899 by the outright purchase of the London Tramways Company Limited, together with the others as they fell due in the first decade of the twentieth century.

Progressive capital expenditure from 1896 to 1906, divided into the sums involved for both north and south sections is shown below in the first table, while from 1907 onwards it is shown in the second table as a single figure for the whole of the system.

Year	Section	Total Sum	Year	Section	Total Sum
1896	North	£ 108,091			
1897		£ 108,091			
1898		£ 850,861			
1899		£ 817,739	1899	South	£ 880,705
1900		£ 817,739	1900		£ 892,816
1901		£ 845,385	1901		£ 901,528
1902		£ 845,385	1902		£ 896,971
1903		£ 849,530	1903		£1,504,464
1904		£ 854,034	1904		£2,167,235
1905		£ 871,536	1905		£2,666,699
1906		£1,118,166	1906		£3,070,829

From 1906 the two sections were combined.

Year	Total Sum	Year	Total Sum	Year	Total Sum
1907	£ 6,946,310	then		1926	nil return
1908	£ 8,414,591	1919	£13,273,991	1927	£17,246,967
1909	£ 9,483,562	1920	£14,128,052	1928	£17,569,636
1910	£10,709,504	1921	nil return	1929	£17,821,825
1911	£11,618,813	1922	£15,525,057	1930	£18,126,719
1912	£12,193,648	1923	£16,326,430	1931	£18,762,368
1913	£12,947,926	1924	£16,497,850	1932	£19,324,944
1914	£13,357,203	1925	£17,025,583	1933	£19,530,452

Due to war conditions, the 1915-1918 figures were not published.

Income and Expenditure

Throughout its existence the Council showed a working surplus on receipts as against expenditure. In some years, however, after certain obligatory payments such as sinking fund and other debt charges had been made, it was left with a deficiency. In these years, recourse had to be made to using reserve funds or by calling on the ratepayers.

Income and Expenditure Account

LCC (Southern) Tramways

Year	Gross Income	Expenditure	Net Income
1899	£ 101,905	£ 86,948	£ 14,957
1900	£ 468,898	£ 375,907	£ 92,991
1901	£ 463,062	£ 400,351	£ 62,711
1902	£ 462,133	£ 409,623	£ 52,510
1903	£ 444,699	£ 397,081	£ 47,618
1904	£ 536,219	£ 443,986	£ 92,233
1905	£ 682,095	£ 503,087	£ 179,008
1906	£ 792,813	£ 579,468	£ 213,345

LCC Tramways

Year	Gross Income	Expenditure	Net Income
1907	£1,413,055	£1,075,094	£ 337,961
1908	£1,671,861	£1,170,115	£ 501,746
1909	£1,845,798	£1,201,419	£ 644,379
1910	£2,019,123	£1,233,821	£ 785,302
1911	£2,232,216	£1,337,624	£ 894,592
1912	£2,366,128	£1,421,468	£ 944,660
1913	£2,251,729	£1,511,845	£ 739,884
1914	£2,268,668	£1,614,687	£ 653,981
then			
1919	£3,578,256	£2,858,414	£ 719,842
1920	£4,282,114	£3,680,899	£ 601,215
1921	figures not available		
1922	£5,156,509	£4,597,330	£ 559,179
1923	£4,898,066	£4,038,027	£ 860,039
1924	£4,394,276	£3,848,822	£ 545,454
1925	£4,197,769	£3,976,802	£ 220,967
1926	figures not available		
1927	£4,036,470	£3,823,533	£ 212,937
1928	£4,232,755	£3,692,451	£ 540,304
1929	£4,315,214	£3,615,491	£ 699,723
1930	£4,404,074	£3,546,158	£ 857,916
1931	£4,313,879	£3,536,894	£ 776,985
1932	£4,176,094	£3,516,760	£ 659,334
1933	£4,073,417	£3,394,220	£ 679,197
1933*	£1,100,000		

* The estimate made for the three months from 1st April 1933 until the undertaking was handed over to the LPTB on 1st July, suggested

that the numbers of passengers would be likely to be about 170 million giving a gross income of about £1,100,000. Working on averages of previous years, it could have been expected that net income would be about £200,000.

A further burden imposed upon the Council was that municipal rates had to be paid for every section of track in every street in every borough. As, an example, in the financial year 1921-22, the sum of £79,871. 3. 9d was paid under this head. Where the overhead wires were used, an extra small sum had to be paid for every pole planted. Even stop sign poles were not exempt - they had to be paid for as well!

Miscellaneous Statistics

Year	Car Miles	Electric Cars	Horse Cars	Horses	Units of Power	Passenger Tickets § Sold
1899*	2,416,671		434	3,957	+ 87 buses	25,650,482
1900*	10,208,161		435	4,076	+ 90 buses	117,992,713
1901*	10,399,058		410	4,159	+ 55 buses	118,281,320
1902*	10,371,866		449	4,148	incl. buses	119,880,559
1903*	10,110,940		517	4,035		109,615,496
1904*	11,536,534	306	290	2,012	5,919,404	133,139,085
1905*	14,081,397	401	227	1,440	16,478.997	164,818,560
1906*	15,817,562	414	216	1,515	21,140,484	185,512,421
1907	30,130,297	671	723	5,868	32,782,702	314,227,090
1908	35,561,189	965	621	4,100	57,362,842	372,515,754
1909	39,119,472	1,170	516	3,123	77,446,427	412,913,841
1910	43,160,186	1,326	127	1,416	96,812,256	451,439,216
1911	48,101,570	1,551	107	1,009	111,527,301	504,715,326
1912	50,457,812	1,583	96	733	122,307,298	533,440,233
1913	53,943,104	1,673	74	584	143,875,604	512,652,653
1914	59,209,289	1,726	56	329	159,518,772	522,952,640
1915	n/a	n/a	n/a	n/a	n/a	550,479,993
1916	n/a	n/a	n/a	n/a	n/a	545,273,397
1917	n/a	n/a	n/a	n/a	n/a	586,127,976
1918	n/a	n/a	n/a	n/a	n/a	593,516,141
1919	48,052,801	1,667	9		103,336,432	636,157,361
1920	53,156,060	1,667	9		119,563,443	685,124,156
1921	n/a	n/a	n/a	n/a	n/a	689,452,036
1922	59,532,087	1,775	2		123,683,417	688,151,316
1923	63,381,367	1,852	2		134,990,784	733,811,367
1924	64,118,565	1,852	2		147,817,326	689,015,086
1925	68,068,216	1,852			143,330,158	682,595,733
1926	n/a	n/a			n/a	691,472,969
1927	68,922,232	1,832			150,720,714	678,422,989
1928	71,644,159	1,819			161,276,025	714,175,261
1929	70,658,768	1,817			167,342,079	713,035,141
1930	70,923,718	1,800			172,644,923	722,888,777
1931	70,300,328	1,834			173,900,291	713,642,686
1932	70,325,579	1,712			191,046,588	689,050,407
1933	69,553,012	1,713			193,923,847	677,011,212
1933**	17,300,000	1,713			48,400,000	169,252,800

§   Total tickets sold, 17,448,404,193.
   Total passenger places occupied including use of return, transfer and all-day tickets about 20,000 million.
*   Information as at 31st March each year.
   Does not include any company undertakings.
   Until 1906, figures show electrified and southern system only.
**   Estimated figures for the period 1st April - 31st July 1933.

964

Tramways Department Head Office

The Head Office of the LCC Tramways was established at 301/303 Camberwell New Road, which was previously the office of the London Tramways Company. With the expansion of the tramway undertaking, the accommodation had, by the end of 1904 become somewhat over-crowded. In April 1906, this lack of working space caused the Council to convert the covered way entrance at the east end of the building into additional office accommodation.

At the same time, a reorganisation was taking place on the tramway system north of the Thames. Included in the hand-over of the North Metropolitan Tramways Company were several offices, two of these being at 62 Finsbury Pavement, E.C. and at Paul Street, Finsbury which between them served as the company main offices. The premises at Finsbury Pavement belonged to the Metropolitan Electric Tramways (who had purchased the tramway company assets in Middlesex), while the Paul Street building was leased to the company. The Council took an extended option on both premises in March 1906, deciding to use those at Finsbury Pavement as a new Head Office for the Tramways Department. Formalities completed, the department moved there in June 1906, the premises at Camberwell then becoming the Southern Divisional Offices of the LCCT, but continuing to house the ticket section until 1910. The newly formed Northern Division had its offices installed at the Finsbury Pavement address, where it remained until December 1919, when it was removed to Hackney car shed.

Such was the rate of expansion of the Tramways Department that, by December 1908, both the Head Office and the Paul Street extension were full, requiring the use of additional temporary premises at Evelyn House, Moorgate, taken on a three-year lease as from Christmas 1908 at a rent of £650 per annum. From this time on, Head Office was moved on several occasions, as is shown in the following table:-

1899 to June 1906	303 Camberwell New Road, Camberwell.
1906 to February 1918	62 Finsbury Pavement, Finsbury.
1918 to February 1923	23 Belvedere Road, Lambeth.
1923 to December 1928	Old Education Offices, Victoria Embankment. (except for ticket sections, as described)
1928 to July 1933	23 Belvedere Road, Lambeth.

Probably the best known address so far as the LCC Tramways was concerned was No. 23 Belvedere Road. However, this was but one of a number of properties in and around Belvedere Road to be used by various sections of the Tramways Department over the course of many years.

The County Hall

After the formation of the London County Council in 1889, it became necessary to provide adequate accommodation for the many people who would provide services for the new county. A site, known as Pedlar's Acre, Lambeth was purchased in the early years of the twentieth century upon which to construct a new County Hall. This site, fronting on to the River Thames, almost opposite Westminster Hall, had as its eastern boundary the street known as Belvedere Road, which was included in the area of the purchased site. Building work on the new edifice started in 1912 with King George V laying the foundation stone, but was incomplete when the war of 1914 began. Following the armistice of 1918, work was re-started on the project, taking many years to complete. During the course of the second phase of construction, the buildings in Belvedere Road were included as part of the new development, even though they were to retain their separate identities and means of access.

Building work resulted in the removal of the Tramways Department out of and back again into No. 23. The final move coincided with the removal of the ticket checking section and other ancillary departments into other premises in south London. An exception was an emergency breakdown tender and crew stationed at No. 23 and whose chargehand moved, in November 1930, to live on site in a flat on the second floor of No. 27. After the ticket checking section moved away in September 1928, the work of reconstruction and adaptation of the buildings for Head Office staff commenced, and proceeded day and night. As seen above, the removal of headquarters into the refurbished premises took place in December, where the staff were then to remain until the undertaking was transferred to the L P T B on 1st July 1933.

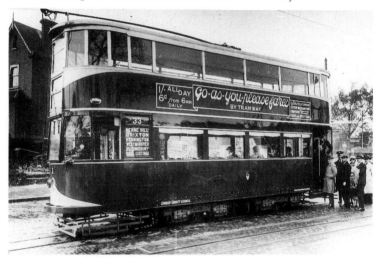

LCC Tramways No. 1 ("Bluebird"), put into service in 1932, stands at Manor House terminus of service 33. It was the only example of what was intended to be a new fleet of modern cars. (*LCC official view*)

Chapter 56
London Transport Takes Over

At midnight on 30th June/1st July 1933 the London County Council Tramways ceased to exist. The whole undertaking became part of the assets of the London Passenger Transport Board. On 1st July, every car in the fleet was seen to belong to the new owner, as paper notices had been affixed to each vehicle during the night, showing the name and address of the new Board. At the front nearside ends was seen "London Passenger Transport Board" and at the back ends "55 Broadway, S.W.1." However, apart from this, everything else on the LCC system appeared outwardly to be the same as it had previously been. But this was not to last for very long.

That a great change had occurred was much more noticeable on the small systems which operated around the edge of London, such as those of Bexley UDC Tramways and Erith Council Tramways. On those two sections, a number of ex-LCC class M cars had been transferred within a week of the new Board taking over, to replace a number of well worn cars and also to add to the fleets of both lines. Within three months of the takeover, all the cars previously owned by Bexley had gone, together with a dozen from Erith, all replaced by class M cars in red livery. Class E/1 cars of 1929 construction soon began to appear in the Walthamstow area, while several of the Walthamstow large and fairly new bogie cars turned up on services working out of Hollway car shed. Next, it was the turn of Croydon, where most of their older cars were replaced by ex-LCC cars.

Within two years, plans were being made for the replacement of several tramway routes by trolleybuses, from Hounslow and Hampton Court to Shepherds Bush and Hammersmith; from Plumstead to Dartford and from Abbey Wood to Erith and Bexleyheath, together with an extension of trolleybus overhead wiring from Abbey Wod and Plumstead to Woolwich Ferry, the new vehicles working alongside the existing tramways; from Sutton to Croydon and Crystal Palace. With these conversions, the ex-LCC routes and services suffered minor changes. Service 26 ceased to work between Hammersmith and Kew Bridge, while in the south-east, service 40 was withdrawn between Abbey Wood and Woolwich, although services 36 and 38 continued to work alongside the new trolleybuses.

Gradually, over almost the next five years, trolleybuses replaced almost all of the trams on the north side of the Thames. With these conversions, many of the cars of classes E and M were withdrawn and taken to Walthamstow, where they were broken up on open ground at the back of the car shed. Similar work also went on in Hampstead car shed as from the beginning of 1938. The two tram routes between the north end of Kingsway Subway, one to "The Angel", Islington, Holloway and "Archway Tavern", the other to Manor House, where it left the Holloway line about half a mile north of "The Angel", however, survived. Services 33 and 35 were to remain in operation until 1952.

On the south side, the only other ex-LCC conversions were between Putney, Wandsworth, Tooting Broadway and Tooting Junction, and between Wandsworth, Battersea "Prince's Head" and Clapham Junction. Holloway and Wandsworth car sheds became joint tram and trolleybus depots. Some of the class E cars removed from service as a result of these conversions were dismantled at Purley car shed formerly belonging to Croydon Corporation, while others were dealt with at the ex-SMET depot at Aurelia Road, Mitcham.

At the beginning of the tram to trolleybus conversion programme, it was not intended that all the tramways would be abandoned - not at least in the foreseeable future. It was expected in 1935 that much of the tramway system would be in use for up to another ten years. To cater for this, a modernisation programme was initiated, in which up to 1,000 tramcars, nearly all in the ex-LCC fleet, were to be rehabilitated up to a standard said to approach that provided by the latest cars of 1930/31 and the new trolleybuses. In the event, due to another change of plan, by which the trolleybuses would replace trams much more quickly, only 154 were upgraded, although a start was made in providing vestibule screens for the remainder of the cars which would be likely to stay in service for several more years.

Then came the 1939 war, which was to drag on until 1945. After the completion of the north side conversions, all further work stopped. Many of the cars taken out of service were moved to Hampstead car shed, access tracks being retained for this purpose. Other cars were taken to Purley shed, where they were stored. This proved to be a wise decision as, before long, many of them had to be returned to service to replace cars destroyed or seriously damaged as a result of the bombing of London. Purley was also used as a store for damaged cars. At the end of the war, many of those left in store were "sold out of service", with some ending up as holiday homes, while others were put to use as garden sheds and outhouses.

Following the end of hostilities, the Board decided that no more new trolleybus overhead would be erected, but as soon as conditions would permit, the remainder of the trams would be replaced with diesel engine motor omnibuses. This programme began in 1950 and took two years to complete. The first trams to go were those working between Wandsworth, Clapham Junction and central London and, at about three-monthly intervals, working roughly from west to east, all the rest were replaced. At the beginning of this phase, a number of cars taken into Board service from Metropolitan Electric Tramways and London United Tramways were sold to Leeds City Tramways, where, in that city, they were to join several of the class HR/2 cars which had been purchased by Leeds before the war.

For those remaining in London it was to be a fiery end. A large site was secured at Penhall Road, Charlton, where tracks were laid, upon which those cars taken out of service would stand until handed over to the demolition contractor. This temporary depot came to be known as the "Tramatorium" because of its regular use as a burning ground for most of the cars. The policy adopted was that the oldest and less roadworthy cars were to be disposed of first. This involved the transfer of newer and better cars to the services which were still to remain. Over the next two years, many of the "1922" and "1929" class E/1 cars, all of the class E/3 cars together with those of class HR/2 which had trolley poles, gravitated eastwards and ended up on services working out of New Cross and Abbey Wood depots. Those of class HR/2 which were not trolley fitted, were taken to Penhall Road in October 1951 when the Dulwich services were converted. The last of London's trams went there following the closure of services 36, 38, 40, 44, 46 and 72 on the night of 5th July 1952.

Five cars and much memorabilia "escaped" the fires. Class E/1 car, No. 1025, was preserved by London Transport, cleaned up and placed in their museum, where it still stands, while snowbroom No. 022 was saved and eventually handed over to and restored by members of the London County Council Tramways Trust to its original condition as class B car No. 106. It is now working in service on the line of the National Tramway Museum, Crich, Derbyshire. LCC experimental car No. 1, which had also been sold to Leeds, was brought back to London after the Leeds system closed and, after being on display in the London Transport Museum, was presented to the Tramway Museum Society with the object of preserving the car and eventually restoring it to working order. It is at present standing as a static exhibit at the Museum, painted in London Transport livery.

Another E/1, No. 1622, sold by London Transport in 1946 and used as a holiday home, was brought back by the same band of enthusiasts who had rebuilt No. 106, and is currently being restored by them. Finally, No. 1858, of LCC class HR/2, was saved from the torch by Peter J. Davis, a member of this History Group, who purchased it from London Transport, and had it placed in secure surroundings at Chessington Zoo in Surrey, where it stood for some years as a mute reminder of London's electric tramways. It was subsequently taken to the East Anglia Transport Museum at Carlton Colville, Lowestoft, where it has been restored to working order and is now in service on the line of that museum.

It is almost inconceivable that any of the horse cars should have survived, but several did and are all in various stages of preservation. An ex-London Tramways Company car was rescued from a farm in Kent several years ago, where it had been doing duty as a tool store. The car body, still standing on its original wheels had been stored in a barn and, although without its platforms and upper works, it is in a reasonable condition. It is now part of the London Transport Collection and is awaiting restoration. A similar car is at the National Tramway Museum, but present plans with regard to its eventual restoration are unclear.

A North Metropolitan Tramways Company car, No. 39, is at present preserved in "kit form" by the London County Council Tramways Trust, having been dismantled many years ago as a first move towards its preservation and eventual restoration. Parts of this are on loan to the Tramway Museum, Crich, for display purposes. Several other examples have been located over the years, one of which, North Metropolitan Tramways No. 707 is being prepared for restoration by an enthusiast in the Thames Valley area. Others are reported to be standing in several locations in the southern counties, but nothing is known about the condition of any of them.

With regard to the removal of the many miles of tram track from the streets, this work was carried out in the years before the 1939 war in something approaching a leisurely manner. Often, the rails were covered up with tar compound, under which they remained for many years. In some of the outer areas, sections of track still remain, buried beneath new road surfaces. Some sections of disused conduit track, particularly pointwork, which were still in the road during the 1939 war, were lifted as required to replace sections in other parts of London which were damaged by bombing. With the complete abandonment of the tramways, all but a couple of sections of the tracks in what was the London County Council area were eventually lifted.

The Kingsway Subway, however, is still largely intact. Apart from the southern end of it being adapted for use as a one-way road for motor traffic, most of the remainder is in much the same condition as it was after the last tram ran through it in April 1952. Even the northern ramp is still there, complete with its conduit tracks, and protected from the activities of Londoners by a pair of rusting iron gates, although plans are now being made to cover the area and use it as part of the roadway.

Several other visual reminders of the vast tramway system of the LCC remain. The first of these, Greenwich generating station, is still standing and supplies power, albeit on a much reduced scale, to the Underground railways in East London. But in 1991, it seems that even this monument to A. L. C. Fell, may be under threat of closure. The second, the buildings of the Central Repair Depot at Charlton, another memorial to Fell, together with its approach road aptly (and belatedly) named "Felltram Way", are still in the condition that they were at the end of the tramways, but parts of the depot premises are now in use as warehouses for private industry. Lastly, several of the car sheds are still being used for various industrial purposes, but are clearly and unmistakeably LCC Tramway buildings.

What of the London County Council itself, that early example of a socially – minded authority, who sought to provide the citizens of its county area with a public transport system which, in its day, was recorded as being second-to-none in all respects? It too, was replaced by a body known as the Greater London Council, which itself has been abolished by parliament, a predecessor of which created the London County Council in the first place. The centre of power of the LCC, County Hall, standing on the south bank of the Thames almost opposite the Palace of Westminster, may possibly end its days as a hotel !

The London Tramways History Group

G. E. Baddeley, B. Connelly, P. J. Davis, C. E. Holland, D. W. K. Jones, M. B. Leahy, G. W. Morant, E. R. Oakley, C. S. Smeeton, C. L. Withey. The Light Rail Transit Association.
The Tramway & Light Railway Society.

Appendix

BIBLIOGRAPHY

The Public Record Office, Kew. Documents and Papers

Board of Trade Papers relating to the introduction of Tramways in London.

Applications to the Board of Trade for Provisional Orders.

Board of Trade Papers relating to Inspections of Tramways.

Board of Trade (later Ministry of Transport) Annual Returns for Tramways.

Board of Trade (later Ministry of Transport) Accident Reports.

Board of Trade Reports to the House of Commons, various years since 1871.

London Traffic Advisory Committee Reports and Minutes.

Metropolitan Police Reports.

Ministry of Munitions Reports and Documents, 1914 - 1919.

Ministry of Transport Reports, 1919 - 1932.

House of Lords Library Papers

Parliamentary Bills and Acts.

Greater London Record Office, Islington, London N. 1.

Local Government Reports

Metropolitan Board of Works:-

Annual Reports, 1860 - 1888.

Report of the Parliamentary Committee on Tramway Schemes for the year 1871.

London County Council:-

Highways Committee Reports, 1889 - 1933.

Tramways belonging to Local Authorities, 1890.

Minutes of Council Meetings.

Annual Reports, General and Financial.

Presented Papers and Documents.

Tramway Legislation Report, 1899.

Tramway Development Report, 1914.

Various Borough Council Reports on Tramways.

Tramway Museum Society Library Papers

Various Reports.

The British Library, Colindale

Technical Papers and Journals

The Electrical Review.

The Municipal Journal.

The Light Railway & Tramway Journal.

The Tramway & Railway Express.

Tramway & Railway World.

The Contract Journal.

The Electrician.

The Engineer.

Engineering.

Various Local Newspapers.

Books

Baddeley, G. E. B. Com., M.C.I.T.	Tramways of Croydon	L.R.T.A./T.L.R.S.	1983
Baddeley, G. E. & Oakley, E. R.	Current Collection Methods for Tramway & Trolleybus Systems	Nemo Productions	1975
Barker, T. C. & Robbins, R. M.	A History of London Transport, Volume I.	George Allen & Unwin	1963
Bett, W. H. & Gillham, J. C.	Great British Tramway Networks	L.R.T.A.	1957
Clark, D. K.	Tramways, Their Construction & Working	Crosby, Lockwood & Co.	1878
Claydon, G. B. C.B., Ll.B., M.I.T.A.	H. M. Railway Inspectorate	L.R.T.A. ("Tramway Review")	1984
Dover, A. T. M.I.E.E., A.A.I.E.E.	Electric Traction	Pitman	1929
Gibbon, Sir Gwilym & Bell, R. W.	History of the L.C.C. 1899 - 1939	L.C.C.	1939
Guilmartin, G. H.	Bare Empty Sheds	T.L.R.S.	1986
Harper, C. G.	Round And About London By Tram	E. J. Burrows	1924 & 1929
Hopkins, A. Bassett	Tramway Legislation in London	L.C.C.	1890
Jackson, E. W.	Achievement, a Short History of the L.C.C.	Longmans	1965
Klapper, C. M.C.I.T.	Golden Age of Tramways	Routledge & Kegan Paul	1961
Millar, A. A.M.I.C.E.	The Electrical Reconstruction of the South London Tramways on the Conduit System	Institution of Civil Engineers	1904
Price, J. H.	Hurst, Nelson Tramcars	Price/Nemo	1977
	The British Electric Car Co.	Price/Nemo	1978
	Mountain & Gibson	Price/Nemo	1980
	Tramcar, Carriage & Wagon Builders of Birmingham	Price/Nemo	1982
Smeeton, C. S.	Metropolitan Electric Tramways, Volume I.	L.R.T.A./T.L.R.S.	1984
	-do- Volume II.		1986
"Southeastern"	Tramways of Woolwich & Southeast London	L.R.T.A.	1963
"Rodinglea"	Tramways of East London	L.R.T.A.	1967
"Kennington"	L.C.C. Tramways Handbook	T.L.R.S.	1970

London County Council Publications

Official Tramways Guide	1908
	1909
	1911
The Pullman Review	1932
The London Holidaymaker	1932
Staff Magazines, Various Issues	
Tramways Maps & Guides	1912 - 1933

Published Papers

Bett, W. H.	Some Notes on the "Effra Road" Tickets of the L.C.C. Tramways and Their Successors		
		T.T.S./L.R.T.A.	1951

Dunbar, C. S. F.C.I.T.	Idealism & Competition	L.R.T.A.	1967
	Tramways in Wandsworth & Battersea	L.R.T.A.	1971
	London's Tramway Subway	L.R.T.A.	1975
Oakley, E. R. & Withey, C. L.	Improving London's Trams, 1932 - 1937	L.R.T.A.	1988
Willsher, M. J. D. B. Sc., A.L.A.	The L.C.C. Trailers	L.R.T.A.	1981

Unpublished Material

| Morant A. W. | London's Tramways, Up To 1915 |
| McCall, A. W. | L.C.C.T. Routes & Services, 1913 - 1933 |

Walter Gratwicke Memorial Lectures, Tramway & Light Railway Society

Wilson, F. E. M.C.I.T., F.P.W.I.	Tramway Permanent Way, With Special Reference to the L C C Tramways	1970
Lee, C. E. F.C.I.T.	Some Tramway Pioneers, Known & Unknown	1971
Dunbar, C. S. F.C.I.T.	Fossilised by Statute - Trams and the Law	1972
Jenson, A. G. M.B.E., F.R.I.B.A.	Tramway Architecture	1973
Price, J. H.	The Brush Electrical Engineering Company and its Tramcars	1975
Goodwyn, A. M.	Evolution of the British Electric Tramcar Truck	1976
Baddeley, G. E. B.Com., M.C.I.T.	Tramcar Liveries	1977
Oakley, E. R.	The British Horse Tram Era	1978
Bond, A. W. O.B.E., F.C.A.	The British Tram, History's Orphan	1979
Smeeton, Cyril S.	Modernisation Of The London Company Tramways	1986

ACTS OF PARLIAMENT

The law as prescribed with regard to the construction and operation of tramways in Britain was quite rigid in its application, requiring the authority of Parliament to every proposal made. In the first place, the promoters were obliged to present each set of proposals to Parliament in a document known as a Bill, prepared on behalf of the applicant by a Parliamentary Agent. The Bill contained considerable detail regarding the proposed method and costs of construction, style of operation and form of motive power, together with rules for passengers and staff. This was followed by a detailed description of the lines to be constructed and the routes to be followed, all entered into the document as a number of "Tramways". On its passage through the House of Commons Committee stages, objections to some or all of its content contained in the Bill could be heard, which sometimes resulted in the deletion of certain clauses, and often, one or more of the proposed Tramways also being struck out. Eventually, once agreement had been reached and the Bill had been "read" a third time, the Passed Bill would then go to the House of Lords for ratification, finally emerging as an Act of Parliament once the Royal Assent had been given.

General Acts of Parliament

The Metropolis Management Act, 1855, established the Metropolitan Board of Works.
The Local Government Act, 1888, established the London County Council as from 1st April 1889, but the Council took office on 21st March 1889.
The Local Government Act, 1899, established the Metropolitan Borough Councils, of which there were 28.

Acts Affecting the London County Council

When the London County Council decided to become a tramway operator, it first of all had to submit a Bill to Parliament, requesting that it be allowed to take over the powers previously enjoyed by the Metropolitan Board of Works, which were, that when any "tramway" had been in existence for a period of twenty-one years (that is, from the date of the authorising Act), the Board was empowered to purchase that "tramway" within a six months' time limit, or at seven year intervals thereafter.

London County Tramways Act, 1896 (59-60 Vic. Ch. li) authorised the transfer of these rights to the Council, and giving the necessary powers to proceed with the purchase of parts of three of the companies then operating within the LCC area.

London County Tramways Act, 1900 (63-64 Vic. Ch. cclxx).
Royal Assent, 6th August 1900. It authorised the construction of new lines for operation in north London as horse tramways only, and also provided for the electrification of the lines from Tooting to various London termini.

London County Tramways (Electrical Powers) Act, 1900 (63-64 Vic. Ch. ccxxxviii).
It authorised the Council to work their tramways by electric power.

London County Council (Tramways & Improvements) Act, 1901 (1 Edw. 7. Ch. cclxxxi).
Royal Assent, 17th August 1901. An Act to enable the Council to construct new tramways and to reconstruct and alter tramways in the County of London, to work tramways by electric traction and to make street improvements and for other purposes.

London County Council (Subways & Tramways) Act, 1902 (2 Edw. 7. Ch. ccxviii).
Royal Assent, 8th August 1902. This Act authorised the construction of Kingsway Subway throughout, but restricted the tramway to be built only between Southampton Row and Aldwych Station.

London County Council (Tramways & Improvements) Act, 1902 (2 Edw. 7. Ch. ccxix).
Royal Assent, 8th August 1902. The Act enabled the Council to construct new tramways in London and to work them by electric traction, to make street improvements, to acquire lands for a station for generating electricity and for use in connection with their tramway undertaking.

London County Council (Tramways & Improvements) Act, 1903 (3 Edw. 7. Ch. ccxix).
Royal Assent, 11th August 1903. An Act to enable the Council to construct new tramways in London and for other purposes.
Powers had been called for to construct the line along Victoria Embankment, but due to much opposition, the section was struck from the Act. It did, however, empower the Council to acquire and use lands for building a generating station or stations.

London County Council (Tramways & Improvements) Act, 1904 (4 Edw. 7. Ch. ccxxxi).
Royal Assent, 15th August 1904. An Act to enable the Council to construct and work new tramways and to alter and reconstruct existing tramways in London; to make street improvements in London and Kent; to empower the Metropolitan Borough of Woolwich to construct a new street and for other purposes; to enable the LCC to have power of purchase of that part of the Bexley Tramways in High Street, Plumstead; to enable the LCC to purchase the tramways of the London, Camberwell & Dulwich Tramways Company.

London County Council (Tramways & Improvements) Act, 1906 (6 Edw. 7. Ch. clxxxi).
Royal Assent, 4th August 1906. An Act ... for the construction ... of tramways; the deviation subway; construction ... of the Vauxhall Tramways for working by electric power; purchase of lands for and erection of car sheds and sub-stations, etc.
This included powers to construct the extension to the subway line and connect it up with a new line along Victoria Embankment.

London County Council (Tramways & Improvements) Act, 1907 (7 Edw. 7. Ch. clxiv).
Royal Assent, 21st August 1907. An Act to empower the Council to construct and work new tramways and to alter and reconstruct existing tramways and to make street improvements and other works in London and for other purposes.

London County Council (Tramways & Improvements) Act, 1908 (8 Edw. 7. Ch. lxxviii).
Royal Assent, 21st August 1908. An Act to empower the Council to construct and work new tramways and to alter and reconstruct existing tramways, etc., in north and south London.

London County Council (Tramways & Improvements) Act, 1909 (9 Edw. 7. Ch. lxxv).
Royal Assent, 16th August 1909. An Act to empower the Council to construct and work new tramways and to alter and reconstruct existing tramways and make a new street and to make street improvements and other works, and to purchase the Highgate Hill Tramways.

**London County Council (Tramways & Improvements) Act, 1910
(10 Edw. 7. & 1 Geo. 5. Ch. cxxviii).**
Royal Assent, 3rd August 1910. An Act to empower the Council to construct and work new tramways and to alter and reconstruct existing tramways in north and south London.

London County Council (Tramways & Improvements) Act, 1911 (1-2 Geo. 5. Ch. cvi).
Royal Assent, 18th August 1911. An Act to empower the Council to construct and work new tramways and to alter and reconstruct existing tramways, and for other purposes. This included quadrupling the tracks along Dog Kennel Hill, Dulwich.

London County Council (Tramways & Improvements) Act, 1912 (2-3 Geo. 5. Ch. cvi).
Royal Assent, 7th August 1912. An Act to empower the Council to construct and work new tramways, to alter and reconstruct existing tramways, to make improvements and other works. It also allowed the use of trailer cars on tramways in south London.

London County Council (Tramways & Improvements) Act, 1913 (3-4 Geo. 5. Ch. cii).
Royal Assent, 15th August 1913. An Act to empower the Council to construct and work new tramways, to make street improvements and other works in both north and south London. It also authorised the carriage of standing passengers in the cars at certain times of the day.

London County Council (Tramways & Improvements) Act, 1914 (4-5 Geo. 5. Ch. cxlix).
Royal Assent, 7th August 1914. An Act to empower the Council to construct and work a new tramway (in Eltham), to make street improvements and other works.

London County Council (Tramways & Improvements) Act, 1915 (5-6 Geo. 5. Ch. civ).
Royal Assent, 28th October 1915. An Act to empower the Council to construct and work new tramways in north London, to alter and reconstruct existing tramways, to make street improvements and other works.

London County Council (Tramways & Improvements) Act, 1920 (10-11 Geo. 5. Ch. clxxii).
Royal Assent, 23rd December 1920. An Act to empower the Council to make street improvements and for other works, including the widening of Old Street, Kingsland Road, Cable Street and Brook Street.

London County Council (General Powers) Act, 1921 (13-14 Geo. 5. Ch. vii).
No tramway content.

London County Council (Tramways & Improvements) Act, 1922 (12-13 Geo. 5. Ch. lxxx).
Royal Assent, 4th August 1922. An Act to empower the Council to construct and work new tramways, to alter and reconstruct an existing tramway and for other purposes of the tramway undertaking, and for street improvements and works connected therewith. This included provision for the construction of the Amhurst Park tramway.

London County Council (General Powers) Act, 1923 (13-14 Geo. 5. Ch. vii).
Royal Assent, 17th May 1923. An Act to empower the Council to be possessed of an extension of time in which to undertake the completion of the tramways and other works authorised by the:-
                    London County Council (Tramways & Improvements) Act, 1915:
                    London County Council (Tramways & Improvements) Act, 1920:

London County Council (Tramways & Improvements) Act, 1924 (14-15 Geo. 5. Ch. xl).
Royal Assent, 14th July 1924. An Act to empower the Council to construct and equip a new tramway and for other purposes. The line across Southwark Bridge was authorised.

London County Council (Tramways & Improvements) Act, 1925 (15-16 Geo. 5. Ch. xliii).
Royal Assent, 31st July 1925. An Act to empower the Council to construct and work new tramways and for street improvements and works connected therewith. Authorised was the line through the new Downham Estate to Grove Park.

London County Council (General Powers) Act, 1926 (16-17 Geo. 5. Ch. cxviii).
Royal Assent, 4th August 1926. The Act authorised further extensions of time allowed for the completion of works provided for in the Acts of 1915, 1920, 1923 and 1924.

London County Council (General Powers) Act, 1927 (17-18 Geo. 5. Ch. xxii).
Royal Assent, 29th June 1927. An Act to confer further powers upon the London County Council and upon the City of London and upon the Metropolitan Borough Councils and for other purposes. Its purpose was to authorise the reconstruction of the tramways at the junction of Whitechapel High Street, Whitechapel Road, Leman Street, Commercial Road and Commercial Street.

**London County Council (Tramway Subway & Improvements) Act, 1928
(18-19 Geo. 5. Ch. xxxix).**
Royal Assent, 2nd July 1928. An Act to empower the Council to enlarge their Tramway Subway and to reconstruct the tramways therein and adjacent thereto, and to make street improvements, etc.

London County Council (General Powers) Act, 1929 (19-20 Geo. 5. Ch. lxxxvii).
Royal Assent, 10th May 1929. The Act authorised the construction of a new line along Westhorne Avenue, Eltham.

London County Council (Improvements) Act, 1930 (21 Geo. 5. Ch. vi).
Royal Assent, 19th December 1930. A comprehensive Act was obtained to authorise the Council to completely re-arrange the tramway layout at the "Elephant & Castle" junction. This was intended to form a "ring road", some sections of which were to be formed by existing streets and the tracks retained, while other tracks were to be laid in a new street to be formed. This plan would have meant that a number of properties would have had to be demolished in order to undertake the work. As is now known, this was not carried out at the time, resulting in the tramways remaining on their old alignments.

London County Council (Vauxhall Cross Improvement) Act, 1931 (21-22 Geo. 5. Ch. lv).
Royal Assent, 8th July 1931. A comprehensive and complex re-arrangement of the road junction at Vauxhall had been designed with the intention of easing the flow of traffic across this busy crossing. It also included the complete recasting of the tramway tracks in the area. In this case, after much delay, the works were started, but not during the time that the LCC operated the tramways. It was left to the LPTB to carry out the trackwork.

STATISTICS.

London Tramways Company

YEAR	CAPITAL			LINE OPEN		GROSS INCOME	EXPENDITURE	NET INCOME	PASSENGERS	CAR MILES	CARS	HORSES	BUSES
	AUTHᴰ	PAID UP	EXPᴰ	MLS	CH								
	£	£	£			£	£	£					
1871			263,664	14	20	47,429	32,386	14,593		890,000	102		
1872			294,022	17	20	105,558	75,138	30,420	11,098,224	1,859,584	106		
1873			336,057	18	00	112,127	81,767	30,360	11,791,498	1,892,323	106		
1874			396,900	18	00	120,161	86,071	34,090	13,164,025	1,953,013	116		
1875			421,799	20	20	140,608	112,836	27,772	15,790,967	2,497,643	129		
1876			419,125	20	20	136,574	103,918	32,656	15,595,536	2,329,703	132	1,316	
1877													
1878	440,000	431,050	419,124	20	38	152,343	126,056	26,287	18,735,326				
1879	460,000	439,950	430,707	20	20	158,508	152,321	6,187	26,741,198	2,686,227	169		
1880	510,000	509,950	448,953	20	20	167,879	158,222	9,657	24,993,944	3,263,746	192	1,565	
1881	510,000	509,950	444,444	19	50	182,775	155,813	26,962	29,746,462	3,728,172	209	1,764	
1882						230,868	186,032	44,836	40,544,125	4,624,839	261	2,161	
1883	610,000	599,230	518,421	19	50	253,014	196,966	56,048	46,021,951	5,382,351	236	2,378	
1884	610,000	607,050	528,377	19	50	259,680	201,866	57,814	50,578,803	5,654,325	242	2,557	
1885	610,000	610,000	555,243	19	50	261,078	203,241	57,837	52,180,082	6,080,746	242	2,599	32
1886	610,000	610,000	565,057	19	50	268,185	206,293	61,892	53,911,910	6,165,967	245	2,644	38
1887	610,000	610,000	573,159	19	50	266,502	209,911	56,591	53,819,711	6,435,288	257	2,618	37
1888	610,000	610,000	566,939	19	50	274,011	213,664	60,347	55,997,860	6,326,124	267	2,706	40
1889	660,000	628,340	579,687	19	50	300,220	223,702	76,518	60,534,994	6,816,031	287	3,211	51
1890	660,000	660,000	615,022	21	58	315,729	252,846	62,883	62,385,588	7,522,710	312	3,287	50
1891	760,000	706,090	652,885	22	20	326,482	285,210	41,272	66,793,790	8,061,975	342	3,107	53
1892	910,000	852,653	767,571	23	30	336,144	264,386	71,758	71,170,959	7,428,922	345	2,937	53
1893	910,000	860,000	818,533	23	30	349,072	278,032	71,040	80,539,109	7,863,997	354	3,060	58
1894	910,000	860,000	829,324	23	20	357,000	273,925	83,075	83,455,433	7,973,107	384	3,310	66
1895	910,000	910,000	835,144	23	20	393,912	303,640	90,272	95,435,902	8,582,546	395	3,476	60
1896	910,000	910,000	881,053	24	01	414,418	332,054	82,364	102,435,717	9,298,638	410	3,828	86
1897	910,000	910,000	896,353	24	01	435,461	350,459	84,912	109,345,904	9,720,852	429	3,835	80
1898	910,000	910,000	882,622	24	01	228,207	158,618	69,589	56,676,141	4,935,097	435	3,808	80
1899	SEE LCC SOUTHERN AREA SYSTEM												

To LCC 31st December 1898.

Annual periods from 1st April of preceding year to 31st March of year shown.

London Deptford & Greenwich Tramways Company

YEAR	CAPITAL			LINE OPEN		GROSS INCOME	EXPENDITURE	NET INCOME	PASSENGERS	CAR MILES	CARS	HORSES	BUSES
	AUTHᴰ	PAID UP	EXPᴰ	MLS	CH								
	£	£	£			£	£	£					
1880	87,500	34,588	21,249						402,867	56,384	16	133	
1881		84,810	73,025	3	21	1,955	5,791	Loss 4,016					
1882													
1883	162,500	159,225	157,095	4	72	18,111	20,368	Loss 2,257	3,776,220	134,070	32	267	
1884		162,383	157,226			21,704	19,456	2,248	4,721,670	623,618		243	
1885						22,457	20,647	1,810	5,230,811	612,367		238	
1886		162,390	163,164			22,834	18,583	4,251	5,350,592	586,328		230	
1887		162,389				23,740	19,373	4,367	5,563,892	599,520		248	
1888						23,518	20,626	2,892	5,546,611	632,378		237	
1889			166,812			23,782	20,456	3,326	5,474,213	534,450		199	
1890	212,500		167,205			24,474	19,745	4,729	5,602,415	530,434		217	
1891			167,314			24,583	20,740	3,849	5,626,763	524,066		215	
1892	252,500					24,781	21,039	3,742	5,516,994	531,241	24	219	
1893			172,186			25,438	21,007	4,431	5,649,292	533,018		217	
1894			167,784			26,769	21,416	5,353	5,971,614	551,896		236	
1895		162,390	169,366			28,431	22,549	5,882	6,513,898	596,763		242	
1896		162,389	168,772			30,094	23,530	6,564	7,165,609	621,975		250	
1897			169,157			30,373	24,487	5,886	7,255,962	613,426	26	285	
1898		162,386	168,926			31,813	25,922	5,891	7,471,478	710,795		281	
1899			169,364			32,467	25,766	6,701	7,658,408	713,594	31	282	
1900		162,349				30,815	26,733	4,082	7,152,485	703,245		294	
1901		162,350	170,954			31,200	28,769	2,431	8,334,498	740,169		300	
1902			171,388			29,275	28,882	393	8,115,350	745,991	42	300	
1903			171,611			28,542	27,879	663	8,172,523	740,159		296	
1904			171,785			28,509	27,257	1,252	8,356,675	799,323		300	
1905		162,350	165,502	4	72	13,773	14,122	Loss 349	3,962,546	366,996		300	

To LCC 7th July 1904

Annual periods from 1st April of preceding year to 31st March of year shown.

YEAR	CAPITAL			LINE OPEN		GROSS INCOME	EXPEND-ITURE	NET INCOME	PASSENGERS	CAR MILES	CARS	HOR-SES	BUS-ES
	AUTHD	PAID UP	EXPD	MLS	CH	£	£	£					
South London Tramways Company	£	£	£			£	£	£					
1880	181,000	51,680											
1881	145,000	74,855	72,095	2	37	3,215	5,691	Loss 2,476	647,836	121,234	28	108	
1882													
1883	306,000	287,300	268,518	10	00	25,218	26,140	Loss 922	5,392,656	684,062	50	416	17
1884	366,000	320,380	314,052	13	00	50,624	52,930	Loss 2,306	10,224,561	1,397,196	96	719	
1885		335,328	330,258			66,536	69,444	Loss 2,908	13,284,660	1,906,856	88	797	
1886		346,390	329,580			66,397	60,893	5,504	12,560,012	1,704,057	82	734	20
1887		355,732	342,167	12	72	70,153	61,758	8,395	13,151,239	1,681,232		808	
1888		362,747	333,300			70,757	61,935	8,822	14,235,251	1,770,458		762	17
1889		366,794	361,325			70,370	61,075	9,295	15,089,182	1,722,138	84	764	
1890		366,960	365,444			74,063	63,647	10,416	16,154,451	1,767,314	86	785	18
1891			368,130			74,381	70,575	3,806	16,237,482	1,752,226		788	16
1892		366,810	365,983			76,384	70,050	6,334	15,607,907	1,697,743		715	
1893		366,860	388,621	12	70	74,602	67,637	6,965	14,536,938	1,609,472	85	731	17
1894		366,360	368,297			78,221	69,807	8,414	16,758,386	1,725,776		773	15
1895			371,152			78,891	66,382	12,509	16,880,599	1,763,573		781	16
1896		365,360	370,993			85,168	69,730	15,438	18,301,885	1,833,167		846	20
1897			370,733			89,213	73,113	16,100	19,098,780	1,977,030	84	881	22
1898			373,107			90,877	74,025	16,852	20,585,995	2,064,102		903	
1899			372,634			93,479	77,659	15,820	21,946,662	2,110,807	85	908	24
1900			373,000			78,461	62,693	15,768	18,687,446	1,663,885	87	749	
1901		365,860	368,031			76,270	64,836	11,434	17,969,659	1,670,475		734	
1902			368,226			73,324	66,294	7,030	17,043,193	1,662,264	95	737	
1903	366,000		361,838			30,117	24,296	5,821	6,985,969	641,301	95	751	

To LCC 21st November 1902.

Annual periods from 1st April of preceding year to 31st March of year shown.

YEAR	CAPITAL			LINE OPEN		GROSS INCOME	EXPEND-ITURE	NET INCOME	PASSENGERS	CAR MILES	CARS	HOR-SES	BUS-ES
	AUTHD	PAID UP	EXPD	MLS	CH	£	£	£					
Woolwich & Southeast London Tramways Company	£	£	£			£	£	£					
1881	60,000	22,149	20,333	1	46	297	1,064	Loss 767	43,228	4,312	6	41	
1882													
1883	75,000	55,864	52,302	4	63	7,617	8,936	Loss 1,319	1,101,616	200,965	11	146	
1884	80,000	77,798	75,239			10,316	11,261	Loss 945	1,543,954	281,293	21	175	
1885	90,000	79,345	75,860			11,869	11,576	293	1,888,379	290,028	15	151	
1886		80,251	77,180			12,517	11,377	1,140	2,058,531	296,342		152	
1887	78,000	69,239	70,140	4	77	12,744	10,667	2,077	2,101,514	303,777		152	
1888			70,395			12,858	10,900	1,958	2,120,058	310,812		154	
1889			70,335			13,722	11,396	2,376	2,279,123	316,728		151	
1890		72,220	71,938			14,968	11,920	3,048	2,481,196	321,435		156	
1891		72,239	73,637			15,293	12,368	2,925	2,523,767	322,671		158	
1892			73,071			15,881	13,741	2,140	2,646,211	350,739	20	180	
1893			73,620			15,877	13,617	2,260	2,636,065	333,522		166	
1894		72,689	73,084			16,190	14,001	2,189	2,974,035	333,342		160	
1895		72,579	73,008			16,275	13,577	2,698	2,875,346	341,514		164	
1896			74,126			17,641	13,639	4,002	3,137,930	356,166	24	178	
1897			74,835			18,472	13,789	4,683	3,324,047	370,683	25	190	
1898			76,174	4	70	19,633	14,980	4,653	3,534,416	388,836		193	
1899			76,906			21,395	15,947	5,448	3,874,805	403,263		201	
1900			77,804			23,079	16,633	6,444	4,195,774	433,980	29	210	
1901			78,338			24,813	17,581	7,232	4,465,828	444,330	31	218	
1902			78,309			23,146	18,729	4,687	4,267,716	446,166	33	209	
1903			78,075			22,171	19,320	2,851	4,067,782	447,120	33	204	
1904			77,819			21,589	18,881	2,768	4,006,892	449,406	32	200	
1905													

To LCC 1st June 1905.

Annual periods from 1st April of preceding year to 31st March of year shown.

South Eastern Metropolitan Tramways Company

YEAR	CAPITAL			LINE OPEN		GROSS INCOME	EXPEND-ITURE	NET INCOME	PASSENGERS	CAR MILES	CARS	HOR-SES	BUS-ES
	AUTHD £	PAID UP £	EXPD £	MLS	CH	£	£	£					
1884-5	75,000		4,000										
1886-8	62,500												
1889													
1890											7	---	
1891		10,800	62,500	2	45	1,131	780	351	220,313	19,175	10	(80)	
1892		62,500				9,936	8,337	1,599	1,881,075	201,670	10	(80)	
1893						10,643	8,486	2,157	2,018,824	198,820	10	(90)	
1894						11,171	8,937	2,234	2,094,355	202,275	12	(100)	
1895						11,678	9,340	2,338	2,189,844	208,439	10	(90)	
1896						12,879	9,871	3,008	2,454,732	216,123	12	(100)	
1897						14,077	11,188	2,889	2,625,447	250,318	12	(100)	
1898		To LCC 31st March 1902.				14,834	11,792	3,062	2,803,107	246,733	12	(100)	
1899						16,433	12,020	4,413	3,097,179	260,801	12	(100)	
1900						16,626	12,203	4,423	3,100,573	257,800	12	(100)	
1901	124,000					17,337	12,860	4,477	3,252,330	263,020	12	(100)	
1902	104,500	62,500	62,500	2	45	12,021	10,133	1,888	2,310,163	186,045	12	(100)	

Horses hired from Thomas Tilling Ltd.

London, Camberwell & Dulwich Tramways Company — Annual periods from 1st April of preceding year to 31st March of year shown.

YEAR	CAPITAL			LINE OPEN		GROSS INCOME	EXPEND-ITURE	NET INCOME	PASSENGERS	CAR MILES	CARS	HOR-SES	BUS-ES
1883	37,500												
1884	75,000	20,030	20,000	2	71								
1885		20,000	20,000										
1886-9													
1890	25,000	30,150	30,150										
1891-5							Line non-operational.						
1896	93,759	40,390	51,310			260	374	Loss 114	46,905	6,815	4	(20)	
1897		40,410	50,898			1,637	2,208	Loss 571	315,405	54,483	4	(12)	
1898		41,875	52,906			1,400	1,662	Loss 262	291,565	40,509	4	(16)	
1899		42,175	53,216			2,232	2,487	Loss 255	463,469	42,491	5?	(24)	
1900		42,175	53,216			1,339	1,371	Loss 32	283,245	28,396	6?	(30)	
1901	94,750	42,675	53,216	2	71		No Annual Returns submitted.						
1902-4	To LCC 15th August 1904.												

Horses hired.

London Southern Tramways Company

YEAR	CAPITAL			LINE OPEN		GROSS INCOME	EXPEND-ITURE	NET INCOME	PASSENGERS	CAR MILES	CARS	HOR-SES	BUS-ES
	AUTHD £	PAID UP £	EXPD £	MLS	CH	£	£	£					
1883	112,500	40,000											
1884		84,050	77,559	3	31	2,266	2,707	Loss 241	445,966	80,770	12	96	
1885	127,500	86,240	84,063	3	74	8,778	8,280	498	1,562,089	286,969	20	119	
1886		87,040	87,750			10,703	10,026	677	1,802,536	341,719			
1887		112,500	84,063			11,097	10,378	719	1,858,213	343,737			
1888			113,360			13,699	14,051	Loss 352	2,260,012	446,363		170	
1889				5	60	14,632	13,086	1,546	2,366,762	449,272			
1890			111,560			14,746	12,617	2,129	2,420,720	454,151			
1891			111,870			15,471	12,878	2,593	2,536,732	462,349			
1892			111,969			15,584	14,010	1,574	2,596,615	457,985			
1893						16,264	14,820	1,444	2,726,348	463,514			
1894			112,349			16,987	13,613	1,374	2,841,157	471,970		168	
1895			112,474			17,726	15,061	2,665	3,010,281	478,522	26		
1896			115,289			21,388	17,221	4,167	4,003,105	497,967		224	
1897						23,997	19,539	4,458	4,625,3405	542,686	32	229	
1898			118,081			26,093	21,026	5,067	5,833,714	585,163		248	
1899			120,236			28,924	23,122	5,862	6,898,914	646,150		263	
1900			122,901			27,032	25,839	1,193	7,440,934	706,233		308	
1901			122,201			26,139	24,171	1,965	6,454,657	654,522	33	275	
1902						24,297	26,698	Loss 2,401	6,490,656	684,554		292	
1903						25,365	26,972	Loss 1,607	6,463,185	666,025		283	
1904						25,097	25,008	89	6,114,154	620,154		287	
1905						24,283	24,761	Loss 478	5,943,504	637,082		290	
1906			125,433			23,139	25,631	Loss 2,492	5,704,357	684,858	32	293	

To LCC 20th December 1906.

Annual periods from 1st April of preceding year to 31st March of year shown.

Harrow Road & Paddington Tramway

YEAR	CAPITAL			LINE OPEN		GROSS INCOME	EXPEND-ITURE	NET INCOME	PASSENGERS	CAR MILES	CARS	HOR-SES	BUS-ES
	AUTHD £	PAID UP £	EXPD £	MLS	CH	£	£	£					
1888	75,000												
1889		55,324	72,810	1	61	07,548	06,779	0,769	1,232,941	200,087	15	110	
1890		75,000	74,337			09,526	07,852	1,674	1,684,740	216,675		122	
1891		73,800	75,159			10,025	07,791	2,234	1,786,292	211,565		114	
1892			76,035			10,202	08,413	1,789	1,849,151	221,850		111	
1893	105,000	73,960	80,329	2	68	10,826	09,178	1,648	1,976,936	218,851	19	110	
1894		76,950	80,877			11,106	09,192	1,914	2,066,688	223,246		113	
1895		77,450	79,584			11,224	09,155	2,069	2,113,483	234,291		110	
1896		78,350	78,467			12,472	09,103	3,369	2,346,093	257,587		117	
1897			78,600			12,948	09,165	3,783	2,469,030	260,043	16	139	
1898	78,350		78,649			13,912	09,511	4,401	2,620,926	263,875		147	
1899		77,850	78,751	2	67	14,867	10,283	4,584	2,828,656	271,903	18	150	
1900			80,010			14,547	10,072	4,475	2,762,946	286,150	21	158	
1901			80,313			14,404	11,205	3,199	2,737,986	205,372		157	
1902			79,939			13,919	11,481	2,438	2,713,056	278,424	22	152	
1903			82,326			14,693	11,227	3,466	2,843,681	210,595		153	
1904	158,350		84,974			14,812	11,250	3,562	2,862,536	312,130		159	
1905			85,409			14,359	10,678	3,681	2,840,325	305,305	19	159	
1906			84,700	2	67	13,792	10,916	2,876	2,673,891	302,113		140	

Subsequent annual figures included in Metropolitan Electric Tramways Ltd. returns.

Annual periods from 1st April of preceding year to 31st March of year shown.

Highgate Hill Tramway

YEAR	CAPITAL			LINE OPEN		GROSS INCOME	EXPEND-ITURE	NET INCOME	PASSENGERS	CAR MILES	CARS	HOR-SES	BUS-ES
	AUTHD £	PAID UP £	EXPD £	MLS	CH	£	£	£					
1883	100,500	30,500	51,150										
1884-5	130,500	60,047	59,227			5,007	4,911	96	729,800	77,445			
1886	130,500	60,047	59,227			3,908	4,414	Loss 506	642,083	104,331			
1887	130,000	60,407	59,227			3,850	4,307	Loss 457	671,421	87,937			
1888	130,000	60,407	59,227			3,499	4,075	Loss 576	609,769	74,204			
1889-90	No return.												
1891	30,000	22,208	21,991			3,974	3,815	159	681,424	84,767			
1892-3	No return.												
1894-6	Line closed.												
1897	16,000	16,000	16,000			1,318	1,180	138	303,039	17,777			
1898						4,796	4,454	342	1,129,973	99,348			
1899	16,000	16,000	16,000			5,126	4,599	527	1,198,446	99,294			
1900	16,000	16,000	16,000			5,172	4,625	747	1,206,754	100,179			
1901	16,000	16,000	16,038			5,073	4,889	184	1,182,251	96,979			
1902	16,000	16,000	16,027			4,796	4,173	623	1,122,855	91,255			
1903	16,300	16,300	16,204			4,532	4,003	529	1,059,815	92,787			
1904	16,300	16,300	16,058			4,562	4,314	248	1,069,180	93,860			
1905	16,300	16,300	16,580			4,909	4,198	711	1,140,395	91,132			
1906-9	No return.												

Annual periods from 1st April of preceding year to 31st March of year shown.

(LINE OPEN: 57 chains long only.)

(CARS: Total of ten cable cars, including passenger carrying "dummies". To LCC 24th August 1909.)

North London Suburban Tramway

Undertaking in liquidation December 1889.

Sold by Order of Court to North Metropolitan Tramways in August 1891.

YEAR	CAPITAL			LINE OPEN		GROSS INCOME	EXPEND-ITURE	NET INCOME	PASSENGERS	CAR MILES	CARS	HOR-SES	STEAM TRAM ENGINES
	AUTHD £	PAID UP £	EXPD £	MLS	CH	£	£	£					
1880	100,000	38,190	9,267			948	3,484	Loss 2,536	212,912	36,479		74	
1881	100,000	52,600	49,593										
1882													
1883	143,750	87,383	84,182	5	64	8,316	10,078	Loss 1,762	1,134,869	272,424	20	112	
1884	143,750	87,925	87,108	5	64	8,924	8,675	249	1,187,017	229,943	20	101	14
1885	143,750	101,799	101,281	5	64	8,106	7,025	1,081	1,171,784	220,264	20	2	15
1886	168,750	133,213	133,611	7	63	10,755	8,816	1,939	1,553,440	296,612	20	1	15
1887	183,750	158,653	154,507	9	73	14,104	10,212	3,892	1,989,264	363,626	27	1	23
1888	183,750	178,525	176,393	9	73	15,436	12,947	2,489	2,154,864	391,582	27	2	25
1889	183,750	183,466	183,261	9	73	16,229	15,066	563	2,300,444	405,563	27	3	25
1890	183,750	183,466	183,261	9	73	17,250	16,609	641	1,777,709	246,227	27	3	25
1891	183,750	183,466	183,261	9	73	14,297	18,681	Loss 4,384	2,512,221	185,014	27	3	25

London Street Tramways Company

YEAR	CAPITAL			LINE OPEN		GROSS INCOME	EXPEND-ITURE	NET INCOME	PASSENGERS	CAR MILES	CARS	HORSES	BUS-ES
	AUTHᴰ	PAID UP	EXPᴰ	MLS	CH								
	£	£	£			£	£	£					
1870-77	156,250	150,000	150,000	5	52								
1878	200,000	175,000	150,000	5	52	49,482	39,334	10,148	5,761,583		54	382	
1879	200,000	175,000	161,445	7	38	51,765	45,914	5,851	6,278,568		58	467	
1880	230,000	224,000	211,487	9	24	58,259	51,189	7,070	7,294,738	1,070,080	64	519	
1881	230,000	224,000	229,756	9	24	66,811	54,951	11,860	7,757,055	1,153,466	64	518	
1882													
1883	304,000	249,000	229,756	9	67	75,625	59,286	16,339	11,179,934	1,222,169	75	606	
1884	316,500	249,000	237,178	9	67	84,354	65,793	18,561	13,079,352	1,381,401	75	644	
1885	316,500	250,000	253,330	9	76	86,133	65,413	20,720	13,527,814	1,483,683	75	665	
1886	416,500	300,000	287,522	10	65	86,520	67,113	19,407	13,649,553	1,516,719	80	723	
1887	491,500	300,000	339,717	11	77	99,980	77,890	22,090	17,443,149	1,781,689	105	942	
1888	491,500	357,000	400,121	11	79	109,943	94,129	15,814	20,586,353	2,242,618	110	1,087	
1889	586,000	362,500	428,966	13	40	116,396	93,802	22,594	21,396,428	2,322,255	110	1,078	
1890	586,500	379,500	433,794	13	40	126,442	101,081	25,361	23,976,706	2,449,436	124	1,127	
1891	586,500	382,500	434,608	13	40	130,242	107,220	23,002	24,661,974	2,468,381	126	1,139	
1892	586,500	382,500	435,774	13	40	133,753	116,666	17,087	23,865,075	2,510,134	134	1,183	
1893	586,500	382,500	436,094	13	37	135,558	122,266	23,292	24,745,863	2,466,113	134	1,186	
1894	586,500	382,500	436,145	13	37	143,001	112,278	21,723	24,753,416	2,482,105	136	1,181	
1895	586,500	382,500	437,223	13	37	131,597	111,884	19,713	24,791,465	2,505,338	136	1,223	
1896	586,500	294,500	318,480	9	9	140,492	110,992	29,500	27,830,858	2,621,567	136	1,282	
1897	586,500	294,500	312,406	9	9	140,343	111,470	28,873	28,065,481	2,719,953	139	1,287	
1898	Included in North Metropolitan Tramways Company returns.												

First sections of lines to LCC and leased back
to Company on 3rd August 1895.
Remainder to LCC and leased back to North Metropolitan
Tramways Company 13th October 1897.

Annual periods from 1st April of preceding
year to 31st March of year shown.

North Metropolitan Tramways Company

YEAR	CAPITAL			LINE OPEN		GROSS INCOME	EXPEND-ITURE	NET INCOME	PASSENGERS	CAR MILES	CARS	HOR-SES	BUS-ES
	AUTHᴰ	PAID UP	EXPᴰ	MLS	CH								
	£	£	£			£	£	£					
1870-77	762,500	720,004	686,999	30	40								
1878	962,500	720,004		30	40	252,514	192,724	59,790	28,510,099		169	1,830	
1879	962,500	834,806	892,571	32	20	252,723	208,264	44,459	29,021,281	4,027,049	203	2,062	
1880	962,500	844,864	930,998	33	60	278,587	218,817	60,400	32,171,418	4,451,217	223	2,094	
1881	1,012,500	870,000	947,775	34	63	284,026	221,366	62,660	32,452,331	4,574,023	223	2,057	
1882													
1883	1,077,500	912,338	1,019,485	34	63	293,601	220,036	73,565	33,846,387	4,662,102	241	2,173	
1884	1,077,500	970,304	1,086,032	35	43	299,505	222,726	76,779	34,745,194	5,062,604	253	2,474	
1885	1,240,000	1,036,656	1,135,274	35	70	302,858	225,323	77,535	36,139,300	5,399,445	285	2,506	
1886	1,240,000	1,090,282	1,194,437	37	69	311,206	228,466	82,740	38,968,929	5,927,451	307	2,681	
1887	1,277,500	1,188,604	1,248,131	40	24	334,559	246,605	87,894	43,907,239	6,400,439	325	2,986	
1888	1,277,500	1,201,225	1,271,451	40	24	345,881	252,223	93,658	48,209,714	6,945,668	335	3,008	
1889	1,277,500	1,267,590	1,289,684	41	58	373,173	266,524	106,649	58,637,711	7,016,685	335	3,849	
1890	1,402,500	1,277,479	1,330,651	41	58	405,292	294,432	110,860	69,715,528	7,196,900	342	3,346	
1891	1,402,500	1,315,250	1,390,888	41	73	415,316	310,880	104,436	72,837,073	7,409,120	356	3,590	
1892	1,552,500	1,370,613	1,429,730	51	55	446,362	351,185	95,177	77,642,583	7,656,478	397	3,733	
1893	1,552,500	1,384,627	1,445,534	51	55	456,018	357,944	98,074	79,732,696	7,962,786	409	3,792	
1894	1,552,500	1,384,627	1,460,094	51	55	459,914	362,663	97,251	82,627,342	8,266,543	431	4,043	
1895	1,552,500	1,384,627	1,518,504	51	55	470,717	370,873	99,844	92,018,492	8,972,027	457	4,117	
1896	1,552,500	1,384,711	1,553,483	51	55	516,739	414,632	102,107	103,675,569	9,724,907	472	4,737	
1897	1,552,500	1,384,711	1,563,889	51	55	542,938	428,981	113,957	109,886,630	10,466,394	499	4,917	
Tracks in London purchased by LCC and leased to company.						Figures include cars and horses purchased from London Street Tramways.							
1898	1,677,500	1,029,293	1,148,195	16	00	681,653	610,449	71,204	139,096,427	13,259,849	673	7,167	
1899	1,677,500	1,090,865	1,169,759	16	00	758,778	700,622	58,156	159,575,696	15,303,178	702	7,345	
1900	1,677,500	1,042,565	1,183,088	16	00	762,616	711,846	50,770	157,904,650	15,366,737	696	7,605	21
1901	1,677,500	1,040,865	1,204,296	16	00	776,737	742,568	34,169	160,676,347	16,282,248	711	7,722	21
1902	1,677,500	1,037,365	1,206,916	16	00	777,214	767,919	9,295	160,209,397	16,662,465	730	7,329	21
1903	1,810,500	1,037,365	954,039	7	53	729,406	700,848	28,558	150,412,344	15,505,907	668	6,380	
1904	1,810,500	1,037,365	947,620	2	10	330,821	311,818	19,003	68,454,670	6,993,864	665	6,495	
1905	1,810,500	1,037,365	952,655	2	10	629,118	601,186	27,932	130,673,957	13,938,748	687	6,536	
1906	1,810,500	1,018,565	897,347	2	10	636,972	538,694	98,278	131,871,635	13,904,557	678	6,192	
East Ham area only.										All London assets to LCC 1st April 1906.			
1907	1,810,500	940,065	70,409	0	60	240,830	136,901	103,929	32,522,750	3,593,157	6	55	
1908	1,810,500	550,834	70,309	0	60	15,437	6,521	8,916	1,958,499	122,492	6	51	
1909						2,591	2,770	Loss 179	398,307	37,800	6	51	

Annual periods from 1st April of preceding
year to 31st March of year shown.

Passenger, Works & Road Vehicles (LCC Tramways)

Passenger Cars and Works Cars

Year End March	Electric D/Deck 8-wh	Electric D/Deck 4-wh	Electric S/Dk 8-wh	Trailer 4-wh	Horse Cars Pair	Horse Cars One	Horses	Works Stores	Works Water	Sand	Electric Broom	Electric Plough	Electric Snow
1904	201	105			290		2012		1				
1905	201	200	13		227		1440		5				
1906	201	200	26		216		1515	6	6				
1907	445	200	50		723	Not in use	5868	8	5				
1908	715	200	50		621	3	4100	8	4+1*				
1909	920	200	50		516	3	3123	8	4+1*	2			
1910	1076	200	50		127	3	1416	8	4+1*	2			
1911	1251	250	50	1	107	3	1009	8	4+1*	2			
1912	1283	250	50	1	96	3	733	8	4+1*	2			
1913	1323	300	50	2	74	PE3	584 ¶						
1914	1376	300	50	8	56	PE3	329 ¶						
1915					37		¶						
1916							¶						
1917				120			¶						
1918	1376	241		158			¶	8	4				
1919	1376	241		158	9		¶	8	4				
1920				158	9		¶						
1921	1426	299		158			¶	10	4				
1922	1501	301	50	158	2		¶	10	4				
1923	1501	301	50	158	2		¶	8	4+2*				
1924	1501	301	50	158	2		¶	8	4+2*				
1925	1501	301	50					8	6*				
1926	1501	281	50					8	6*				
1927	1501	268	50					8	6*		17	3	
1928	1505	264	48					8	6*		17	16	
1929	1553	247						9	6*		21	16	
1930	1660	174						9	6*		21	16	
1931	1612	100						9	6*		21	16	
1932	1615	98									21	18	
1933											21	18	

¶ Horses supplied on contract. Mainly by Thomas Tilling
* Including 1 or 2 rail grinders
PE: Petrol-electric cars

Road Vehicles (Horse Drawn) and Mechanical

Year End March	Carts Vans	Lorries	Brakes	Towers	Horse Other	Snow Swpr	Horses	Motor Cars	Motor Vans	Lorries Petrol	Lorries Steam	Towers
1904	103	3	12	3	11	11	Included in totals in passenger cars section	1		4+1¶		
1905	115	3	14	3	10	15		4		4+1¶		
1906	258	6	28	3	21	15		5		4+1¶	5	
1907	170	5	24	4	27	15		5		4+1¶	5	
1908	232	20	22	4	9	15		6		4+1¶	5	
1909	227	21	20	3	10	10		6		4		
1910	215	17	20	3	11	11		8		7	5	
1911	199	17	20	4	11	11		8		7	5	
1912	199	17	20	4	5	11		8		11	5	
1913	203	17	20	5	5	11		8		11+2*	11	
1914				5						11+2*		
1915												
1916	No details available											
1917	No details available											
1918	No details available											
1919	No details available			4				8				
1920				4				8		9+2*		
1921				4				10		13+2*		
1922				5				9		25+2*	11	
1923				5				9		24+2*	11	
1924				5				13		25§+1*	18	
1925				5				13		24§+1*	18	
1926				5				13		26	18	
1927				5				11		32	18	
1928				5				18	^	32	18	
1929				5				18	^	33	18	
1930				5				18	^	33	18	
1931				5				18	^	35	18	
1932				5				18	^	39	18	
1933				5				18	^	37+4**	16	

Mechanical Towers: 4 electric → / 1 petrol-electric → (4 elec / 3 elec / 1 petrol-electric)

¶ Rail grinder.
* "Auto-carriers"
§ Includes 2 "Lorries" (electric) trailer tractors"
** 4 Petrol-electric lorries

From LCC Statistical Records

Index

Volume I, pages 1 - 488.   Volume II, pages 489 - 986.

Volume I, pages 1 - 488.   Volume II, pages 489 - 986.

Volume I, pages 1 - 488.   Volume II, pages 489 - 986.